The Prentice Hall Textbook Reader

specific topic
general topic
2|15   class
2|16 — 2|21
2|22   class

Timothy C. Brown, Ed.D.

Riverside Community College

Upper Saddle River, New Jersey 07458

© 2005 by PEARSON EDUCATION, INC.
Upper Saddle River, New Jersey 07458

ISBN 0-13-184895-X

Printed in the United States of America

Contents

Introduction

A JUSTIFICATION FOR A TEXTBOOK READER

College reading courses offer students an opportunity to improve their reading skills. Many of these courses require reading a textbook similar to the text you have for this class. The goal of a college reading course is to build reading skills sufficient for comprehending readings found in the textbooks required for your content-area classes. After previewing your textbook for this class, you will see that many of the reading skills are applied in single paragraphs or short essays. Also, in addition to learning basic reading skills such as determining the main idea, successful college readers can also call on a variety of strategies, which can be applied to different textbooks depending on the subject matter. The purpose of this textbook reader is to provide you an opportunity to practice applying different reading strategies, many of which you will be taught in your reading class. The selected chapters included in this reader were taken from current college textbooks from many different content areas. Your textbook, when used in conjunction with this reader, will allow for a more authentic application of reading skills and strategies to be applied to content-area reading.

TEXT EXPLICIT VS. TEXT IMPLICIT INFORMATION

Authors can choose to state the idea they intend for you to understand or they can suggest the idea and rely on you to draw an appropriate conclusion about the idea they intended for you to understand. Both approaches are seen in textbooks. When the author states the idea directly in the print, the idea is referred to as text explicit. When the author chooses to suggest an idea, and rely on the reader's ability to draw a conclusion, this is called text implicit.

READING COMPREHENSION

Reading comprehension consists of two very important mental processes. The first one is most commonly known as *understanding* ideas in print. The second, and most often left out, is *retaining* those ideas. In the case of textbook reading, merely understanding an idea in print may have very little value unless the concept is personalized in some way and remembered. Also, it's unlikely that you would ever be able to personalize and remember a concept that you did not understand or that did not make sense.

METACOMPREHENSION

Metacomprehension is the awareness of and conscious control over your own understanding or lack of understanding. In other words, are you aware of what you did or did not understand from the chapter you just completed reading? Sounds easy, right? However, you would be surprised how easy it is to think you understand a concept that you really do not. Have you ever been called on in class to explain a concept that you are certain you understand from a reading and then find that you are unable to put it into words? If so, then not only did you have low comprehension, but you also had low metacomprehension.

COMPREHENSION STRATEGIES

In this reader you will find nine different comprehension strategies which can be applied when reading a chapter in a textbook. They are all slightly different, and which one you use may be a matter of personal preference, the format of the textbook, or the content area the textbook deals with. The strategies are:

1. K-W-L
2. M.U.R.D.E.R.
3. P.L.A.N.
4. Plan-Do-Review
5. P.O.R.P.E
6. Q.A.R.
7. Semantic Web
8. S.Q.3.R.
9. S. Q. Study the Problem 3. R. (Modified for Math)

Each strategy will be explained in detail with examples. Then, you will have the opportunity to apply the strategy to authentic textbook chapters taken from various subjects and included in this reader. There will be keys for you to compare your responses in order to evaluate how effective the strategy was for you.

METACOGNITION

You may be asking yourself, "Why do I need a strategy, why can't I just read the textbook?" In the past, have you ever been given a textbook assignment and then proceeded to read the chapter(s) at home, then, after you have finished, realized you don't remember anything about what you just spent two hours reading? If that has happened to you it is because you were reading passively rather than actively. In other words, sometime during those two hours when you were reading, you stopped understanding what you were reading but you were not even aware that it happened. When this occurs, you are usually forced to reread, and rereading expository text a second or third time can be frustrating as well as time consuming.

A more effective approach to reading textbooks is monitoring your comprehension. You think about what you should be thinking while you are reading. Strategies such as the ones included in this textbook reader can help you accomplish this task. So, rather than passively recognizing words from left to right across a page, you are recognizing the author's thoughts, linking those thoughts to some of your own, thus not only understanding what you are reading, but remembering the material as well.

3-STEP APPROACH TO READING

The reading process can be broken down into three steps. The first step is what should be done in *preparation* to reading. This step is called the "pre-read." The second step is what should be done *while* you are reading. This step is called the "through-read." The last step is what should be done *after you are finished* reading and that step is called the "post-read." Each step in succession is essential to reading comprehension. Remember, "comprehension" is more than understanding, it is also your ability to retain what you understood.

Your ability to remember what you read is dependent upon what it is that you already know. You remember new ideas by linking them to ideas that you are already familiar with. Therefore, it is important to identify what you know about a subject before engaging in reading about it. Pre-reading activities are designed to *activate* what prior knowledge you already hold about a particular topic. As you are reading you must continuously recognize new ideas presented by the author and *associate* them to ideas you already know. Through-reading activities force you to link new knowledge with knowledge you already have. In the end, you as the reader must be able to account for what you have learned. In some cases you will *assimilate* the author's new ideas into your own, but when the author's ideas cause you to reject current and replace with new knowledge, you must *accommodate* those new ideas. Post-reading activities help you sort out or account for what was assimilated and what was accommodated.

BRAINSTORMING

Almost all of the strategies introduced in this reader will require some amount of brainstorming. Simply put, brainstorming is an activity designed to help you identify what ideas you already have (prior knowledge) which in some way relate to the topic (subject) of what you are preparing to read. In order to do so, you must have an "activator" or a "trigger." The trigger is the topic. If you are unsure what the topic of the chapter is, quickly preview the headings in the chapter and ask yourself what those headings have in common; whatever that is will be the topic. To brainstorm effectively, it is important just to let your mind go. Do not try to screen your ideas while brainstorming. Be satisfied that if the idea occurred to you as you considered the topic, it will be useful later while reading.

SUMMARIZING

Summarizing is an important skill to help you determine the extent to which you have processed new information gathered from your reading. Summaries include the topic, points, and supporting ideas included in the reading, but a summary is written in your words, not those of the author. As discussed earlier in this introduction, you will only retain ideas that are meaningful to you. The author's ideas as expressed in his/her words were meaningful to the author. But for you to make those ideas meaningful to you, they must be transposed into your own prior knowledge. Once this has taken place, you have personalized this new information and you should be absolutely capable of reviewing the information included in the reading using your own language and expressions. Your ability to summarize is the true test as to whether or not you have learned.

READING RATE

Reading rate is a term that is often misunderstood. For some, reading rate refers to how fast your eyes are able to fixate on words or groups of words from left to right across the page. For others, reading rate means how quickly one can read and comprehend a particular chapter in a textbook. One's ability to recognize words or groups of words in print does not necessarily lead to comprehension. What we find is that there are a number of factors which heavily influence how quickly one can read and comprehend. Among these are the amount of prior knowledge the reader has about the topic and the purpose for which the reader is reading the chapter. You should keep in mind that reading rate and reading comprehension levels are inversely related. Generally the higher the reading rate, the lower the comprehension level will be.

SUMMARY

Textbook reading is not recreational reading. In novels, for example, authors use various techniques to "hook" the reader. Textbook authors do not use such devices. The purpose of a textbook is to aid in instruction, thus using expository text as opposed to narrative text. If the interest level for the reader is low, or if the reader possesses limited prior knowledge about the subject, textbook reading presents some difficult challenges. A metacognitive approach to reading can help you monitor your comprehension so that you are aware when it breaks down and fix it then rather than continuing for hours and then being forced to reread.

Looking at reading as a sequential three-step process will help you to better understand the mental processes which lead to effective reading. You will find that each strategy discussed in the coming pages has pre-reading activities, through-reading activities, and post-reading activities. Each is important for good reading comprehension. Remember the goal is not simply to pass your reading class; it is to take the skills and strategies that you learn in class and apply them to reading the textbooks required for the content-area classes you will need to earn your certificate or degree.

Nine Comprehension Strategies

K-W-L

The K-W-L strategy was created by Donna Ogle in 1986. The objective of the strategy is to facilitate metacognitive thought processes as you are reading. The strategy can be illustrated by a simple chart consisting of three columns. The first column is labeled "K" which stands for *what you know already* about the topic of the chapter. The second or middle column is labeled "W" which stands for *what you think you will learn*. The third and final column is labeled "L" which stands for *what you actually did learn*.

To fill the "K" column, simply brainstorm all of the different ideas which exist in your prior knowledge relative to the topic. Remember the topic is the person, place, or thing the chapter is about. If you find that you possess limited prior knowledge about a topic, try going to the Internet and do search using the topic as the keyword.

The key to the K-W-L strategy are the questions you raise in the "W" column. Those questions allow you to make associations while you are reading. If you ask a question the author does not answer somewhere in the reading, you will be unable to make an association. The most reliable way to create questions is by taking each of the headings and converting it into a question. Try using words like *who*, *what*, *when*, *where*, *why*, or *how*. Both the "K" and "W" column are completed as part of the pre-reading process. While reading, you will always read the question to yourself prior to reading the text beneath the heading.

The "L" column is completed in the post-read. After you have finished reading the chapter, you simply go back and answer each question in your *own words*. Remember; do not try to answer the questions as you think the author would answer them. Answer them how you would answer them now that you have read the chapter. This way you can be sure that you learned and retained the ideas the author was trying to convey in the text. If you find that you are unable to answer a question, you can go back and reread only that section and then try to answer that question again.

You can modify the K-W-L strategy if you need to by including one additional column. The column is called the "H" column and it stands for *how can you learn more about this topic if you want to or need to or how can I apply what I have learned*. For example, if you are going to write a research paper on the topic, thinking about how you might be able to find more information would be useful to you. However, in the case of readings in science, you may have to use what you have learned in a demonstration or experiment, in which case considering how to practice what you have learned may be important. In either case, the "H" column is a post-reading activity.

M.U.R.D.E.R.

Although you may want to become violent with your textbook from time to time, this acronym is not to be associated with violence but rather as a study system for textbook learning. M.U.R.D.E.R. stands for *mood*, *understand*, *recall*, *digest*, *expand* and *review*. It is adapted from a study guide used at St. Thomas University.

Mood. Setting your mood to study is too often underemphasized. A positive frame of mind prior to sitting down and reading your textbook is important. If you look at the reading as drudgery or something that you will ultimately fail at, it is likely that you will do just that. Look at every new reading assignment as an opportunity to become better in some way or as meeting another challenge in the pursuit of your college degree. If something is bothering you that may prevent you from establishing a positive attitude, perhaps you should put off the reading until you have reconciled whatever is troubling you. Decide what environment creates the least amount of anxiety for you and then read there. It doesn't have to be quiet; music does not have to be a distraction, it can sometime enhance the environment. Be physically comfortable, but reading in bed before you normally go to sleep may not be the best time to read a textbook.

Understand. Use a highlighter to identify any information in the reading that you find difficult to understand. You can either come back and reread that section later or ask your instructor to help explain the idea in a different way.

Recall. After you have completed the reading, write a summary of the chapter being sure to use your own words. Again, it is important to summarize your thoughts as they relate to the reading and not simply those of the author. Be sure to include in your summary the topic, the points the author made about the topic, and the major support for those points.

Digest. After you have written your summary, go back and reread any print you highlighted. Often after you have read the entire chapter something that seemed difficult to understand early in the chapter is more easily understood now that you have finished the chapter. If after rereading, the information remains unclear, perhaps you can e-mail your instructor and ask for clarification. In addition, you may also be able to locate the e-links to websites in the chapter and visit those sites for more information.

Expand. This is the key step in this strategy. Here you formulate three kinds of questions:

1. If I could speak to the author, what questions would I ask or what criticism would I offer?
2. How could I apply this material to what I am interested in?
3. How could I make this information interesting and understandable to other students?

If you are able to develop complete answers to these questions or similar questions, you have gone beyond the print and have begun to personalize the new information you have now acquired. Once it becomes **yours**, now it is part of your **prior knowledge** that can be triggered again and again to help you prepare to read and learn more from additional chapters in this textbook or others.

Review. Think about what strategies helped you understand and/or retain information in the past and apply these to your current studies

P.L.A.N.

This study-reading strategy consists of four steps that students use before, during, and after reading. It was developed for college students by reading faculty at Southwest Texas State University in 1992.

Predict. Using different typographical elements of the printed text titles, headings, subheadings, graphic illustrations, marginal annotations, and boldface type, try to predict or forecast what you think the content and structure of the chapter will be before you begin to read. It is best to graphically illustrate these predictions in a map.

Locate. Now that you have predicted what you believe the content of the chapter will be, you need to assess (activate) your prior knowledge. In this assessment, you are trying to determine the "gaps" between what you already know and what you think the author is going to try to explain. This will allow you to make a key decision about reading the chapter which will ultimately affect your reading rate. That question is, what does your comprehension level need to be for this chapter? Or to put it another way, how closely do I need to read this material?

Add. Following the reading, return to your map and, using metacomprehension, briefly explain the new concepts in your own words or confirm or extend the existing concepts that you had before you read.

Note. At this stage you can choose what you want to do with the new information. You can reproduce the map from memory, reorganize the information perhaps in an outline, or summarize the information in paragraph form.

PLAN-DO-REVIEW

Plan-Do-Review Cycle

Plan to Read

- Preview the selection
- Clarify your specific purpose for reading
- Activate prior knowledge
- Estimate how difficult the material is for you

Do the Reading

- Monitor your comprehension as you read
- Restate ideas in your own words
- Compare what you are reading to what you know
- Answer questions

If you don't understand, stop and clarify

- Define unfamiliar words
- Review graphics

- Read surrounding paragraphs
- Seek help

Review What You Read

- Answer questions
- Determine what else you need to know and repeat the cycle if necessary
- Test yourself
- Participate in a study group
- Consolidate and integrate information

P.O.R.P.E.

This strategy is an approach to studying textbook materials in which you create and answer essay questions. It can be a time-consuming process, but it is an excellent tool for preparing for essay exams. It can be broken down into five steps. To some extent the success of this strategy relies on the grading scheme of the instructor. *Since grading essay questions is somewhat subjective, it is recommended that before using this strategy, consult with your teacher.*

The goals for using P.O.R.P.E. are to:

- Organize key concepts of chapters
- Predict possible test questions
- Determine how well you really understand the concepts addressed in the chapter

Step 1. Plan. You must have read the chapter, predicted which concepts are the most important and most likely to be included in test questions, and finally have identified sources including:

- Instructor's syllabus
- Chapter questions or study guides
- Chapter headings or boldface/italicized print
- Ideas stressed in the instructor's lectures

Step 2. Organize. Organize information in such a way that you can generate questions and answers. Maps, review sheets, and charts are just some of the ways you may want to organize this information. Be sure you:

- Predict enough questions
- Focus on large important issues
- Relate detailed information to the larger more general concepts
- Outline the information in the order that you think you will present it

Step 3. Rehearse.

- Commit to memory the organization of answers to each of your predicted questions
- Verbalize your answers out loud
- Write your answers out on paper
- Repeat this process until you are confident you can complete this under the pressure of the actual exam

Step 4. Practice. From long-term memory, practice answering questions under simulated exam conditions including:

- time of day the exam will be taken
- the length of time that will be allotted to the exam or perhaps each question

Step 5. Evaluate. Evaluate your own work by asking the following questions:

- Do I have enough concrete examples?
- Are my answers complete, accurate, and appropriate?
- Is there anything I should study (going back to step #3) before taking the exam?

Q.A.R.

Q.A.R. is a reading strategy developed by Raphael and Pearson in 1985. With this strategy your teacher will create comprehension questions according to where the information needed to answer each question is located.

- Text explicit
- Text implicit
- Information based entirely on your prior knowledge

After you have read and answered each question, you will indicate whether the information required for answering the question is textually explicit information, textually implicit information, or information entirely from your own background knowledge.

Q.A.R. will help you to:

- Monitor your comprehension of the text in the chapter
- Provide yourself a purpose for your reading
- Allow you to assess your comprehension level
- Help you to elaborate on and critically think about the author's ideas
- Help you see the important role your prior knowledge plays in your ability to bring meaning to textbook print

Using Q.A.R.

- Select your textbook chapter.
- Before you begin reading, ask your instructor to create 2–3 of these questions for you in each category without revealing the categories.
- After you have finished reading, answer the questions in your own words and categorize them according to where the information used to answer the question came from.

SEMANTIC WEB

The Semantic Web, sometimes referred to as mapping, is particularly useful when you are asked to read expository text that is not highly organized. In other words, there are few or no headings or subheadings from which you can make questions as in the K-W-L strategy. You may remember the K-W-L facilitates comprehension by using questions to help the reader make associations while reading. The Semantic Web uses the reader's ability to predict to make associations during reading. The reader's ability to predict is heavily influenced by prior knowledge.

The Semantic Web is a graphic illustration of the reader's prior knowledge about the topic **before** reading. Your prior knowledge can be activated by a series of trigger words. Those trigger words can be found in the *Foreword* or *Introduction* to the reading. Normally three to four trigger words are adequate. You should choose them with care because they must actually trigger what you know. If you choose a word that does not activate any prior knowledge, it serves no purpose. Do not choose unfamiliar terms.

As you are brainstorming, cluster your ideas around the trigger word. Once you have activated all of your prior knowledge relative to each trigger word, and then make a prediction about what the topic is and what the author might say about the topic. Now you are ready to read. An example of what your map might look like is found on the next page.

As a post-reading activity, you should revisit your map beginning with your prediction. Undoubtedly, you will have to modify some. Do so and then ask yourself, what supporting examples, reasons, or facts do I remember that support this idea? Add those to your map. Upon completion, you should have a graphic organizer that effectively illustrates what information you assimilated and what accommodation for new information you made.

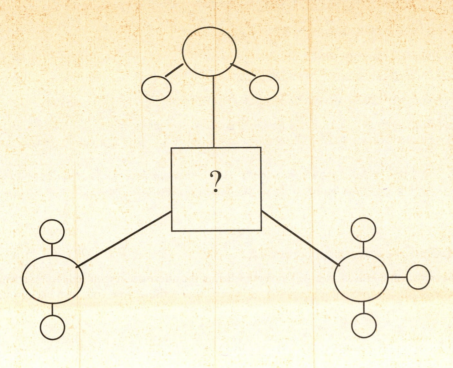

S. Q. 3. R.

Created by Francis P. Robinson in 1941, the S.Q.3.R. method of study is one of the most common and easily adaptable study techniques for college students. You can follow all steps as written, or modify them to best fit your learning styles. It has also been modified for mathematics.

There are five components to this strategy:

1. Survey
2. Question
3. Read
4. Recite
5. Review

Survey. Gather the information necessary to set expectations as to what you will learn and to utilize all the typographical tools which may be available.

- Read the title—and start to consider the topic of the chapter.
- Read the introduction and/or summary—focusing on the most important points the author seems to be making about the topic.
- Notice each boldface heading and subheading—think about the information following each heading and sub-heading and how it relates to the topic. Try to create a mental structure in your mind for the topic.
- Notice any graphics—charts, maps, diagrams, etc. are there to make a point—study them before you read so you do not have to interrupt your reading of the chapter. Go back to them after you have completed the reading and be sure you understand the data represented.
- Notice reading aids—italics, bold face print, chapter objective, end-of-chapter questions—all of these are aids to comprehension that are included by design from the author or publisher of the textbook.

Question. Help yourself make associations as you read.

One section at a time, turn the boldface heading into as many questions as you think will be answered in that section. Use words like *who, what, when, where, why, how* and *which*. Be sure to ask questions that you are confident the author will answer. If the author does not answer the question, change the question.

Read. Fortify the mental structure you initiated in the "Survey" with supporting information in the text.

Read each section (one at a time) after reading the question back to yourself. Look for the answers; if you need to back up, do so.

Recite. Answer your questions in your own words.

After each section, stop, recall your questions, and see if you can answer them from memory. If not, look back again (as often as necessary) but don't go on to the next section until you can answer the questions.

Review. Determine what you still don't know and continue building that information into your memory.

Once you've finished the entire chapter using the preceding steps, go back over all the questions from all the headings. In this step, focus on what you have not yet learned. Do not spend time going over the material that you feel confident you know.

S. Q. Study the Problems 3. R. (Modified for Math)

The traditional S.Q.3.R. system was recently modified for math applications by Patty Self and Taryn Emmerich at Florida International University.

There are 6 components:

1. Survey
2. Question
3. Study the Problems
4. Read
5. Recite
6. Review

Survey. Preview what the chapter is about by:

*   Reading the introduction and conclusion
*   Reading questions provided by the author
*   Looking at the problems at the end of the chapter
*   Identifying and looking up any new terms or theorems
*   Reviewing any learned formulas or equations you may need to know

Question. After you have previewed the chapter, and using what you have already learned in class, develop some questions on new material you may be confused about or a problem–solution you are curious about. Try to formulate one or two questions for each section of the chapter that you are confident will be addressed by the author in the text of that section.

Read. Read to answer the questions that you formulated during the previous phase. Write down the answers to the questions. Make notes and marginal annotations on supplemental information that relates to the answers to your questions.

Study the Problems.

*   Look back at the problems presented in the text
*   Analyze it by putting abstract formulas in your own words
*   Ask yourself these three questions
    o   What concepts, formulas, and rules were applied?
    o   What methods were used to solve the problems? Why was that method used?
    o   What was the first step? Second step? And so on . . .
    o   Have any steps been combined?
    o   What differences and similarities are there between the examples in the textbook and the homework assignment?
*   Draw diagrams and labels as necessary

Recite.

*   Go over what you have just done and try to verbalize
*   Putting the problem solving into your own words will help you remember what to do on different problems
*   Focus on the process, not specifically the answer

- Ask yourself these questions
  - o What concepts, formulas, and rules did I apply to solve the problem?
  - o What methods did I use?
  - o How did I begin? Walk yourself through the problem out loud.
  - o Can I do this problem another way? Can I simplify it?
  - o Does this problem compare with others from class or homework?
- Talk out the problems, then write down your explanations in your notes.

Review. After a period of one or two days:
- Look back over your chapter and your notes
- Recite again how you solved each problem
- Review the vocabulary terms, symbols, and formulas
- List and study the concepts and formulas that are most important from the chapter

You may need to review multiple times before your next class or test. This step should be the easiest because you were actively learning the material along the way.

Peter the Great (r. 1682–1725), seeking to make Russia a military power, reorganized the country's political and economic structures. His reign saw Russia enter fully into European power politics. The Apotheosis of Tsar Peter the Great 1672–1725 by unknown artist, 1710. Historical Museum, Moscow, Russia/E.T. Archive

CHAPTER 15

SUCCESSFUL AND UNSUCCESSFUL PATHS TO POWER (1686–1740)

*T*HE LATE SEVENTEENTH AND EARLY *eighteenth centuries witnessed significant shifts of power and influence among the states of Europe. Nations that had been strong lost their status as significant military and economic units. Other countries that in some cases had figured only marginally in international relations came to the fore. Great Britain, France, Austria, Russia, and Prussia emerged during this period as the powers that would dominate Europe until at least World War I. Their political and economic dominance occurred at the expense of Spain, the United Netherlands, Poland, Sweden, and the Ottoman Empire. Equally essential to their rise was the weakness of the Holy Roman Empire after the Treaty of Westphalia (1648), which ended the Thirty Years' War.*

The successful competitors for international power were those states that created strong central political authorities. Farsighted observers in the late seventeenth century already understood that in the future those domains that would become or remain great powers must imitate the political and military organization of Louis XIV's France. Strong monarchy alone could impose unity of purpose on the state. The turmoil of seventeenth-century civil wars and aristocratic revolts had impressed people with the value of a firm centralized monarch as the guarantor of minimum domestic tranquility.

Imitation of French absolutism involved more than belief in a strong centralized monarchy; it usually also required building a standing army, organizing an efficient tax structure to support the army, and establishing a bureaucracy to collect the taxes. Moreover, the political classes of the country—especially the nobles— had to be converted to a sense of duty and loyalty to the central government that was more intense than their loyalty to other competing political and social institutions.

The waning powers were those that failed to achieve such effective organization. They were unable to employ their political, economic, and human resources to resist external aggression or to overcome the forces of domestic dissolution. Internal and external failures were closely related. If a state did not maintain or establish a central political authority with sufficient power over the nobility, the cities, the guilds, and the church, it could not raise a strong army to defend its borders or its economic interests. More often than not, the key element leading to success or failure was the character, personality, and energy of the monarch.

The Maritime Powers

Central and Eastern Europe and the Ottoman Empire

Russia Enters the European Political Arena

In Perspective

481

KEY TOPICS

- The Dutch Golden Age
- French aristocratic resistance to the monarchy
- Early-eighteenth-century British political stability
- Power and decline of the Ottoman Empire
- The efforts of the Habsburgs to secure their holdings
- The emergence of Prussia as a major power under the Hohenzollerns
- The efforts of Peter the Great to transform Russia into a powerful centralized nation along Western lines

The Maritime Powers

In western Europe, Britain and France emerged as the dominant powers. This development represented a shift of influence away from Spain and the United Netherlands. Both of the latter countries had been powerful and important during the sixteenth and seventeenth centuries, but they became politically and militarily marginal during the eighteenth century. Neither, however, disappeared from the map, and both retained considerable economic vitality and influence. Spanish power declined after the War of the Spanish Succession. (See Chapter 13.) The case of the Netherlands was more complicated.

THE NETHERLANDS: GOLDEN AGE TO DECLINE

The seven provinces that became the United Provinces of the Netherlands were the single genuinely new state to appear on the European scene during the early modern period. They emerged as a nation after revolting against Spain in 1572. Spain acknowledged their autonomy only in a truce in 1609, though other European powers had recognized Dutch independence in the 1580s. The Netherlands won formal independence from Spain in the Treaty of Westphalia (1648). These eighty years of on-again, off-again warfare forged much of the national identity of the Netherlands. During the middle of the seventeenth century, the Dutch fought a series of naval wars with England. Then, in 1672, the armies of Louis XIV invaded the Netherlands. William III, the *stadtholder* of Holland, the most important of the United Provinces, rallied the Dutch and eventually led the entire European coalition against France. As a part of that strategy, he answered the invitation of Protestant English aristocrats in 1688 to assume, along with his wife Mary who was the daughter of King James II, the English throne. (See Chapter 13.)

During both the seventeenth and eighteenth centuries, the political and economic life of the Netherlands differed from that of the rest of Europe. The other major nations pursued paths toward strong central government, generally under monarchies, as with France, or in the case of England, under a strong parliamentary system. By contrast, the Netherlands was formally a republic. Each of the provinces retained considerable authority, and the central government, embodied in the States General that met in the Hague, exercised its authority through a kind of ongoing negotiation with the provinces. Prosperous and populous Holland dominated the States General. The Dutch deeply distrusted monarchy and the ambitions of the House of Orange. Nonetheless, when confronted with major military challenges, the Dutch would permit the House of Orange and, most notably, William III to assume dominant leadership. These political arrangements proved highly resilient and allowed the republic to establish itself permanently in the European state system during the seventeenth century. When William died in 1702 and the wars with France ended in 1714, the Dutch reverted to their republican structures.

Although the provinces making up the Netherlands were traditionally identified with the Protestant cause in Europe during their revolt against Spain and the wars against Louis XIV, extensive toleration marked Dutch religious life. The Calvinist Reformed Church was the official church of the nation, and most of the political elite belonged to it, but it was not an established church. There were always a significant number of Roman Catholics and Protestants living in the Netherlands who did not belong to the Reformed Church. The country also became a haven for Jews driven out of other lands, particularly those who had been expelled from Spain. Consequently, while other European states attempted to impose a single religion on their people or tore themselves apart in religious conflict, in the Netherlands peoples of differing religious faiths lived together peacefully.

Urban Prosperity   Beyond the climate of religious toleration, what most amazed seventeenth-century contemporaries about the Dutch Republic was its economic prosperity. While the rest of Europe fought over religion, the Dutch attained a high standard of living. Their remarkable economic achievement was built on the foundations of urbanization, transformed agriculture, extensive trade and finance, and an overseas commercial empire. (See "Art & the West: Rachel Ruyseh, *Flower Still Life*," p. 510.)

In the Netherlands, more people lived in cities than in any other area of Europe. By 1675, in Holland, the province where Amsterdam was located, at least 60 percent of the population were urban dwellers. Not until after the onset of industrialization in the late eighteenth century would such urbanization occur elsewhere, and then notably in England. Trade, manufacture, shipbuilding, and finance were the engine of Dutch urban prosperity.

This urban concentration had been made possible by key transformations in Dutch farming that served as the model for the rest of Europe. During the seventeenth century, the Dutch drained and reclaimed much land from the sea. The Dutch were able to use this reclaimed terrain for highly profitable farming because their shipping interests dominated the Baltic trade, which provided them with a steady supply of grain. The availability of this cheap grain meant that Dutch farmers could use their land to produce more profitable dairy products and beef. Dutch farmers also diversified into the cultivation of cash products such as tulip bulbs. So successful was tulip cultivation, that for a few years in the late 1630s, market speculation led to the sale of tulip bulbs at astounding prices.

The Baltic grain trade was just one example of the Dutch acting as the chief trading nation of Europe. Their fishermen dominated the market for herring and supplied much of the Continent's dried fish. The Dutch also supplied textiles to many parts of Europe. Dutch ships appeared in harbors all over the Continent, with their captains purchasing goods that they then transported and resold at a profit to other nations. Or such goods might be returned to the Netherlands, stored, and then sold later at more advantageous prices. Many of the handsome merchant houses lining the canals of Amsterdam had storage facilities on their upper floors. The overseas trades also supported a vast domestic industry of shipbuilding and ship supplies.

All of this trade, commerce, and manufacturing was supported by the most advanced financial system of the day. Capital could be more easily raised in Amsterdam than anyplace else in the seventeenth century. Shares traded easily and often speculatively in the Amsterdam bourse. Dutch capital financed economic life outside its own borders.

The final foundation of Dutch prosperity was the Dutch seaborne empire. During the late sixteenth and early seventeenth centuries, Dutch traders established a major presence in East Asia, particularly in spice-producing areas of Java, the Moluccas, and

In the mid–eighteenth century, when this picture of the Amsterdam Exchange was painted, Amsterdam had replaced the cities of Italy and south Germany as the leading banking center of Europe. Amsterdam retained this position until the late eighteenth century. Painting by Hiob A. Berckheyde, *The Amsterdam Exchange.* Canvas 85 × 105 cm. Coll. Museum Boijmans Van Beuningen, Rotterdam, The Netherlands, Inv. no. 1043

Sri Lanka. The vehicle for this penetration was the Dutch East Indies Company (chartered in 1602), shares of which traded on the Amsterdam bourse. The Dutch East Indies Company eventually displaced Portuguese dominance in the spice trade of East Asia and for many years prevented English traders from establishing a major presence there. Initially, the Dutch had only wanted commercial dominance of the spice trade, but in time, that goal led them to move toward producing the spices themselves, which required them to control many of the islands that today constitute Indonesia. The Netherlands remained the colonial master of this region until after World War II.

Economic Decline The decline in political influence of the United Provinces of the Netherlands occurred within the eighteenth century. After the death of William III of Britain in 1702, the various local provinces prevented the emergence of another strong *stadtholder.* Unified political leadership therefore vanished. During the earlier long wars with Louis XIV and Britain, naval supremacy had slowly but steadily passed to the British. The fishing industry declined, and the Dutch lost their technological superiority in shipbuilding. Countries between which Dutch ships had once carried goods now traded directly with each other. For example, the British began to use their own vessels in the Baltic traffic with Russia.

Similar stagnation overtook the Dutch domestic industries, such as textile finishing, papermaking, and glassblowing. The disunity of the provinces and the absence of vigorous leadership hastened this economic decline and prevented action that might have slowed or halted it.

What saved the United Provinces from becoming completely insignificant in European affairs was their continued financial dominance. Well past the middle of the eighteenth century, their banks continued to finance European trade. Moreover, the Amsterdam bourse remained an important financial institution because, as we see later in this chapter, both France and England experienced disastrously excessive and politically disruptive stock speculations in the early eighteenth century, which made them fearful to invest in shares.

FRANCE AFTER LOUIS XIV

Despite its military reverses in the War of the Spanish Succession, France remained a great power. It was less strong in 1715 than in 1680, but it still possessed the largest European population, an advanced, if troubled, economy, and the administrative structure bequeathed it by Louis XIV. Moreover, even if France and its resources had been drained by the last of Louis's wars, the other major states of Europe were similarly debilitated. What France required was economic recovery and consolidation, wiser political leadership, and a less ambitious foreign policy. It did enjoy a period of recovery, but its leadership was at best indifferent. Louis XIV was succeeded by his five-year-old

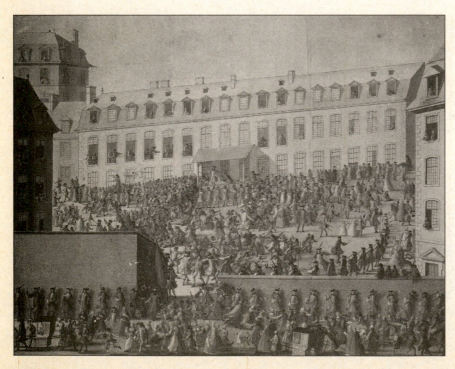

The impending collapse of John Law's bank triggered a financial panic throughout France. Desperate investors, such as those shown here in the city of Rennes, sought to exchange their paper currency for gold and silver before the banks' supply of precious metals was exhausted.
Collection Musée de Bretagne, Rennes

great-grandson Louis XV (r. 1715–1774). The young boy's uncle, the duke of Orléans, became regent and remained so until his death in 1720. The regency, marked by financial and moral scandals, further undermined the faltering prestige of the monarchy.

John Law and the Mississippi Bubble The duke of Orléans was a gambler, and for a time he turned over the financial management of the kingdom to John Law (1671–1729), a Scottish mathematician and fellow gambler. Law believed an increase in the paper-money supply would stimulate France's economic recovery. With the permission of the regent, he established a bank in Paris that issued paper money. Law then organized a monopoly, called the Mississippi Company, on trading privileges with the French colony of Louisiana in North America.

The Mississippi Company also took over the management of the French national debt. The company issued shares of its own stock in exchange for government bonds, which had fallen sharply in value. To redeem large quantities of bonds, Law encouraged speculation in Mississippi Company stock. In 1719, the price of the stock rose handsomely. Smart investors, however, took their profits by selling their stock in exchange for paper money from Law's bank, which they then sought to exchange for gold. The bank, however, lacked enough gold to redeem all the paper money brought to it.

In February 1720, all gold payments were halted in France. Soon thereafter, Law himself fled the country. The Mississippi Bubble, as the affair was called, had burst. The fiasco brought disgrace on the government that had sponsored Law. The Mississippi Company was later reorganized and functioned profitably, but fear of paper money and speculation marked French economic life for decades.

Renewed Authority of the *Parlements* The duke of Orléans made a second decision that also lessened the power of the monarchy: He attempted to draw the French nobility once again into the decision-making processes of the government. Louis XIV had filled his ministries and bureaucracies with persons from non-noble families. The regent, under pressure from the nobility, tried to restore a balance. He set up a system of councils on which nobles were to serve along with bureaucrats. The years of idle noble domestication at Versailles, however, had worked too well, and the nobility seemed to

Cardinal Fleury (1653–1743) was the tutor and chief minister of Louis XV from 1726 to 1743. Fleury gave France a period of peace and prosperity, but was unable to solve the state's long-term financial problems. This portrait is by Hyacinthe Rigaud. © Réunion des Musées Nationaux/Art Resource, N.Y.

lack both the talent and the desire to govern. The experiment failed.

Despite this failure, the great French nobles did not surrender their ancient ambition to assert their rights, privileges, and local influence over those of the monarchy. The chief feature of eighteenth-century French political life was the attempt of the nobility to use its authority to limit the power of the monarchy. The most effective instrument in this process was the *parlements*, or courts dominated by the nobility.

The French *parlements* were different from the English Parliament. These French courts, the most important of which was the *Parlement* of Paris, could not legislate. Rather, they had the power to recognize or not to recognize the legality of an act or law promulgated by the monarch. By long tradition, their formal approval had been required to make a royal law valid. Louis XIV had often restricted stubborn, uncooperative *parlements*. In another major political blunder, however, the duke of Orléans had formally approved the full reinstitution of the *parlements'* power to allow or disallow laws. Thereafter, the growing financial and moral weakness of the monarchy allowed these aristocratic judicial institutions to reassert their authority. This situation meant that until the revolution in 1789 the *parlements* became natural centers for aristocratic resistance to royal authority.

Administration of Cardinal Fleury   In 1726, Cardinal Fleury (1653–1743) became the chief minister of the French court. He was the last of the great clerics who loyally and effectively served the French monarchy. Like his seventeenth-century predecessors, the cardinals Richelieu and Mazarin, Fleury was a realist. He understood the political ambition and incapacity of the nobility and worked quietly to block their undue influence. He was also aware of the precarious financial situation of the royal treasury. The cardinal, who was seventy-three years old when he came to office, was determined to give the country a period of peace. He surrounded himself with able assistants who tried

Under Louis XV (r. 1715–1774) France suffered major defeats in Europe and around the world and lost most of its North American empire. Louis himself was an ineffective ruler, and during his reign, the monarchy encountered numerous challenges from the French aristocracy.   Corbis

to solve France's financial problems. Part of the national debt was repudiated. New industries enjoying special privileges were established and roads and bridges built. On the whole, the nation prospered, but Fleury could never draw sufficient tax revenues from the nobles or the church to put the state on a stable financial footing.

Fleury died in 1743, having unsuccessfully attempted to prevent France from intervening in the war that was then raging between Austria and Prussia. The cost of this intervention was to undo all his financial pruning and planning.

Another failure must also be attributed to this elderly cleric. Despite his best efforts, he had not trained Louis XV to become an effective monarch. Louis XV possessed most of the vices and almost none of the virtues of his great-grandfather Louis XIV. He wanted to hold on to absolute power, but was unwilling to work the long hours required. He did not choose many wise advisers after Fleury. He was tossed about by the gossip and intrigues of the court. His personal life was scandalous. Louis XV was not an evil person, but a mediocre one. And in a monarch, mediocrity was unfortunately often a greater fault than vice. Consequently, it was not a lack of resources or military strength that plagued France, but the absence of political leadership to organize, direct, and inspire its people.

GREAT BRITAIN: THE AGE OF WALPOLE

In 1713, Britain had emerged as a victor over Louis XIV, but the nation required a period of recovery. As an institution, the British monarchy was not in the degraded state of the French monarchy, yet its stability was not certain.

The Hanoverian Dynasty   In 1714, the Hanoverian dynasty, as designated by the Act of Settlement (1701), came to the throne. Almost immediately, George I (r. 1714–1727) faced a challenge to his new title. The Stuart pretender James Edward (1688–1766), the son of James II, landed in Scotland in December 1715. His forces marched southward, but met defeat less than two months later. Although militarily successful against the pretender, the new dynasty and its supporters saw the need for consolidation.

Whigs and Tories   During the seventeenth century, England had been one of the most politically restive countries in Europe. The closing years of

Queen Anne's reign (1702–1714) had seen sharp clashes between the political factions of Whigs and Tories over whether to end the war with France. The Tories had urged a rapid peace settlement and after 1710 had opened negotiations with France. During the same period, the Whigs were seeking favor from the elector of Hanover, the future George I, who would soon be their monarch. His concern for French threats to his domains in Hanover made him unsympathetic to the Tory peace policy. In the final months of Anne's reign, some Tories, fearing they would lose power under the waiting Hanoverian dynasty, opened channels of communication with the Stuart pretender; a few even rallied to his cause.

Under these circumstances, George I, on his arrival in Britain, clearly favored the Whigs. Previously, the differences between the Whigs and the Tories had been vaguely related to principle. The Tories emphasized a strong monarchy, low taxes for landowners, and firm support of the Anglican church. The Whigs supported monarchy, but wanted Parliament to retain final sovereignty. They favored urban commercial interests as well as the prosperity of the landowners. They encouraged a policy of religious toleration toward the Protestant nonconformists in England. Socially, both groups supported the status quo.

Neither group was organized like a modern political party. Outside Parliament, each party consisted of political networks based on local connections and economic influence. Each group acknowledged a few national spokesmen, who articulated positions and principles. After the Hanoverian accession and the eventual Whig success in achieving the firm confidence of George I, the chief difference between the Whigs and the Tories for almost forty years was that one group had access to public office and patronage and the other did not. This early Hanoverian proscription of Tories from public life was one of the most prominent features of the age.

The Leadership of Robert Walpole   The political situation after 1715 remained in flux, until Robert Walpole (1676–1745) took over the helm of government. Though previously active in the House of Commons since the reign of Queen Anne and a cabinet minister, what gave Walpole special prominence under the new dynasty was a British financial scandal similar to the French Mississippi Bubble.

Management of the British national debt had been assigned to the South Sea Company, which exchanged government bonds for company stock. As in the French case, the price of the stock soared, only to crash in 1720 when prudent investors sold their holdings and took their speculative profits. Parliament intervened and, under Walpole's leadership, adopted measures to honor the national debt. To most contemporaries, Walpole had saved the financial integrity of the country and had thus proved himself a person of immense administrative capacity and political ability.

George I gave Walpole his full confidence. For this reason, Walpole has often been regarded as the first prime minister of Great Britain and the originator of the cabinet system of government. Walpole generally demanded that all the ministers in the cabinet agree on policy, but he could not prevent frequent public differences among them. Unlike a modern English prime minister, he was not chosen by the majority of the House of Commons. The real sources of his power were the personal support of the king, first George I and later George II (r. 1727–1760), his ability to handle the House of Commons, and his ironfisted control of government patronage, which bought support for himself and his policies from people who wanted jobs, appointments, favors, and government contracts. Such corruption supplied the glue of political loyalty.

Walpole's favorite slogan was *Quieta non movere* (roughly, "Let sleeping dogs lie"). To that end, he pursued peace abroad and supported the status quo at home. In this regard he much resembled Cardinal Fleury.

The Structure of Parliament   The structure of the eighteenth-century British House of Commons aided Walpole in his pacific policies. It was neither a democratic nor a representative body. Each of the counties into which Britain was divided elected two members. (See "Lady Mary Wortley Montagu Advises Her Husband on Election to Parliament.") But if the more powerful landed families in a county agreed on the candidates, there was no contest. Most members, however, were elected from a variety of units called *boroughs*. A few boroughs were large enough for elections to be relatively democratic, but most had few electors. For example, a local municipal corporation or council of only a dozen members might have the right to elect a member of Parliament. In Old Sarum, one of the most famous corrupt, or "rotten," boroughs, the Pitt family simply bought up those pieces of property to which a vote was attached and thus in effect owned a seat in the House of Commons. Through proper electoral management, which involved favors to the electors, the House of Commons could be controlled.

Sir Robert Walpole (1676–1745), far left, is shown talking with the Speaker of the House of Commons. Walpole, who dominated British political life from 1721 to 1742, is considered the first prime minister of Britain.   Mansell/Time Pix

The structure of Parliament and the manner in which the House of Commons was elected meant the owners of property, especially wealthy nobles, dominated the government of England. They did not pretend to represent people and districts or to be responsive to what would later be called public opinion. They regarded themselves as representing various economic and social interests, such as the West Indian interest, the merchant interest, and the landed interest. These owners of property were suspicious of an administrative bureaucracy controlled by the crown or its ministers. To diminish royal influence, they or their agents served as local government administrators, judges, militia commanders, and tax collectors. In this sense, the British nobility and large landowners actually did govern the nation. And because they regarded the Parliament as the political sovereign, there was no absence of central political authority and direction. Consequently, the supremacy of Parliament gave Britain the unity that strong central monarchy provided elsewhere in Europe.

These parliamentary structures also helped strengthen the financial position of the British government, which, under William III, had learned much about government finance from Dutch practices. The British monarch could not raise taxes the way his continental counterparts could, but the British government consisting of the monarch and Parliament could and did raise vast sums of tax revenue and loans to wage war throughout the eighteenth century. All Britons paid taxes; there were virtually no exemptions. The British credit market was secure through the regulation of the Bank of England, founded in 1693. This strong system of finance and tax collection was one of the cornerstones of eighteenth-century British power.

Freedom of Political Life   British political life was genuinely more free than that on the Continent. There were real limits on the power of Robert Walpole. Parliament could not wholly ignore popular

LADY MARY WORTLEY MONTAGU ADVISES HER HUSBAND ON ELECTION TO PARLIAMENT

In this letter of 1714, Lady Mary Wortley Montagu discussed with her husband the various paths that he might follow to gain election to the British House of Commons. Note her emphasis on knowing the right people and on having large amounts of money to spend on voters. Eventually, her husband was elected to Parliament in a borough that was controlled through government patronage.

■ *What are the various ways in which candidates and their supporters used money to campaign? What role did friendships play in the campaigning? How important do the political ideas or positions of the candidates seem to be? Women could not vote in eighteenth-century parliamentary elections. Was there some other influence they exerted?*

You seem not to have received my letters, or not to have understood them: you had been chose undoubtedly at York, if you had declared in time; but there is not any gentleman or tradesman disengaged at this time; they are treating every night. Lord Carlisle and the Thompsons have given their interest to Mr. Jenkins. I agree with you of the necessity of your standing this Parliament, which, perhaps, may be more considerable than any that are to follow it; but, as you proceed, 'tis my opinion, you will spend your money and not be chose. I believe there is hardly a borough unengaged. I expect every letter should tell me you are sure of some place; and, as far as I can perceive you are sure of none. As it has been managed, perhaps it will be the best way to deposit a certain sum in some friend's hands, and buy some little Cornish borough: it would, undoubtedly, look better to be chose for a considerable town; but I take it to be now too late. If you have any thoughts of Newark, it will be absolutely necessary for you to enquire after Lord Lexington's interest; and your best way to apply yourself to Lord Holdernesse, who is both a Whig and an honest man. He is now in town, and you may enquire of him if Brigadier Sutton stands there; and if not, try to engage him for you. Lord Lexington is so ill at the Bath, that it is a doubt if he will live 'till the elections; and if he dies, one of his heiresses, and the whole interest of his estate, will probably fall on Lord Holdernesse.

'Tis a surprize to me, that you cannot make sure of some borough, when a number of your friends bring in so many Parliament-men without trouble or expense. 'Tis too late to mention it now, but you might have applied to Lady Winchester, as Sir Joseph Jekyl did last year, and by her interest the Duke of Bolton brought him in for nothing; I am sure she would be more zealous to serve me, than Lady Jekyl.

From Lord Wharncliffe, ed., *Letters and Works of Lady Mary Wortley Montagu*, 3rd ed., Vol. 1 (London: 1861), p. 211.

political pressure. Even with the extensive use of patronage, many members of Parliament maintained independent views. Newspapers and public debate flourished. There was freedom of speech and association. There was no large standing army. Those Tories barred from political office and the Whig enemies of Walpole could and did openly oppose his policies—which would have been far more difficult on the Continent.

For example, in 1733, Walpole presented a scheme to the House of Commons to expand the scope of the excise tax, a tax that resembled a modern sales tax. The outcry in the press, on the public platforms, and in the streets was so great that he eventually withdrew the measure. What the British regarded as their traditional political rights raised a real and potent barrier to the power of the government. Again, in 1739, the public outcry over the alleged Spanish treatment of British merchants in the Caribbean pushed Britain into a war that Walpole opposed and deplored. He left office in 1742.

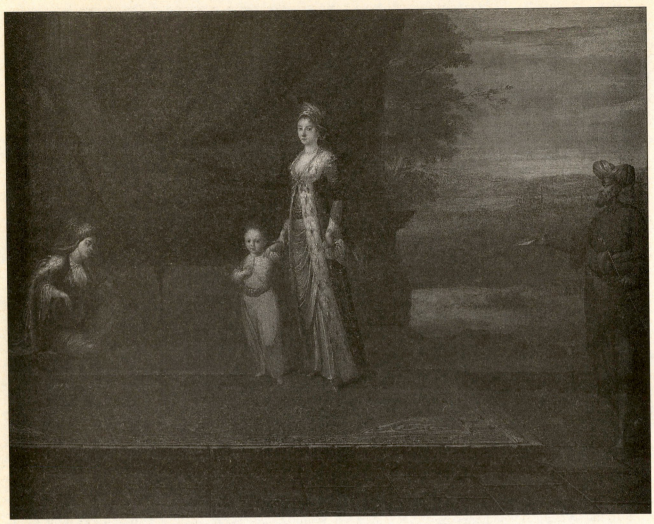

Lady Mary Wortley Montagu (1689–1762) was a famous writer of letters and an extremely well-traveled woman of the eighteenth century. As the document on p. 489 suggests, she was also a shrewd and tough-minded political adviser to her husband. By courtesy of the National Portrait Gallery, London

Central and Eastern Europe and the Ottoman Empire

The major factors in the shift of political influence among the maritime nations were naval strength, economic progress, foreign trade, and sound domestic administration. The conflicts among them occurred less in Europe than on the high seas and in their overseas empires. These nations existed in well-defined geographical areas with established borders. Their populations generally accepted the authority of the central government.

Central and eastern Europe were different. The entire region was economically much less advanced than western Europe. Except for the Baltic ports, the economy was agrarian. There were fewer cities and many more large estates populated by serfs. The states in this region did not possess overseas empires; nor did they engage in extensive overseas trade of any kind, except for the supply of grain to western Europe, grain more often than not carried on west European ships.

Changes in the power structure normally involved changes in borders or in the prince who ruled a particular area. Military conflicts took place at home rather than overseas. The political structure of this region, which lay largely east of the Elbe River, was very "soft." The almost constant warfare of the seventeenth century had led to a habit of temporary and shifting political loyalties. The princes and aristocracies of small states and principalities were unwilling to subordinate

This etching by Hogarth is the last of a series of four that satirizes the notoriously corrupt English electoral system. In the others, Hogarth shows the voters going to the polls after having been bribed and intoxicated with free gin. (Voting was then in public. The secret ballot was not introduced in England until 1872.) This fourth etching, Chairing the Member, *shows the triumphal procession of the victorious candidate, which is clearly turning into a brawl.*
William Hogarth, "Chairing the Member." Etching. Metropolitan Museum of Art, Harris Brisbane Dick Fund, 1932. 32.35 (214).

themselves to a central monarchical authority. Consequently, the political life of the region and the kind of state that emerged there were different from those of western Europe.

During the last half of the seventeenth century, the region of central and eastern Europe began to assume the political and social contours that would characterize it for the next two centuries. After the Peace of Westphalia, the Austrian Habsburgs recognized the basic weakness of the position of the Holy Roman Emperor and started to consolidate their power outside Germany. At the same time, Prussia emerged as a factor in North German politics and as a major challenger to Habsburg domination of Germany. Most important, Russia at the opening of the eighteenth century became a military and naval power of the first order. These three states (Austria, Prussia, and Russia) achieved their new status largely as a result of the political decay or military defeat of Sweden, Poland, and the Ottoman Empire.

SWEDEN: THE AMBITIONS OF CHARLES XII

Under Gustavus Adolphus II (r. 1611–1632), Sweden had played an important role as a Protestant combatant in the Thirty Years' War. During the rest of the seventeenth century, Sweden had consolidated its control of the Baltic, thus preventing Russian possession of a Baltic port and permitting Polish and German access to the sea only on Swedish terms. The Swedes also possessed one of the better armies in Europe. Sweden's economy, however, based primarily on the export of iron, was not strong enough to ensure continued political success.

In 1697, Charles XII (r. 1697–1718) came to the throne. He was headstrong, to say the least, and

France and Great Britain in the Early Eighteenth Century	
1713	Treaty of Utrecht ends the War of the Spanish Succession
1714	George I becomes king of Great Britain and establishes the Hanoverian dynasty
1715	Louis XV becomes king of France
1715–1720	Regency of the duke of Orléans in France
1720	Mississippi Bubble bursts in France and South Sea Bubble bursts in Great Britain
1720–1742	Robert Walpole dominates British politics
1726–1743	Cardinal Fleury serves as Louis XV's chief minister
1727	George II becomes king of Great Britain
1733	Excise-tax crisis in Britain

perhaps insane. In 1700, Russia began a drive to the west against Swedish territory. The Russian goal was a foothold on the Baltic. In the resulting Great Northern War (1700–1721), Charles XII led a vigorous and often brilliant campaign, but one that eventually resulted in the defeat of Sweden. In 1700, he defeated the Russians at the Battle of Narva, but then he turned south to invade Poland. The conflict dragged on, and the Russians were able to strengthen their forces.

In 1708, the Swedish monarch began a major invasion of Russia, but became bogged down in the harsh Russian winter. The next year, his army was decisively defeated at the Battle of Poltava. Thereafter, the Swedes could maintain only a holding action against their enemies. Charles himself sought refuge in Turkey and did not return to Sweden until 1714. He was killed under uncertain circumstances four years later while fighting the Danes in Norway.

The Great Northern War came to a close in 1721. Sweden had exhausted its military and economic resources and had lost its monopoly on the Baltic coast. Russia had conquered a large section of the eastern Baltic, and Prussia had gained a part of Pomerania. Internally, after the death of Charles XII, the Swedish nobles were determined to reassert their power over the monarchy. They did so, but then quarreled among themselves. Sweden played a very minor role in European affairs thereafter.

THE OTTOMAN EMPIRE

Now that it no longer exists, it is difficult to realize the enormous importance and geographical magnitude of the Ottoman Empire. Governing a remarkably diverse collection of peoples that ranged from Baghdad across the Arabian peninsula, Anatolia, the Balkan peninsula, and North Africa from Egypt to Algiers, the **Ottoman Empire** was the largest and most stable political entity to arise in or near Europe after the collapse of the Roman Empire. It had achieved this power between the eleventh and early sixteenth centuries as Ottoman tribes migrated eastward from the steppes of Asia. In 1453, they conquered Constantinople, thus putting an end to the Byzantine Empire. By the early seventeenth century only cities in China were larger than the Ottoman capital and only the emperors of China governed a larger area than the Ottoman sultan supported by his administrative bureaucracy and army.

The Ottoman Empire was the dominant political power in the Muslim world, after 1516 administering the holy cities of Mecca and Medina as well as Jerusalem, and arranging the safety of Muslim pilgrimages to Mecca. Yet its population was exceedingly diverse ethnically, linguistically, and religiously with significant numbers of Orthodox and Roman Catholic Christians and after the late fifteenth century many thousands of Jews from Spain. The Ottomans extended considerable religious toleration to their subjects, indeed far more toleration than existed anywhere in Europe. The Ottoman sultans governed their empire through units, called **millets**, of officially recognized religious communities. Various laws and regulations applied to the persons who belonged to a particular millet rather than to a particular administrative territory. Non-Islamic persons in the empire, known as *dhimmis*, or followers of religions tolerated by law, could practice their religion and manage their internal community affairs through their own religious officials, but were second-class citizens generally unable to rise in the service of the empire. *Dhimmis* paid a special poll tax (*jizyah*), could not serve in the military, and were prohibited from wearing certain colors. Their residences and places of worship could not be as large as those of Muslims. Over the years, however, they often attained economic success because they possessed the highest level of commercial skills in the empire. Because the Ottomans discouraged their various peoples from interacting with each other, the Islamic population rarely acquired these and other skills from their non-Islamic neighbors. Thus, for example, when the Ottomans negotiated with European powers, their Greek subjects almost invariably served as the interpreters.

The Ottoman dynasty also kept itself separated from the most powerful families of the empire by recruiting military leaders and administrative officers from groups whom the sultans believed would be personally loyal to them. For example, through a practice known as the *devshirme*, the Ottomans until the end of the seventeenth century recruited their most elite troops from Christian communities usually in the Balkans. Christian boys so recruited were raised as Muslims and organized into elite military units, the most famous of which were infantry troops called *Janissaries*. It was thought these troops would be extremely loyal to the sultan and the state because they owed their life and status to the sultan. As a result of this policy, entry into the elite military organizations and advancement in the administrative structures of the empire remained generally closed to the native Islamic population and most especially to members of the most elite Islamic families. Instead, in addition to the army, thousands of persons usually from the outer regions of the empire who were technically slaves of the sultan filled government posts and achieved major political influence and status. Thus in contrast to the situation in Europe, few people from the socially leading families in the empire gained military, administrative, or political experience in the central institutions of the empire, but remained primarily linked to local government in provincial cities. Paradoxically, many people in the Ottoman Empire believed it was better to be a favored slave than a free subject.

Again in contrast to the long-standing tension between church and state in Europe, Islamic religious authorities played a significant and enduring role in the political, legal, and administrative life of the Ottoman Empire. The dynasty saw itself as one of the chief protectors of Islamic law (*Shari'a*) and the Sunni traditions of the Islamic faith as well as its holy places. Islamic scholars, or *Ulama*, dominated not only Ottoman religious institutions but also schools and courts of law. There essentially existed a trade-off between Ottoman political and religious authorities. Through what was known as "the circle of equity," the sultan and his administrative officials would consult these Islamic scholars for advice with regard to how their policies and the behavior of their subjects accorded with Islamic law and the Qur'an. In turn, the Ulama would support the Ottoman state while the latter deferred to their judgments. This situation would prove a key factor in the fate of

the Ottoman Empire. From the late seventeenth century onward, the Ulama urged Ottoman rulers to conform to traditional life even as the empire confronted a rapidly changing and modernizing Europe. At the same time the Janissaries also resisted any changes that might undermine their own privileged status.

From the fifteenth century onward, the Ottoman Empire had tried to push further westward into Europe. Even after its naval defeat in 1571 at the Battle of Lepanto, the empire retained control of the eastern Mediterranean and the lands bordering it. Still determined to move toward the west, the Ottomans made their deepest military invasion into Europe in 1683, when they unsuccessfully besieged Vienna (see Map 15–1). Although that defeat proved to be decisive, many observers at the time thought it the result only of an overreach of power by the Ottomans rather than as a symptom of a deeper decline, which was actually the case.

Gradually, from the seventeenth century onward, the authority of the grand vizier, the major political figure after the sultan, began to grow. This development meant that more and more authority lay with the administrative and military bureaucracy. Rivalries for power among army leaders and nobles, as well as their flagrant efforts to enrich themselves, weakened the effectiveness of the government. About the same time local elites in the various provincial cities of the empire began to assert their own influence. They did not so much reject imperial authority as quietly renegotiate its

In 1683 the Ottomans laid siege to Vienna. Only the arrival of Polish forces under King John III Sobieski (r. 1674–1696) saved the Habsburg capital. © Bettmann/Corbis

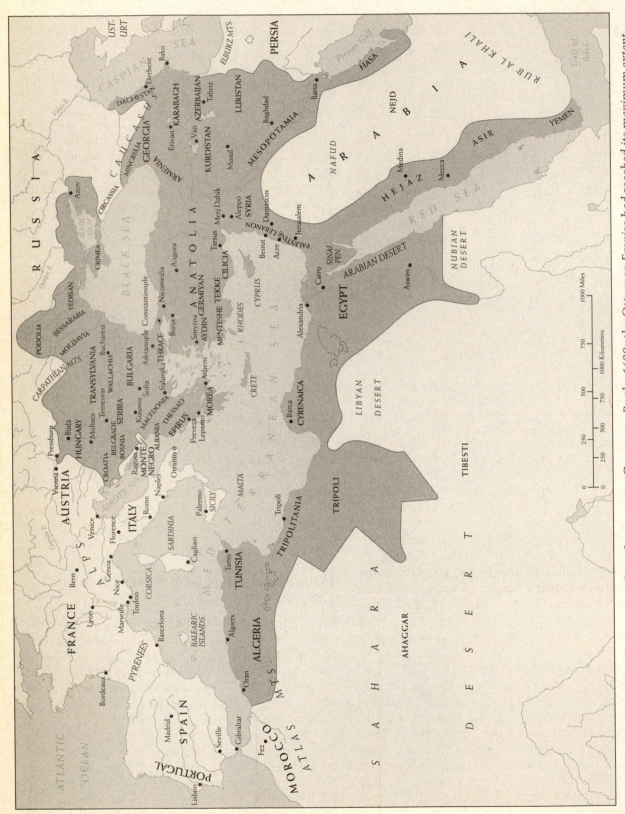

MAP 15–1 THE OTTOMAN EMPIRE IN THE LATE SEVENTEENTH CENTURY   By the 1680s the Ottoman Empire had reached its maximum extent, but the Ottoman failure to capture Vienna in 1683 marked the beginning of a long and inexorable decline that ended with the empire's collapse after World War I.

conditions. For example, in the outer European provinces, such as Transylvania, Wallachia, and Moldavia (all parts of modern Romania), the empire depended on the goodwill of local rulers, who paid tribute, but never submitted fully to imperial authority. The same was true in Egypt, Algeria, Tunisia, and elsewhere.

External factors also accounted for both the blocking of Ottoman expansion in the late seventeenth century and then its slow decline thereafter. During the European Middle Ages the Islamic world had far outdistanced Europe in learning, science, and military prowess. From the fifteenth century onward, however, Europeans had begun to make rapid advances in technology, wealth, and scientific knowledge. For example, they designed ships for the difficult waters of the Atlantic and thus eventually opened trade routes to the East around Africa and reached the American continents. As trade expanded, Europeans achieved new commercial skills, founded trading posts in South Asia, established the plantation economies and precious metal mines of the Americas, and became much wealthier. By the seventeenth century, Europeans, particularly the Dutch and Portuguese, imported directly from Asia or America commodities such as spices, sugar, and coffee that they had previously acquired through the Ottoman Empire. By sailing around the Cape of Good Hope in Africa, the Europeans literally circumnavigated the Middle East, which could not match the quantity of raw goods and commodities available in South Asia. During the same decades Europeans developed greater military and naval power and new weapons.

The Ottoman defeats at Lepanto and Vienna had occurred at the outer limits of their expansion. Then, however, during the 1690s, the Ottomans unsuccessfully fought a league of European states including Austria, Venice, Malta, Poland, and Tuscany joined by Russia, which, as we see later in this chapter, was emerging as a new aggressive power to the north. In early 1699, the defeated Ottomans negotiated the Treaty of Carlowitz, which required them to surrender significant territory lying not at the edges but at the very heart of their empire in Europe, including most of Hungary, to the Habsburgs, Poland, and Venice. This treaty meant not only the loss of territory but also of the revenue the Ottomans had long drawn from those regions. From this time onward, Russia and the Ottomans would duel for control of regions around the Black Sea with Russia achieving ever greater success by the close of the eighteenth century.

Despite these defeats, the Ottomans remained deeply inward looking, continuing to regard themselves as superior to the once underdeveloped European West. Virtually no works of the new European science were translated into Arabic or Ottoman Turkish. Few Ottoman subjects traveled in Europe. The Ottoman leaders, isolated from both their own leading Muslim subjects and from Europe, failed to understand what was occurring far beyond their immediate borders, especially European advances in military technology. When during the eighteenth century the Ottoman Empire began to recognize the new situation, it tended to borrow European technology and import foreign advisers, thus failing to develop its own infrastructure. Moreover, the powerful influence of the Ulama worked against imitation of Christian Europe. Although traditionally opposed to significant interaction with non-Muslims, they did eventually allow non-Muslim teachers into the empire and approved alliances with non-Muslim powers. But the Ulama limited such relationships. For example, in the middle of the eighteenth century, the Ulama persuaded the sultan to close a school of technology and to abandon a printing press he had opened. This influence by Muslim religious teachers occurred just as governments, such as that of Peter the Great, and secular intellectuals across Europe through the influence of the Enlightenment (see Chapter 18) were increasingly diminishing the influence of the Christian churches in political and economic affairs. Consequently, intellectual circles in Europe began to view the once much-feared Ottoman Empire as a declining power and Islam as a backward-looking religion.

POLAND: ABSENCE OF STRONG CENTRAL AUTHORITY

In no other part of Europe was the failure to maintain a competitive political position so complete as in Poland. In 1683, King John III Sobieski (r. 1674–1696) had led a Polish army to rescue Vienna from the Turkish siege. Following that spectacular effort, however, Poland became a byword for the dangers of aristocratic independence.

The Polish monarchy was elective, but the deep distrust and divisions among the nobility prevented their electing a king from among themselves. Sobieski was a notable exception. Most of the Polish monarchs were foreigners and were the tools of foreign powers. The Polish nobles did have a central legislative body called the **Sejm**, or diet. It included only the nobles and specifically excluded representatives from corporate bodies, such as the towns. In the diet, however, there existed a practice known as the *liberum veto*, whereby the staunch opposition of any single member, who might have been bribed by a foreign power, could require the body to disband. Such opposition was termed "exploding the diet." This practice was most often the work of a group of dissatisfied nobles rather than of one person. Nonetheless, the requirement of unanimity was a major stumbling block to effective government. The price of this noble liberty would eventually be the disappearance of Poland from the map of Europe during the latter half of the eighteenth century.

THE HABSBURG EMPIRE AND THE PRAGMATIC SANCTION

The close of the Thirty Years' War with the Treaty of Westphalia marked a fundamental turning point in the history of the Austrian Habsburgs. Previously, allied with the Spanish branch of the family, they had hoped to dominate all of Germany and to return it to the Catholic fold. They did not achieve either goal, and the decline of Spanish power

meant that in future diplomatic relations the Austrian Habsburgs were on their own.

After 1648, the Austrian Habsburgs retained the title of Holy Roman Emperor, but their political effectiveness depended less on force of arms than on the cooperation that the emperor could elicit from the over three hundred corporate political entities in the empire, including those that were Protestant, whose representatives met in the imperial diet that from 1663 until the empire was dissolved in 1806 sat at Regensburg.

Consolidation of Austrian Power While concentrating on their hereditary Austrian holdings among the German states, the Habsburgs also began to consolidate their power and influence within their other hereditary possessions. (See Map 15–2.) These included, first, the Crown of Saint Wenceslas, encompassing the kingdom of Bohemia (in the modern Czech Republic and Slovakia) and the duchies of Moravia and Silesia and, second, the Crown of Saint Stephen, which included Hungary, Croatia, and Transylvania. In the middle of the seventeenth century, much of Hungary remained occupied by the Ottoman Empire

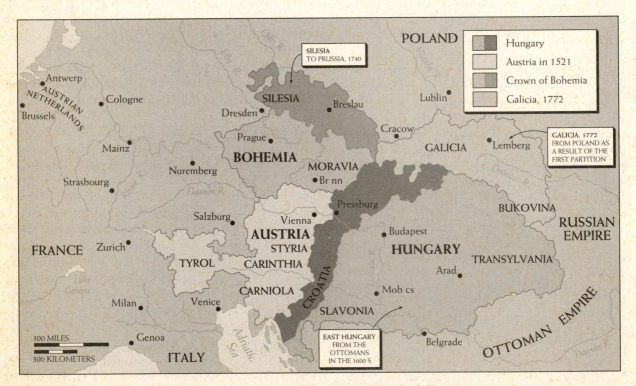

MAP 15–2 THE AUSTRIAN HABSBURG EMPIRE, 1521–1772 *The empire had three main units: Austria, Bohemia, and Hungary. Expansion was mainly eastward: East Hungary from the Ottomans (seventeenth century) and Galicia from Poland (1772). Meantime, Silesia was lost, but the Habsburgs retained German influences as Holy Roman emperors.*

and only came under Habsburg rule in 1699 through the Treaty of Carlowitz.

In the early eighteenth century, the Habsburgs extended their domains further, receiving the former Spanish (thereafter Austrian) Netherlands, Lombardy in northern Italy, and, briefly, the kingdom of Naples in southern Italy through the Treaty of Utrecht in 1713. During the eighteenth and nineteenth centuries, the Habsburgs' power and influence in Europe were based primarily on their territories outside Germany.

In the second half of the seventeenth century and later, the Habsburgs faced immense problems in these hereditary territories. In each, they ruled by virtue of a different title and had to gain the cooperation of the local nobility. There was almost no common basis for political unity among peoples of such diverse languages, customs, and geography. The Habsburgs established various central councils to chart common policies for their far-flung domains. Virtually all of these bodies dealt with only part of the Habsburgs' holdings. Repeatedly, the Habsburgs had to bargain with nobles in one part of their empire to maintain their position in another. The most difficult of these were the largely Calvinist **Magyar** nobility of Hungary.

Despite all these internal difficulties, Leopold I (r. 1658–1705) rallied his domains to resist the advances of the Ottomans and the aggression of Louis XIV, achieved Ottoman recognition of his sovereignty over Hungary in 1699, and began the suppression of a long Magyar rebellion that lasted from 1703 to 1711. He also conquered much of the Balkan Peninsula and western Romania. These southeastward extensions allowed the Habsburgs to hope to develop Mediterranean trade through the port of Trieste. Habsburg expansion at the cost of the Ottoman Empire helped them compensate for their loss of domination over the Holy Roman Empire. The new strength in the East gave them somewhat greater political leverage in Germany. Leopold I was succeeded by Joseph I (r. 1705–1711), who continued Leopold's policies.

(problem heir)

The Habsburg Dynastic Problem   When Charles VI (r. 1711–1740) succeeded Joseph, he had no male heir, and there was only the weakest of precedents for a female ruler of the Habsburg domains. Charles feared that on his death the Austrian Habsburg lands might fall prey to the surrounding powers, as had those of the Spanish Habsburgs in 1700. He was determined to prevent that disaster and to provide his domains with the semblance of legal

unity. To those ends, he devoted much of his energy throughout his reign to seeking the approval of his family, the estates of his realms, and the major foreign powers for a document called the **Pragmatic Sanction**. *(solution)*

This instrument provided the legal basis for a single line of inheritance within the Habsburg dynasty through Charles VI's daughter Maria Theresa (r. 1740–1780). Other members of the Habsburg family recognized her as the rightful heir. The nobles of the various Habsburg domains did likewise after extracting various concessions from Charles. So, when Charles VI died in October 1740, he believed he had secured legal unity for the Habsburg Empire and a safe succession for his daughter. *(more conflict)*

Charles VI had indeed established a permanent line of succession and the basis for future legal bonds within the Habsburg holdings. He had failed, however, to protect his daughter from foreign aggression, either through the Pragmatic Sanction or, more importantly, by leaving her a strong army and a full treasury. Less than two months after his death, the fragility of the foreign agreements became apparent. In December 1740, Frederick II of Prussia invaded the Habsburg province of Silesia. Maria Theresa had to fight to defend her inheritance.

PRUSSIA AND THE HOHENZOLLERNS

The Habsburg achievement had been to draw together into an uncertain legal unity a collection of domains possessed through separate feudal titles. The achievement of the Hohenzollerns of Brandenburg-Prussia was to acquire a similar collection of titular holdings and then to forge them into a centrally administered unit. They subordinated every social class and most economic pursuits to the strengthening of the single institution that united their far-flung realms: the army. They thus made the term *Prussian* synonymous with administrative rigor and military discipline.

A State of Disconnected Territories   The rise of Prussia is the story of the extraordinary Hohenzollern family, which had ruled the German territory of Brandenburg since 1417. (See Map 15–3.) Through inheritance, the family had acquired the duchy of Cleves and the counties of Mark and Ravensburg in 1609, the duchy of East Prussia in 1618, and the duchy of Pomerania in 1637. Except for Pomerania, none of these lands was contiguous with Brandenburg. East Prussia lay inside

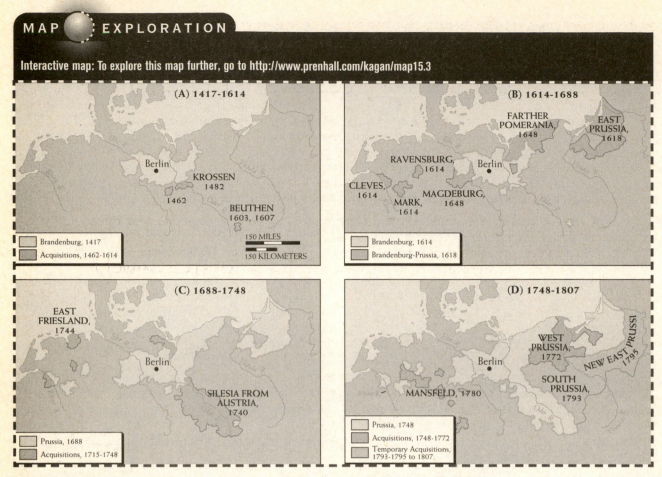

MAP ● **EXPLORATION**

Interactive map: To explore this map further, go to http://www.prenhall.com/kagan/map15.3

MAP 15–3 EXPANSION OF BRANDENBURG-PRUSSIA *In the seventeenth century, Brandenburg-Prussia expanded mainly by acquiring dynastic titles in geographically separated lands. In the eighteenth century, it expanded through aggression to the east, seizing Silesia in 1740 and various parts of Poland in 1772, 1793, and 1795.*

Poland and outside the authority of the Holy Roman Emperor. All of the territories lacked good natural resources, and many of them were devastated during the Thirty Years' War. At Westphalia the Hohenzollerns lost part of Pomerania to Sweden, but were compensated by receiving three more bishoprics and the promise of the archbishopric of Magdeburg when it became vacant, as it did in 1680. By the late seventeenth century, the scattered Hohenzollern holdings represented a block of territory within the Holy Roman Empire second in size only to that of the Habsburgs.

Frederick William, the Great Elector The person who began to forge these separated regions and diverse nobles into a modern state was Frederick William (r. 1640–1688), who became known as the Great Elector. (The ruler of Brandenburg was called an *elector* because he was one of the princes who

elected the Holy Roman Emperor.) He established himself and his successors as the central uniting power by breaking the local noble estates, organizing a royal bureaucracy, and establishing a strong army. (See "The Great Elector Welcomes Protestant Refugees from France.")

Between 1655 and 1660, Sweden and Poland engaged in a war that endangered the Great Elector's holdings in Pomerania and East Prussia. Frederick William had neither the military nor the financial resources to confront this threat. In 1655, the Brandenburg estates1 refused to grant him new taxes; however, he proceeded to collect the required taxes by military force. In 1659, a different grant of taxes, originally made in 1653, elapsed; Frederick William continued to collect them, as well as those he had imposed by his own authority. He used the money to build up an army that allowed him to continue to enforce his will without

THE GREAT ELECTOR WELCOMES PROTESTANT REFUGEES FROM FRANCE

The Hohenzollern dynasty of Brandenburg-Prussia pursued a policy of religious toleration. The family itself was Calvinist, whereas most of its subjects were Lutherans. When Louis XIV of France revoked the Edict of Nantes in 1685, Frederick William, the Great Elector, seized the opportunity to invite French Protestants into his realms. As his proclamation indicates, he wanted to attract persons with productive skills who could aid the economic development of his domains.

■ *In reading this document, do you believe religious or economic concerns more nearly led the elector of Brandenburg to welcome the French Protestants? What specific privileges did the elector extend to them? To what extent were these privileges a welcoming measure, and to what extent were they inducements to emigrate to Brandenburg? In what kind of economic activity does the elector expect the French refugees to engage?*

We, Friedrich Wilhelm, by Grace of God Margrave of Brandenburg . . .

Do hereby proclaim and make known to all and sundry that since the cruel persecutions and rigorous ill-treatment in which Our co-religionists of the Evangelical-Reformed faith have for some time past been subjected in the Kingdom of France, have caused many families to remove themselves and to betake themselves out of the said Kingdom into other lands, We now . . . have been moved graciously to offer them through this Edict . . . a secure and free refuge in all Our Lands and Provinces. . . .

Since Our Lands are not only well and amply endowed with all things necessary to support life, but also very well-suited to the reestablishment of all kinds of manufactures and trade and traffic by land and water, We permit, indeed, to those settling therein free choice to establish themselves where it is most convenient for their profession and way of living. . . .

The personal property which they bring with them, including merchandise and other wares, is to be totally exempt from any taxes, customs dues, licenses, or other imposts of any description, and not detained in any way. . . .

As soon as these Our French co-religionists of the Evangelical-Reformed faith have settled in any town or village, they shall be admitted to the domiciliary rights and craft freedoms customary there, gratis and without payments of any fee; and shall be entitled to the benefits, rights, and privileges enjoyed by Our other, native, subjects, residing there. . . .

Not only are those who wish to establish manufacture of cloth, stuffs, hats, or other objects in which they are skilled to enjoy all necessary freedoms, privileges and facilities, but also provision is to be made for them to be assisted and helped as far as possible with money and anything else which they need to realize their intention. . . .

Those who settle in the country and wish to maintain themselves by agriculture are to be given a certain plot of land to bring under cultivation and provided with whatever they need to establish themselves initially. . . .

From C. A. Macartney, ed., *The Habsburg and Hohenzollern Dynasties in the Seventeenth and Eighteenth Centuries* (New York: Walker, 1970), pp. 270–273.

the approval of the nobility. Similar threats and coercion took place against the nobles in his other territories.

There did occur, however, an important political and social trade-off between the elector and his various nobles: In exchange for their obedience to the Hohenzollerns, the **Junkers** received the right to demand obedience from their serfs. Frederick William also tended to choose as the local administrators of the tax structure men who would normally have been members of the noble estates. He thus coopted potential opponents into his service.

Austria and Prussia in the Late Seventeenth and Early Eighteenth Centuries	
1640–1688	Reign of Frederick William, the Great Elector
1658–1705	Leopold I rules Austria and resists the Turkish invasions
1683	Turkish siege of Vienna
1688–1713	Reign of Frederick I of Prussia
1699	Peace treaty between Turks and Habsburgs
1711–1740	Charles VI rules Austria and secures agreement to the Pragmatic Sanction
1713–1740	Frederick William I builds up the military power of Prussia
1740	Maria Theresa succeeds to the Habsburg throne
1740	Frederick II violates the Pragmatic Sanction by invading Silesia

His taxes fell most heavily on the backs of the peasants and the urban classes.

Frederick William I, King of Prussia Yet, even with the considerable accomplishments of the Great Elector, the house of Hohenzollern did not possess a crown. The achievement of a royal title was one of the few state-building accomplishments of Frederick I (r. 1688–1713). This son of the Great Elector was the least "Prussian" of his family during these crucial years. He built palaces, founded Halle University (1694), patronized the arts, and lived luxuriously. In 1701, however, at the outbreak of the War of the Spanish Succession, he put his valuable, well-trained army at the disposal of the Habsburg Holy Roman Emperor. In exchange for this loyal service, the emperor permitted Frederick to assume the title of "King in Prussia." Thereafter Frederick became Frederick I, and he passed the much-desired royal title to his son Frederick William I in 1713.

Frederick William I (r. 1713–1740) was both the most eccentric and one of the most effective Hohenzollerns. His political aims seem to have been the consolidation of an obedient, compliant bureaucracy and the establishment of a bigger army. He initiated a policy of *Kabinett* government, which meant that lower officials submitted all relevant documents to him in his office, or *Kabinett*. Then he alone examined the papers, made his decisions, and issued his orders. He thus skirted the influence of ministers and ruled alone.

Frederick William I organized the bureaucracy along military lines. He united all departments under the *General-Ober-Finanz-Kriegs-und-Domänen-Direktorium*, more happily known to us as the General Directory. He imposed taxes on the nobility and changed most remaining feudal dues into monetary payments. He sought to transform feudal and administrative loyalties into a sense of duty to the monarch as a political institution rather than as a person. He once described the perfect royal servant as an intelligent, assiduous, and alert person who after God values nothing higher than his king's pleasure and serves him out of love and for the sake of honor rather than money and who in his conduct solely seeks and constantly bears in mind his king's service and interests, who, moreover, abhors all intrigues and emotional deterrents.[1]

Service to the state and the monarch was to become impersonal, mechanical, and, in effect, unquestioning.

The Prussian Army During Frederick William's reign, the size of the army grew from about 39,000 in 1713 to more than 80,000 in 1740. It was the third or fourth largest army in Europe, whereas Prussia ranked thirteenth in population. Rather than using recruiters, the king made each canton or local district responsible for supplying a quota of soldiers.

After 1725, Frederick William I always wore an officer's uniform. He formed one regiment from the tallest soldiers he could find in Europe. Separate laws applied to the army and to civilians. Laws, customs, and royal attention made the officer corps the highest social class of the state. Military service attracted the sons of Junkers. Thus, the army, the Junker nobility, and the monarchy were forged into a single political entity. Military priorities and values dominated Prussian government, society, and daily life as in no other state of Europe. It has often been said that whereas other nations possessed armies, the Prussian army possessed its nation.

Although Frederick William I built the best army in Europe, he avoided conflict. He wanted to drill his soldiers, but not to order them into battle. The army was for him a symbol of Prussian power and unity, not an instrument to be used for foreign adventures or aggression.

---

[1] Quoted in Hans Rosenberg, *Bureaucracy, Aristocracy, and Autocracy* (Boston: Beacon Press, 1958), p. 93.

At his death in 1740, he passed to his son Frederick II, later known as "the Great" (r. 1740–1786), this superb military machine, but he could not also pass on the wisdom to refrain from using it. Almost immediately on coming to the throne, Frederick II upset the Pragmatic Sanction, invaded Silesia, and thus crystallized the Austrian-Prussian rivalry for control of Germany that would dominate central European affairs for over a century.

Russia Enters the European Political Arena

Though ripe with consequences for the future, the rise of Prussia and the new consolidation of the Austrian Habsburg domains seemed to many at the time only another shift in the long-troubled German scene. The emergence of Russia, however, as an active European power was a wholly new factor in European politics. Previously, Russia had been considered part of Europe only by courtesy, and before 1673 it did not send permanent ambassadors to western Europe, though it had sent various diplomatic missions since the fifteenth century. Geographically and politically, it lay on the periphery. Hemmed in by Sweden on the Baltic and by the Ottoman Empire on the Black Sea, Russia had no warm-water ports. Its chief outlet for trade to the west was Archangel on the White Sea, which was ice free for only part of the year. What Russia did possess was a vast reserve of largely undeveloped natural and human resources.

BIRTH OF THE ROMANOV DYNASTY

The reign of Ivan the Terrible, which had begun so well and closed so frighteningly, was followed by anarchy and civil war known as the "Time of Troubles." In 1613, hoping to restore stability, an assembly of nobles elected a seventeen-year-old boy named Michael Romanov (r. 1613–1654) as tsar. Thus began the dynasty that, despite palace revolutions, military conspiracies, assassinations, and family strife, ruled Russia until 1917.

Michael Romanov and his two successors, Aleksei (r. 1654–1676) and Theodore II (r. 1676–1682), brought stability and modest bureaucratic centralization to Russia. The country remained, however, weak and impoverished. After years of turmoil, the bureaucracy was still largely controlled by the *boyars*, the old nobility. This administrative apparatus could barely suppress a revolt of peasants and Cossacks (horsemen who lived on the steppe frontier) under Stepan Razin in 1670–1671. Furthermore, the government and the tsars faced the danger of mutiny from the *streltsy*, or guards of the Moscow garrison.

PETER THE GREAT

In 1682, another boy—ten years old at the time—ascended the fragile Russian throne as co-ruler with his half brother. His name was Peter (r. 1682–1725), and Russia would never be the same after him. He and the sickly Ivan V had come to power on the shoulders of the *streltsy*, who expected to be rewarded for their support. Much violence and bloodshed had surrounded the disputed succession. Matters became even more confused when the boys' sister, Sophia, was named regent. Peter's followers overthrew her in 1689. From that date onward, Peter ruled personally, although in theory he shared the crown until Ivan died in 1696. The dangers and turmoil of his youth convinced Peter of two things: first, the power of the tsar must be made secure from the jealousy of the *boyars* and the greed of the *streltsy*; second, the military power of Russia must be increased. In both respects, he self-consciously resembled Louis XIV of France, who had experienced the turmoil of the *Fronde* during his youth and resolved to establish a strong monarchy safe from the nobility and defended by a powerful army.

Northwestern Europe, particularly the military resources of the maritime powers, fascinated Peter I, who eventually became known as Peter the Great. In 1697, he made a famous visit in transparent disguise to western Europe. There he dined and talked with the great and the powerful, who considered this almost seven-foot-tall ruler crude. He spent his happiest moments on the trip inspecting shipyards, docks, and the manufacture of military hardware in England and the Netherlands. While Peter traveled in northwestern Europe, he had ordered other Russians to travel elsewhere on the Continent to learn languages and new commercial and military skills. An imitator of the first order, Peter returned to Moscow determined to copy what he had seen abroad, for he knew warfare would be necessary to make Russia a great power. But he understood his goal would require him to confront the long-standing power and traditions of the Russian nobles.

TAMING THE STRELTSY AND BOYARS

In 1698, prior to Peter's return from abroad, the *streltsy* had rebelled. On his return, Peter brutally suppressed the revolt with private tortures and public executions, in which Peter's own ministers took part. Approximately a thousand of the rebels were put to death, and their corpses remained on public display to discourage future disloyalty. (See "Encountering the Past: Public Executions.")

The new military establishment that Peter built would serve the tsar and not itself. He introduced effective and ruthless policies of conscription, drafting an unprecedented 130,000 soldiers during the first decade of the eighteenth century and almost 300,000 troops by the end of his reign. He had adopted policies for the officer corps and general military discipline patterned on those of west European armies.

Peter also determined to make a sustained attack on the *boyars* and their attachment to traditional Russian culture. After his European journey, he personally shaved the long beards of the court *boyars*

and sheared off the customary long hand-covering sleeves of their shirts and coats, which had made them the butt of jokes among other European courts. During the 1690s, Peter had gradually stopped granting *boyar* status to new individuals. Throughout his reign he made numerous major decisions in both foreign and domestic policy without consulting the *boyars*. Consequently, Peter faced considerable opposition from troublesome and potentially seditious factions of court nobility. Never able fully to dominate them, he became highly skilled at balancing one group off against another while never completely excluding any as he set about to organize Russian government and military forces along the lines of the more powerful European states.

DEVELOPING A NAVY

When Peter came to the throne, Russia had no real navy. One historian has described the building of a Russian navy as "Peter the Great's most revolutionary innovation."[2] The creation of a navy was one part of Peter's strategy to secure warm-water ports that would allow Russia to trade with the West and to influence European affairs.

In the mid-1690s, he oversaw the construction of ships to protect his interests in the Black Sea against the Ottoman Empire. In 1695, he began a war with the Ottomans and captured Azov on the Black Sea in 1696.[3] Part of the reason for Peter's trip to western Europe in 1697 was to learn how to build still better warships, this time for combat on the Baltic. The construction of a Baltic fleet, largely constructed on the Finnish coast, was essential in the Great Northern War with Sweden, a struggle that over the years accounted for many of Peter's major steps toward westernizing his realm.

RUSSIAN EXPANSION IN THE BALTIC: THE GREAT NORTHERN WAR

Following the end of the Thirty Years' War in 1648, Sweden had consolidated its control of the Baltic, thus preventing Russian possession of a port on that sea and permitting Polish and German access to the sea only on Swedish terms. The Swedes also had one of the better armies in Europe. Sweden's economy, however, based primarily on the export

---

[2]Simon Dixon, *The Modernization of Russia, 1676–1825* (Cambridge: Cambridge University Press, 1999), p. 35.

[3]Although Peter had to return Azov to the Ottomans in 1711, its recapture became a goal of Russian foreign policy. See Chapter 18.

Public Executions

Executions—the judicial taking of life—are the most stringent exercise of authority. In early modern Europe most executions were held in public before crowds of onlookers.

The ritual of the public execution changed little from the close of the Middle Ages through the end of the eighteenth century. Executions were carried out by professional executioners, a trade that was often passed from father to son. Hanging was the most common method, but the condemned could also be "broken on the wheel" (have their bones fractured and then be strangled), burned at the stake, beheaded, or buried alive with a stake driven through their heart (a penalty often reserved for women in central Europe). The condemned person was taken in a procession from prison to the place of execution. Normally a clergyman accompanied the prisoner—a sign that church and state agreed the death penalty was appropriate. The crowds before whom the judgment would be read and the condemned person permitted to speak expected the penalty to be carried out efficiently, without any more suffering than necessary. Careless or inept executioners could provoke a riot. Often, however, a carnival atmosphere surrounded the proceedings. Hawkers sold food and drink or pamphlets and woodcuts about the criminal. As a warning the bodies or heads of common criminals and political offenders were frequently left to rot in a public place after the execution.

For centuries most Europeans appear to have accepted the need for these executions and to have gained satisfaction, if not enjoyment, from watching them. Order had to be maintained and crime punished. Retribution was a valid social and religious norm, and although some of the common people may have resented the power of the state and the way local social elites enforced the law, it was ordinary people, then as now, who were most often the victims of crime. Moreover, most of those who were executed appear to have committed what their societies regarded as terrible crimes—murder, incest, rape, treason, banditry. In condemning these offenders to death, the courts thus upheld the law and the expectations of the local communities, both of which were harsh. The courts also understood, however, that too frequent imposition of the death penalty might lead to public disapproval and unrest.

From the early 1600s onward, the number of executions actually carried out declined across Europe. Hard service—rowing naval galleys, imprisonment, and, in Britain, being shipped to Australia—became substitutes for execution. Although some thinkers during the Enlightenment condemned capital punishment itself (see Chapter 18), public executions continued throughout Europe during the nineteenth century. From the late nineteenth century onward, however, executions in Europe increasingly occurred within prisons. The last public execution occurred in France in 1939. The law might still require execution for certain crimes, but the state no longer considered it edifying—or even decent—for the public to witness it. Executions were no longer a public spectacle.

After World War II, the nations of Western Europe began to do away with the death penalty in reaction to the Nazi Holocaust and as a result of campaigns for its abolition. Since 1998, no state can be a member of the European Union unless it abolishes the death penalty.

■ *Why did most Europeans support public executions in the early modern period? Why did support for capital punishment eventually weaken in Europe?*

Julius R. Ruff, *Violence in Early Modern Europe, 1500–1800* (Cambridge: Cambridge University Press, 2001); V. A. C. Gatrell, *The Hanging Tree: Execution and the English People, 1770–1868* (Oxford: Oxford University Press, 1994); Richard J. Evans, *Rituals of Retribution: Capital Punishment in Germany, 1600–1987* (Oxford: Oxford University Press, 1996)

The execution of Colonel Turner   © Bettmann/Corbis

503

of iron, was not strong enough to ensure continued political success.

In 1697, Charles XII (r. 1697–1718) came to the throne. He was headstrong, to say the least, and perhaps insane. In 1700, Peter the Great began a drive to the west against Swedish territory to gain a foothold on the Baltic. In the resulting Great Northern War (1700–1721), Charles XII led a vigorous and often brilliant campaign defeating the Russians at the Battle of Narva (1700). As the conflict dragged on, however, Peter was able to strengthen his forces. By 1709, he decisively defeated the Swedes at the Battle of Poltava. Thereafter, the Swedes could maintain only a holding action against their enemies. Charles himself sought refuge in Turkey and did not return to Sweden until 1714. He was killed under uncertain circumstances four years later while fighting the Danes in Norway. When the Great Northern War came to a close in 1721, the Peace of Nystad confirmed the Russian conquest of Estonia, Livonia, and part of Finland. Henceforth, Russia possessed ice-free ports and a permanent influence on European affairs.

FOUNDING ST. PETERSBURG

At one point, the domestic and foreign policies of Peter the Great intersected. This was at the site on the Gulf of Finland where he founded his new capital city of St. Petersburg in 1703. There he built government structures and compelled the *boyars* to construct town houses. He thus imitated those European monarchs who had copied Louis XIV by constructing smaller versions of Versailles. The founding of St. Petersburg went beyond establishing a central imperial court, however; it symbolized a new Western orientation of Russia and Peter's determination to hold his position on the Baltic coast. He had begun the construction of the city and had moved the capital there even before his

Vūe des bords de la Neva en descendant la riviere entre le Palais d'hyver de Sa Majesté Imperiale & les batimens de l'Academie des Sciences

Peter the Great built St. Petersburg on the Gulf of Finland to provide Russia with better contact with western Europe. He moved Russia's capital there from Moscow in 1712. This is an eighteenth-century view of the city. The Granger Collection

victory over Sweden was assured. Moreover, he and his successors employed architects from western Europe for many of the most prominent buildings in and around the city. Consequently, St. Petersburg looked different from other Russian cities. Both in Peter's day and later, many Russians saw St. Petersburg as a kind of illegitimate west European growth on Russian culture that symbolized Peter's autocracy and rejection of traditional Russian life and government.

REORGANIZING DOMESTIC ADMINISTRATION

Hard upon his successes in the war against Sweden, Peter in 1711 created a Senate of nine members. The Senate, which replaced the former Privy Chancellery, was to direct virtually all aspects of government when the tsar was away with the army. The purpose of this and other more local administrative reforms was to establish a bureaucratic structure that could support an efficient military establishment.

The Senate was also intended to represent the authority of the tsar against intriguing court nobles. The membership of the Senate would shift as Peter's political favorites changed. Over time, however, the Senate itself would become a center for intrigue and possible opposition to Peter's policies. These would come to a head in a conspiracy involving Peter's son.

THE CASE OF PETER'S SON ALEKSEI

Peter's son Aleksei had been born to his first wife whom he had divorced in 1698. Peter was jealous of the young man, who had never demonstrated strong intelligence or ambition, and feared that Aleksei might undertake sedition by gathering court factions around him or by cooperating with foreign rulers. Over the years Peter had constantly quarreled with Alexsei, criticizing the young man's shortcomings as a future ruler. (See "Peter the Great Tells His Son to Acquire Military Skills.") By 1716, Peter was becoming convinced that his opponents looked to Aleksei as a focus for their possible sedition while Russia remained at war with Sweden.

Late that year Aleksei undertook a secret visit to Vienna where he appears to have entered into a vague military plot with the Habsburg emperor Charles VI against Peter's interests in the Great Northern War. There is evidence that Sweden itself was interested in furthering this conspiracy. Nothing actually came of these secret conversations, however, although Aleksei remained under the protection of Charles VI until late in 1717 when the emperor decided the whole affair was too dangerous. Much compromised, Alexsei then returned to Russia surrounded by rumors and suspicions.

Peter, who was investigating official corruption, realized his son might become a rallying point for those he accused. Early in 1718, when Aleksei reappeared in St. Petersburg, the tsar began to look into his son's relationships with Charles VI and with Russian nobles including members of the Senate opposed to Peter's policies. Peter discovered that although any actual conspiracy probably did not extend beyond Aleksei and Charles VI, had those two moved against him, numerous Russian nobles, administrators, and churchmen might have joined them. During this six-month investigation Peter personally interrogated Aleksei, who was eventually condemned to death and died under mysterious circumstances on June 26, 1718. The case of the tsar's son had enormous ramifications for the rest of Peter's reign.

REFORMS OF PETER THE GREAT'S FINAL YEARS

The difficulties between Peter and his son were much more than a tragic family quarrel. The interrogations surrounding Aleksei had revealed greater degrees of court opposition than Peter had suspected. Recognizing he could not eliminate his numerous opponents the way he had attacked the *streltsy* in 1698, Peter undertook radical administrative reforms designed to bring the nobility and the Russian Orthodox Church more closely under the authority of persons loyal to the tsar. As an historian has commented recently, "The case of Aleksei was the greatest spur to Peter's reform in the history of the reign, greater even than the Northern War."[4]

Administrative Colleges In December 1717, while his son was returning to Russia, Peter reorganized his domestic administration to sustain his own personal authority and to fight rampant corruption. To achieve this goal, Peter looked to Swedish institutions called *colleges*—bureaus of several persons operating according to written instructions rather than departments headed by a single minister. These colleges, eight of which he

[4]Peter Bushkovitch, *Peter the Great: The Search for Power, 1671–1725* (Cambridge: Cambridge University Press, 2001), p. 425.

PETER THE GREAT TELLS HIS SON TO ACQUIRE MILITARY SKILLS

Enormous hostility existed between Peter the Great and his son Aleksei. Peter believed his son was not prepared to inherit the throne. In October 1715, he composed a long letter to Aleksei in which he berated him for refusing to take military matters seriously. The letter indicates how an early-eighteenth-century ruler saw the conduct of warfare as a fundamental part of the role of a monarch. Peter also points to Louis XIV of France as a role model. Peter and Aleksei did not reach an agreement. Aleksei died under mysterious circumstances in 1718, with Peter possibly responsible for his death.

■ *How did Peter use the recent war with Sweden to argue for the necessity of his son acquiring military skills? What concept of leadership does Peter attempt to communicate to his son? Why did Peter see military prowess as the most important ability in a ruler?*

You cannot be ignorant of what is known to all the world, to what degree our people groaned under the oppression of the Swede before the beginning of the present war. . . . You know what it has cost us in the beginning of this war . . . to make ourselves experienced in the art of war, and to put a stop to those advantages which our implacable enemies obtained over us. . . .

But you even will not so much as hear warlike exercises mentioned: though it was by them that we broke through that obscurity in which we were involved, and that we make ourselves known to nations, whose esteem we share at present.

I do not exhort you to make war without lawful reasons: I only desire you to apply yourself to learn the art of it: for it is impossible well to govern without knowing the rules and discipline of it, was it for no other end than for the defense of the country. . . .

You mistake, if you think it is enough for a prince to have good generals to act under his order. Everyone looks upon the head; they study its inclinations and conform themselves to them: all the world own this. . . .

You have no inclination to learn war. You do not apply yourself to it, and consequently you will never learn it: And how then can you command others, and judge of the reward which those deserve who do their duty, or punish others who fail of it? You will do nothing, nor judge of anything but by the assent and help of others, like a young bird that holds up his bill to be fed. . . .

If you think there are some, whose affairs do not fail of success, though they do not go to war themselves; it is true: But if they do not go themselves, yet they have an inclination for it, and understand it.

For instance, the late King of France did not always take the field in person; but it is known to what degree he loved war, and what glorious exploits he performed in it, which make his campaigns to be called the theatre and school of the world. His inclinations were not confined solely to military affairs, he also loved mechanics, manufacture and other establishment, which rendered his kingdom more flourishing than any other whatsoever.

From Friedrich C. Weber, *The Present State of Russia* (London, 1722), 2:97–100; *The Global Experience*, 3/3rd ed., Vol. 2 by P. F. Riley, © 1998. Reprinted by permission of Prentice Hall, Inc., Upper Saddle River, NJ.

imposed on Russian administration, were to look after matters such as the collection of taxes, foreign relations, war, and economic affairs. Each college was to receive advice from a foreigner. Peter used his appointive power to balance the influence in these colleges between nobles and persons he was certain would be personally loyal to himself. The presence of the colleges to some degree balanced the influence of the Senate where Aleksei had sympathizers.

Table of Ranks Peter made another major administrative reform with important consequences when in 1722 he published a **Table of Ranks** intended to draw the nobility into state service. That table equated a person's social position and privileges with his rank in the bureaucracy or the military, rather than with his lineage among the traditional landed nobility, many of whom continued to resent the changes Peter had introduced into Russia. Peter thus made the social standing of individual *boyars* a function of their willingness to serve the central state. Earlier tsars had created some service nobles on the basis of merit, but none had envisioned drawing all nobles into state service. Unlike Prussian Junkers, however, the Russian nobility never became perfectly loyal to the state. They repeatedly sought to reassert their independence and their control of the Russian imperial court and to bargain with later tsars over local authority and the nobles' dominance of the serfs.

Achieving Secular Control of the Church Peter also moved to suppress the independence of the Russian Orthodox Church. Here Peter was confronting a problem that had arisen both in the turbulent decades preceding his reign and from the sympathy some church leaders had displayed toward Aleksei.

The history of the Russian Orthodox Church of this era is extremely complicated. In the mid–seventeenth century, a reformist movement led by Patriarch Nikon had introduced changes into church texts and ritual. A group of Russian Orthodox Christians, known as the **Old Believers**, strongly opposed these changes. Although condemned by the hierarchy, the Old Believers persisted in their opposition. Thousands committed suicide rather than submit to the new rituals. In response to this traditionalist opposition, church leaders began to advocate both popular preaching and a more Western form of clerical education, including the teaching of Latin. In that respect, like Peter, they were modernizers, but they moved too slowly to please the tsar. Consequently, by 1700 he had begun to appoint his own bishops, especially Ukrainians, many of whom had been trained in European schools. But both reform-minded Ukrainian and Russian-born bishops objected to Peter's heavy-handed influence on religious matters. Those objections lay behind their sympathy for the tsar's son.

After Aleksei's death, Peter set about curtailing the capacity of the Russian Orthodox Church to oppose his interference in its affairs and to meddle in politics. In 1721, he simply abolished the

position of *patriarch*, the bishop who had been head of the church. In its place he established a government department called the *Holy Synod*, which consisted of several bishops headed by a layman, called the *procurator general*. This body would govern the church in accordance with the tsar's secular requirements. This ecclesiastical re-organization, which drew on German Lutheran models, was the most radical transformation of a traditional institution in Peter's reign. It produced further futile opposition from the Old Believers, who saw the tsar as leading the church into new heresy. Peter's policy toward the Russian church stood in sharp contrast to the Ottoman sultans' contemporary policy of deference to the Muslim Ulama.

For all the numerous decisive actions Peter had taken since 1718, he still had not settled on a successor. Consequently, when he died in 1725, there was no clear line of succession to the throne. For more than thirty years, soldiers and nobles again determined who ruled Russia. Peter had laid the foundations of a modern Russia, but not the foundations of a stable state.

IN PERSPECTIVE

By the second quarter of the eighteenth century, the major European powers were not nation-states in which the citizens felt themselves united by a shared sense of community, culture, language, and history. Rather, they were monarchies in which the personality of the ruler and the personal relationships of the great noble families exercised considerable influence over public affairs. The monarchs, except in Great Britain, had generally succeeded in making their power greater than the nobility's. The power of the aristocracy and its capacity to resist or obstruct the policies of the monarch were not destroyed, however.

In Britain, of course, the nobility had tamed the monarchy, but even there tension between nobles and monarchs would continue throughout the rest of the century.

In foreign affairs, the new arrangement of military and diplomatic power established early in the century prepared the way for two long conflicts. The first was a commercial rivalry for trade and overseas empire between France and Great Britain. During the reign of Louis XIV, these two nations had collided over the French bid for dominance in Europe. During the eighteenth century, they dueled for control of commerce on other continents. The second arena of warfare was in central Europe, where Austria and Prussia fought for the leadership of the German states.

Behind these international conflicts and the domestic rivalry of monarchs and nobles, however, the society of eighteenth-century Europe began to change. The character and the structures of the societies over which the monarchs ruled were beginning to take on some features associated with the modern age. These economic and social developments would eventually transform the life of Europe to a degree beside which the state building of the early-eighteenth-century monarchs paled.

REVIEW QUESTIONS

1. Why did Britain and France remain leading powers in western Europe while the United Netherlands declined?

2. How did the structure of British government change under the leadership of Robert Walpole?

3. Compare and contrast the weakening of the Ottoman Empire with the rise of Russia under Peter the Great.

4. How were the Hohenzollerns able to forge their diverse landholdings into the state of Prussia? How did the Habsburgs try to resolve their problems? Were the Habsburgs as successful as the Hohenzollerns?

5. Why did Sweden, the Ottoman Empire, and Poland decline?

6. How and why did Russia emerge as a great power? What were Russia's domestic problems before Peter the Great came to power? To what extent did his reforms succeed? What problems did his son cause? Compare and contrast Peter the Great with Louis XIV of France.

7. How did the problems and uncertainties of who would and could succeed to the thrones of the various states constitute one of the major political and diplomatic problems of European politics between approximately 1685 and 1740?

SUGGESTED READINGS

T. M. Barker, *Army, Aristocracy, Monarchy: Essays in War, Society and Government in Austria, 1618–1780* (1982). Examines the intricate power relationships among these major institutions.

J. Black, *Eighteenth-Century Europe, 1700–1789* (1990). An excellent survey.

C. R. Boxer, *The Dutch Seaborne Empire* (1965). Remains the best treatment of the subject.

J. Brewer, *The Sinews of Power: War, Money and the English State, 1688–1783* (1989). An extremely important study of the financial basis of English power.

P. Bushkovitch, *Peter the Great: The Struggle for Power, 1671–1725* (2001). Replaces all previous studies.

J. C. D. Clark, *English Society: 1688–1832: Social Structure and Political Practice during the Ancien Régime* (1985). An important, controversial work that emphasizes the role of religion in English political life.

N. Davis, *God's Playground*, Vol. 1 (1991). Excellent on prepartition Poland.

J. De Vries and A. van der Woude, *The First Modern Economy* (1997). An account of Holland comparing it to other European nations.

W. Doyle, *The Old European Order, 1660–1800* (1992). The most thoughtful treatment of the subject.

R. J. W. Evans, *The Making of the Habsburg Monarchy, 1550–1700: An Interpretation* (1979). Places much emphasis on intellectual factors and the role of religion.

F. Ford, *Robe and Sword: The Regrouping of the French Aristocracy after Louis XIV* (1953). Remains important for political, social, and intellectual history.

C. J. Ingrao, *The Habsburg Monarchy, 1618–1815* (1994). The best recent survey.

J. I. Israel, *The Dutch Republic, Its Rise, Greatness, and Fall, 1477–1806* (1995). The major survey of the subject.

R. A. Kann and Z. V. David, *The Peoples of the Eastern Habsburg Lands, 1526–1918* (1984). A helpful overview of the subject.

D. McKay, *The Great Elector: Frederick William of Brandenburg-Prussia* (2001). An account of the origins of Prussian power.

D. McKay and H. M. Scott, *The Rise of the Great Powers, 1648–1815* (1983). Now a standard survey.

G. Parker, *The Military Revolution: Military Innovation and the Rise of the West (1500–1800)* (1988). A major work.

S. Schama, *An Embarrassment of Riches: An Interpretation of Dutch Culture in the Golden Age* (1987). Lively and controversial.

P. F. Sugar, *Southeastern Europe under Ottoman Rule, 1354–1804* (1977). An extremely clear presentation.

DOCUMENTS CD-ROM

Rachel Ruysch, *Flower Still Life*: Flowers, Commerce, and Morality

Rachel Ruysch, Dutch, 1664–1750, *Flower Still Life* (1956.57).   The Toledo Museum of Art, Toledo, Ohio; Purchased with funds from the Libbey Endowment, Gift of Edward Drummond Libbey

510

Paintings often are intended to convey more than first meets the eye. Such is more or less obvious in allegorical scenes in which themes appear in the guise of ancient gods or other mythological figures. But a painting of objects of everyday life arranged on tables, known as a still life, can also hold deep symbolic and cultural meaning. From the Middle Ages onward, particular flowers had religious meaning, but during the seventeenth century flowers took on more worldly associations.

Rachel Ruysch (1664–1750) was a Dutch woman artist living in Amsterdam who specialized in depicting elaborate arrangements of flowers. These paintings stand as very beautiful images, but they are also much more. The floral still life portrayed flowers usually raised from bulbs, a major Dutch commercial enterprise. Several decades before Ruysch completed this particular painting, *Flower Still Life* (after 1700), a financial mania had gripped Holland, with speculation in rare tulip bulbs reaching enormous extravagance before the bubble burst. Consequently, a painting such as this one from the early eighteenth century—and there were hundreds of such still-life floral works executed in seventeenth- and eighteenth-century Holland—would have recalled that event.

The flowers in this and other Dutch floral paintings represent work and commerce, not the natural bounty of the Dutch countryside. Commercial growers and traders brought such flowers to the Netherlands from its overseas empire and trading partners, and the flowers came to symbolize Dutch interaction with the most far-flung regions of the globe.

The variety of flowers in the bowl suggests wealth and abundance; these are valuable species, not humble objects of ordinary life. And never, except on canvas, would these flowers have bloomed at one time. Only the painter can gather them together in a single place at a single moment, in effect overcoming the cycle of nature.

Paintings such as this one have been called "a dialogue between this newly affluent society and its material possessions" and "an expression of how the phenomenon of plenty is to be viewed and understood."[5] These rich still-life paintings allowed the Calvinist Dutch to accommodate a morality that emphasized frugality and abstinence with life in the single wealthiest society in Europe. The melancholy surrounding the images conveys a lesson in the vanity and transience of earthly beauty and richness. All of these beautiful, valuable, rare natural objects, whether flowers or food, will soon decay. The flowers in this bowl, so stunning at the peak of their blossoming, will in a matter of days wilt and eventually rot. The insects buzzing about the flowers will also disappear. Even the empty snail shells on the table suggest that earthly life is only temporary. Similarly, the shadows in so many of the floral arrangements suggest the shadows that surround human life and the transience of both light and life. Yet, by owning a painting of an exquisite, diverse collection of flowers, one could possess an object of great beauty that would itself not decay.

The amazing attention to detail in Ruysch's work reflects the growth in botanical observation and knowledge during the previous century. Van Leeuwenhoek, the inventor of the microscope, hired artists to draw the organisms he could see through the instrument. That invention, as well as other Dutch optical achievements, such as the magnifying glass, led many artists to paint with enormous attention to detail.

Many of the most important illustrators of botanical manuals and other works of natural history were women. Among the leading figures was Anna Maria Sibylla Merian (1647–1717), a German woman who moved to the Netherlands and traveled to the Dutch colony of Surinam to study both plants and insects. Her work would have been enormously helpful to Ruysch, who would only rarely have worked from an actual bowl of real flowers.

■ *What does Ruysch's* Flower Still Life *tell us about the importance of flowers and commerce in seventeenth-century Holland? How does the painting indicate advances in botanical observations? How does the work deal with Calvinist morality and the richness and beauty of art?*

[5]Norman Bryson, *Looking at the Overlooked: Four Essays on Still Life Painting* (Cambridge, MA: Harvard University Press, 1990), p. 104.

Sources: Norman Bryson, *Looking at the Overlooked: Four Essays on Still Life Painting* (Cambridge, MA: Harvard University Press, 1990); Mariët Westermann, *A Worldly Art: The Dutch Republic, 1585–1718* (Upper Saddle River, NJ, and New York: Prentice Hall and Harry N. Abrams, 1990); Marilyn Stokstad, *Art History*, rev. ed. (Upper Saddle River, NJ, and New York: Prentice Hall and Harry N. Abrams, 1999), pp. 798–801.

CHECKING YOUR COMPREHENSION

Choose the best answer for each of the following questions.

1. Which of the following factors was not significant in the diminished power and influence of the United Netherlands during the eighteenth century after the death of William III of Britain?
    a. Local provinces prevented the emergence of a *stadtholder*.
    b. The Dutch lost their technology and superiority in shipbuilding.
    c. Pursuing a territorial war with Spain.
    d. Stagnation overtook many domestic industries such as textile finishing.

2. Which of the descriptions below would be a fair assessment of the leadership philosophy of Robert Walpole of Britain in the mid-eighteenth century?
    a. revolutionary
    b. status quo
    c. reformation
    d. parliamentarian

3. The Ottoman Empire was arguably was the largest and most stable political entity to arise near Europe since the fall of the Roman Empire. Which of the following made this empire so historically significant?
    a. the size of its geographical region
    b. the cultural and religious diversity among its people
    c. the ferocity of its invasions into the territories of its neighbors
    d. the longevity of its existence

4. How would you characterize the accomplishments of Peter the Great in Russia during the eighteenth century?
    a. modernizer
    b. war monger
    c. religious zealot
    d. traditionalist

Identify the following statements as true or false.

5. What plagued France during the eighteenth century was not lack of resources or military strength, but rather a lack of leadership from its monarch.

6. The single most important factor in the disappearance of Poland from Europe was termed "*liberum veto*" or "exploding the diet."

Answer the following questions.

7. Compare and contrast the Habsburg Empire and the Ottoman Empire in how each approached the rule of people of very diverse language, customs, and geography.

8. It wasn't until the late seventeenth century under Peter the Great that Russia began to develop ships. Why do you think Romanov or either of his successors did not place any importance on developing a naval armada?

Discussion and Critical Thinking Question

9. The United States is arguably recognized as possessing the best armed forces in the world today. Would you say, in light of the most recent conflicts in Iraq, that the leadership of our armed forces is more alike or different than the leadership of Frederick William over the Prussian Army?

NOTES

Learning

Nearly every organism must learn to survive in its environment. Indeed, the ability to adapt to the environment is often the key to determining which organisms survive long enough to pass on their genes to future generations. According to the evolutionary perspective, learning is an adaptive behavior that supports *natural selection*. We have already examined the physical structures (Chapter 2) and sensory and perceptual processes (Chapter 3) that we use to interact with our environment. In some cases our responses to environmental stimuli, such as reflexively blinking in response to a puff of air, are routine, very brief in duration, and do not enter consciousness. In other instances our awareness is critical when it comes to responding to and interacting with our environment. For example, we need to remember how to call 911 to summon the fire department, how to program our VCR to record a television program, and how to stop the bleeding from a severe cut. Similarly, once a field rat has found a way into a farmer's corn crib, it is helpful for the rat to remember how to return to this food source in the future. These longer-lasting effects of interacting with the environment are the focus of this chapter and the next. In short, they are what we mean when we speak of *learning*. In this chapter we discuss several basic forms of learning.

WHAT IS LEARNING?

For a person who has grown up in a small Nebraska town, driving in big-city traffic can be an anxiety-provoking experience. The furious pace and the large number of vehicles on the road can be overwhelming at first; with cars to the left, to the right, and almost in the trunk there is little sanity in sight! After several months of driving to and from work during the height of rush hour in Chicago, however, Linda, who grew up in a small town, has become a "real pro" at driving in big-city traffic. *Why would Linda's improved driving ability be considered an example of learning?*

Most psychologists define **learning** as a relatively permanent change in behavior or the potential to make a response that occurs as a result of some experience (Hergenhahn & Olson, 2001; Mazur, 1998). This definition distinguishes learned behaviors from those that occur automatically in response to external events, like shivering in a cold wind or sweating when it is hot. By including the concept of experience in the definition of learning, we distinguish between learned behaviors and behaviors that become possible as our physical capabilities develop—that is, *maturation*. For example, when you were 6 months old it is unlikely that you were able to walk. Around your first birthday (or shortly after), the ability to walk emerged. Did it occur as a result of learning? As we will see, the answer is no. When you were 2 years old, you did not have the strength to lift a 5-pound weight. By the time you were 10, however, lifting 5 pounds was easy. You did not have to learn anything to be able to walk or to pick up the 5-pound weight. As a result of the process of maturation, your muscles and nerves had developed to the point that you were able to walk and to lift the weight.

To return to our question, why would Linda's improved driving ability in Chicago be considered an example of learning? Unless Linda was very young at the time she

Definition clue

learning
A relatively permanent change in behavior or the potential to make a response that occurs as a result of experience

began big-city driving, we can rule out maturation as a cause for the change in her behavior. Likewise, the change in Linda's driving behavior is not an automatic response, like shivering in a cold wind or blinking when a puff of air is directed toward your eyes. Rather, the repeated experience of rush-hour city driving has brought about a change in her behavior; she has *learned*.

In Chapter 3 we discussed how psychologists study color vision in animals such as Ruby the elephant. Ruby's painting also provides us with a good example of learning. Initially, the sound of the word "paint" had no meaning, and Ruby made no response to it. After the word was associated (paired) with one of her favorite activities, Ruby began to squeal when her trainer said "paint." Ruby had learned that this word signaled the opportunity to engage in an enjoyable activity. The elephant's response is an example of a relatively permanent change in behavior that occurs as a result of experience; she has *learned*.

In this chapter we first discuss two of the three basic types of learning, *classical* (or respondent) *conditioning* and *operant* (or instrumental) *conditioning*. Later in the chapter we will explore more cognitively oriented perspectives on learning along with the third basic type of learning, *observational* learning or modeling. Keep in mind that the word *conditioning* refers to the fact that the learner forms an association, usually between a stimulus and a response or between two stimuli.

CLASSICAL CONDITIONING

A psychology class is participating in an unusual demonstration. The instructor passes a can of powdered lemonade mix around the room; each student puts a spoonful of the powder on a sheet of paper. Once all students have their own lemonade powder, they are instructed to wet one of their fingers. When the instructor says "now," each student puts a small amount of lemonade powder on his or her tongue with the moistened finger. The effect of putting lemonade powder on the tongue is predictable: The mouth puckers, and saliva begins to flow. The instructor has the students repeat this procedure several times during the class period until all the lemonade powder is gone. Before the class period ends, the instructor says "now" without warning. The students' mouths pucker, and saliva flows. *What is the purpose of this class demonstration?*

This demonstration is an example of *classical conditioning*, which has become so closely associated with the Russian scientist Ivan Pavlov (1849–1936) that it is often called *Pavlovian conditioning*. Pavlov was a physiologist whose work was so well respected that he received a Nobel Prize in Medicine in 1904 for his research on digestion. Although Pavlov conducted much of his research with dogs, examples of classical conditioning can be found in many human behaviors. **Classical conditioning** is a form of learning that occurs when two stimuli—a neutral stimulus and an unconditioned stimulus—that are "paired" (presented together) become associated with each other. For example, the sight of McDonald's golden arches and the smell and taste of a juicy burger have occurred together, and as a result many people associate the golden arches with tasty fast food.

Basic Elements of Classical Conditioning

We have said that the procedure for establishing classical conditioning is to present two events—called *stimuli*—so that the pairing of these two events causes a human participant or animal to make an association between them. At the start of conditioning, the first event, which in a laboratory setting may be the presentation of a light or a tone, is neutral—that is, not currently associated with the response to be established.

classical conditioning
Learning that occurs when two stimuli—a conditioned stimulus (originally a neutral stimulus) and an unconditioned stimulus—are paired and become associated with each other

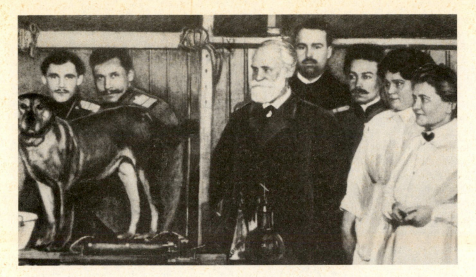

Ivan Pavlov's research on digestion was so well regarded that he was awarded the Nobel Prize in 1904. In the course of his research, he surgically brought the opening of the salivary gland to the outside of the dog's skin so the secretion of saliva could be seen and measured. Over time, Pavlov and his research team noticed that the dogs began salivating to stimuli other than food. The precision of the laboratory provided Pavlov with the setting in which he could investigate the components of what became known as classical conditioning.

What was the neutral stimulus in the lemonade example at the start of this section? Keep reading and you will find out. When this **neutral stimulus (NS)** is presented, the participant may notice that it is there, but it does not cause any particular reaction. By presenting the second event, called an **unconditioned stimulus (UCS),** after the NS, however, we transform the NS into a **conditioned stimulus (CS).** The NS becomes a CS because it is repeatedly paired with a UCS. This pairing eventually causes the participant to establish an association between the two events; the CS comes to *predict* the occurrence of the UCS. In the lemonade powder example the word "now" was the NS; it became a CS after it was paired with the lemonade powder.

As the term suggests, the UCS automatically produces a reaction; the participant does not have to be trained to react to it. The UCS never fails to produce the same reaction. Food in your mouth causes you to salivate; touching a hot stove causes you to jerk your hand away; a puff of air to your eye causes you to blink. In psychological terms, the UCS elicits, or calls forth, a response. The reaction that is elicited by the UCS is called the **unconditioned response (UCR).** If you have a feeling that we have already discussed this type of response, you are correct. These UCRs are reflexes, like those we described in Chapter 2. You do not have to learn a UCR; all organisms come equipped by nature with a number of built-in responses, which generally have survival value. For example, you do not learn to jerk your hand away when you touch a hot stove; you pull it away automatically. It is a built-in (unconditioned) response. As part of a routine physical examination, a physician may use a small rubber hammer to hit an area just below your knee. When your lower leg kicks up, the physician knows that particular reflex (called knee flexion) is working properly (see Chapter 2). Now, what is the UCR in the lemonade powder example?

When a participant associates the NS (for example, a light or a tone) with the UCS, the NS is transformed into a CS that can elicit a response similar to the UCR (for example, a little less saliva). The response caused by the CS is known as the **conditioned response (CR).** When the CS elicits the CR, we say that classical conditioning has occurred. Ivan Pavlov (1927) used food as the UCS in his pioneering studies. While a metronome was ticking (CS), he placed a small amount of meat powder (UCS) into a hungry dog's mouth. The meat powder caused the dog to begin salivating (UCR). Later, when just the sound of the ticking metronome was presented, the dog salivated (CR).

Let's return to the earlier demonstration in which lemonade powder was associated with the word "now" (Cogan & Cogan, 1984) so that you can experience classical conditioning firsthand. Consider what occurred naturally (UCS–UCR) and what was learned (CS–CR) and complete the blanks in this sentence to see if you can

neutral stimulus (NS)
Stimulus that, before conditioning, does not elicit a particular response

unconditioned stimulus (UCS)
Event that automatically produces a response without any previous training

conditioned stimulus (CS)
Neutral stimulus that acquires the ability to elicit a conditioned response after being paired with an unconditioned stimulus

unconditioned response (UCR)
Reaction that is automatically produced when an unconditioned stimulus is presented

conditioned response (CR)
Response elicited by a conditioned stimulus that has been paired with an unconditioned stimulus; is similar to the unconditioned response

apply the terminology just described to the demonstration. "The CS, _____, paired with the UCS, _____, results in the UCR, _____." The CS is the word "now." The lemonade powder is the UCS; it automatically elicits the unconditioned response (UCR) of puckering and salivating. Initially the word "now" is a neutral stimulus. After it is paired with the lemonade powder several times, however, it becomes a CS and now elicits the conditioned response (CR) of puckering and salivating.

Let's put these elements together in another example. Suppose that your younger brother is just tall enough to reach a hot skillet on the stove. He grabs it and immediately drops it. His pain is obvious and intense, and you try to comfort him. Finally his tears stop, and you put the incident out of your mind. Three days later, however, the same skillet is again on the stove. Your brother enters the kitchen, sees the skillet, and begins to cry. Clearly, the skillet has taken on a new meaning for him, demonstrating that some stimuli are so memorable that they produce learning without the need for repeated pairing.

In classical conditioning terms, initially the skillet was an NS (does not cause any particular response); after conditioning, it became the CS. The intense heat was the UCS, which always elicits pain and an avoidance response. Those responses—the pain and jerking the hand away or dropping the skillet—constitute the UCR. Remember that the classical conditioning sequence involves first presenting the NS and then following it with the UCS. If these two events are associated, the NS becomes a CS that signals that the UCS is on its way.

After a conditioning experience of this type, when the CS is encountered alone, it produces a response—the CR—that is very similar to the UCR. In our example, the sight of the skillet reminds your brother of the pain he experienced. The classical conditioning sequence for this situation is presented in diagrammatic form in Figure 5-1.

The UCS does not have to be a painful event like heat, electric shock, or hitting your finger with a hammer (Capaldi & Sheffer, 1992; Owens, Capaldi, & Sheffer, 1993). A wide variety of stimuli can serve as a UCS; their associated responses are

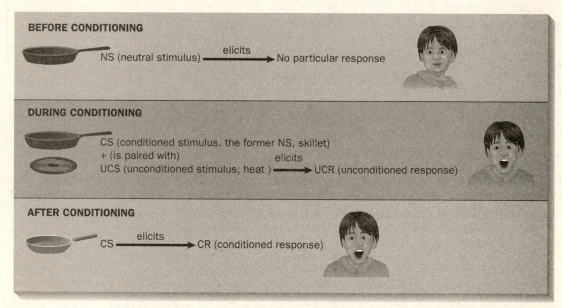

FIGURE 5-1 Using our symbols, we can describe classical conditioning in the following manner: *Before Conditioning*: The NS originally does not elicit a specific response. *During Conditioning*: The NS (now called the CS) is presented just before the UCS. The UCS automatically elicits a UCR. *After Conditioning*: Later, when the CS is presented by itself, a CR, which is similar to the UCR, occurs. In short, a new response, the CR, has been conditioned to the CS because the CS has been paired with the UCS.

TABLE 5-1

Common Unconditioned Stimuli (UCS) and Their Associated Unconditioned Responses (UCR).

The associations between these stimuli and responses are built-in or innate. Each of the responses can be elicited from the organism by using the appropriate stimulus.

UCS	UCR
Voluntary muscles	
sharp or hot stimuli	jerk away and cry
blows, shock, burns	withdrawal
gentle caresses	relaxation and calm
object touches lip	sucking
food in mouth	swallowing
object touches hand	grasping
novel stimulation	reflexive orienting
Circulatory system	
high temperature	sweating, flushing
sudden loud noise	blanching, pounding heart
Digestive system	
good food	salivation
bad food	sickness, nausea, vomiting
Respiratory system	
irritation in nose	sneeze
throat clogged	cough
allergens	asthma attack
Emotional system	
painful blow	fear
sexual stimulation	erotic feeling
Reproductive system	
genital stimulation	vaginal lubrication, penile erection, orgasm
nipple stimulation	milk release (in lactating women)

Source: Baldwin & Baldwin, 2001

reflexes that are often crucial for basic biological functioning, survival, and reproduction (Baldwin & Baldwin, 2001). For example, a bite of your favorite food when you are hungry automatically causes you to salivate. Food in your mouth is the UCS; salivation is the UCR. The positive feelings you experience when you receive a kiss or a hug are also examples of UCS. Table 5-1 contains a list of common UCSs and UCRs; as you will see such stimuli and responses are found throughout our bodily systems. What is important about classical conditioning is that organisms learn to respond not only to the original UCS, they learn to respond to other CSs that become associated with our reflexes (Baldwin & Baldwin, 2001).

Obviously, psychologists do not hide in restaurants waiting to present a tone while you are eating, nor do most instructors take lemonade powder to class with them. Yet people become classically conditioned in much the same way that Pavlov's dogs did. For example, the sights and sounds that accompany meals can become conditioned stimuli.

For many people, the unique decor of a restaurant, an advertisement, or a menu may act as a CS. Have you ever found yourself salivating as you looked at the tempting pictures in an advertisement or browsed up and down the aisles of a grocery store? Numerous examples of classical conditioning of CRs exist in everyday life. Is there a particular song (CS) that prompts you to recall a happy moment (CR)? Do you know someone who purchases cars only of a certain color because that color was associated in the past with a favorite car?

Hands On

Conditioning Your Friends

The ease by which classical conditioning is demonstrated in class can be duplicated in real life. This demonstration rests on the premise that most people have been conditioned to flinch (the startle response) when we see someone stick a balloon with a pin. (The pin is the CS, the bang is the UCS, and the startle response is the UCR.) Use the following procedure to surprise your friends and observe classical conditioning at the same time.

You will need about 20 good-quality balloons and a needle. Any sharp sewing needle will do, but for especially dramatic effect a foot-long needle is best. Blow up 15 to 20 balloons. Then have a friend pop 5 or 6 of them with the needle. Next have your friends watch you use the needle to pop 5 or 6 more balloons. Once you have popped several of them, stick the needle into an area of the balloon where there is less tension (the nipple or around the knot). Because there is less tension at these points, the rubber is relatively thick, and the balloon does not pop when it is stuck. Your friends will still flinch, however. Why? They have been conditioned to expect a loud bang. If you use a foot-long needle, you can make the effect even more dramatic by passing the needle completely through the balloon (enter at the nipple and exit at the knot, see photographs below).

Psychological Detective

Think of your own examples of classical conditioning. You will probably find it easiest to start with the UCS, then decide what the UCR is, and finally determine what CSs might readily occur in the presence of the UCS. Think of a food smell that makes you remember a pleasant childhood memory—perhaps cookies baking or the cinnamon smell of hot apple pie. Do you think of a particular event, and does your mouth water? The food you enjoy is the UCS. What is the UCR? The CS? The CR? (See some possible answers at the end of the chapter.)

Dr. Edie McClellan prepares to demonstrate that a needle can be put through a balloon and not pop it. When the needle approaches the balloon (A), many students flinch—a conditioned response based on past experiences of hearing the noise as a pin was pushed into a balloon. Sticking the needle through the thick part of the balloon allows the needle to be passed entirely through the balloon without popping it (B).

A

B

Classical Conditioning Processes

Pavlov's research revealed several important processes of classical conditioning besides those discussed so far. These findings fall into two general categories: *acquisition*, or how we develop CRs, and *extinction*, or how we eliminate those responses.

Acquisition. Acquisition is the training stage during which a particular response (for example, salivating or blinking) is learned (occurs after a CS is presented). Several factors influence the acquisition of CRs. Among them are the order in which the CS and UCS are presented, the intensity of the UCS, and the number of times the CS and UCS are paired (Barker, 2001). We now take a closer look at each of these factors.

Sequence of CS-UCS Presentation. The sequence in which the CS and UCS are presented influences the strength of the conditioning. The optimum sequence is for the CS to precede the UCS and remain until the UCS is presented. This particular sequence is often called *forward conditioning*. Other sequences, such as the UCS preceding the CS (that is, *backward conditioning*), produce weaker conditioning.

Strength of the UCS. The stronger the UCS, the stronger the conditioning (Holloway & Domjan, 1993). When Pavlov gave his dogs a small amount of meat powder, they did not salivate as much as they did when he gave them a large amount of meat powder. The hot skillet your younger brother grabbed on the stove was a painful and salient stimulus. Stronger UCSs elicit stronger UCRs; weaker UCSs elicit weaker UCRs.

Number of CS-UCS Pairings. The more times the CS and UCS are presented together, the stronger the CR becomes. It is easy to conduct research on the relation between the CS and the UCS when we can use a laboratory setup such as Pavlov's. Under such conditions, the number of times the CS and UCS are presented can be determined precisely. The effects of varying numbers of CS-UCS pairings, however, can also be demonstrated in real life. If your little brother grabs the hot skillet more than once, the chances are good that his CR to the skillet will be stronger. If you have eaten at an exceptionally fine restaurant several times, your conditioned responses to the sight of the restaurant and its menu will be stronger than they would be if you had eaten there only once before. Figure 5-2 displays several patterns of classical conditioning acquisition; as you can see, as the percentage of pairings increases, acquisition of the CR becomes stronger.

Extinction. Once a CR has been acquired, what can be done to extinguish or eliminate that response? The easiest procedure is to present the CS without the UCS and record how strong the CR is and how many times or how long we can present the CS alone before the CR disappears. The number of times the CS is presented without the UCS is a very important factor in eliminating the CR. When Pavlov repeatedly sounded the tone (CS) without giving the dog any meat powder (UCS), the number of drops of saliva produced gradually decreased each time the tone was sounded. Similarly, if your brother grabs the skillet several times when it is cold, his fear will decrease a little each time.

PAVLOV
KNOCK,
DO NOT
RING BELL,
DOGS
INSIDE

 5.1

SNIF
SNIF...

SPLOIT...

DOG

EVEN **PAVLOV'S** DOG WOULDN'T SALIVATE AT THIS!

FIGURE 5-2 Acquisition patterns in classical conditioning when the UCS is presented at different percentages on trials (a series of presentations of stimuli). Within a given trial, the CS and UCS were paired 25% to 100% of the time. Some participants received the CS and UCS on every presentation during a trial; in other cases, the UCS was presented with the CS only 25% of the time. Across trials, greater pairing of the UCS with the CS led to stronger conditioning, that is, more frequent occurrence of the CR.

Source: Hartman & Grant, 1960.

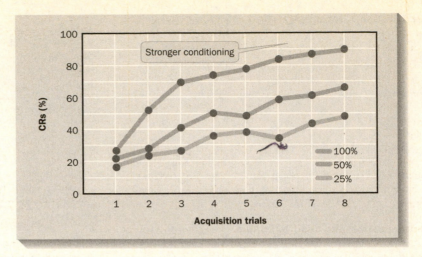

extinction
A general term for the reduction and elimination of behaviors; in classical conditioning extinction occurs when repeated presentation of the CS alone leads to a reduction in the strength of the CR

spontaneous recovery
Reappearance of an extinguished CR after the passage of time

Extinction is a general term for a reduction and disappearance of a behavior; in the case of classical conditioning, extinction occurs when repeated presentation of the CS alone leads to a decrease in the strength of the CR (Schreurs, 1993). The stronger the CR, the longer extinction takes. What takes place during acquisition influences the process of extinction. For example, the stronger the UCS and the more frequently it is presented during acquisition, the longer it will take to extinguish the CR.

Spontaneous Recovery. At times a classical conditioning participant seems to "forget" that extinction has occurred. Consider Pavlov's dog once again. Only the CS (a bell in this case) has been presented to the dog several times during its daily extinction session. The CR (salivation) has decreased until it appears that the dog is not salivating at all. When the dog is returned to its cage, we might conclude that the extinction process is complete. When the CS is presented on the following day, however, the dog begins to salivate once more. Pavlov (1927) called this phenomenon **spontaneous recovery** because the CR recovers some of the strength it lost during the previous extinction session. This process is diagrammed in Figure 5-3. The amount of spontaneous recovery will decrease from day to day until the CR finally does not occur at the start of a session. At this point extinction of the response is probably complete.

Spontaneous recovery is not limited to laboratory experiments; it occurs in real-life situations as well. For example, let's say you went skiing last winter and on the second day you had a very bad fall. After summoning as much courage and

FIGURE 5-3 Extinction occurs when the tone (CS) is presented without meat powder (UCS). By the end of each daily extinction session, the CR is quite weak. It regains some strength, however, by the start of the next session, a phenomenon known as spontaneous recovery. By the end of extinction, the CR is quite low, and the amount of spontaneous recovery may be undetectable.

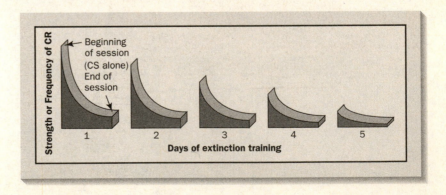

determination as possible, you put your skis on and went back out on the slopes for the next 2 days. Thankfully, there were no additional spills on those days; your fear seemed to be extinguished. Now, a full year later, you have returned to the ski resort. You experience some apprehension as you pull on your ski boots. You thought the fear had disappeared—that it had been extinguished—by the time you were finished skiing last year, but a bit seems to have returned (spontaneous recovery) this year.

Figure 5-4 illustrates the relations among acquisition, extinction, and spontaneous recovery. Consult this figure as you read this section to provide you with the "big picture" of all of the elements and processes involved in classical conditioning.

Generalization and Discrimination.

Suppose that several days after your little brother made the mistake of grabbing the hot skillet, the two of you are walking through the housewares section of a department store when he starts crying and refuses to walk any farther. You note where he is looking and see a display of skillets. Is he afraid of them also? Yes, he is, and the more those skillets resemble the one at home, the greater is his fear.

When a response occurs to stimuli that are similar to a CS, **generalization** has occurred. The effects of classical conditioning may be applied (generalized) to other stimuli that are similar to the original CS; they "spread" from the original stimulus to others. For example, although Pavlov's dogs were conditioned to salivate in response to a specific tone (CS), they also salivated when other tones were presented (see Figure 5-5). Someone who has acquired a fear of snakes, might react with fear when seeing a piece of rope lying on the ground a few feet away. The similarity of the snake to the rope elicits the fear response (CR), which has generalized from the snake. Suppose your favorite color is red and whenever you see it you feel warm all over. You might have a similar, perhaps somewhat muted, reaction to various shades of red.

It is easy to see how generalization occurs. If you have ever been stung by a wasp, you probably have a healthy respect for all flying insects, especially those that resemble

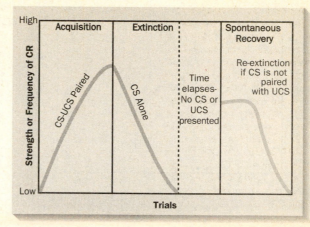

FIGURE 5-4 The basic phases of classical conditioning. In the acquisition or training phase, the CS and UCS are paired together and lead to the UCR. This pairing eventually leads to production of the CR following the CS. Repeated presentation of the CS alone leads to extinction. Following the passage of time, presentation of the CS alone may lead to spontaneous recovery of the CR.

generalization
Occurrence of responses to stimuli that are similar to a CS

A bad fall on a ski slope can result in a classically conditioned fear. Getting up and "hitting the slopes" immediately after such a fall is one of the best ways to extinguish the fear. The extinction may be "forgotten" over the summer, resulting in spontaneous recovery of the fear response when you hit the slopes once again the following year.

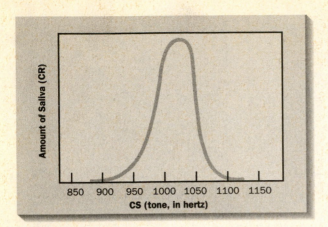

FIGURE 5-5 Generalization occurs when organisms respond to stimuli that are similar to the original CS. As Pavlov discovered, dogs would salivate to tones that are similar to the original CS. Tones that were less similar to the original CS were less likely to lead to the CR of salivation.

wasps. Your response has generalized from one stimulus to many others. But if you are not stung every time you encounter a flying insect, many of these generalized responses will be extinguished. Thus, as children we quickly discover that butterflies and moths do not sting, whereas hornets and bees do. We therefore come to fear the stinging insects but not the others. In other words, we learn to distinguish or discriminate between conditioned stimuli that accurately predict the occurrence of the UCS and those that do not (Bouton & Brooks, 1993; Nakajima, 1993). Through this process of **discrimination,** we have extinguished our fear of insects that do not sting but have retained our fear of insects that do.

Generalization and discrimination work in opposite ways. Whereas generalization makes you more likely to respond to a number of similar stimuli, discrimination narrows your response to the appropriate stimulus and no other. Discrimination thus requires stimuli that are clearly distinguishable. For example, if you could not easily distinguish between insects that sting and those that do not, imagine how apprehensive you would be whenever you went outdoors.

Pavlov (1928) understood this principle and investigated it. First, he trained a group of dogs to discriminate between a circle and an ellipse; the circle was always associated with food. Once this association was made, Pavlov changed the ellipse over a series of presentations until it was indistinguishable from the circle.

Psychological Detective

What behavior(s) did Pavlov's dogs show when confronted by these two indistinguishable stimuli? Write down your answer before reading further.

Because the dogs were unable to discriminate between the two stimuli, they salivated to both of them. They displayed other behaviors that did not occur when they were able to discriminate between the two stimuli. They whined and yelped, became agitated, and tried to escape from their harnesses. To Pavlov's surprise, these behaviors continued outside the experimental room. Pavlov called these inappropriate behaviors *experimental neuroses* and believed that they occurred when an animal or human attempted to solve a discrimination task that could not be solved. This analysis provides a clue concerning a possible origin of some abnormal behaviors in humans (see Chapter 12; Baumrind, 1983). As the next section shows, such agitation and apprehension can influence our motivated behavior.

Applications of Classical Conditioning: Phobias and Beyond

In 1913, John B. Watson proclaimed that psychologists should study only directly observable behaviors. As we saw in Chapter 1, Watson's approach to psychology was called *behaviorism*. According to the behaviorists, the main business of psychology is the study of behaviors such as jogging in the park, running through an airport to catch a flight, and even expressing emotion. Anything having to do with thinking, feeling, or consciousness was not considered an appropriate subject of psychological study because those processes could not be observed directly. The behaviorists' goal was to discover which observable stimuli elicit which responses (observable behaviors). In pursuit of this goal, John Watson and his assistant, Rosalie Rayner, classically conditioned 9-month-old "Little Albert" to fear a white rat (Watson & Rayner, 1920). At first Albert

discrimination
Occurrence of responses only to a specific CS

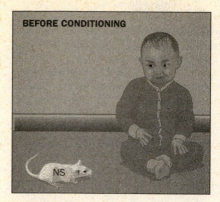
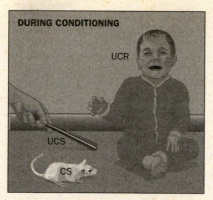
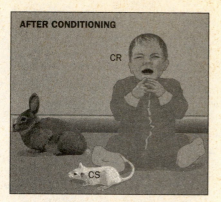

FIGURE 5-6   Conditioning "Little Albert" to fear a white rat. *Before conditioning*: Originally Little Albert had no fear of the white rat (the NS for Little Albert); the rat had no fear of Little Albert (the NS for the rat). *During conditioning*: While Little Albert is playing with the rat, John Watson strikes a steel bar. The loud noise (UCS) elicits a startle and fear response (UCR). The white rat (now the CS) is associated with the loud noise for Little Albert. Little Albert (now the CS) is associated with the loud noise for the rat. *After conditioning*: Later, the white rat elicits fear in Little Albert. Other objects, such as a rabbit, that are similar to the white rat now elicit fear in Little Albert, and the boy, in turn, elicits fear in the rat.

showed no fear of the rat and even allowed it to crawl on him. (You can view a filmed segment of this research on the CD that accompanies this text.) While Little Albert was playing with the rat, Watson hit a steel rod with a hammer, making a sudden, deafening noise. Not surprisingly, Albert was startled and scared. Each time the loud noise was paired with the presence of the rat, Albert cried in fear. After several pairings of the two stimuli, Albert started crying at the sight of the rat, even when there was no noise, and he eventually came to fear any object that resembled a rat, such as a white rabbit and even the white whiskers on a Santa Claus mask. Albert developed a phobia for rats and ratlike objects. Unfortunately, no one followed Albert throughout his life; hence we do not know how long these phobias plagued him.

Let's analyze the elements of Little Albert's fear. What UCS was used? What was the UCR? What were the CS and the CR? While you think about these questions, remember that the rat was also exposed to a frightening situation. For both Little Albert and the rat, the UCS was the loud noise. The UCR was the state of being startled and scared. For Albert, the CS was the rat; for the rat, the CS was Albert. The CR for both of them was fear of an object that signaled that a loud noise might follow. These relations are diagrammed in Figure 5-6.

Many of the unconditioned responses we make have an emotional component that is either pleasurable or aversive. When a reflex is elicited, it often brings up emotional responses, as was the case with Little Albert. As we have seen, some of these emotional reactions are pleasurable (for example, involving food and sex), whereas others are aversive (for example, painful stimuli). These pleasure and pain components of our reflexes can be traced back to our basic biological survival functions (Keltner & Haidt, 1999; Levenson, 1999).

Psychological Detective

Although the Watson and Rayner study is important because it was one of the first efforts to show that an emotional reaction like fear could be classically conditioned (resulting in a *conditioned fear response*), it raises questions about the ethics of psychological research (see Chapter 1). Was it acceptable for Watson and Rayner purposely

[Handwritten margin notes:]
watson hit a steel
Albert starts to fear
for rats and ratlike objects
when he was child.
Phobia can come to
everyone when we was child
Phobia can come to the
child through images
fear of images is a kind
of Phobia

to frighten Little Albert so intensely? Would you allow such an experiment to be conducted with your child? Would such a procedure be acceptable if the child's parents authorized it? Write down your responses and the reasons for them before reading further.

John B. Watson (left), his research assistant Rosalie Rayner (right) and Little Albert were part of one of the most well known research efforts in psychology. The findings showed how classical conditioning could be responsible for the development of phobias. This research, however, raised many ethical questions; it could not be conducted under the ethics code in place today.

The Ethical Principles of Psychologists and Code of Conduct, published by the American Psychological Association (2002), would probably say "no" to all of our questions. If Watson and Rayner were to conduct their research with Little Albert in the 21st century, they would have difficulty meeting the ethical standards you read about in Chapter 1.

Despite the questionable ethics exhibited in the Little Albert research, classical conditioning has been a focus of attention in our efforts to understand phobias since the 1920s. Consider the case of Scott, who was 3 years old when he was locked in an abandoned refrigerator by his playmates and nearly died from suffocation. Ever since then, he has avoided closed spaces. Now, 30 years later, he is still deathly afraid of closed spaces and anything that reminds him of them. He cannot stand to ride in an elevator and always takes the stairs, even in tall buildings. Even seeing a picture of a refrigerator makes him break out in a cold sweat. If you were unaware of Scott's background, his intense fear of closed spaces, such as elevators, compact cars, and small rooms might seem strange. Although you may not fear closed spaces to the same degree as Scott, chances are good that you are afraid of certain other objects or situations that most people do not fear. How do we acquire many of these apparently unrealistic, irrational fears?

Many of our fears and anxieties may have been classically conditioned, as in the case of Scott's fear of closed spaces. Because he was locked in an abandoned refrigerator when he was a child and nearly died, Scott now fears anything that remotely resembles a closed space. He has a condition known as a *phobia*; more specifically, he is suffering from *claustrophobia* (*claustrop*, "enclosed place"; *phobos*, "fear"). A **phobia** is an irrational fear of an activity, object, or situation, that is out of proportion to the actual danger it poses. Because phobias create so much anxiety that they interfere with normal functioning, they are classified as *anxiety disorders* (see Chapter 12). Other people with phobias may not be able to recall a specific event that is the cause of the phobia. Thus many phobias exert their influence in a seemingly mysterious and potentially detrimental manner.

As you might expect, phobias can interfere with a person's daily activities. For example, a salesperson suffering from *glossophobia* (fear of speaking) would not do very well in the business world where meeting and greeting clients are the order of the day. A psychiatrist, Joseph Wolpe (1915–1997), developed a treatment, known as *systematic desensitization*, to help eliminate phobias (Rachman, 2000). Basically, systematic desensitization involves classically conditioning a desired response, relaxation, to the phobic stimuli; it has been quite successful in treating a range of phobias (Hoffmann & Odendal, 2001; Schneider & Nevid, 1993; Ventis, Higbee, & Murdock, 2001). For example, using this procedure a person with claustrophobia, like Scott, is conditioned to relax in enclosed spaces. We discuss systematic desensitization in greater detail in Chapter 13.

Classical Conditioning and Our Motives.   As the discussion of Little Albert and the development of phobias reveals, classical conditioning has a lot more to say about human and animal behavior than you might think based on its origins in research on salivation. As a result of his conditioning, Little Albert was motivated to avoid rats and other furry animals. As we will see next, classical conditioning can lead organisms to develop a range of other behaviors that can have long-lasting influences. Even though Jim did not have cats as pets when he was a child, his friends persuaded him to adopt the cute stray kitten he found last week. Jim is now convinced this was a very bad idea. Each evening, when Jim has settled into his favorite chair to watch the evening news,

phobia
Irrational fear of an activity, object, or situation that is out of proportion to the actual danger posed

the kitten launches a sneak attack. After a week of this behavior, Jim becomes tense as soon as he sits in his favorite chair, whether the kitten is in the room or not. The sound of the evening news increases his anxiety. When Jim leaves the room, he immediately feels better.

What is the relation among the kitten's attacks, Jim's tension and anxiety, and motivation? Parts of the story about Jim and his cat may sound familiar. Can we describe the cat's sneak attack in psychological terms that you have already learned? Would certain responses automatically follow such an attack? If you said that pain, fear, or anxiety would follow, we would agree. What kind of stimuli automatically elicit a response? If you are thinking that unconditioned stimuli (UCSs) elicit unconditioned responses (UCRs), you are right again. What about Jim's favorite chair and the evening news program? What role do they serve? After these stimuli have been associated with cat attacks several times, they cause Jim to become tense and anxious. These are conditioned stimuli (CSs), and the tension and anxiety they produce are conditioned responses (CRs).

How is Jim's conditioned anxiety related to motivation? Through the process of classical conditioning, Jim's favorite chair and the evening news have become CSs that elicit tension and anxiety. Jim finds these feelings of tension and anxiety unpleasant and is motivated to reduce them when they occur by leaving the room. Motives that are acquired through the process of classical conditioning are called **learned motives.** Many other motives are acquired in this manner. Phobias are excellent examples of learned motives. Classical conditioning appears to be at the core of many of these unusual fears.

The same procedure and logic can be applied to the learning of goals and incentives. The importance of many of the goals and incentives that motivate our behavior is also learned through classical conditioning; hence they are termed **learned goals (incentives).** Consider money, diamonds, gold, and concert tickets. An infant's response to these objects will quickly convince you that they do not possess intrinsic value; we must learn their value before their acquisition is reinforcing.

Trends in Classical Conditioning: After Pavlov

Our conception of classical conditioning has changed dramatically since Pavlov's time. We now know that conditioning is not an automatic process that simply links conditioned stimuli and unconditioned stimuli. Psychologists now place more emphasis on what information the CS seems to tell or convey to the participant.

Contingency Theory. One principle that has emerged from this continued research is that the better the CS predicts the occurrence of the UCS, the stronger the conditioning will be (Bolles, 1979; Rescorla, 1968). (Recall that we encountered the importance of predictability when we discussed the sequence of CS-UCS presentation on page 187). A study of classical conditioning in two groups of rats illustrates this point (Rescorla, 1968). For the first group the CS (tone) was always *followed by* the UCS (a shock). The animals in this group were called the *contingent group* because the occurrence of shock always followed (was contingent on) the tone. The animals in the second group heard the tone *before* or *after* the shock was presented. These animals were called the *noncontingent group* because the occurrence of shock did not always follow (was not contingent on) the tone. Because the tone perfectly predicted the UCS for the *contingent* animals, classical conditioning was strong. Classical conditioning was weaker for the *noncontingent* animals because the CS did not always precede the UCS.

This relation should not be surprising. As we have seen, a strong and predictable CS is the goal of the acquisition or training process during which an association between the CS and UCS is formed. A particular CS predicts that a particular UCS is about to occur. For Pavlov's dogs, for example, the sound of the ticking metronome reliably predicted the delivery of meat powder. Conversely, when we undertake extinction, we try to convince the participant that the CS will no longer be followed by—will no longer predict—the UCS (Delemater, 1995). The more reliable the CS is in predicting the UCS, the harder it will be to extinguish the CR. As the next section shows,

learned motives
Motives that are learned or acquired, usually through classical conditioning

learned goals (incentives)
Goals or incentives that are learned, usually through classical conditioning

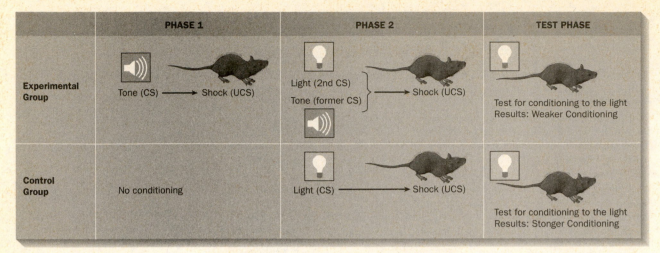

FIGURE 5-7 Research on the phenomenon of *blocking* has convincingly demonstrated that the pairing of the CS and UCS is not the only factor involved in classical conditioning. The timing of the pairing can lead to results in which prior pairings can *block* the effect of a particular CS.

Source: Kamin, 1969

however, conditioned stimuli do not automatically become associated with unconditioned stimuli, even if they are predictable.

Blocking.　If classical conditioning simply involves the pairing of a CS and a UCS, the time at which the pairing occurs should not make any difference. But the timing of the pairing does matter. Consider the following research. One group of rats was classically conditioned by presenting a tone (CS) and following it with an electric shock (UCS) (Kamin, 1969). Once a response to the tone was conditioned, a second CS (a light) was also presented before the shock. A second group of animals received only pairings of the light and the shock. The researcher then tested the strength of conditioning to the light. This experimental arrangement is shown in Figure 5-7.

Conditioning was weaker for the animals that received tone–shock pairings before tone and light were paired with shock. The animals that received only the light–shock pairing demonstrated stronger conditioning. The conditioning of the tone before presenting the light had blocked or reduced the conditioning of the light.

If you consider predictability again, this result makes sense. If the tone had already been established as a predictable CS, another predictable CS was not needed (Barnett, Grahame, & Miller, 1993; Williams, 1994). For the animals that had already received tone-and-shock pairings, the result was **blocking** of the light–and–shock association. Because light was the only CS presented to the other group of animals, it was conditioned strongly.

Evolution and Classical Conditioning: Taste-Aversion Learning and Preparedness

Suppose that you have just moved to a large metropolitan area, which is quite different from the small town you left behind. For example, the variety of restaurants is amazing. Last night some friends took you to a seafood restaurant. The décor and atmosphere of the restaurant were intriguing; the taste of the food was delightful and unlike any you had ever had. Unfortunately, however, during the night you came down with the stomach flu that had been going around. For the rest of the night you were nauseated or worse—not a pleasant experience. These events may not seem to involve learning, but

blocking
Situation in which the condition-ability of a CS is weakened when it is paired with a UCS that has previously been paired with another CS

classical conditioning took place: You were conditioned to avoid seafood. But why? As it turns out, "The brain is not equally sensitive to all types of stimuli. Some types of stimuli are much more important for survival than others, and evolutionary processes have prepared the brain to locate some types of causal correlations more easily than others" (Baldwin & Baldwin, 2001, p. 24).

Taste Aversion.   Does becoming nauseated after eating a food that is unusual to you have anything to do with learning? The notion of predictability is helpful once again. Whenever a person or animal becomes ill after consuming a food with a novel taste (taste-aversion), that taste (CS) may become a predictor of illness.

Taste-aversion learning involves the development of an aversion to (dislike of) a flavor that has been associated with illness (Batsell & Best, 1992, 1993). In the mid-1960s, John Garcia and his colleagues demonstrated that when a novel flavor was used as the CS and illness or nausea was the UCR, rats developed an intense aversion to the flavor, which has become known as the *Garcia effect.* Classical conditioning of a tone and food occurs best when the tone is sounded one-half second before the food is presented, but strong taste aversions can be conditioned when illness occurs more than an hour after the taste is experienced (Garcia, Ervin, & Koelling, 1966). When Garcia's research was first reported, it was greeted with much skepticism because it did not seem to follow established principles of classical conditioning. The significant amount of time between the presentation of the CS and the UCS was at odds with what researchers had learned from decades of laboratory research. As a result, Garcia's research was refused publication in the major journal devoted to animal behavior. It is credit to his persistence that his work was not only accepted, it is considered classic in demonstrating that "an animal's evolutionary inheritance places limits on what it can learn" (Leahey, 2001, p. 288).

There are two points of interest in these taste-aversion results. First, the flavor had to be novel for it to become associated with the illness. A flavor that has been consumed many times does not predict illness. Second, the time between the onset of the CS (taste) and the onset of the UCS (illness) can be quite lengthy, yet strong conditioning still occurs.

Preparedness.   Certain stimuli, such as flavors, can be associated with certain unconditioned responses, such as illness, more easily than they can be associated with other UCRs, such as electric shock. Animals seem to be biologically ready or *prepared* to associate certain CSs with certain UCSs (Seligman, 1970). Some events seem to go together naturally, whereas others do not. For humans and many animal species, taste and illness form one such natural pairing; presenting a tone or light CS with an electric shock is another natural pair. If instead we try to pair the tone or light CS with illness or the taste CS with an electric shock, we get very weak conditioning (Garcia & Koelling, 1966; see Figure 5-8). Other pairings also are learned quite easily. For example, humans, as well as many household pets, seem prepared to associate the sight of lightning (CS) with the sound of thunder. **Preparedness** occurs when some species are more biologically ready to form certain associations; it may explain why some phobias are learned so easily (see Chapter 12). We do not seem prepared, however, to associate loud noises with nausea or illness.

Psychological Detective

Preparedness may differ according to the species that is being tested. For example, birds use color, rather than taste, as an important cue in food selection. In birds, how would you determine whether color can be conditioned to an illness UCS more easily than a taste? Give this question some thought, and diagram an experiment to test it before proceeding.

---

taste-aversion learning
Development of a dislike or aversion to a flavor or food that has been paired with illness

preparedness
Theory that organisms are biologically ready or prepared to associate certain conditioned stimuli (CSs) with certain unconditioned stimuli (UCSs)

FIGURE 5-8 Whether rats develop taste aversions depends on the stimuli and the responses involved. *Group 1* was shocked while drinking bright, noisy water: They developed an aversion to water. *Group 2* drank the same water and received radiation that caused nausea: They did not develop an aversion to water. *Group 3* drank a saccharin solution and were shocked: They did not develop an aversion to saccharin. *Group 4* drank a saccharin solution and were irradiated (nausea): They developed an aversion to saccharin. There are natural relations between events and the pain the rats experienced. When pain comes from "out there" rats search for external predictors (light and noise associated with drinking water). Nausea is experienced internally, so rats associate it with an internal stimulus—saccharin. Through evolution, organisms have been *prepared* to make some associations more readily than others.

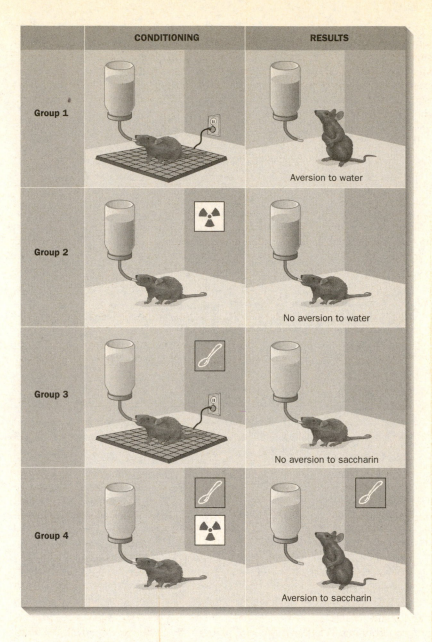

In a study designed to answer this question, investigators first presented blue, sour-tasting water (CS) to quail and then made the birds ill temporarily by giving them a nausea-producing drug (Wilcoxin, Dragoin, & Kral, 1971). After the birds became ill they had a strong aversion to the blue color but not to the sour taste. These findings suggest that the quail were unprepared—or "contraprepared"—to make the taste-illness association. Preparedness theory suggests one important means by which animals adapt to their environments: They learn to avoid potentially dangerous stimuli that have made them ill on a previous occasion. Avoiding such substances increases their chances of survival. With their keen eyesight, birds are more likely to discriminate stimuli on the basis of color, whereas rats and mice, whose eyesight is poor, are likely to discriminate on the basis of taste. Preparedness theory is an excellent example of the evolutionary perspective at work: Animals are prepared to make associations that help them adapt to the environments they inhabit.

As we noted earlier, humans also form taste aversions quite readily. Think of the times you have been nauseated after eating. In most of these cases, had you just consumed a novel food or beverage? Will you ever consume that food or drink again? Chances are pretty good that you are saying "never," and you may be right. Such experiences are surprisingly common. In one survey of undergraduates, 65% of the students reported having at least one food aversion. Most of these food aversions developed several hours after eating food associated with sickness (Logue, Ophir, & Strauss, 1981). What's more, such aversions do not extinguish very easily; they can last for 50 years or more (Garb & Stunkard, 1974).

Sometimes taste aversions have detrimental effects. For example, children undergoing chemotherapy for cancer often develop very strong food aversions that prevent proper eating. Psychologists have applied their knowledge of taste-aversion learning to this problem (Bernstein, 1978; Bernstein & Webster, 1980, 1982). In one study, children were allowed to eat an unusually flavored ice cream (called "Mapletof") shortly before receiving nausea-producing chemotherapy. Later these patients ate less Mapletof ice cream than did a second group of patients whose treatment consisted of surgery rather than drug therapy. Children in the second group had also eaten some Mapletof ice cream before treatment. Because their treatment did not produce nausea, however, these patients did not associate the ice cream flavor with illness. Clearly the taste–illness pairing is crucial for the development of taste aversion.

Subsequent research demonstrated that consumption of the Mapletof ice cream *before* chemotherapy greatly reduced the patients' reluctance to consume their normal diet. After chemotherapy, patients who had previously eaten the Mapletof ice cream and had formed a taste aversion to this flavor were more willing to consume their normal diet than were patients who had not eaten any Mapletof ice cream. The formation of a taste aversion to the Mapletof ice cream tended to block the formation of taste aversions to other foods and thus helped the patients maintain their normal diet without becoming nauseated.

Learning by Various Species.

In 1950, psychologist Frank Beach published an article titled *The Snark Was a Boojum*. Beach's message was straightforward: Comparative psychology should be based on studies of numerous species. He examined 613 research articles and found that 50% of them dealt with the rat, despite the fact that the rat represented only .001% of all living creatures. Failure to heed this caution could result in comparative psychology fading away, just like the hunters in Lewis Carroll's *Alice in Wonderland* who encountered a snark that was a boojum.

Beach's cautions are as relevant today as they were in 1950. In many respects psychology has become the science of the white rat and the American, male, college sophomore. These two types of participants appear far more often in the published research literature than other types of participants (Jones, 1994; Lee & Hall, 1994; Marin, 1994).

Our intent is to alert you to the fact that psychologists should be concerned about looking for such influences in the area of basic learning processes such as classical and operant conditioning. Why is it difficult to point to such influences when basic learning processes are considered?

Part of the answer concerns the nature of the material: basic learning processes. Most researchers and students probably assume that basic processes apply to all animal species and people in all cultures; hence cross-species and cross-cultural studies are not needed. This assumption may be true, but we will never know for sure until such studies are conducted.

A second reason for the lack of comparative and cross-cultural data concerns the orientation of the researchers. This area of psychology traditionally has been very concerned with the methodology that is used in the experiments and in the creation of theories to account for the behaviors and phenomena that are observed. These interests shift attention away to the specifics involved in the conduct of the experiments and away from investigating cross-species and cross-cultural effects. Keep these concerns in mind as you read about basic learning processes. The future, we hope, will see a change in this state of affairs.

STUDY TIP

After reading the section on the elements of classical conditioning, brainstorm in a group of three. Think of five additional examples, not mentioned in the text, of ways in which human behavior is conditioned. Discuss each behavior and how the conditioning occurred.

REVIEW SUMMARY

1. Learning occurs when experience produces a relatively permanent change in behavior.

2. Classical conditioning involves pairing an **unconditioned stimulus (UCS),** which automatically elicits an **unconditioned response (UCR),** with a **conditioned stimulus (CS),** which is neutral at the start of conditioning. Several pairings during an acquisition phase lead to a situation in which the CS presented by itself elicits a **conditioned response (CR).**

3. When the UCS is intense and presented more frequently, stronger classical conditioning is produced.

4. The classically conditioned response is eliminated or extinguished when the UCS is removed or not presented; this process is called **extinction. Spontaneous recovery** of the CR occurs when time is allowed to pass between extinction sessions.

5. Generalization occurs when CRs are elicited by stimuli that are similar to the CS. **Discrimination** is the opposing process; it involves responding only to the appropriate CS.

6. John Watson and Rosalie Rayner demonstrated that emotions can be learned by classically conditioning 9-month-old Little Albert to fear a white rat. This child exhibited a **phobia,** which is a fear for certain activities, objects, or situations. The research conducted by Watson and Rayner would not be considered ethical by present-day standards.

7. Learned motives and **learned goals** (or learned incentives) are acquired through classical conditioning.

8. Our understanding of classical conditioning has been subject to revision since Pavlov introduced the basic processes. For example, although the association of CS with UCS is important in establishing conditioning, the real key is the degree to which the CS predicts occurrence of the UCS. Previous trials of a CS-UCS pairing can serve to **block** the effectiveness of a second CS.

9. For many species, the pairing of a novel taste with the experience of illness results in learning an aversion to that taste. **Taste-aversion learning** occurs readily in humans; birds, however, more readily associate a color with illness. **Preparedness** is evident when some species are more likely to form certain associations than others.

✓ CHECK YOUR PROGRESS

1. Have you ever found yourself salivating while walking through the bakery section of a supermarket? What was the UCS? the CS? the CR?

2. Complete the following:
   a. Before conditioning, the _____ is automatically elicited by the _____.
   b. The CR is strengthened if the _____ and _____ are paired frequently.
   c. Extinction of a classically conditioned response involves presentation of only the _____. In other words, the _____ is removed.
   d. Extinction causes the _____ to grow gradually _____.

3. State which aspect of classical conditioning is illustrated by each of the following situations:
   a. A tone sounds; half a second later, a puff of air is delivered to your eye and you blink. Once the conditioned eye blink has been established, the puff of air is discontinued and the tone is presented by itself a number of times.
   b. As a child you had the misfortune of being stung by a bee. In addition to the pain of the sting, your body reacted strongly. Your breathing became difficult and you were rushed to the hospital for treatment. Twenty years later you have a fear of bees and other flying insects.
   c. Your roommate went to a new pizza restaurant for dinner and developed a severe case of intestinal flu later that night. The pizza restaurant lost a customer.

   d. Children who play with large plastic bags sometimes become trapped inside the bag and nearly suffocate. If they are fortunate enough to be rescued, they will probably have a conditioned fear of closed spaces.

4. What was the conditioned stimulus (CS) in the case of Little Albert?
   a. rat
   b. hammer
   c. small toy
   d. loud noise

5. In classical conditioning, what automatically produces a reaction?
   a. CS
   b. CR
   c. UCS
   d. UCR

6. For the past few months, Sara has been using a perfume called Passion. Her boyfriend, Jim, really likes the perfume. In fact, on several occasions, he has passed women who were wearing Passion and had the same reaction: his heart rate increased. In this example, the perfume is the _____ and Jim's increased heart rate is the _____.
   a. CS, UCS
   b. CS, CR
   c. UCS, UCR
   d. UCS, UR

7. Taste aversions seem to be specific examples of what type of learning?

   a. insight learning
   b. vicarious learning
   c. operant conditioning
   d. classical conditioning

8. Last week Ted saw a movie that vividly depicted a serial killer's gruesome murders. When school began, Ted had an uncomfortable feeling when one of his teachers walked into class. After class, he realized that the teacher had a striking resemblance to the killer. Ted's reaction to the teacher is an example of

   a. extinction.
   b. acquisition.
   c. discrimination.
   d. generalization.

9. Why is Little Albert such a well-known individual in the history of psychology?

   a. He outlined key elements of classical conditioning in his research on dogs.
   b. A serious bout of the flu led him to discover the major principles of taste-aversion learning.
   c. He was the subject of research that illustrated how classical conditioning can explain the development of phobias.
   d. After he developed a strong aversion to needles, pins, and injections he found a way to use hypnosis to overcome such reactions.

10. Which of the following illustrates an unconditioned response?

   a. A large ice cream sundae.
   b. Your favorite ice cream shop.
   c. Salivation when you taste an ice cream sundae.
   d. Salivation when you see your favorite ice cream shop.

ANSWERS: 1. UCS—the taste of the bakery goods you've eaten before   CS—the sight and smell of the bakery goods   CR—salivation **2. a.** UCR, UCS **b.** CS, UCS **c.** CS, UCS **d.** CR, weaker **3. a.** extinction **b.** generalization **c.** taste aversion **d.** conditioned fear response or phobia **4. a 5. c 6. b 7. d 8. d 9. c 10. c**

OPERANT CONDITIONING

Bob's roommate, Greg, is a complete slob. In Bob's view, the condition of Greg's room is Greg's business, but the condition of the bathroom they share is another matter. Almost every week they have major arguments about cleaning the bathroom, and Bob ends up doing the cleaning. When the unfairness of the situation is more than Bob can stand, he tries a new approach. Whenever Greg does anything to help clean the apartment, Bob praises him: "Good job, Greg; the apartment really looks great." Gradually Greg begins helping on a more regular basis, and one week he even offers to clean the bathroom. *What technique did Bob use to get Greg to help clean the apartment?*

We will now discuss the second basic type of learning, operant conditioning. In **operant conditioning**, also known as *instrumental conditioning*, an organism operates on its environment to produce a change (Leahey & Harris, 2001). In other words, the organism's behavior is *instrumental*—it results in a change in the environment. As you will see, the type of change that is produced is a critical element of this type of learning.

Reinforcers: The Basic Concept of Operant Conditioning

Probably no one has been associated more closely with operant conditioning than the late Harvard psychologist B. F. Skinner (1904–1990), who has been described as the most famous psychologist who has ever lived (Fowler, 1990). Skinner was strongly influenced by John B. Watson's behavioral view of psychology (see page 190). As we have seen, Watson believed that if we could understand how to predict and control behavior, we would know all there was to know about psychology. Skinner therefore

operant conditioning
Learning that occurs when the participant must make a response to produce a change in the environment

FIGURE 5-9 (A) An operant conditioning chamber, or Skinner box. Pecking the circular disk or "key" is the target response that delivers a food reinforcer for the pigeon. (B) The cumulative recorder automatically logs the participant's responses.

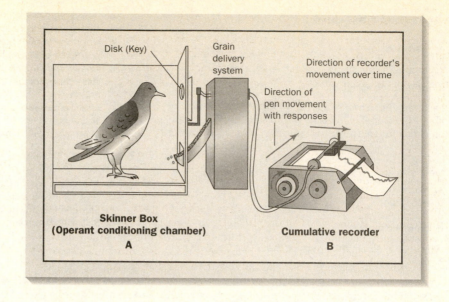

began to look for the stimuli that control behavior. To isolate those effects, he developed a special testing environment called an *operant conditioning chamber*, which is usually referred to as a *Skinner box* (see Figure 5-9). Although Skinner relied on the use of animals such as rats and pigeons, his ideas can be applied to human behavior. The advantage of the Skinner box and laboratory studies is that they allow researchers to exert a great deal of control in their research and thus they are in a better position to identify the actual influences on behavior.

Let's take a moment to return to the question we posed earlier: How did Bob convince Greg to help clean their apartment? The answer is that he praised his behavior, thus using what Skinner called a *reinforcer*.

In some cases, operant behavior may result in the delivery of a stimulus or an event. When you insert money into a soda machine, for example, you receive a cold drink. When Greg cleaned the apartment, he received praise. In other instances, the operant behavior may result in the elimination of a stimulus or an event. For example, you have probably learned the quickest way to eliminate the sound your alarm clock makes early in the morning. Such events, or reinforcers, are at the heart of operant conditioning. Thus we can define a **reinforcer** as an event or stimulus that makes the behavior it follows more likely to occur again (Skinner, 1938). For example, obtaining a cold drink from the soda machine and eliminating the annoying sound of your alarm clock are both reinforcers. The behavior that a reinforcer follows can be thought of as the *target response*—it is the behavior that we want to strengthen or increase. Reinforcers can be either positive or negative; in either instance, they can serve to increase the occurrence of the target response.

B. F. Skinner training a rat in a Skinner box.

reinforcer
Event or stimulus that increases the frequency of the response that it follows

positive reinforcer
Event or stimulus presented after the target response that increases the likelihood that this response will occur again

Positive and Negative Reinforcers. **Positive reinforcers** are events or stimuli such as food, water, money, and praise that are presented after the target response occurs. They are generally considered desirable and pleasant and are therefore sought by people and animals alike. For example, a real estate agent earns a commission for each house she sells; the commissions reinforce her efforts to sell as many houses as possible. Your little brother is allowed to watch cartoons on Saturday mornings after he has cleaned his room; as a result, he cleans his room every Saturday. We hope that you have been praised for receiving good grades on psychology tests; the praise should encourage you to study even harder in the future.

Psychological Detective

Can a positive reinforcer encourage unethical behavior? Consider the problem of cheating. Children are taught that cheating is wrong, but this behavior persists in most segments of our society. Why? Take a few moments to analyze the behavior of cheating in operant conditioning terms. Be sure to write down the target response and the reinforcers.

Suppose a student consults a concealed cheat sheet during a test or passes answers to a friend. The target responses here are the acts of cheating. The reinforcer is receiving a high (or passing) grade. Because the grade is given (presented), it is a positive reinforcer. Do threats of punishment counteract this behavior? The answer appears to be no; the number of students who admit to having cheated on examinations is quite high: As many as 40% to 95% of college students surveyed have reported having cheated at some time (Burnett, Rudolph, & Clifford, 1998; Davis et al., 1992; Davis & Ludvigson, 1995); consequently, cheating is a serious concern on college campuses (McCabe et al., 2001; Whitley & Spiegel, 2002). There is growing concern that current expansion of distance learning formats may make it even easier to cheat (Kennedy et al., 2000). What's more, detection rates are very low—frequently less than 2 percent (Haines et al., 1986). Thus a very small number of cheaters are caught, and even fewer are punished. The prospect of achieving an easy grade, coupled with a relatively low chance of getting caught, can be a powerful reinforcer of cheating on tests. The same analysis also applies to other familiar events. For example, the number of people who receive tickets for speeding on the highway is very low, relative to the number of people who speed.

When students see the word *negative*, they tend to assume that a behavior will decrease. Don't get caught up in this misconception, which has been called one of the major mistakes made by students of psychology (Leahey & Harris, 2001; McConnell, 1990). Both positive and negative reinforcers make the target response more likely to occur again. **Negative reinforcers** are events or stimuli that are removed because a response has occurred. Examples of negative reinforcement include playing music to reduce boredom, cleaning your room so that your roommate will stop complaining that you're a slob, and turning off the alarm clock to stop that annoying sound. In these situations something stopped (boredom) or was removed (criticism) because you performed a target response. What response will occur the next time these unpleasant situations arise? If the negative reinforcer has been effective, the target response that terminated it is likely to occur again. The operation of positive and negative reinforcers is diagrammed in Figure 5-10.

negative reinforcer
Event or stimulus removed after the target response, thereby increasing the likelihood that this response will occur again

When rates of detection and punishment are very low, cheating rates may be very high.

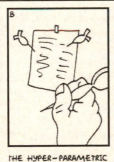

WHICH IS THE BEST WAY TO ANSWER MULTIPLE-CHOICE QUESTIONS?

A — THE DICHOTOMOUS-MONETARY METHOD (COIN TOSSING)

B — THE HYPER-PARAMETRIC AERODYNAMIC MISSILE METHOD (BASED ON RESEARCH BY NASA)

C — SYMBOLIC PROTEST AGAINST STIFLING OF ARTISTIC EXPRESSION INHERENT IN TESTING KNOWLEDGE WITH MULTIPLE-CHOICE QUESTIONS

D — NONE OF THE ABOVE

E — HELP FROM ABOVE

Psi Chi Newsletter. Reprinted with the permission of Psi Chi.

POSITIVE REINFORCER

Target response (cleaning room) is made

Reinforcing stimulus (money) is presented

Target response (cleaning room) occurs again

NEGATIVE REINFORCER

Target response (taking medication) is made

Unpleasant stimulus (pain) is removed

Target response (taking medication) occurs again

FIGURE 5-10 Diagram of the operation of positive and negative reinforcers. In the top panel, the target response of cleaning the room is reinforced with money (a positive reinforcer) resulting in *positive reinforcement* (increase in the target response). In the bottom panel the target response (taking medication for a painful headache) removes the pain (a negative reinforcer) resulting in *negative reinforcement* (an increase in use of the medication). Note that both positive and negative reinforcement lead to increases in the frequency of target responses.

Primary and Secondary (Conditioned) Reinforcers. A **primary reinforcer** is an event or stimulus that has innate (that is, biological) reinforcing properties; you do not have to learn that such stimuli are reinforcers. For a hungry person, food is a primary reinforcer. Water is another primary reinforcer, especially on a very hot day; and the rest provided by sleep, which is welcome, refreshing, and too often insufficient for our needs, is a third example of a primary reinforcer. Needless to say, not all events or stimuli that might follow a behavior will necessarily satisfy some biological need such as hunger, thirst, or sleep. A **secondary reinforcer** is a stimulus that acquires reinforcing properties by being associated with a primary reinforcer. Because you must learn that such stimuli are reinforcers, they are also called conditioned reinforcers. Money may be the best example of a secondary reinforcer. By itself, money has no intrinsic value; children learn that money can be exchanged for primary reinforcers such as ice cream. We also use money to purchase other foods, beverages, and a place to catch up on our sleep, whether it is our apartment, a house, or a hotel room.

primary reinforcer
Stimulus that has innate reinforcing properties

secondary reinforcer
Stimulus that acquires reinforcing properties by being associated with a primary reinforcer

Contingencies and Behavior

Skinner coined the term *operant conditioning* because the behaviors we emit (as opposed to behaviors that are elicited) *operate* on the environment in some way. These changes in the environment determine what happens to a given target behavior. As previously mentioned, if a behavior is followed by a positive reinforcer—as when a student answers a question and the professor says "Excellent!"—the behavior tends to increase in the future. Why? There is a contingency established here: If a student answers a question, then the professor will say "Excellent." Contingencies take the form of "If _____ then _____" relations. Skinner noted that there is a contingency established between the behavior and the outcomes: If a student gives a good answer the professor will say "Excellent." In other cases, such as punishment, the contingency is different: If a child runs into the street, his parents may spank him. Take a moment to think about some of the contingencies that exist in your environment. As you think about these contingencies, you may realize that the final behavior does not always occur right from the start. For example, it is not likely that you learned to drive after just one ride around the block. How does Skinner explain how we develop more complex behaviors, which may not exist before training begins?

When you start training a rat in a Skinner box (see page 200), you should not expect much from the rat. The rat will not begin pressing the lever or bar as soon as it enters this new environment. You may have to help it to learn to press the lever or bar to receive food. The technique you will use is a form of operant conditioning called **shaping.** Shaping involves reinforcing successive responses that more closely resemble the desired target response; in other words, you are using the method of *successive approximations*. When using this method, we generally withhold reinforcement until the animal engages in a behavior that comes closer to the desired target response. Although the concept of shaping is reasonably clear, actually doing the job may be difficult. The timing of reinforcement presentation is crucial; if reinforcers are not presented at exactly the right moment, an inappropriate response may be shaped.

For a rat learning to press a lever for food, the sequence of events might go as follows: When the rat is near the food dish, you drop a piece of food into it. Eating the food reinforces the behavior of approaching the dish. Once the rat has learned where the food is, you begin offering reinforcers only when the rat goes near the response lever. Gradually you make your response requirements more demanding until the rat must actually touch the lever to receive the reinforcement. Once the rat has started touching the lever, you can require that the lever be pressed before the reinforcement is given. In this way you have gradually made the response that produces reinforcement more closely resemble (*successively approximate*) the target response of pressing the lever. In short, you have *shaped* the rat's response.

5.2

Perhaps the best known cases of shaping involves a patient who was admitted to a mental hospital at the age of 21 with the diagnosis of schizophrenia; he had been "completely mute almost immediately upon commitment" (Isaacs, Thomas, & Goldiamond, 1960). In fact, he did not say a word for 19 years! No one had been able to coax a single word out of him. He lived day in and day out without uttering a word, staring ahead with a fixed gaze. One day, a psychologist accidentally dropped a pack of chewing gum. The patient's eyes turned to focus on the gum and then returned to their fixed gaze. Finally, there was some small sign of responsiveness. The psychologist decided that gum could be used as a reinforcer. For the first two weeks, the psychologist held up the gum in front of the patient, waiting for some sign of visual contact. Once the response occurred, he was given some gum. Then, the psychologist withheld gum until the patient responded with both visual contact and lip movement. Through a painstaking process of shaping, the patient eventually said "Gum, please"; these were his first words in 19 years. Another case of mutism in a 7th-grade boy who had been selectively mute since kindergarten was treated using a variety of behavioral techniques (Rye & Ullman, 1999).

Shaping has a wide range of applications and is an especially effective tool derived from operant conditioning principles. If teachers find that their students are not able

shaping
A form of operant conditioning in which a desired response is taught by reinforcement of successive responses that more closely resemble the target response

to provide correct answers to questions posed in class, they praise partial answers and even effort. Gradually, they can raise expectations so students have to give more complete responses to earn praise (Eggen & Kauchak, 2001). If you have ever seen bears roller skating, seals catching balls, dolphins "flying" through hoops, or pigeons playing ping pong, you have been entertained by the results of a long series of steps that shaped these behaviors (Coren, 1999). When you stop to think about the range of behaviors we engage in every day, especially the more complex ones, you can see how important shaping can be. Driving a car, playing the piano, and typing are all behaviors that we probably learned through shaping.

Psychological Detective

Whether or not we realize it, shaping techniques have been used to help us acquire many new behaviors. Think about behaviors such as talking, writing, and driving a car. These behaviors were gradually shaped through the appropriate delivery of reinforcers. Remember when you learned to drive? How were your driving skills when you first started driving? How are they now? In which ways were those skills shaped? Recall these behaviors and events and relate them to our discussion of operant conditioning before you read further.

Most of the behaviors of animals we see in shows and theme parks do not occur in their natural habitats. Animal trainers use operant conditioning methods, especially shaping, to train raccoons, seals, whales, dolphins, and other creatures. The key to shaping is to break down complex behaviors into smaller and easier behaviors and then to reinforce successive approximations to the ultimate, more complex behavior.

The first time you sat behind the wheel, you were probably unable to drive around the block or parallel park like an experienced driver. To drive around the block, you had to become accustomed to the rear-view mirrors, use the turn signals, apply the brakes, and perhaps shift gears. Then there was parallel parking, which required much practice. Your instructor reinforced good driving techniques with phrases like "Good job," "Excellent," and "Way to go." Gradually your skills improved until you could maneuver your car into a small space without any difficulty.

Now recall the case of the roommates Bob and Greg, who had trouble keeping their apartment clean. Bob was shaping Greg's behavior. At first he praised anything Greg did to help keep the apartment clean. Gradually he reserved his praise for greater efforts, until finally Greg was cleaning the apartment on a regular basis.

The Premack Principle. Imagine that you are a music teacher in a middle school where your students love to play modern, jazz–rock compositions. Unfortunately, they are less than enthusiastic when it comes to playing the standard works of music that are part of the curriculum (Eggen & Kauchak, 2001). How would you use the principles of operant conditioning to deal effectively with this situation? One clever way of addressing this problem involves use of the *Premack Principle* named after the psychologist David Premack (1965). Premack determined that the opportunity to participate in a preferred activity (playing jazz in this case) could reinforce less preferred activities (playing the standard music pieces). What Premack described in operant conditioning terms has been known for some time as "Grandma's Rule" ("First eat your vegetables, and then you can have dessert"). There are numerous other examples including these:

- completion of homework (less preferred activity) is reinforced by the opportunity to play (preferred activity)
- football players get to run new plays (preferred activity) after they have run their required laps (less preferred activity)
- raking and bagging the leaves on Saturday (less preferred activity) is reinforced by the opportunity to play a video game (preferred activity).

Schedules of Reinforcement

In an operant conditioning chamber, the experimenter can deliver reinforcers, such as a piece of food for a hungry rat or pigeon, according to a preset pattern. Figure 5-9 (p. 200) shows an instrument, known as a *cumulative recorder*, that logs the participant's responses. The results sheet, known as a **cumulative record,** shows the rate of responding in a series of operant conditioning trials; the steeper the line, the higher the rate of responding. Keep in mind that a cumulative recorder keeps track of the accumulation of target responses over time; hence the term *cumulative*.

Psychological Detective

Suppose you are looking at the cumulative record of a rat that is being trained in a Skinner box. As you hold the rat in your hand, you scan the record and note something interesting. Across several days, the record shows a straight, horizontal line. What is likely to have happened to the rat's target response?

This particular rat has stopped responding. The fact that you are holding it, of course, indicates that the animal is still alive. The researcher put this rat on a schedule that led to the reduction and elimination of the behavior (extinction).

The preset pattern or plan for delivering reinforcement is known as a **schedule of reinforcement.** Schedules of reinforcement are important determinants of behavior (Shull & Lawrence, 1998). Once a target response has been shaped, the experimenter can arrange to have the reinforcer delivered according to a specific schedule. A researcher can create many plans or schedules for delivering reinforcers; however, we can describe the most basic schedules or reinforcement as falling into two categories: *continuous* and *intermittent* (partial) reinforcement. What this means is that reinforcement will follow every target behavior or it will follow the target behavior only at times.

Continuous Reinforcement. As noted earlier, a schedule of reinforcement is a preset pattern or plan for delivering reinforcement. The most basic schedule of reinforcement is **continuous reinforcement,** in which the participant is given a reinforcement after each target response occurs. For example, a rat in a Skinner box receives a food pellet for each bar press; a salesperson receives a commission for each car sold; a soda machine delivers a cold drink each time you put money in it. A continuous schedule of reinforcement produces a reasonably high rate of responding. Once the reinforcer loses its effectiveness, however, the response rate drops quickly. Thus food pellets reinforce responding in a hungry rat, but they are not effective after the rat has eaten a large number of them.

Intermittent (Partial) Reinforcement. In schedules of reinforcement that do not involve the use of continuous reinforcement, some responses are not reinforced. The term **intermittent (or partial) reinforcement** is used to describe these noncontinuous patterns of delivering reinforcement. There are two main types of intermittent schedules: *ratio* and *interval*.

Ratio Schedules. When a **ratio schedule** is in effect, the number of responses determines whether the participant receives reinforcement. In some cases the exact number of responses that must be made to receive a reinforcer is specified. For example, a pigeon may be required to peck a key 5 times before grain (a positive reinforcer) is presented. When the number of responses required to produce a reinforcer is specified, the arrangement is

cumulative record
Results of a series of operant conditioning trials, shown as rate of responding

schedule of reinforcement
Preset pattern for delivering reinforcement

continuous reinforcement
Reinforcement that follows every target response

intermittent (or partial) reinforcement
Reinforcement that does not follow every target response

ratio schedule
Reinforcement schedule in which reinforcement is based on the number of responses; number may be set (fixed-ratio [FR] schedule) or may vary from one reinforcement to the next (variable-ratio [VR] schedule)

"Actually, he's easy to train, everytime I press the buzzer, he brings me food."

Reprinted by permission of Jerry Marcus.

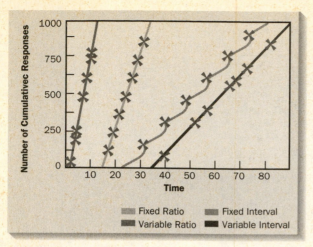

FIGURE 5-11 Examples of fixed-ratio (FR) and variable ratio (VR) response patterns. The steeper the slope of the line, the higher the rate of responding. Note that the responding ceases (flat line) for a brief period after reinforcement has been delivered under the demanding FR schedule. This pause does not occur when the VR schedule is in effect.

interval schedule
Reinforcement schedule based on the passage of time and in which a single response at the end of the designated interval is reinforced; intervals may be set (fixed interval [FI] schedule) or may vary from one reinforcement to the next (variable-interval [VI] schedule)

known as a *fixed-ratio (FR) schedule*. Requiring a pigeon to peck 5 times to receive reinforcement is designated as a "fixed-ratio 5" (FR5) schedule. A continuous reinforcement schedule can be thought of as a "fixed-ratio 1" (FR1) schedule.

On other occasions we may not want to specify the exact number of responses. Sometimes the reinforcer will be delivered after 15 responses, sometimes after 35 responses, sometimes after 10 responses, and so forth. Because the exact number of responses required for a reinforcer is not specified, this arrangement is called a *variable-ratio (VR) schedule*. Typically the average number of responses is used to indicate the type of variable-ratio schedule. In our example, in which the values 15, 35, and 10 were used, the average number of responses would be 20 [(15 + 35 + 10)/3 = 20]. This particular schedule would be designated as a "variable-ratio 20" (VR20) schedule.

Whether we are dealing with a VR or FR schedule, our participants usually make many responses. Frequent responding makes good sense in these situations: The more responses are made, the more frequently participants receive reinforcers. Although both FR and VR schedules produce many responses, VR schedules tend to produce the highest rates of responding. These differences in rates of responding are shown in Figure 5-11.

When an FR schedule is in effect, the participant may pause for a brief period after the reinforcement has been delivered. This *postreinforcement pause* typically does not occur when a VR schedule is used. When an FR schedule is used, the reinforcer seems to serve as a signal to take a short break. If you were responding on an FR schedule, you might be thinking, "Five more responses until I get the reinforcer, then I'll rest for a bit before I start responding again."

Suppose that you have a job stuffing envelopes. For every 200 envelopes you stuff, you receive $10 (a positive reinforcer). To earn as much money as possible, you work very hard and stuff as many envelopes as possible. Every time the 200th envelope is completed, however, you stop for a minute to straighten the stack and count how many piles of 200 envelopes you have completed (Mazur, 1998).

The duration of the postreinforcement pause is not the same for all FR schedules; the higher the schedule (the greater the number of responses required to produce a reinforcer), the longer the pause. In addition, the more time expended in responding, the longer the postreinforcement pause will be.

Now consider a case in which there is no postreinforcement pause. Last year Barbara and some of her friends spent their spring break in Las Vegas. The slot machines proved to be Barbara's downfall. Sometimes the jackpot bell rang and she collected a potful of quarters, which encouraged her to continue playing. Before she knew it, she had been putting quarters into the "one-armed bandit" for 6 hours straight. When she counted her winnings and losses, she had spent $250 just to win $33. Why did Barbara put so much money into the slot machine?

The answer is that slot machines "pay off" on a VR schedule. As Barbara put quarter after quarter into the machine, she was probably thinking, "Next time the bell will ring, and I'll get the jackpot." She knew that she would receive a reward (hitting the jackpot) at some point, but because slot machines operate on a variable schedule, she could not predict when she would be rewarded. If you have ever become "hooked" on playing the lottery, you can understand this process. Keep in mind that VR schedules of reinforcement can lead to high rates of responding in a Skinner box or in front of a one-armed bandit in Las Vegas.

Interval Schedules. The second type of intermittent (partial) schedule of reinforcement, the interval schedule, involves the passage of time. When an **interval schedule**

TABLE 5-2

Reinforcement Schedules and Examples

Continuous	A teacher "walks students through" the steps for solving simultaneous equations. They are liberally praised at each step as they first learn the solution.
Fixed-ratio	The algebra teacher announces, "As soon as you've done two problems in a row correctly, you may start on your homework assignments so that you'll be able to finish by the end of class."
Variable-ratio	Students volunteer to answer questions by raising their hands and are called on at random.
Variable-interval	Students are given unannounced quizzes.
Fixed-interval	Students are given a quiz every Friday.

is in effect, responses are reinforced only after a certain interval of time has passed. As with ratio schedules, there are two basic types of interval schedules, fixed-interval and variable-interval. Table 5-2 lists some common examples of the schedules of reinforcement that we are discussing.

Under a *fixed-interval (FI) schedule*, a constant period of time must pass before a response is reinforced. Responses made before the end of that period are not reinforced. No matter how many times you check your mailbox, you will not receive mail until it is time for the daily mail delivery. Under an FI schedule, participants try to estimate the passage of time and make most of their responses toward the end of the interval, when they will be reinforced. If your mail always is delivered between 3:00 and 3:30 P.M., you won't start looking for it until close to that time. Participants (humans or animals), however, tend to make what are called *anticipatory responses* before the end of the interval. Suppose a turkey for Thanksgiving dinner is scheduled to roast for 4 hours. How many of us can resist opening the oven door before the 4 hours, especially as the end of the 4-hour time period approaches? In general, however, the longer participants stay on an FI schedule, the better they become at timing their responses.

When reinforcement occurs on a *variable-interval (VI) schedule*, the participant never knows the exact length of time that must pass before a response is reinforced; the time interval changes after every reinforcement. Because a response can be reinforced at any time, it makes sense for the participant to maintain a steady—but not especially high—rate of responding. Think of the times you have called a friend on the phone only to get voice mail. You probably did not start redialing at a frantic pace. Most likely you initially called back a few minutes later, and then a few minutes after that if you were not successful, and so on. You could not determine whether your friend was having several short conversations or a lengthy one—that is, you did not know when your dialing would be reinforced by the sound of a ringing telephone. Only time would tell. At some point your friend hung up, and you were able to get through. As time passed, your chances of getting through got better and better.

The average amount of time that must elapse before a response produces reinforcement under a VI schedule influences the rate of responding; the longer the interval, the lower the rate of responding. For example, pigeons reinforced on a VI 2-minute schedule responded between 60 and 100 times per minute, whereas pigeons reinforced on a VI 7-minute schedule responded 20 to 70 times per minute (Catania & Reynolds, 1968). The characteristic response patterns for FI and VI schedules are shown in Figure 5-12.

The Study Chart on the next page compares classical and operant conditioning. Check your understanding of these basic forms of learning before reading further.

FIGURE 5-12 On a fixed-interval (FI) schedule, most responses are made toward the end of the interval when a response will be reinforced. Once the reinforcer has been delivered and the interval begins again, the rate of responding decreases drastically. Under the variable-interval (VI) schedule, the participant cannot predict the end of the interval and therefore cannot judge when to respond. A low, steady rate of responding is maintained.

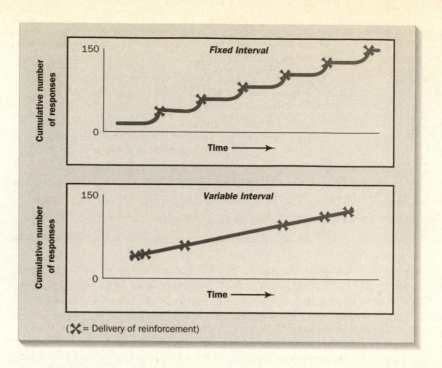

The Partial Reinforcement Effect

Every day you look in your mailbox for a letter from a friend. After 3 months of looking, you are finally convinced your friend is not going to write; no letters have come, and there is no reason to expect any. Completely removing the reinforcer—in this case, your friend's letters—from the operant conditioning situation eventually results in *extinction*, or elimination, of the operantly conditioned response. There are some basic similarities between the way extinction is produced in classical conditioning (by omitting the UCS) and the way it is produced in operant conditioning (by removing the reinforcer).

So why is it so difficult to stop playing a slot machine once you have started? As you saw earlier in this chapter, intermittent or partial reinforcement schedules can produce very high rates of responding. This outcome is especially true of ratio schedules, in which the harder the participants work, the more reinforcement they receive. Because partial reinforcement schedules involve making a number of responses that are not reinforced, it may be difficult to tell when reinforcement has been discontinued completely and when it has merely been delayed. Because Barbara cannot tell whether the slot machine is broken or whether it will pay off the next time she puts in a quarter, she continues to play. Many players stop only when all their money is gone. Gambling is not the only behavior occurring on a partial schedule of reinforcement. Do you know a friend who has a lucky seat in class? Do you know someone who carries a rabbit's foot for luck? Do you own a "lucky" hat that you must wear to the big game? These are all examples of behaviors that could be described as superstitious. A critical thinker might collect data to determine that any supposed relation between the lucky seat and grades does not hold up to scrutiny, but few of us check the data. Superstitious behaviors are generally reinforced on partial schedules of reinforcement just like slot machines, and they are difficult to stop (Vyse, 1997).

Do you see a general pattern concerning extinction and operant conditioning? If reinforcement is delivered in a predictable manner, it should be easier to tell when it has been discontinued and when extinction has begun. Hence extinction should occur more rapidly following FR training than following VR training. Likewise, extinction

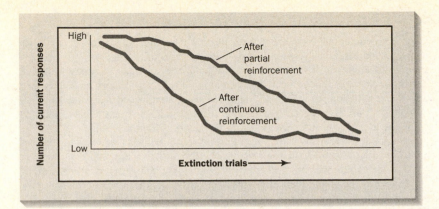

FIGURE 5-13 Extinction of a bar-press response after continuous and partial reinforcement training in a Skinner box.

should occur more rapidly following FI training than following VI training. What's more, it should be even easier to extinguish responding that has been conditioned through the use of continuous reinforcement than responding that has been conditioned through any partial or intermittent schedule.

These facts have been verified experimentally. The **partial reinforcement effect** states that extinction of operant behavior is more difficult after partial or intermittent reinforcement than after continuous reinforcement. Have you ever taken pity on a hungry, stray cat and put out some food for it? Sometimes when it comes to your door you feed it, and other times you don't. When you finally decide you are never going to feed the cat again, you find it will not go away. The cat has been reinforced on an intermittent or partial schedule of reinforcement. It will return again and again for quite some time. Figure 5-13 shows differences in extinction after continuous and partial reinforcement training in a Skinner box.

partial reinforcement effect
Phenomenon in which extinction of an operant response following partial or intermittent reinforcement takes longer than extinction following continuous reinforcement

STUDY CHART

Comparison of Classical and Operant Conditioning

Basic Process	Classical Conditioning	Operant Conditioning
	An unconditioned stimulus (UCS) causes an unconditioned response (UCR); after pairing a conditioned stimulus (CS) with the UCS several times, the CS comes to elicit a conditioned response (CR).	Reinforcement (positive and negative) is used to shape a target response; once the response is established, a schedule of reinforcement (fixed or variable, interval or ratio) may be implemented to maintain it.
Training—Acquisition of a new response.	The CS and UCS are paired; after several pairings the CS comes to elicit a CR.	Because the target response is followed by a reinforcer, its probability or rate increases.
Extinction—Probability or frequency of a conditioned response is decreased.	The CS is presented alone, and a decrease in the CR is observed.	Reinforcement is discontinued and the rate of responding gradually decreases.
Generalization—Responses are made to stimuli other than those used in training.	Stimuli similar to the CS elicit the CR.	Responding occurs when stimuli similar to the discriminative stimulus are presented.
Discrimination—Responses are made only to stimuli used in training.	Stimuli that are similar to the CS do not elicit a CR.	Only the discriminative stimulus results in responding.

discriminative stimulus
Stimulus or signal telling the participant that responding will be reinforced

punisher
Stimulus that produces a decrease in responding; may take the form of presentation of a stimulus or termination of a stimulus

law of effect
Thorndike's view that reinforcers promote learning, whereas punishers lead to the unlearning of responses

punishment
The process of using a punisher to decrease response rate

Operant Conditioning and Stimulus Control

Bringing a behavior under stimulus control means that a particular stimulus or signal tells the participant that its responses will be reinforced (Fetterman, 1993). In an operant conditioning chamber, for example, a green light or a tone can be a signal to a rat that pressing the lever will be reinforced. Such a signal is called a **discriminative stimulus.** When the light or tone is present, lever presses are reinforced under the schedule of reinforcement that the rat has experienced during training. When the discriminative stimulus is absent, the responses are not reinforced, and extinction occurs.

A vast number of discriminative stimuli are found in the real world. The "Open" sign in a store window is a discriminative stimulus signaling that the response of reaching for the door handle will be reinforced by your being able to enter the store and shop. The color of the traffic light at an intersection signals that the response of stopping your car (red) or proceeding through the intersection (green) will be reinforced by safe arrival at your destination. Your friend's mood serves as a signal that a response such as telling a joke or making a sympathetic remark will be appreciated.

Punishment: The Opposite of Reinforcement

We have seen that the effect of a reinforcer (either positive or negative) is to increase the likelihood of a target response. A **punisher** has the opposite effect: to decrease the likelihood or rate of responding of a target response.

Everyone seems to have an opinion about the usefulness and desirability of punishment. In the early 1900s, educator E. L. Thorndike developed an influential theory of learning. One of the main components of that theory was the **law of effect** (Thorndike, 1911), which stated that presenting a "satisfier" (a reinforcer) leads to the strengthening or learning of new responses, whereas presenting an "annoyer" (a punisher) leads to the weakening or unlearning of responses. Thorndike later concluded that punishment might not be effective, but he may have been premature in dismissing the influence of punishment. We now turn our attention to different types of punishers as well as some guidelines for using punishment effectively.

As you can see in Figure 5-14, punishers may be 1) aversive stimuli or events that are presented, or 2) pleasant stimuli or events that are removed. Remember that reinforcement (positive or negative) *increases* the rate of responding, whereas **punishment** *decreases* the rate of responding. For example, if a rat in an operant conditioning chamber receives an electric shock after pressing a lever, its rate of responding decreases. Similarly, if a child is scolded for playing in the street, that behavior is likely to occur less often. These are examples of punishment. Other examples of punishment include taking away a child's allowance, grounding a teenager, or swatting your cat for scratching the furniture. Note that punishment decreases or suppresses behavior, it rarely eliminates behavior as is the case in extinction.

The "open" sign is a discriminative stimulus signaling that the response of pulling the door handle will be reinforced by your being able to enter Mother Myrick's for an afternoon snack.

Psychological Detective

We have examined how to present reinforcers to obtain a high rate of responding. How can punishment be administered in order to maximize its effects? Select a behavior that you or society find undesirable that you would like to see decreased and then formulate specific answers to this question and write them down before reading further.

If punishment is to be used effectively, there are several procedures that should be followed (Azrin & Holz, 1966; Axelrod & Apsche, 1983):

1. The punisher should be delivered (positive) or taken away (negative) *immediately after the response that is to be eliminated.* Slapping your cat for digging up your African violets while you were out will have no effect except perhaps to make you

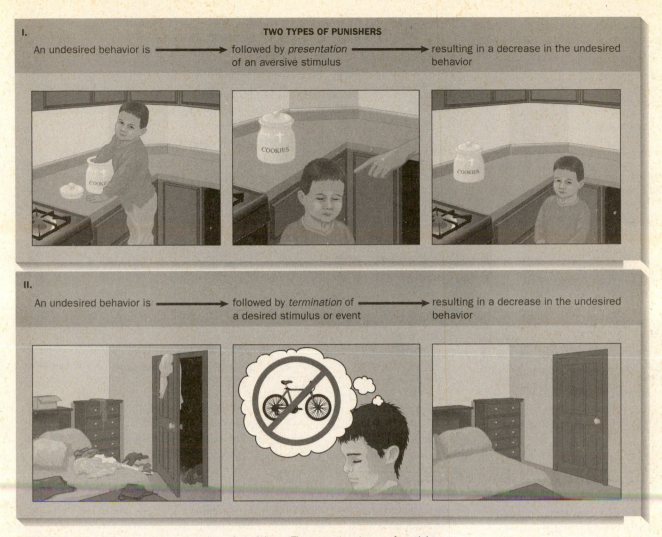

FIGURE 5-14 Diagram of the operation of punishers. There are two types of punishers: a) presenting an aversive stimulus (negative reinforcer) such as scolding, b) removing a desired stimulus (positive reinforcer) such as use of the bicycle. In both cases the end result is punishment or a decrease in the response rate of the behavior.

feel better. Why not? The cat will not see any connection between the earlier, undesirable behavior and the current punishment.

2. The punisher should be *strong enough to make a real difference*. Being grounded for two days may not matter very much, but being grounded for two months is a different story. Most people consider the use of extremely strong punishers, particularly those involving physical or violent punishment, unacceptable, if not ethically wrong. We do not want to inflict so much punishment that real damage results.

3. The punishment should be administered *after each and every undesired target response*. Punishment is not as effective when you do not punish all of the undesired responses; it must be administered consistently. Thus if you want to stop a child from using "bad" or offensive language, you should punish the child every time he or she uses it. Permitting even one episode of the undesired behavior to occur after previous punishment greatly decreases the effectiveness of the punishment.

Positive and Negative Reinforcement Compared with Punishment

Reinforcement	Results in an increase in responding
POSITIVE	A stimulus is presented after a target response; an increase in responding occurs (e.g., receiving good grades increases the amount of time one studies).
NEGATIVE	A stimulus is removed after a target response; an increase in responding occurs (e.g., if playing music reduces boredom, the frequency of playing music increases).
Punishment	**Results in a decrease in responding**
POSITIVE	A stimulus is presented after a target response; a decrease in responding occurs (e.g., washing a child's mouth out with soap for cursing reduces the number of curse words the child says).
NEGATIVE	A stimulus is removed after a target response; a decrease in responding occurs (e.g., Saturday morning cartoon privileges are taken away because the child's chores have not been completed).

4. There should be *no unauthorized escape from the punisher*. If the punishment is not applied uniformly, its effects will be weakened. Rats are very clever; frequently they learn how to hang upside down from the top of a cage to avoid an electric shock to their feet.

5. If you use punishment, be prepared for the possibility of *aggressive responding*. Rats do not like to be shocked, children do not like to have their television privileges taken away, and spankings can elicit behaviors other than crying. Children who are spanked may retaliate by kicking and biting. Note that aggressive responding may be directed toward a person, an animal, or an object that cannot retaliate, such as a pet dog or cat; such behavior is called *displaced aggression*. Nor does aggressive behavior always end when the punishment ends. As a child, did you ever try to "get even" with your parents after being punished? In short, punishment can teach a child to use force or other violence against people.

6. Provide an *alternative desired behavior* that can gain a reinforcer for the person. Giving a child a spanking for playing in the street may not be especially effective if there is nowhere else to play. Clearly, it is very difficult to use punishment effectively. Perhaps the best solution is to reinforce an alternate desired behavior. The use of "redirecting" as a disciplinary technique in child-care settings provides an example. When a child engages in an inappropriate behavior, the child is removed from the "scene" and given another, appropriate activity to engage in. Praising the child for success in this appropriate activity is reinforcement of an alternate, desired behavior.

The Study Chart above summarizes the difference between reinforcement and punishment.

STUDY TIP

Create an outline summarizing the basic points of the material on the Skinner Box, shaping, and schedules of reinforcement.

R E V I E W   S U M M A R Y

1. **Operant conditioning** occurs when an organism performs a target response that is followed by a reinforcer, which increases the probability that the behavior (target response) will occur again.

2. All reinforcers increase the frequency of the response they follow. **Positive reinforcers** are presented after the target response has been made; **negative reinforcers** are withdrawn or taken away after the target response has been made.

Primary reinforcers (for example, food) satisfy basic biological needs; **secondary (conditioned) reinforcers** (for example, money) acquire their power to reinforce behavior by being associated with primary reinforcers.

3. Complex responses may be acquired gradually through the process of **shaping** (*successive approximations*). Psychologists can keep track of the rate of responding by using a *cumulative record*, which keeps track of all target responses made by an organism across time.

4. Once a behavior has been acquired, it may be reinforced according to a particular **schedule of reinforcement.** When a **ratio schedule** is in effect, the number of responses is important. *Fixed-ratio (FR) schedules* require that a set number of responses be made before a reinforcer is delivered; *variable-ratio (VR) schedules* require that the participant perform differing numbers of responses to obtain a reinforcer. With an **interval**

schedule, a certain amount of time must pass before a response is reinforced. With a *fixed-interval (FI) schedule,* the time interval is constant; the time interval changes after each reinforcer is delivered when a *variable-interval (VI) schedule* is used. Ratio schedules generally produce higher rates of responding than interval schedules.

5. Operant responses that are not reinforced each time during training take much longer to extinguish than ones that have received continuous reinforcement. This phenomenon is known as the **partial** (intermittent) **reinforcement effect.**

6. A discriminative stimulus signals that responses will be reinforced. Behavior is said to be under stimulus control when responding occurs only when the discriminative stimulus is present.

7. The opposite of reinforcement, **punishment,** involves presentation or withdrawal of stimuli called **punishers,** which results in a suppression of the target behavior.

✓CHECK YOUR PROGRESS

1. For each of the following situations, find the response that is being reinforced, identify the reinforcer, and determine which schedule of reinforcement is being used.

   a. Playing the lottery has become so popular that people line up to buy lottery tickets. Sometimes they win, and sometimes they lose.

   b. A friend has a part-time job making telephone calls to convince people to sign up for a credit card. For every 25 new customers who sign up, your friend receives a bonus.

   c. Each morning, rain or shine, your dog, McDuff, comes to the back door to wait for his breakfast.

   d. Every time Alan experiences a headache, he takes the medication that his physician prescribed and the pain is relieved enough that he can go about his daily routine without any problems.

2. For each of the following situations, indicate whether a positive or negative reinforcer is being used.

   a. A rat presses a bar to turn off an electric foot shock.

   b. A child digs through a new box of cereal to get a prize.

   c. A teenager pretends to be sick in order to receive extra attention.

   d. A student pretends to be sick in order to avoid having to make a presentation in class.

3. For each of the following, indicate whether partial reinforcement is involved. If it is, indicate the likely schedule of reinforcement.

   a. Receiving praise for each good grade you make.

   b. Sometimes getting caught for speeding.

   c. Having never been caught for cheating in high school.

   d. Occasionally finding money on the ground as you walk to class.

   e. Playing basketball on a team that won 3 out of 15 games last year.

f. Driving around and around a full parking lot until someone leaves and you can park your car.

4. Explain why learning to play the piano would be an example of shaping. What would the reinforcer or reinforcers be in this situation?

5. In which type of conditioning is the learner's behavior important in bringing about the learning?

   a. backward conditioning

   b. classical conditioning

   c. operant conditioning

   d. Pavlovian conditioning

6. What is an event or stimulus that makes the behavior it follows more likely to occur?

   a. reinforcer

   b. punishment

   c. conditioned stimulus

   d. unconditioned stimulus

7. What is the graph that shows the pattern of a rat's responding in a Skinner box?

   a. shaping record

   b. response pattern

   c. cumulative record

   d. reinforcement pattern

8. The effect of _____ is to decrease the likelihood or rate of a target response.

   a. punishment

   b. positive reinforcement

   c. negative reinforcement

   d. intermittent reinforcement

9. What is the partial reinforcement effect?

    a. Extinction after continuous reinforcement is more difficult.

    b. Extinction after partial reinforcement is more difficult.

    c. Learning under continuous reinforcement is more difficult.

    d. Learning under partial reinforcement is more difficult.

10. What two opposing processes are involved in creating discriminative stimuli?

    a. shaping and cognition

    b. discrimination and generalization

    c. positive and negative reinforcement

    d. observational learning and modeling

ANSWERS: 1. *Lottery example:* **a.** Buying lottery tickets is the response that is being reinforced; **b.** Money is the reinforcer; **c.** A variable ratio schedule is being used. *Telephone call:* **a.** Making telephone calls is the response that is being reinforced; **b.** The bonus is the reinforcer; **c.** A fixed ratio schedule is being used. *McDuff waiting for breakfast:* **a.** McDuff coming to the door is the response that is being reinforced; **b.** Food is the reinforcer; **c.** A fixed interval schedule is being used. *Headache example:* **a.** Taking medication is the behavior that is being reinforced; **b.** Relief from pain is the reinforcer; **c.** A continuous schedule of reinforcement is involved. **2. a.** Negative reinforcer **b.** Positive reinforcer **c.** Positive reinforcer **d.** Negative reinforcer **3. a.** Partial reinforcement is not used; this is a continuous reinforcement schedule. **b.** Punishment, not reinforcement, is involved. **c.** Partial reinforcement is not useful; this is a continuous reinforcement schedule. **d.** Partial reinforcement is involved. A fixed interval schedule is involved. **e.** Partial reinforcement is involved. A variable interval schedule is involved. **4.** Beginning piano students do not possess the required skills to play immediately. Musical skills—such as left- and right-hand dexterity and coordination, phrasing, and tempo—are acquired gradually. Praise from the music teacher and significant others is one source of reinforcement; the student's own feelings of accomplishment is another source of reinforcement. **5.** c **6.** a **7.** c **8.** a **9.** b **10.** b

COGNITIVE AND SOCIAL PERSPECTIVES ON LEARNING

The door to the garage was ajar and Mary became frightened; she was afraid that someone might be trying to rob the house. Trembling, she peeked into the garage to discover that her 3-year-old son was in the driver's seat, fiddling with the car key. Suddenly the engine started to run and Mary made a dash to the car to prevent an accident. At a family gathering several weeks after this event, Mary was discussing what had happened; family members seemed quite surprised that a 3-year-old could start the car. One of Mary's cousins, Sally, is a psychology major who had some ideas concerning what happened that day. *How would psychologists explain how this 3-year-old managed to start the car?*

We encountered contingency theory and blocking in our study of classical conditioning (see pages 193–194). These processes suggest that classical conditioning is not a simple mechanical process; rather, mental activity or thought processes (cognition) are involved to some degree. The relation of cognition to basic learning processes, such as insight learning and latent learning, has been studied for many decades.

The Role of Cognition

Two of the most compelling examples of how cognitive factors are involved in learning are insight learning and latent learning. We will discuss these next.

insight learning
sudden grasp of a concept or the solution to a problem that results from perceptual restructuring; typically characterized by an immediate change in behavior

Insight Learning. The importance of cognition to operant conditioning can be seen in the process known as insight learning. **Insight learning** is a form of operant conditioning in which we restructure our perceptual stimuli (we see things in a different way), make an instrumental (operant) response, and generalize this behavior to other situations. In short, it is not blind, trial-and-error learning that develops gradually but a type of learning that occurs suddenly and relies on cognitive processes. It is the "aha!" experience we have when we suddenly solve a problem.

Research by the Gestalt psychologist (see Chapter 1) Wolfgang Köhler (1927) exemplifies insight learning. Using chimpanzees as his test animals, Köhler gave them the following problem. A bunch of bananas was suspended out of reach of the chimps. To reach the bananas, the chimps had to stack three boxes on top of one another and then put together the pieces of a jointed pole to form a single, longer pole. After several unsuccessful attempts at jumping and trying to reach the bananas, Köhler's star pupil, Sultan, appeared to survey the situation (mentally rearrange the stimulus elements that were present) and solve the problem in the prescribed manner. Köhler believed that Sultan had achieved insight into the correct solution of the problem.

Consider the solution of a particularly difficult math problem. You struggle and struggle to solve the problem, without success. In frustration you set the problem aside and turn to another assignment. All of a sudden you understand what is required to work the math problem successfully; you've had an "aha!" experience. How you perceive the situation has changed; insight has occurred. Once this problem has been solved, you are able to solve others like it. Similarly, one of the authors of this book works on word puzzles; the daily newspaper carries two of them almost every day. Sometimes he struggles to rearrange the mixed up letters to form words, and sometimes the answers appear almost instantly. Quite often (especially after he takes a brief break from the puzzle), the answer seems to occur quickly, as insight has been achieved.

Thus cognitive processes are important in helping us to adapt to our environment. As we shall see, other organisms—even rats—may use cognitive processes as they go about their daily activities.

Latent Learning. Psychologist Edward C. Tolman presented persuasive evidence for the use of cognitive processes in basic learning in his study of maze learning by rats (Tolman & Honzik, 1930). Tolman is associated most often with his study of **latent learning**, which occurs when learning has taken place but is not demonstrated. In one of Tolman's most famous studies, three groups of rats learned a complex maze that had many choices and dead ends. One group of rats was always reinforced with food for successfully completing the maze. These animals gradually made fewer and fewer errors until, after 11 days of training, their performance was nearly perfect. A second group was never reinforced; the rats continued to make numerous errors. The third (latent-learning) group of animals did not receive reinforcement for the first 10 days of training. On the 11th day, reinforcement was provided. The behavior of these animals on the 12th day is of crucial importance. If learning occurs in a gradual, trial-and-error manner, the rats' performance on the 12th day should not have differed much from their performance on the 11th day. If, however, the rats used cognitive processes to learn to navigate the maze, they would exhibit dramatic behavior changes.

In fact, on the 12th day these rats solved the maze as quickly as the rats who had been continually reinforced (see Figure 5-15). How did these rats learn so quickly? Tolman argued that by wandering through the maze for 10 days before the introduction of reinforcement, these animals had formed a cognitive map of the maze. In other words, they had learned to solve the maze, but this knowledge had remained latent (unused) until reinforcement was introduced on the 11th day. Then, on the 12th day, these rats demonstrated that they knew how to get to the location of the reinforcement. Their latent learning had manifested itself. The implications of this finding are clear: It is possible to learn a behavior, yet that learning is not directly observed.

Observational Learning

As the previous discussion suggests, our behavior and the behavior of other animals is not just mechanically stamped in or out. There is a degree of cognitive activity or processing of information that is involved when we learn. Consider the following example.

latent learning
Learning that has occurred but is not demonstrated

FIGURE 5-15 Results of Tolman and Honzik's maze running experiment are not easily explained by operant conditioning concepts. This research was a significant contributor to the development of more cognitively oriented views of how organisms learn.
Source: Tolman & Honzik, 1930.

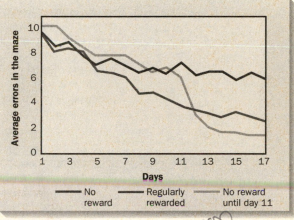

STUDY TIP

Create a visual organizer that shows behaviors with cognitive requirements (insight learning, latent learning, and so on) and their most important elements.

observational learning (modeling)
Learning that occurs through watching and imitating the behaviors of others

Imagine that you have given permission for your 6-year-old son and 8-year-old daughter to participate in a psychological experiment at the local university. During the experiment each child watches an adult play with a large inflatable doll that can double as a punching bag. Because the doll's base contains sand, the doll bounces back when it is punched and then is ready for more punches. The adult gives the doll a merciless beating; then each child is given an opportunity to play with the doll. What can this experiment tell us about learning?

For many years psychologists believed a participant must actually perform an operant response for learning to occur. In the early 1960s, Albert Bandura and his colleagues changed this view (Bandura, Ross, & Ross, 1963). As you will recall from Chapter 1, they found that children who observed an adult hitting and punching an inflatable Bobo doll were likely to repeat those behaviors when they were given a chance to play with the doll. Control participants, who had not observed the adult model, behaved less aggressively. Because the children made no responses while they were watching, the researchers concluded that simply observing the behavior and reinforcement (or punishment) of another participant could result in learning (Bandura, 1977). Such learning is termed **observational learning** or modeling. Because the observation of other people is a central factor in this form of learning, this approach is often called social learning theory.

While a great deal of concern has been raised concerning the possible effects of learning violence from television, a more recent concern focuses on video games, which can be highly violent. Researchers Craig Anderson and Karen Dill (2000) found that playing violent games was positively correlated with aggressive behavior and delinquency in children. The cautions we raised concerning correlational evidence in Chapter 1 should lead you to wonder if there is a causal relationship here. In a second study, the researchers found that exposing a random sample of children to a graphically violent video game had a direct and immediate impact on their aggressive thoughts and behavior. What's more, a review of the literature on the effects of video game violence led researchers (Anderson & Bushman, 2001) to the following conclusion:

> The results clearly support the hypothesis that exposure to violent video games poses a public-health threat to children and youth, including college-age individuals. Exposure is positively associated with heightened levels of aggression in young adults and children, in experimental and nonexperimental designs, and in males and females. Exposure is negatively associated with prosocial behavior (p. 358).

New York Yankee and Hall of Fame baseball player, Yogi Berra, once said "You can learn a lot by watching." There is growing concern that many young people are modeling the violence they see in movies and video games. Today's video games are realistic, attractive, exciting, and captivating. The challenge in the future may be to design games that are as equally attractive and exciting yet provide opportunities to model prosocial and non-violent forms of behavior.

TABLE 5.3

Major Effects of Vicarious Consequences

Vicarious Reinforcement	Vicarious Punishment
• Conveys information about which behaviors are appropriate in which settings	• Conveys information about which behaviors are inappropriate in which settings
• Arousal of the emotional responses of pleasure and satisfaction in the observer	• Tends to exert restraining influence on imitation of modeled behavior
• After repeated reinforcements, incentive-motivational effects are generated; behavior acquires functional value	• Tends to devalue the model's status because the behavior did not lead to a reinforcement

Adapted from Gredler, 2001.

If you stop to think about it, observational learning is the main way we learn about our culture and its customs and traditions. Let's return to the vignette that opened this section. Observational learning is most likely how Mary's 3-year-old son learned to start the car. He has most likely observed his mother and father put the key in the ignition and turn it hundreds if not thousands of times.

One of the keys to observational learning appears to be that the participant identifies with the person being observed. If we put ourselves in the other person's place for a moment, we are better able to imagine the effects of the reinforcer or punisher. This phenomenon is called *vicarious reinforcement* or *vicarious punishment*. Table 5-3 describes the major effects of vicarious (through another) consequences and their implications for learning.

Observational learning is a widespread phenomenon. For example, it is even found among a number of animals. For example, rats that observed the extinction behavior of other rats subsequently stopped responding more rapidly than rats that did not observe extinction performance (Heyes, Jaldow, & Dawson, 1993). In another experiment, monkeys reared in a laboratory didn't fear snakes. After watching another group of monkeys react fearfully to snakes, however, the nonfearful monkeys developed a pronounced fear of snakes (Cook et al., 1985).

Attempts to influence behavior through observational learning occur every day. Turn on the television and you are bombarded with commercials, which are nothing more than a form of observational learning. If you drive this kind of car, wear these clothes, use this brand of perfume, shower with this soap, use this shampoo, and eat this kind of breakfast, you will be rich, famous, powerful, sexy, and so forth, just like the models in the commercials.

According to the social learning theory proposed by Bandura (1986), for observational learning to be effective, the following conditions must be present:

1. You must pay attention to what the other person is doing and what happens to him or her.

2. You probably will not make the modeled response immediately, so you need to store a memory of the situation you have observed. For example, catchy advertising jingles that run through our heads continuously help us remember a particular commercial and its message (see Chapter 6).

3. You must be able to repeat or reproduce the behavior you observed. It might be wonderful to dream of owning a Porsche, but most of us will never be able to reproduce the behaviors needed to obtain one, regardless of how often we watch the commercial.

4. Your motivational state must be appropriate to the behavior you have learned through observation. Watching numerous commercials of people drinking a particular soft drink will not normally cause you to purchase one if you are not thirsty.

5. You must pay attention to discriminative stimuli. Sometimes we do not choose the best time and place to imitate someone else's behavior. For example, it would not be wise for teenagers to model some of their peers' behaviors at the dinner table.

STUDY TIP

Rewrite in your own words, and provide two examples to illustrate, the conditions necessary for effective observational learning.

Observational learning has also been used to reduce or eliminate phobias. For example, adults with an intense fear of snakes were shown live models handling live snakes (Bandura, Blanchard, & Ritter, 1969). These individuals were then encouraged to handle the snakes themselves. A final test indicated that they had less fear of snakes than those people who had watched a film of people handling snakes and a control group who had received no treatment.

We have presented this chapter's various concepts and principles separately to make your learning and understanding easier. In reality, classical conditioning, operant conditioning, observational learning, and punishment are not mutually exclusive. They can, and do, occur simultaneously.

REVIEW SUMMARY

1. **Insight learning** involves restructuring our perceptual stimuli to achieve the solution to a problem. Such perceptual restructuring and solutions typically occur rapidly.

2. **Latent learning** occurs when learning has taken place but is not demonstrated until a later time.

3. **Observational learning** takes place when we observe and identify with the behaviors of others. Advertisements and television commercials appeal to this process. Televised violence may result in observational learning and lead to an increase in violent behaviors.

✓ CHECK YOUR PROGRESS

1. Which of the following situations involve(s) observational learning?

   a. Learning to drive by taking a driver education course that emphasizes behind-the-wheel experience
   b. Pushing the remote control to change channels on the television
   c. Using a video to learn how to play golf
   d. Seeing friends go by on their motorcycles, saying to yourself, "I bet I can do that" and trying it
   e. Salivating every time you pass your favorite restaurant

2. Concern has been raised about violence in television and films because of research evidence about

   a. modeling.
   b. classical conditioning.
   c. operant conditioning.
   d. negative reinforcement.

3. Which of the following is the best summary of the evidence on the relation between video game violence and aggression?

   a. To date, only correlational research has been reported.
   b. There is little relation between the two; extreme cases are highlighted in the media.

   c. Although the correlational research finds an association, no laboratory research support any conclusion beyond an association.
   d. Both correlational and laboratory-based research support the existence of a relation between the two.

4. After running rats through mazes, Tolman found evidence for

   a. modeling.
   b. latent learning.
   c. classical conditioning.
   d. vicarious conditioning.

5. Which of the following is another common name for the approach that Bandura described in his famous research involving Bobo dolls?

   a. modeling
   b. latent learning
   c. cognitive imagery
   d. respondent conditioning

6. Evidence offered by Wolfgang Köhler supported the existence of the phenomenon of

   a. insight learning.
   b. operant conditioning.

c. respondent conditioning
d. vicarious conditioning

7. You are given the assignment of writing a paper on the work of Wolfgang Köhler, Edward Tolman, and Albert Bandura. Which of the following would be the best summary of the main points you will make in your paper?

a. Reinforcers are important in all forms of learning.
b. Learning is the result of either operant or classical conditioning.
c. Some cognitive processing of information occurs when we learn.
d. The primary ways in which we learn can be traced to our reflex actions.

ANSWERS: 1. a. Not observational learning **b.** Not observational learning **c.** Observational learning **d.** Observational learning **e.** Not observational learning **2.** a **3.** d **4.** d **5.** b **6.** a **7.** c

---

ANSWERS To Psychological Detective on Classical Conditioning

PAGE 186

For the food example, the UCS is the food in your mouth, and the UCR is salivation that occurs when the food is in your mouth. The CS is the name of the food that is spoken to you, and the CR is the salivation that occurs when you hear the name of your favorite food. In the example of Scott's fear of closed spaces, the UCS is being locked in the abandoned refrigerator and the UCR is nearly suffocating. Anything that resembles a closed space is the CS, and the fear he has to closed spaces is the CR.

CHECKING YOUR COMPREHENSION

Choose the best answer for each of the following questions.

1. Which of the following reactions would be considered the result of classical conditioning?
   a. shivering in a cold wind
   b. a baby taking a first step
   c. salivation at the site of a thick juicy steak
   d. sweating when feelings of anxiety take over

2. Which of these behaviors is consistent with operant conditioning?
   a. a real estate agent trying to sell as many houses as possible which results in higher commissions
   b. your brother cleaning his room every Saturday so he can watch cartoons for an hour following
   c. turning off your alarm clock to avoid listening to an annoying sound
   d. all of these are consistent with operant conditioning.

3. Which of the following behaviors is unlikely to be the result of observational learning?
   a. domestic violence
   b. starting the car
   c. respect for authority
   d. success at word puzzles

Match the researcher to the learning theory he is associated with.

4. Tolman   a. Observational learning
5. Kolher   b. Insight learning
6. Pavlov   c. Latent learning
7. Skinner   d. Operant conditioning
                   e. Classical conditioning

Identify the following statements as true or false.

8. Classical conditioning involves pairing an unconditioned stimulus (UCS), which automatically elicits an unconditioned response (UCR), with a conditioned stimulus (CS), which is neutral at the start of conditioning.

9. Shaping involves reinforcing random responses that more closely resemble the desired target response.

Answer the following questions.

10. Compare and contrast *generalization* with *discrimination* and give behavioral examples of both.

11. There are differences of opinion as to the effectiveness of punishment on changing learned behaviors. There is some agreement on guidelines of punishment. What are those guidelines?

Discussion and Critical Thinking Question

12. While on a vacation trip to Las Vegas, you find yourself obsessed with playing the quarter slot machines. Considering the behavior is the result of *partial reinforcement effect*, as a critical thinker what might you do to interrupt the partial schedule of reinforcement?

NOTES

22 CHAPTER

STATE AND LOCAL POLITICS
Who Governs?

W

HO PAVES OUR ROADS, RUNS OUR SCHOOLS, SHAPES WELFARE POLICY, DECIDES WHO GOES TO PRISON OR GETS probation, and levies property and sales taxes? Most of these policies are determined by elected and appointed officials in our states and localities. Many of the most critical domestic and economic issues facing the United States today are decided by our state and local officials. Such challenging responsibilities as overseeing the transition from welfare to work, maintaining prisons and jails (over 90 percent of the people incarcerated in America are in state and local facilities, not federal prisons), and bringing the residents of the inner cities in our large metropolitan areas into the economic mainstream require imaginative leadership and thoughtful public policy making at the state and local levels of government as well as in Washington, D.C.

Most state and local governments currently face big deficits. In 2003, New Jersey had a deficit of $5.3 billion, and New York a shortfall of $5.1 billion; New York City's was $4.7 billion. Each responds differently, based on its own set of problems (especially those stemming from the September 11, 2001, terorist attacks), history, and the leadership of elected officials. New Jersey's governor, James E. McGreevey, cut funding for state agencies and building construction, whereas New York's governor, George E. Pataki, is drawing on hundreds of millions of dollars that the state squirreled away during the economic boom of the 1990s and reserved "for a rainy day," which Pataki said has turned out to be more like a "monsoon."[1]

State and local governments flourished long before there was a national government. Indeed, the framers of our Constitution shaped the national government largely according to their practical experience with colonial and state governments. What happens today in state and local governments continues to influence the policies of the national government. The reverse, of course, is also true: The national government and its policies have an important impact on local and state government. The national government's activities—such as the war against international terrorism, diplomatic maneuvers in the Middle East, key Supreme Court decisions, and major congressional debates and investigations—receive such great publicity that we often overlook the countless ways governments closer to home affect our lives.

Studying state and local governments to find out how they operate and who governs them is a challenge. It is one thing to study our national system, vast and complex as it is; it is something else to study 50 separate state governments, each with its own legislature, executive, and judiciary and each with its own intricate politics and political traditions. Moreover, state and local governments are only part of a much larger picture. To discuss the government of the state of Mississippi or of the city of Detroit without mentioning race, the government of New York City or of Los Angeles without noting the politics of ethnic groups, or the government of Texas without referring to the cattle and oil industries would be to ignore the real dynamics of the political process. State and local governments, like the national government, are more than organizational charts. They are systems of politics and people with their own unique histories. The great variations among the states and localities—in population, economic resources, and environment—make comparisons and generalizations difficult.

Still, every government system is part of a larger social system. A government is a structure and a process that resolves, or at least manages, conflicts. It regulates, distributes, and sometimes redistributes property and wealth. It is also a means for achieving certain goals and performing services desired both by those who govern and by the governed. It operates in the context of an economic system, class structure, and lifestyle that are often more important than the structure of the government itself or even the nature of its political processes. The interrelations among the economic, social, and political systems are complex and hard to unscramble, and it is difficult to decide which is cause and which is effect.[2]

This already complex picture is complicated further by the fact that more than 87,500 cities, counties, towns, villages, school districts, water control districts, and other governmental units are piled one on top of another within the states. If all states or cities or towns were alike, the task might be manageable. But of course they are not. Each city, like each state, has distinct characteristics.[3]

Who Has the Power?

How can we grasp the operations and problems of state and local government without becoming bogged down in endless detail? We can do so by focusing on the core components of democratic governance: citizen participation, liberty, constitutional checks and balances, representation, and responsible leadership. Further, we can address several questions that throw light on all these problems: Who governs? How much influence or control is in the hands of the business community? Does political power tend to gravitate toward a relatively small number of people? If so, who are these people? Do they work closely together, or do they oppose each other? Do the same people or factions shape the agenda for public debate and dominate all decision making? Or do some sets of leaders decide certain questions and leave other questions to other leaders or simply to chance?

In 1924, two sociologists from Columbia University, Robert and Helen Lynd, decided to study a typical American city as though they were anthropologists investigating a tribe in Africa or Indonesia. For two years, they lived in Muncie, Indiana—at that time a city of 38,000 residents—asking questions and watching how people made their living, raised their children, used their leisure time, and joined in civic and social associations. The Lynds reported that despite the appearance of democratic rule, a social and economic elite actually ran things.[4] Their work stimulated studies in all kinds of communities to find out whether power is concentrated in the hands of the few, is dispersed among the many, or operates in some other way.

Relying on a mix of research methods, social scientists since the Lynds' time have studied patterns of power in communities and arrived at a variety of findings. Floyd Hunter, a sociologist who analyzed Atlanta in the 1950s, found a relatively small and stable group of top policy makers drawn largely from the business class. This elite operated through secondary leaders who sometimes modified policy, but the power of the elite was almost always important.[5] In contrast, Robert Dahl and his graduate students at Yale studied New Haven at the same time and concluded that although some people had a great deal of influence, there was no permanent elite. Instead, there were shifting coalitions of leaders who sometimes disagreed among themselves but who always had to keep in mind what the public would accept when making decisions.[6]

Rule by a Few or Rule by the Many?

One group of investigators, chiefly sociologists such as Hunter, have been concerned with **social stratification** in the political system—how politics is affected by divisions among socioeconomic groups or classes in a community. These social scientists assume that political influence is a function of social stratification. They try to find out who governs particular communities by asking various citizens to identify the people who are most influential. Then they study those influential people to determine their social characteristics, their roles in decision making, and the interrelations among them and between them and the rest of the citizens. Using this technique, they find that the upper socioeconomic groups make up the *power elite,* that elected political leaders are subordinate to that elite, and that the major conflicts within the community are between the upper and the lower socioeconomic classes.

Other investigators question these findings and raise objections to the research techniques used. They contend that the evidence in social stratification studies does not support the conclusion that communities are run by a power elite. Rather, the notion of a power elite is merely a reflection of the techniques used and the assumptions made by stratification theorists. Instead of studying the activities of those who are thought to have "clout," these researchers insist, one should study how decisions are actually made.

Researchers who conduct *community power* studies analyzing the making of decisions usually find a relatively open, pluralistic power structure. Some people do have more influence than others, but that influence is shared among many people and tends to be limited to particular issues and areas. For example, those who decide how the public schools are run may have little influence over other economic policies. In many communities and for many issues, there is no identifiable group of influential people. Policies emerge not from the actions of a small group but rather from the unplanned and unanticipated consequences of the behavior of a relatively large number of people, especially from the countless contending groups that form and win access to those who make the important decisions. According to community power theorists, the social structure of the community is certainly one factor, but not the determining factor in how goods and services are distributed.

Comparing power elite and community power studies highlights the fact that how we ask questions often influences the answers we get. If we ask highly visible and actively involved citizens for their opinions of who is powerful, we find that they name a relatively small number of people as the real holders of power. But if we study dozens of local events and decisions, we find that a variety of people are involved—different people in different policy areas.

Other studies of local politics suggest that local values, traditions, and the structure of governmental organizations also determine which issues get on the local agenda.[7] Thus tobacco, mining, or steel interests may be so dominant in some areas that tax, regulation, or job safety policies are kept off the local policy agenda for fear of offending the "powers that be." Those "powers" may indeed go to great lengths to prevent what they deem to be adverse policies. This type of research alerts us to weigh carefully the possibility that defenders of the status quo can mobilize power resources in such a way that nondecisions may be more important than decisions. In effect, these researchers tell us not only to study who

Local communities often give special status and recognition to prominent local business people and other community leaders. Here, Limestone County Commission Chairman Stanley Meneffe, Dura Coat Founder Mike Hoag, Huntsville Mayor Loretta Spencer, and Huntsville-Madison County Chamber of Commerce Chairman Clay Vandiver break ground in Greenbrier, Alabama for a building that will employee 150 people.

social stratification
Divisions in a community among socio-economic groups or classes.

governs but also to study the procedures and rules of the game. They urge us to determine which groups or interests would gain and which would lose by political decisions.[8]

On many economic policy matters, local corporations and business elites are involved. Studies of cities in Michigan and of Atlanta employing refined and contextual analysis of political decision making concluded that business elites are indeed important, but they are not necessarily the controlling factor in city governance:

> There is, then, no controlling hand in community politics. No conspiracy of business and government exists. Business interests do not invariably dominate government policy even where a single industry dominates the community. However, the giant industrial companies do provide the backdrop against which the public policy process operates in the industrial city. They are always there, seldom intervening in specific policy matters but never far from the calculations of policy makers.[9]

Studies of states and communities have now produced enough findings that we can see how formal government institutions, social structure, economic factors, and other variables interact in a working political system.

The Stakes in the Political Struggle

The national government has become the driving force behind the nation's economic strength and security. It assumes major responsibility for protecting civil rights, fighting inflation and unemployment, regulating sectors with great economic power, and subsidizing weaker sectors of the economy—not to mention matters of war and peace. State and local governments cannot claim so central a role. Yet the role of states and localities is increasing over a range of domestic policies, even though they diverge in their priorities and policies as a result of the maze of interests in each state. In response to health concerns and budget deficits, for example, seven states charge more than $1 per pack of cigarettes in taxes, while about half charge just 33 cents or less, with Virginia the lowest at 2.5 cents (see Figure 22-1).

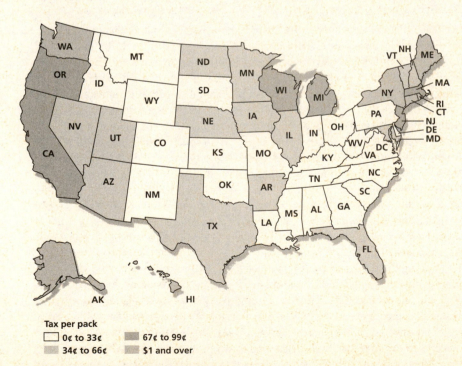

Tax per pack
☐ 0¢ to 33¢   ▨ 67¢ to 99¢
▨ 34¢ to 66¢   ▨ $1 and over

FIGURE 22–1   State Taxes on Tobacco Products.

SOURCE: "Sinful Tax?" *New York Times,* March 17, 2002, p. WK5.

Since World War II, state and local government activities have increased much faster than the nondefense activities of the federal government. In the past decade, the federal government has been downsizing while state and local governments have been growing. Six times as many people work for state and local governments—18 million—than work for the Federal government, which has fewer than 3 million civilian employees.[10] States have had to assume greater responsibilities for raising taxes, setting economic and social priorities, and administering most welfare and job creation programs as a result of cutbacks in federal funds and devolution of responsibilities to the states.

State and local governments deal more directly with the average person than the national government does, because neighborhood, school, and housing problems are closely regulated at the state and local levels. The points at which people come into contact with government services and officials most often concern schools, streets and highways, parks and playgrounds, police and fire protection, zoning, and health care. But even in these areas, the mix of national, state, and local programs and responsibilities is such that it is often hard to isolate which level of government does what to or for whom. Also, there are some national-to-individual relationships that bypass state and local governments altogether, such as the Internal Revenue Service, the U.S. Postal Service, and Social Security.

Government reaches into many trivial aspects of our lives, such as restrictions on our pets.

The Maze of Interests

Special-interest groups can be found in varying forms in every state and locality. For example, industrial Rhode Island has farm organizations, and rural Wyoming has trade unions. Influential economic pressure groups and political action committees, organized to raise and disburse campaign funds to candidates for public office, operate in the states much as they do nationally. They try to build up the membership of their organizations, they lobby the state capitals and city halls, they educate and organize the voters, and they support their political friends in office and oppose their enemies. They also face the same internal problems all groups face: maintaining unity, dealing with subgroups that break off in response to special needs, and balancing democracy with discipline.

One great difference, however, is that group interests can be concentrated in states and localities, whereas their strength tends to be diluted in the national government. Big business does not really run things in Washington, D.C., any more than Wall Street, the Catholic Church, or the American Legion does. But in some states and localities, certain interests do clearly dominate because they represent the social and economic majorities of the area. Few politicians in Wisconsin will attack dairy farmers, few candidates for office in Florida will oppose benefits for senior citizens, and few officeholders in Idaho will support gun control. In other areas, industries such as timber or energy are influential because of their role in the local economy.

It is the range and variety of these local groups that give American politics its special flavor, excitement, and challenge: auto unions and manufacturers in Michigan, corn and hog farmers in Iowa, gas and oil dealers in Texas, gun owners in New Hampshire and Idaho, tobacco farmers in North Carolina and Virginia, poultry growers in Arkansas, Boeing and Microsoft in the Seattle area, coal miners in West Virginia, and sheep ranchers in Utah. However, the power of these groups should not be exaggerated.

We have to be cautious about lumping all workers, all business people, all teachers, all Hispanics, or all African Americans together. The union movement is sometimes sharply divided among the truckers, building trades, machinists, auto workers, and so on. The business community is often divided between big industrial, banking, and commercial firms on the one hand and small merchants on the other. In New England, Irish and Italian fraternal societies express the opinions of their respective groups on public issues; other organizations speak for people of French Canadian or Polish descent. New England politicians fear the power of ethnic groups to influence elections, especially primaries, yet there are plenty of examples of "Yankees" winning in heavily ethnic areas. Similarly, Asian American, Latino, and African American communities are playing an increasingly important role in elections in states such as California, Florida, and Texas.

Pet Peeves

Some areas of life might seem far removed from any government—having a dog or a cat as a pet, for example. But a dog needs a license and a collar, it must be confined, and it must be inoculated. And if anyone thinks that cats are beyond the reach of the law, they should remember Adlai E. Stevenson's famous veto of the "cat bill" when he was governor of Illinois. The bill would have imposed fines on cat owners who let their pets run off their premises, and it would have allowed cat haters to trap them. Stevenson said:

> I cannot agree that it should be declared public policy of Illinois that a cat visiting a neighbor's yard or crossing the highway is a public nuisance. It is in the nature of cats to do a certain amount of unescorted roaming. . . . I am afraid this bill could only create discord, recrimination, and enmity. . . . We are all interested in protecting certain varieties of birds. . . . The problem of cat versus bird is as old as time. If we attempt to resolve it by legislation, who knows but what we may be called upon to take sides as well in the age-old problem of dog versus cat, bird versus bird, or even bird versus worm.*

So the governor sided with cat supporters over bird lovers while staying neutral between bird lovers and worm diggers. Such incidents illustrate how the complex workings of modern society can lead to government intervention in or overregulation of our lives.

*Governor Adlai Stevenson, veto message to members of the State Assembly, Springfield, Illinois, 1949.

Compared to the other considerations affecting voters' choices, the ethnic factor may be small. Still, even a small percentage of the populace voting according to their ethnic interests can have a decisive effect on an election. Much depends on the character of the candidates and their personal appeal. Any group, no matter how strong, must cope with a variety of cross pressures, including a general sense that the voter does not vote for "one of our own" on that ground alone.

Other interests that are more specialized may also have a close relationship with local government. Many businesspeople sell products to the state or perform services for it: milk dealers, printers, contractors, parking meter manufacturers, computer and communications technology firms, makers of playground equipment, textbook publishers, and so on. They often organize formally or informally to improve their relations with purchasing officials. At the local level, developers and home builders and their lawyers press for zoning and planning commission action. Millions of dollars are often at stake, and the resulting action or inaction frequently shapes both the economic growth and the environmental quality of a community.

Business interests are inevitably involved in city and county politics and policy making. As one study of Atlanta found, the business elite is rarely a passive or reluctant partner in setting local priorities. "Atlanta's postwar political experience is a story of active business-elite efforts to make the most of their economic and organizational resources in setting the terms on which civic cooperation occurs."[11] Businesses everywhere depend on local governments for parking, good roads and transportation, safety, urban renovations, and much more. Business elites get involved in long-range community planning, are keenly interested in who gets elected, and are ever watchful of changes in taxation structures.

Another type of interest group intimately concerned with public policy is the professional association. States license barbers, beauticians, architects, lawyers, doctors, teachers, accountants, dentists, and many other occupational groups. You will find representatives from the Beauticians Aid Association, the Funeral Directors and Embalmers Association, the Institute of Dry Cleaning, and the Association of Private Driver-Training Schools lobbying at the statehouse. Associations representing such groups are concerned with the nature of the regulatory laws and the makeup of the boards that do the regulating. They are especially concerned about the rules for admission to their profession or trade and about the way in which professional misconduct is defined and punished. Stiffening licensing requirements for physicians will decrease the supply of new doctors, for example, and thereby raise the incomes of those in practice. Bar associations, for the same reason, closely monitor licensing standards for the legal profession and the appointment of judges.

Today, other groups of citizens are also likely to organize to influence decisions in the state capital: those who are pro-life and those who are pro-choice, those who want stiffer sentences for drunken driving, and those who favor three-strikes-and-you're-out legislation to send repeat criminals to jail for life. Right to Life groups, Planned Parenthood, antismoking groups, animal rights activists, and prison guards are also well organized. Increasingly significant are environmental groups such as the Sierra Club, both in forging public policies and as forces in election contests.

Lobbyists at the Statehouse

Many businesses, especially larger corporations, employ lobbyists, public relations specialists, political consultants, or law firms to represent them.[12] One of the growth businesses in state politics is consulting, usually by specialized lawyers or former state legislators. For a fee, lobbyists push desired bills through the legislature or block unwanted ones. This kind of activity again raises the question of who has clout or who governs. Clearly, those who can hire skilled lobbyists and other experts to shape the public agenda often wield more influence than unorganized citizens, who rarely even follow state and regional governmental decision making.

Lobbyists are present in every state capital, and they are there to guide through the legislature a small handful of bills their organization wants passed or to stop those their organization wants defeated.[13] Legislators process hundreds or even thousands of bills each year, in addition to doing casework on behalf of constituents and worrying about reelections. Shrewd lobbyists usually get a chance—sometimes several chances—to influence the fate of their few bills.

There is a widespread impression that lobbyists have freer rein in state legislatures than they do in the U.S. Congress and, what is more, that bribes or informal payoffs by lobbyists are cruder and more obvious in state legislatures. Certainly lobbying restrictions in the states are more relaxed than at the federal level, although in some of the larger

Professions and occupations of various types are regulated by the government through licensing and standards.

Ethics Laws in the States: A Comparison

- *No contributions from lobbyists:* Seven states completely ban lobbyists from contributing to campaigns at any time.

- *No contributions from lobbyists during legislative sessions:* 23 states prohibit lobbyists from making contributions during a legislative session.

- *Gifts and expenditure limitations:* 25 states restrict the monetary value of gifts a public employee may receive.

- *Investigatory authority:* Agencies that may initiate an investigation of ethics violations on their own volition result in ten times the number of investigations per year as those that may only investigate in response to a formal complaint.

SOURCE: *The Book of the States, 2000–2001* (Council of State Governments, 2000), p. 397.

states they may be even more stringent. There is less media coverage of state politics in many states than is focused on national politics in Washington, D.C.

Corruption of legislators and state officials is usually hard to prove. Exposure of scandals in several states pushed many legislatures to curb election abuses and pass ethics codes with stringent conflict-of-interest provisions.[14] Several legislatures have enacted comprehensive financial disclosure laws, and today most state governments are more open, professional, and accountable than in the past.[15] Former President Jimmy Carter, who served in the Georgia Senate and then became governor, recalled that only a "tiny portion" of the 259 members of the Georgia legislature were not good or honest people. But Carter found that "it is difficult for the common good to prevail against the intense concentration of those who have a special interest, especially if the decisions are made behind locked doors."[16]

In a few states, one corporation or organization may exercise considerable influence; in others, a "big three" or "big four" dominate politics. But in most states, there is competition among organizations; no single group or coalition of groups stands out. In no state does only one organization control legislative politics, although the powerful Anaconda Company once came close in Montana. For example, some 400 lobbyists are registered in Arkansas. Of these, 125 represent utilities; more than 200 represent individual businesses, industry, or professions; nine represent labor interests; eight work on behalf of senior citizens; and three lobby for environmental interests. The Arkansas Power and Light Company, the railroads, the poultry and trucking industries, the teachers, and the state Chamber of Commerce are the most effective lobbyists. "It is still true that ordinarily those with greater economic resources, greater numbers, and higher status have far more impact than those who lack these attributes," writes political scientist Diane Blair. "Nevertheless, an increasingly complex economy has produced many more actors in the political system, and especially when there is division among the economic elite, some of the lesser voices can be heard."[17]

In Michigan, about 1,250 lobbyists are registered with the state, including representatives of the "big three" automakers, the United Auto Workers, the AFL-CIO, the Michigan Education Association, the Michigan Manufacturers Association, the city of Detroit, the Michigan Chamber of Commerce, certain conservation and environmental groups, and various antitax groups.[18]

Not to be overlooked are the growing number of groups and media outlets that view themselves as "watchdogs" of the public policy process. Groups such as the League of Women Voters, Common Cause, and various citizens' groups regularly monitor state politics for questionable fund-raising or lobbying practices. Their "watchdog" efforts are sometimes aided by reporters who cover state capitals.

Participation Patterns in Small and Medium-Sized Cities

Although it is widely believed that citizens feel "closer" to city and county governments than they do to the more remote national government in Washington, D.C., citizens generally take less interest in, vote less often in, and are less informed about their local governments than they are about the national government. There are understandable reasons for the lower involvement in local government. Although issues about where to locate a garbage dump or a prison or how to deal with police brutality can arouse considerable heat, most of the time local governments are preoccupied with relatively noncontroversial routine matters, such as keeping the roads in shape, providing fire and police service, attracting businesses that can create more jobs, or applying for state and federal financial assistance.

Local communities want to keep their tax rates down and promote their cities as "nice places" in which to live, work, and raise families. Mayors and city officials generally try to avoid controversy and the kind of criticism that will divide a community. Although they do not always succeed, they go to considerable lengths to be reasonable and work for the good of the community. Few aggressively seek to alter the status quo. They do not, as a rule, try to promote equality by redistributing various resources to needier citizens. **Redistributive policies** are programs to shift wealth or benefits from one segment of the population to another, usually from the rich to the poor. Local officials tend to believe that this is the task of the national or state authorities—if they think it should be done at all. Typically, they say their communities do not have the funds for such programs. They might add, "Go see the governor" or "Go talk to your member of Congress." This may be good advice, because various programs (educational loans, unemployment compensation, disability assistance, and so on) explicitly designed to help the less fortunate are administered at the state or federal level.

Neighborhood groups sometimes become involved in protecting their neighborhoods and petitioning for improvements. One concern that often activates neighborhood groups is the possibility that "undesirable" facilities might be located in their neighborhood, such as drug rehabilitation clinics, prisons, dumps, or homeless shelters. Although attendance at local government meetings is usually low, the announcement of a land-fill area or a prison construction project often stimulates the reaction that local officials call NIMBY, an acronym for "Not In My Back Yard!"

Don Wright/Don Wright, Inc.

The Role of Local Media

Most communities have only one newspaper, and in small communities it is often a weekly. Some newspapers and local radio and television stations do a good job of covering city and county politics, but this is the exception rather than the rule. Reporters assigned to cover local politics are often inexperienced beginners, yet they provide the only news that citizens get about their city council or zoning board. Even the best of them have difficulty conveying the full complexities of what is going on in a column or two of newsprint.

Some local newspapers enjoy a cozy relationship with elected local officials. Sometimes the owners or editors are social friends or golfing buddies of local officials. Friendships and mutual interests develop, and close scrutiny of what goes on in city hall takes a back seat to city boosterism. In effect, "newspapers boost their hometown, knowing that its prosperity and expansion aid their own. Harping on local faults, investigating dirty politics, revealing unsavory scandals, and stressing governmental inefficiencies only provide readily available documentary material to competing cities."[19]

Editors and station managers recognize that their readers or listeners are more interested in state or national news, and especially in sports, than in what is going on at municipal planning meetings or county commission sessions. Much of what takes place in local government is rather dull. It may be important to some people, yet it strikes the average person as decidedly less exciting than what goes on at the White House or whether Congress has finally solved the Social Security problem or whether their stocks have gone up or down or whether the New York Jets or the Los Angeles Lakers won last night. We have dozens of ways to find out about Congress and the White House, but we usually have only one source for stories about the mayor or sheriff or school board. Of course, we could attend board meetings or even talk with our mayor, but that is not what most people are likely to do.

Apathy in Grassroots America

Voter apathy in local elections is summed up in the bumper sticker "DON'T VOTE. IT ONLY ENCOURAGES THEM." Many important political and economic transactions in communities are ignored by the press and citizens. Charter revision and taxation often galvanize only those directly affected by the new taxes or regulations. Even New England town meetings have difficulty getting people to participate—despite the fact that decisions made at these meetings have major consequences for local tax rates and the quality of the schools, the police force, and the parks and recreational areas. Thomas Jefferson once proclaimed the town meeting to be the noblest, wisest instrument yet devised for the

redistributive policies
Governmental tax and social programs that shift wealth or benefits from one segment of the population to another, often from the rich to the poor.

WE THE PEOPLE

What One Person Can Accomplish

T. Willard Fair.

Urban League leader T. Willard Fair is a committed problem solver for his Liberty City community in Miami. He is recognized as a one-man force trying to rid Liberty City of drug dealers. In the late 1980s, Fair started a private-public collaboration to improve the quality of life in this inner-city community. Among many other results, his efforts led to 3,500 arrests, the breakup of 27 crack houses, the towing of many abandoned vehicles, and the trimming of trees to expose shaded areas where drug deals were made. But above all, Fair was able to get his neighbors in Liberty City to band together and have faith that their neighborhood could be rid of its pushers.

Fair started the program after reading about a young woman who had been shot. Residents were too fearful of drug dealers to cooperate with police. Fair became a catalyst for change, enlisting the help of government and school officials, police and fire officers, churches, residents, and local businesses. He also persuaded the national drug program to share some funds, and he raised other funds by whatever means he could. By the early 1990s, he could declare, along with the Liberty City residents, that their 70-square-block, drug-free zone was "off limits" to what he calls "the drug boys."

Fair has received over 100 awards, including Florida's Outstanding Citizen Award, for his dedication and efforts in community building, combating crime, and promoting education among inner-city children. He remains the president of the Urban League of Greater Miami.

SOURCE: Catherine Foster, "One Man Rallies a Neighborhood Against Pushers," *Christian Science Monitor,* June 11, 1992, p.7.

School board meetings in Austin, Texas do not usually draw a crowd, but when the topic of sex education was discussed, a vocal and concerned crowd turned out.

conduct of public affairs, but today most towns find that only about 2 or 3 percent of the population cares enough to come.[20]

The major reason for grassroots apathy is that local politics simply does not interest the average person. Most people are content to leave politics and political responsibilities to a relatively small number of activists while they pursue their own private concerns—their bowling leagues, their children's Little League or soccer games, golf, or fishing. In a healthy democracy, we can expect that most people will be involved with their families and jobs; other than voting occasionally, they tend to leave civic responsibilities to a relatively small number of their fellow citizens. This is probably a reasonable choice. It may also be an indication of satisfaction with the state of the community.

Cynicism about the effectiveness and fairness of local political processes is sometimes reflected in the politics of protest—mass demonstrations, economic boycotts, even civil disorders—to make demands on government. When certain issues become intense, people become politically active. African Americans, Hispanics, gays, and others form political organizations to present their grievances and marshal votes. Neighborhood organizations work for better housing and enforcement of inspection ordinances and to prevent crime and drug dealing.

Civic Initiatives in Local Governments

Just as there will always be indifference toward politics and apathy about government, so too will there always be creative, entrepreneurial people who are willing to step forward and find new ways of solving problems. States such as Oregon and Minnesota seem to encourage a climate of innovation and civic enterprise, and a wider look at the United States finds buoyant, optimistic, creative problem solvers in nearly every corner of the nation.

Enterprising local activists have advocated and implemented cost-saving energy programs, environmental cleanup campaigns, recycling and solar energy initiatives, job training centers, AIDS prevention efforts, housing for the elderly, tutoring for the illiterate, housing for the poor, and hundreds of other problem-solving and opportunity-enhancing community efforts.[21] In almost every case, they create partnerships with elected officials at city hall, sometimes with the Urban League or Chamber of Commerce, and often with local foundations and business corporations.

Sometimes it takes a tragedy to get community groups mobilized. Such a tragic event happened in Boston when gang members burst into the funeral of a young man. "In the presence of the mourners, the gang killed one of those in attendance," writes the Reverend Eugene Rivers of the Azusa Christian Community.

Not all citizens are apathetic. These young people are spending their free time rehabilitating a community center.

> That brazen act told us we had to do more. Now. That young man's death galvanized us, and soon the Ten Point Coalition was reaching out to at-risk youth. Our mission was to pair the holy and the secular, to do whatever it took to save our kids. The black churches worked hand-in-hand with the schools, courts, police, and social service agencies. We called on anyone and everyone who had the means to help our children. We formed programs for teens, neighborhood watches, and patrols. . . . We established ourselves in the neighborhood, standing on the same street corner where the drug dealers once stood. We tracked down the thieves, dealers, and gangs. We tried to give people a chance, but if they wouldn't take it, we staked our claim and ran them out of our neighborhood.[22]

There are persistent debates about how to solve social, economic, and racial problems in our large metropolitan areas. Some people contend that government can't undertake this task and that private initiatives can be more effective. Others insist that state and local governments are best suited to deal with these challenges. Still others contend that imaginative public-private collaboration is needed to fashion the strategies and mobilize the resources to revive our cities and bring about greater opportunity. Whatever the merits of such contending interpretations, it is clear that neighborhood organizations and spirited civic renewal are critical to the vitality of local government.[23]

Challenges for State and Local Governments

Most states and communities are confronting testing times. Virtually all of the states and major cities face serious budget problems and increasing demands for services. People don't like tax increases, but they also want better schools, a clean environment, and safe roads.[24] About one-third of our inner-city governments and school systems are in financial distress. The cycle of poverty in the inner cities remains one of the greatest threats to the economic health of the country. Cities, though, often cannot raise enough funds through local taxes to create jobs and housing. Federal and state initiatives have attempted to create economic opportunities for inner-city residents. Community development banks, "empowerment zones," Head Start, charter schools, and national service (Americorp) programs have all been tried in an attempt to bring residents of depressed inner cities into the economic mainstream. But these efforts have been inadequate and must compete with other demands on financially pressed states and localities.

The following central issues in the states and local communities command the attention of the country. They vary depending on location, of course, yet these urgent challenges are part of the unfinished business of a government by the people:

- *People want more services* yet at the same time would like to see their taxes cut. City and state officials are constantly trying to do more with less and introduce

Local residents often form groups to handle and discuss issues that are important to their neighborhood, as illustrated by this gathering of Neighborhood Watch volunteers.

efficiencies into city and state operations. Voters in many communities have enacted spending limits that constrain growth in public budgets.

- *Racism still exists in many communities.* As our nation has become more diverse, most Americans have learned to appreciate the strength that comes from multiple cultures and races. Yet the Ku Klux Klan and other racist groups still thrive in many areas, and bigotry and discrimination persist.

- *Drugs, gangs, and drug-related crime impose tough policy challenges.* The costs of corrections and prisons have skyrocketed in recent years, yet gangs, drugs, and crime are still a menace in our urban areas. Most state and local "wars on drugs" have failed, and the ravages of drug abuse are enormously costly to the nation. Drug abusers lose their jobs; they make our streets, schools, and neighborhoods unsafe; they add to our welfare rolls; they make it necessary for states to build more prisons; and in numerous ways they undermine the vitality of a great many cities and towns.

- *Poverty in the inner cities persists.* We have extremes of rich and poor within metropolitan regions, and often the wealthier suburbs turn their backs on the problems and poverty of the older cities. Indifference to these inequalities and lack of opportunities may undermine a sense of community and fairness in America.

- *We need to guarantee the best possible education for all our young people.* Parents are demanding better education and more parental involvement. Many communities are experimenting with educational choice and competition, school vouchers, and charter schools. Improving the public schools is necessary, but their resources and the salaries of teachers are often too low to attract and retain the best-qualified teachers. State and local governments have the responsibility to pay for public education, so educational reform and the search for excellent teachers and learning processes will remain a top state and local priority.

- *Environmental regulation, land use, and recycling are also major challenges at the local level.* Every city and state wants economic growth and economic opportunities for its workers and businesses, but many forms of economic development impose costs in terms of the quality of air, water, landscapes, and health. Local officials face tough decisions about the need to balance economic and environmental concerns.

- *Health care costs and delivery are challenges to all levels of government.* Health care reform has been an important policy issue for many years. Some states have experimented with universal health care; others have worked to control costs. Many of the uninsured end up obtaining health care in emergency rooms in local public hospitals, which in turn seek funding from the local and state governments.

For more information on these and other issues confronting state and local governments go to our home page at www.prenhall.com/burns, or to the Web site of the Council of State Governments at www.csg.org, or that of the National Conference of State Legislatures at www.ncsl.org.

Summary

1. Many of the most critical domestic and economic issues facing the United States today are decided at the state and local levels of government.

2. Studies of states and communities have investigated how formal government institutions, social structure, economic factors, and local traditions interact to create a working political system. Some studies find that a power elite dominates, whereas community power studies find pluralism and diverse interest groups competing for influence over a range of policy areas. Special-interest groups operate in every state and locality, but their influence varies.

3. Although it is widely believed that local governments are "closer to the people" than the national government, voting and other forms of participation at the local level are low.

4. Innovative programs at the local level address problems in education, the environment, crime and violence, and ways to improve community life. Local civil action is one of the most important forms of citizen participation in politics.

Key Terms

social stratification   redistributive policies

Further Reading

THAD L. BEYLE, ED., *State Government: CQ's Guide to Current Issues and Activities, 2001–2002* (CQ Press, 2001).

BUZZ BISSINGER, *A Prayer for the City* (Random House, 1997).

PAUL BRACE, *State Government and Economic Performance* (Johns Hopkins University Press, 1993).

ALLAN CIGLER AND BURDETT LOOMIS, EDS., *Interest Group Politics,* 5th ed. (CQ Press, 1998).

FRANK J. COPPA, *County Government* (Praeger, 2000).

THOMAS E. CRONIN AND ROBERT D. LOEVY, *Colorado Politics and Government: Governing the Centennial State* (University of Nebraska Press, 1993).

E. J. DIONNE JR., ED. *Community Works: The Revival of Civil Society in America* (Brookings Institution, 1998).

THOMAS D. DYE, *Politics in States and Communities,* 10th ed. (Prentice Hall, 2000).

ROBERT S. ERIKSON, GERALD C. WRIGHT, AND JOHN P. MCIVER, *Statehouse Democracy: Public Opinion and Policy in the American States* (Cambridge University Press, 1993).

JOEL GARREAU, *Edge City: Life on the New Frontier* (Doubleday, 1991).

STEPHEN GOLDSMITH, *The Twenty-First Century City* (Regnery, 1997).

VIRGINIA GRAY, RUSSELL HANSON, AND HERBERT JACOB, EDS., *Politics in the American States,* 7th ed. (CQ Press, 1999).

JONATHAN HARRIS, *A Civil Action* (Vintage, 1996).

DENNIS R. JUDD AND PAUL KANTOR, EDS., *Politics of Urban American: A Reader* (Addison-Wesley, 1997).

DANIEL KEMMIS, *The Good City and the Good Life* (Houghton Mifflin, 1995).

DAVID L. KIRP, JOHN P. DWYER, AND LARRY A. ROSENTHAL, *Our Town: Race, Housing, and the Soul of Suburbia* (Rutgers University Press, 1997).

MADELEINE KUNIN, *Living a Political Life* (Vintage, 1995).

TOM LOFTUS, *The Art of Legislative Politics* (CQ Press, 1994).

JOHN O. NORQUIST, *The Wealth of Cities* (Addison-Wesley, 1998).

ALAN ROSENTHAL, *The Third House: Lobbyists and Lobbying in the States,* 2d ed. (CQ Press, 2001).

TODD SWANSTROM AND DENNIS R. JUDD, EDS., *City Politics: Private Power and Public Policy,* 3d ed. (Addison-Wesley, 2002).

JOSEPH F. ZIMMERMAN, *The New England Town Meeting: Democracy in Action* (Praeger, 1999).

See also the *State Politics and Policy Quarterly* and the Web site of the Council of State Governments at www.csg.org.

CHECKING YOUR COMPREHENSION

Choose the best answer for each of the following questions.

1. Which of the following would you expect to find influencing local government?
   a. upper socioeconomic groups
   b. special interest groups
   c. local traditions and values
   d. All of these, at one time or another, can influence local government

2. Which of these would not serve as a explanation for voter apathy?
   a. satisfaction with the current state of affairs
   b. a willingness to leave the responsibility of governing to a few
   c. a preference for pursuing one's own private interests
   d. the growth of neighborhood associations

3. Which of the following is most likely to lead to a local political-action group stepping forward?
   a. regional transportation
   b. tariffs on imported goods
   c. demand for services
   d. AIDS Research

4. Most states and local municipalities are facing
   a. budget problems and increasing demands for service.
   b. a divided community.
   c. high crime rates.
   d. All of these

Identify the following statements as true or false.

5. Citizens feel closer to city and county governments than they do to the more remote national government in Washington D.C.

6. Local governments tend to believe that redistributive policies are the task of national and state authorities and consequently defer to the governor or members of Congress on issues surrounding assistance for the less fortunate.

Answer the following questions.

7. What effect might the growing number of "watchdog" groups have on lobbying activities at the state legislature level? Can you think of a recent example in your state?

8. What are some of the reasons why local newspapers may not accurately depict local politics or fairly assess the effectiveness of local government?

Discussion and Critical Thinking Question

9. People who step forward and try to find new ways of solving problems in their community usually create partnerships with local organizations like the Chamber of Commerce, local foundations, or business groups. Identify a problem that is confronting your community: If you were to step forward to try to find a way to address it, who might you partner with and why?

learning objectives

After reading this chapter, you should be able to

- Describe the realities of prison life and sub-culture from the inmate's point of view
- Explain the concept of prisonization
- Describe the realities of prison life from the correctional officer's point of view
- Describe the causes of riots, and list the stages through which prison riots progress
- Explain the nature of the hands-off doctrine, and discuss the status of that doctrine today

- Discuss the legal aspects of prisoners' rights, and explain the consequences of precedent-setting U.S. Supreme Court cases in the area of prisoners' rights
- Explain the balancing test established by the U.S. Supreme Court as it relates to the rights of prisoners
- Explain state-created rights within the context of corrections.
- Describe the major problems and issues facing prisons today

Prisons are necessary for punishment. Too often, how-ever, inmates leave them unprepared to take up pro-ductive roles in their communities.

—President George W. Bush[1]

Our policy of confining large numbers of offenders seems to have been ineffective in reducing the violent crime rate.

—John H. Kramer, Executive Director, Pennsylvania Commission on Sentencing

12

Prison Life

Introduction

for many years, prisons and prison life could be described by the phrase "out of sight, out of mind." Very few citizens cared about prison conditions, and those unfortunate enough to be locked away were regarded as lost to the world. By the mid-twentieth century, however, this attitude started to change. Concerned citizens began to offer their services to prison administrations, neighborhoods began accepting work-release prisoners and halfway houses, and social scientists initiated a serious study of prison life.

This chapter describes the realities of prison life today, including prisoner lifestyles, prison subcultures, sexuality in prison, prison violence, and prisoners' rights and grievance procedures. We will discuss both the inmate world and the staff world. A separate section on women in prison details the social structure of women's prisons, daily life in those facilities, and the various types of female inmates. We begin with a brief overview of early research on prison life.

Research on Prison Life—Total Institutions

In 1935, Hans Reimer, Chairman of the Department of Sociology at Indiana University, set the tone for studies of prison life when he voluntarily served three months in prison as an incognito participant-observer.[2] Reimer reported the results of his studies to the American Prison Association, stimulating many other, albeit less spectacular, efforts to examine prison life. Other early studies include Donald Clemmer's *The Prison Community* (1940),[3] Gresham M. Sykes's *The Society of Captives: A Study of a Maximum Security Prison* (1958),[4] Richard A. Cloward and Donald R. Cressey's *Theoretical Studies in Social Organization of the Prison* (1960),[5] and Cressey's edited volume, *The Prison: Studies in Institutional Organization and Change* (1961).[6]

These studies and others focused primarily on maximum-security prisons for men. They treated correctional institutions as formal or complex organizations and employed the analytic techniques of organizational sociology, industrial psychology, and administrative science.[7] As modern writers on prisons have observed, "The prison was compared to a primitive society, isolated from the outside world, functionally integrated by a delicate system of mechanisms, which kept it precariously balanced between anarchy and accommodation."[8]

Key Concepts

[TERMS]

balancing test
civil death
grievance procedure

hands-off doctrine
prison argot
prisonization

prison subculture
total institution

[CASES]

Block v. *Rutherford*
Bounds v. *Smith*
Cruz v. *Beto*
Estelle v. *Gamble*
Helling v. *McKinney*
Houchins v. *KQED, Inc.*

Hudson v. *Palmer*
Johnson v. *Avery*
Jones v. *North Carolina*
   Prisoners' Labor Union
Katz v. *U.S.*
Newman v. *Alabama*

Pell v. *Procunier*
Pennsylvania Department
   of Corrections v. *Yeskey*
Ruiz v. *Estelle*
Sandin v. *Conner*
Wolff v. *McDonnell*

total institutions

Enclosed facilities, separated from society both socially and physically, where the inhabitants share all aspects of their lives daily.

Another approach to the study of prison life was developed by Erving Goffman, who coined the term **total institutions** in a 1961 study of prisons and mental hospitals.[9] Goffman described total institutions as places where the same people work, recreate, worship, eat, and sleep together daily. Such places include prisons, concentration camps, mental hospitals, seminaries, and other facilities in which residents are cut off from the larger society either forcibly or willingly. Total institutions are small societies. They evolve their own distinctive values and styles of life and pressure residents to fulfill rigidly prescribed behavioral roles.

Generally speaking, the work of prison researchers built on findings of other social scientists who discovered that any group with similar characteristics, subject to confinement in the same place at the same time, develops its own subculture with specific components that govern hierarchy, behavioral patterns, values, and so on. Prison subcultures, described in the next section, also provide the medium through which prison values are communicated and expectations are made known. Learn more about prison research via **Library Extra! 12–1** at cjbrief.com.

Library extra

The Male Inmate's World

prison subculture

The values and behavioral patterns characteristic of prison inmates. Prison subculture has been found to be surprisingly consistent across the country.

Two social realities coexist in prison settings. One is the official structure of rules and procedures put in place by the wider society and enforced by prison staff. The other is the more informal but decidedly more powerful inmate world.[10] The inmate world, best described by its pervasive immediacy in the lives of inmates, is controlled by **prison subculture.** The realities of prison life—including a large and often densely packed inmate population which must look to the prison environment for all its needs—mean that prison subculture is not easily subjected to the control of prison authorities.

Prison subcultures develop independently of the plans of prison administrators, and inmates entering prison discover a social world not mentioned in the handbooks prepared by correctional staff. Inmate concerns, values, roles, and even language weave a web of social reality into which new inmates step and in which they must participate. Those who try to remain aloof soon find themselves subjected to dangerous ostracism and may even be suspected of being in league with the prison administration.

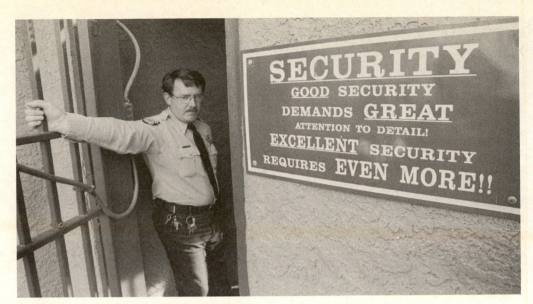

A notice posted on a prison fence. Custody and security remain the primary concerns of prison staffers throughout the country—a fact reinforced by this notice.
Mike Fiala, CORBIS

The socialization of new inmates into the prison subculture has been described as a process of "prisonization."[11] **Prisonization** refers to the learning of convict values, attitudes, roles, and even language. By the time the process is complete, new inmates have become "cons." The values of the inmate social system are embodied in a code whose violation can produce sanctions ranging from ostracism and avoidance to physical violence and homicide.[12] Gresham M. Sykes and Sheldon L. Messinger recognized five elements of the prison code in 1960:[13]

1. Don't interfere with the interests of other inmates. Never rat on a con.
2. Don't lose your head. Play it cool and do your own time.
3. Don't exploit inmates. Don't steal. Don't break your word. Be right.
4. Don't whine. Be a man.
5. Don't be a sucker. Don't trust the guards or staff.

Some criminologists have suggested that the prison code is simply a reflection of general criminal values. If so, these values are brought to the institution rather than created there. Either way, the power and pervasiveness of the prison code require convicts to conform to the worldview held by the majority of prisoners.

Stanton Wheeler closely examined the concept of prisonization in an early study of the Washington State Reformatory.[14] Wheeler found that the degree of prisonization experienced by inmates tends to vary over time. He described changing levels of inmate commitment to prison norms and values by way of a U-shaped curve. When an inmate first enters prison, Wheeler said, the conventional values of outside society are of paramount importance. As time passes, inmates adopt the lifestyle of the prison. However, within the half year prior to release, most inmates begin to demonstrate a renewed appreciation of conventional values. Learn more about both the positive and negative impact of imprisonment at **Library Extra! 12–2** at cjbrief.com.

Different prisons share aspects of a common inmate culture;[15] prison-wise inmates who enter a new facility far from their home will already know the ropes. **Prison argot**, or language, provides one example of how widespread prison subculture can be. The terms used to describe inmate roles in one institution are generally understood in others. The word *rat*, for example, is prison slang for an informer. Popularized by crime movies of the 1950s, the term is understood today by members of the wider society. Other words common to prison argot are shown in the CJ Exhibit on the next page. View an online prisoner's dictionary via **Web Extra! 12–1** at cjbrief.com.

prisonization

The process whereby newly institutionalized offenders come to accept prison lifestyles and criminal values. Although many inmates begin their prison experience with only a few values that support criminal behavior, the socialization experience they undergo while incarcerated leads to a much wider acceptance of such values.

Library | **extra** |

prison argot

The slang characteristic of prison subcultures and prison life.

WEB | **extra** |

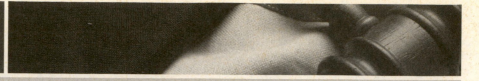

CJ Exhibit

PRISON ARGOT: THE LANGUAGE of CONFINEMENT

Writers who have studied prison life often comment on prisoners' use of a special language or slang termed *prison argot*. This language generally describes the roles assigned by prison culture to types of inmates as well as to prison activities. This box lists a few of the many words and phrases identified in studies by different authors. The first group of words are characteristic of men's prisons; the last few have been used in women's prisons.

MEN'S PRISON SLANG

Ace duce: Best friend
Badge (or bull, hack, the man, or screw): A correctional officer
Banger (or burner, shank, or sticker): A knife
Billy: A white man
Boneyard: The conjugal visiting area
Cat-J (or J-cat): A prisoner in need of psychological or psychiatric therapy or medication
Cellie: Cellmate
Chester: A child molester
Dog: A homeboy or friend
Fag: A male inmate who is believed to be a "natural" or "born" homosexual
Featherwood: A white prisoner's woman
Fish: A newly arrived inmate
Gorilla: An inmate who uses force to take what he wants from others

Homeboy: A prisoner from one's hometown or neighborhood
Ink: Tattoos
Lemon squeezer: An inmate who masturbates frequently
Man walking: A phrase used to signal that a guard is coming
Merchant (or peddler): One who sells when he should give
Peckerwood (or wood): A white prisoner
Punk: A male inmate who is forced into a submissive role during homosexual relations
Rat (or snitch): An inmate who squeals (provides information about other inmates to the prison administration)
Schooled: Knowledgeable in the ways of prison life
Shakedown: A search of a cell or of a work area
Tree jumper: A rapist
Turn out: To rape or make into a punk
Wolf: A male inmate who assumes the dominant role during homosexual relations

WOMEN'S PRISON SLANG

Cherry (or cherrie): A female inmate who has not yet been introduced to lesbian activities
Fay broad: A white female inmate
Femme (or mommy): A female inmate who plays the female role during lesbian relations
Safe: The vagina, especially when used for hiding contraband
Stud broad (or daddy): A female inmate who assumes the male role during lesbian relations

SOURCES: Gresham Sykes, *The Society of Captives* (Princeton, NJ: Princeton University Press, 1958); Rose Giallombardo, *Society of Women: A Study of a Woman's Prison* (New York: John Wiley, 1966); and Richard A. Cloward et al., *Theoretical Studies in Social Organization of the Prison* (New York: Social Science Research Council, 1960). For a more contemporary listing of prison slang terms, see Reinhold Aman, *Hillary Clinton's Pen Pal: A Guide to Life and Lingo in Federal Prison* (Santa Rosa, CA: Maledicta Press, 1996); Jerome Washington, *Iron House: Stories from the Yard* (Ann Arbor, MI: QED Press, 1994); Morrie Camhi, *The Prison Experience* (Boston: Charles Tuttle, 1989); and Harold Long, *Survival in Prison* (Port Townsend, WA: Loompanics, 1990).

The Evolution of Prison Subcultures

Prison subcultures change constantly. Like any other American subculture, they evolve to reflect the concerns and experiences of the wider culture, reacting to new crime-control strategies and embracing novel opportunities for crime. The AIDS epidemic of the last two decades, for example, has brought about changes in prison sexual behavior, at least for a segment of the inmate population, while the emergence of a high-tech criminal group has further differentiated convict types. Because of such changes, John Irwin, as he was completing his classic study entitled *The Felon* (1970), expressed worry that his book was already obsolete.[16] *The Felon,* for all its insights into prison subcultures, follows in the descriptive tradition of works by Clemmer and Reimer. Irwin recognized that by 1970, prison subcultures had begun to reflect the cultural changes sweeping America. A decade later, other investigators of prison subcultures were able to write, "It was no longer meaningful to speak of a single inmate culture or even subculture. By the time we began our field research . . . it was clear that the unified, oppositional convict culture, found in the sociological literature on prisons, no longer existed."[17]

Charles Stastny and Gabrielle Tyrnauer, describing prison life at Washington State Penitentiary in 1982, discovered four clearly distinguishable subcultures: (1) official, (2) traditional, (3) reform, and (4) revolutionary.[18] Official culture was promoted by the staff and by the administrative rules of the institution. Enthusiastic participants in official culture were mostly correctional officers and other staff members, although inmates were also well aware of the normative expectations official culture imposed on them. Official culture affected the lives of inmates primarily through the creation of a prisoner hierarchy based on sentence length, prison jobs, and the "perks" which cooperation with the dictates of official culture could produce. Traditional prison culture, described by early writers on the subject, still existed, but its participants spent much of their time lamenting the decline of the convict code among younger prisoners. Reform culture was unique at Washington State Penitentiary. It was the result of a brief experiment with inmate self-government during the early 1970s. Elements of prison life which evolved during the experimental period sometimes survived the termination of self-government and were eventually institutionalized in what Stastny and Tyrnauer called "reform culture." Such elements included inmate participation in civic-style clubs, citizen involvement in the daily activities of the prison, banquets, and inmate speaking tours. Revolutionary culture built on the radical political rhetoric of the disenfranchised and found a ready audience among minority prisoners who saw themselves as victims of society's basic unfairness. Although they did not participate in it, revolutionary inmates understood traditional prison culture and generally avoided running afoul of its rules.

The Functions of Prison Subcultures

How do social scientists and criminologists explain the existence of prison subcultures? Although people around the world live in groups and create their own cultures, in few cases does the intensity of human interaction approach the level found in prisons. As we discussed in Chapter 11, many of today's prisons are densely crowded places where inmates can find no retreat from the constant demands of staff and the pressures of fellow prisoners. Prison subcultures, according to some authors, are fundamentally an adaptation to deprivation and confinement. They are a way of addressing the psychological, social, physical, and sexual needs of prisoners living within a highly controlled and regimented institutional setting.

What are some of the deprivations prisoners experience? In *The Society of Captives*, Sykes called felt deprivations the "pains of imprisonment."[19] The pains of imprisonment—the frustrations induced by the rigors of confinement—form the nexus of a deprivation model of prison subculture. Sykes said that prisoners are deprived of (1) liberty, (2) goods and services, (3) heterosexual relationships, (4) autonomy, and (5) personal security and that these deprivations lead to the development of subcultures intended to ameliorate the personal pains which accompany deprivation.

In contrast to the deprivation model, the importation model of prison subculture suggests that inmates bring with them values, roles, and behavior patterns from the outside world. Such external values, second nature as they are to career offenders, depend substantially on the criminal worldview. When offenders are confined, these external elements shape the social world of inmates.

The social structure of the prison, a concept that refers to accepted and relatively permanent social arrangements, is another element which shapes prison subculture. Clemmer's early prison study recognized nine structural dimensions of inmate society. He said that prison society could be described in terms of[20]

- Prisoner–staff dichotomy
- Three general classes of prisoners
- Work gangs and cell-house groups
- Racial groups

It is better to prevent crimes than to punish them.

—Cesare Bonesana, Marchese Di Beccaria

- Type of offense
- Power of inmate "politicians"
- Degree of sexual abnormality
- Record of repeat offenses
- Personality differences due to preprison socialization

Clemmer's nine structural dimensions are probably still descriptive of prison life today. When applied in individual situations, they designate an inmate's position in the prison "pecking order" and create expectations of the appropriate role for that person. Prison roles serve to satisfy the needs of inmates for power, sexual performance, material possessions, individuality, and personal pleasure and to define the status of one prisoner relative to another. For example, inmate leaders, sometimes referred to as "real men" or "toughs" by prisoners in early studies, offer protection to those who live by the rules. They also provide for a redistribution of wealth inside prison and see to it that the rules of the complex prison-derived economic system—based on barter, gambling, and sexual favors—are observed. For an intimate multimedia portrait of life behind bars, visit **Web Extra! 12–2** at cjbrief.com.

Prison Lifestyles and Inmate Types

Prison society is strict and often unforgiving. Even so, inmates are able to express some individuality through the choice of a prison lifestyle. John Irwin was the first well-known author to describe prison lifestyles, viewing them (like the subcultures of which they are a part) as adaptations to the prison environment.[21] Other writers have since elaborated on these coping mechanisms. Listed in the paragraphs that follow are some of the types of prisoners that researchers have described.

- *The mean dude.* Some inmates adjust to prison by being mean. They are quick to fight, and when they fight, they fight like wild men (or women). They give no quarter and seem to expect none in return. Other inmates know that such prisoners are best left alone. The mean dude is frequently written up and spends much time in solitary confinement.

    Some prisoners occupy the mean dude role in prison as they did when they were free. Certain personality types, such as the psychopath, may feel a natural attraction to this role. On the other hand, prison culture supports the role of the mean dude in

A San Diego, California, inmate showing off his physique. Some inmates attempt to adapt to prison life by acting tough. During the mid-1990s, the states and the federal government moved to ban weight-lifting programs in prison on the belief that they contradict the punishment goal of imprisonment.
Armineh Johannes, SIPA Press

two ways: (1) by expecting inmates to be tough and (2) through the prevalence of the idea that only the strong survive inside prison.

A psychologist might say that the mean dude is acting out against the fact of captivity, striking out at anyone he (or she) can. This role is most common in male institutions and in maximum-security prisons. It is found less frequently as inmates progress to lower security levels.

■ *The hedonist.* Some inmates build their lives around the limited pleasures which can be had within the confines of prison. The smuggling of contraband, homosexuality, gambling, drug running, and other officially condemned activities provide the center of interest for prison hedonists. Hedonists generally have an abbreviated view of the future, living only for the "now." Such a temporal orientation is probably characteristic of the personality type of all hedonists, both inside the prison and out.

■ *The opportunist.* The opportunist takes advantage of the positive experiences prison has to offer. Schooling, trade training, counseling, and other self-improvement activities are the focal points of the opportunist's life in prison. Opportunists are the "do-gooders" of the prison subculture. They are generally well liked by prison staff, but other prisoners shun and mistrust them because they come closest to accepting the role which the staff defines as "model prisoner." Opportunists may also be religious, a role adaptation described below.

■ *The retreatist.* Prison life is rigorous and demanding. Badgering by the staff and actual or feared assaults by other inmates may cause some prisoners to attempt psychological retreat from the realities of imprisonment. Such inmates may experience neurotic or psychotic episodes, become heavily involved in drug and alcohol abuse, or even attempt suicide. Depression and mental illness are the hallmarks of the retreatist personality in prison. The best hope for the retreatist, short of release, is protective custody combined with therapeutic counseling.

■ *The legalist.* The legalist is the "jailhouse lawyer." Just like the mean dude, the legalist fights confinement. The weapons in this fight are not fists or clubs, however, but the legal writ. Convicts facing long sentences, with little possibility for early release through the correctional system, are most likely to turn to the courts in their battle against confinement.

■ *The radical.* Radical inmates picture themselves as political prisoners. Society and the successful conformists who populate it are seen as oppressors who have forced criminality on many "good people" through the creation of a system which distributes wealth and power inequitably. The radical inmate speaks a language of revolution and may be versed in the writings of the "great" revolutionaries of the past.

The inmate who takes on the radical role is unlikely to receive much sympathy from prison staff. Radical rhetoric tends to be diametrically opposed to staff insistence on accepting responsibility for problematic behavior.

■ *The colonist.* Some inmates think of prison as their home. They "know the ropes," have many "friends" inside, and may feel more comfortable institutionalized than on the streets. They typically hold either positions of power or respect (or both) among the inmate population. These are the prisoners who don't look forward to leaving prison. Most colonizers grow into the role gradually and only after having spent years behind bars. Once released, some colonizers have been known to commit new crimes to return to prison.

■ *The religious.* Some prisoners profess a strong religious faith. They may be "born-again" Christians, committed Muslims, or even satanists or witches (perhaps affiliated with the Church of Wicca). Religious inmates frequently attend services, may form prayer groups, and sometimes ask the prison administration to allocate meeting facilities or to create special diets to accommodate their claimed spiritual needs.

While it is certainly true that some inmates have a strong religious faith, staff members are apt to be suspicious of the overly religious prisoner. The tendency is to view such prisoners as "faking it" to demonstrate a fictitious rehabilitation and thereby gain sympathy for an early release.

Convicted murderer Henry Lee Lucas. Lucas, who confessed to 600 murders, later recanted, and in 1998 his death sentence was commuted to life in prison by then-Governor George W. Bush of Texas. Prison inmates adopt diverse coping strategies, and Lucas claims to have found God.
AP/Wide World Photos

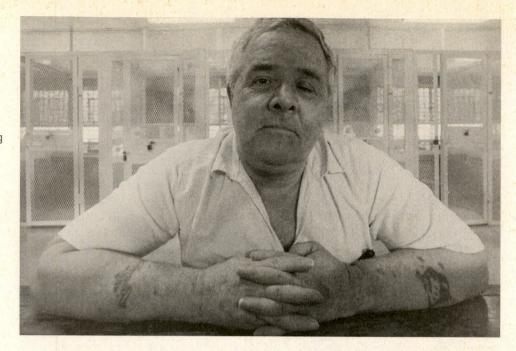

■ *The realist.* The realist is a prisoner who sees confinement as a natural consequence of criminal activity. Time spent in prison is an unfortunate cost of doing business. This stoic attitude toward incarceration generally leads the realist to "pull his (or her) own time" and to make the best of it. Realists tend to know the inmate code, are able to avoid trouble, and continue in lives of crime once released.

Homosexuality in Prison

Homosexual behavior inside prisons is both constrained and encouraged by prison subculture. One Houston woman, whose son is serving time in a Texas prison, explained the path to prison homosexuality this way: "Within a matter of days, if not hours, an unofficial prison welcome wagon sorts new arrivals into those who will fight, those who will pay extortion cash of up to $60 every two weeks, and those who will be servants or slaves. 'You're jumped on by two or three prisoners to see if you'll fight,'" said the woman. "If you don't fight, you become someone's girl, until they're tired of you and they sell you to someone else."[22]

Sykes's early study of prison argot found many words describing homosexual activity. Among them were the terms *wolf, punk,* and *fag.* Wolves were aggressive men who assumed the masculine role in homosexual relations. Punks were forced into submitting to the female role, often by wolves. The term *fag* described a special category of men who had a natural proclivity toward homosexual activity and effeminate mannerisms. While both wolves and punks were fiercely committed to their heterosexual identity and participated in homosexuality only because of prison conditions, fags generally engaged in homosexual lifestyles before their entry into prison and continued to emulate feminine mannerisms and styles of dress once incarcerated.

Prison homosexuality depends to a considerable degree on the naïveté of young inmates experiencing prison for the first time. Even when newly arrived inmates are protected from fights, older prisoners looking for homosexual liaisons may ingratiate themselves by offering cigarettes, money, drugs, food, or protection. At some future time, these "loans" will be called in, with payoffs demanded in sexual favors. Because the inmate code requires the repayment of favors, the "fish" who tries to resist may quickly find himself face-to-face with the brute force of inmate society.

Prison rape represents a special category of homosexual behavior behind bars. Estimates of the incidence of prison rape are both rare and dated. Survey-based studies vary consid-

A group of male inmates dressed as women in a California institution. Homosexuality is common in both men's and women's prisons.
Rasmussen, SIPA Press

erably in their findings. One such study found 4.7% of inmates in the Philadelphia prison system willing to report sexual assaults.[23] Another survey found that 28% of prisoners had been targets of sexual aggressors at least once during their institutional careers.[24]

While not greatly different from other prisoners, a large proportion of sexual aggressors are characterized by low education and poverty, having grown up in a broken home headed by the mother, and having a record of violent offenses. Victims of prison rape tend to be physically slight, young, white, nonviolent offenders from nonurban areas.[25] Lee H. Bowker, summarizing studies of sexual violence in prison, provides the following observations:[26]

■ Most sexual aggressors do not consider themselves to be homosexuals.

■ Sexual release is not the primary motivation for sexual attack.

■ Many aggressors must continue to participate in gang rapes to avoid becoming victims themselves.

■ The aggressors have themselves suffered much damage to their masculinity in the past.

As in cases of heterosexual rape, sexual assaults in prison are likely to leave psychological scars long after the physical event is over.[27] The victims of prison rape live in fear, may feel constantly threatened, and can turn to self-destructive activities.[28] At the very least, victims question their masculinity and undergo a personal devaluation. In some cases, victims of prison sexual attacks turn to violence. Frustrations, long bottled up through abuse and fear, may explode and turn the would-be rapist into a victim of prison homicide.

A comprehensive review of rape inside male prisons was published in 2001 by Human Rights Watch. Entitled *No Escape: Male Rape in U.S. Prisons*,[29] the 378-page report involved three years of research and interviews with more than 200 prisoners in 34 states. Researchers found that prisoners "fitting any part of the following description" are more likely to become rape victims: "young, small in size, physically weak, white, gay, first offender, possessing 'feminine' characteristics such as long hair or a high voice; being unassertive, unaggressive, shy, intellectual, not street-smart, or 'passive;' or having been convicted of a sexual offense against a minor." The researchers also noted that "prisoners with several overlapping characteristics are much more likely than other prisoners to be targeted for abuse."

Perpetrators of prison rape were found to be young (generally 20 to 30 years old), larger or stronger than their victims, and "generally more assertive, physically aggressive, and more at home in the prison environment" than their victims. Rapists were also found to be "street smart" and were frequently gang members who were well established in the inmate hierarchy and who had been convicted of violent crimes. The report concluded that to reduce the incidence of prison rape, "prison officials should take considerably more care in matching cell mates, and that, as a general rule, double-celling should be avoided." Learn more about male rape in U.S. prisons at **Library Extra! 12–3** at cjbrief.com.

Library extra

The Female Inmate's World

As Chapter 11 showed, more than 93,000 women were imprisoned in state and federal correctional institutions throughout the United States in 2001, accounting for 6.6% of all prison inmates.[30] Texas had the largest number of female prisoners (12,369), exceeding even the federal government.[31] Figure 12–1 provides a breakdown of the total American prison population by gender and ethnicity. Most female inmates are housed in centralized state facilities known as women's prisons, which are dedicated exclusively to incarcerating female felons. Many states, however, particularly those with small populations, continue to keep female prisoners in special wings of what are otherwise institutions for men.

While there are still far more men imprisoned across the nation than women (approximately 15 men for every woman), the number of female inmates is rising.[32] In 1981, women made up only 4% of the nation's overall prison population, but the number of female inmates nearly tripled during the 1980s and is continuing to grow at a rate greater than that of male inmates.

Some professionals working with imprisoned women attribute the rise in female prison populations largely to drugs.[33] Approximately 33% of all women in prison are there explicitly for drug offenses. Other estimates, however, say that the impact of drugs on the imprisonment of women is far greater than a simple reading of the figure indicates. Warden Robert Brennan of a New York City jail for women estimates that drugs—either directly or

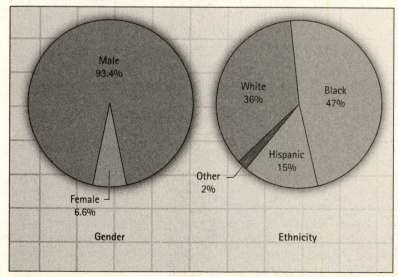

FIGURE 12–1

Prison Inmates by Gender and Ethnicity in State and Federal Prisons, 2001.

SOURCE: Paige M. Harrison and Allen J. Beck, *Prisoners in 2001* (Washington, D.C.: Bureau of Justice Statistics, 2002).

indirectly—account for the imprisonment of around 95% of the inmates there. Drug-related offenses committed by women include larceny, burglary, fraud, prostitution, embezzlement, and robbery, as well as other crimes stimulated by the desire for drugs. In fact, incarcerated women most frequently list (1) trying to pay for drugs, (2) attempting to relieve economic pressures, and (3) exercising poor judgment as the reasons for their arrest.[34]

Another reason for the rapid growth in the number of women behind bars may be the demise, over the last two or three decades, of the "chivalry factor." The chivalry factor, so called because it was based on an archaic cultural stereotype that depicted women as helpless or childlike compared to men, allegedly lessened the responsibility of female offenders in the eyes of some male judges and prosecutors, resulting in fewer active prison sentences for women involved in criminal activity. Recent studies show that the chivalry factor is now primarily of historical interest. In jurisdictions examined, the gender of convicted offenders no longer affects sentencing practices except insofar as it may be tied to other social variables. In a comprehensive study of gender differences in sentencing, B. Keith Crew observes, "A woman does not automatically receive leniency because of her status of wife or mother, but she may receive leniency if those statuses become part of the official explanation of her criminal behavior (for example, she was stealing to feed her children, or an abusive husband forced her to commit a crime)."[35]

Although there may be no one typical prison for women and no perfectly average female inmate, the American Correctional Association's 1990 report by the Task Force on the Female Offender found that female inmates and the institutions which house them could be generally described as follows:[36]

- Most prisons for women are located in towns with fewer than 25,000 inhabitants.
- A significant number of facilities were not designed to house female inmates.

A female inmate being housed in the segregation unit of a Rhode Island correctional facility because of disciplinary problems. The number of women in prison is growing steadily.
Richard Falco, Black Star

■ The number of female offenders being sent to prison is rising.

■ Most facilities that house female inmates also house men.

■ Few facilities for women have programs especially designed for female offenders.

■ Few major disturbances or escapes are reported among female inmates.

■ Substance abuse among female inmates is very high.

■ Few work assignments are available to female inmates.

■ The number of female inmates without a high school education is very high.

Statistics show that the average age of female inmates is 29 to 30, most are black or Hispanic (57%), most come from single-parent or broken homes, and half have other family members who are incarcerated.[37] The typical female inmate is a high school dropout (50%), who left school either because she was bored or because of pregnancy (34%). She has been arrested two to nine times (55%) and has run away from home between one and three times (65%). Thirty-nine percent report using drugs to make themselves feel better emotionally, while 28% have attempted suicide at least once. Sixty-two percent were single parents with one to three children prior to incarceration, and many have been physically or sexually abused.[38]

Eighty percent of women entering prison are mothers, and 85% of those women had custody of their children at the time of admission. One out of four women entering prison has either recently given birth or is pregnant. In 2000, more than 1.5 million American children had mothers who were confined in prison or jail.[39] Moreover, the number of women in prison who were parents of minor children more than doubled during the 1990s.[40]

Critics charge that female inmates face a prison system designed for male inmates and run by men. Hence pregnant inmates, many of whom are drug users, malnourished, or sick, often receive little prenatal care—a situation that risks additional complications. Separation from their children is a significant deprivation for many women. Although husbands or boyfriends may assume responsibility for the children of imprisoned spouses or girlfriends, this outcome is the exception to the rule. Eventually, a large proportion of children are released by their imprisoned mothers into foster care or are put up for adoption.

Some states do offer parenting classes for female inmates with children. In a national survey of prisons for women, 36 states responded that they provide parenting programs which deal with caretaking, reducing violence toward children, visitation problems, and related issues.[41] Some offer play areas furnished with toys, while others attempt to alleviate difficulties attending mother-child visits. The typical program studied meets for two hours per week and lasts from four to nine weeks.

Other meaningful prison programs for women are often lacking, perhaps because the ones which are in place were originally based on traditional models of female roles which left little room for substantive employment opportunities. Many trade-training programs still emphasize low-paying jobs, such as cook, beautician, or laundry machine operator. Classes in homemaking are not uncommon.

> We must remember always that the doors of prisons swing both ways.
>
> —**Mary Belle Harris,** *first federal female warden*

Social Structure in Women's Prisons

"Aside from sharing the experience of being incarcerated," says Professor Marsha Clowers of the John Jay College of Criminal Justice, "female prisoners have much in common. They are likely to be black or Hispanic, poor, uneducated, abuse survivors, single parents, and in poor health."[42] Shared social characteristics may lead to similar values and behaviors. One type of behavior identified by early prison researchers as characteristic of a fair number of incarcerated women concerns the way that female inmates construct organized pseudo-families. Typical of such studies are D. Ward and G. Kassebaum's *Women's Prison: Sex and Social Structure* (1966),[43] Esther Heffernan's *Making It in Prison: The Square, the Cool, and the Life* (1972),[44] and Rose Giallombardo's *Society of Women: A Study of Women's Prisons* (1966).[45]

Giallombardo, for example, examined the Federal Reformatory for Women at Alderson, West Virginia, spending a year gathering data in the early 1960s. Focusing closely on the

CJ News

CHILD SLEEPOVERS at PRISON REVIEWED

YORK, Neb. (AP)—Once a month, Jessica Davis spends five nights in a row with her 2-year-old daughter—behind prison walls.

She is just one of dozens of mother prisoners who participate in an overnight visitation program that Gov. Mike Johanns wants changed after a convicted murderer requested that her 6-year-old stay overnight with her.

Johanns said last week the policy at the Nebraska Correctional Center for Women in York will be changed to prohibit women serving life sentences from participating, and he ordered a review of the entire overnight program to begin Tuesday.

Davis, 19, serving up to two years in prison for second-degree assault, said she is bothered that some children will not be allowed to spend the night with their mothers. She and her daughter read books, watch movies, play with stuffed animals and enjoy an outdoor playground during the sleepovers.

"It's given me that chance to be able to bond with my daughter," she said. "It gives her that security knowing that I am OK."

But Bruce Faust doesn't want his ex-wife, Kimberly Faust, to enjoy such a luxury with their 6-year-old son. Faust was convicted in November [2000] of killing her estranged husband's girlfriend, Shannon Bluhm, and a passer-by who tried to save her.

She wants the 6-year-old to stay overnight with her at the prison, where she is serving two life sentences without the possibility of parole.

Bruce Faust has custody of the couple's two sons, ages 6 and 11. He has said he does not object to the boys visiting their mother, but does not think the 6-year-old should stay overnight.

Johanns stepped in after *Chicago Tribune* columnist Bob Greene wrote about the situation and urged people to contact the governor. Johanns received more than 1,000 e-mails, faxes and phone calls.

On Thursday, he took away Faust's right to have the son sleep over, saying the policy will no longer apply to inmates who face no possibility of parole. The move is to take effect within two weeks.

Harold Clarke, prison director, said the program was the first of its kind in the country and has a proven track record.

"Not one kid has had a bad experience in this program," Clarke said.

Of the 267 inmates at York, prison officials estimate about 40 to 50 are mothers. Clarke said more than 95 percent of the women will be leaving the prison within three years, making it important to have a program that will help them be better parents once they leave.

Johanns said the overnight program has merits for women who will be paroled.

The prison resembles a college campus. Red-brick housing units are spread out in a semicircle, inside which inmates walk freely. The entire campus is ringed by a barbed-wire fence.

Under the policy, children ages 1 to 8 are allowed to spend nights with their mothers. The rooms they share are small, with just enough space for a metal cabinet to hang clothes, a bed and cot for the child, and a night stand.

Down the hall from the rooms is a nursery equipped with all the basics—rocking chairs, playpens, swings for the children and toys.

Inmate Cherie Carter reading a book with her three-year-old daughter, Onisha, at the Nebraska Correctional Center for Women in York. Onisha was at the prison as part of an overnight visitation program that Nebraska Governor Mike Johanns wants revised.

AP/Wide World Photos

(continued)

The overnight stays are on the third floor of one of the housing units. They are isolated from inmates on the first and second floor, who are part of the general population.

In a separate building, mothers and their children can play with a variety of board games, read from a small Library of books, bake at a kitchenette, or watch videos. Outside is a playground equipped with all the basics.

"There are no bars here," said inmate Amanda Wardlow-Stubblefield, who has three children ages 2 to 13. "It seems like a small community."

SOURCE: Associated Press, "Child Sleepovers at Prison Reviewed," September 3, 2001. Reprinted with permission of the Associated Press.
For the latest in crime and justice news, visit the Talk Justice news feed at http://www.crimenews.info.

social formation of families among female inmates, she entitled one of her chapters "The Homosexual Alliance as a Marriage Unit." In it, she described in great detail the sexual identities assumed by women at Alderson and the symbols they chose to communicate those roles. Hairstyle, dress, language, and mannerisms were all used to signify "maleness" or "femaleness." Giallombardo detailed "the anatomy of the marriage relationship from courtship to 'fall out,' that is, from inception to the parting of the ways, or divorce."[46] Romantic love at Alderson was of central importance to any relationship between inmates, and all homosexual relationships were described as voluntary. Through marriage, the "stud broad" became the husband and the "femme" the wife.

Studies attempting to document the extent of inmate involvement in prison "families" have produced varying results. Some have found as many as 71% of female prisoners involved in the phenomenon, while others have found none.[47] The kinship systems described by Giallombardo and others, however, extend beyond simple "family" ties to the formation of large, intricately related groups involving a large number of nonsexual relationships. In these groups, the roles of "children," "in-laws," "grandparents," and so on may be explicitly recognized. Even "birth order" within a family can become an issue for kinship groups.[48] Kinship groups sometimes occupy a common household—usually a prison cottage or a dormitory area. The descriptions of women's prisons provided by authors like Giallombardo show a closed society in which social interaction—including expectations, normative forms of behavior, and emotional ties—is regulated by an inventive system of artificial relationships which mirror those of the outside world.

Female inmates in Sheriff Joe Arpaio's "equal opportunity jail" in Maricopa County, Arizona, being inspected by a correctional officer before leaving for chain gang duty. Not all states make use of chain gangs, and only a few use female inmates on chain gangs.
Jack Kurtz, The Image Works

114

Recent studies provide additional details about the nature of sexual behavior in women's prisons. A 1998 study of the Central California Women's Facility, for example, found that most of the staff and inmates alike claimed that "everybody was involved" in homosexual behavior. When inmates were interviewed individually, however, and asked to provide some details about the extent of their involvement in such behavior, many denied any lesbian activity.

A 2001 study of a women's correctional facility in the southeastern United States found that female inmates asked about their preincarceration sexual orientation gave answers that were quite different than when they were asked about their sexual orientation while incarcerated.[49] In general, 64% of inmates interviewed reported being exclusively heterosexual; 28% said they were bisexual; and 8% said that they were lesbians before being incarcerated. In contrast, these same women reported sexual orientations while incarcerated of 55% heterosexual; 31% bisexual; and 13% lesbian. Researchers found that same-sex sexual behavior within the institution was more likely to occur in the lives of young inmates who had had such experiences before entering prison. The study also found that female inmates tended to become more involved in lesbian behavior the longer they were incarcerated.

Finally, a significant aspect of sexual activity far more commonly found in women's prisons than in prisons for men involves sexual misconduct between staff and inmates. While a fair amount of such behavior is attributed to the exploitation of female inmates by male correctional officers acting from positions of power, some studies suggest that female inmates may sometimes attempt to manipulate unsuspecting male officers into illicit relationships in order to gain favors.[50]

Types of Female Inmates

As in institutions for men, the subculture of women's prisons is multidimensional. Esther Heffernan, for example, found that three terms used by the female prisoners she studied—the *square,* the *cool,* and the *life*—were indicative of three styles of adaptation to prison life.[51] Square inmates had few early experiences with criminal lifestyles and tended to sympathize with the values and attitudes of conventional society. Cool prisoners were more likely to be career offenders. They tended to keep to themselves and generally supported inmate values. Women who participated in the life subculture were quite familiar with lives of crime. Many had been arrested repeatedly for prostitution, drug use, theft, and so on. They were full participants in the economic, social, and familial arrangements of the prison. Heffernan believed that the life offered an alternative lifestyle to women who had experienced early and constant rejection by conventional society. Within the life, women could establish relationships, achieve status, and find meaning in their lives. The square, the cool, and the life represented subcultures to Heffernan because individuals with similar adaptive choices tended to relate closely to one another and to support the lifestyle characteristic of that type.

Recently, the social structure of women's prisons has been altered by the arrival of "crack kids," as they are called in prison argot. Crack kids, whose existence highlights generational differences among female offenders, are streetwise young women with little respect for traditional prison values, for their elders, or even for their own children. Known for frequent fights and for their lack of even simple domestic skills, these young women quickly estrange many older inmates, some of whom call them "animalescents."

Violence in Women's Prisons

Some authors have suggested that violence in women's prisons is less frequent than it is in institutions for men. Lee Bowker observes that "except for the behavior of a few 'guerrillas,' it appears that violence is only used in women's prisons to settle questions of dominance and subordination when other manipulative strategies fail to achieve the desired effect."[52] It appears that few homosexual liaisons are forced, perhaps representing a general aversion among women to such victimization in wider society. At least one study, however, has shown the use of sexual violence in women's prisons as a form of revenge against inmates who are overly vocal in their condemnation of lesbian practices among other prisoners.[53]

Not all abuse occurs at the hands of inmates. In 1992, 14 correctional officers, ten men and four women, were indicted for the alleged abuse of female inmates at the 900-bed Women's Correctional Institute in Hardwick, Georgia. The charges resulted from affidavits filed by 90 female inmates alleging "rape, sexual abuse, prostitution, coerced abortions, sex for favors, and retaliation for refusal to participate" in such activities.[54] One inmate who was forced to have an abortion after becoming pregnant by a male staff member said, "As an inmate, I simply felt powerless to avoid the sexual advances of staff and to refuse to have an abortion."[55]

To address the problems of imprisoned women, including violence, the Task Force on the Female Offender recommended a number of changes in the administration of prisons for women.[56] Among those recommendations were these:

- Substance-abuse programs should be available to female inmates.
- Female inmates need to acquire greater literacy skills, and literacy programs should form the basis on which other programs are built.
- Female offenders should be housed in buildings without male inmates.
- Institutions for women should develop programs for keeping children in the facility in order to "fortify the bond between mother and child."
- To ensure equal access to assistance, institutions should be built to accommodate programs for female offenders.

Learn more about women in prison and their special needs via **Library Extras! 12–4** and **12–5** at cjbrief.com.

The Staff World

The flip side of inmate society can be found in the world of the prison staff, which includes many people working in various professions. Staff roles encompass those of warden, psychologist, counselor, area supervisor, program director, instructor, correctional officer, and—in some large prisons—physician and therapist.

According to the American Correctional Association (ACA), approximately 350,000 people are employed in corrections,[57] with the majority performing direct custodial tasks in state institutions. On a per capita basis, the District of Columbia has the most state and local corrections employees (53.3 per every 10,000 residents), followed by Texas (43.8).[58] Across the nation, 70% of correctional officers are white, 22% are black, and slightly over 5% are Hispanic.[59] Women account for 20% of all correctional officers, with the proportion of female officers increasing at around 19% per year.[60] The ACA encourages correctional agencies to "ensure that recruitment, selection, and promotion opportunities are open to women."

Correctional officers, generally considered to be at the bottom of the staff hierarchy, may be divided into cell-block guards and tower guards; others are assigned to administrative offices, where they perform clerical tasks. The inmate-to-staff ratio in state prisons averages around 4.1 inmates for each correctional officer.[61]

Like prisoners, correctional officers undergo a socialization process that helps them function by the official and unofficial rules of staff society. In a now-classic study, Lucien X. Lombardo described the process by which officers are socialized into the prison work world.[62] Lombardo interviewed 359 correctional personnel at New York's Auburn Prison and found that rookie officers quickly had to abandon preconceptions of both inmates and other staff members. According to Lombardo, new officers learn that inmates are not the "monsters" much of the public makes them out to be. On the other hand, rookies may be seriously disappointed in their experienced colleagues when they realize that the ideals of professionalism, often emphasized during early training, rarely translate into reality. The pressures of the institutional work environment, however, soon force most correctional personnel to adopt a united front when relating to inmates.

One of the leading formative influences on staff culture is the potential threat that inmates pose. Inmates far outnumber correctional personnel in every institution, and the hostility they feel for guards is only barely hidden even at the best of times. Correctional personnel know that however friendly inmates may appear, a sudden change in institutional climate—as can happen in anything from simple disturbances in the yard to full-blown riots—can quickly and violently unmask deep-rooted feelings of mistrust and hatred.

As in years past, prison staffers are still most concerned with custody and control. Society, especially under the just deserts philosophy of criminal sentencing, expects correctional staff to keep inmates in custody; this is the basic prerequisite of successful job performance. Custody is necessary before any other correctional activities, such as instruction or counseling, can be undertaken. Control, the other major staff concern, ensures order, and an orderly prison is thought to be safe and secure. In routine daily activities, control over almost all aspects of inmate behavior becomes paramount in the minds of most correctional officers. It is the twin interests of custody and control that lead to institutionalized procedures for ensuring security in most facilities. The enforcement of strict rules; body and cell searches; counts; unannounced shakedowns; the control of dangerous items, materials, and contraband; and the extensive use of bars, locks, fencing, cameras, and alarms all support the staff's vigilance in maintaining security.

Types of Correctional Officers

Staff culture, in combination with naturally occurring personality types, gives rise to a diversity of correctional officer types. Like the inmate typology we've already discussed, correctional staff can be classified according to certain distinguishing characteristics. Among the most prevalent types are these:

- *The dictator.* Some officers go by the book; others go beyond it, using prison rules to enforce their own brand of discipline. The guard who demands signs of inmate subservience, from constant use of the word *sir* or *ma'am* to free shoe shines, is one type of dictator. Another goes beyond legality, beating or macing inmates for even minor infractions or perceived insults. Dictator guards are bullies. They find their counterpart in the "mean dude" inmate described earlier.

  Dictator guards may have sadistic personalities and gain ego satisfaction through the feelings of near omnipotence which come from the total control of others. Some may be fundamentally insecure and employ a false bravado to hide their fear of inmates. Officers who fit the dictator category are the most likely to be targeted for vengeance should control of the institution temporarily fall into the hands of the inmates.

- *The friend.* Friendly officers try to fraternize with inmates. They approach the issue of control by trying to be "one of the guys." They seem to believe that they can win inmate cooperation by being nice. Unfortunately, such guards do not recognize that fraternization quickly leads to unending requests for special favors, from delivering mail to bending "minor" prison rules. Once a few rules have been "bent," the officer may find that inmates have the upper hand through the potential for blackmail.

  Many officers have amiable relationships with inmates. In most cases, however, affability is only a convenience which both sides recognize can quickly evaporate. "Friendly officers," as the term is being used here, are *overly* friendly. They may be young and inexperienced. On the other hand, they may simply be possessed of kind and idealistic personalities built on successful friendships in free society.

- *The merchant.* Contraband could not exist in any correctional facility without the merchant officer. The merchant participates in the inmate economy, supplying drugs, pornography, alcohol, and sometimes even weapons to inmates who can afford to pay for them.

Probably only a very few officers consistently perform the role of merchant, although a far larger proportion may occasionally turn a few dollars by smuggling some item through the gate. Low salaries create the potential for mercantile corruption among many otherwise straight-arrow officers. Until salaries rise substantially, the merchant will remain an institutionalized feature of most prisons.

■ *The turnkey.* The turnkey officer cares little for what goes on in the prison. Officers who fit this category may be close to retirement, or they may be alienated from their jobs for various reasons. Low pay, the view that inmates are basically worthless and incapable of changing, and the boring routine of "doing time" all combine to numb the professional consciousness of even young officers.

The term *turnkey* comes from prison argot, where it means a guard who is there just to open and shut doors and who cares about nothing other than getting through his or her shift. Inmates do not see the turnkey as a threat, nor is such an officer likely to challenge the status quo in institutions where merchant guards operate.

■ *The climber.* The climber is apt to be a young officer with an eye for promotion. Nothing seems impossible to the climber, who probably hopes eventually to be warden or program director or to hold some high-status position within the institutional hierarchy. Climbers are likely to be involved in schooling, correspondence courses, and professional organizations. They may lead a movement toward unionization for correctional personnel and tend to see the guard's role as a "profession" which should receive greater social recognition.

Climbers have many ideas. They may be heavily involved in reading about the latest confinement or administrative technology. If so, they will suggest many ways to improve prison routine, often to the consternation of complacent staff members.

Like the turnkey, climbers turn a blind eye toward inmates and their problems. They are more concerned with improving institutional procedures and with their own careers than they are with the treatment or day-to-day control of inmates.

■ *The reformer.* The reformer is the do-gooder among officers, the person who believes that prison should offer opportunities for personal change. The reformer tends to lend

Freedom or Safety? You Decide

On August 27, 2001, Amric Singh Rathour, a Sikh who was born and raised in New York City, was fired by the New York City Police Department (NYPD) while in training because he refused to remove his turban while in uniform. The Sikh religion mandates the wearing of turbans and beards by adult males as a sign of their faith. Rathour's termination letter cited a provision of the NYPD dress code that requires all uniformed officers to wear department-approved hats. Rathour later filed a civil suit against his former employer alleging religious discrimination.

Although turbaned correctional officers are a rarity, some have pointed to the possibility of similar lawsuits in the corrections arena. One example of a way for agencies and busi-nesses to avoid legal action comes from the resolution of a religious bias claim brought against United Airlines by a turban-wearing Sikh employee in 2001. Although airline regulations banned the wearing of headgear by employees while indoors, company officials were able to avoid civil liability by offering the man six alternative jobs where he could wear a turban.

YOU DECIDE

How might dress codes relate to public safety? Should agencies have the authority to enforce dress codes without fear of civil liability if those codes enhance public safety? What if they merely enforce uniformity of appearance? How does the idea of dress codes apply to correctional agencies?

SOURCES: The Sikh Coalition, Office of Community Relations, "Petition to Mayor Bloomberg: Allow Turban Sikhs to Serve as Officers in the NYPD"; Web posted at http://www.petitiononline.com/Sikh NYPD; accessed January 10, 2003; and Bureau of National Affairs, Inc., "Religious Bias, Indoor Head-Gear Ban, Offering Six Other Jobs to Turban-Wearing Sikh Sufficient Accommodation," *Employment Discrimination Report,* Vol. 18, p. 469; Web posted at http://www.bna.com/current/edr/topa.htm; accessed January 10, 2003.

a sympathetic ear to the personal needs of inmates and is apt to offer "armchair" counseling and suggestions. Many reformers are motivated by personal ideals, and some of them are highly religious. Inmates tend to see the reformer guard as naive but harmless. Because the reformer actually tries to help, even when help is unsolicited, he or she is the most likely of all the guard types to be accepted by prisoners.

The Professionalization of Correctional Officers   *problem*

Correctional officers have generally been accorded low occupational status. Historically, the role of prison guard required minimal formal education and held few opportunities for professional growth and career advancement. Such jobs were typically low paying, frustrating,

CJ Exhibit

AMERICAN CORRECTIONAL ASSOCIATION CODE of ETHICS

PREAMBLE

The American Correctional Association expects of its members unfailing honesty, respect for the dignity and individuality of human beings and a commitment to professional and compassionate service. To this end, we subscribe to the following principles:

- Members shall respect and protect the civil and legal rights of all individuals.

- Members shall treat every professional situation with concern for the welfare of the individuals involved and with no intent to personal gain.

- Members shall maintain relationships with colleagues to promote mutual respect within the profession and improve the quality of service.

- Members shall make public criticisms of their colleagues or their agencies only when warranted, verifiable, and constructive.

- Members shall respect the importance of all disciplines within the criminal justice system and work to improve cooperation with each segment.

- Members shall honor the public's right to information and share information with the public to the extent permitted by law subject to individuals' right to privacy.

- Members shall respect and protect the right of the public to be safeguarded from criminal activity.

- Members shall refrain from using their positions to secure personal privileges or advantages.

- Members shall refrain from allowing personal interest to impair objectivity in the performance of duty while acting in an official capacity.

- Members shall refrain from entering into any formal or informal activity or agreement which presents a conflict of interest or is inconsistent with the conscientious performance of duties.

- Members shall refrain from accepting any gifts, service, or favor that is or appears to be improper or implies an obligation inconsistent with the free and objective exercise of professional duties.

- Members shall clearly differentiate between personal views/statements and views/statements/positions made on behalf of the agency or association.

- Members shall report to appropriate authorities any corrupt or unethical behaviors in which there is sufficient evidence to justify review.

- Members shall refrain from discriminating against any individual because of race, gender, creed, national origin, religious affiliation, age, disability, or any other type of prohibited discrimination.

- Members shall preserve the integrity of private information; they shall refrain from seeking information on individuals beyond that which is necessary to implement responsibilities and perform their duties; members shall refrain from revealing nonpublic information unless expressly authorized to do so.

- Members shall make all appointments, promotions, and dismissals in accordance with established civil service rules, applicable contract agreements, and individual merit, and not in furtherance of partisan interests.

- Members shall respect, promote, and contribute to a workplace that is safe, healthy, and free of harassment in any form.

Adopted August 1975 at the 105th Congress of Correction. Revised August 1990 at the 120th Congress of Correction. Revised August 1994 at the 124th Congress of Correction.

SOURCE: American Correctional Association. Reprinted with permission. Visit the American Correctional Association at http://www.corrections.com/aca.

and often boring. Growing problems in our nation's prisons, including emerging issues of legal liability, however, increasingly require a well-trained and adequately equipped force of professionals. As correctional personnel have become better trained and more proficient, the old concept of guard has been supplanted by that of correctional officer.

Many states and a growing number of large-city correctional systems try to eliminate individuals with potentially harmful personality characteristics from correctional officer applicant pools. New York, New Jersey, Ohio, Pennsylvania, and Rhode Island, for example, all use some form of psychological screening in assessing candidates for prison jobs.[63]

Although only a few states utilize psychological screening, all make use of training programs intended to prepare successful applicants for prison work. New York, for example, requires trainees to complete six weeks of classroom-based instruction, 40 hours of rifle range practice, and six weeks of on-the-job training. Training days begin around 5 A.M. with a mile run and conclude after dark with study halls for students who need extra help. To keep pace with rising inmate populations, the state has often had to run a number of simultaneous training academies.[64]

Prison Riots

> Whilst we have prisons it matters little which of us occupies the cells.
>
> —George Bernard Shaw
> (1856–1950)

The ten years between 1970 and 1980 have been called the "explosive decade" of prison riots.[65] The decade began with a massive uprising at Attica Prison in New York State in September 1971. The Attica riot resulted in 43 deaths, and more than 80 men were wounded. The "explosive decade" ended in 1980 at Santa Fe, New Mexico. There, in a riot at the New Mexico Penitentiary, 33 inmates died, the victims of vengeful prisoners out to eliminate rats and informants. Many of the deaths involved mutilation and torture. More than 200 other inmates were beaten and sexually assaulted, and the prison was virtually destroyed.

Prison riots did not stop with the end of the explosive 1970s. For 11 days in 1987, the Atlanta (Georgia) Federal Penitentiary was under the control of inmates. The institution was heavily damaged, and inmates had to be temporarily relocated while it was rebuilt. The Atlanta riot followed on the heels of a similar, but less intense, disturbance at the federal detention center at Oakdale, Louisiana. Both outbreaks were attributed to the dissatisfaction of Cuban inmates, most of whom had arrived in the mass exodus known as the Mariel boat lift.[66] Easter Sunday 1993 marked the beginning of an 11-day rebellion at the 1,800-inmate Southern Ohio Correctional Facility in Lucasville, Ohio—one of the country's toughest maximum-security prisons. When the riot ended, nine inmates and one correctional officer were dead. The officer had been hung. The close of the riot—involving a parade of 450 inmates—was televised as prisoners had demanded. Among other demands were (1) no retaliation by officials, (2) review of medical staffing and care, (3) review of mail and visitation rules, (4) review of commissary prices, and (5) better enforcement against what the inmates called "inappropriate supervision."[67]

Riots related to inmate grievances over perceived disparities in federal drug-sentencing policies and the possible loss of weight-lifting equipment occurred throughout the federal prison system in October 1995. Within a few days, the unrest led to a nationwide lockdown of 73 federal prisons. Although fires were set and a number of inmates and guards were injured, no deaths resulted. In February 2000, a riot between 200 black and Hispanic prisoners in California's infamous Pelican Bay State Prison led to the death of one inmate. Fifteen other inmates were wounded. Finally, in November 2000, 32 inmates took a dozen correctional officers hostage at the privately run Torrance County Detention Facility in Estancia, New Mexico. Two of the guards were stabbed and seriously injured, while another eight were beaten. The riot was finally quelled after an emergency response team threw tear-gas canisters into the area where the prisoners had barricaded themselves.[68]

Causes of Riots

It is difficult to explain satisfactorily why prisoners riot, despite study groups which attempt to piece together the "facts" leading up to an incident. After the riot at Attica in 1971, for example, the New York State Special Commission of Inquiry filed a report which recom-

A Broad River (South Carolina) Correctional Institution inmate being subdued following a riot in 1995. A new rule limiting hair length sparked the riot, which resulted in five staff members being stabbed. Three others were taken hostage.
AP/Wide World Photos

mended the creation of inmate advisory councils, changes in staff titles and uniforms, and other institutional improvements. The report emphasized "enhancing [the] dignity, worth, and self-confidence" of inmates. In a final report on the violence at Santa Fe in 1980, the New Mexico attorney general blamed a breakdown in informal controls and the subsequent emergence of a new group of violent inmates among the general prison population.[69]

Researchers have suggested a variety of causes for prison riots.[70] Among them are these:

- An insensitive prison administration and neglected inmates' demands. Calls for "fairness" in disciplinary hearings, better food, more recreational opportunities, and the like may lead to riots when ignored.
- The lifestyles most inmates are familiar with on the streets. It should be no surprise that prisoners use organized violence when many of them are violent people.
- Dehumanizing prison conditions. Overcrowded facilities, the lack of opportunity for individual expression, and other aspects of total institutions culminate in explosive situations of which riots are but one form.
- To regulate inmate society and redistribute power balances among inmate groups. Riots provide the opportunity to "cleanse" the prison population of informers and rats and to resolve struggles among power brokers and ethnic groups within the institution.
- "Power vacuums" created by changes in prison administration, the transfer of influential inmates, or court-ordered injunctions which significantly alter the informal social control mechanisms of the institution.

Although riots are difficult to predict in specific institutions, some state prison systems appear ripe for disorder. The Texas prison system, for example, is home to a number of gangs, among whom turf violations can easily lead to widespread disorder. Gang membership among inmates in the Texas prison system, practically nonexistent in 1983, was estimated at over 1,200 in 1992.[71] The Texas Syndicate, the Aryan Brotherhood of Texas, and the Mexican Mafia (sometimes known as La Eme, Spanish for the letter *M*) are probably the largest gangs functioning in the Texas prison system. Each has around 300 members.[72] Other gangs known to operate in some Texas prisons include Aryan Warriors, Black Gangster Disciples (mostly in midwestern Texas), the Black Guerrilla Family, the Confederate Knights of America, and Nuestra Familia, an organization of Hispanic prisoners.

Gangs in Texas grew rapidly in part because of the power vacuum created when a court ruling ended the "building tender" system.[73] Building tenders were tough inmates who were given almost free reign by prison administrators in keeping other inmates in line, especially in many of the state's worst prisons. The end of the building tender system dramatically increased demands on the Texas Department of Criminal Justice for increased abilities and professionalism among its guards and other prison staff.

The "real" reasons for any riot are probably specific to the institution and may not allow for easy generalization. However, it is no simple coincidence that the "explosive decade" of prison riots coincided with the growth of the revolutionary prisoner subculture referred to earlier. As the old convict code began to give way to an emerging perception of social victimization among inmates, it was probably only a matter of time until those perceptions turned to militancy. Seen from this perspective, riots are more a revolutionary activity undertaken by politically motivated cliques than spontaneous and disorganized expressions stemming from the frustrations of prison life.

Stages in Riots and Riot Control

Riots are generally unplanned and tend to occur spontaneously, the result of some relatively minor precipitating event. Once the stage has been set, prison riots tend to evolve through five phases: (1) explosion, (2) organization into inmate-led groups, (3) confrontation with authority, (4) termination through negotiation or physical confrontation, and (5) reaction and explanation, usually by investigative commissions.[74] Donald Cressey points out that the early explosive stages of a riot tend to involve "binges" during which inmates exult in their newfound freedom with virtual orgies of alcohol and drug use or sexual activity.[75] Buildings are burned, facilities are wrecked, and old grudges between individual inmates and inmate groups are settled, often through violence. After this initial explosive stage, leadership changes tend to occur. New leaders emerge who, at least for a time, may effectively organize inmates into a force that can confront and resist officials' attempts to regain control of the institution. Bargaining strategies then develop, and the process of negotiation begins.

In the past, many correctional facilities depended on informal procedures to quell disturbances, often drawing on the expertise of seasoned correctional officers who were veterans of past skirmishes and riots. Given the large size of many of today's institutions, the rapidly changing composition of inmate and staff populations, and increasing tensions caused by overcrowding and the movement toward reduced inmate privileges, the "old guard" system can no longer be depended on to quell disturbances. Hence most modern facilities have incident-management procedures and systems in place in case a disturbance occurs. Such systems remove the burden of riot control from the individual officer, depending instead on a systematic and deliberate approach developed to deal with a wide variety of correctional incidents.

Prisoners' Rights

In May 1995, Limestone Prison inmate Larry Hope was handcuffed to an Alabama hitching post after arguing with another inmate while working on a chain gang near an interstate highway.[76] Hope was released two hours later, after a supervising officer determined that Hope had not instigated the altercation. During the two hours that he was coupled to the post, Hope was periodically offered drinking water and bathroom breaks, and his responses to those offers were recorded on an activity log. Because of the height of the hitching post, however, his arms grew tired, and it was later determined that whenever he tried moving his arms to improve his circulation, the handcuffs cut into his wrists, causing pain and discomfort.

One month later, Hope was punished more severely after he had taken a nap during the morning bus ride to the chain gang's work site. When the bus arrived, he was slow in responding to an order to exit the vehicle. A shouting match soon led to a scuffle with an officer, and four other guards intervened and subdued Hope, handcuffing him and placing him in leg irons for transportation back to the prison. When he arrived at the facility, officers made him take off his shirt and again put him on the hitching post. He stood in the sun for approximately seven hours, sustaining a sunburn. Hope was given water only once or twice during that time and was provided with no bathroom breaks. At one point, an officer taunted him about his thirst. According to Hope: "[The guard] first gave water to some dogs, then brought the water cooler closer to me, removed its lid, and kicked the cooler over, spilling the water onto the ground."

Eventually Hope filed a civil suit against three officers, claiming that he experienced "unnecessary pain" and that the "wanton infliction of pain . . . constitutes cruel and unusual punishment forbidden by the Eighth Amendment." His case eventually reached the U.S. Supreme Court, and on June 27, 2002, the Court found that Hope's treatment was "totally without penological justification" and constituted an Eighth Amendment violation. The Court ruled, "Despite the clear lack of emergency, respondents knowingly subjected [Hope] to a substantial risk of physical harm, unnecessary pain, unnecessary exposure to the sun, prolonged thirst and taunting, and a deprivation of bathroom breaks that created a risk of particular discomfort and humiliation."

In deciding the *Hope* case, the Court built on almost 40 years of precedent-setting decisions in the area of prisoners' rights. It may be surprising, but prior to the 1960s, American courts had taken a neutral approach—commonly called the **hands-off doctrine**—toward the running of prisons. Judges assumed that prison administrators were sufficiently professional in the performance of their duties to balance institutional needs with humane considerations. The hands-off doctrine rested on the belief that defendants lost most of their rights upon conviction, suffering a kind of **civil death.** Many states defined the concept of civil death through legislation which denied inmates the right to vote, to hold public office, and even to marry. Some states made incarceration for a felony a basis for uncontested divorce at the request of the noncriminal spouse. Aspects of the old notion of civil death are still reality in a number of jurisdictions today, and the Sentencing Project says that 3.9 million American citizens across the nation are barred from voting because of previous felony convictions.[77]

Although the concept of civil death has not entirely disappeared, the hands-off doctrine ended in 1970, when a federal court declared the entire Arkansas prison system to be unconstitutional after hearing arguments that it constituted a form of cruel and unusual punishment.[78] The court's decision resulted from what it judged to be pervasive overcrowding and primitive living conditions. Longtime inmates claimed that a number of other inmates had been beaten or shot to death by guards and buried over the years in unmarked graves on prison property. An investigation did unearth some skeletons in old graves, but their origin was never resolved.

Detailed media coverage of the Arkansas prison system gave rise to suspicions about correctional institutions everywhere. Within a few years, federal courts intervened in the running of prisons in Florida, Louisiana, Mississippi, New York City, and Virginia.[79] In 1975, in a precedent-setting decision, U.S. District Court Judge Frank M. Johnson issued an order banning the Alabama Board of Corrections from accepting any more inmates. Citing a population which was more than double the capacity of the state's system, Judge Johnson enumerated 44 standards to be met before additional inmates could be admitted to prison. Included in the requirements were specific guidelines on living space, staff-to-inmate ratios, visiting privileges, the racial makeup of staff, and food service modifications.

hands-off doctrine

A policy of nonintervention with regard to prison management that U.S. courts tended to follow until the late 1960s. For the past 30 years, the doctrine has languished as judicial intervention in prison administration dramatically increased, although there is now some evidence of a return to a new hands-off era.

civil death

The legal status of prisoners in some jurisdictions who are denied the opportunity to vote, hold public office, marry, or enter into contracts by virtue of their status as incarcerated felons. While civil death is primarily of historical interest, some jurisdictions still limit the contractual opportunities available to inmates.

The Legal Basis of Prisoners' Rights

In 1974, the U.S. Supreme Court case of *Pell* v. *Procunier*[80] established a "balancing test" which, although originally addressing only First Amendment rights, eventually served as a general guideline for all prison operations. In *Pell,* the Court ruled that the "prison inmate retains those First Amendment rights that are not inconsistent with his status as a prisoner or with the legitimate penological objectives of the corrections system."[81] In other words, inmates have rights, much the same as people who are not incarcerated, provided that the legitimate needs of the prison for security, custody, and safety are not compromised. Other courts have declared that order maintenance, security, and rehabilitation are all legitimate concerns of prison administration but that financial exigency and convenience are not. As the **balancing test** makes clear, we see reflected in prisoners' rights a microcosm of the individual-rights-versus-public-order dilemma found in wider society.

Further enforcing the legal rights of prisoners is the Civil Rights of Institutionalized Persons Act (CRIPA) of 1980.[82] The law, which has been amended over time, applies to all adult and juvenile state and local jails, detention centers, prisons, mental hospitals, and other care facilities (such as those operated by a state, county, or city for the physically challenged or chronically ill). Section 1997a of the act, entitled "Initiation of Civil Actions," reads as follows:

> Whenever the Attorney General has reasonable cause to believe that any State, political subdivision of a State, official, employee, or agent thereof, or other person acting on behalf of a State or political subdivision of a State is subjecting persons residing in or confined to an institution . . . to egregious or flagrant conditions which deprive such persons of any rights, privileges, or immunities secured or protected by the Constitution or laws of the United States . . . and that such deprivation is pursuant to a pattern or practice of resistance to the full enjoyment of such rights, privileges, or immunities, the Attorney General, for or in the name of the United States, may institute a civil action in any appropriate United States district court against such party for such equitable relief as may be appropriate.

balancing test

A principle, developed by the courts and applied to the corrections arena by *Pell* v. *Procunier* (1974), which attempts to weigh the rights of an individual, as guaranteed by the Constitution, against the authority of states to make laws or to otherwise restrict a person's freedom in order to protect the state's interests and its citizens.

Huttonsville Correctional Center (West Virgina) inmates Thomas Casey (left) and Robert McCabe review statutes in the prison's law library. McCabe and Casey are known to others in the institution as jailhouse lawyers, and help their peers in the preparation of legal writs: They also represent other inmates in in-house disciplinary actions.
Courtesy Huttonsville Correctional Center

Significantly, the most recent version of CRIPA also states:[83]

> No action shall be brought with respect to prison conditions under section 1983 of this title, or any other Federal law, by a prisoner confined in any jail, prison, or other correctional facility until such administrative remedies as are available are exhausted.

Prisoners' rights, because they are constrained by the legitimate needs of imprisonment, can be thought of as conditional rights rather than absolute rights. The Second Amendment to the U.S. Constitution, for example, grants citizens the right to bear arms. The right to arms is, however, necessarily compromised by the need for order and security in prison, and we would not expect a court to rule that inmates have a right to weapons. Prisoners' rights must be balanced against the security, order-maintenance, and treatment needs of correctional institutions.

Conditional rights, because they are subject to the exigencies of imprisonment, bear a strong resemblance to privileges, which should not be surprising since "privileges" were all that inmates officially had until the modern era. The practical difference between a privilege and a conditional right is that privileges exist only at the convenience of granting institutions and can be revoked at any time for any reason. The rights of prisoners, on the other hand, have a basis in the Constitution and in law external to the institution. Although the institution may restrict such rights for legitimate correctional reasons, those rights may not be infringed without good cause that can be demonstrated in a court of law. Mere institutional convenience does not provide a sufficient legal basis for the denial of rights.

The past two decades have seen many lawsuits brought by prisoners challenging the constitutionality of some aspect of confinement. As mentioned in Chapter 9, suits filed by prisoners with the courts are generally called writs of *habeas corpus* and formally request that the person detaining a prisoner bring him or her before a judicial officer to determine the lawfulness of the imprisonment. The American Correctional Association says that most prisoner lawsuits are based on "1. the Eighth Amendment prohibition against cruel and unusual punishment; 2. the Fourteenth Amendment prohibition against the taking of life, liberty, or property without due process of law; and 3. the Fourteenth Amendment provision requiring equal protection of the laws."[84] Aside from appeals by inmates which question the propriety of their convictions and sentences, such constitutional challenges represent the bulk of legal action initiated by the imprisoned. State statutes and federal legislation, however, including Section 1983 of the Civil Rights Act of 1871, provide other bases for challenges to the legality of specific prison conditions and procedures.

> The Privilege of the Writ of Habeas Corpus shall not be suspended, unless when in Cases of Rebellion or Invasion the public Safety may require it.
>
> —*Article I, Section 9, Clause 2, of the U.S. Constitution*

Precedents in Prisoners' Rights

The U.S. Supreme Court has not yet spoken with finality on a number of prisoners' rights questions. Nonetheless, high court decisions of the last few decades and a number of lower-court findings can be interpreted to identify the existing conditional rights of prisoners, as shown in Table 12–1. A number of especially significant Supreme Court decisions are discussed in the pages which follow.

> The person of a prisoner sentenced to imprisonment in the State prison is under the protection of the law, and any injury to his person, not authorized by law, is punishable in the same manner as if he were not convicted or sentenced.
>
> —*Section 2650 of the California Penal Code*

Communications

In the case of *Procunier* v. *Martinez* (1974),[85] the Supreme Court ruled that a prisoner's mail may be censored if it is necessary to do so for security purposes. In *McNamara* v. *Moody* (1979),[86] however, a federal court upheld the right of an inmate to write vulgar letters to his girlfriend in which he made disparaging comments about the prison staff. The court reasoned that the letters may have been embarrassing to prison officials but that they did not affect the security or order of the institution. However, libelous materials have generally not been accorded First Amendment protection in or out of institutional contexts.

Concerning inmate publications, legal precedent has held that prisoners have no inherent right to publish newspapers or newsletters for use by other prisoners, although many institutions do permit and finance such periodicals.[87] Publications originating from outside of prison, such as newspapers, magazines, and special-interest tracts, have generally been

Table 12-1 | The Conditional Rights of Inmates

Religious Freedom

A right of assembly for religious services and groups
A right to attend services of other religious groups
A right to receive visits from ministers
A right to correspond with religious leaders
A right to observe religious dietary laws
A right to wear religious insignia

Freedom of Speech

A right to meet with members of the press[1]
A right to receive publications directly from the publisher
A right to communicate with nonprisoners

Access to Legal Assistance

A right to have access to the courts[2]
A right to visits from attorneys
A right to have mail communications with lawyers[3]
A right to communicate with legal assistance organizations
A right to consult "jailhouse lawyers"[4]
A right to assistance in filing legal papers, which should include one of the following:
- Access to an adequate law library
- Paid attorneys
- Paralegal personnel or law students

Medical Treatment

A right to sanitary and healthy conditions
A right to medical attention for serious physical problems
A right to required medications
A right to treatment in accordance with "doctor's orders"

Protection

A right to food, water, and shelter
A right to protection from foreseeable attack
A right to protection from predictable sexual abuse
A right to protection against suicide

Institutional Punishment and Discipline

An absolute right against corporal punishments (unless sentenced to such punishments)
A limited right to due process prior to punishment, including the following:
- Notice of charges
- A fair and impartial hearing
- An opportunity for defense
- A right to present witnesses
- A written decision

[1]But not beyond the opportunities afforded for inmates to meet with members of the general public.

[2]As restricted by the Prison Litigation Reform Act of 1996.

[3]Mail communications are generally designated as privileged or nonprivileged. Privileged communications include those between inmates and their lawyers or court officials and cannot legitimately be read by prison officials. Nonprivileged communications include most other written communications.

[4]Jailhouse lawyers are inmates with experience in the law, usually gained from filing legal briefs in their own behalf or in the behalf of others. Consultation with jailhouse lawyers was ruled permissible in the Supreme Court case of *Johnson* v. *Avery*, 393 U.S. 483 (1968), unless inmates are provided with paid legal assistance.

532

protected when mailed directly from the publisher, although magazines which depict deviant sexual behavior can be banned according to *Mallery* v. *Lewis* (1983)[88] and other precedents. Nudity by itself is not necessarily obscene, and federal courts have held that prisons cannot ban nude pictures of inmates' wives or girlfriends.[89]

Religious Practice

The Supreme Court case of *Cruz* v. *Beto* (1972)[90] established that inmates must be given a "reasonable opportunity" to pursue their faith, even if it differs from traditional forms of worship. Meeting facilities must be provided for religious use when those same facilities are made available to other groups of prisoners for other purposes,[91] but no group can claim exclusive use of a prison area for religious reasons.[92] The right to assemble for religious purposes, however, can be denied to inmates who use such meetings to plan escapes or who take the opportunity to dispense contraband. Similarly, prisoners in segregation can be denied the opportunity to attend group religious services.[93]

Although prisoners cannot be made to attend religious services,[94] records of religious activity can be maintained to administratively determine dietary needs and eligibility for passes to religious services outside of the institution.[95] In *Dettmer* v. *Landon* (1985),[96] a federal district court held that an inmate who claimed to practice witchcraft must be provided with the artifacts necessary for his worship services. Included were items such as sea salt, sulfur, a quartz clock, incense, candles, and a white robe without a hood. The district court's opinion was later partially overturned by the U.S. Court of Appeals for the Fourth Circuit. The appellate court recognized the Church of Wicca as a valid religion but held that concerns over prison security could preclude inmates' possession of dangerous items of worship.[97]

Drugs and dangerous substances have not been considered permissible even when inmates claimed they were a necessary part of their religious services.[98] Prison regulations prohibiting the wearing of beards, even those grown for religious reasons, were held acceptable for security reasons in the 1985 federal court case of *Hill* v. *Blackwell*.[99]

Visitation

Visitation and access to the news media are other areas which have come under court scrutiny. Maximum-security institutions rarely permit "contact" visits, and some have on occasion suspended all visitation privileges. In the case of *Block* v. *Rutherford* (1984),[100] the U.S. Supreme Court upheld the policy of the Los Angeles County Central Jail, which prohibited all visits from friends and relatives. The Court agreed that the large jail population and the conditions under which visits might take place could combine to threaten the security of the jail.

In *Pell* v. *Procunier* (1974),[101] discussed earlier in regard to the balancing test, the Court found in favor of a California law which denied prisoners the opportunity to hold special meetings with members of the press. The Court reasoned that media interviews could be conducted through regular visitation arrangements and that most of the information desired by the media could be conveyed through correspondence. In *Pell*, the Court also held that any reasonable policy of media access was acceptable so long as it was administered fairly and without bias.

In a later case, the Court ruled that news personnel cannot be denied correspondence with inmates but also ruled that they have no constitutional right to interview inmates or to inspect correctional facilities beyond the visitation opportunities available to the public.[102] This equal-access policy was set forth in *Houchins* v. *KQED, Inc.* (1978) by Justice Potter Stewart, who wrote, "The Constitution does no more than assure the public and the press equal access once government has opened its doors."[103]

Access to the Courts and to Legal Assistance

Access to the courts[104] and to legal assistance is a well-established right of prisoners. The right of prisoners to petition the court was recognized in *Bounds* v. *Smith* (1977),[105] which, at the time, was a far-reaching Supreme Court decision. While attempting to define "access," the Court in *Bounds* imposed on the states the duty of assisting inmates in the preparation and filing of legal papers. Assistance could be provided through trained personnel knowledgeable in the law or via law libraries in each institution, which all states have since built. In 1996, however, in the case of *Lewis* v. *Casey*,[106] the U.S. Supreme Court repudiated part of the *Bounds* decision, saying, "[S]tatements in *Bounds* suggesting that prison authorities must also enable the prisoner to discover grievances, and to litigate effectively once in court . . . have no antecedent in this Court's pre-*Bounds* cases, and are now disclaimed." In *Lewis,* the Court overturned earlier decisions by a federal district court and by the Ninth Circuit Court of Appeals. Both lower courts had found in favor of Arizona inmates who had complained that state prison law libraries provided inadequate legal research facilities, thereby depriving them of their right of legal access to the courts, as established by *Bounds*. In turning back portions of *Bounds,* the majority in *Lewis* wrote that inmates raising such claims need to demonstrate "widespread actual injury" to their ability to access the courts, not merely "isolated instances of actual injury." "Moreover," wrote the justices, "*Bounds* does not guarantee inmates the wherewithal to file any and every type of legal claim, but requires only that they be provided with the tools to attack their sentences . . . and to challenge the conditions of their confinement."

In an earlier case, *Johnson* v. *Avery* (1968),[107] the Court had ruled that prisoners under correctional supervision have a right to consult "jailhouse lawyers" for advice when assistance from trained professionals is not available. Other court decisions have established that inmates have a right to correspond with their attorneys[108] and with legal assistance organizations. Such letters, however, can be opened and inspected for contraband[109] (but not read) by prison authorities in the presence of the inmate. The right to meet with hired counsel for reasonable lengths of time has also been upheld.[110] Indigent defendants must be provided with stamps for the purpose of legal correspondence,[111] and inmates cannot be disciplined for communicating with lawyers or for requesting legal help. Conversations between inmates and their lawyers can be monitored, although any evidence thus obtained cannot be used in court.[112] Inmates do not, however, have the right to an appointed lawyer, even when indigent, if no judicial proceedings have been initiated against them.[113]

Medical Care

The historic Supreme Court case of *Estelle* v. *Gamble* (1976)[114] specified prison officials' duty to provide for inmates' medical care. In *Estelle,* the Court concerned itself with "deliberate indifference" on the part of the staff toward a prisoner's need for serious medical attention. "Deliberate indifference" can mean a wanton disregard for the health of inmates. Hence while poor treatment, misdiagnosis, and the like may constitute medical malpractice, they do not necessarily constitute deliberate indifference.[115] In 1992, in *Hudson* v. *McMillan,*[116] the Court clarified the concept of "deliberate indifference" by holding that it requires both actual knowledge and disregard of risk of harm.

Two years later, in the case of *Farmer* v. *Brennan* (1994),[117] the Court found that even when a prisoner is harmed, and even when prison officials knew that a risk of harm existed, they cannot be held liable for that harm if they took appropriate steps to mitigate the risk of its happening. The case involved Dee Farmer, a preoperative transsexual with obvious feminine characteristics who had been incarcerated with other males in the federal prison system. While mixing with other inmates, Farmer was beaten and raped by a fellow prisoner. Subsequently, he sued correctional officials, claiming that they had acted with deliberate indifference to his safety because they knew that the penitentiary had a violent environment as well as a history of inmate assaults and because they should have known that Farmer would be particularly vulnerable to sexual attack. Although both a federal district court and the U.S. Court of Appeals for the seventh circuit agreed with Farmer, the U.S. Supreme Court sent Farmer's case back to a lower court for rehearing after clarifying what it said was necessary to establish deliberate indifference. "Prison officials," wrote the justices, "have a duty under the Eighth Amendment to provide humane conditions of confinement. They must ensure that inmates receive adequate food, clothing, shelter, and medical care and must protect prisoners from violence at the hands of other prisoners. However, a constitutional violation occurs only where . . . the official has acted with 'deliberate indifference' to inmate health or safety." The Court continued, "A prison official may be held liable under the Eighth Amendment for acting with 'deliberate indifference' to inmate health or safety only if he knows that inmates face a substantial risk of serious harm and disregards that risk by failing to take reasonable measures to abate it."[118]

Two other cases, *Ruiz* v. *Estelle* (1982)[119] and *Newman* v. *Alabama* (1972),[120] have had a substantial impact on the rights of prisoners to medical attention. In *Ruiz,* the Texas Department of Criminal Justice was found lacking in its correctional medical treatment programs. The court ordered an improvement in record keeping, physical facilities, and general medical care while it continued to monitor the progress of the department. In *Newman,* Alabama's prison medical services were found to be so inadequate as to be "shocking to the conscience." Problems with the Alabama program included[121]

- Not enough medical personnel
- Poor physical facilities for medical treatment
- Poor administrative techniques for dispersal of medications
- Poor medical records
- A lack of medical supplies
- Poorly trained or untrained inmates who provided some medical services and performed minor surgery
- Medically untrained personnel who determined the need for treatment

Part of the issue of medical treatment is the question of whether inmates can be forced to take medication. A 1984 state court case held that inmates could be medicated against their will in an emergency.[122] The court did recognize that unwanted medications designed to produce only psychological effects, such as tranquilizers, might be refused more readily than life-sustaining drugs.[123] In the 1984 federal court case of *Bee* v. *Greaves,*[124] the Tenth Circuit Court of Appeals ruled that "less restrictive alternatives" should be considered before the administration of antipsychotic drugs to in-custody pretrial detainees. In 1990, in the case of *Washington* v. *Harper,*[125] the U.S. Supreme Court held that prisoners can refuse the involuntary administration of antipsychotic drugs unless government officials can demonstrate an "overriding justification" as to why administration of the drugs is necessary. Under *Harper,* an inmate in a correctional institution "may be treated involuntarily with antipsychotic drugs where there is a determination that the inmate is dangerous to himself or others and the treatment is in the inmate's medical interest."

In 1993, the U.S. Supreme Court indicated that environmental conditions of prison life which pose a threat to inmate health may have to be corrected. In *Helling* v. *McKinney,*[126] Nevada inmate William McKinney claimed that exposure to secondary cigarette smoke circulating in his cell was threatening his health, in violation of the Eighth Amendment's prohibition against cruel and unusual punishment. The Court, in ordering that a federal district court provide McKinney with the opportunity to prove his allegations, held that "an injunction cannot be denied to inmates who plainly prove an unsafe, life-threatening condition on the ground that nothing yet has happened to them." In effect, the *Helling* case gave notice to prison officials that they are responsible not only for "inmates' current serious health problems" but also for maintaining environmental conditions under which health problems might be prevented from developing.

In 1998, in the case of *Pennsylvania Department of Corrections* v. *Yeskey,*[127] the Supreme Court held that the Americans with Disabilities Act (ADA) of 1990[128] applies to prisons and to prison inmates. In May 1994, Ronald Yeskey was sentenced to serve 18 to 36 months in a Pennsylvania correctional facility. The sentencing court recommended that he be placed in Pennsylvania's Motivational Boot Camp for first-time offenders, the successful completion of which would have led to his release on parole in just six months. When Yeskey was refused admission because of his medical history of hypertension, he sued the Pennsylvania Department of Corrections and several state officials, alleging that his exclusion violated Title II of the ADA, which prohibits a "public entity" from discriminating against a "qualified individual with a disability" on account of that disability. Lawyers for the state of Pennsylvania argued that state prisoners are not covered by the ADA. The Supreme Court ruled, however, that "state prisons fall squarely within Title II's statutory definition of 'public entity,' which includes 'any . . . instrumentality of a State . . . or local government.'"

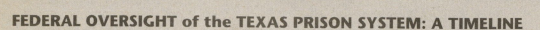

CJ Exhibit

FEDERAL OVERSIGHT of the TEXAS PRISON SYSTEM: A TIMELINE

1972: Inmate David Ruiz and several other prisoners file a civil rights suit against the Texas Department of Corrections (now called the Texas Department of Criminal Justice), alleging constitutional violations.

October 2, 1978–September 20, 1979: The Ruiz case is tried in Houston.

December 10, 1980: U.S. District Court Judge William Wayne Justice finds that confinement in the Texas prison system constitutes cruel and unusual punishment. He cites overcrowding, understaffing, brutality by guards and inmate-guards known as building tenders, substandard medical care, and uncontrolled physical abuse among inmates.

January 12, 1981: The judge orders improvements to be made to the system and sets deadlines.

April 19, 1981: Judge Justice appoints a special master to supervise compliance with his order.

April 1982: The state agrees to halt the building tender system and to hire additional correctional officers.

January–June 1983: The Texas legislature passes laws intended to reduce the prison population.

November 1987: Texas voters authorize $500 million in bonds for prison construction.

March 31, 1990: The special master's office is closed.

November 1990: Texas voters approve $672 million in bonds to build 25,300 prison beds and 12,000 drug- and alcohol-treatment beds.

February 1992: Inmates' attorneys and the Texas Board of Criminal Justice reach an agreement. Texas Attorney General Dan Morales rejects it.

May 1, 1992: Morales offers a settlement proposal.

July 14, 1992: Inmates' attorneys accept the proposal.

December 11, 1992: Judge Justice signs the settlement.

January 21, 1999: Judge Justice begins a hearing to determine whether Texas prisons should be freed of federal court oversight.

March 1, 1999: Judge Justice decides to maintain oversight of the prison system.

March 20, 2001: The 5th U.S. Circuit Court of Appeals reverses Judge Justice's ruling, ending oversight but giving him 90 days to review the matter.

June 18, 2001: Judge Justice says that the Texas prison system has improved but that oversight is still needed in the areas of "conditions of confinement in administrative segregation, the failure to provide reasonable safety to inmates against assault and abuse, and the excessive use of force by correctional officers." Judge Justice discontinues federal oversight of other aspects of the prison system, including health services and staffing.

SOURCE: Adapted from Ed Timms, "Judge to Lessen Oversight of Texas Prisons," *Dallas Morning News,* June 19, 2001. Reprinted with permission. Web posted at http://www.dallasnews.com/archive. Accessed March 12, 2002.

Privacy

Many court decisions, including the Tenth Circuit case of *U.S.* v. *Ready* (1978)[129] and the U.S. Supreme Court decisions of *Katz* v. *U.S.* (1967)[130] and *Hudson* v. *Palmer* (1984),[131] have held that inmates cannot have a reasonable expectation to privacy while incarcerated. Palmer, an inmate in Virginia, claimed that Hudson, a prison guard, had unreasonably destroyed some of his personal (noncontraband) property following a cell search. Palmer's complaint centered on the lack of due process which accompanied the destruction. The Court disagreed, saying that the need for prison officials to conduct thorough and unannounced searches precludes inmate privacy in personal possessions. In *Block* v. *Rutherford* (1984),[132] the Court established that prisoners do not have a right to be present during a search of their cells.

Some lower courts, however, have begun to indicate that body-cavity searches may be unreasonable unless based on a demonstrable suspicion or conducted after prior warning has been given to the inmate.[133] They have also indicated that searches conducted simply to "harass or humiliate" inmates are illegitimate.[134] These cases may be an indication that the Supreme Court will eventually recognize a limited degree of privacy in prison cell searches, especially those which uncover legal documents and personal papers prepared by the prisoner.

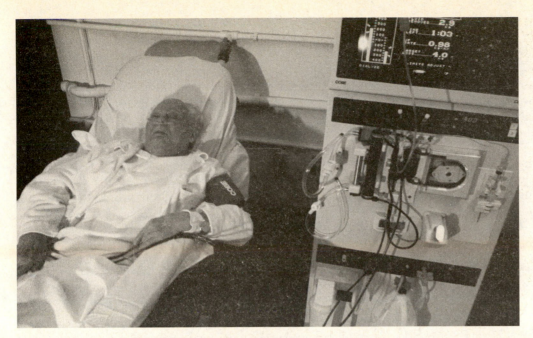

Inmate Santos Pagon undergoing kidney dialysis at Laurel Highlands Prison in Pennsylvania. Court decisions over the years have established a firm set of inmate rights. Among them is the right to necessary health care.
Mark Petersen, CORBIS/SABA Press Photos, Inc.

Grievance and Disciplinary Procedures

A major area of inmate concern is the hearing of grievances. Complaints may arise in areas as diverse as food service (quality of food or special diets for religious purposes or health regimens), interpersonal relations between inmates and staff, denial of privileges, and alleged misconduct levied against an inmate or a guard.

In 1972, the National Council on Crime and Delinquency developed a Model Act for the Protection of Rights of Prisoners, which included the opportunity for grievances to be heard. The 1973 National Advisory Commission on Criminal Justice Standards and Goals called for the establishment of responsible practices for the hearing of inmate grievances. Finally, in 1977, in the case of *Jones* v. *North Carolina Prisoners' Labor Union*,[135] the Supreme Court held that prisons must establish some formal opportunity for the airing of inmate grievances. Soon, formal grievance plans were established in prisons in an attempt to divert inmate grievances away from the courts.

Today, all sizable prisons have an established **grievance procedure** whereby an inmate files a complaint with local authorities and receives a mandated response. Modern grievance procedures range from the use of a hearing board composed of staff members and inmates to a single staff appointee charged with the resolution of complaints. Inmates who are dissatisfied with the handling of their grievance can generally appeal beyond the local prison.

Disciplinary actions by prison authorities may also require a formalized hearing process, especially when staff members bring charges of rule violations against inmates which might result in some form of punishment being imposed on them. In a precedent-setting decision in the case of *Wolff* v. *McDonnell* (1974),[136] the Supreme Court decided that sanctions could not be levied against inmates without appropriate due process. The *Wolff* case involved an inmate who had been deprived of previously earned "good-time" credits because of misbehavior. The Court established that "good-time" credits were a form of "state-created right(s)," which, once created, could not be "arbitrarily abrogated."[137] *Wolff* was especially significant because it began an era of court scrutiny of what came to be called *state-created liberty interests*. State-created liberty interests were said to be based on the language used in published prison regulations and were held, in effect, to confer due process guarantees on prisoners. Hence if a prison regulation said that a disciplinary hearing should be held before a prisoner could be sent to solitary confinement and that the hearing should permit a discussion of the evidence for and against the prisoner, courts interpreted that regulation to mean that the prisoner had a state-created right to a hearing and that sending him or her

grievance procedure

A formalized arrangement, usually involving a neutral hearing board, whereby institutionalized individuals have the opportunity to register complaints about the conditions of their confinement.

to solitary confinement in violation of the regulation was a violation of a state-created liberty interest. In later court decisions, state-created rights and privileges were called *protected liberties* and were interpreted to include any significant change in a prisoner's status.

In the interest of due process, and especially where written prison regulations governing the hearing process exist, courts have generally held that inmates going before disciplinary hearing boards are entitled to (1) notice of the charges brought against them, (2) the chance to organize a defense, (3) an impartial hearing, and (4) the opportunity to present witnesses and evidence in their behalf. A written statement of the hearing board's conclusions should be provided to the inmate.[138] In the case of *Ponte* v. *Real* (1985),[139] the Supreme Court held that prison officials must provide an explanation to inmates who are denied the opportunity to have a desired witness at their hearing. The case of *Vitek* v. *Jones* (1980)[140] extended the requirement of due process to inmates about to be transferred from prisons to mental hospitals.

So that inmates will know what is expected of them as they enter prison, the American Correctional Association recommends that "a rulebook that contains all chargeable offenses, ranges of penalties and disciplinary procedures [be] posted in a conspicuous and accessible area; [and] a copy . . . given to each inmate and staff member."[141]

A Return to the Hands-Off Doctrine?

Many state-created rights and protected liberties may soon be a thing of the past. In June 1991, an increasingly conservative U.S. Supreme Court signaled the beginning of what appears to be at least a partial return to the "hands-off" doctrine of earlier times. The case, *Wilson* v. *Seiter*,[142] involved a 1983 suit brought against Richard P. Seiter, Director of the Ohio Department of Rehabilitation and Correction, and Carl Humphreys, Warden of the Hocking Correctional Facility (HCF) in Nelsonville, Ohio. In the suit, Pearly L. Wilson, a felon incarcerated at HCF, alleged that a number of the conditions of his confinement constituted cruel and unusual punishment in violation of the Eighth and Fourteenth Amendments to the U.S. Constitution. Specifically, Wilson cited overcrowding, excessive noise, insufficient locker storage space, inadequate heating and cooling, improper ventilation, unclean and inadequate restrooms, unsanitary dining facilities and food preparation, and housing with mentally and physically ill inmates. Wilson asked for a change in prison conditions and sought $900,000 from prison officials in compensatory and punitive damages.

Both the federal district court in which Wilson first filed affidavits and the Sixth Circuit Court of Appeals held that no constitutional violations existed because the conditions cited by Wilson were not the result of malicious intent on the part of officials. The U.S. Supreme Court agreed, noting that the "deliberate indifference" standard applied in *Estelle* v. *Gamble* (1976)[143] to claims involving medical care is similarly applicable to other cases in which prisoners challenge the conditions of their confinement. In effect, the Court created a standard which effectively means that all future challenges to prison conditions by inmates, which are brought under the Eighth Amendment, must show "deliberate indifference" by the officials responsible for the existence of those conditions before the Court will hear the complaint.

The written opinion of the Court in *Wilson* v. *Seiter* is telling. Writing for the majority, Justice Antonin Scalia observed that "if a prison boiler malfunctions accidentally during a cold winter, an inmate would have no basis for an Eighth Amendment claim, even if he suffers objectively significant harm. If a guard accidentally stepped on a prisoner's toe and broke it, this would not be punishment in anything remotely like the accepted meaning of the word."

Although the criterion of deliberate indifference is still evolving, it is likely that such indifference could be demonstrated by petitioners able to show that prison administrators have done nothing to alleviate life-threatening prison conditions after those conditions had been called to their attention. Even so, critics of *Wilson* are concerned that the decision may excuse prison authorities from the need to improve living conditions within institutions on the basis of simple budgetary constraints. Four of the justices themselves recognized the potential held by *Wilson* for a near return to the days of the hands-off doctrine.

Although concurring with the Court's majority, Justices Byron White, Thurgood Marshall, Harry Blackmun, and John Paul Stevens noted their fear that "[t]he ultimate result of today's decision [may be] that 'serious deprivations of basic human needs' . . . will go unredressed due to an unnecessary and meaningless search for 'deliberate indifference.'"

In the 1995 case of *Sandin* v. *Conner*,[144] the U.S. Supreme Court took a much more definitive stance in favor of a new type of hands-off doctrine and voted 5 to 4 to reject the argument that any state action taken for a punitive reason encroaches on a prisoner's constitutional due process right to be free from the deprivation of liberty. The Court effectively set aside substantial portions of earlier decisions, such as *Wolff* v. *McDonnell* (1974)[145] and *Hewitt* v. *Helms* (1983),[146] which, wrote the justices, focused more on procedural issues than on those of "real substance." As a consequence, the majority opinion held, past cases like these have "impermissibly shifted the focus" away from the nature of a due process deprivation to one based on the language of a particular state or prison regulation. "This shift in focus," the justices wrote, "has encouraged prisoners to comb regulations in search of mandatory language on which to base entitlements to various state-conferred privileges." As a result, the Court said, cases like *Wolff* and *Hewitt* "created disincentives for States to codify prison management procedures in [order to avoid lawsuits by inmates], and . . . led to the involvement of federal courts in the day-to-day management of prisons."

In *Sandin,* Demont Conner, an inmate at the Halawa Correctional Facility in Hawaii, was serving an indeterminate sentence of 30 years to life for numerous crimes, including murder, kidnapping, robbery, and burglary. Conner alleged in a lawsuit in federal court that prison officials had deprived him of procedural due process when a hearing committee refused to allow him to present witnesses during a disciplinary hearing and then sentenced him to segregation for alleged misconduct. An appellate court agreed with Conner, concluding that an existing prison regulation which instructed the hearing committee to find guilt in cases where a misconduct charge is supported by substantial evidence meant that the committee could not impose segregation if it did not look at all the evidence available to it.

The Supreme Court, however, reversed the decision of the appellate court, holding that while "such a conclusion may be entirely sensible in the ordinary task of construing a statute defining rights and remedies available to the general public, [i]t is a good deal less sensible in the case of a prison regulation primarily designed to guide correctional officials in the administration of a prison." The Court concluded that "such regulations [are] not designed to confer rights on inmates" but are meant only to provide guidelines to prison staff members. Hence, based on *Sandin,* it appears that inmates in the future will have a much more difficult time challenging the administrative regulations and procedures imposed on them by prison officials, even when stated procedures are not explicitly followed. "The *Hewitt* approach," wrote the majority in *Sandin,* "has run counter to the view expressed in several of our cases that federal courts ought to afford appropriate deference and flexibility to state officials trying to manage a volatile environment. . . . The time has come," said the Court, "to return to those due process principles that were correctly established and applied" in earlier times.

The Prison Litigation Reform Act of 1996

Only about 2,000 petitions per year concerning inmate problems were filed with the courts in 1961, but by 1975 the number of filings had increased to around 17,000, and in 1996 prisoners filed 68,235 civil rights lawsuits in federal courts nationwide.[147] Some inmate-originated suits seemed patently ludicrous and became the subject of much media coverage in the mid-1990s.[148] One such suit involved Robert Procup, a Florida State Prison inmate serving time for the murder of his business partner. Procup repeatedly sued Florida prison officials—once because he got only one roll with his dinner; again because he didn't get a luncheon salad; a third time because prison-provided TV dinners didn't come with a drink; and a fourth time because his cell had no television. Two other well-publicized cases involved an inmate who went to court asking to be allowed to exercise religious freedom by attending prison chapel services in the nude and an inmate who, thinking he could become pregnant via homosexual relations, sued prison doctors who wouldn't provide him with birth-control pills. An infamous example of seemingly frivolous inmate lawsuits was one brought by inmates claiming religious freedoms and demanding that members of the

Church of the New Song, or CONS, be provided steak and Harvey's Bristol Cream every Friday in order to celebrate communion. The CONS suit stayed in various courts for ten years before finally being thrown out.[149]

The huge number of inmate-originated lawsuits in the mid-1990s created a backlog of cases in many federal courts and was targeted by the media and by some citizens' groups as an unnecessary waste of taxpayers' money. The National Association of Attorneys General, which supports efforts to restrict frivolous inmate lawsuits, estimated that lawsuits filed by prisoners cost states more than $81 million a year in legal fees alone.[150]

In 1996, the federal Prison Litigation Reform Act (PLRA) became law.[151] The PLRA is a clear legislative effort to restrict inmate filings to worthwhile cases and to reduce the number of suits brought by state prisoners in federal courts. The PLRA

- Requires inmates to exhaust their prison's grievance procedure before filing a lawsuit
- Requires judges to screen all inmate complaints against the federal government and to immediately dismiss those deemed frivolous or without merit
- Prohibits prisoners from filing a lawsuit for mental or emotional injury unless they can also show there has been physical injury
- Requires inmates to pay court filing fees. Prisoners who don't have the needed funds can pay the filing fee over a period of time through deductions to their prison commissary accounts
- Limits the award of attorneys' fees in successful lawsuits brought by inmates
- Revokes the credits earned by federal prisoners toward early release if they file a malicious lawsuit
- Mandates that court orders affecting prison administration cannot go any further than necessary to correct a violation of a particular inmate's civil rights
- Makes it possible for state officials to have court orders lifted after two years unless there is a new finding of a continuing violation of federally guaranteed civil rights
- Mandates that any court order requiring the release of prisoners due to overcrowding be approved by a three-member court before it can become effective

The U.S. Supreme Court has upheld provisions of the PLRA on a number of occasions. In 1997, for example, in the case of *Edwards* v. *Balisok*,[152] the Supreme Court made it harder to successfully challenge prison disciplinary convictions, holding that, under the PLRA, prisoners cannot sue for damages under 42 U.S.C. § 1983 for loss of good-time until they sue in state court and get their disciplinary conviction set aside.[153] In *Booth* v. *Churner* (2001),[154] the U.S. Supreme Court held that under the PLRA, "an inmate seeking only [monetary] damages must complete any prison administrative process capable of addressing the inmate's complaint and providing some form of relief [before filing his or her grievance with a federal court], even if the process does not make specific provision for monetary relief." The case involved Timothy Booth, a Pennsylvania inmate who had filed a Section 1983 action in federal district court seeking financial compensation from the state based on the claim that corrections officers had violated his Eighth Amendment right to be free from cruel and unusual punishment by assaulting him, using excessive force against him, and denying him medical attention to treat his injuries. Similarly, in the case of *Porter* v. *Nussle* (2002),[155] the U.S. Supreme Court held that a Connecticut inmate had inappropriately brought a Section 1983 complaint directly to federal district court without first having filed an inmate grievance as required by Connecticut Department of Correction procedures. In *Porter,* the Court held that the PLRA's exhaustion requirement applies to all inmate suits about prison life, whether they involve general circumstances or particular episodes and whether they allege excessive force or some other wrong.

According to a 2002 Bureau of Justice Statistics study, the PLRA has been effective in reducing the number of frivolous lawsuits filed by inmates alleging unconstitutional prison conditions.[156] The study found that the filing rate of inmates' civil rights petitions in federal courts had been cut in half four years after passage of the act.

CJ Careers

SUPPORT POSITIONS AVAILABLE: U.S. CUSTOMS SERVICE

Typical Positions

Criminal investigator, special agent, customs inspector, canine enforcement officer, and import specialist. Support positions include intelligence research specialist, computer operator, auditor, customs aide, investigative assistant, and clerk.

Employment Requirements

Applicants must (1) be U.S. citizens, (2) pass an appropriate physical examination, (3) pass a personal background investigation, (4) submit to urinalysis testing for the presence of controlled substances, (5) have at least three years of work experience, and (6) be under 35 years of age. Appointment at the GS-7 level also requires (1) one year of specialized experience (for example, "responsible criminal investigative or comparable experience"), (2) a bachelor's degree with demonstration of superior academic achievement (a 3.0 grade point average in all courses completed at time of application, a 3.5 grade point average for all courses in the applicant's major field of study, rank in the upper third of the applicant's undergraduate class, or membership in a national honorary scholastic society), or (3) one year of successful graduate study in a related field.

Other Requirements

Applicants for special agent positions must (1) be willing to travel frequently, (2) be able to work overtime, (3) be able to work under stressful conditions, and (4) be willing to carry weapons and be able to qualify regularly with firearms. Applicants will not be hired for the position of criminal investigator or special agent if they have any chronic disease or condition affecting the respiratory, cardiovascular, gastrointestinal, musculoskeletal, digestive, nervous, endocrine, or genitourinary system that would impair full performance of the duties required of the position. Because required duties involve responsibility for the safety of others under trying conditions, successful applicants must possess emotional and mental stability. Proficiency in a foreign language may be used as a selective placement factor for certain positions.

Salary

Successful candidates are typically hired at GS-5 or GS-7, depending on education and work experience.

Benefits

Benefits include (1) 13 days of sick leave annually, (2) two and a half to five weeks of paid vacation and ten paid federal holidays each year, (3) federal health and life insurance, and (4) a comprehensive retirement program.

Direct Inquiries To:

Office of Human Resources
U.S. Customs Service
1301 Constitution Ave., N.W.
Washington, DC 20229
Phone: (800) 944-7725
Website: http://www.customs.gov

SOURCE: U.S. Customs Service
For additional career information in the criminal justice field, visit http://cjbrief.com/careers.

Opponents of the PLRA fear that it might stifle the filing of meritorious suits by inmates facing real deprivations. According to the ACLU, for example, "The Prison Litigation Reform Act . . . attempts to slam the courthouse door on society's most vulnerable members. It seeks to strip the federal courts of much of their power to correct even the most egregious prison conditions by altering the basic rules which have always governed prison reform litigation. The PLRA also makes it difficult to settle prison cases by consent decree, and limits the life span of any court judgment."[157] The ACLU is leading a nationwide effort to have many provisions of the PLRA overturned. So far, however, the effort has borne little fruit.

Issues Facing Prisons Today

> To return to society discharged prisoners unreformed is to poison it with the worst elements possible.
>
> —Zebulon R. Brockway[j]

Prisons are society's answer to a number of social problems. They house outcasts, misfits, and some highly dangerous people. While prisons provide a part of the answer to the question of crime control, they also face problems of their own. A few of those special problems are described here.

AIDS

Chapter 6 discussed the steps that police agencies are taking to deal with health threats from acquired immunodeficiency syndrome (AIDS). In 2001, the Justice Department reported finding 25,757 cases of AIDS among inmates of the nation's prisons[158]—more than a 12-fold increase over 1987, when surveys were first conducted. At the time of the most recent survey, 3.4% of all female state prison inmates tested positive for HIV infection, as did 2.1% of male prisoners. Some states have especially high rates of HIV infection among their prisoners. Almost 10% of New York prison inmates, for example, are HIV-positive. Of all HIV-positive inmates, 24% exhibit symptoms of AIDS.[159] Jail populations exhibit a similar prevalence of HIV infection. In both prisons and jails, the highest incidence of infection is found among inmates being held on drug charges (2.9%), while property offenders (2.4%) and violent criminals (1.9%) have somewhat lower rates. Those who reported having shared a needle to use drugs prior to arrest had the highest infection rate (7.7%).[160]

The incidence of HIV infection among the general population stands at 120 cases per 100,000, according to a recent report by the Centers for Disease Control. Among inmates, however, best estimates place the reported HIV-infection rate at 600 cases per 100,000[161]—five times as great. A few years ago, AIDS was the leading cause of death among prison inmates.[162] Today, however, the number of inmates who die from AIDS (or, more precisely, from AIDS-related complications like pneumonia or Kaposi's sarcoma) is much lower than it has been in the past. The introduction of drugs like protease inhibitors and useful combinations of antiretroviral therapies have reduced inmate deaths from AIDS by 75% since 1995.[163]

Some inmates are infected in prison, while others carry the HIV virus into prison with them. Authorities say the virus is spread behind bars through homosexual activity (including rape), intravenous drug use, and the sharing of tainted tattoo and hypodermic needles. The fact that inmates tend to have histories of high-risk behavior before entering prison, especially intravenous drug use, probably means that many are infected before being incarcerated.

A report by the National Institute of Justice suggests that correctional administrators can use two types of strategies to reduce the transmission of AIDS.[164] One strategy relies on medical technology to identify seropositive inmates and to segregate them from the rest of the prison population. Mass screening and inmate segregation, however, may be prohibitively expensive. They may also be illegal. Some states specifically prohibit HIV-antibody testing without the informed consent of the person tested.[165] The related issue of confidentiality may be difficult to manage, especially when the purpose of testing is to segregate infected inmates from others. In addition, civil liability may result if inmates are falsely labeled as infected or if inmates known to be infected are not prevented from spreading the disease. Only Alabama and South Carolina still segregate all known HIV-infected inmates,[166] but more limited forms of separation are practiced elsewhere. Many state prison systems have denied HIV-positive inmates jobs, educational opportunities, visitation privileges, conjugal visits, and home furloughs, causing some researchers to conclude that "inmates with HIV and AIDS are routinely discriminated against and denied equal treatment in ways that have no accepted medical basis."[167] In 1994, for example, a federal appeals court upheld a California prison policy that bars inmates who are HIV-positive from working in food-service jobs.[168] In contrast, in 2001, the Mississippi Department of Correction ended its policy of segregating HIV-positive prisoners from other inmates in educational and vocational programs.

The second strategy is one of prevention through education. Educational programs teach both inmates and staff members about the dangers of high-risk behavior and suggest ways to avoid HIV infection. A National Institute of Justice (NIJ) model program recommends the use of simple, straightforward messages presented by knowledgeable and approachable trainers.[169] Alarmism, says NIJ, should be avoided. One survey found that 98% of state and federal prisons provide some form of AIDS/HIV education and that 90% of jails do as well—although most such training is oriented toward correctional staff rather than inmates.[170] Learn more about HIV in prisons and jails via **Library Extra! 12–6** at cjbrief.com. Inmate medical problems in general are discussed in **Library Extra! 12–7.**

Geriatric Offenders

Chapter 2 described the involvement of older people in crime. As noted in that chapter, crimes committed by the elderly, like most other crimes, have recently been on the decline. Nonetheless, the significant expansion of America's retiree population has led to an increase in the number of elderly people who are behind bars. In fact, crimes of violence are what brings most older people into the correctional system. According to one early study, 52% of inmates who were over the age of 50 when they entered prison had committed violent crimes, compared with 41% of younger inmates.[171] On January 1, 2002, 40,200 inmates aged 55 or older were housed in state and federal prisons. The number of prisoners older than 55 increased more than 300% between 1990 and 2002.[172] Similarly, the per capita rate of incarceration for inmates aged 55 and over now stands at 154 per 100,000 residents of like age and, until very recently, had steadily increased.

Some authors have interpreted prison statistics on older inmates to presage the growth of a "geriatric delinquent" population, freed by age and retirement from jobs and responsibilities. Such people, say these authors, may turn to crime as one way of averting boredom and adding a little spice to life.[173] Prison statistics on geriatric offenders, however, probably require a more cautious interpretation. They are based on relatively small numbers, and much of the increase in imprisonment among the elderly may be due to the rapid growth of the older population in this country; even greater increases are expected over the next three decades. Advances in health care have lengthened life expectancy and have made those added years more active than ever before. Finally, World War II baby boomers are now reaching their late middle years, which probably means that present trends in criminal involvement among the elderly can be expected to continue.

Of course, not all of today's elderly inmates were old when they entered prison. Because of harsh sentencing laws passed throughout the country in the 1990s, a small but growing number of inmates (10%) will serve 20 years or more in prison, and 5% will never be released.[174] This means that many inmates who enter prison when they are young will grow old behind bars. Hence the "graying" of America's prison population has a number of causes: "(1) the general aging of the American population, which is reflected inside prisons; (2) new sentencing policies such as 'three strikes,' 'truth in sentencing' and 'mandatory minimum' laws that send more criminals to prison for longer stretches; (3) a massive prison building boom that took place in the 1980s and 1990s, and which has provided space for more inmates, reducing the need to release prisoners to alleviate overcrowding; and (4) significant changes in parole philosophies and practices,"[175] with state and federal authorities phasing out or canceling parole programs, thereby forcing jailers to hold inmates with life sentences until they die.

Elderly inmates inside the geriatric unit of Texas's Estelle Prison. Geriatric inmates are becoming an increasingly large part of the inmate population.
Andrew Lichtenstein, The Image Works

Long-termers and geriatric inmates have special needs. They tend to suffer from handicaps, physical impairments, and illnesses not generally encountered among their more youthful counterparts. Unfortunately, few prisons are equipped to deal adequately with the medical needs of aging offenders. Some large facilities have begun to set aside special sections to care for elderly inmates with "typical" disorders, such as Alzheimer's disease, cancer, or heart disease. Unfortunately, such efforts have barely kept pace with the problems that geriatric offenders present. The number of inmates requiring round-the-clock care is expected to increase dramatically over the next two decades.[176]

Even the idea of rehabilitation takes on a new meaning where geriatric offenders are concerned. What kinds of programs are most useful in providing the older inmate with the tools needed for success on the outside? Which counseling strategies hold the greatest promise for introducing socially acceptable behavior patterns into the long-established lifestyles of elderly offenders about to be released? There are few answers to these questions. Learn about some of

the oldest prisoners in America via **Web Extra! 12–3** at cjbrief.com, and read a letter from William Heirens, who has been locked up for more than 50 years, via **Web Extra! 12–4.**

Mentally Ill Inmates

The mentally ill are another type of inmate with special needs. Some mentally ill inmates are neurotic or have personality problems, which increase tension in prison. Others have serious psychological disorders that may have escaped diagnosis at trial or that did not provide a legal basis for the reduction of criminal responsibility. A fair number of offenders develop psychiatric symptoms while in prison.

Inmates suffering from significant mental illnesses account for a substantial number of those imprisoned. A 2002 lawsuit brought by a New York advocacy group on behalf of mentally ill prisoners in New York's penal institutions put the number of inmates suffering from psychiatric illnesses at 16,000 (out of a total state prison population of 67,000). The suit alleges that problem inmates with psychiatric illnesses are often isolated, exacerbating their condition and resulting in a "cycle of torment" for inmates unable to conform to prison regimens.[177]

In contrast to the allegations made by the lawsuit, a 2000 Bureau of Justice Statistics (BJS) survey of public and private state-level adult correctional facilities (excluding jails) found that 51% of such institutions provide 24-hour mental health care, while 71% provide therapy and counseling by trained mental health professionals as needed.[178] A large majority of prisons distribute psychotropic medications (when such medications are ordered by a physician), and 66% have programs to help released inmates obtain community mental health services. According to the BJS, 13% of state prisoners were receiving some type of mental health therapy at the time of the survey, and 10% were receiving psychotropic medications (including antidepressants, stimulants, sedatives, and tranquilizers).

Unfortunately, few state-run correctional institutions have any substantial capacity for the in-depth psychiatric treatment of inmates who are seriously mentally disturbed. A number of states, however, do operate facilities that specialize in psychiatric confinement of convicted criminals. The BJS reports that state governments throughout the nation operate 12 facilities devoted exclusively to the care of mentally ill inmates and that another 143 prisons report psychiatric confinement as one specialty among other functions that they perform.

As mentioned previously, the U.S. Supreme Court has ruled that mentally ill inmates can be required to take antipsychotic drugs, even against their wishes.[179] A 1999 study by the BJS found that the nation's prisons and jails hold an estimated 283,800 mentally ill inmates (16% of those confined) and that 547,800 such offenders are on probation.[180] The govern-

ment study also found that 40% of mentally ill inmates receive no treatment at all. For more details about the report, visit **Web Extra! 12–5** at cjbrief.com.

Mentally deficient inmates constitute still another group with special needs. Some studies estimate the proportion of mentally deficient inmates at about 10%.[181] Retarded inmates are less likely than other inmates to complete training and rehabilitative programs successfully. They also evidence difficulty in adjusting to the routines of prison life. As a consequence, they are likely to exceed the averages in proportion of sentence served.[182] Only seven states report special facilities or programs for the mentally retarded inmate.[183] Other

CJ Futures

TECHNOCORRECTIONS

The technological forces that have made cell phones ubiquitous are beginning to converge with the forces of law and order to create what some have called *technocorrections*. Members of the correctional establishment—the managers of the jail, prison, probation, and parole systems and their sponsors in elected office—are seeking more cost-effective ways to increase public safety as the number of people under correctional supervision continues to grow. Technocorrections is being defined by a correctional establishment that seeks to take advantage of all the potential offered by the new technologies to reduce the costs of supervising criminal offenders and to minimize the risk they pose to society.

Emerging technologies in three areas will soon be central elements of technocorrections: electronic tracking and location systems, pharmacological treatments, and genetic and neurobiological risk assessments. While these technologies may significantly increase public safety, we must also be mindful of the threats they pose to democratic principles. The critical challenge will be to learn how to take advantage of new technological opportunities applicable to the corrections field while minimizing their threats.

TRACKING AND LOCATION SYSTEMS

Electronic tracking and location systems are the technology perhaps most familiar to correctional practitioners today. Most states use electronic monitoring—either with the older bracelets that communicate through a device connected to telephone lines or with more modern versions based on cellular or satellite tracking. With such technology, correctional officials can continuously track offenders' locations and use that information to supervise their movements. As this technology expands, it will enable correctional officials to define geographic areas from which offenders are prohibited and to furnish tracking devices to potential victims (such as battered spouses). The devices will set "safe zones" that trigger alarms or warning notices when the offender approaches.

Tiny cameras might also be integrated into tracking devices to provide live video of offenders' locations and activities. Miniature electronic devices implanted in the body to signal the location of offenders at all times, to create unique identifiers that trigger alarms, and to monitor key bodily functions that affect unwanted behaviors are under development and are close to becoming reality.[1]

PHARMACOLOGICAL TREATMENTS

Pharmacological breakthroughs—new "wonder drugs" being developed to control behavior in correctional and noncorrectional settings—will also be a part of technocorrections. Correctional officials are already familiar with some of these drugs, which are currently used to treat mentally ill offenders. Yet these drugs could also be used to control mental conditions affecting undesirable behaviors even for offenders who are not mentally ill. Research into the relationship between levels of the neurotransmitter serotonin and violent behavior continues to be refined. Findings to date seem to indicate that people who have low levels of serotonin are more prone than others to impulsive, violent acts, especially when they abuse alcohol.[2] Not long ago, the National Academy of Sciences (NAS) recommended a new emphasis in biomedical research on violence as a means to understand the biological roots of violent behavior.[3] The NAS reports that research findings from animal and human studies "point to several features of the nervous system as promising sites" for discovering reliable biological "markers" for violent behavior and designing preventive therapies.[4]

It is only a matter of time before research findings in this area lead to the development of drugs to control neurobiological processes. These drugs could become correctional tools to manage violent offenders and perhaps even to prevent violence. Such advances are related to the third area of technology that will affect corrections: genetic and neurobiological risk-assessment technologies.

RISK-ASSESSMENT TECHNOLOGIES

Correctional officials today are familiar with the DNA profiling of offenders, particularly sex offenders. This is just the beginning of the correctional application of gene-related technologies, however. The Human Genome Project, supported by the National Institutes of Health and the Department of Energy, should be completed by the time this book goes to press. The goal of the Human Genome Project is creation of a map of the 3 billion chemical bases that make up human DNA. The map is being constructed by high-powered "sequencer" machines that can analyze human DNA faster than any human researcher can.[5] Emerging as a powerhouse of the high-tech economy, the biotechnology industry will drive developments in DNA-based risk assessment.

Gene "management" technologies are already widely used in agriculture and are increasingly used in medicine. The progression is likely to continue with applications in psychiatric and behavioral management. Researchers are investigating the genetic—or inherited—basis of behavior, including antisocial and criminal behavior. Studies of twins, for example, have revealed similarities in behavior attributable to a genetic effect.[6] Eventually, the genetic roots of human behavior could be profiled.

Neurobiological research is taking the same path, although thus far no neurobiological patterns specific enough to be reliable biological markers for violent behavior have been uncovered. Is it possible that breakthroughs in these areas will lead to the development of risk-assessment tools that use genetic or neurobiological profiles to identify children

(continued)

who have a propensity toward addiction or violence? Might they also be capable of identifying individuals with a propensity for sex offending? We may soon be able to link genetic and neurobiological traits with social and environmental factors to reliably predict who is at risk for addiction, sex offending, violent behavior, or crime in general.

Attempts will surely be made to develop genetic or neurobiological tests for assessing risks posed by individuals. This is already done for the risk of contracting certain diseases. Demand for risk assessments of individuals will come from correctional officials under pressure to prevent violent recidivism. Once under correctional control, specific offenders could be identified, on the basis of such testing and risk assessment, as likely violent recidivists. The group so classified could be placed under closer surveillance or declared a danger to themselves and society and be civilly committed to special facilities for indeterminate periods. In other words, incarceration could assume a more preventive role.

"Preventive incarceration" is already a reality for some convicted sex offenders. More than a dozen states commit certain sex offenders to special "civil commitment" facilities after they have served their prison sentences because of a behavioral or mental abnormality that makes them dangerous.[7] This happens today with no clear understanding of the nature of the abnormality. It is not difficult to imagine what might be done to justify preventive incarceration if this "abnormal" or criminal behavior could be explained and predicted by genetic or neurobiological profiling.

SOURCE: Adapted from Tony Fabelo, *"Technocorrections": The Promises, the Uncertain Threats* (Washington, D.C.: National Institute of Justice, 2000).

[1]"Microchip Implants Closer to Reality," *Futurist,* Vol. 33, No. 8 (October 1999), p. 9.

[2]Sheryl Stolberg, "Scientific Studies Are Generating Controversy," *Austin American-Statesman,* January 16, 1994.

[3]Albert J. Reiss, Jr., and Jeffrey A. Roth, eds., *Understanding and Preventing Violence* (Washington, D.C.: National Academy Press, 1993). Reiss and Roth call for "systematic searches for neurobiologic markers for persons with elevated potentials for violent behavior" (p. 24).

[4]Ibid., p. 12. Reiss and Roth caution, however, that "the generalizability of experimental findings from other animal species to humans is not always straightforward" (p. 116).

[5]Walter Isaacson, "The Biotech Century," *Time,* January 11, 1999, p. 42; and Michael D. Lemonick and Dick Thompson, "Racing to Map Our DNA," *Time,* January 11, 1999, p. 44.

[6]G. Carey and D. Goldman, "The Genetics of Antisocial Behavior," in D. M. Stoff et al., eds., *Handbook of Antisocial Behavior* (New York: John Wiley, 1997), pp. 243–254.

[7]See *Kansas* v. *Hendricks,* 521 U.S. 346 (1997), in which the Court approved such a practice. In the case of *Kansas* v. *Crane* (122 S.Ct. 867 [2002]), however, the U.S. Supreme Court ruled that the Constitution does not permit commitment of certain types of dangerous sexual offenders without a "lack-of-control determination."

state systems "mainstream" such inmates, making them participate in regular activities with other inmates.

Texas, one state which does provide special services for retarded inmates, began the Mentally Retarded Offender Program (MROP) in 1984. Inmates in Texas are given a battery of tests that measure intellectual and social adaptability skills, and prisoners who are identified as retarded are housed in special satellite correctional units. The Texas MROP program provides individual and group counseling, along with training in adult life skills.

Learn more about prison issues in general via **Web Extra! 12–6** at cjbrief.com.

Summary

Prisons are small, self-contained societies which are sometimes described as *total institutions*. Studies of prison life have detailed the existence of prison subcultures, or inmate worlds, replete with inmate values, social roles, and lifestyles. New inmates who are socialized into prison subculture are said to undergo the process of prisonization. This involves, among other things, learning the language of prison, commonly called *prison argot*.

Prison subcultures are very influential, and both inmates and staff must reckon with them. Given the large and often densely packed inmate populations which characterize many of today's prisons, prison subcultures are not easily subject to the control of prison authorities. Complicating life behind bars are numerous conflicts of interest between inmates and staff. Lawsuits, riots, violence, and frequent formal grievances are symptoms of such differences.

For many years, courts throughout the nation assumed a "hands-off" approach to prisons, rarely intervening in the day-to-day administration of prison facilities. That changed in the late 1960s, when the U.S. Supreme Court began to identify inmates' rights mandated by the U.S. Constitution. Rights identified by the Court include the right to physical integrity, an absolute right to be free from unwarranted corporal punishments, certain religious rights, and procedural rights, such as those involving access to attorneys and to the courts. The conditional rights of prisoners, which have repeatedly been supported by the U.S. Supreme Court, mandate professionalism among prison administrators and require vigilance in the provision of correctional services. The era of prisoners' rights was sharply curtailed in 1996, with the passage of the Prison Litigation Reform Act, spurred on by a growing recognition of the legal morass resulting from unregulated access to federal courts by inmates across the nation. The legislation, in concert with other restrictions sanctioned by the U.S. Supreme Court, has substantially limited inmate access to federal courts.

Today's prisons are miniature societies, reflecting the problems and challenges which exist in the larger society of which they are a part. HIV-infected inmates, geriatric offenders, and the mentally ill constitute special groups within the inmate population which require additional attention.

DISCUSSION QUESTIONS

1. What are prison subcultures, and how do they influence prison life? How do they develop, and what purpose do they serve?

2. What does *prisonization* mean? Describe the U-shaped curve developed by Stanton Wheeler to illustrate the concept of prisonization.

3. What are the primary concerns of prison staff? Do you agree that those concerns are important? What other goals might staff members focus on?

4. What causes prison riots? Through what stages do most riots progress? How might riots be prevented?

5. What is the hands-off doctrine? What is the status of that doctrine today?

6. What are the commonly accepted rights of prisoners in the United States? Where do these rights come from? What U.S. Supreme Court cases are especially significant in this regard? Do inmates have too many rights? Explain.

7. Explain the balancing test established by the Supreme Court in deciding issues of prisoners' rights. How might such a test apply to the emerging area of inmate privacy?

8. What does the term *state-created rights* mean within the context of corrections? What might be the future of state-created rights?

9. What are some of the special problems that prisons face today? What new problems might the future bring?

To participate in an online discussion on these topics and others, go to the Global Town Meeting electronic message board for Chapter 12 on the *Criminal Justice: A Brief Introduction* Companion Website at cjbrief.com.

WEB QUEST!

Visit the Cybrary, and search for "jobs," "careers," and "employment." What criminal justice–related employment sites can you find? Explore some of the sites you find, and consider the possibility of a career in corrections. Document the sources you used, and list the URLs and the date you accessed each. Then answer these questions:[184]

What is the difference between a job and a career?
What career opportunities are available in corrections?

Why is career planning important? How can you develop an effective career plan?
What is the difference between education and training?
Why are education and training important to building a career in corrections?
What role might professionalism play in building your career?
What traits must you have to achieve your goals and to be successful in a career in corrections?

E-mail your answers to your instructor if asked to do so.

To complete this Web Quest! online, go to the Web Quest! module in Chapter 12 of the *Criminal Justice: A Brief Introduction* Companion Website at cjbrief.com.

LIBRARY EXTRAS!

Library Extra! 12–1   *Prisons Research at the Beginning of the Twenty-first Century* (NIJ, 2001).
Library Extra! 12–2   *Prison Use and Social Control* (NIJ, 2000).
Library Extra! 12–3   *No Escape: Male Rape in U.S. Prisons* (Human Rights Watch, 2001).
Library Extra! 12–4   *Women Offenders: Programming Needs and Promising Approaches* (NIJ, 1998).
Library Extra! 12–5   *Women in Prison* (BJS, current volume).
Library Extra! 12–6   *HIV in Prisons and Jails* (BJS, current volume).
Library Extra! 12–7   *Medical Problems of Inmates* (NIJ, 2001).

To explore these resources online, go to the Library Extras! area of the *Criminal Justice: A Brief Introduction* Companion Website at cjbrief.com. You should also check the author's "Late Picks" online for newly released documents and updated Library Extras! You can find Late Picks at http://cjbrief.com/latepicks.htm.

NOTES

i. Zebulon R. Brockway, *The Ideal of a True Prison System for a State* (1865). Reprinted in the *Journal of Correctional Education,* Vol. 46, No. 2 (1995), pp. 68–74.

1. Web posted at http://www.whitehouse.gov/news/reports/faithbased.html. Accessed November 2, 2001.
2. Hans Reimer, "Socialization in the Prison Community," *Proceedings of the American Prison Association, 1937* (New York: American Prison Association, 1937), pp. 151–155.
3. Donald Clemmer, *The Prison Community* (Boston: Holt, Rinehart and Winston, 1940).
4. Gresham M. Sykes, *The Society of Captives: A Study of a Maximum Security Prison* (Princeton, NJ: Princeton University Press, 1958).
5. Richard A. Cloward, Donald R. Cressey, et al., *Theoretical Studies in Social Organization of the Prison* (New York: Social Science Research Council, 1960).
6. Donald R. Cressey, ed., *The Prison: Studies in Institutional Organization and Change* (New York: Holt, Rinehart and Winston, 1961).
7. Lawrence Hazelrigg, ed., *Prison within Society: A Reader in Penology* (Garden City, NY: Anchor, 1969), preface.

8. Charles Stastny and Gabrielle Tyrnauer, *Who Rules the Joint? The Changing Political Culture of Maximum-Security Prisons in America* (Lexington, MA: Lexington Books, 1982), p. 131.
9. Erving Goffman, *Asylums: Essays on the Social Situation of Mental Patients and Other Inmates* (Garden City, NY: Anchor, 1961).
10. For a firsthand account of the prison experience, see Victor Hassine, *Life without Parole: Living in Prison Today* (Los Angeles: Roxbury, 1996); and W. Rideau and R. Wikberg, *Life Sentences: Rage and Survival behind Prison Bars* (New York: Times Books, 1992).
11. The concept of prisonization is generally attributed to Clemmer, *The Prison Community,* although Quaker penologists of the late eighteenth century were actively concerned with preventing "contamination" (the spread of criminal values) among prisoners.
12. Gresham M. Sykes and Sheldon L. Messinger, "The Inmate Social System," in Richard A. Cloward, Donald R. Cressey, et al., *Theoretical Studies in Social Organization of the Prison* (New York: Social Science Research Council, 1960), pp. 5–19.
13. Ibid., p. 5.
14. Stanton Wheeler, "Socialization in Correctional Communities," *American Sociological Review,* Vol. 26 (October 1961), pp. 697–712.

15. Sykes, *The Society of Captives,* p. xiii.
16. Stastny and Tyrnauer, *Who Rules the Joint?* p. 135.
17. Ibid.
18. Ibid.
19. Sykes, *The Society of Captives.*
20. Clemmer, *The Prison Community,* pp. 294–296.
21. John Irwin, *The Felon* (Englewood Cliffs, NJ: Prentice Hall, 1970).
22. Joseph L. Galloway, "Into the Heart of Darkness," *U.S. News* online, March 8, 1999. Web posted at http://www.usnews.com/usnews/issue/990308/8pris.htm. Accessed March 20, 2000.
23. Alan J. Davis, "Sexual Assaults in the Philadelphia Prison System and Sheriff's Vans," *Trans-Action,* Vol. 6 (December 1968), pp. 8–16.
24. Daniel Lockwood, "Sexual Aggression among Male Prisoners," unpublished dissertation (Ann Arbor, MI: University Microfilms International, 1978).
25. Lee H. Bowker, *Prison Victimization* (New York: Elsevier, 1980).
26. Ibid., p. 42.
27. Ibid., p. 1.
28. Hans Toch, *Living in Prison: The Ecology of Survival* (New York: Free Press, 1977), p. 151.
29. Joanne Mariner, *No Escape: Male Rape in U.S. Prisons* (New York: Human Rights Watch, 2001). Web posted at http://www.hrw.org/reports/2001/prison/report.html. Accessed September 23, 2002.
30. Paige M. Harrison and Allen J. Beck, *Prisoners in 2001* (Washington, D.C.: Bureau of Justice Statistics, 2002).
31. Ibid.
32. Some of the information in this section comes from the American Correctional Association, Task Force on the Female Offender, *The Female Offender: What Does the Future Hold?* (Washington, D.C.: St. Mary's Press, 1990); and "The View from behind Bars," *Time* (fall 1990, special issue), pp. 20–22.
33. Merry Morash, Timothy S. Bynum, and Barbara A. Koons, *Women Offenders: Programming Needs and Promising Approaches,* NIJ Research in Brief (Washington, D.C.: National Institute of Justice, 1998).
34. ACA, *The Female Offender.*
35. B. Keith Crew, "Sex Differences in Criminal Sentencing: Chivalry or Patriarchy?" *Justice Quarterly,* Vol. 8, No. 1 (March 1991), pp. 59–83.
36. ACA, *The Female Offender.*
37. Ibid.
38. Mary Jeanette Clement, "National Survey of Programs for Incarcerated Women," paper presented at the annual meeting of the Academy of Criminal Justice Sciences, Nashville, Tennessee, March 1991.
39. Mary K. Shilton, *Resources for Mother-Child Community Corrections* (Washington, D.C.: Bureau of Justice Assistance, 2001), p. 3.
40. Ibid.
41. Clement, "National Survey of Programs for Incarcerated Women," pp. 8–9.
42. Marsha Clowers, "Dykes, Gangs, and Danger: Debunking Popular Myths about Maximum Security Life," *Journal of Criminal Justice and Popular Culture,* Vol. 9, No. 1 (2001), pp. 22–30.
43. D. Ward and G. Kassebaum, *Women's Prison: Sex and Social Structure* (London: Weidenfeld and Nicolson, 1966).
44. Esther Heffernan, *Making It in Prison: The Square, the Cool, and the Life* (London: Wiley-Interscience, 1972).
45. Rose Giallombardo, *Society of Women: A Study of Women's Prisons* (New York: John Wiley, 1966).
46. Ibid., p. 136.
47. For a summary of such studies (including some previously unpublished), see Lee H. Bowker, *Prisoner Subcultures* (Lexington, MA: Lexington Books, 1977), p. 86.
48. Giallombardo, *Society of Women,* p. 162.
49. Mary Koscheski and Christopher Hensley, "Inmate Homosexual Behavior in a Southern Female Correctional Facility," *American Journal of Criminal Justice,* Vol. 25, No. 2 (2001), pp. 269–277.
50. See, for example, Margie J. Phelps, "Sexual Misconduct between Staff and Inmates," *Corrections Technology and Management,* Vol. 12 (1999).
51. Heffernan, *Making It in Prison.*
52. Bowker, *Prison Victimization,* p. 53.
53. Giallombardo, *Society of Women.*
54. "Georgia Indictments Charge Abuse of Female Inmates," *USA Today,* November 16, 1992, p. 3A.
55. Ibid.
56. ACA, *The Female Offender,* p. 39.
57. American Correctional Association, "Correctional Officers in Adult Systems," in *Vital Statistics in Corrections* (Laurel, MD: ACA, 2000).
58. Sidra Lea Gifford, *Justice Expenditure and Employment in the United States, 1999* (Washington, D.C.: BJS, 2002), p. 8.
59. Ibid. "Other" minorities round out the percentages to a total of 100%.
60. Ibid.
61. ACA, "Correctional Officers in Adult Systems."
62. Lucien X. Lombardo, *Guards Imprisoned: Correctional Officers at Work* (New York: Elsevier, 1981), pp. 22–36.
63. Leonard Morgenbesser, "NY State Law Prescribes Psychological Screening for CO Job Applicants," *Correctional Training* (winter 1983), p. 1.
64. "A Sophisticated Approach to Training Prison Guards," *Newsday,* August 12, 1982.
65. Stastny and Tyrnauer, *Who Rules the Joint?* p. 1.
66. See Frederick Talbott, "Reporting from behind the Walls: Do It before the Siren Wails," *The Quill* (February 1988), pp. 16–21.
67. "Ohio Prison Rebellion Is Ended," *USA Today,* April 22, 1993, p. 2A.
68. "Guards Hurt in Prison Riot," Associated Press wire service, November 11, 2000.
69. Office of the Attorney General, *Report of the Attorney General on the February 2 and 3, 1980, Riot at the Penitentiary of New Mexico* (two parts) (Santa Fe, NM: Office of the Attorney General, June and September 1980).
70. See, for example, American Correctional Association, *Riots and Disturbances in Correctional Institutions* (College Park, MD: ACA, 1981); Michael Braswell et al., *Prison Violence in America* (Cincinnati: Anderson, 1985); and R. Conant, "Rioting, Insurrectional and Civil Disorderliness," *American Scholar,* Vol. 37 (summer 1968), pp. 420–433.

71. Robert S. Fong, Ronald E. Vogel, and S. Buentello, "Prison Gang Dynamics: A Look Inside the Texas Department of Corrections," in A. V. Merlo and P. Menekos, eds., *Dilemmas and Directions in Corrections* (Cincinnati: Anderson, 1992).

72. Ibid.

73. *Ruiz* v. *Estelle*, 503 F.Supp. 1265 (S.D. Texas, 1980).

74. Vernon Fox, "Prison Riots in a Democratic Society," *Police*, Vol. 26, No. 12 (December 1982), pp. 35–41.

75. Donald R. Cressey, "Adult Felons in Prison," in Lloyd E. Ohlin, ed., *Prisoners in America* (Englewood Cliffs, NJ: Prentice Hall, 1972), pp. 117–150.

76. The facts in this story are taken from *Hope* v. *Pelzer*, No. 01-309 (U.S. Supreme Court, decided June 27, 2002).

77. "Convictions Bar 3.9 Million from Voting," Associated Press wire service, September 22, 2000.

78. *Holt* v. *Sarver*, 309 F.Supp. 362 (E.D. Ark. 1970).

79. Vergil L. Williams, *Dictionary of American Penology: An Introduction* (Westport, CT: Greenwood, 1979), pp. 6–7.

80. *Pell* v. *Procunier*, 417 U.S. 817, 822 (1974).

81. Ibid.

82. Title 42 U.S.C.A. 1997, Public Law 104-150.

83. Section 1997e.

84. American Correctional Association, *Legal Responsibility and Authority of Correctional Officers: A Handbook on Courts, Judicial Decisions and Constitutional Requirements* (College Park, MD: ACA, 1987), p. 8.

85. *Procunier* v. *Martinez*, 416 U.S. 396 (1974).

86. *McNamara* v. *Moody*, 606 F.2d 621 (5th Cir. 1979).

87. *Luparar* v. *Stoneman*, 382 F.Supp. 495 (D. Vt. 1974).

88. *Mallery* v. *Lewis*, 106 Idaho 227 (1983).

89. See, for example, *Pepperling* v. *Crist*, 678 F.2d 787 (9th Cir. 1981).

90. *Cruz* v. *Beto*, 405 U.S. 319 (1972).

91. *Aziz* v. *LeFevre*, 642 F.2d 1109 (2d Cir. 1981).

92. *Glasshofer* v. *Thornburg*, 514 F.Supp. 1242 (E.D. Pa. 1981).

93. See, for example, *Smith* v. *Coughlin*, 748 F.2d 783 (2d Cir. 1984).

94. *Campbell* v. *Cauthron*, 623 F.2d 503 (8th Cir. 1980).

95. *Smith* v. *Blackledge*, 451 F.2d 1201 (4th Cir. 1971).

96. *Dettmer* v. *Landon*, 617 F.Supp. 592, 594 (D.C. Va. 1985).

97. *Dettmer* v. *Landon*, 799 F.2d 929 (4th Cir. 1986).

98. *Lewellyn (L'Aquarius)* v. *State*, 592 P.2d 538 (Okla. Crim. App. 1979).

99. *Hill* v. *Blackwell*, 774 F.2d 338, 347 (8th Cir. 1985).

100. *Block* v. *Rutherford*, 486 U.S. 576 (1984).

101. *Pell* v. *Procunier*, 417 U.S. 817, 822 (1974).

102. *Houchins* v. *KQED, Inc.*, 438 U.S. 11 (1978).

103. Ibid.

104. For a Supreme Court review of the First Amendment right to petition the courts, see *McDonald* v. *Smith*, 105 S.Ct. 2787 (1985).

105. *Bounds* v. *Smith*, 430 U.S. 817, 821 (1977).

106. *Lewis* v. *Casey*, 516 U.S. 804 (1996).

107. *Johnson* v. *Avery*, 393 U.S. 483 (1968).

108. *Bounds* v. *Smith*, 430 U.S. 817, 821 (1977).

109. *Taylor* v. *Sterrett*, 532 F.2d 462 (5th Cir. 1976).

110. *In re Harrell*, 87 Cal. Rptr. 504, 470 P.2d 640 (1970).

111. *Guajardo* v. *Estelle*, 432 F.Supp. 1373 (S.D. Texas, 1977).

112. *O'Brien* v. *U.S.*, 386 U.S. 345 (1967); and *Weatherford* v. *Bursey*, 429 U.S. 545 (1977).

113. *U.S.* v. *Gouveia*, 104 S.Ct. 2292, 81 L.Ed. 2d 146 (1984).

114. *Estelle* v. *Gamble*, 429 U.S. 97 (1976).

115. Ibid., pp. 105–106.

116. *Hudson* v. *McMillan*, 503 U.S. 1 (1992).

117. *Farmer* v. *Brennan*, 114 S.Ct. 1970, 128 L.Ed. 2d 811 (1994).

118. Ibid.

119. *Ruiz* v. *Estelle*, 679 F.2d 1115 (5th Cir. 1982).

120. *Newman* v. *Alabama*, 349 F.Supp. 278 (M.D. Ala. 1972).

121. Adapted from ACA, *Legal Responsibility and Authority of Correctional Officers*, pp. 25–26.

122. *In re Caulk*, 35 CrL 2532 (New Hampshire S.Ct. 1984).

123. Ibid.

124. *Bee* v. *Greaves*, 744 F.2d. 1387 (10th Cir. 1984).

125. *Washington* v. *Harper*, 494 U.S. 210 (1990).

126. *Helling* v. *McKinney*, 113 S.Ct. 2475, 125 L.Ed. 2d 22 (1993).

127. *Pennsylvania Department of Corrections* v. *Yeskey*, 524 U.S. 206, 209 (1998).

128. 42 U.S.C. § 12132.

129. *U.S.* v. *Ready*, 574 F.2d 1009 (10th Cir. 1978).

130. *Katz* v. *U.S.*, 389 U.S. 347, 88 S.Ct. 507, 19 L.Ed. 2d 576 (1967).

131. *Hudson* v. *Palmer*, 468 U.S. 517 (1984).

132. *Block* v. *Rutherford*, 104 S.Ct. 3227, 3234–35 (1984).

133. *U.S.* v. *Lilly*, 576 F.2d 1240 (5th Cir. 1978).

134. *Palmer* v. *Hudson*, 697 F.2d 1220 (4th Cir. 1983).

135. *Jones* v. *North Carolina Prisoners' Labor Union*, 433 U.S. 119, 53 L.Ed. 2d 629, 641 (1977).

136. *Wolff* v. *McDonnell*, 94 S.Ct. 2963 (1974).

137. Ibid.

138. Ibid.

139. *Ponte* v. *Real*, 471 U.S. 491, 105 S.Ct. 2192, 85 L.Ed. 2d 553 (1985).

140. *Vitek* v. *Jones*, 445 U.S. 480 (1980).

141. American Correctional Association, Standard 2-4346. See ACA, *Legal Responsibility and Authority of Correctional Officers*, p. 49.

142. *Wilson* v. *Seiter*, 501 U.S. 294 (1991).

143. *Estelle* v. *Gamble*, 429 U.S. 97, 106 (1976).

144. *Sandin* v. *Conner*, 63 U.S.L.W. 4601 (1995).

145. *Wolff* v. *McDonnell*, 94 S.Ct. 2963 (1974).

146. *Hewitt* v. *Helms*, 459 U.S. 460 (1983).

147. Laurie Asseo, "Inmate Lawsuits," Associated Press wire service, May 24, 1996; and Bureau of Justice Statistics, "State and Federal Prisoners Filed 68,235 Petitions in U.S. Courts in 1996," press release, October 29, 1997.

148. See, for example, "The Great Prison Pastime," *20/20*, ABC News, September 24, 1993, which is part of the video library available to instructors using this textbook.

149. Ibid.

150. Asseo, "Inmate Lawsuits."

151. Public Law 104-134. Although the PLRA was signed into law on April 26, 1996, and is fre-

quently referred to as the Prison Litigation Reform Act of 1996, the official name of the act is the Prison Litigation Reform Act of 1995.

152. *Edwards* v. *Balisok,* 520 U.S. 641 (1997).
153. American Civil Liberties Union, *Prisoners' Rights—An ACLU Position Paper,* fall 1999. Web posted at http://www.aclu.org/library/PrisonerRights.pdf. Accessed March 5, 2002.
154. *Booth* v. *Churner,* U.S. Supreme Court, No. 99-1964 (decided May 29, 2001).
155. *Porter* v. *Nussle,* 534 U.S. 516 (2002).
156. John Scalia, *Prisoner Petitions Filed in U.S. District Courts, 2000, with Trends 1980-2000* (Washington, D.C.: Bureau of Justice Statistics, 2002).
157. American Civil Liberties Union, *Prisoners' Rights.*
158. Laura M. Maruschak, *HIV in Prisons and Jails, 1999* (Washington, D.C.: Bureau of Justice Statistics, 2001).
159. Ibid.
160. Ibid.
161. Ibid., p. 4.
162. Dennis Cauchon, "AIDS in Prison: Locked Up and Locked Out," *USA Today,* March 31, 1995, p. 6A.
163. Maruschak, *HIV in Prisons and Jails, 1999,* p. 5.
164. Theodore M. Hammett, *AIDS in Correctional Facilities: Issues and Options,* 3d ed. (Washington, D.C.: National Institute of Justice, 1988), p. 37.
165. At the time of this writing, California, Massachusetts, New York, Wisconsin, and the District of Columbia were among those jurisdictions.
166. "Mississippi Eases Policy of Separating Inmates with HIV," *Corrections Journal,* Vol. 5, No. 6 (2001), p. 5.
167. Cauchon, "AIDS in Prison."
168. See "Court Allows Restriction on HIV-Positive Inmates," in *Criminal Justice Newsletter,* Vol. 25, No. 23 (December 1, 1994), pp. 2–3.
169. Ibid.
170. Darrell Bryan, "Inmates, HIV, and the Constitutional Right to Privacy: AIDS in Prison Facilities," *Corrections Compendium,* Vol. 19, No. 9 (September 1994), pp. 1–3.
171. Lincoln J. Fry, "The Older Prison Inmate: A Profile," *Justice Professional,* Vol. 2, No. 1 (spring 1987), pp. 1–12.

172. Harrison and Beck, *Prisoners in 2001.*
173. See, for example, Georgette Bennett, *Crimewarps* (New York: Random House, 1989), p. 61.
174. Bureau of Justice Statistics, "The Nation's Prison Population Grew by 60,000 Inmates Last Year," press release, August 15, 1999.
175. Jim Krane, "Demographic Revolution Rocks U.S. Prisons," APB Online, April 12, 1999. Web posted at http://www.apbonline.com/safestreets/oldprisoners/mainpris0412.html. Accessed January 5, 2000.
176. Ronald Wikbert and Burk Foster, "The Longtermers: Louisiana's Longest Serving Inmates and Why They've Stayed So Long," paper presented at the annual meeting of the Academy of Criminal Justice Sciences, Washington, D.C., 1989, p. 51.
177. *Disability Advocates, Inc.* v. *New York State Office of Mental Health,* filed in Federal District Court (NY 2002).
178. Allen J. Beck and Laura M. Maruschak, *Mental Health Treatment in State Prisons, 2000,* BJS Special Report (Washington, D.C.: Bureau of Justice Statistics, 2001), p. 1, from which most of the information in this paragraph and the next is derived.
179. *Washington* v. *Harper,* 494 U.S. 210 (1990).
180. Paula M. Ditton, *Mental Health and Treatment of Inmates and Probationers* (Washington, D.C.: Bureau of Justice Statistics, 1999).
181. Robert O. Lampert, "The Mentally Retarded Offender in Prison," *Justice Professional,* Vol. 2, No. 1 (spring 1987), p. 61.
182. Ibid., p. 64.
183. George C. Denkowski and Kathryn M. Denkowski, "The Mentally Retarded Offender in the State Prison System: Identification, Prevalence, Adjustment, and Rehabilitation, "*Criminal Justice and Behavior,* Vol. 12 (1985), pp. 55–75.
184. The questions in this Web Quest! were adapted from "Building Your Career in Corrections," *Keeper's Voice,* Vol. 18, No. 1. Web posted at http://www.oict.org/public/toc.efm?series-KV. Accessed February 20, 2002.

CHECKING YOUR COMPREHENSION

Choose the best answer for each of the following questions.

1. Which of the following would not be elements of a prison subculture?
   a. hierarchy
   b. behavioral patterns
   c. population density
   d. values

2. The "hands off" doctrine essentially held that:
   a. prison administrators were in a better position to determine the rules of incarceration than the courts.
   b. prisoners, upon conviction, forfeited most of their Constitutional rights and suffered "civil death."
   c. incarceration for a felony was a basis for uncontested divorce from spouses.
   d. All of these are consistent with the "hands off" doctrine.

3. Which of the following "prisoner's rights" has not been guaranteed by the courts?
   a. communications
   b. visitation
   c. medical care
   d. access to legal assistance

Identify the following statements as true or false.

4. Wheeler's U-shaped curve as it applies to "prisonization" always includes a stage of revolt.

5. Just like prisoners, correctional officers undergo a socialization process that helps them function by the official and unofficial rules of the prison subculture.

6. The conditional rights of a prisoner are actually privileges which can be withheld by the correctional institution without cause.

Answer the following questions.

7. What are some of the common causes for prison riots? Discuss some of the reforms which may be necessary to curtail the incidents of prison riots in the future.

8. What are some of the issues facing prisons today? Discuss some of the solutions for these issues.

Discussion and Critical Thinking Question

9. Construct an argument either for or against female correctional institutions having facilities for keeping children so their mothers can continue to nurture the bond between a mother and child.

NOTES

3

OHM'S LAW, ENERGY, AND POWER

Georg Simon Ohm (1787–1854) experimentally found that voltage, current, and resistance are all related in a specific way. This basic relationship, known as *Ohm's law,* is one of the most fundamental and important laws in the fields of electricity and electronics. In this chapter, Ohm's law is examined, and its use in practical circuit applications is discussed and demonstrated by numerous examples.

In addition to Ohm's law, the concepts and definitions of energy and power in electric circuits are introduced and the Watt's law power formulas are given. A general approach to troubleshooting using the analysis, planning, and measurement (APM) method is also introduced.

CHAPTER OUTLINE

CHAPTER OBJECTIVES

- Explain Ohm's law
- Use Ohm's law to determine voltage, current, or resistance
- Define *energy* and *power*
- Calculate power in a circuit
- Properly select resistors based on power consideration
- Explain energy conversion and voltage drop
- Discuss power supplies and their characteristics
- Describe a basic approach to troubleshooting

KEY TERMS

- Ohm's law
- Linear
- Energy
- Power
- Joule (J)
- Watt (W)
- Kilowatt-hour (kWh)
- Watt's law
- Power rating
- Voltage drop
- Ampere-hour rating
- Efficiency
- Troubleshooting
- Half-splitting

■ ■ ■ APPLICATION ASSIGNMENT PREVIEW

As a technician working in the engineering development lab of an electronics company, you are assigned the task of modifying an existing test fixture for use in a new application. The test fixture is a resistance box with an array of switch-selectable resistors of various values. Your job will be to determine and specify the changes to be made in the existing circuit and develop a procedure to test the box once the modifications have been made. To complete the assignment, you will

1. Determine color-coded resistor values.
2. Determine resistor power ratings.
3. Draw the schematic of the existing circuit.
4. Draw the schematic to meet the new requirements.
5. Use Watt's law power formulas to determine required power ratings.
6. Use Ohm's law to determine resistor values to meet specifications.

After studying this chapter, you should be able to complete the application assignment.

WWW.   VISIT THE COMPANION WEBSITE
Study Aids for this chapter are available at
http://www.prenhall.com/floyd

3–1   OHM'S LAW

Ohm's law describes mathematically how voltage, current, and resistance in a circuit are related. Ohm's law can be written in three equivalent forms; the formula you use depends on the quantity you need to determine. In this section, you will learn each of these forms.

After completing this section, you should be able to

■ **Explain Ohm's law**

■ Describe how voltage (V), current (I), and resistance (R) are related

■ Express I as a function of V and R

■ Express V as a function of I and R

■ Express R as a function of V and I

Ohm determined experimentally that *if the voltage across a resistor is increased, the current through the resistor will increase; and, likewise, if the voltage is decreased, the current will decrease.* For example, if the voltage is doubled, the current will double. If the voltage is halved, the current will also be halved. This relationship is illustrated in Figure 3–1, with relative meter indications of voltage and current.

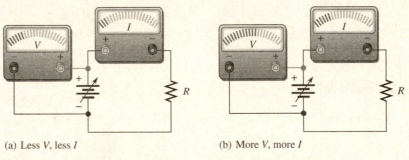

(a) Less V, less I (b) More V, more I

▲ **FIGURE 3–1**

Effect on the current of changing the voltage with the resistance at a constant value.

 Ohm's law also shows that *if the voltage is kept constant, less resistance results in more current, and more resistance results in less current.* For example, if the resistance is halved, the current doubles. If the resistance is doubled, the current is halved. This concept is illustrated by the meter indications in Figure 3–2, where the resistance is increased and the voltage is held constant.

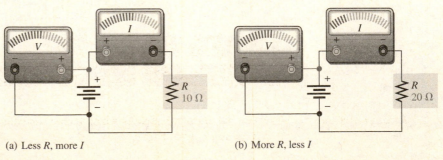

(a) Less R, more I (b) More R, less I

▲ **FIGURE 3–2**

Effect on the current of changing the resistance with the voltage at a constant value.

Formula for Current

Ohm's law can be stated as follows:

$$I = \frac{V}{R}$$

Equation 3-1

This formula describes the relationship illustrated by the action in the circuits of Figures 3–1 and 3–2.

For a constant resistance, if the voltage applied to a circuit is increased, the current will increase; and if the voltage is decreased, the current will decrease.

$$I = \frac{V}{R}$$

Increase *V, I* increases

$$I = \frac{V}{R}$$

Decrease *V, I* decreases

R constant

For a constant voltage, if the resistance in a circuit is increased, the current will decrease; and if the resistance is decreased, the current will increase.

$$I = \frac{V}{R}$$

Increase *R, I* decreases

$$I = \frac{V}{R}$$

Decrease *R, I* increases

V constant

Using Equation 3–1, you can calculate the current in amperes if you know the values of voltage in volts and resistance in ohms.

EXAMPLE 3-1

Using the Ohm's law formula in Equation 3–1, verify that the current through a 10 Ω resistor increases when the voltage is increased from 5 V to 20 V.

Solution   The following calculations show that the current increases from 0.5 A to 2 A. The calculator sequence for each calculation is also shown, based on the TI-86 set in the ENG mode.

For *V* = 5 V,

$$I = \frac{V}{R} = \frac{5\text{ V}}{10\text{ }\Omega} = \textbf{0.5 A}$$

For *V* = 20 V,

$$I = \frac{V}{R} = \frac{20\text{ V}}{10\text{ }\Omega} = \textbf{2 A}$$

*Related Problem**   Show that the current decreases when the resistance is increased from 5 Ω to 20 Ω and the voltage is a constant 10 V.

---

* Answers are at the end of the chapter.

Formula for Voltage

Ohm's law can also be stated another equivalent way. By multiplying both sides of Equation 3–1 by R and transposing terms, you obtain an equivalent form of Ohm's law, as follows:

Equation 3–2

$$V = IR$$

With this formula, you can calculate voltage in volts if you know the current in amperes and resistance in ohms.

EXAMPLE 3–2

Use the Ohm's law formula in Equation 3–2 to calculate the voltage across a 100 Ω resistor when the current is 2 A.

Solution

$$V = IR = (2 \text{ A})(100 \text{ Ω}) = \mathbf{200 \text{ V}}$$

Related Problem   Find the voltage across a 1.0 kΩ resistor when the current is 1 mA.

Formula for Resistance

There is a third equivalent way to state Ohm's law. By dividing both sides of Equation 3–2 by I and transposing terms, you obtain the following formula:

Equation 3–3

$$R = \frac{V}{I}$$

This form of Ohm's law is used to determine resistance in ohms if you know the values of voltage in volts and current in amperes.

Remember, the three formulas—Equations 3–1, 3–2, and 3–3—are all equivalent. They are simply three different ways of expressing Ohm's law.

EXAMPLE 3–3

Use the Ohm's law formula in Equation 3–3 to calculate the resistance in a circuit when the voltage is 12 V and the current is 0.5 A.

Solution

$$R = \frac{V}{I} = \frac{12 \text{ V}}{0.5 \text{ A}} = \mathbf{24 \text{ Ω}}$$

Related Problem   Find the resistance when the voltage is 9 V and the current is 10 mA.

The Linear Relationship of Current and Voltage

In resistive circuits, current and voltage are linearly proportional. **Linear** means that if one is increased or decreased by a certain percentage, the other will increase or decrease by the same percentage, assuming that the resistance is constant in value. For example, if the voltage across a resistor is tripled, the current will triple. If the voltage is reduced by half, the current will decrease by half.

EXAMPLE 3–4

Show that if the voltage in the circuit of Figure 3–3 is increased to three times its present value, the current will triple in value.

▶ **FIGURE 3–3**

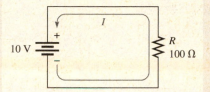

Solution   With 10 V, the current is

$$I = \frac{V}{R} = \frac{10\,V}{100\,\Omega} = 0.1\,A$$

If the voltage is increased to 30 V, the current will be

$$I = \frac{V}{R} = \frac{30\,V}{100\,\Omega} = 0.3\,A$$

The current went from 0.1 A to 0.3 A when the voltage was tripled to 30 V.

Related Problem   If the voltage in Figure 3–3 is quadrupled, will the current also quadruple?

A Graph of Current Versus Voltage

Let's take a constant value of resistance, for example, 10 Ω, and calculate the current for several values of voltage ranging from 10 V to 100 V in the circuit in Figure 3–4(a). The current values obtained are shown in Figure 3–4(b). The graph of the *I* values versus the *V* values is shown in Figure 3–4(c). Note that it is a straight line graph. This graph shows that a change in voltage results in a linearly proportional change in current. No matter what value *R* is, assuming that *R* is constant, the graph of *I* versus *V* will always be a straight line.

▼ **FIGURE 3–4**

Graph of current versus voltage for the circuit in part (a).

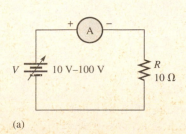

(a)

V	I
10 V	1 A
20 V	2 A
30 V	3 A
40 V	4 A
50 V	5 A
60 V	6 A
70 V	7 A
80 V	8 A
90 V	9 A
100 V	10 A

$$I = \frac{V}{10\,\Omega}$$

(b)

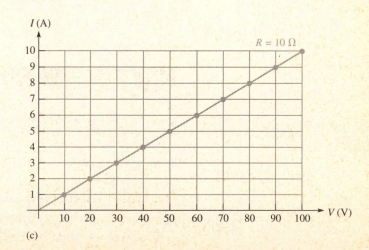

(c)

A Graphic Aid for Ohm's Law

You may find the graphic aid in Figure 3–5 helpful for applying Ohm's law. It is a way to remember the formulas.

▶ FIGURE 3–5

A graphic aid for the Ohm's law formulas.

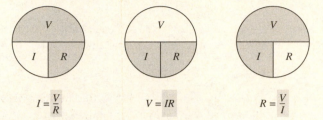

$$I = \frac{V}{R} \qquad V = IR \qquad R = \frac{V}{I}$$

**SECTION 3–1
REVIEW**

Answers are at the end of the chapter.

1. Briefly state Ohm's law in words.

2. Write the Ohm's law formula for calculating current when voltage and resistance are known.

3. Write the Ohm's law formula for calculating voltage when current and resistance are known.

4. Write the Ohm's law formula for calculating resistance when voltage and current are known.

5. If the voltage across a resistor is tripled, does the current increase or decrease? By how much?

6. There is a fixed voltage across a variable resistor, and you measure a current of 10 mA. If you double the resistance, how much current will you measure?

7. What happens to the current in a linear circuit where both the voltage and the resistance are doubled?

3–2 APPLICATION OF OHM'S LAW

This section provides examples of the application of Ohm's law for calculating voltage, current, and resistance in electric circuits. You will also see how to use quantities expressed with metric prefixes in circuit calculations.

After completing this section, you should be able to

■ **Use Ohm's law to determine voltage, current, or resistance**

■ Use Ohm's law to find current when you know voltage and resistance

■ Use Ohm's law to find voltage when you know current and resistance

■ Use Ohm's law to find resistance when you know voltage and current

■ Use quantities with metric prefixes

Determining *I* When You Know *V* and *R*

In these examples you will learn to determine current values when you know the values of voltage and resistance. In these problems, the formula $I = V/R$ is used. In order to get current in amperes, you must express the value of V in volts and the value of R in ohms.

EXAMPLE 3–5

How many amperes of current are in the circuit of Figure 3–6?

▶ FIGURE 3–6

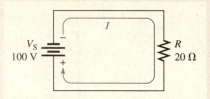

Solution Use the Ohm's law formula $I = V/R$ to find the current. Substitute the values for the source voltage and resistance shown in the figure.

$$I = \frac{V_S}{R} = \frac{100\text{ V}}{20\ \Omega} = 5\text{ A}$$

There are 5 A of current in this circuit.

Related Problem What is the current in Figure 3–6 if the voltage is reduced to 50 V?

Open file E03-05 on your Multisim CD-ROM. Connect the multimeter to the circuit and verify the value of current calculated in this example.

In electronics, resistance values of thousands or millions of ohms are common. As you learned in Chapter 1, large values of resistance are indicated by the metric system prefixes *kilo* (k) and *mega* (M). Thus, thousands of ohms are expressed in kilohms (kΩ), and millions of ohms are expressed in megohms (MΩ). The following examples illustrate how to use kilohms and megohms when you use Ohm's law to calculate current.

EXAMPLE 3–6

Calculate the current in milliamperes for the circuit of Figure 3–7.

▶ FIGURE 3–7

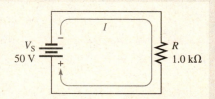

Solution Remember that 1.0 kΩ is the same as $1.0 \times 10^3\ \Omega$. Use the formula $I = V/R$ and substitute 50 V for V and $1.0 \times 10^3\ \Omega$ for R.

$$I = \frac{V_S}{R} = \frac{50\text{ V}}{1.0\text{ k}\Omega} = \frac{50\text{ V}}{1.0 \times 10^3\ \Omega} = 50 \times 10^{-3}\text{ A} = 50\text{ mA}$$

5	0	÷	1	EE	3	ENTER	50/1ᴇ3
							50ᴇ⁻3

Related Problem   If the resistance in Figure 3–7 is increased to 10 kΩ, what is the current?

> Open file E03-06 on your Multisim CD-ROM. Connect the multimeter to the circuit and verify the value of current calculated in this example.

In Example 3–6, the current is expressed as 50 mA. Thus, *when volts (V) are divided by kilohms (kΩ), the current is in milliamperes (mA).*

When volts (V) are divided by megohms (MΩ), the current is in microamperes (μA), as Example 3–7 illustrates.

EXAMPLE 3–7

Determine the amount of current in microamperes for the circuit of Figure 3–8.

▶ **FIGURE 3–8**

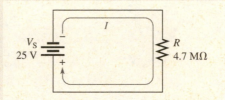

Solution   Recall that 4.7 MΩ equals $4.7 \times 10^6 \, \Omega$. Use the formula $I = V/R$ and substitute 25 V for V and $4.7 \times 10^6 \, \Omega$ for R.

$$I = \frac{V_S}{R} = \frac{25 \text{ V}}{4.7 \text{ M}\Omega} = \frac{25 \text{ V}}{4.7 \times 10^6 \, \Omega} = 5.32 \times 10^{-6} \text{ A} = \mathbf{5.32 \; \mu A}$$

```
25/4.7E6
        5.31914893617E-6
```

Related Problem   If the resistance in Figure 3–8 is decreased to 1.0 MΩ, what is the current?

> Open file E03-07 on your Multisim CD-ROM. Connect the multimeter to the circuit and verify the value of current calculated in this example.

Small voltages, usually less than 50 V, are common in electronic circuits. Occasionally, however, large voltages are encountered. For example, the high-voltage supply in a television receiver is around 20,000 V (20 kV). Transmission voltages generated by the power companies may be as high as 345,000 V (345 kV).

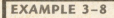

EXAMPLE 3–8

How much current in microamperes is there through a 100 MΩ resistor when 50 kV are applied across it?

Solution Divide 50 kV by 100 MΩ to get the current. Substitute 50×10^3 V for 50 kV and 100×10^6 Ω for 100 MΩ in the formula for current. V_R is the voltage across the resistor.

$$I = \frac{V_R}{R} = \frac{50 \text{ kV}}{100 \text{ M}\Omega} = \frac{50 \times 10^3 \text{ V}}{100 \times 10^6 \text{ }\Omega} = 0.5 \times 10^{-3} \text{ A} = 500 \times 10^{-6} = \textbf{500 } \boldsymbol{\mu}\textbf{A}$$

```
50E3/100E6
      500E-6
```

Related Problem How much current is there through 10 MΩ when 2 kV are applied?

Determining *V* When You Know *I* and *R*

In these examples you will see how to determine voltage values when you know the current and resistance using the formula $V = IR$. To obtain voltage in volts, you must express the value of I in amperes and the value of R in ohms.

EXAMPLE 3–9

In the circuit of Figure 3–9, how much voltage is needed to produce 5 A of current?

▶ FIGURE 3–9

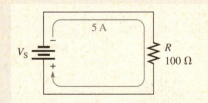

Solution Substitute 5 A for I and 100 Ω for R into the formula $V = IR$.

$$V_S = IR = (5 \text{ A})(100 \text{ }\Omega) = \textbf{500 V}$$

Thus, 500 V are required to produce 5 A of current through a 100 Ω resistor.

Related Problem How much voltage is required to produce 8 A in the circuit of Figure 3–9?

EXAMPLE 3–10

How much voltage will be measured across the resistor in Figure 3–10?

▶ **FIGURE 3–10**

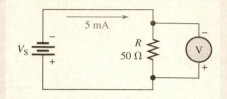

Solution Note that 5 mA equals 5×10^{-3} A. Substitute the values for I and R into the formula $V = IR$.

$$V_R = IR = (5 \text{ mA})(50 \text{ }\Omega) = (5 \times 10^{-3} \text{ A})(50 \text{ }\Omega) = \textbf{250 mV}$$

When milliamperes are multiplied by ohms, the result is millivolts.

Related Problem Change the resistor in Figure 3–10 to 22 Ω and determine the voltage required to produce 10 mA.

EXAMPLE 3–11

The circuit in Figure 3–11 has a current of 10 mA. What is the source voltage?

▶ **FIGURE 3–11**

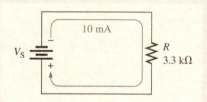

Solution Note that 10 mA equals 10×10^{-3} A and that 3.3 kΩ equals 3.3×10^3 Ω. Substitute these values into the formula $V = IR$.

$$V_S = IR = (10 \text{ mA})(3.3 \text{ k}\Omega) = (10 \times 10^{-3} \text{ A})(3.3 \times 10^3 \text{ }\Omega) = \textbf{33 V}$$

When milliamperes and kilohms are multiplied, the result is volts.

Related Problem What is the voltage in Figure 3–11 if the current is 5 mA?

Determining R When You Know V and I

In these examples you will see how to determine resistance values when you know the voltage and current using the formula $R = V/I$. To find resistance in ohms, you must express the value of V in volts and the value of I in amperes.

EXAMPLE 3–12

In the circuit of Figure 3–12 how much resistance is needed to draw 3 A of current from the battery?

▶ FIGURE 3–12

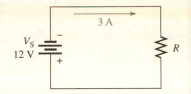

Solution   Substitute 12 V for V and 3 A for I into the formula $R = V/I$.

$$R = \frac{V_S}{I} = \frac{12\ \text{V}}{3\ \text{A}} = \mathbf{4\ \Omega}$$

Related Problem   How much resistance is required to draw 3 mA from the battery in Figure 3–12?

EXAMPLE 3–13

The ammeter in Figure 3–13 indicates 5 mA of current and the voltmeter reads 150 V. What is the value of R?

▶ FIGURE 3–13

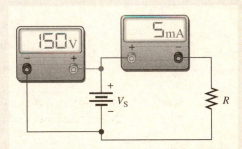

Solution   Note that 5 mA equals 5×10^{-3} A. Substitute the voltage and current values into the formula $R = V/I$.

$$R = \frac{V_S}{I} = \frac{150\ \text{V}}{5\ \text{mA}} = \frac{150\ \text{V}}{5 \times 10^{-3}\ \text{A}} = 30 \times 10^{3}\ \Omega = \mathbf{30\ k\Omega}$$

Thus, if volts are divided by milliamperes, the resistance will be in kilohms.

Related Problem   Determine the value of R if $V_S = 50$ V and $I = 500$ mA in Figure 3–13.

**SECTION 3–2
REVIEW**

1. $V = 10$ V and $R = 4.7 \, \Omega$. Find I.
2. If a 4.7 MΩ resistor has 20 kV across it, how much current is there?
3. How much current will 10 kV across a 2 kΩ resistance produce?
4. $I = 1$ A and $R = 10 \, \Omega$. Find V.
5. What voltage do you need to produce 3 mA of current in a 3 kΩ resistance?
6. A battery produces 2 A of current into a 6 Ω resistive load. What is the battery voltage?
7. $V = 10$ V and $I = 2$ A. Find R.
8. In a stereo amplifier circuit there is a resistor across which you measure 25 V, and your ammeter indicates 50 mA of current through the resistor. What is the resistor's value in kilohms? In ohms?

3–3   ENERGY AND POWER

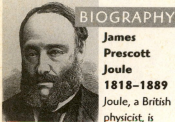

BIOGRAPHY

**James Prescott Joule
1818–1889**

Joule, a British physicist, is known for his research in electricity and thermodynamics. He formulated the relationship that states that the amount of heat energy produced by an electrical current in a conductor is proportional to the conductor's resistance and the time. The unit of energy is named in his honor. (Photo credit: Library of Congress.)

When there is current through a resistance, electrical energy is converted to heat or other form of energy, such as light. A common example of this is a light bulb that becomes too hot to touch. The current through the filament that produces light also produces unwanted heat because the filament has resistance. Power is a measure of how fast energy is being used; electrical components must be able to dissipate a certain amount of energy in a given period of time.

After completing this section, you should be able to

■ **Define energy and power**

■ Express power in terms of energy

■ State the unit of power

■ State the common units of energy

■ Perform energy and power calculations

■ **Energy is the ability to do work.**

■ **Power is the rate at which energy is used.**

In other words, power, symbolized by P, is a certain amount of energy, symbolized by W, used in a certain length of time (t), expressed as follows:

Equation 3–4

$$P = \frac{W}{t}$$

Energy is measured in **joules (J),** time is measured in seconds (s), and power is measured in watts (W). Note that an italic W is used to represent energy in the form of work and a nonitalic W is used for watts, the unit of power.

Energy in joules divided by time in seconds gives power in watts. For example, if 50 J of energy are used in 2 s, the power is 50 J/2 s = 25 W. By definition,

One watt is the amount of power when one joule of energy is used in one second.

Thus, the number of joules used in 1 s is always equal to the number of watts. For example, if 75 J are used in 1 s, the power is $P = W/t = 75$ J/1 s = 75 W.

EXAMPLE 3–14

An amount of energy equal to 100 J is used in 5 s. What is the power in watts?

Solution

$$P = \frac{\text{energy}}{\text{time}} = \frac{W}{t} = \frac{100 \text{ J}}{5 \text{ s}} = \textbf{20 W}$$

Related Problem   If 100 W of power occurs for 30 s, how much energy in joules is used?

Amounts of power much less than one watt are common in certain areas of electronics. As with small current and voltage values, metric prefixes are used to designate small amounts of power. Thus, milliwatts (mW) and microwatts (μW) are commonly found in some applications.

In the electrical utilities field, kilowatts (kW) and megawatts (MW) are common units. Radio and television stations also use large amounts of power to transmit signals. Electric motors are commonly rated in horsepower (hp) where 1 hp = 746 W.

EXAMPLE 3–15

Express the following powers using appropriate metric prefixes:

(a) 0.045 W   (b) 0.000012 W

(c) 3500 W   (d) 10,000,000 W

Solution   (a) $0.045 \text{ W} = 45 \times 10^{-3} \text{ W} = \textbf{45 mW}$

(b) $0.000012 \text{ W} = 12 \times 10^{-6} \text{ W} = \textbf{12 } \boldsymbol{\mu}\textbf{W}$

(c) $3500 \text{ W} = 3.5 \times 10^{3} \text{ W} = \textbf{3.5 kW}$

(d) $10,000,000 \text{ W} = 10 \times 10^{6} \text{ W} = \textbf{10 MW}$

Related Problem   Express the following amounts of power in watts without metric prefixes:

(a) 1 mW   (b) 1800 μW   (c) 3 MW   (d) 10 kW

The Kilowatt-hour (kWh) Unit of Energy

Since power is the rate at which energy is used, power utilized over a period of time represents energy consumption. If you multiply power in watts and time in seconds, you have energy in joules, symbolized by *W*.

$$W = Pt$$

Equation 3–5

The joule has been defined as the unit of energy. However, there is another way to express energy. Since power is expressed in watts and time can be expressed in hours, a unit of energy called the kilowatt-hour (kWh) can be used.

When you pay your electric bill, you are charged on the basis of the amount of energy you use. Because power companies deal in huge amounts of energy, the most practical unit is the **kilowatt-hour.** *You use a kilowatt-hour of energy when you use the equivalent of* *1000 W of power for 1 h.* For example, a 100 W light bulb burning for 10 h uses 1 kWh of energy.

$$W = Pt = (100 \text{ W})(10 \text{ h}) = 1000 \text{ Wh} = 1 \text{ kWh}$$

EXAMPLE 3–16

Determine the number of kilowatt-hours (kWh) for each of the following energy consumptions:

(a) 1400 W for 1 hr   (b) 2500 W for 2 h   (c) 100,000 W for 5 h

Solution

(a) 1400 W = 1.4 kW
$$W = Pt = (1.4 \text{ kW})(1 \text{ h}) = \textbf{1.4 kWh}$$

(b) 2500 W = 2.5 kW
$$\text{Energy} = (2.5 \text{ kW})(2 \text{ h}) = \textbf{5 kWh}$$

(c) 100,000 W = 100 kW
$$\text{Energy} = (100 \text{ kW})(5 \text{ h}) = \textbf{500 kWh}$$

Related Problem   How many kilowatt-hours of energy are used by a 250 W light bulb burning for 8 h?

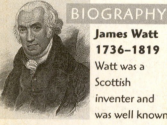

BIOGRAPHY

**James Watt
1736–1819**

Watt was a Scottish inventer and was well known for his improvements to the steam engine, which made it practical for industrial use. Watt patented several inventions, including the rotary engine. The unit of power is named in his honor. (Photo credit: Library of Congress.)

Table 3–1 lists the typical power rating in watts for several household appliances. You can determine the maximum kWh for various appliances by using the power rating in Table 3–1 converted to kilowatts times the number of hours it is used.

▶ TABLE 3–1

APPLIANCE	POWER RATING (WATTS)
Air conditioner	860
Blow dryer	1300
Clock	2
Clothes dryer	4800
Dishwasher	1200
Heater	1322
Microwave oven	800
Range	12,200
Refrigerator	1800
Television	250
Washing machine	400
Water heater	2500

EXAMPLE 3–17

During a typical 24-hour period, you use the following appliances for the specified lengths of time:

air conditioner: 15 hours   microwave oven: 15 minutes

blow dryer: 10 minutes   refrigerator: 12 hours

clock: 24 hours   television: 2 hours

clothes dryer: 1 hour   water heater: 8 hours

dishwasher: 45 minutes

Determine the total kilowatt-hours and the electric bill for the time period. The rate is 10 cents per kilowatt-hour.

Solution Determine the kWh for each appliance used by converting the watts in Table 3–1 to kilowatts and multiplying by the time in hours:

air conditioner: $0.860 \text{ kW} \times 15 \text{ h} = 12.9 \text{ kWh}$

blow dryer: $1.3 \text{ kW} \times 0.167 \text{ h} = 0.217 \text{ kWh}$

clock: $0.002 \text{ kW} \times 24 \text{ h} = 0.048 \text{ kWh}$

clothes dryer: $4.8 \text{ kW} \times 1 \text{ h} = 4.8 \text{ kWh}$

dishwasher: $1.2 \text{ kW} \times 0.75 \text{ h} = 0.9 \text{ kWh}$

microwave: $0.8 \text{ kW} \times 0.25 \text{ h} = 0.2 \text{ kWh}$

refrigerator: $1.8 \text{ kW} \times 12 \text{ h} = 21.6 \text{ kWh}$

television: $0.25 \text{ kW} \times 2 \text{ h} = 0.5 \text{ kWh}$

water heater: $2.5 \text{ kW} \times 8 \text{ h} = 20 \text{ kWh}$

Now, add up all the kilowatt-hours to get the total energy for the 24-hour period.

Total energy $= (12.9 + 0.217 + 0.048 + 4.8 + 0.9 + 0.2 + 21.6 + 0.5 + 20) \text{ kWh}$
$= \textbf{61.165 kWh}$

At 10 cents/kilowatt-hour, the cost of energy to run the appliances for the 24-hour period is

Energy cost $= 61.165 \text{ kWh} \times 0.1 \text{ \$/kWh} = \textbf{\$6.12}$

Related Problem In addition to the appliances, suppose you used two 100 W light bulbs for 2 hours and one 75 W bulb for 3 hours. Calculate your cost for the 24-hour period for both appliances and lights.

SECTION 3–3 REVIEW

1. Define *power*.
2. Write the formula for power in terms of energy and time.
3. Define *watt*.
4. Express each of the following values of power in the most appropriate units:
   (a) 68,000 W   (b) 0.005 W   (c) 0.000025 W
5. If you use 100 W of power for 10 h, how much energy (in kilowatt–hours) have you used?
6. Convert 2000 W to kilowatts.
7. How much does it cost to run a heater (1322 W) for 24 hours if energy cost is 9¢ per kilowatt-hour?

3–4 POWER IN AN ELECTRIC CIRCUIT

The generation of heat, which occurs when electrical energy is converted to heat energy, in an electric circuit is often an unwanted by-product of current through the resistance in the circuit. In some cases, however, the generation of heat is the primary purpose of a circuit as, for example, in an electric resistive heater. In any case, you must always deal with power in electrical and electronic circuits.

After completing this section, you should be able to

■ **Calculate power in a circuit**

■ Determine power when you know I and R

■ Determine power when you know V and I

■ Determine power when you know V and R

▶ **FIGURE 3–14**

Power dissipation in an electric circuit is seen as heat given off by the resistance. The power dissipation is equal to the power produced by the voltage source.

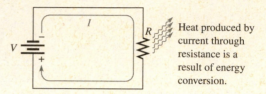

Heat produced by current through resistance is a result of energy conversion.

When there is current through a resistance, the collisions of the electrons as they move through the resistance give off heat, resulting in a conversion of electrical energy to thermal energy as indicated in Figure 3–14. There is always a certain amount of power dissipated in an electrical circuit, and it is dependent on the amount of resistance and on the amount of current, expressed as follows:

Equation 3–6

$$P = I^2R$$

You can get an equivalent expression for power in terms of voltage and current by substituting $I \times I$ for I^2 and V for IR.

$$P = I^2R = (I \times I)R = I(IR) = (IR)I$$

Equation 3–7

$$P = VI$$

where P is in watts when V is in volts and I is in amperes.

You obtain another equivalent expression by substituting V/R for I (Ohm's law).

$$P = VI = V\left(\frac{V}{R}\right)$$

Equation 3–8

$$P = \frac{V^2}{R}$$

 The three power formulas in Equations 3–6, 3–7, and 3–8 are also known as **Watt's law.** An aid for using both Ohm's law and Watt's law is found in the summary, Figure 3–27, at the end of the chapter.

Using the Appropriate Power Formula

To calculate the power in a resistance, you can use any one of the three equivalent Watt's law power formulas, depending on what information you have. For example, assume that you know the values of current and voltage; in this case, calculate the power with the formula $P = VI$. If you know I and R, use the formula $P = I^2R$. If you know V and R, use the formula $P = V^2/R$.

EXAMPLE 3–18

Calculate the power in each of the three circuits of Figure 3–15.

▶ **FIGURE 3–15**

The ground symbols in these diagrams were introduced in Section 2–6.

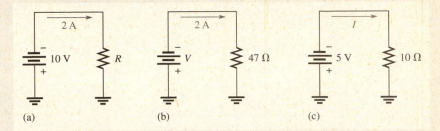

(a)   (b)   (c)

Solution In circuit (a), V and I are known. The power is determined as follows with calculator sequences also shown:

$$P = VI = (10 \text{ V})(2 \text{ A}) = \textbf{20 W}$$

In circuit (b), I and R are known. Therefore,

$$P = I^2R = (2 \text{ A})^2(47 \text{ } \Omega) = 188 \text{ W}$$

In circuit (c), V and R are known. Therefore,

$$P = \frac{V^2}{R} = \frac{(5 \text{ V})^2}{10 \text{ } \Omega} = \textbf{2.5 W}$$

Related Problem Determine the power in each circuit of Figure 3–15 for the following changes: In circuit (a), I is doubled and V remains the same; in circuit (b), R is doubled and I remains the same; in circuit (c), V is halved and R remains the same.

EXAMPLE 3–19

A 100 W light bulb operates on 120 V. How much current does it require?

Solution Use the formula $P = VI$ and solve for I by first transposing the terms to get I on the left side of the equation.

$$VI = P$$

Divide both sides of the equation by V to get I by itself.

$$\frac{\cancel{V}I}{\cancel{V}} = \frac{P}{V}$$

The V's cancel on the left, leaving

$$I = \frac{P}{V}$$

Substitute 100 W for P and 120 V for V.

$$I = \frac{P}{V} = \frac{100 \text{ W}}{120 \text{ V}} = 0.833 \text{ A} = \textbf{833 mA}$$

Related Problem   A light bulb draws 545 mA from a 110 V source. What is the power dissipated?

**SECTION 3–4
REVIEW**

1. If there are 10 V across a resistor and a current of 3 A through it, what is the power dissipated?
2. If there is a current of 5 A through a 47 Ω resistor, what is the power dissipated?
3. How much power is produced by 20 mA through a 5.1 kΩ resistor?
4. Five volts are applied to a 10 Ω resistor. What is the power dissipated?
5. How much power does a 2.2 kΩ resistor with 8 V across it produce?
6. What is the resistance of a 55 W bulb that draws 0.5 A?

3–5   THE POWER RATING OF RESISTORS

As you know, a resistor gives off heat when there is current through it. There is a limit to the amount of heat that a resistor can give off, which is specified by its power rating.

After completing this section, you should be able to

■ **Properly select resistors based on power consideration**

■ Define *power rating*

■ Explain how physical characteristics of resistors determine their power rating

■ Check for resistor failure with an ohmmeter

The **power rating** is the maximum amount of power that a resistor can dissipate without being damaged by excessive heat buildup. The power rating is not related to the ohmic value (resistance) but rather is determined mainly by the physical composition, size, and shape of the resistor. All else being equal, the larger the surface area of a resistor, the more power it can dissipate. *The surface area of a cylindrically shaped resistor is equal to the length (l) times the circumference (c)*, as indicated in Figure 3–16. The area of the ends is not included.

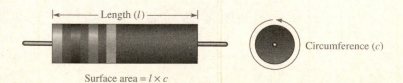

Surface area = $l \times c$

▲ **FIGURE 3–16**

The power rating of a resistor is directly related to its surface area.

Metal-film resistors are available in standard power ratings from ⅛ W to 1 W, as shown in Figure 3–17. Available power ratings for other types of resistors vary. For example, wirewound resistors have ratings up to 225 W or greater. Figure 3–18 shows some of these resistors.

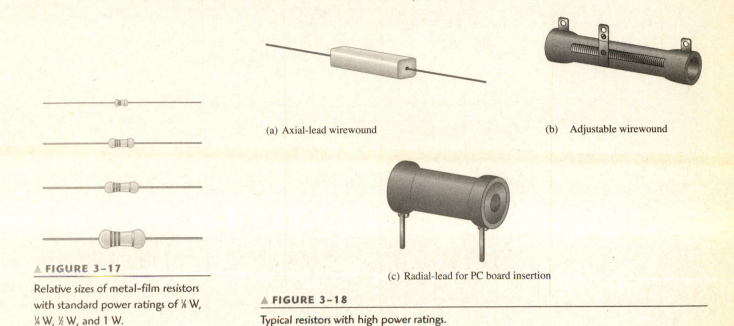

(a) Axial-lead wirewound

(b)   Adjustable wirewound

(c) Radial-lead for PC board insertion

▲ **FIGURE 3–17**

Relative sizes of metal–film resistors with standard power ratings of ⅛ W, ¼ W, ½ W, and 1 W.

▲ **FIGURE 3–18**

Typical resistors with high power ratings.

Selecting the Proper Power Rating for an Application

When a resistor is used in a circuit, its power rating should be greater than the maximum power that it will have to handle. Generally, the next higher standard value is used. For example, if a metal-film resistor is to dissipate 0.75 W in a circuit application, its rating should be the next higher standard value which is 1 W.

EXAMPLE 3–20

Choose an adequate power rating (⅛ W, ¼ W, ½ W, or 1 W) for each of the metal-film resistors represented in Figure 3–19.

▶ **FIGURE 3–19**

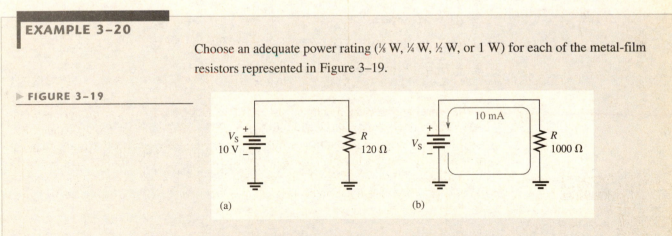

(a)

(b)

Solution   For the circuit in Figure 3–19(a), the actual power is

$$P = \frac{V_S^2}{R} = \frac{(10\text{ V})^2}{120\text{ }\Omega} = \frac{100\text{ V}^2}{120\text{ }\Omega} = 0.833\text{ W}$$

Select a resistor with a power rating higher than the actual power dissipation. In this case, a **1 W resistor** should be used.

For the circuit in Figure 3–19(b), the actual power is

$$P = I^2R = (10 \text{ mA})^2(1000 \text{ }\Omega) = 0.1 \text{ W}$$

A ⅛ W (**0.125 W**) **resistor** should be used in this case.

Related Problem   A certain resistor is required to dissipate 0.25 W (¼ W). What standard rating should be used?

Resistor Failures

When the power dissipated in a resistor is greater than its rating, the resistor will become excessively hot. As a result, either the resistor will burn open or its resistance value will be greatly altered.

A resistor that has been damaged because of overheating can often be detected by the charred or altered appearance of its surface. If there is no visual evidence, a resistor that is suspected of being damaged can be checked with an ohmmeter for an open or increased resistance value. Recall that a resistor should be disconnected from the circuit to measure resistance.

EXAMPLE 3–21

Determine whether the resistor in each circuit of Figure 3–20 has possibly been damaged by overheating.

▶ **FIGURE 3–20**

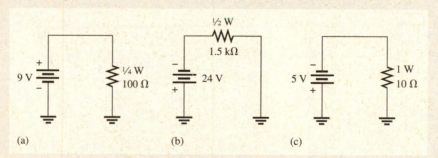

(a)   (b)   (c)

Solution   For the circuit in Figure 3–20(a),

$$P = \frac{V^2}{R} = \frac{(9 \text{ V})^2}{100 \text{ }\Omega} = 0.81 \text{ W}$$

The rating of the resistor is ¼ W (0.25 W), which is insufficient to handle the power. The resistor has been overheated and *may* be burned out, making it an open.

For the circuit in Figure 3–20(b),

$$P = \frac{V^2}{R} = \frac{(24 \text{ V})^2}{1.5 \text{ k}\Omega} = 0.384 \text{ W}$$

The rating of the resistor is ½ W (0.5 W), which is sufficient to handle the power.

For the circuit in Figure 3–20(c),

$$P = \frac{V^2}{R} = \frac{(5 \text{ V})^2}{10 \text{ }\Omega} = 2.5 \text{ W}$$

The rating of the resistor is 1 W, which is insufficient to handle the power. The resistor has been overheated and *may* be burned out, making it an open.

Related Problem A ¼ W, 1.0 kΩ resistor is connected across a 12 V battery. Will it overheat?

Checking a Resistor with an Ohmmeter

A typical digital multimeter and an analog multimeter are shown in Figure 3–21(a) and 3–21(b), respectively. For the digital meter in Figure 3–21(a), you use the round function switch to select ohms (Ω). You do not have to manually select a range because this particular meter is autoranging and you have a direct digital readout of the resistance value. The large round switch on the analog meter is called a *range switch*. Notice the resistance (OHMS) settings on both meters.

For the analog meter in part (b), each setting indicates the amount by which the ohms scale (top scale) on the meter is to be multiplied. For example, if the pointer is at 50 on the ohms scale and the range switch is set at ×10, the resistance being measured is 50 × 10 Ω = 500 Ω. *If the resistor is open, the pointer will stay at full left scale (∞ means infinite) regardless of the range switch setting.*

(a) Digital

(b) Analog

◄ **FIGURE 3–21**

Typical portable multimeters. (Photography courtesy of B&K Precision Corp.)

SECTION 3–5 REVIEW

1. Name two important parameters associated with a resistor.
2. How does the physical size of a resistor determine the amount of power that it can handle?
3. List the standard power ratings of metal-film resistors.
4. A resistor must handle 0.3 W. What standard size metal-film resistor should be used to dissipate the energy properly?
5. If the pointer indicates 8 on the ohmmeter scale and the range switch is set at ×1k, what resistance is being measured?

3-6 ENERGY CONVERSION AND VOLTAGE DROP IN A RESISTANCE

As you have seen, when there is current through a resistance, electrical energy is converted to heat energy. This heat is caused by collisions of the free electrons within the atomic structure of the resistive material. When a collision occurs, heat is given off; and the electron gives up some of its acquired energy as it moves through the material.

After completing this section, you should be able to

■ **Explain energy conversion and voltage drop**

■ Discuss the cause of energy conversion in a circuit

■ Define *voltage drop*

■ Explain the relationship between energy conversion and voltage drop

Figure 3–22 illustrates charge in the form of electrons flowing from the negative terminal of a battery, through a circuit, and back to the positive terminal. As they emerge from the negative terminal, the electrons are at their highest energy level. The electrons flow through each of the resistors that are connected together to form a current path (this type of connection is called series, as you will learn in Chapter 4). As the electrons flow through each resistor, some of their energy is given up in the form of heat. Therefore, the electrons have more energy when they enter a resistor than when they exit the resistor, as illustrated in the figure by the decrease in the intensity of the red color. When they have traveled through the circuit back to the positive terminal of the battery, the electrons are at their lowest energy level.

Recall that voltage equals energy per charge ($V = W/Q$) and that charge is a property of electrons. Based on the voltage of the battery, a certain amount of energy is imparted to all of the electrons that flow out of the negative terminal. The same number of electrons flow at each point throughout the circuit, but their energy decreases as they move through the resistance of the circuit.

In Figure 3–22, the voltage at the left end of R_1 is equal to W_{enter}/Q, and the voltage at the right end of R_1 is equal to W_{exit}/Q. The same number of electrons that enter R_1 also exit R_1, so Q is constant. However, the energy W_{exit} is less than W_{enter}, so the voltage at the right end of R_1 is less than the voltage at the left end. This is a **voltage drop** across the resistor.

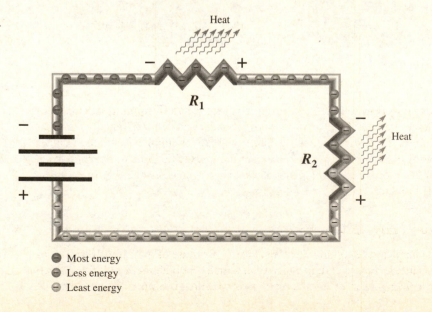

▶ **FIGURE 3–22**

A loss of energy by electrons (charge) as they flow through a resistance creates a voltage drop because voltage equals energy divided by charge.

Heat

R_1

Heat

R_2

● Most energy
● Less energy
● Least energy

The voltage at the right end of R_1 is less negative (or more positive) than the voltage at the left end. So, the voltage drop is indicated by $-$ and $+$ signs (the $+$ implies a less negative or more positive voltage).

The electrons have lost some energy in R_1 and now they enter R_2 with a reduced energy level. As they flow through R_2, they lose more energy, resulting in another voltage drop across R_2.

**SECTION 3–6
REVIEW**

1. What is the basic reason for energy conversion in a resistor?
2. What is a voltage drop?
3. What is the polarity of a voltage drop in relation to current direction?

3–7   POWER SUPPLIES

A power supply is a device that provides power to a load. Recall that a load is any electrical device or circuit that is connected to the output of the power supply and draws current from the supply.

After completing this section, you should be able to

■ **Discuss power supplies and their characteristics**

■ Define *ampere-hour rating*

■ Discuss power supply efficiency

Figure 3–23 shows a block diagram of a power supply with a loading device connected to its output. The load can be anything from a light bulb to a computer. The power supply produces a voltage across its two output terminals and provides current through the load, as indicated in the figure. The product IV_{OUT} is the amount of power produced by the supply and consumed by the load. For a given output voltage (V_{OUT}), more current drawn by the load means more power from the supply.

▶ **FIGURE 3–23**

Block diagram of power supply and load.

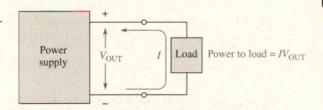

HANDS ON TIP

An electronic power supply provides both output voltage and current. You should make sure the voltage range is sufficient for your applications. Also, you must have sufficient current capacity to assure proper circuit operation. The current capacity is the maximum current that a power supply can provide to a load at a given voltage.

Power supplies range from simple batteries to regulated electronic circuits where an accurate output voltage is automatically maintained. A battery is a dc power supply that converts chemical energy into electrical energy. Electronic power supplies normally convert 110 V ac (alternating current) from a wall outlet into a regulated dc (direct current) voltage at a level suitable for electronic components. A regulated voltage is one that remains essentially constant with changes in input voltage or load.

Ampere-hour Ratings of Batteries

Batteries convert chemical energy into electrical energy. Because of their limited source of chemical energy, batteries have a certain capacity that limits the amount of time over which they can produce a given power level. This capacity is measured in ampere-hours (Ah). The

ampere-hour rating determines the length of time that a battery can deliver a certain amount of current to a load at the rated voltage.

A rating of one ampere-hour means that a battery can deliver one ampere of current to a load for one hour at the rated voltage output. This same battery can deliver two amperes for one-half hour. The more current the battery is required to deliver, the shorter the life of the battery. In practice, a battery usually is rated for a specified current level and output voltage. For example, a 12 V automobile battery may be rated for 70 Ah at 3.5 A. This means that it can supply 3.5 A for 20 h at the rated voltage.

EXAMPLE 3–22

For how many hours can a battery deliver 2 A if it is rated at 70 Ah?

Solution The ampere-hour rating is the current times the number of hours, x.

$$70 \text{ Ah} \times (2 \text{ A})(x \text{ h})$$

Solving for the number of hours, x, yields

$$x = \frac{70 \text{ Ah}}{2 \text{ A}} = \textbf{35 h}$$

Related Problem A certain battery delivers 10 A for 6 h. What is its minimum Ah rating?

Power Supply Efficiency

An important characteristic of electronic power supplies is efficiency. **Efficiency** is the ratio of the output power, P_{OUT}, to the input power, P_{IN}.

Equation 3–9
$$\text{Efficiency} = \frac{P_{OUT}}{P_{IN}}$$

Efficiency is often expressed as a percentage. For example, if the input power is 100 W and the output power is 50 W, the efficiency is $(50 \text{ W}/100 \text{ W}) \times 100\% = 50\%$.

All electronic power supplies are energy converters and require that power be put into them in order to get power out. For example, an electronic dc power supply might use the ac power from a wall outlet as its input. Its output is usually regulated dc voltage. The output power is *always* less than the input power because some of the total power is used internally to operate the power supply circuitry. This internal power dissipation is normally called the *power loss*. The output power is the input power minus the power loss.

Equation 3–10
$$P_{OUT} = P_{IN} - P_{LOSS}$$

High efficiency means that very little power is dissipated in the power supply and there is a higher proportion of output power for a given input power.

EXAMPLE 3–23

A certain electronic power supply requires 25 W of input power. It can produce an output power of 20 W. What is its efficiency, and what is the power loss?

Solution
$$\text{Efficiency} = \left(\frac{P_{OUT}}{P_{IN}}\right)100\% = \left(\frac{20 \text{ W}}{25 \text{ W}}\right)100\% = \textbf{80\%}$$

$$P_{LOSS} = P_{IN} - P_{OUT} = 25 \text{ W} - 20 \text{ W} = \textbf{5 W}$$

Related Problem A power supply has an efficiency of 92%. If P_{IN} is 50 W, what is P_{OUT}?

1. When a loading device draws an increased amount of current from a power supply, does this change represent a greater or a smaller load on the supply?

2. A power supply produces an output voltage of 10 V. If the supply provides 0.5 A to a load, what is the power output?

3. If a battery has an ampere–hour rating of 100 Ah, how long can it provide 5 A to a load?

4. If the battery in Question 3 is a 12 V device, what is its power output for the specified value of current?

5. An electronic power supply used in the lab operates with an input power of 1 W. It can provide an output power of 750 mW. What is its efficiency?

3–8 INTRODUCTION TO TROUBLESHOOTING

Technicians must be able to diagnose and repair malfunctioning circuits and systems. In this section, you learn a general approach to troubleshooting using a simple example. Troubleshooting coverage is an important part of this textbook, so you will find a troubleshooting section in many of the chapters as well as troubleshooting problems for skill building.

After completing this section, you should be able to

- **Describe a basic approach to troubleshooting**
- List three steps in troubleshooting
- Explain what is meant by half-splitting
- Discuss and compare the three basic measurements of voltage, current, and resistance

Troubleshooting is the application of logical thinking combined with a thorough knowledge of circuit or system operation to correct a malfunction. The basic approach to troubleshooting consists of three steps: *analysis, planning,* and *measuring.* We will refer to this 3-step approach as APM.

Analysis

The first step in troubleshooting a circuit is to analyze clues or symptoms of the failure. The analysis can begin by determining the answer to certain questions:

1. Has the circuit ever worked?

2. If the circuit once worked, under what conditions did it fail?

3. What are the symptoms of the failure?

4. What are the possible causes of failure?

Planning

The second step in the troubleshooting process, after analyzing the clues, is formulating a logical plan of attack. Much time can be saved by proper planning. A working knowledge of the circuit is a prerequisite to a plan for troubleshooting. If you are not certain how the circuit is supposed to operate, take time to review circuit diagrams (schematics), operating instructions, and other pertinent information. A schematic with proper voltages marked at various test points is particularly useful. Although logical thinking is perhaps the most important tool in troubleshooting, it rarely can solve the problem by itself.

Measuring

The third step is to narrow the possible failures by making carefully thought out measurements. These measurements usually confirm the direction you are taking in solving the problem, or they may point to a new direction that you should take. Occasionally, you may find a totally unexpected result.

An Example

The thought process that is part of the APM approach is best illustrated with a simple example. Suppose you have a string of 8 decorative lamps connected in series to a 120 V source, as shown in Figure 3–24. Assume that this circuit worked properly at one time but stopped working after it was moved to a new location. When plugged in at the new location, the lamps fail to turn on. How do you go about finding the trouble?

▶ **FIGURE 3–24**

A string of bulbs connected to a voltage source.

The Analysis Thought Process   You may think like this as you proceed to analyze the situation:

- Since the circuit worked before it was moved, the problem could be that there is no voltage at the new location.
- Perhaps the wiring was loose and pulled apart when moved.
- It is possible that a bulb is burned out or loose in its socket.

With this reasoning, you have considered possible causes and failures that may have occurred. The thought process continues:

- The fact that the circuit once worked eliminates the possibility that the original circuit was improperly wired.
- If the fault is due to an open path, it is very unlikely that there is more than one break which could be either a bad connection or a burned out bulb.

You have now analyzed the problem and are ready to plan the process of finding the fault in the circuit.

The Planning Thought Process   The first part of your plan is to measure for voltage at the new location. If the voltage is present, then the problem is in the string of lights. If voltage is not present, check the circuit breaker at the distribution box in the house. Before resetting breakers, you should think about why a breaker may be tripped. Let's assume that you find the voltage is present. This means that the problem is in the string of lights.

The second part of your plan is to measure either the resistance in the string of lights or to measure voltages across the bulbs. The decision whether to measure resistance or voltage is a toss-up and can be made based on the ease of making the test. Seldom is a troubleshooting plan developed so completely that all possible contingencies are included. You will frequently need to modify the plan as you go along.

The Measurement Process   You proceed with the first part of your plan by using a multimeter to check the voltage at the new location. Assume the measurement shows a voltage of 120 V. Now you have eliminated the possibility of no voltage. You know that, since you have voltage across the string and there is no current because no bulb is on, there must be an open in the current path. Either a bulb is burned out, a connection at the lamp socket is broken, or the wire is broken.

Next, you decide to locate the break by measuring resistance with your multimeter. Applying logical thinking, you decide to measure the resistance of each half of the string instead of measuring the resistance of each bulb. By measuring the resistance of half the bulbs at once, you can possibly reduce the effort required to find the open. This technique is a common troubleshooting procedure called **half-splitting**.

Once you have identified the half in which the open occurs, as indicated by an infinite resistance, you use half-splitting again on the faulty half and continue until you narrow the fault down to a faulty bulb or connection. This process is shown in Figure 3–25, assuming for purposes of illustration that the seventh bulb is burned out.

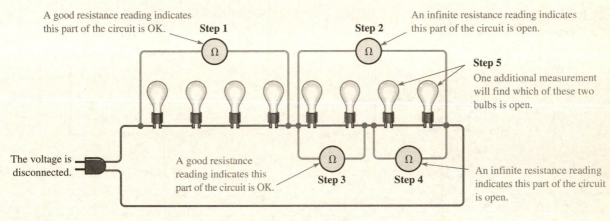

▲ **FIGURE 3–25**

Illustration of the half-splitting troubleshooting process. The numbered steps indicate the sequence in which the multimeter is moved from one position to another.

As you can see in the figure, the half-splitting approach in this particular case takes five measurements to identify the open bulb. If you had decided to measure each bulb individually and had started at the left, you would have needed seven measurements. So, sometimes half-splitting saves steps; sometimes it doesn't. The number of steps required depends on where you make your measurements and in what sequence.

Unfortunately, most troubleshooting is more difficult than this example. However, analysis and planning are essential for effective troubleshooting in any situation. As measurements are made, the plan is often modified; the experienced troubleshooter narrows the search by fitting the symptoms and measurements into a probable cause. In some cases, low-cost equipment is simply discarded when troubleshooting and repair costs are comparable to replacement costs.

Comparison of V, R, and I Measurements

As you know from Section 2–7, you can measure voltage, current, or resistance in a circuit. To measure voltage, place the voltmeter in parallel across the component; that is, place one lead on each side of the component. This makes voltage measurements the easiest of the three types of measurements.

To measure resistance, connect the ohmmeter across a component; however, the voltage must be first disconnected, and sometimes the component itself must be removed from the circuit. Therefore, resistance measurements are generally more difficult than voltage measurements.

To measure current, place the ammeter in series with the component; that is, the ammeter must be in line with the current path. To do this you must disconnect a component lead or a wire before you connect the ammeter. This usually makes a current measurement the most difficult to perform.

APPLICATION ASSIGNMENT

PUTTING YOUR KNOWLEDGE TO WORK

In this assignment, an existing resistance box that is to be used as part of a test setup in the lab is to be checked out and modified. Your task is to modify the circuit so that it will meet the requirements of the new application. You will have to apply your knowledge of Ohm's law and Watt's law in order to complete this assignment.

The specifications are as follows:

1. Each resistor is switch selectable and only one resistor is selected at a time.

2. The lowest resistor value is to be 10 Ω.

3. Each successively higher resistance in the switch sequence must be a decade (10 times) increase over the previous one.

4. The maximum resistor value must be 1.0 MΩ.

5. The maximum voltage across any resistor in the box will be 4 V.

6. Two additional resistors are required, one to limit the current to 10 mA ± 10% with a 4 V drop and the other to limit the current to 5 mA ± 10% with a 4 V drop.

Step 1: Inspect the Existing Resistance Box

The existing resistance box is shown in both top and bottom views in Figure 3–26. The switch is a rotary type. The resistors all have a power rating of 1 W.

Step 2: Draw the Schematic

From Figure 3–26, determine the resistor values and draw the schematic for the existing circuit so that you will know what you have to work with. Determine the resistor numbering from the R labels on the top view.

▶ FIGURE 3–26

(a) Top view

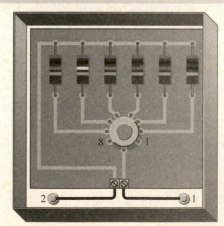

(b) Bottom view

Step 3: Modify the Schematic to Meet New Requirements

Change the schematic from Step 2 so the circuit will accomplish the following:

1. One resistor at a time is to be connected by the switch between terminals 1 and 2 of the box.

2. Provide switch selectable resistor values beginning with 10 Ω and increasing in decade increments to 1.0 MΩ.

3. Each of the resistors from Step 1 must be selectable by a sequence of adjacent switch positions in ascending order.

4. In addition to the resistors in Step 1, there must be two switch-selectable resistors, one is in switch position 1 (shown in Figure 3–26, bottom view) and must limit the current to 10 mA ± 10% with a 4 V drop and the other is in switch position 8 and must limit the current to 5 mA ± 10% with a 4 V drop.

5. All the resistors must be standard values with 10% tolerance and have a sufficient power rating for the 4 V operating requirement. See Appendix A for standard resistor values.

Step 4: Modify the Circuit

State the modifications that must be made to the existing box to meet the specifications and develop a detailed list of the changes including resistance values, power ratings, wiring, and new components. You should number each point in the schematic for easy reference.

Step 5: Develop a Test Procedure

After the box has been modified to meet the new specifications, it must be tested to see if it is working properly. Determine how you would test the resistance box and what instruments you would use and then detail your test procedure in a step-by-step format.

Step 6: Troubleshoot the Circuit

When an ohmmeter is connected across terminals 1 and 2 of the resistance box, determine the most likely fault in each of the following cases:

1. The ohmmeter shows an infinitely high resistance when the switch is in position 3.

2. The ohmmeter shows an infinitely high resistance in all switch positions.

3. The ohmmeter shows an incorrect value of resistance when the switch is in position 6.

Application Assignment Review

1. Explain how you applied Watt's law to this application assignment.

2. Explain how you applied Ohm's law to this application assignment.

3. How did you determine the power ratings of the resistors in the existing box?

SUMMARY

- Voltage and current are linearly proportional.
- Ohm's law gives the relationship of voltage, current, and resistance.
- Current is directly proportional to voltage.
- Current is inversely proportional to resistance.
- A kilohm (kΩ) is one thousand ohms.
- A megohm (MΩ) is one million ohms.
- A microampere (μA) is one-millionth of an ampere.
- A milliampere (mA) is one-thousandth of an ampere.
- Use $I = V/R$ to calculate current.
- Use $V = IR$ to calculate voltage.
- Use $R = V/I$ to calculate resistance.
- One watt equals one joule per second.
- Watt is the unit of power, and joule is the unit of energy.
- The power rating of a resistor determines the maximum power that it can handle safely.

- Resistors with a larger physical size can dissipate more power in the form of heat than smaller ones.

- A resistor should have a power rating as high or higher than the maximum power that it is expected to handle in the circuit.

- Power rating is not related to resistance value.

- A resistor usually opens when it overheats and fails.

- Energy is equal to power multiplied by time.

- The kilowatt-hour is a unit of energy.

- An example of one kilowatt-hour is one thousand watts used for one hour.

- A power supply is an energy source used to operate electrical and electronic devices.

- A battery is one type of power supply that converts chemical energy into electrical energy.

- An electronic power supply converts commercial energy (ac from the power company) to regulated dc at various voltage levels.

- The output power of a power supply is the output voltage times the load current.

- A load is a device that draws current from the power supply.

- The capacity of a battery is measured in ampere-hours (Ah).

- One ampere-hour equals one ampere used for one hour, or any other combination of amperes and hours that has a product of one.

- An electronic power supply with a high efficiency has a smaller percentage power loss than one with a lower efficiency.

- The formula wheel in Figure 3–27 gives the Ohm's law and Watt's law relationships.

- APM (analysis, planning, and measurement) provides a logical approach to troubleshooting.

- The half-splitting method of troubleshooting generally results in fewer measurements.

▶ FIGURE 3–27

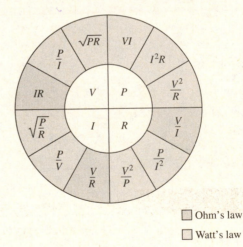

☐ Ohm's law
☐ Watt's law

KEY TERMS   Key terms and other bold terms in the chapter are defined in the end-of-book glossary.

Ampere-hour rating A number given in ampere-hours (Ah) determined by multiplying the current (A) times the length of time (h) a battery can deliver that current to a load.

Efficiency The ratio of the output power to the input power of a circuit, expressed as a percent.

Energy The ability to do work. The unit is the joule (J).

Half-splitting A troubleshooting procedure where one starts in the middle of a circuit or system and, depending on the first measurement, works toward the output or toward the input to find the fault.

Joule (J) The unit of energy.

Kilowatt-hour (kWh) A common unit of energy used mainly by utility companies.

Linear Characterized by a straight-line relationship.

Ohm's law A law stating that current is directly proportional to voltage and inversely proportional to resistance.

Power The rate of energy usage.

Power rating The maximum amount of power that a resistor can dissipate without being damaged by excessive heat buildup.

Troubleshooting A systematic process of isolating, identifying, and correcting a fault in a circuit or system.

Voltage drop The difference in the voltage at two points due to energy conversion.

Watt (W) The unit of power. One watt is the power when 1 J of energy is used in 1 s.

Watt's law A law that states the relationships of power to current, voltage, and resistance.

FORMULAS

3–1	$I = \dfrac{V}{R}$	Ohm's law for current
3–2	$V = IR$	Ohm's law for voltage
3–3	$R = \dfrac{V}{I}$	Ohm's law for resistance
3–4	$P = \dfrac{W}{t}$	Power equals energy divided by time.
3–5	$W = Pt$	Energy equals power multiplied by time.
3–6	$P = I^2R$	Power equals current squared times resistance.
3–7	$P = VI$	Power equals voltage times current.
3–8	$P = \dfrac{V^2}{R}$	Power equals voltage squared divided by resistance.
3–9	$\text{Efficiency} = \dfrac{P_{OUT}}{P_{IN}}$	Power supply efficiency
3–10	$P_{OUT} = P_{IN} - P_{LOSS}$	Output power

SELF-TEST

Answers are at the end of the chapter.

1. Ohm's law states that
   (a) current equals voltage times resistance
   (b) voltage equals current times resistance
   (c) resistance equals current divided by voltage
   (d) voltage equals current squared times resistance

2. When the voltage across a resistor is doubled, the current will
   (a) triple   (b) halve   (c) double   (d) not change

3. When 10 V are applied across a 20 Ω resistor, the current is
   (a) 10 A   (b) 0.5 A   (c) 200 A   (d) 2 A

4. When there are 10 mA of current through a 1.0 kΩ resistor, the voltage across the resistor is
   (a) 100 V   (b) 0.1 V   (c) 10 kV   (d) 10 V

5. If 20 V are applied across a resistor and there are 6.06 mA of current, the resistance is
   (a) 3.3 kΩ   (b) 33 kΩ   (c) 330 Ω   (d) 3.03 kΩ

6. A current of 250 μA through a 4.7 kΩ resistor produces a voltage drop of

   (a) 53.2 V   (b) 1.175 mV   (c) 18.8 V   (d) 1.175 V

7. A resistance of 2.2 MΩ is connected across a 1 kV source. The resulting current is approximately

   (a) 2.2 mA   (b) 455 μA   (c) 45.5 μA   (d) 0.455 A

8. Power can be defined as

   (a) energy   (b) heat
   (c) the rate at which energy is used   (d) the time required to use energy

9. For 10 V and 50 mA, the power is

   (a) 500 mW   (b) 0.5 W   (c) 500,000 μW   (d) answers (a), (b), and (c)

10. When the current through a 10 kΩ resistor is 10 mA, the power is

    (a) 1 W   (b) 10 W   (c) 100 mW   (d) 1 mW

11. A 2.2 kΩ resistor dissipates 0.5 W. The current is

    (a) 15.1 mA   (b) 227 μA   (c) 1.1 mA   (d) 4.4 mA

12. A 330 Ω resistor dissipates 2 W. The voltage is

    (a) 2.57 V   (b) 660 V   (c) 6.6 V   (d) 25.7 V

13. The power rating of a resistor that is to handle up to 1.1 W should be

    (a) 0.25 W   (b) 1 W   (c) 2 W   (d) 5 W

14. A 22 Ω half-watt resistor and a 220 Ω half-watt resistor are connected across a 10 V source. Which one(s) will overheat?

    (a) 22 Ω (b) 220 Ω (c) both   (d) neither

15. When the needle of an analog ohmmeter indicates infinity, the resistor being measured is

    (a) overheated   (b) shorted   (c) open   (d) reversed

TROUBLESHOOTING: SYMPTOM AND CAUSE

The purpose of these exercises is to help develop thought processes essential to troubleshooting. Answers are at the end of the chapter.

Determine the cause for each set of symptoms. Refer to Figure 3–28.

1. *Symptom:* The ammeter reading is zero, and the voltmeter reading is 10 V.

   Cause:

   (a) R is shorted.

   (b) R is open.

   (c) The voltage source is faulty.

2. *Symptom:* The ammeter reading is zero, and the voltmeter reading is 0 V.

   Cause:

   (a) R is open.

   (b) R is shorted.

   (c) The voltage source is turned off or faulty.

▶ **FIGURE 3–28**

The meters indicate the correct readings for this circuit.

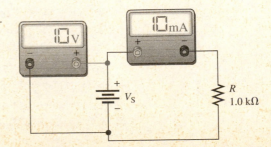

3. *Symptom:* The ammeter reading is 10 mA, and the voltmeter reading is 0 V.

   Cause:

   (a) The voltmeter is defective.

   (b) The ammeter is faulty.

   (c) The voltage source is turned off or faulty.

4. *Symptom:* The ammeter reading is 1 mA, and the voltmeter reading is 10 V.

   Cause:

   (a) The voltmeter is defective.

   (b) The resistor value is higher than it should be.

   (c) The resistor value is lower than it should be.

5. *Symptom:* The ammeter reading is 100 mA, and the voltmeter reading is 10 V.

   Cause:

   (a) The voltmeter is defective.

   (b) The resistor value is higher than it should be.

   (c) The resistor value is lower than it should be.

PROBLEMS

Answers to odd-numbered problems are at the end of the book.

BASIC PROBLEMS

SECTION 3-1   Ohm's Law

1. The current in a circuit is 1 A. Determine what the current will be when

   (a) the voltage is tripled

   (b) the voltage is reduced by 80%

   (c) the voltage is increased by 50%

2. The current in a circuit is 100 mA. Determine what the current will be when

   (a) the resistance is increased by 100%

   (b) the resistance is reduced by 30%

   (c) the resistance is quadrupled

3. The current in a circuit is 10 mA. What will the current be if the voltage is tripled and the resistance is doubled?

SECTION 3-2   Application of Ohm's Law

4. Determine the current in each case.

   (a) $V = 5$ V, $R = 1.0$ Ω **(b)** $V = 15$ V, $R = 10$ Ω

   (c) $V = 50$ V, $R = 100$ Ω **(d)** $V = 30$ V, $R = 15$ kΩ

   (e) $V = 250$ V, $R = 4.7$ MΩ

5. Determine the current in each case.

   (a) $V = 9$ V, $R = 2.7$ kΩ **(b)** $V = 5.5$ V, $R = 10$ kΩ

   (c) $V = 40$ V, $R = 68$ kΩ **(d)** $V = 1$ kV, $R = 2$ kΩ

   (e) $V = 66$ kV, $R = 10$ MΩ

6. A 10 Ω resistor is connected across a 12 V battery. How much current is there through the resistor?

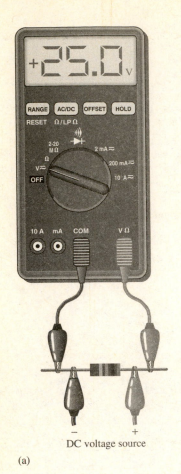

(a)

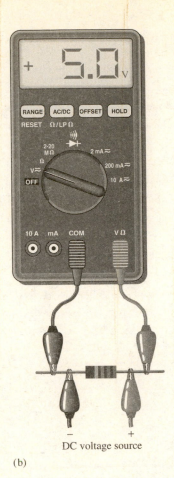

(b)

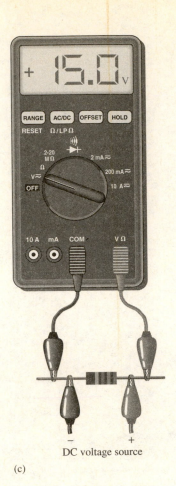

(c)

▲ FIGURE 3–29

7. A resistor is connected across the terminals of a dc voltage source in each part of Figure 3–29. Determine the current in each resistor.

8. Calculate the voltage for each value of I and R.

   (a) $I = 2$ A, $R = 18$ Ω   (b) $I = 5$ A, $R = 47$ Ω

   (c) $I = 2.5$ A, $R = 620$ Ω   (d) $I = 0.6$ A, $R = 47$ Ω

   (e) $I = 0.1$ A, $R = 470$ Ω

9. Calculate the voltage for each value of I and R.

   (a) $I = 1$ mA, $R = 10$ Ω   (b) $I = 50$ mA, $R = 33$ Ω

   (c) $I = 3$ A, $R = 4.7$ kΩ   (d) $I = 1.6$ mA, $R = 2.2$ kΩ

   (e) $I = 250$ μA, $R = 1.0$ kΩ   (f) $I = 500$ mA, $R = 1.5$ MΩ

   (g) $I = 850$ μA, $R = 10$ MΩ   (h) $I = 75$ μA, $R = 47$ Ω

10. Three amperes of current are measured through a 27 Ω resistor connected across a voltage source. How much voltage does the source produce?

11. Assign a voltage value to each source in the circuits of Figure 3–30 to obtain the indicated amounts of current.

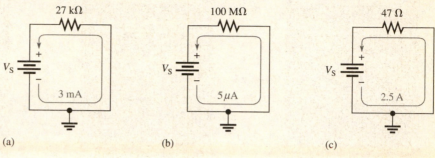

(a)   (b)   (c)

▲ FIGURE 3–30

12. Calculate the resistance for each value of V and I.
   (a) $V = 10$ V, $I = 2$ A   (b) $V = 90$ V, $I = 45$ A
   (c) $V = 50$ V, $I = 5$ A   (d) $V = 5.5$ V, $I = 10$ A
   (e) $V = 150$ V, $I = 0.5$ A

13. Calculate R for each set of V and I values.
   (a) $V = 10$ kV, $I = 5$ A   (b) $V = 7$ V, $I = 2$ mA
   (c) $V = 500$ V, $I = 250$ mA   (d) $V = 50$ V, $I = 500$ μA
   (e) $V = 1$ kV, $I = 1$ mA

14. Six volts are applied across a resistor. A current of 2 mA is measured. What is the value of the resistor?

15. Choose the correct value of resistance to get the current values indicated in each circuit of Figure 3–31.

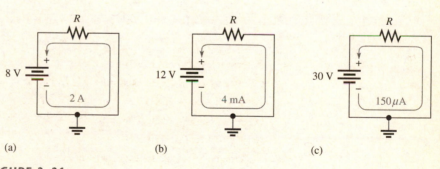

(a)   (b)   (c)

▲ FIGURE 3–31

SECTION 3–3 Energy and Power

16. What is the power when energy is used at the rate of 350 J/s?

17. What is the power in watts when 7500 J of energy are used in 5 h?

18. Convert the following in kilowatts:
   (a) 1000 W   (b) 3750 W   (c) 160 W   (d) 50,000 W

19. Convert the following to megawatts:
   (a) 1,000,000 W   (b) 3×10^6 W   (c) 15×10^7 W   (d) 8700 kW

20. Convert the following to milliwatts:

    (a) 1 W   **(b)** 0.4 W   **(c)** 0.002 W   **(d)** 0.0125 W

21. Convert the following to microwatts:

    (a) 2 W   **(b)** 0.0005 W   **(c)** 0.25 mW   **(d)** 0.00667 mW

22. Convert the following to watts:

    (a) 1.5 kW   **(b)** 0.5 MW   **(c)** 350 mW   **(d)** 9000 μW

SECTION 3–4   Power in an Electric Circuit

23. If a resistor has 5.5 V across it and 3 mA through it, what is the power dissipation?

24. An electric heater works on 115 V and draws 3 A of current. How much power does it use?

25. How much power is produced by 500 mA of current through a 4.7 kΩ resistor?

26. Calculate the power handled by a 10 kΩ resistor carrying 100 μA.

27. If there are 60 V across a 620 Ω resistor, what is the power dissipation?

28. A 56 Ω resistor is connected across the terminals of a 1.5 V battery. What is the power dissipation in the resistor?

29. If a resistor is to carry 2 A of current and handle 100 W of power, how many ohms must it be? Assume that the voltage can be adjusted to any required value.

30. Convert 5×10^6 watts used for 1 minute to kWh.

31. Convert 6700 watts used for 1 second to kWh.

32. How many kilowatt-hours do 50 W use for 12 h equal?

SECTION 3–5   The Power Rating of Resistors

33. A 6.8 kΩ resistor has burned out in a circuit. You must replace it with another resistor with the same resistance value. If the resistor carries 10 mA, what should its power rating be? Assume that you have available resistors in all the standard power ratings.

34. A certain type of power resistor comes in the following ratings: 3 W, 5 W, 8 W, 12 W, 20 W. Your particular application requires a resistor that can handle approximately 8 W. Which rating would you use? Why?

SECTION 3–6   Energy Conversion and Voltage Drop in a Resistance

35. For each circuit in Figure 3–32, assign the proper polarity for the voltage across the resistor.

▶ FIGURE 3–32

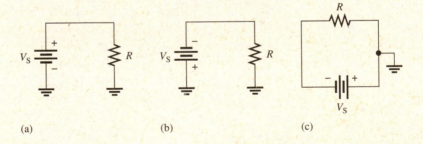

   (a)   (b)   (c)

SECTION 3–7   Power Supplies

36. A 50 Ω load consumes 1 W of power. What is the output voltage of the power supply?

37. A battery can provide 1.5 A of current for 24 h. What is its ampere-hour rating?

38. How much continuous current can be drawn from an 80 Ah battery for 10 h?

39. If a battery is rated at 650 mAh, how much current will it provide for 48 h?

40. If the input power is 500 mW and the output power is 400 mW, what is the power loss? What is the efficiency of this power supply?

41. To operate at 85% efficiency, how much output power must a source produce if the input power is 5 W?

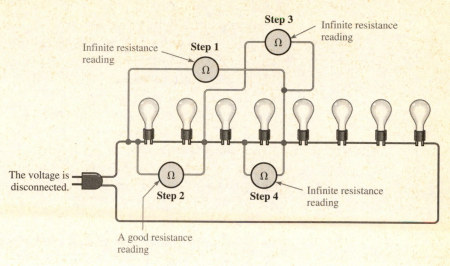

Step 3
Infinite resistance reading
Ω

Infinite resistance reading
Step 1
Ω

The voltage is disconnected.
Step 2
Ω

Step 4
Ω
Infinite resistance reading

A good resistance reading

▲ **FIGURE 3–33**

SECTION 3–8 **Introduction to Troubleshooting**

42. In the light circuit of Figure 3–33, identify the faulty bulb based on the series of ohmmeter readings shown.

43. Assume you have a 32-light string and one of the bulbs is burned out. Using the half-splitting approach and starting in the left half of the circuit, how many resistance measurements will it take to find the faulty bulb if it is seventeenth from the left. Remember, you don't know which bulb is faulty.

ADVANCED PROBLEMS

44. A certain power supply provides a continuous 2 W to a load. It is operating at 60% efficiency. In a 24 h period, how many kilowatt-hours does the power supply use?

45. The filament of a light bulb in the circuit of Figure 3–34(a) has a certain amount of resistance, represented by an equivalent resistance in Figure 3–34(b). If the bulb operates with 120 V and 0.8 A of current, what is the resistance of its filament?

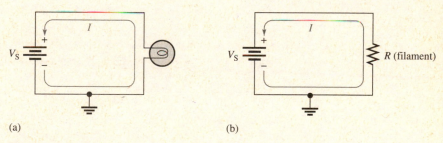

(a)

V_S

I

(b)

V_S

I

R (filament)

▲ **FIGURE 3–34**

46. A certain electrical device has an unknown resistance. You have available a 12 V battery and an ammeter. How would you determine the value of the unknown resistance? Draw the necessary circuit connections.

47. A variable voltage source is connected to the circuit of Figure 3–35. Start at 0 V and increase the voltage in 10 V steps up to 100 V. Determine the current at each voltage value, and plot a graph of V versus I. Is the graph a straight line? What does the graph indicate?

▶ FIGURE 3–35

Variable V R 100 Ω

48. In a certain circuit, $V_S = 1$ V and $I = 5$ mA. Determine the current for each of the following voltages in a circuit with the same resistance:

  (a) $V_S = 1.5$ V   (b) $V_S = 2$ V   (c) $V_S = 3$ V

  (d) $V_S = 4$ V   (e) $V_S = 10$ V

49. Figure 3–36 is a graph of current versus voltage for three resistance values. Determine R_1, R_2, and R_3.

▶ FIGURE 3–36

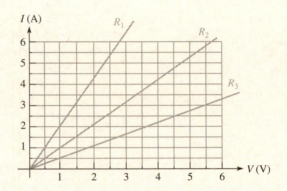

50. You are measuring the current in a circuit that is operated on a 10 V battery. The ammeter reads 50 mA. Later, you notice that the current has dropped to 30 mA. Eliminating the possibility of a resistance change, you must conclude that the voltage has changed. How much has the voltage of the battery changed, and what is its new value?

51. If you wish to increase the amount of current in a resistor from 100 mA to 150 mA by changing the 20 V source, by how many volts should you change the source? To what new value should you set it?

52. By varying the rheostat (variable resistor) in the circuit of Figure 3–37, you can change the amount of current. The setting of the rheostat is such that the current is 750 mA. What is the resistance value of this setting? To adjust the current to 1 A, to what resistance value must you set the rheostat? The rheostat must never be adjusted to 0 Ω. Why?

▶ FIGURE 3–37

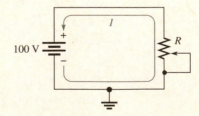

100 V I R

53. A certain resistor has the following color code: orange, orange, red, gold. Determine the maximum and minimum currents you should expect to measure when a 12 V source is connected across the resistor.

54. A 6 V source is connected to a 100 Ω resistor by two 12 ft lengths of 18-gauge copper wire. Refer to Table 2–4 to determine the following:

    (a) current   **(b)** resistor voltage   **(c)** voltage across each length of wire

55. A certain appliance uses 300 W. If it is allowed to run continuously for 30 days, how many kilowatt-hours of energy does it use?

56. At the end of a 31-day period, your utility bill shows that you have used 1500 kWh. What is the average daily power?

57. A certain type of power resistor comes in the following ratings: 3 W, 5 W, 8 W, 12 W, 20 W. Your particular application requires a resistor that can handle approximately 10 W. Which rating would you use? Why?

58. A 12 V source is connected across a 10 Ω resistor for 2 min.

    (a) What is the power dissipation?

    (b) How much energy is used?

    (c) If the resistor remains connected for an additional minute, does the power dissipation increase or decrease?

59. The rheostat in Figure 3–38 is used to control the current to a heating element. When the rheostat is adjusted to a value of 8 Ω or less, the heating element can burn out. What is the rated value of the fuse needed to protect the circuit if the voltage across the heating element at the point of maximum current is 100 V?

▶ **FIGURE 3–38**

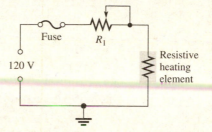

MULTISIM TROUBLESHOOTING PROBLEMS

CD–ROM file circuits are shown in Figure 3–39.

60. Open file P03-60 on your CD-ROM. Determine whether or not the circuit is operating properly. If not, find the faulty part.

61. Open file P03-61 on your CD-ROM. Determine whether or not the circuit is operating properly. If not, find the faulty part.

62. Open file P03-62 on your CD-ROM. Determine whether or not the circuit is operating properly. If not, find the faulty part.

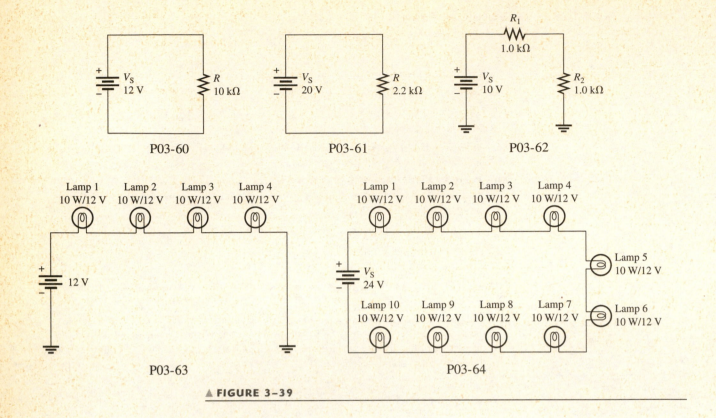

P03-60   P03-61   P03-62

P03-63   P03-64

▲ FIGURE 3–39

63. Open file P03-63 on your CD-ROM. Determine whether or not the circuit is operating properly. If not, find the faulty part.

64. Open file P03-64 on your CD-ROM. Determine whether or not the circuit is operating properly. If not, find the faulty part.

ANSWERS

SECTION REVIEWS

SECTION 3–1   Ohm's Law

1. Ohm's law states that current varies directly with voltage and inversely with resistance.

2. $I = V/R$ 3. $V = IR$ 4. $R = V/I$

5. The current increases; three times when V is tripled

6. Doubling R cuts I in half to 5 mA.

7. No change in I if V and R are doubled.

SECTION 3–2   Application of Ohm's Law

1. $I = 10\ \text{V}/4.7\ \Omega = 2.13\ \text{A}$

2. $I = 20\ \text{kV}/4.7\ \text{M}\Omega = 4.26\ \text{mA}$

3. $I = 10\ \text{kV}/2\ \text{k}\Omega = 5\ \text{A}$

4. $V = (1\ \text{A})(10\ \Omega) = 10\ \text{V}$

5. $V = (3\ \text{mA})(3\ \text{k}\Omega) = 9\ \text{V}$

6. $V = (2\ \text{A})(6\ \Omega) = 12\ \text{V}$

7. $R = 10\ \text{V}/2\ \text{A} = 5\ \Omega$

8. $R = 25\ \text{V}/50\ \text{mA} = 0.5\ \text{k}\Omega = 500\ \Omega$

SECTION 3–3   **Energy and Power**

   1. Power is the rate at which energy is used.

   2. $P = W/t$

   3. Watt is the unit of power. One watt is the power when 1 J of energy is used in 1 s.

   4. **(a)** 68,000 W = 68 kW   **(b)** 0.005 W = 5 mW   **(c)** 0.000025 = 25 μW

   5. (100 W)(10 h) = 1 kWh

   6. 2000 W = 2 kW

   7. (1.322 kW)(24 h) = 31.73 kWh; (0.09 \$/kWh)(31.73 kWh) = \$2.86

SECTION 3–4   **Power in an Electric Circuit**

   1. $P = (10\ V)(3\ A) = 30\ W$

   2. $P = (5\ A)^2(47\ \Omega) = 1175\ W$

   3. $P = (20\ mA)^2(5.1\ k\Omega) = 2.04\ W$

   4. $P = (5\ V)^2/10\ \Omega = 2.5\ W$

   5. $P = (8\ V)^2/2.2\ k\Omega = 29.1\ mW$

   6. $R = 55\ W/(0.5\ A)^2 = 220\ \Omega$

SECTION 3–5   **The Power Rating of Resistors**

   1. Two resistor parameters are resistance and power rating.

   2. A larger resistor physical size dissipates more energy.

   3. Standard ratings of metal-film resistors are 0.125 W, 0.25 W, 0.5 W, and 1 W.

   4. At least a 0.5 W rating to handle 0.3 W

   5. $8 \times 1k = 8\ k\Omega$

SECTION 3–6   **Energy Conversion and Voltage Drop in a Resistance**

   1. Energy conversion in a resistor is caused by collisions of free electrons with the atoms in the material.

   2. Voltage drop is the difference in the voltage at two points due to energy conversion.

   3. Voltage drop is negative to positive in the direction of current.

SECTION 3–7   **Power Supplies**

   1. An increased amount of current represents a greater load.

   2. $P_{OUT} = (10\ V)(0.5\ A) = 5\ W$

   3. 100 Ah/5 A = 20 h

   4. $P_{OUT} = (12\ V)(5\ A) = 60\ W$

   5. Efficiency = (750 mW/1000 mW)100% = 75%

SECTION 3–8   **Introduction to Troubleshooting**

   1. Analysis, Planning, and Measuring

   2. Half-splitting identifies the fault by successively isolating half of the remaining circuit.

   3. Voltage is measured across a component. Current is measured in series with the component.

■   **Application Assignment**

   1. Watt's law was used to find power ratings ($P = V^2/R$).

   2. Ohm's law was used to find the two additional resistors ($R = V/I$).

   3. Power ratings were determined by the relative sizes of the resistors, given the range of values.

RELATED PROBLEMS FOR EXAMPLES

3–1 $I_1 = 10\ \text{V}/5\ \Omega = 2\ \text{A}; I_2 = 10\ \text{V}/20\ \Omega = 0.5\ \text{A}$

3–2   1 V

3–3   900 Ω

3–4   Yes

3–5   2.5 A

3–6   5 mA

3–7   25 μA

3–8   200 μA

3–9   800 V

3–10   220 mV

3–11   16.5 V

3–12   4 kΩ

3–13   100 Ω

3–14   3000 J

3–15   **(a)** 0.001 W   **(b)** 0.0018 W

       (c) 3,000,000 W   **(d)** 10,000 W

3–16   2 kWh

3–17 $6.12 + $.06 = 6.18

3–18   **(a)** 40 W

       (b) 376 W

       (c) 625 mW

3–19   60 W

3–20   0.5 W (½ W)

3–21   No

3–22   60 Ah

3–23   46 W

SELF-TEST

1. (b)   **2.** (c)   **3.** (b)   **4.** (d)   **5.** (a)   **6.** (d)   **7.** (b)

8. (c)   **9.** (d)   **10.** (a)   **11.** (a)   **12.** (d)   **13.** (c)   **14.** (a)

15. (c)

TROUBLESHOOTING: SYMPTOM AND CAUSE

1. (b)

2. (c)

3. (a)

4. (b)

5. (c)

CHECKING YOUR COMPREHENSION

Choose the best answer for each of the following questions.

1. Which of the following is not a formula from which Ohm's Law can be written?
    a. I=V/R
    b. V= IR
    c. R=V/I
    d. V= I/R

2. What would be the energy cost for using a blow dryer with a power rating of 1300 for an hour at a cost of 10 cents a kilowatt hour?
    a. 10 cents
    b. 15 cents
    c. 17 cents
    d. 19 cents

3. Which of the following is not one of the three steps in troubleshooting?
    a. identify the source of the problem
    b. analyze symptoms of the failure
    c. formulating a logical plan of attack
    d. narrow the possibility of failure by carefully thinking out measurements

Identify the following statements as true or false.

4. All else being equal, the smaller the surface area of a resistor, the more power it can dissipate.

5. Ampere-hour rating determines the length of time a battery can deliver a certain amount of current to a load at the rated voltage.

Answer the following questions.

6. Explain Ohm's Law by describing how voltage (v), current (c), and resistance (r) are related.

7. Define the terms "energy" and "power" and discuss how the two concepts are related.

8. Explain the relationship between energy conversion and voltage drop.

Discussion and Critical Thinking Question

9. Discuss the significance of both George Simon Ohm and James Watts in terms of their contributions to the practical applications and uses for electricity today.

➤ *An engraving of New Yorkers celebrating their party's national convention at Madison Square Garden in 1888 conveys the popular enthusiasm and mass participation that characterized American politics in the late nineteenth century.*

Politics and Government 20
1877–1900

> Cincinnati, Ohio
> September 28, 1884
>
> Dear Fanny,
>
> Will has been appointed chief supervisor and so has to take means to prevent fraud at the election. He must appoint assistants for each ward.
>
> Horace
> October 12, 1884
>
> Dear Father,
>
> Will has no time for anything but the election and his duties as chief supervisor. . . . I am afraid the election will be a stormy one & violence will not surprise me. I am one of a citizens' committee of the 18th ward and we propose to be on hand from 6 in the morning till the votes are counted at night.
>
> Horace
> October 22, 1884
>
> Dear Mother,
>
> We had an exciting time election day. The Democrats tried to introduce their Southern methods into northern elections and succeeded in one or two wards, but in general the U.S. Deputy Marshals managed to keep the scoundrels

629

quiet. The negroes in many precincts voted at the risk of their lives. I saw a man shot & killed about fifteen feet from me at our polling place. . . . He drew a pistol on a Deputy Marshal but the Deputy was too quick for him.

Horace
October 22, 1884

Dear Father,

In the 5th, 8th, and 19th Wards the marshals were utterly useless and were soon overpowered. The police did nothing except to set on [incite] the crowd. . . . The negroes were driven away from the polls, beaten and wounded and exposed to as much abuse as they could have been south of Mason's and Dixon's line. No colored votes were polled in those precincts after twelve o'clock.

Will

William H. Taft Papers, Manuscript Division, Library of Congress.

Horace and Will Taft wrote regularly to their parents and sister Fanny to keep them informed of the 1884 congressional election in their hometown of Cincinnati. Alphonso, Louise, and Fanny Taft, all staunch Republicans, were desperate for such political news. Alphonso's high standing in his party had led to important political appointments, first to President Ulysses S. Grant's cabinet and then as American minister to Austria. Now in Vienna, they eagerly awaited news of their party's success.

As the Taft brothers reported, voters in the city had a complicated and difficult journey to the polls, and some did not reach their destination. The lead-up to the election had electrified the city, as rabid partisans had staged competing torchlight parades, with thousands of uniformed marchers organized into companies, brigades, and divisions; orators had stirred the huge crowds for hours with patriotic, religious, and cultural bombast. And amid such excitement, the election itself did produce the violence Horace had expected. The Republican brothers condemned the Democrats for intimidating African Americans and others likely to vote Republican, "importing" Democratic voters from other states and "colonizing" them in Cincinnati, and using the local police force as a partisan organization to frighten or arrest Republicans attempting to reach the ballot box.

But there was a Democratic version of events as well. The U.S. marshals so praised by Horace had been appointed by Republican federal officials under Will's supervision. And many of those marshals were merely thugs, paid and armed by the Lincoln Club, a local Republican campaign organization, and often interested simply in improving Republican election prospects. As Will conceded, they first "drove from the city the night before election" hundreds of Democrats they alleged might commit election fraud. On election day itself they sought to incite violence in the city's Irish wards to keep other Democratic voters from the polls, and they made mass arrests of others trying to vote, often claiming that they were Kentucky Democrats who had crossed the Ohio River to "colonize" Cincinnati's election. Several times deputies fired point-blank into Democratic crowds around the polls. As Will admitted to his father about those deputies, "it is attended with risk to furnish revolvers to men who are close to or belong to the criminal class."

"The Democrats are so mad at not being able to perpetrate these frauds," Will concluded with unwitting irony, "that they are trying to get even by crying fraud at us."

Not all American elections in the late nineteenth century were as riotous as this Cincinnati contest. (And both Democrats and Republicans were eventually convicted of illegal voting and election fraud, while Alphonso Taft congratulated his two sons for the "risk and labor" they had undertaken in the election.) But in many ways it suggested much about

630

American politics at the time. From the military-style campaign to the rough act of voting itself, elections were a masculine business—although women were intensely interested. Marked by pageantry and hoopla, campaigns attracted mass participation but often avoided substantive policy issues. The two major political parties shaped campaigns and controlled elections, which were usually tumultuous if not always violent. Partisan divisions overlapped with ethnic, racial, and other social divisions, and the question of suffrage was a contested one. Partisanship often determined both the membership and the activities of government agencies, even those nominally charged with the maintenance of public order. The lack of a common national election day, which allowed Kentuckians to vote in Cincinnati's October election without missing their own, reflected localism—the belief that local concerns took precedence over national concerns. One newspaper even denied the legitimacy of federal involvement in the city's elections, declaring that federal deputies "can all be kicked and cuffed about like ordinary citizens, and will be compelled to take their chances with common people on election day."

These features of late-nineteenth century politics would eventually be transformed in significant ways. But while they endured, they shaped not only campaigns and elections but the form and role of government as well. As for William Howard Taft, he moved up the political ladder, eventually becoming President of the United States. His success, he explained, stemmed from his father's reputation, his own loyalty to his party, and keeping his "plate the right side up when offices were falling."

KEY TOPICS

- The exuberant partisan politics and the close balance between parties in the late nineteenth century

- The inability of a weak federal government to address problems of America's industrializing economy

- The pressure for civil service reform

- The tariff issue

- Monetary policy and the call for free silver

- Agricultural protest and the emergence of the Populist party

- The end of political stalemate after the election of 1896

THE STRUCTURE AND STYLE OF POLITICS

Politics in the late nineteenth century was an absorbing activity. Campaigns and elections expressed social values as they determined who held the reins of government. Political parties dominated political life. They organized campaigns, controlled balloting, and held the unswerving loyalty of most of the electorate. While the major parties worked to maintain a sense of unity and tradition among their followers, third parties sought to activate those the major parties left unserved. Other Americans looked outside the electoral arena to fulfill their political goals.

CAMPAIGNS AND ELECTIONS

Political campaigns and elections generated remarkable public participation and enthusiasm. They constituted a major form of entertainment at a time when recreational opportunities were limited. Campaign pageantry absorbed communities large and small. In cities and towns across the nation, thousands of men in elaborate uniforms marched in massive torchlight parades to demonstrate partisan enthusiasm. The small town of Emporia, Kansas, once witnessed a campaign rally of twenty thousand people, several times its population. A parade of wagons stretched 5 miles, reported the proud local newspaper. "When the head of the procession was under the equator the tail was

Chronology

1867 Patrons of Husbandry (the Grange) is founded.

1869 Massachusetts establishes the first state regulatory commission.

1873 Silver is demonetized in the "Crime of '73."

1874 Woman's Christian Temperance Union is organized.

1875 U.S. Supreme Court, in *Minor v. Happersett,* upholds denial of suffrage to women.

1876 Greenback Party runs presidential candidate.

1877 Rutherford B. Hayes becomes president after disputed election.

Farmers' Alliance is founded.

Supreme Court, in *Munn v. Illinois,* upholds state regulatory authority over private property.

1878 Bland-Allison Act obliges the government to buy silver.

1880 James A. Garfield is elected president.

1881 Garfield is assassinated; Chester A. Arthur becomes president.

1883 Pendleton Civil Service Act is passed.

1884 Grover Cleveland is elected president.

1886 Supreme Court, in *Wabash v. Illinois,* rules that only the federal government, not the states, can regulate interstate commerce.

1887 Interstate Commerce Act is passed.

1888 Benjamin Harrison is elected president.

1890 Sherman Antitrust Act is passed.

McKinley Tariff Act is passed.

Sherman Silver Purchase Act is passed.

National American Woman Suffrage Association is organized.

Wyoming enters the Union as the first state with woman suffrage.

1892 People's Party is organized.

Cleveland is elected to his second term as president.

1893 Depression begins.

Sherman Silver Purchase Act is repealed.

1894 Coxey's Army marches to Washington.

Pullman strike ends in violence.

1895 Supreme Court, in *Pollock v. Farmers' Loan and Trust Company,* invalidates the federal income tax.

Supreme Court, in *United States v. E.C. Knight Company,* limits the Sherman Antitrust law to commerce, excluding industrial monopolies.

1896 William Jennings Bryan is nominated for president by Democrats and Populists.

William McKinley is elected president.

1900 Currency Act puts U.S. currency on the gold standard.

coming around the north pole." Political picnics and camp meetings served a comparable function in rural areas. Attending party meetings and conventions, listening to lengthy speeches appealing to group loyalties and local pride, gathering at the polls to watch the voting and the counting, celebrating victory and drowning the disappointment of defeat—all these provided social enjoyment and defined popular politics.

The excitement of political contests prompted the wife of Chief Justice Morrison Waite to write longingly on election day, 1876, "I should want to vote all day." But women—though they often identified with and endorsed a political party—could not vote at all in national elections. Justice Waite himself had just a year earlier written the unanimous opinion of the Supreme Court (in *Minor v. Happersett*) that the Constitution did not confer suffrage on women. Men generally believed that weakness and sentimentality disqualified women from the fierce conflicts of the public realm.

Virtually all men participated in politics. In many states, even immigrants not yet citizens were eligible to vote and flocked to the polls. African Americans voted regularly in the North and irregularly in the South before being disfranchised at the end of the century. Overall, turnout was remarkably high, averaging nearly 80 percent of eligible voters in presidential elections between 1876 and 1900, a figure far greater than ever achieved thereafter (see Figure 20-1).

Political parties mobilized this huge electorate. They kept detailed records of voters, transported them to the polls, saw that they were registered where necessary, and sometimes even paid their poll taxes or naturalization fees to make them eligible. With legal regulations and public machinery for elections negligible, parties dominated the campaigns and elections. Many states did not have meaningful registration laws, making it difficult to determine voter eligibility. Until the 1890s, most states had no laws to ensure secrecy in voting, and balloting often took place in open rooms or on sidewalks. Election clerks and judges were not public officials but partisans chosen by the political parties.

Nor did public authorities issue official ballots. Instead voters used party tickets, strips of paper printed by the parties. These had only the names of the candidates of the party issuing them and often varied in size and color. The voter's use of a ballot thus revealed his party allegiance. Tickets were distributed by paid party workers known as peddlers or hawkers, who stationed themselves near the polls, each trying to force his ticket on prospective voters. These contending hawkers contributed greatly to election day chaos. Fighting and intimidation were so commonplace at the polls that one state supreme court ruled in 1887 that they were "acceptable" features of elections.

As the court recognized, the open and partisan aspects of the electoral process did not necessarily lead to election fraud, however much they shaped the nature of political participation. In these circumstances, campaigns and elections provided opportunities for men to demonstrate publicly their commitment to their party and its values, thereby reinforcing their partisan loyalties.

Nonvoting women, too, often exhibited their partisanship in this exciting political environment. Women wrote partisan literature and gave campaign speeches; Anna Dickinson, one of the period's most popular orators, was hired by the Republican National Committee to campaign in the East and Midwest. Sometimes partisan women acted together with men; other times they worked through separate women's organizations. J. Ellen Foster established the Woman's National Republican Association in 1888 and built it into an organizing machine for the Republican Party with numerous state and local clubs. In these partisan groups women discussed and circulated party literature and devised plans to influence elections. Their partisanship was so deeply embedded that they remained loyal Republicans even when their party repudiated woman suffrage. "What discourages me about women," noted suffragist Susan B. Anthony, was that they care more for "[their] political party . . . than for [their] own political rights."

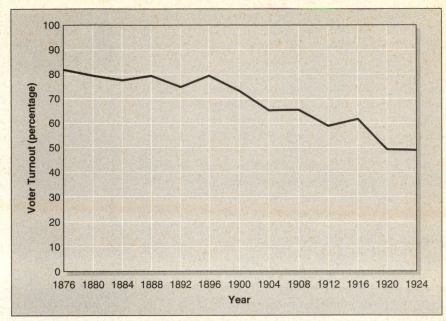

FIGURE 20-1   Voter Turnout in Presidential Elections, 1876–1924
The exciting partisan politics of the late nineteenth century produced very high voter turnouts, but as party competition declined and states enacted more restrictive voting regulations, popular participation in elections fell in the twentieth century.

PARTISAN POLITICS

A remarkably close balance prevailed between the two major parties in the elections of this era. Democrats and Republicans had virtually the same level of electoral support, one reason they worked so hard to get

The campaign pageantry of a Republican parade in Canton, Ohio, in 1896 illustrates the central role played by political parties in entertaining, organizing, and mobilizing voters. Over a century later, parties have lost many of their functions and much of their popular support.

out the vote (see Map 20-1). Control of the presidency and Congress shifted back and forth between them. Rarely did either party control both branches of government at once.

The party balance also gave great influence to New York, New Jersey, Ohio, and Indiana, whose evenly divided voters controlled electoral votes that could swing an election either way. Said one New York politician, "We need the entire Republican vote, and this means work and attention in every school district in the State." Both parties tended to nominate presidential and vice presidential candidates from those states to woo their voters. The parties also concentrated campaign funds and strategy on the swing states. Thus the Republican presidential candidate James Garfield of Ohio commented during the election campaign in 1880: "Nothing is wanting except an immediate and liberal supply of money for campaign expenses to make Indiana certain. With a victory there, the rest is easy." Garfield narrowly carried Indiana by six thousand votes and the nation by nine thousand, out of 9.2 million cast. His victory was not the outcome of a contest over great issues but of carefully organized, tightly balanced parties mobilizing their supporters.

Party loyalty. Interrelated regional, ethnic, religious, and local factors determined the party affiliations of most Americans. Economic issues, although important to the politics of the era, generally did not decide party ties. Farmers, for example, despite often shared economic concerns, affiliated with both major parties. Like religious belief and ethnic identity, partisan loyalty was largely a cultural trait passed from parents to children—a situation that helps to explain the electoral stability of most communities.

Republicans were strongest in the North and Midwest, where they benefited from their party's role as the defender of the Union in the Civil War. "Republicanism in [Iowa] is not a logical conviction," reported one journalist in 1884; "it is a baleful fanaticism. . . . The war is still in progress in this region. . . . The women are worse than the men; they are intolerant, ferocious, implacable." But not all Northerners voted for the Grand Old Party, or GOP. The Republican Party appealed primarily to old-stock Americans and other Protestants, including those of German and Scandinavian descent. African Americans, loyal to the party that had emancipated and enfranchised the slaves of the South, also supported the GOP where they could vote. Democrats were strongest in the South, where they stood as the defender of the traditions of the region's white population. But Democrats also drew support in the urban Northeast, especially from Catholics and recent immigrants.

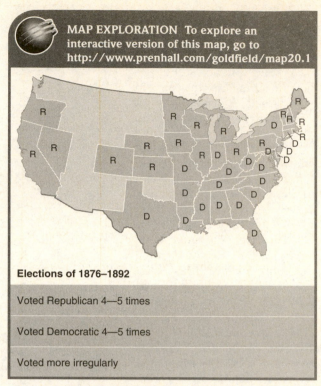

MAP EXPLORATION To explore an interactive version of this map, go to http://www.prenhall.com/goldfield/map20.1

Elections of 1876–1892

Voted Republican 4—5 times

Voted Democratic 4—5 times

Voted more irregularly

MAP 20-1   **The Two-Party Stalemate of the Late Nineteenth Century**
Strong parties, staunch loyalties, and an evenly divided electorate made for exciting politics but often stalemated government in the late nineteenth century. Most states voted consistently for one of the major parties, leaving the few swing states like New York and Indiana the scenes of fierce partisan battles.

Party identities. Each major party thus consisted of a complex coalition of groups with differing traditions and interests. One observer of the Democratic Party in California described it as "a sort of Democratic happy family, like we see in the prairie-dog villages, where owls, rattlesnakes, prairie dogs, and lizards all live in the same hole." This internal diversity often provoked conflict and threatened party stability. To hold its coalition together, each party identified itself with a theme that appealed broadly to all its constituents, while suggesting that it was menaced by the members and objectives of the opposing party.

Republicans identified their party with nationalism and national unity and attacked the Democrats as an "alliance between the embittered South and the slums of the Northern cities." They combined a "bloody shirt" appeal to the memories of the Civil War with campaigns for immigration restriction and cultural uniformity. Seeing a threat to American society in efforts by Catholic immigrants to preserve their ethnic and cultural traditions, for example, Republican legislatures in several states in the 1880s and 1890s enacted laws regulating parochial schools, the use of foreign languages, and alcohol consumption.

Democrats portrayed themselves as the party of limited government and "personal liberties," a theme that appealed both to the racism of white Southerners and the resentment immigrants felt about the nativist meddling the Republicans favored. The Democrats' commitment to personal liberties had limits. They supported the disfranchisement of African Americans, the exclusion of Chinese immigrants, and the dispossession of American Indians. Nevertheless, their emphasis on traditional individualism and localism proved popular.

The partisan politics of both major parties culminated in party machines, especially at the local level. Led by powerful bosses, such as the Democrat Richard Croker of New York and the Republican George Cox of Cincinnati, these machines controlled not only city politics but also municipal government. Party activists used well-organized ward clubs to mobilize working-class voters, who were rewarded by municipal jobs and baskets of food or coal doled out by the machine. Such assistance was often necessary, given the lack of public welfare systems, but to buy votes the machine also sold favors. Public contracts and franchises were peddled to businesses whose high bids covered kickbacks to the machine.

Third parties.   The partisan politics of the era left room for several third parties, organized around specific issues or groups. The **Prohibition Party** persistently championed the abolition of alcohol but also supported electoral reforms such as woman suffrage, economic reforms such as railroad regulation and income taxes, and social reforms including improved race relations. It won as many as a quarter of a million votes, drawn mostly from Republicans, and its strong showing in New York may have cost the GOP the presidential election in 1884.

Some farmers and workers, fed up with the major parties, formed larger but shorter-lived third parties. These parties charged that Republicans and Democrats had failed to respond to economic problems caused by industrialization or, worse still, had deliberately promoted powerful business interests at the expense of ordinary Americans. The **Greenback Party** of the 1870s denounced "the infamous financial legislation which takes all from the many to enrich the few." Its policies of labor reform and currency inflation (to stimulate and democratize the economy) attracted

supporters from Maine to Texas. Other significant third parties included the Anti-Monopoly party, the Union Labor party, and, most important, the People's or **Populist Party** of the 1890s. Although third parties often won temporary success at the local or regional level, they never permanently displaced the major parties or undermined traditional voter allegiances.

ASSOCIATIONAL POLITICS

Associations of like-minded citizens, operating outside the electoral arena, played an increasingly important role in late-nineteenth-century politics. These organizations worked to achieve public policies beneficial to their members. Farmers organized many such groups, most notably the Patrons of Husbandry, known familiarly as the Grange (see Chapter 17). Established in 1867, with both women and men eligible for membership, the Grange had 22,000 local lodges and nearly a million members by 1875. Its campaign for public regulation of the rates charged by railroads and grain elevators helped convince midwestern states to pass the so-called **Granger laws**. The Grange also sought reforms in the nation's financial system. Although it inspired the formation of small independent farmers' parties in the Midwest and on the Pacific coast, the Grange itself remained nonpartisan.

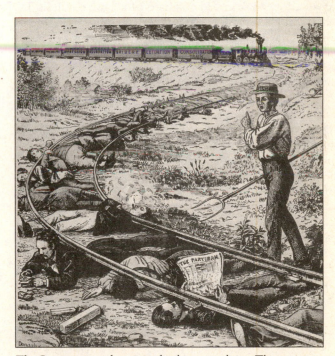

The Grange rejected partisanship but not politics. This sympathetic cartoon shows a Granger trying to warn Americans blindly absorbed in partisan politics of the dangers of onrushing industrialization.

To the Grangers' dismay, industrialists also formed pressure groups. Organizations such as the American Iron and Steel Association and the American Protective Tariff League lobbied Congress for high tariff laws and made campaign contributions to friendly politicians of both parties. A small group of conservative reformers known derisively as **Mugwumps** (the term derives from the Algonquian word for "chief") objected to both tariffs and the government regulations farmers favored as interfering with "natural" economic laws. They devoted most of their efforts, however, to campaigning for honest and efficient government through civil-service reform. They organized the National Civil Service Reform

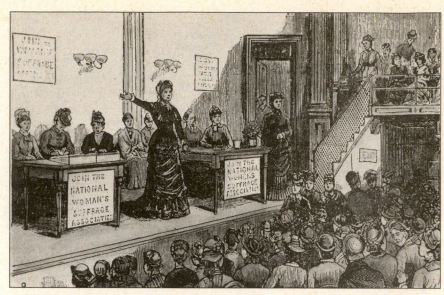

A meeting in 1880 of the National Woman Suffrage Association protested the exclusion of women from electoral politics. Susan B. Anthony noted with regret that "to all men woman suffrage is only a side issue."

League to publicize their plans, lobby Congress and state legislatures, and endorse sympathetic candidates. Other pressure groups focused on cultural politics. The rabidly anti-Catholic American Protective Association, for example, agitated for laws restricting immigration, taxing church property, and inspecting Catholic religious institutions.

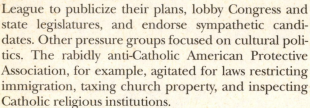

Women as activists.

Women were also active in associational politics. Susan B. Anthony and others formed groups to lobby Congress and state legislatures for constitutional amendments extending the right to vote to women. The leading organizations merged in 1890 as the **National American Woman Suffrage Association**. Despite the opposition of male politicians of both major parties, suffragists had succeeded by the mid-1890s in gaining full woman suffrage in four western states—Wyoming, Colorado, Idaho, and Utah—and partial suffrage (the right to vote in school elections) in several other states, east and west.

Other women influenced public issues through social service organizations. Although the belief that women belonged in the domestic sphere limited their involvement in electoral politics, it furnished a basis for political action focused on welfare and moral reform. With petition campaigns, demonstrations, and lobbying, women's social service organizations sought to remedy poverty and disease, improve education and recreation, and provide day nurseries for the children of workingwomen. The Illinois Woman's Alliance—

organized in 1888 by suffragists, women assemblies of the Knights of Labor, and middle-class women's clubs—investigated the conditions of women and children in workshops and factories, campaigned successfully for protective labor legislation and compulsory school-attendance laws, and obtained greater representation of women on the Chicago school board. The Woman's Municipal League, organized in New York City in 1894, described itself as a "political club" for women concerned with "education, sanitation, public health, and police and fire protection."

Women also combined domesticity and politics in the temperance movement. Alcoholism, widespread in American society, was regarded as a major cause of crime, wife abuse, and broken homes. The temperance movement thus invoked women's presumed moral superiority to address a real problem that fell within their accepted sphere. The Woman's Christian Temperance Union (WCTU) gained a massive membership by campaigning for restrictive liquor laws. It helped secure prohibition or local-option laws in a dozen states and was particularly successful in persuading legislatures to require temperance education in the public schools.

Under the leadership of Frances Willard, the WCTU built on traditional women's concerns to develop an important critique of American society. Reversing the conventional view, Willard argued that alcohol abuse was a result, not a cause, of poverty and social disorder. Under the slogan of "Home Protection," the WCTU inserted domestic issues into the political sphere with a campaign for social and economic reforms far beyond temperance. It particularly sought to strengthen and enforce laws against rape. Willard bitterly noted that twenty states fixed the age of consent at ten and that "in Massachusetts and Vermont it is a greater crime to steal a cow" than to rape a woman. The WCTU also pushed for improved health conditions, reached out to the Knights of Labor to support workplace reforms, and lobbied for federal aid to education, particularly as a means to provide schooling for black children in the South. It eventually supported woman suffrage as well, on the grounds that women needed the vote to fulfill their duty to protect home, family, and morality. The organization further expanded its political activities in 1887 by making Ada Bittenbender, a Nebraska attorney, its Superintendent on Legislation, and she established an effective office in Washington, testifying before Congress, drafting model legislation, and otherwise developing lobbying techniques that other special interest groups have subsequently followed.

THE LIMITS OF GOVERNMENT

Despite the popular enthusiasm for partisan politics and the persistent pressure of associational politics, government in the late nineteenth century was neither active nor productive by present standards. The receding government activism of the Civil War and Reconstruction years coincided with a resurgent belief in localism and **laissez-faire** policies. In addition, a Congress and presidency divided between the two major parties, a small and inefficient bureaucracy, and judicial restraints joined powerful private interests to limit the size and objectives of the federal government.

THE WEAK PRESIDENCY

The presidency was a weak and restricted institution. The impeachment of President Johnson at the outset of Reconstruction had undermined the office. President Grant clearly subordinated it to the legislative branch by deferring to Congress on appointments and legislation. Other factors contributed as well. The men who filled the office between 1877 and 1897—Republicans Rutherford B. Hayes (1877–1881), James A. Garfield (1881), and Chester A. Arthur (1881–1885); Democrat Grover Cleveland (1885–1889 and 1893–1897); and Republican Benjamin Harrison (1889–1893)—were all honest and generally capable. Each had built a solid political record at the state or federal level. But they were all conservatives, with a narrow view of the presidency, and proposed few initiatives. The most aggressive of them, Cleveland, used

his energy in a singularly negative fashion, vetoing two-thirds of all the bills Congress passed, more than all his predecessors combined. Cleveland once vetoed a relief measure for drought-stricken Texas farmers with the statement that "though the people support the Government, the Government should not support the people." This attitude limited government action.

The presidents of this era viewed their duties as chiefly administrative. They made little effort to reach out to the public or to exert legislative leadership. In 1885, Woodrow Wilson, at the time a professor of history and government, described "the business of the president" as "not much above routine" and concluded that the office might "not inconveniently" be made purely administrative, its occupant a sort of tenured civil servant. (Wilson, who helped transform the presidency into a powerful office in the twentieth century, took a very different view when he became president himself in 1913.) Benjamin Harrison devoted as many as six hours a day to dealing with office seekers, and Garfield lamented, "My day is frittered away by the personal seeking of people, when it ought to be given to the great problems which concern the whole country."

The presidency was also hampered by its limited control over bureaus and departments, which responded more directly to Congress, and by its small staff. Indeed, the president's staff consisted of no more than a half-dozen secretaries, clerks, and telegraphers. As Cleveland complained, "If the President has any great policy in mind or on hand he has no one to help him work it out."

THE INEFFICIENT CONGRESS

Congress was the foremost branch of the national government. It exercised authority over the federal budget, oversaw the cabinet, debated public issues, and controlled legislation. Its members were often state and national party leaders, who were strong-willed and, as one senator conceded, "tolerated no intrusion from the President or from anybody else."

But Congress was scarcely efficient. Its chambers were noisy and chaotic, and members rarely devoted their attention to the business at hand. Instead, they played cards, read newspapers, or sent a page to get fruit or tobacco from the vendors who lined the hallways of the capitol. The repeated shifts in party control of Congress also impeded effective action. So, too, did the loss of experienced legislators to rapid turnover. In some Congresses, a majority of members were first-termers.

Procedural rules, based on precedents from a simpler time and manipulated by determined partisans, hindered congressional action. Some rules restricted the introduction of legislation; others prevented its passage. The most notorious rule required that a quorum be not only present but voting. When the House was narrowly divided along party lines, the minority could block all business simply by refusing to answer when the roll was called.

But as a nationalizing economy required more national legislation, business before Congress grew relentlessly (see Figure 20-2). The expanding scale of congressional work prompted a gradual reform of procedures and the centralization of power in the Speaker of the House and the leading committees. These changes did not, however, create a coherent program for government action.

THE FEDERAL BUREAUCRACY AND THE SPOILS SYSTEM

Reflecting presidential weakness and congressional inefficiency, the federal bureaucracy remained small and limited in the late nineteenth century. There were little more than fifty thousand government employees in 1871, and three-fourths of them were local postmasters scattered across the nation. Only six thousand, from President Grant to janitors, worked in Washington. The number of federal employees doubled to 100,000 in 1881 and grew again to 157,000 in 1891 and to 239,000 in 1901. It was still the postal service, however, that absorbed most of this increase.

FIGURE 20-2   **Increase in Congressional Business, 1871–1901**
Industrialization, urbanization, and western expansion brought increased demands for government action, but the party stalemate, laissez-faire attitudes, and inefficient public institutions often blocked effective responses.

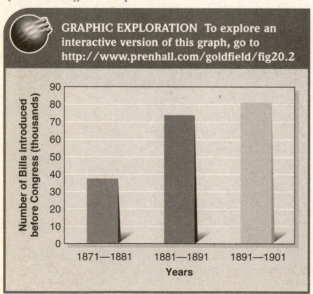

GRAPHIC EXPLORATION To explore an interactive version of this graph, go to http://www.prenhall.com/goldfield/fig20.2

The system for selecting and supervising federal officials had developed gradually in the first half of the century. Known as the spoils system, its basic principle was that victorious politicians awarded government jobs to party workers, with little regard for qualifications, and ousted the previous employees. Appointees then typically promised part of their salary and time to the political interests of their patron or party. The spoils system played a crucial role in all aspects of politics. It enabled party leaders to strengthen their organizations, reward loyal party service, and attract the political workers needed to mobilize the electorate. Supporters described it as a democratic system that offered opportunities to many citizens and prevented the emergence of an entrenched bureaucracy.

Critics, however, charged that the system was riddled with corruption, abuse, and inefficiency. Rapid turnover bred instability; political favoritism bred incompetence. One secretary of the navy, appointed at the behest of Indiana's Republican machine, was said to have exclaimed during his first official inspection of a ship: "Why, the thing's hollow!" Certainly the spoils system was ineffective for filling positions that required special clerical skills, such as typing, or scientific expertise like that required by the Weather Bureau (established in 1870) or the U.S. Geological Survey (established in 1879). Even worse, the spoils system also absorbed the president and Congress in unproductive conflicts over patronage.

INCONSISTENT STATE GOVERNMENT

State governments were more active than the federal government. Considered closer and more responsible to the people, they had long exercised police power and regulatory authority. They collected taxes for education and public works, and they promoted private enterprise and public health. Still, they did little by today's standards. Few people thought it appropriate for government at any level to offer direct help to particular social groups. Some state governments contracted in the 1870s and 1880s following the wartime activism of the 1860s. Newly elected Democratic governors hewed to their party's narrow view of government, and new state constitutions restricted the scope of public authority. California's constitution of 1879, for example, limited the state government's authority so sharply that one wit even proposed abolishing the legislature, "and any person who shall be guilty of suggesting that a Legislature be held, shall be punished as a felon without the benefit of clergy."

But state governments gradually expanded their role in response to the stresses produced by industrialization. Following the lead of Massachusetts in 1869, a majority of states had by the turn of the century created commissions to investigate and regulate industry. Public intervention in other areas of the industrial economy soon followed. One observer noted in 1887 that state governments enacted many laws and established numerous state agencies in "utter disregard of the laissez-faire principle." In Minnesota, for example, the state helped farmers by establishing a dairy commission, prohibiting the manufacture or sale of margarine, creating a bureau of animal industry, and employing state veterinarians. In the lumber industry, state officials oversaw every log "from the woods to the saw-mill." State inspectors examined Minnesota's steam boilers, oil production, and sanitary conditions. Other laws regulated railroads, telegraphs, and dangerous occupations, prohibited racial discrimination in inns, and otherwise protected the public welfare.

Not all such agencies and laws were effective, nor were all state governments as diligent as Minnesota's. Southern states, especially, lagged, and one Midwesterner complained that his legislature merely "meets in ignorance, sits in corruption, and dissolves in disgrace every two years." Still, the widening scope of state action represented a growing acceptance of public responsibility for social welfare and economic life and laid the foundation for more effective steps in the early twentieth century.

PUBLIC POLICIES AND NATIONAL ELECTIONS

Several great issues dominated the national political arena in the late nineteenth century, including civil service reform, tariffs, and business and financial regulation. Civil-service reform attracted relatively little popular interest, but Americans argued passionately about even the smallest details of tariff, regulatory, and financial legislation. Rarely, however, did these issues clearly and consistently separate the major political parties. Instead, they divided each party into factions along regional, interest, and economic lines. As a consequence, these leading issues often played only a small role in determining elections and were seldom resolved by government action.

CIVIL SERVICE REFORM

Reform of the spoils system emerged as a prominent issue during the Hayes administration. Such reformers as the Mugwumps wanted a professional civil service, based on merit and divorced from politics. They wanted officeholders to be selected on the basis of competitive written examinations and protected from removal on political grounds. They expected such a

system to promote efficiency, economy, and honesty in government. But they also expected it to increase their own influence and minimize that of "mere politicians." As one Baltimore Mugwump said, civil-service reform would replace ignorant and corrupt officeholders with "gentlemen . . . who need nothing and want nothing from government except the satisfaction of using their talents," or at least with "sober, industrious . . . middle-class persons who have taken over . . . the proper standards of conduct."

Not all Americans agreed with such haughty views. The *New York Sun* denounced "the proposition that men shall be appointed to office as the result of examinations in book learning and that they shall remain in office during life. . . . We don't want an aristocracy of office-holders in this country." And a Midwestern newspaper declared, "A free land develops free men. They will accept no dictation from men who claim superior virtue or superior wisdom."

President Hayes favored civil-service reform but did not fully renounce the spoils system. He rewarded

In this 1881 cartoon, the evil spirit of partisanship threatens a government clerk hesitating to kick back an assessed portion of his salary to the party in power. Civil service reformers wanted to eliminate political factors in staffing the federal bureaucracy.

those who had helped to elect him, permitted party leaders to name or veto candidates for the cabinet, and insisted that his own appointees contribute funds to Republican election campaigns. But he rejected the claims of some machine leaders and office seekers and proposed reforms, which Congress promptly blocked. He struck a blow for change, however, when he fired Chester A. Arthur from his post as New York customs-house collector after an investigation pronounced Arthur's patronage system "unsound in principle, dangerous in practice, . . . and calculated to encourage and perpetuate the official ignorance, inefficiency, and corruption. . . ."

The weakness of the civil-service reformers was dramatically underscored in 1880 when the Republicans, to improve their chances of carrying the crucial state of New York, nominated Arthur for vice president on a ticket headed by James Garfield of Ohio. They won, and Garfield immediately found himself enmeshed in the demands of the unreformed spoils system. He once complained to his wife, "I had hardly arrived before the door-bell began to ring and the old stream of office-seekers began to pour in. They had scented my coming and were lying in wait for me like vultures for a wounded bison. All day long it has been a steeple chase, I fleeing and they pursuing." Within a few months of his inauguration in 1881, Garfield was assassinated by a disappointed and crazed office seeker, and Arthur became president.

Public dismay over this tragedy finally spurred changes in the spoils system. Arthur himself urged Congress to act, and in 1883, it passed the **Pendleton Civil Service Act**. This measure prohibited federal employees from soliciting or receiving political contributions from government workers and created the Civil Service Commission to administer competitive examinations to applicants for government jobs. The act gave the commission jurisdiction over only about 10 percent of federal positions but contained a provision that allowed presidents to extend its authority. And subsequent presidents did so, if sometimes only to prevent their own appointees from being turned out by a succeeding administration. A professional civil service free from partisan politics gradually emerged, strengthening the executive branch's ability to handle its increasing administrative responsibilities.

The new emphasis on merit and skill rather than party ties opened new opportunities to women. Federal clerks were nearly exclusively male as late as 1862, but by the early 1890s, women held a third of the clerical positions in the executive departments in Washington. These workers constituted the nation's first substantial female clerical labor force. Their work in public life challenged the conventional belief that a woman's ability and personality limited her to the domestic sphere. To succeed, clerks had to be assertive and competent, to acquire managerial skills, and to think of their careers as permanent, not temporary. Julia Henderson described her work as an examiner of accounts in the Interior Department in 1893 as "brain work of a character that requires a knowledge not only of the rulings of this Department, but also those of the Treasury, Second Auditor, Second Comptroller, and Revised Statutes; demanding the closest and most critical attention, together with a great deal of legal and business knowledge."

THE POLITICAL LIFE OF THE TARIFF

Americans debated heatedly over tariff legislation throughout the late nineteenth century. This complex issue linked basic economic questions to partisan, ideological, and regional concerns. Tariffs on imported goods provided revenue for the federal government and protected American industry from European competition. They thus promoted industrial growth but often allowed favored industries to garner high profits. By the 1880s, tariffs covered four thousand items and generated more revenue than the government needed to carry on its limited operations.

Reflecting its commitment to industry, the Republican Party vigorously championed protective tariffs. Party leaders also claimed that American labor benefited from tariff protection. "Reduce the tariff, and labor is the first to suffer," declared William McKinley of Ohio. Most Democrats, by contrast, favored tariff reduction, a position that reflected their party's relatively laissez-faire outlook. They argued that lower tariffs would encourage foreign trade and, by reducing the treasury surplus, minimize the temptation for the government to pursue activist policies. They pointed out the discriminatory effects of high tariffs, which benefited some interests, such as certain manufacturers, but hurt others, such as some farmers, while raising the cost of living for all (see the Overview table, "Arguments in the Tariff Debates").

The differences between the parties, however, were often more rhetorical than substantial. They disagreed only about how high tariffs should be and what interests they should protect. Regardless of party position, congressmen of both parties voted for tariffs that would benefit their districts. California Democrats called for protective duties on wool and raisins, products produced in California; Massachusetts Republicans, to aid their state's shoe manufacturers, supported tariffs on shoes but opposed tariffs on leather. A Democratic senator from Indiana, elected on a campaign pledge to reduce tariffs, summed up the prevailing rule succinctly: "I am a

Overview

Arguments in the Tariff Debates

Area Affected	High-Tariff Advocates	Low-Tariff Advocates
Industry	Tariffs promote industrial growth.	Tariffs inflate corporate profits.
Employment	Tariffs stimulate job growth.	Tariffs restrict competition.
Wages and prices	Tariffs permit higher wages.	Tariffs increase consumer prices.
Government	Tariffs provide government revenue.	Tariffs violate the principle of laissez-faire and produce revenues that tempt the government to activism.
Trade	Tariffs protect the domestic market.	Tariffs restrict foreign trade.

protectionist for every interest which I am sent here by my constituents to protect."

In the 1884 campaign, the Republican presidential candidate, James G. Blaine, maintained that prosperity and high employment depended on high duties. The Democrats' platform endorsed a lowered tariff, but their candidate, New York governor Grover Cleveland, generally ignored the issue. Unable to address this and other important issues, both parties resorted to scandalmongering. The Democrats exploited Blaine's image as a beneficiary of the spoils system, which convinced the Mugwumps to bolt to Cleveland. Blaine's nomination, resolved the Massachusetts Mugwumps, was "an insult to the conscience of the country." Republicans responded by exposing Cleveland as the father of an illegitimate child. One observer called the election "a more bitter, personal, and disgusting campaign than we have ever seen."

Cleveland continued to avoid the tariff issue for three years after his election, until the growing treasury surplus and rising popular pressure for tariff reduction prompted him to act. He devoted his entire 1887 annual message to attacking the "vicious, inequitable, and illogical" tariff, apparently making it the dominant issue of his 1888 reelection campaign. Once again, however, the distinctive political attribute of the period—intense and organized campaigning between closely balanced parties—forced both Democrats and Republicans to blur their positions. Cleveland proposed a Democratic platform that ignored his recent message and did not even use the word tariff. When the party convention adopted a tariff-reduction plank, Cleveland complained bitterly and named high-tariff advocates to manage his campaign. "What a predicament the party is placed in," lamented one

Texas Democrat, with tariff reform "for its battle cry and with a known protectionist . . . as our chairman." Cleveland won a slightly larger share of popular votes than his Republican opponent, Benjamin Harrison of Indiana, but Harrison carried the electoral college, indicating the decisive importance of strategic campaigning, local issues, and large campaign funds rather than great national issues.

The triumphant Republicans raised tariffs to unprecedented levels with the McKinley Tariff Act of 1890. McKinley praised the law as "protective in every paragraph and American on every page," but it provoked a popular backlash that helped return the Democrats to power. Still, the Democrats made little effort to push tariff reform. The *Atlanta Constitution* mused about such tariff politics in a bit of doggerel:

It's funny 'bout this tariff—how they've lost it
　　or forgot;
They were rushing it to Congress once; their
　　collars were so hot
They could hardly wait to fix it 'till we harvested a crop;
Was it such a burnin' question that they had
　　to let it drop?

THE BEGINNINGS OF FEDERAL REGULATION

While business leaders pressed for protective tariffs and other public policies that promoted their interests, they otherwise used their great political influence to insure governmental laissez-faire. Popular pressure nonetheless compelled Congress to take the first steps toward the regulation of business with the passage of the **Interstate Commerce Act** in 1887 and the **Sherman Antitrust Act** in 1890.

The rapid growth of great industrial corporations and their disruptive effects on traditional practices and values profoundly alarmed the public (see Chapter 18). Farmers condemned the power of corporations over transportation facilities and their monopolization of industries affecting agriculture, from those that manufactured farm machinery to those that ran flour mills. Small business owners suffered from the destructive competition of corporations, workers were exploited by their control of the labor market, and consumers felt victimized by high prices. The result was a growing demand to rein in the corporations.

Popular concern focused first on the nation's railroads, the preeminent symbol of big business. Both farm groups and business shippers complained of discriminatory rates levied by railroads. Consumers condemned the railroads' use of pooling arrangements to suppress competition and raise rates. The resulting pressure was responsible for the Granger laws enacted in several midwestern states in the 1870s to regulate railroad freight and storage rates.

At first, the Supreme Court upheld this legislation, ruling, in *Munn v. Illinois* (1877), that state governments had the right to regulate private property when it was "devoted to a public use." But in 1886, the Court ruled in *Wabash, St. Louis, and Pacific Railway Company v. Illinois* that only the federal government could regulate interstate commerce. This decision effectively ended state regulation of railroads but simultaneously increased pressure for congressional action. "Upon no public question are the people so nearly unanimous as upon the proposition that Congress should undertake in some way the regulation of interstate business," concluded a Senate committee. With the support of both major parties, Congress in 1887 passed the Interstate Commerce Act.

The act prohibited rebates, discriminatory rates, and pooling and established the **Interstate Commerce Commission (ICC)** to investigate and prosecute violations. The ICC was the first federal regulatory agency. But its powers were too limited to be effective. Senator Nelson Aldrich of Rhode Island, a leading spokesman for business interests, described

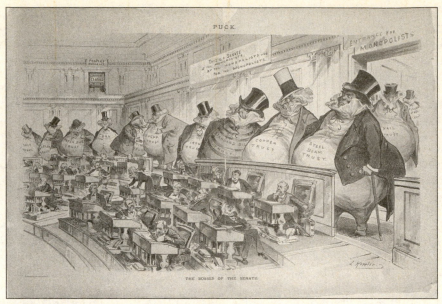

"The Bosses of the Senate," a political cartoon of 1889, depicts the popular belief that huge corporate trusts controlled the government and corrupted public policy. This conviction helped fuel the demand for antitrust legislation but may not have been allayed by the weaknesses of the Sherman Act.

the law as an "empty menace to great interests, made to answer the clamor of the ignorant." Presidents did little to enforce it, and railroads continued their objectionable practices. They frustrated the commission by refusing to provide required information and endlessly appealing its orders to a conservative judiciary. In its first fifteen years, only one court case was decided in favor of the ICC. Not surprisingly, then, popular dissatisfaction with the railroads continued into the twentieth century. Californian Frank Norris, in his novel *The Octopus* (1901), likened them to "a gigantic parasite fattening upon the lifeblood of an entire commonwealth."

Many people saw railroad abuses as indicative of the dangers of corporate power in general and demanded a broader federal response. As with railroad regulation, the first antitrust laws—laws intended to break up or regulate corporate monopolies—were passed by states. Exposés of the monopolistic practices of such corporations as Standard Oil forced both major parties to endorse national antitrust legislation during the campaign of 1888. In 1890, Congress enacted the Sherman Antitrust Act with only a single vote in opposition. But this near unanimity concealed real differences over the desirability and purpose of the law. Although it emphatically prohibited any combination in restraint of trade (any attempt to restrict competition), it was otherwise vaguely written and hence weak in its ability to prevent abuses. The courts further weakened the act, and presidents of both parties made little effort to enforce it. Essentially still unfettered, large corporations remained an ominous threat in the eyes of many Americans.

THE MONEY QUESTION

Persistent wrangling over questions of currency and coinage made monetary policy the most divisive political issue in the late nineteenth century. President Garfield suggested the complexities of this subject when he wryly declared that a member of Congress had been committed to an asylum after "he devoted himself almost exclusively to the study of the currency, became fully entangled with the theories of the subject, and became insane." Despite the sometimes arcane and difficult nature of the money question, millions of Americans adopted positions on it and defended them with religious ferocity.

Creditors, especially bankers, as well as conservative economists and many business leaders favored limiting the money supply. They called this a **sound money** policy and insisted that it would insure economic stability, maintain property values, and retain investor confidence. Farmers and other debtors complained that this deflationary monetary policy would exacerbate the trend toward depressed prices in the American economy. They feared that it would depress already low crop prices, drive debtors further into debt, and restrict economic opportunities. They favored expanding the money supply to match the country's growing population and economy. They expected this inflationary policy to raise prices, stimulate the economy, reduce debt burdens, and increase opportunities.

The conservative leadership of both major parties supported the sound money policy, but their rank-and-file membership, especially in the West and the South, included many inflationists. As a result, the parties avoided confronting each other on the money issue.

The conflict between advocates of sound money and inflation centered on the use of paper money— "greenbacks"—and silver coinage. The greenback controversy had its roots in the Civil War. To meet its expenses during the war, the federal government issued $450 million in greenbacks—paper money backed only by the credit of the United States, not by gold or silver, the traditional basis of currency. After the war, creditors demanded that these greenbacks be withdrawn from circulation. Debtors and other Americans caught up in a postwar depression favored retaining the greenbacks and even expanding their use.

In 1875, sound money advocates in Congress enacted a deflationary law that withdrew some greenbacks from circulation and required that the remainder be convertible into gold after 1878. This action forced the money issue into electoral politics. Outraged inflationists organized the Greenback Party. They charged that the major parties had "failed to take the side of the people" and instead supported the "great moneyed institutions." The Greenbackers polled more than a million votes in 1878 and elected fourteen members of Congress, nearly gaining the balance of power in the House. As the depression faded, however, so did interest in the greenback issue, and the party soon withered.

The silver issue.　　Inflationists then turned their attention to the silver issue, which would prove more enduring and disruptive. Historically, the United States had been on a bimetallic standard; that is, it used both gold and silver as the basis of its currency. But after the 1840s, the market price of silver rose above the currency value assigned to it by the government. Silver miners and owners began to sell the metal for commercial use rather than to the government for coinage, and little silver money circulated. In 1873, Congress passed a law "demonetizing" silver, making gold the only standard for American currency. Gold-standard supporters hoped that the law would promote international trade by aligning U.S. financial policy with that of Great Britain, which insisted on gold-based currency. But they also wanted to prevent new silver discoveries in the American West from expanding the money supply.

Indeed, silver production soon boomed, flooding the commercial market and dropping the value of the metal. Dismayed miners wanted the Treasury Department to purchase their surplus silver on the old terms and demanded a return to the bimetallic system. More important, the rural debtor groups seeking currency inflation joined in this demand, seeing the return to silver coinage as a means to reverse the long deflationary trend in the economy. Many passionately denounced the "Crime of '73" as a conspiracy of eastern bankers and foreign interests to control the money system to the detriment of ordinary Americans.

Again, both major parties equivocated. Eastern conservatives of both parties denounced silver; Southerners and Westerners demanded **free silver**, meaning unlimited silver coinage. One New York Democrat complained that western and southern members of his party were "mad as wild Texas steers on this silver dollar business. As we pass each other in the streets they seem to sneer, and hiss through their teeth the words 'gold bug,' and look as if they would like to spit upon [us]."

By 1878, a bipartisan coalition succeeded in passing the Bland-Allison Act. This compromise measure required the government to buy and coin at least $2 million of silver a month. However, the government never exceeded the minimum, and the law had little inflationary effect. Republican President Arthur and Democratic President Cleveland recommended repealing the Bland-Allison Act, but the parties avoided the silver issue in their national platforms, fearing its divisive effect.

As hard times hit rural regions in the late 1880s, inflationists secured passage of the Sherman Silver Purchase Act of 1890. The Treasury now had to buy a larger volume of silver and pay for it with treasury notes redeemable in either gold or silver. But this, too, produced little inflation, because the government did not coin the silver it purchased, redeemed the notes only with gold, and, as western silver production increased further, had to spend less and less to buy the stipulated amount of silver. Debtors of both parties remained convinced that the government favored the "classes rather than the masses." Gold standard advocates (again, of both parties) were even less happy with the law and planned to repeal it at their first opportunity. The division between them was deep and bitter.

THE CRISIS OF THE 1890s

In the 1890s, social, economic, and political pressures created a crisis for both the political system and the government. A third-party political challenge generated by agricultural discontent disrupted traditional party politics. A devastating depression spawned social misery and labor violence. Changing public attitudes led to new demands on the government and a realignment of parties and voters. These developments, in turn, set the stage for important political, economic, and social changes in the new century.

FARMERS PROTEST INEQUITIES

The agricultural depression that engulfed the Great Plains and the South in the late 1880s brought misery and despair to millions of rural Americans. Falling crop prices and rising debt overwhelmed many people already exhausted from overwork and alarmed by the new corporate order. "At the age of 52 years, after a long life of toil, economy, and self-denial, I find myself and family virtual paupers," lamented one Kansan. His family's farm, rather than being "a house of refuge for our declining years, by a few turns of the monopolistic crank has been rendered valueless." To a large extent, the farmers' plight stemmed from conditions beyond control, including bad weather and an international overproduction of farm products. Seeking relief, however, the farmers naturally focused on the inequities of railroad discrimination, tariff favoritism, a restrictive financial system, and apparently indifferent political parties.

Credit inequities.   Angry farmers particularly singled out the systems of money and credit that worked so completely against agricultural interests. Government rules for national banks directed credit into the urbanized North and East at the expense of the rural South and West and prohibited loans on farm property and real estate. As a result, farmers had to turn to other sources of credit and pay higher interest rates. In the West, farmers borrowed from mortgage companies to buy land and machinery.

Declining crop prices made it difficult for them to pay their debts and often required them to borrow more and at higher rates. In hard times, mortgage foreclosures crushed the hopes of many farmers. In the South, the credit shortage interacted with the practices of cotton marketing and retail trade to create the sharecropping system, which trapped more and more farmers, black and white, in a vicious pattern of exploitation. The government's policies of monetary deflation worsened the debt burden for all farmers.

Freight rates and tariffs.   Farmers protested other features of the nation's economic system as well. Railroad freight rates were two or three times higher in the West and South than in the North and East. The near-monopolistic control of grain elevators and cotton brokerages in rural areas left farmers feeling exploited. Protective tariffs on agricultural machinery and other manufactured goods further raised their costs. The failure of political parties and the government to devise effective regulatory and antitrust measures or to correct the inequities in the currency, credit, and tariff laws capped the farmers' anger. By the 1890s, many were convinced that the nation's economic and political institutions were aligned against them.

Farmers organize.   In response, farmers turned to the **Farmers' Alliance**, the era's greatest popular movement of protest and reform. Originating in Texas, the Southern Farmers' Alliance spread throughout the South and across the Great Plains to the Pacific coast. African American farmers organized the Colored Farmers' Alliance. The Northwestern Farmers' Alliance spread westward and northward from Illinois to Nebraska and Minnesota. In combination, these groups constituted a massive grassroots movement committed to economic and ultimately to political reform.

The Farmers' Alliance restricted its membership to men and women of the "producing class" and urged them to stand "against the encroachments of monopolies and in opposition to the growing corruption of wealth and power." At first, the Alliance attempted to establish farmers' cooperatives to market crops and purchase supplies. Although some co-ops worked well, most soon failed because of the opposition of established merchants and other business interests. Railroads suppressed Alliance grain elevators by refusing to handle their wheat. In Leflore County, Mississippi, when members of the Colored Farmers' Alliance shifted their trade to an Alliance store, local merchants provoked a conflict in which state troops killed twenty-five black farmers, including the local leaders of the Colored Alliance.

The Alliance also developed ingenious proposals to remedy rural credit and currency problems. In the South, the Alliance pushed the subtreasury system, which called on the government to warehouse farmers' cotton and advance them credit based on its value (see Chapter 17). In the West, the Alliance proposed a system of federal loans to farmers, using land as security. This land-loan scheme, like the subtreasury system, was a political expression of greenbackism; it would have expanded the money supply while providing immediate relief to distressed farmers. These proposals were immensely popular among farmers, but the major parties and Congress rejected them. The Alliance also took up earlier calls for free silver, government control of railroads, and banking reform, again to no avail. Denouncing the indifference of the major political parties and the institutions of government, William A. Peffer, the influential editor of the Alliance newspaper the *Kansas Farmer*, declared that the "time has come for action. The people will not consent to wait longer. . . . The future is full of retribution for delinquents."

THE PEOPLE'S PARTY

In the West, discontented agrarians organized independent third parties to achieve reforms the major parties had ignored. State-level third parties appeared in the elections of 1890 under many names. All eventually adopted the labels "People's" or "Populist," which were first used by a Kansas party that formed in June 1890. The founders of the Kansas People's Party included members of the Farmers' Alliance, the Knights of Labor, the Grange, and the old Greenback party. The new party's campaign, marked by grim determination and fierce rhetoric, set the model for Populist politics and introduced many of

the movement's leaders. These people, women as well as men, were earnest organizers and powerful orators. One was *Kansas Farmer* editor Peffer. Others included "Sockless Jerry" Simpson, Annie Diggs, and Mary E. Lease.

When hostile business and political leaders attacked the Populist plans as socialistic, Lease retorted, "You may call me an anarchist, a socialist, or a communist. I care not, but I hold to the theory that if one man has not enough to eat three times a day and another has $25,000,000, that last man has something that belongs to the first." Lease spoke as clearly against the colonial status experienced by the South and West: "The great common people of this country are slaves, and monopoly is the master. The West and South are bound and prostrate before the manufacturing East."

The Populist parties proved remarkably successful. They gained control of the legislatures of Kansas and Nebraska and won congressional elections in Kansas, Nebraska, and Minnesota. Their victories came at the expense of the Republicans, who had traditionally controlled politics in these states, and contributed to a massive defeat of the GOP in the 1890 midterm elections after the passage of the McKinley Tariff and the Sherman Silver Purchase Act.

Established interests ridiculed the Populists unmercifully. This hostile cartoon depicts the People's Party as an odd assortment of radical dissidents committed to a "Platform of Lunacy."

A PARTY OF PATCHES.
Grand Balloon Ascension—Cincinnati, May 20th, 1891.

Thereafter, Populists gained further victories throughout the West. In the mountain states, where their support came more from miners than from farmers, they won governorships in Colorado and Montana. On the Pacific coast, angry farmers found allies among urban workers in Seattle, Tacoma, Portland, and San Francisco, where organized labor had campaigned for reform since the 1880s. The Populists elected a governor in Washington, congressmen in California, and legislators in all three states. Even in the Southwest, where territorial status limited political activity, Populist parties emerged. In Oklahoma, the party drew support from homesteaders and tenant farmers; in Arizona, from miners and railroad workers; in New Mexico, from small stockraisers and poor Hispanics threatened by corporate ranches and land companies.

In the South, the Alliance did not initially form third parties but instead attempted to seize control of the dominant Democratic Party by forcing its candidates to pledge support to the Alliance platform. The rural southern electorate then swept these "Alliance Democrats" into office, electing four governors, several dozen members of Congress, and a majority of legislators in eight states.

With their new political power, farmers enacted reform legislation in many western states. New laws regulated banks and railroads and protected poor debtors by capping interest rates and restricting mortgage foreclosures. Others protected unions and mandated improved workplace conditions. Still others made the political system more democratic. Populists were instrumental, for example, in winning woman suffrage in Colorado and Idaho, although the united opposition of Democrats and Republicans blocked their efforts to win it in other states. In the South, the Democratic Party frustrated reform, and most Alliance Democrats repudiated their Alliance pledges and remained loyal to their party and its traditional opposition to governmental activism.

National action. Populists soon realized that successful reform would require national action. They met in Omaha, Nebraska, on July 4, 1892, to organize a national party and nominated former Greenbacker James B. Weaver for president. The party platform, known as the **Omaha Platform**, rejected the laissez-faire policies of the old parties: "We believe that the powers of government—in other words, of the people, should be expanded . . . to the end that oppression, injustice, and poverty shall eventually cease in the land." It demanded government ownership of the railroads and the telegraph and telephone systems, a national currency issued by the government rather than by private banks, the subtreasury system, free

and unlimited silver coinage, a graduated income tax, and the redistribution to settlers of land held by railroads and speculative corporations. Accompanying resolutions endorsed the popular election of senators, the secret ballot, and other electoral reforms to make government more democratic and responsive to popular wishes. When the platform was adopted, "cheers and yells," one reporter wrote, "rose like a tornado from four thousand throats and raged without cessation for 34 minutes, during which women shrieked and wept, men embraced and kissed their neighbors . . . in the ecstasy of their delirium."

The Populists left Omaha to begin an energetic campaign. Weaver toured the western states and with Mary Lease invaded the Democratic stronghold of the South where some Populists, such as Tom Watson of Georgia, tried to mobilize black voters. Southern Democrats, however, used violence and fraud to intimidate Populist voters and cheat Populist candidates out of office. Some local Populist leaders were murdered, and Weaver was driven from the South. One Democrat confessed that Alabama's Populist gubernatorial candidate "carried the state, but was swindled out of his victory . . . with unblushing trickery and corruption." Southern Democrats also appealed effectively to white supremacy, undermining the Populist effort to build a biracial reform coalition.

Elsewhere, too, Populists met disappointment. Midwestern farmers unfamiliar with Alliance ideas and organization ignored Populist appeals and stood by their traditional political allegiances. So did most eastern working-class voters, who learned little of the Populist program beyond its demand for inflation, which they feared would worsen their own conditions.

The Populists lost the election but showed impressive support for a new organization. They garnered more than a million votes (one out of every twelve cast), carried several western states, and won hundreds of state offices throughout the West and in pockets of the South, such as Texas and North Carolina. Populist leaders began immediately working to expand their support, to the alarm of both southern Democrats and northern Republicans.

THE CHALLENGE OF THE DEPRESSION

The emergence of a significant third-party movement was but one of many developments that combined by the mid-1890s to produce a national political crisis. A harsh and lengthy depression began in 1893, cruelly worsening conditions not only for farmers but for most other Americans as well. Labor unrest and violence engulfed the nation, reflecting workers' distress but frightening more comfortable Americans. The persistent failure of the major parties to respond to serious problems contributed mightily to growing popular discontent. Together these developments constituted an important challenge to America's new industrial society and its government.

Although the Populists had not triumphed in 1892, the election nonetheless reflected the nation's spreading dissatisfaction. Voters decisively rejected President Harrison and the incumbent Republicans in Congress; turning again to the other major party, they placed the Democrats in control of Congress and Grover Cleveland back in the White House. But the conservative Cleveland was almost oblivious to the mounting demand for reform. He delivered an inaugural address championing the doctrine of laissez-faire and rejecting government action to solve social or economic problems.

Cleveland's resolve was immediately tested when the economy collapsed in the spring of 1893. Railroad overexpansion, a weak banking system, tight credit, and plunging agricultural prices all contributed to the disaster. So too did a depression in Europe, which reduced American export markets and prompted British investors to sell their American investments for gold. Within a few months, hundreds of banks closed, and thousands of businesses, including the nation's major railroads, went bankrupt. By winter, 20 percent of the labor force was unemployed, and the jobless scavenged for food in a country that had no public unemployment or welfare programs. "Never within memory," said one New York minister, "have so many people literally starved to death as in the past few months."

Churches, local charity societies, and labor unions tried to provide relief but were overwhelmed. Most state governments offered little relief beyond encouraging private charity to the homeless. In Kansas, however, the Populist governor insisted that traditional laissez-faire policies were inadequate: "It is the duty of government to protect the weak, because the strong are able to protect themselves." (See "American Views: A Populist Views American Government.") Cleveland disagreed and showed little sympathy for the struggling. The functions of the government, he said in 1893, "do not include the support of the people."

Appeals for federal action. If Cleveland and Congress had no idea how the federal government might respond to the depression, some thoughtful Americans did. Jacob Coxey, a Populist businessman from Ohio, proposed a government public-works program for the unemployed to be financed with paper money. This plan would improve the nation's infrastructure, create jobs for the unemployed, and pro-

vide an inflationary stimulus to counteract the depression's deflationary effects. In short, Coxey was advocating positive government action to combat the depression. Elements of his plan would be adopted for mitigating economic downturns in the twentieth century; in 1894, it was too untraditional for Congress to consider.

Coxey organized a march of the unemployed to Washington as "a petition with boots on" to support his ideas. **Coxey's Army** of the unemployed, as the excited press dubbed it, marched through the industrial towns of Ohio and Pennsylvania and into Maryland, attracting attention and support. Other armies formed in eastern cities from Boston to Baltimore and set out for the capital. Some of the largest armies organized in the western cities of Denver, San Francisco, and Seattle. Three hundred men in an army from Oakland elected as their commander Anna Smith, who promised to "land my men on the steps of the Capitol at Washington." "I'm not afraid of anything," Smith explained. "I have a woman's heart and a woman's sympathy, and these lead me to do what I have done for these men, even though it may not be just what a woman is expected to do."

Lewis Fry, the organizer of the Los Angeles army, declared: "If the government has a right to make us die in time of war, we have the right to demand of her the right to live in time of peace." Fry's five hundred marchers captured a train to cross the desert regions of the Southwest and were feted and fed by townspeople from Tucson to El Paso. When the Southern Pacific uncoupled the train's locomotive and left the marchers stranded without food or water in West Texas for five days, the governor of Texas threatened to hold the railroad responsible for murder "by torture and starvation." Texas citizens quickly raised funds to speed the army on to St. Louis. From there it marched to Washington on foot.

The sympathy and assistance with which Americans greeted these industrial armies reflected more than anxiety over the depression and unemployment. As one economist noted, what distinguished the Populists and Coxeyites from earlier reformers was their appeal for federal action. Their substantial public support suggested a deep dissatisfaction with the failure of the government to respond to social and economic needs.

Nonetheless, the government acted to suppress Coxey. When he reached Washington with six hundred marchers, police and soldiers arrested him and his aides, beat sympathetic bystanders in a crowd of twenty thousand, and herded the marchers into detention camps. Unlike lobbyists for business and finance, Coxey was not permitted to reach Congress to

AMERICAN VIEWS

A Populist Views American Government

An educator, merchant, and former editor, Lorenzo D. Lewelling became one of the most articulate champions of the Populist party and its principles. Elected governor of Kansas in 1892, he headed what was heralded as "The First People's Party Government on Earth." On January 9, 1893, Lewelling delivered his inaugural address, in which he declared, "I appeal to the people of this great commonwealth to array themselves on the side of humanity and justice." The following passages from that speech sketch out both Lewelling's views of the 1890s and his "dream of the future."

- How does Lewelling's rhetoric reflect the deep divisions of the 1890s?
- What is Lewelling's view of the proper role of government?
- For what does Lewelling criticize the government of the 1890s?
- What does Lewelling mean by his statement that "the rich have no right to the property of the poor"?

The survival of the fittest is the government of brutes and reptiles, and such philosophy must give place to a government which recognizes human brotherhood. It is the province of government to protect the weak, but the government today is resolved into a struggle of the masses with the classes for supremacy and bread, until business, home, and personal integity are trembling in the face of possible want in the family. Feed a tiger regularly and you tame and make him harmless, but hunger makes tigers of men. If it be true that the poor have no right to the property of the rich let it also be declared that the rich have no right to the property of the poor.

It is the mission of Kansas to protect and advance the moral and material interests of all its citizens. It is its especial duty at the present time to protect the producer from the ravages of combined wealth. National legislation has for twenty years fostered and protected the interests of the few, while it has left the South and West to supply the products with which to feed and clothe the world, and thus to become the servants of wealth.

The demand for free coinage has been refused. The national banks have been permitted to withdraw their circulation, and thus the interests of the East and West have been diverged until the passage of the McKinley bill culminated in their diversement. The purchasing power of the dollar has become so great [that] corn, wheat, beef, pork, and cotton have

---

deliver his statement urging the government to assist "the poor and oppressed."

Protecting big business. The depression also provoked labor turmoil. In 1894, there were some 1,400 industrial strikes, involving nearly 700,000 workers, the largest number of strikers in any year in the nineteenth century. Cleveland had no response except to call for law and order. One result was the government's violent suppression of the Pullman strike (see Chapter 18).

In a series of decisions in 1895, the Supreme Court strengthened the bonds between business and government. First, it upheld the use of a court-ordered injunction to break the Pullman strike. As a result, injunctions became a major weapon for courts and corporations against labor unions, until Congress finally limited their use in 1932. Next, in *United States v. E.C. Knight Company*, the Court gutted the Sherman Antitrust Act by ruling that manufacturing, as opposed to commerce, was beyond the reach of federal regulation. The Court thus allowed the American

scarcely commanded a price equal to the cost of production.

The instincts of patriotism have naturally rebelled against these unwarranted encroachments of the power of money. Sectional hatred has also been kept alive by the old powers, the better to enable them to control the products and make the producer contribute to the millionaire; and thus, while the producer labors in the field, the shop, and the factory, the millionaire usurps his earnings and rides in gilded carriages with liveried servants. . . .

The problem of today is how to make the State subservient to the individual, rather than to become his master. Government is a voluntary union for the common good. It guarantees to the individual life, liberty, and the pursuit of happiness. The government then must make it possible for the citizen to enjoy liberty and pursue happiness. If the government fails of these things, it fails in its mission. . . . If old men go to the poor-house and young men go to prison, something is wrong with the economic system of the government.

What is the State to him who toils, if labor is denied him and his children cry for bread? What is the State to the farmer who wearily drags himself from dawn till dark to meet the stern necessities of the mortgage on the farm? What is the State to him if it sanctions usury and other legal forms by which his home is destroyed and his innocent ones become a prey to the fiends who lurk in the shadow of civilization? What is the State to the business man, early grown gray, broken in health and spirit by successive failures; anxiety like a boding owl his constant companion by day and the disturber of his dreams by night? How is life to be sustained, how is liberty to be enjoyed, how is happiness to be pursued under such adverse conditions as the State permits if it does not sanction? Is the State powerless against these conditions?

This is the generation which has come to the rescue. Those in distress who cry out from the darkness shall not be heard in vain. Conscience is in the saddle. We have leaped the bloody chasm and entered a contest for the protection of home, humanity, and the dignity of labor.

The grandeur of civilization shall be emphasized by the dawn of a new era in which the people shall reign, and if found necessary they will "expand the powers of government to solve the enigmas of the times." The people are greater than the law or the statutes, and when a nation sets its heart on doing a great and good thing it can find a legal way to do it.

I have a dream of the future. I have the evolution of an abiding faith in human government, and in the beautiful vision of a coming time I behold the abolition of poverty. A time is foreshadowed when the withered hand of want shall not be outstretched for charity; when liberty, equality, and justice shall have permanent abiding places in the republic.

Source: *People's Party Paper* (Atlanta), January 20, 1893.

Sugar Refining Company, a trust controlling 90 percent of the nation's sugar, to retain its great power. Finally, the Court invalidated an income tax that agrarian Democrats and Populists had maneuvered through Congress. The conservative Court rejected the reform as an "assault upon capital." A dissenting judge noted that the decision gave vested interests "a power and influence" dangerous to the majority of Americans.

Not until 1913, and then only with an amendment to the Constitution, would it be possible to adopt an equitable system of taxation. Surveying these developments, farmers and workers increasingly concluded that the government protected powerful interests while ignoring the plight of ordinary Americans.

Certainly the callous treatment shown workers contrasted sharply with Cleveland's concern for bankers as he managed the government's monetary policy in the depression. Cleveland blamed the economic collapse on the Sherman Silver Purchase Act, which he regarded as detrimental to business confidence and a threat to the nation's gold reserve. He

Jacob Coxey's "Army" of the unemployed marches to Washington, D.C., in 1894. Many such "industrial armies" were organized during the depressed 1890s, revealing dissatisfaction with traditional politics and limited government.

persuaded Congress in 1893 to repeal the law, enraging southern and western members of his own party. These Silver Democrats condemned Cleveland for betraying the public good to "the corporate interests."

Cleveland's policy failed to end the depression. By 1894, the Treasury began borrowing money from Wall Street to bolster the gold reserve. These transactions benefited a syndicate of bankers headed by J.P. Morgan. It seemed to critics that an indifferent Cleveland was helping rich bankers profit from the nation's economic agony. "A set of vampires headed by a financial trust has control of our destiny," cried one rural newspaper.

THE BATTLE OF THE STANDARDS AND THE ELECTION OF 1896

The government's unpopular actions, coupled with the unrelenting depression, alienated workers and farmers from the Cleveland administration and the Democratic party. In the off-year elections of 1894, the Democrats suffered the greatest loss of congressional seats in American history. Populists increased their

vote by 42 percent, making especially significant gains in the South, but the real beneficiaries of the popular hatred of Cleveland and his policies were the Republicans. Denouncing Cleveland's "utter imbecility," they gained solid control of Congress as well as state governments across the North and West. All three parties began to plan for the presidential election of 1896.

As hard times persisted, the silver issue came to overshadow all others. Some Populist leaders, hoping to broaden the party's appeal, had already begun to emphasize silver rather than the more radical but divisive planks of the Omaha Platform. Weaver declared the silver issue "the line upon which the battle should be fought. It is the line of least resistance and we should hurl our forces against it at every point." Many southern and western Democrats, who had traditionally favored silver inflation, also decided to stress the issue, both to undercut the Populists and to distance themselves and their party from the despised Cleveland. ("I hate the very ground that man walks on," said one Alabama Democrat.) In 1895, leading Democrats began using the silver issue to reorganize their party and displace Cleveland and his conservative supporters. They held rallies and conventions across the South and West, distributed silver literature, and argued that free silver would finally end the depression.

McKinley and the Republicans. The dissension among Democrats pleased Republicans. William McKinley, governor of Ohio and author of the McKinley Tariff Act of 1890, emerged as the leader of a crowd of hopeful Republican presidential candidates. His candidacy benefited particularly from the financial backing and political management of Mark Hanna, a wealthy Ohio industrialist. Hanna thought McKinley's passion for high tariffs as the key to revived prosperity would appeal to workers as well as to industry and business. As governor, McKinley had reached out to workers by supporting prolabor legislation and by avoiding the anti-Catholic positions that alienated immigrants from the Republicans. Nonetheless, he shared Hanna's conviction that government should actively promote business interests; he was not Hanna's puppet, as opponents sometimes claimed.

Republicans nominated McKinley on the first ballot at their 1896 convention. Their platform called for high tariffs but also endorsed the gold standard, placating eastern delegates but prompting several western Silver Republicans to withdraw from the party.

Bryan and the Silverites. The Democratic convention met shortly thereafter. Embattled supporters of the gold standard soon learned that the silver crusade had made them a minority in the party. With a fervor that conservatives likened to "scenes of the French Revolution," the Silver Democrats revolutionized their party. They adopted a platform repudiating Cleveland and his policies and endorsing free silver, the income tax, and tighter regulation of trusts and railroads. A magnificent speech supporting this platform by William Jennings Bryan helped convince the delegates to nominate him for president. Bryan was only 36 years old but he had already served in Congress, edited an important newspaper, and gained renown for his oratorical skills and popular sympathies.

Holding their convention last, the Populists now faced a terrible dilemma. The Democratic nomination of Bryan on a silver platform undercut their hopes of attracting into their own ranks disappointed reformers from the major parties. Bryan, moreover, had already worked closely with Nebraska Populists, who now urged the party to endorse him rather than split the silver vote and insure the victory of McKinley and the gold standard. Other Populists

William Jennings Bryan in 1896. A powerful orator of great human sympathies, Bryan was adored by his followers as "the majestic man who was hurling defiance in the teeth of the money power." Nominated three times for the presidency by the Democrats, he was never elected.

argued that fusing—joining with the Democrats—would cost the Populists their separate identity and subordinate their larger political principles to the issue of free silver. After anguished discussion, the Populists nominated Bryan for president but named a separate vice presidential candidate, Tom Watson of Georgia, in an effort to maintain their identity. They hoped the Democrats would reciprocate by replacing their nominee with Watson, but the Democrats ignored the overture. The Populists' strength was in the South and West, regions that Bryan would control anyway. They could offer him little help in the battle for the Midwest and East, what Bryan called "the enemy's country."

Money and oratory. The campaign was intense and dramatic, with each side demonizing the other. Terrified by the thought of Bryan's election, eastern financial and business interests contributed millions of dollars to Hanna's campaign for McKinley. Standard Oil alone provided $250,000, about the same amount as the Democrats' total national expenses. Hanna used these funds to organize an unprecedented kind of campaign. Shifting the emphasis from parades to information, Republicans issued 250 million campaign documents in a dozen languages, warning of economic disaster should Bryan be elected and the bimetallic standard be restored, but promising that McKinley's election would finally end the depression. Republicans were aided by a national press so completely sympathetic that many newspapers not only shaped their editorials but distorted their news stories to Bryan's disadvantage.

Lacking the Republicans' superior resources, the Democrats relied on Bryan's superb speaking ability and youthful energy. Bryan was the first presidential candidate to campaign systematically for election, speaking hundreds of times to millions of voters. By contrast, McKinley stayed home in Canton, Ohio, where he conducted a "front porch" campaign. Explaining his refusal to campaign outside Canton, McKinley said, "I might just as well put up a trapeze . . . and compete with some professional athlete as go out speaking against Bryan." But Hanna brought groups of Republicans from all over the country to visit McKinley every day, and McKinley reiterated his simple promise of prosperity.

In the depression, that appeal proved enough. As the Democratic candidate, Bryan was, ironically, burdened with the legacy of the hated Cleveland administration. The intense campaign brought a record voter turnout. McKinley won decisively by capturing the East and Midwest as well as Oregon and California (see Map 20-2). Bryan carried the traditionally Democratic South and the mountain and plains states, where Populists and silverites dominated. He failed to gain support in either the Granger states of the Midwest or the cities of the East. His silver campaign had little appeal to industrial workers. Hanna realized that Bryan was making a mistake in subordinating other popular grievances to silver: "He's talking silver all the time, and that's where we've got him."

Bryan immediately wrote a personal account of the campaign, which he optimistically titled *The First Battle.* But Bryan and the Democrats would not win subsequent battles, at least not on the issues of the 1890s. The elections of 1894 and 1896 ended the close balance between the major parties. Cleveland's failures, coupled with an economic recovery in the wake of the election of 1896, gained the Republicans a reputation as the party of prosperity and industrial

This Republican campaign poster of 1896 depicts William McKinley standing on sound money and promising a revival of prosperity. The depression of the 1890s shifted the electorate into the Republican column.

progress, firmly establishing them in power for years to come. By contrast, the Democratic party receded into an ineffectual sectional minority dominated by southern conservatives, despite Bryan's liberal views.

The People's party simply dissolved. Demoralized by fusion with the Democrats, who had earlier violently repressed them, many southern Populists dropped out of politics. The Democrats' disfranchisement laws, directed at discontented poor white Southerners as well as poor black Southerners, further undermined the Populists in the South. In the West, the silver tide of 1896 carried many Populists into office, but with their party collapsing, they had no hope of reelection. By 1898, the Populist party had virtually disappeared. Its reform

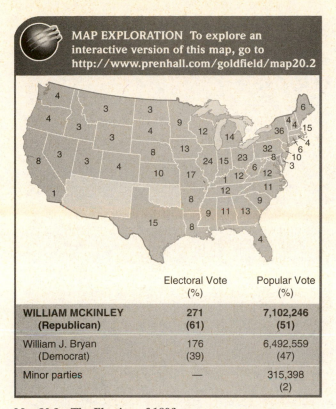

MAP EXPLORATION To explore an interactive version of this map, go to http://www.prenhall.com/goldfield/map20.2

	Electoral Vote (%)	Popular Vote (%)
WILLIAM MCKINLEY (Republican)	**271 (61)**	**7,102,246 (51)**
William J. Bryan (Democrat)	176 (39)	6,492,559 (47)
Minor parties	—	315,398 (2)

MAP 20-2   The Election of 1896
William Jennings Bryan carried most of the rural South and West, but his free silver campaign had little appeal to more urban and industrial regions, which swung strongly to Republican candidate William McKinley.

legacy, however, proved more enduring. The issues it raised would continue to shape state and national politics.

McKinley plunged into his presidency. Unlike his predecessors, he had a definite, if limited, program, consisting of tariff protection, sound money, and overseas expansion. He worked actively to see it through Congress and to shape public opinion, thereby helping establish the model of the modern presidency. He had promised prosperity, and it returned, although not because of the record high tariff his party enacted in 1897 or the Currency Act of 1900, which firmly established the gold standard. Prosperity returned, instead, because of reviving markets and a monetary inflation that resulted from the discovery of vast new deposits of gold in Alaska, Australia, and South Africa. The silverites had recognized that an expanding industrial economy required an expanding money supply. Ironically, the new inflation was greater than the inflation that

would have resulted from free silver. With the return of prosperity and the decline of social tensions, McKinley easily won reelection in 1900, defeating Bryan a second time.

CONCLUSION

In late-nineteenth-century America, politics and government often seemed at cross purposes. Political contests were exciting events, absorbing public attention, attracting high voter turnout, and often raising issues of symbolic or substantive importance. Closely balanced political parties commanded the zealous support of their constituents and wielded power and influence. The institutions of government, by contrast, were limited in size, scope, and responsibility. A weakened presidency and an inefficient Congress, hampered by a restrictive judiciary, were often unable to resolve the very issues that were so dramatically raised in the political arena. The persistent disputes over tariff and monetary policy illustrate this impasse. But the issue that most reflected it was civil-service reform. The patronage system provided the lifeblood of politics but also disrupted government business.

The localism, laissez-faire, and other traditional principles that shaped both politics and government were becoming increasingly inappropriate for America's industrializing society. New challenges were emerging that state and local governments could not effectively solve on their own. The national nature of the railroad network, for example, finally brought the federal government into the regulatory arena, however imperfectly, with the Interstate Commerce Act of 1887. Both the depression of the 1890s and the popular discontent articulated most clearly by the Populist rejection of laissez-faire underscored the need for change and discredited the limited government of the Cleveland administration.

By the end of the decade, the political system had changed. The Republicans had emerged as the dominant party, ending the two-party stalemate of previous decades. Campaign hoopla in local communities had given way to information-based campaigns directed by and through national organizations. A new, activist presidency was emerging. And the disruptive currency issue faded with the hard times that had brought it forth. Still greater changes were on the horizon. The depression and its terrible social and economic consequences undermined traditional ideas about the responsibilities of government and increased public support for activist policies. The stage was set for the Progressive Era..

FROM THEN TO NOW

Political Parties

Few things in contemporary American politics present a sharper contrast to the nineteenth century than the role of political parties. In the late nineteenth century, parties dominated politics. They commanded the allegiance of Americans, controlled the selection of candidates, mobilized voters, shaped voting behavior, provided ballots, and ran elections. They also shaped public policies and, through patronage, staffed government positions. At the beginning of the twenty-first century, parties do virtually none of these things.

This transformation began at the end of the nineteenth century. Extreme partisanship prompted states to assert control over elections. The corruption attributed to party machines led gradually to such changes as nonpartisan municipal elections and increased public control over parties. Restrictions on campaign expenditures reduced the party hoopla that had made politics so exciting and voter turnout so high. The connection between parties and voters declined further as new voters unfamiliar

with the passions and loyalties of the past joined the electorate.

The inability of the major parties to deal effectively with important national problems, so evident in the depression of the 1890s, prompted Americans to find other ways to influence public policy. Associational groups that had acted outside the partisan arena evolved into effective special-interest lobbying groups. Civil-service reform, beginning with the Pendleton Act, steadily reduced party influence in government. So did the growing reliance in the twentieth century on independent regulatory commissions, rather than partisan legislative committees, to make and implement policies.

In recent decades, party decline has accelerated. The introduction and spread of primary elections have stripped parties of their control over nominations. Individual candidates have come increasingly to rely more on personal organizations than on the party apparatus to manage campaigns. Candidates often appeal for

REVIEW QUESTIONS

1. In their letters to their parents, the Taft brothers simply condemned the personal morality and behavior of their Democratic opponents in Cincinnati's election, but there were social and institutional factors that shaped the disorderly nature of elections in the late nineteenth century. What were those factors and how did they operate in American politics?

2. What social and institutional factors determined the role of government? How and why did the role of government change during this period?

3. What factors determined the party affiliation of

American voters? Why did so many third parties develop during this era?

4. How might the planks of the Omaha Platform have helped solve farmers' troubles?

5. What factors shaped the conduct and outcome of the election of 1896? How did that contest differ from earlier elections?

KEY TERMS

Coxey's Army (p. 647)

Farmers' Alliance (p. 644)

Free silver (p. 643)

votes as individuals rather than as party members and communicate directly to voters through the mass media, relying less on the old door-to-door personal campaign requiring party workers. Television, in particular, with its focus on dramatic and personal sound bites, is better at promoting individual candidates than it is at presenting such abstract entities as parties.

Campaign finance reform laws have reduced party control over the funding of campaigns. So too has the rise of political action committees (PACs) as an important source of support for candidates. PACs represent particular interests, not a collection of interests, as parties do. Candidates dependent on specific interests find it harder to make broader partisan appeals.

Polls show fewer and fewer Americans identifying with a particular party and indicate that partisanship has greatly declined as a factor in voting decisions. Americans increasingly regard parties as neither meaningful nor even useful, let alone essential to democratic government. Nearly half of the electorate favors making all elections nonpartisan or even abolishing parties. More and more people believe that interest groups better represent their political needs than parties. At the same time, fewer and fewer Americans bother to vote. Those who do are much more likely than before to split their ticket, voting for candidates of different parties for different offices. This often results in divided government—with the presidency controlled by one party and Congress by the other. The resulting stalemate increases public cynicism about parties.

Of course, parties endure and retain some importance. Election laws favor the two established parties and obstruct independent candidacies. Public funds subsidize party activities, and party coffers harvest unregulated "soft money" campaign contributions. Congress and state legislatures continue to rely on party divisions to organize their leadership and committee structures, and party discipline still influences the way legislators vote. But while such institutional factors guarantee the continued presence of a two-party system, the parties themselves no longer enjoy the influence they had in the nineteenth century.

Granger laws (p. 635)

Greenback Party (p. 635)

Interstate Commerce Act (p. 641)

Interstate Commerce Commission (ICC) (p. 642)

Laissez-faire (p. 637)

Mugwumps (p. 636)

National American Woman Suffrage Association (p. 636)

Omaha Platform (p. 646)

Pendleton Civil Service Act (p. 640)

Populist Party (p. 635)

Prohibition Party (p. 635)

Sherman Antitrust Act (p. 641)

Sound money (p. 643)

RECOMMENDED READING

Cherny, Robert W. *American Politics in the Gilded Age* (1997). An excellent brief analysis, emphasizing the importance of parties in both elections and public policy.

Keller, Morton. *Affairs of State: Public Life in Late Nineteenth Century America* (1977). A detailed and fascinating account of the changing dimensions of government and politics.

McMath, Robert C. Jr. *American Populism: A Social History, 1877–1898* (1993). The best modern history of Populism; balanced and readable.

Summers, Mark. *The Gilded Age* (1997). A useful survey that effectively captures the complexities of the era.

Williams, R. Hal. *Years of Decision: American Politics in the 1890s* (1978). A valuable synthesis of the scholarship on the political currents of the 1890s.

ADDITIONAL SOURCES
The Structure and Style of Politics
Argersinger, Peter H. *Structure, Process, and Party* (1992).

Baker, Paula. "The Domestication of Politics: Women and American Political Society, 1780–1920," *American Historical Review* 89 (1984): 620–647.

Bordin, Ruth. *Frances Willard: A Biography* (1986).

Bordin, Ruth. *Woman and Temperance* (1981).

Edwards, Rebecca. *Angels in the Machinery: Gender in American Party Politics* (1997).

Goldberg, Michael. *An Army of Women: Gender and Politics in Gilded Age Kansas* (1997).

Gustafson, Melanie Susan. *Women and the Republican Party* (2001).

Kleppner, Paul. *The Third Electoral System, 1853–1892* (1979).

McCormick, Richard L. *The Party Period and Public Policy* (1986).

McGerr, Michael. *The Decline of Popular Politics: The American North, 1865–1928* (1988).

Schneirov, Richard. *Labor and Urban Politics* (1998).

Shafer, Byron, and Anthony Badger. *Contesting Democracy* (2001).

Silbey, Joel. *The American Political Nation, 1838–1893* (1991).

The Limits of Government
Aron, Cindy. *Ladies and Gentlemen of the Civil Service: Middle-Class Workers in Victorian America* (1987).

Brock, William R. *Investigation and Responsibility: Public Responsibility in the United States, 1865–1900* (1984).

Campbell, Ballard C. *Representative Democracy: Public Policy and Midwestern Legislatures in the Late Nineteenth Century* (1980).

Garraty, John A. *The New Commonwealth, 1877–1890* (1968).

Hoogenboom, Ari. *Rutherford B. Hayes: Warrior and President* (1996).

Skowronek, Stephen. *Building a New American State: The Expansion of National Administrative Capacities* (1982).

Thompson, Margaret S. *The "Spider Web": Congress and Lobbying* (1985).

White, Leonard D. *The Republican Era* (1958).

Public Policies and National Elections
Hoogenboom, Ari. *Outlawing the Spoils: A History of the Civil Service Movement, 1865–1883* (1961).

Marcus, Robert D. *Grand Old Party: Political Structure in the Gilded Age, 1880–1896* (1971).

Morgan, H. Wayne. *From Hayes to McKinley* (1969).

Reitano, Joanne. *The Tariff Question in the Gilded Age: The Great Debate of 1888* (1995).

Ritter, Gretchen. *Goldbugs and Greenbacks: The Antimonopoly Tradition and the Politics of Finance* (1997).

Socolofsky, Homer E. and Allan B. Spetter. *The Presidency of Benjamin Harrison* (1987).

Sproat, John. *The Best Men: Liberal Reformers in the Gilded Age* (1968).

Summers, Mark. *Rum, Romanism, and Rebellion: The Making of a President, 1884* (2000).

The Crisis of the 1890s
Argersinger, Peter H. *Populism and Politics: W. A. Peffer and the People's Party* (1974).

Clanton, Gene. *Populism: The Humane Preference* (1991).

Glad, Paul. *McKinley, Bryan, and the People* (1964).

Goodwyn, Lawrence. *The Populist Moment* (1978).

Jensen, Richard. *The Winning of the Midwest: Social and Political Conflict, 1888–1896* (1971).

Kousser, J. Morgan. *The Shaping of Southern Politics* (1974).

Larson, Robert W. *Populism in the Mountain West* (1986).

McSeveney, Samuel. *The Politics of Depression* (1972).

Miller, Worth Robert. *Oklahoma Populism* (1987).

Ostler, Jeffrey. *Prairie Populism* (1993).

Ross, William G. *A Muted Fury: Populists, Progressives, and Labor Unions Confront the Courts* (1994).

Schneirov, Richard, Shelton Stromquist, and Nick Salvatore. *The Pullman Strike and the Crisis of the 1890s* (1999).

Schwantes, Carlos A. *Coxey's Army: An American Odyssey* (1985).

Shaw, Barton. *The Wool-Hat Boys: Georgia's Populist Party* (1984).

Welch, Richard. *The Presidencies of Grover Cleveland* (1988).

WHERE TO LEARN MORE
- **Rest Cottage, Evanston, Illinois.** Frances Willard's home, from which she directed the Woman's Christian Temperance Union, is carefully preserved as a museum. The Willard Memorial Library contains more memorabilia and papers of Willard and the WCTU. **www.wctu.org/house.html.**

- **President Benjamin Harrison's Home, Indianapolis, Indiana.** President Harrison's brick Italianate mansion, completed in 1875, has been completely restored with the family's furniture and keepsakes. The former third-floor ballroom serves as a museum with exhibits of many artifacts of the Harrisons' public and private lives. **www.presidentbenjaminharrison.org/.**

- **Fairview, Lincoln, Nebraska.** A National Historic Landmark, Fairview was the home of William Jennings Bryan, who described it as "the Monticello of the West." Faithfully restored to depict the Bryan family's life in the early 1900s, it includes a museum and interpretive center. www.bryanlgh.org/aboutus/fairviewhistory.htm.

- **Susan B. Anthony House National Historic Landmark, Rochester, New York.** This modest house was the home of the prominent suffragist and contains Anthony's original furnishings and personal photographs. www.susanbanthonyhouse.org/main.html.

- **Rutherford B. Hayes Presidential Center, Fremont, Ohio.** This complex contains President Hayes's home, office, and extensive grounds together with an excellent library and museum holding valuable collections of manuscripts, artifacts, and photographs illustrating his personal interests and political career. www.rbhayes.org/.

- **James A. Garfield Home, Mentor, Ohio.** Operated by the Western Reserve Historical Society as a museum, Garfield's home is the site of his successful 1880 front-porch campaign for president. www.nps.gov/jaga/index.htm

 Please refer to the document CD-ROM for primary sources related to this chapter.

CHECKING YOUR COMPREHENSION

Choose the best answer for each of the following questions.

1. The National Women's Temperance Association was a lobbying group for a woman's right to vote. Over what social ill were they founded?
    a. violence against women
    b. freedom to worship
    c. alcohol abuse
    d. employment opportunities

2. Which one of the following circumstances did not, in some way, lead to the limited impact of the federal government in the 1800s?
    a. women's suffrage
    b. the impeachment of President Johnson
    c. repeated shifts of party control of Congress
    d. small and inefficient federal workforce

3. The conflict between advocates of "sound money" and "inflationist's" centered on
    a. the value of greenbacks.
    b. the printing of greenbacks.
    c. the use of Greenbacks.
    d. gold vs. silver coinage.

Identify the following statements as true or false.

4. In the 1800s, women were excluded from politics primarily because men generally believed that weakness and sentimentality disqualified women from the fierce conflicts in the public realm.
5. As the two party systems began to take hold of American politics in the 1800s, economic issues generally did not decide party ties.
6. Partisan politics in the 1800s left little room for a third party to form around specific issues and groups.

Answer the following questions.

7. Explain the debate over the tariff legislation by looking at the argument for those in favor and those opposed.

8. What impact did the Great Depression of 1890 have on the political party system in the late 1800s?

Discussion and Critical Thinking Question

9. The beginnings of federal regulation can be traced back to the 1800s. After reflecting on entities today that are regulated by the federal government (i.e. FCC, interest rates, stem cell research, and others) discuss the pros and cons of the federal government regulation.

NOTES

8
DEVIANT BEHAVIOR

Peyote on the Reservation

Joseph, an 18-year-old Navajo boy, recently joined a 125-year-old Christian sect called the Native American Church that uses the bud of the peyote cactus in its sacred rituals. Although considered a dangerous drug by many people because of the vivid hallucinations it produces, peyote has long been familiar to Native Americans as a traditional means of promoting healing and self-knowledge (Aberle, 1982). Before the reservation era, it was expected that young members of a number of different tribes would engage in "vision quests," periods of prolonged fasting and self-denial that led to hallucinations much like those Joseph is now seeking through peyote. Indeed, in some traditional Native American cultures, youths who were not successful in evoking visions of ancestor spirits were considered deviant, or at least less than full adults. (Lame Deer & Erdoes, 1972)

Coca Cola in Utah

As a Mormon living in a small town in Utah, Susan knows that her spiritual well-being depends on, among other things, following her church's teachings requiring abstinence from drugs—including not only alcohol and tobacco (to say nothing of peyote!), but also caffeine-laden drinks such as tea, coffee, and some soft drinks (Whalen, 1964). But sometimes it's hard to live up to these ideals. Earlier today Susan drank a Coca Cola, and now she can't stop worrying about her lapse into "drug abuse."

Both of these young people have used a mood-altering drug. In each case, some people would consider the behavior wrong while others would see it as perfectly normal. This chapter examines how behaviors such as drug-taking come to be socially de-fined as unacceptable. We also present a number of different explanations for why people engage in such activity.

WHAT IS DEVIANCE?

Deviance consists of behavior, beliefs, or conditions that are viewed by relatively powerful segments of society as serious violations of important norms. Let's look at each element of this definition more closely.

When most Americans think of deviants, they probably visualize drug addicts, rapists, or child molesters. This view emphasizes behaviors that involve *major* violations of *important* norms. People are not generally defined as deviant for such minor violations as not applauding at the end of a play or wearing mismatched clothes.

But note that under the sociological definition, deviance may consist not only of *behaviors*, but also of *beliefs*—atheism and communism come to mind—and *conditions*, such as being physically handicapped, mentally ill, HIV-positive, or morbidly obese (Degher & Hughes, 1991).

Students are frequently uncomfortable with the fact that sociologists classify people who are physically disabled or mentally ill as deviants. Such an interpretation seems unjust: These people did not choose to be different. Yet it is clear that because of their conditions, they are denied full acceptance in society in much the same way as bank robbers and bigamists—people who are generally believed to have chosen to violate norms—are looked down upon. The extent to which an individual's behavior is voluntary may affect how negatively he or she is viewed, but it is not necessary that nonconformity or difference be freely chosen for it to be classified as deviance (Link et al., 1987; Gortmaker et al., 1993; Crandall, 1995).

Along the same lines, note that an individual need not cause appreciable harm to anyone in order to be regarded as deviant. Most mental patients, many drug users, and the vast majority of the members of unconventional religious groups harm no one except,

INTERNET CONNECTIONS

Students sometimes have difficulty understanding the sociological approach to deviant behavior. In addition to your readings in the text, you may wish to review notes on the concept of deviance that will serve as another useful "Introduction to Deviance." Go to:

http://www.umsl.edu/~rkeel/200/200lec.html#disclaim

After you have completed a review of the information, write a brief report on the sociological meaning of deviance.

(handwritten in left margin: definition clue)

arguably, themselves, yet they are clearly deviants in many people's eyes.

Deviance should be differentiated from the related concept of crime, which we discuss in the next chapter. A **crime** is a violation of a formal statute enacted by a legitimate government. Acts such as homicide, arson, or rape are clearly both criminal and deviant. However, some criminals are not treated as deviants, including most traffic offenders and people who cheat on their income taxes. Furthermore, many types of deviance, such as mental illness or not bathing regularly, are not covered by the criminal statutes (see Figure 8.1).

The Relative Nature of Deviance

The vignettes that opened this chapter illustrate an important point: *Deviance is relative.* What is regarded as deviant in one society may be accepted or even honored in another (Goode, 1997). Using peyote is seen as seriously deviant by most citizens of the United States but not by many traditional Native Americans; drinking Coca Cola is mildly deviant for a Mormon, but not for a Catholic or Jew.

Some of the most striking examples of the relative nature of deviance concern sexuality, the topic of Chapter 7. Some cultures are extremely repressed by the standards of most residents of the United States, regarding as seriously deviant many behaviors that we consider quite normal. Among the traditional Cheyenne, for example, a girl who lost her virginity was permanently dishonored and considered unmarriageable (Hoebel, 1978). Residents of Inis Beag, an island off the west coast of Ireland, were even more conservative, traditionally disapproving of nudity even in the marital bed (Messenger, 1971).

On the other hand, about 25 percent of all societies fully accept premarital sex by both genders (Rathaus et al., 1997). In the developed world, the Scandinavians are widely known for their sexual openness. The least sexually repressed people in the world may well be the Polynesians of Mangaia in the Cook Islands; early field work among these people reported intense sexual activity among both women and men, largely devoid of romantic attachment and beginning well before puberty (Marshall, 1971; see Harris, 1995, for a more skeptical account).

What is regarded as deviant also changes over time within any particular society. A hundred years ago, child-rearing practices that would be seen as abusive today ("Spare the rod and spoil the child") were not only accepted but frequently encouraged. Racial discrimination was legal and widely endorsed. And millions of respectable Americans routinely used drugs that are illegal today: Opium was a common ingredient in over-the-counter medications, and Coca Cola originally contained a small dose of cocaine.

People with serious physical disabilities are often treated as deviants. However, a record of outstanding personal achievement can help to overcome the stigma. Former Senator Max Cleland of Georgia is an excellent example.

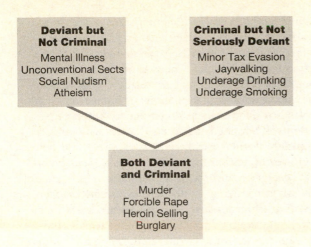

FIGURE 8.1 The Relationship Between Deviance and Criminality.

and groups with high levels of power and prestige. In the United States today, this means that the definition of what is deviant is more heavily shaped by the rich than by the poor, by men than by women, and by whites than by people of color. The definition of deviance is thus a political process: Behaviors that are accepted by the powerful are likely to be regarded as normative, while those that are common among the powerless may well be stigmatized (Schur, 1971).

There is widespread agreement in modern societies that certain types of behaviors, especially predatory crimes like robbery and forcible rape, are seriously deviant. But in other areas where value-

On the other hand, many practices that most people in the United States now take for granted were once regarded as deviant, including participating in lotteries, women smoking and wearing pants in public, and unmarried couples cohabiting.

Deviance is relative in other ways as well. Behavior that is generally acceptable for one gender—such as asking a friend to accompany you to a public restroom—is unacceptable for the other. Similarly, behavior that is strongly encouraged in one subculture may be just as strongly rejected by another. For example, members of street gangs are expected to fight—but the Amish embrace strict norms opposing physical combat.

Deviance also varies by place—language heard in a football locker room would be most unseemly at a church social. Class also matters. Although standards are currently changing, bearing children out of wedlock continues to be more acceptable in the lower class than in the middle and upper strata of U.S. society. Figure 8.2 illustrates how class affects drinking, smoking, and attitudes toward the decriminalization of marijuana.

The extent of these variations in what is considered deviant strongly suggests that *no behavior is inherently deviant*. While some actions, such as incest within the nuclear family, are condemned by nearly all cultures, researchers have not been able to identify any universally deviant behaviors.

Since deviance is a relative concept, the question of who decides what will and will not be considered deviant is a crucial one. In small, traditional societies displaying a very high level of consensus regarding norms and values, it may be reasonable to say that the society as a whole makes this decision. However, in modern societies where disagreement about norms is widespread, deviance is often defined by individuals

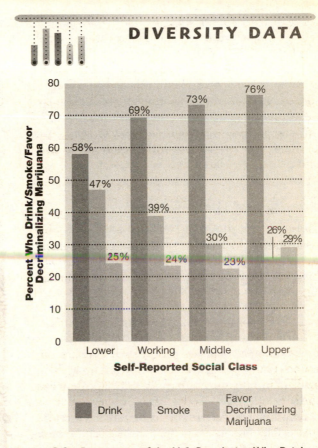

FIGURE 8.2 Percentage of the U.S. Population Who Drink, Smoke, and Support Decriminalizing Marijuana, by Social Class. As self-reported social class position rises, people tend to be more likely to drink and less likely to smoke. Attitudes toward decriminalizing marijuana do not vary sharply by class, although the elite is slightly more supportive of decriminalization than any other class. Given the fact that the upper class tends to have a disproportionate ability to affect the way laws are written, what do these findings suggest about which substances are likely to remain legal?

Source: NORC. General Social Surveys, 1972–2000. Chicago: National Opinion Research Center, 2000. Reprinted by permission of NORC, Chicago, IL.

consensus is lacking, such as attitudes toward recreational drug use, soft-core pornography, and homosexuality, the preferences of the powerful usually dominate. Thus, for example, the primary reason why one drug—say, marijuana—is generally considered deviant, whereas another drug—say, whiskey—is widely accepted, is not because of the relative dangerousness of these substances but rather because the most powerful members of society—typically older, middle- and upper-class white males—are much more likely to relax after work with a few drinks than with a joint. (The *Global Connections* box on page 216 in this chapter discusses how some European nations respond to drugs in very different ways than does the United States).

Finally, *deviance is a cultural universal*. In other words, deviance can be found in every society (Durkheim, 1897/1964). Even in a culture with a high degree of normative consensus and virtually no serious crime, there is occasional misbehavior. However, as the story of Susan (the Mormon girl who indulged in a forbidden soft drink) suggests, in a strongly moralistic society, what outsiders might consider to be a minor type of deviance will likely be viewed as a relatively major violation.

Deviance and Social Control

Sociologists use the term **social control** to refer to measures taken by members of society intended to encourage conformity to norms. In other words, the purpose of social control is to reduce, if not eliminate, deviance (Gibbs, 1989). This can be done in three general ways: through formal social control, informal social control, or internalized normative standards.

Formal social control consists of efforts to discourage deviance made by people such as police officers and college deans whose jobs involve, in whole or in part, punishing nonconformity and rewarding obedience.

Punishments, referred to as **negative sanctions**, are especially important at the formal level. Negative sanctions range from a parking fine or academic probation to the total ostracism of a deviant by an entire community (Hostetler & Huntington, 1971). The ultimate negative formal sanction is, of course, execution.

Formal social control may also involve **positive sanctions** or rewards, such as a good conduct medal or an A on an examination. In either case, the purpose of the sanction is the same: to promote conformity and to discourage deviance.

While formal social control is necessary to restrain the most serious deviants, no society could survive if people conformed only to avoid formal sanctioning. A far more effective way to reduce deviance is through **informal social control**—positive and negative sanc-

tions applied by friends and family. The desire for approval from significant others can be a far stronger motive for conformity than the fear of negative formal sanctions. After all, while the authorities may have a great deal of power over us, it is usually the opinions of those who are closest to us that really matter. The *Then and Now* box on the facing page entitled "Informal Social Control: Shunned at Berkeley" discusses a modern example of informal social control.

However, neither formal nor informal social control is society's main line of defense against deviance. Most conformity results from the *internalization of norms* during the process of moral socialization. Fear of externally imposed sanctions is often far less powerful than the desire to avoid feelings of guilt. Similarly, the pleasure obtained from positive sanctions can rarely compare with the sense of self-esteem that comes from living up to the demands of one's conscience (Berger, 1963:93).

FOUR QUESTIONS ABOUT DEVIANCE

Sociologists who study deviance are generally interested in answering one or more of four important theoretical questions:

1. *Who decides what behaviors, beliefs, and conditions will be defined as deviant?*
2. *What are the social functions of deviance?*
3. *Why do people deviate?*
4. *How do people react to deviants, and how do these reactions in turn affect the behavior of the deviants?*

Later in this chapter, we will explore these issues in some depth. However, before we proceed further, we need to introduce one of the most widely read research studies in the sociology of deviance, William Chambliss's (1973) analysis of two groups of juveniles he called the Saints and the Roughnecks. Despite the fact that this study was carried out more than a generation ago, its central findings remain as valid and relevant as they were when it was first published. We will use this research to illustrate a number of important theoretical points throughout the remainder of the chapter.

The Saints and the Roughnecks were two groups of boys who attended the same high school. The Saints grew up in middle-class families. The other clique, the Roughnecks, came from lower-class backgrounds.

Both groups of boys were fairly seriously delinquent. The Saints cut school regularly, drank excessively, drove recklessly, and committed various acts of petty and not-so-petty vandalism. The Roughnecks, too, were often truant and stole from local stores, got

THEN AND NOW

Informal Social Control: Shunned at Berkeley

Informal means of controlling deviance have been far more common throughout history and often much more effective than the formal controls applied by the police, courts, and prisons. Small, traditional societies, or *Gemeinschafts* (see Chapter 4), relied especially heavily on informal social control.

The Amish are arguably the most traditional subculture that still exists in the United States. They may be viewed as a kind of living fossil, allowing us to experience firsthand something of what it was like to live in a true Gemeinschaft. The Amish custom of *meidung,* or shunning, is a classic example of the sorts of informal social control mechanisms that were widely employed by societies before the industrial era (Wasilchick, 1992). When an Amish individual violates important religious rules, the faithful—including the person's immediate family—are forbidden to speak to that person, eat at the same table with him or her, or even, in the case of a spouse, engage in marital relations. Shunning is the ultimate penalty: Imagine living in a community where everyone behaved as if you no longer existed.

Even in modern *Gesellschaft* societies in which elaborate formal social control mechanisms are present, informal social control remains important. On Memorial Day weekend, 1997, University of California student David Cash and his best friend Jeremy Strohmeyer visited a casino outside Las Vegas. Around 3:30 AM, Strohmeyer lured a 7-year-old girl into a

ladies room. Cash followed, watched as his friend forced the child into a stall, then walked outside. Not long afterward, Strohmeyer rejoined Cash and confessed that he had raped and murdered the girl. Cash had made no effort to stop the assault; nor did he report the crime—out of loyalty to his friend, he later claimed. Strohmeyer was arrested a few days later. To avoid the death penalty, he pleaded guilty and was sentenced to life without parole. But prosecutors could not bring charges against Cash because he had not broken any law (Hammer, 1998).

During his freshman year at Berkeley, Cash went unnoticed. That August, however, he appeared on a popular radio talk show, defended his behavior, and proclaimed, "the university officials are behind me, baby." And they were. Because he had not committed a crime or violated campus codes, university officials (agents of formal social control) had no grounds for expelling him or even reviewing his case. In the chancellor's words, "We cannot set aside due process based upon our outrage over a particular instance." But Berkeley students who learned about the case disagreed. Soon after the talk show, a large demonstration alerted other students to Cash's presence on campus. He was thrown out of a fraternity party and chased to his dormitory room by an angry mob. Overnight, spray-painted graffiti reading EXPEL DAVID CASH appeared all over the campus. The Berkeley student senate passed a bill asking Cash to withdraw voluntarily. Invoking due process, the president of the senate vetoed the

bill. In his words, "David Cash is morally repugnant. But if you don't like him, don't talk to him. That's all you can do."

Cash continued to attend classes at Berkeley, but as an outcast, shunned (in Amish tradition) by fellow students. No one spoke to him, though some students muttered obscenities when he passed by. Everywhere he went, he confronted graffiti calling for his expulsion. He avoided major gatherings. When he walked into a nearby 7-Eleven store, a stranger spat in his face. Thus, when formal social controls failed to satisfy public outrage, Berkeley students applied informal controls.

The shunning of David Cash shows that even in a modern, heterogeneous society, there is a high level of consensus on certain issues, such as child molestation. Berkeley has a reputation as an exceptionally tolerant campus where widely different points of view are respected. But even there, Cash found few defenders. Just as prisons isolate child molesters from other inmates for their own protection, so Cash was accompanied everywhere by a plain-clothes police officer.

1. Do you think Cash would have been more likely to have come to understand the seriousness of his failure to act had he simply been expelled from Berkeley rather than being shunned?

2. Can you think of examples from your own experience of informal social control? Were they effective?

Sources: Wasilchick, 1992; Hammer, 1998.

---

drunk, and fought with other youths. But despite these similarities, the two groups were regarded very differently by social control agents, particularly by the police and school authorities.

The middle-class Saints were perceived as basically good boys. This image was partly a direct reflection of the respectability of their parents, but it was

also influenced by other class-based factors. The Saints had learned during primary socialization to treat authority figures with the appearance of respect. When they cut school, they arranged for fake excuses; when stopped by the police, they were always polite and deferential. Further, since they could afford cars, their deviance was generally carried out in other towns or at least well away from the eyes of their neighbors. When the Saints were caught misbehaving, social control agents consistently made excuses for them.

In contrast, the Roughnecks were viewed as no-good punks heading for trouble. Again, this label was both a direct and an indirect consequence of their class status. Their socialization had not prepared them to sweet-talk the authorities; instead, they tended to be insolent and aggressive when confronted. Lacking the means to own cars, they hung out on a centrally located street corner where everyone in the community could see them. When they were caught in some criminal or deviant act, nobody was inclined to go easy on them.

Which group was more deviant? In the eyes of the community, clearly the Roughnecks. Yet, according to Chambliss, the Saints caused at least as much harm as the Roughnecks, and they probably committed more criminal acts. But the fact that the Roughnecks were labeled as deviant had devastating consequences. Seven of the eight Saints finished college, and most established themselves in careers as doctors, politicians, and businessmen. Two of the seven Roughnecks never graduated from high school, three became heavily involved in criminal activities, and only two achieved stable, respectable community roles.

Now we will return to the four questions that opened this section and explore how sociologists respond to them, making reference to the Saints and Roughnecks as appropriate. This discussion will also illustrate how many sociological explanations of deviance are linked to the major theoretical perspectives that were introduced in Chapter 1.

WHO DEFINES WHAT IS DEVIANT?

The first question sociologists must consider in explaining deviance is how—and by whom—certain behaviors, beliefs, and characteristics come to be understood in a given society as deviant. This question has principally been addressed by conflict theorists (Lynch, 1994). Their answer, in short, is that societal elites control the definition process (Turk, 1977; Chasin, 1997).

You will recall that conflict theory is based on principles first developed by Karl Marx, who maintained that the ruling class in a capitalist society controls all the major institutions and uses them to protect its interests (Lynch & Groves, 1989). Their control of the political institution is especially significant. The legal statutes that define what will be considered criminal deviance clearly reflect the values and interests of the ruling class (Quinney, 1970;

Many behaviors are regarded as more deviant in some cultures than in others. This tourist from San Francisco is taking advantage of the relatively tolerant attitudes toward marijuana use currently prevalent in Holland; back in the United States such a public display of drug use would very likely result in his arrest.

Greenberg, 1981). Crimes committed mostly by the poor—robbery, burglary, larceny, aggravated assault—carry heavy penalties, while offenses most commonly committed by elites, such as price-fixing, dumping hazardous wastes, or maintaining unsafe working conditions, carry lesser penalties (Reiman, 1995). Conflict theorists also charge that the police and courts routinely discriminate in the application of the law, a problem we will take up in Chapter 9 (Arvanites, 1992; Lynch, 1994).

The elite also control the schools and the mass media, two additional important social institutions, and use them to shape people's understandings of what sorts of behaviors and ideas ought to be considered deviant. These definitions are biased in favor of the capitalists' interests and emphasize the seriousness of types of deviance that are especially common among the poor and minorities (Quinney, 1970). Note that these insights concerning how deviance is defined reflect a synthesis of the conflict and symbolic interactionist perspectives.

Richard Quinney is an important modern conflict theorist who has addressed these issues. He notes that the fact that the ruling class defines deviance and enforces laws in a self-serving manner actively promotes norm violation among both the wealthy and the poor (Quinney, 1977). The elite commit what Quinney calls "crimes of domination and repression," which are designed to increase their wealth and power and to control the middle and lower classes, with relative impunity. After all, writes Quinney (1972), ". . . those in power, those who control the legal system, are not likely to prosecute themselves and define their official policies as crime."

At the same time, the poor have little choice but to engage in predatory deviance in order to survive. Most of their acts are property crimes such as larceny and burglary. The lower classes also engage in a great deal of violent personal crime, which Quinney sees as an expression of their anger and frustration. Crime thus makes sense for both the upper class, because they can get away with it, and for the poor, because they have few other options (Gordon, 1973).

According to conflict theorists, mainstream sociologists are too willing to accept the elite's definitions of deviance. As a result, many do not devote sufficient attention to the great harm that results from the misbehavior of elites and from the inequities of the criminal law (Liazos, 1972).

For example, America's current drug laws mandate much more severe penalties for the possession or sale of crack cocaine than for the powdered form of the drug (Smolowe, 1995). Crack is used primarily by lower-class African Americans, while the majority of powdered cocaine offenders are white. The average prison sentence for crack is three to eight times longer, yet the two forms of the drug are, in essence, chemically identical (Kappler et al., 1996). Similarly, the police are much more likely to arrest streetwalkers, who are heavily minority, than to go after call girls, who are mostly white. They also rarely arrest female prostitutes' male customers (Riccio, 1992).

Conflict theory can be applied easily to the Saints and the Roughnecks. The middle-class Saints misbehaved extensively, yet they suffered no lasting consequences because the authorities identified them as "our kind" and treated them with a presumption of innocence. Conversely, the lower-class Roughnecks were defined as members of the "dangerous classes" and treated accordingly. No conflict theorist would be at all surprised by the different paths these two groups traveled after high school.

CRITIQUE Conflict theory's great strength is that it directs our attention to the importance of power in shaping social definitions of deviance. It has also highlighted the biases present in our criminal justice system. Yet the conflict approach enjoys only limited acceptance among sociologists and has had little effect on the general public.

This lack of acceptance is congruent with the central point made by conflict analysis. Most Americans, including many sociologists, have internalized elite definitions of deviance and are thus likely to believe that the conflict perspective is "radical." But this belief may lead sociologists to concentrate their attention on "real" crimes like robbery or assault, crimes committed principally by the poor, while largely overlooking white-collar crimes like the recent Enron scandal which, as conflict theorists are quick to point out, are actually far more costly than any street crime.

There are, however, some real problems with conflict theory (Toby, 1979; Inciardi, 1980; Sparks, 1980; Gibbs, 1987; Gibbons, 1994). First, its observation that the elite often control the definition of deviance makes the most sense with regard to acts such as insider trading or drug use. It is hard to support when applied to predatory crimes such as murder, forcible rape, or robbery, which almost everyone, regardless of class, regards as seriously deviant.

In addition, the primary policy implication of conflict theory is that economic inequality must be substantially reduced in order to prevent the dominant class from distorting the definition of deviance to its own advantage. Most conflict theorists believe that this can only be achieved by a fundamental shift of the U.S. political economy away from capitalism and toward some form of democratic socialism (Pepinsky & Quinney, 1993; Milovanovic, 1996). However, such an economic transformation is not only unlikely to be achieved in the United States (Owomero, 1988), but it also did not appear to be effective in reducing deviance and crime in the old Soviet bloc nations.

WHAT ARE THE FUNCTIONS OF DEVIANCE?

The conflict perspective, as we have just seen, is useful for answering the first of our key questions: Who decides what is deviant? The second question, however, is best addressed by functionalism.

Following the lead of Emile Durkheim, functionalists maintain that any aspect of a society that fails to contribute to its stability tends eventually to fade away. Since deviance is a cultural universal, it follows that although it is socially devalued, it must serve some functions (Durkheim, 1897/1964; Erickson, 1966). There are four especially important positive functions of deviance:

1. *The Boundary Setting Function.* In complex modern societies, the *real* rules are frequently unclear. How often and how much can students cheat before they are expelled? How fast can you really

THEN AND NOW

From Getting High to Getting Drunk: Changing Styles of Campus Deviance

The marijuana "epidemic," as some called it, peaked in the mid-1970s (Akers, 1992). Study after study in this era found that two out of three college students had used pot, up from a mere 5 percent in the mid-1960s. Prior to this era, marijuana use had been largely confined to "outsiders," especially Mexican American laborers and jazz musicians, whom respectable people did not consider "one of us." Use of the drug by these groups merely confirmed their otherness; it was not a cause for public alarm.

When middle-class college students—presumably the best and the brightest American youth and the nation's future leaders—began using marijuana, it was a different story. As part of the hippie rebellion, college students were also experimenting with cocaine, LSD, amphetamines, and other illicit substances. Clearly, the nation's youth were at risk. And so campaigns like DARE and Just Say No were born.

Over time, the use of marijuana and other illicit drugs by college students declined. But a new epidemic was on the horizon. In 1994 the Harvard School of Public Health issued a report on the use of alcohol on college campuses. A survey of 140 campuses found that almost half of all students engaged in "binge drinking" (consuming five or more drinks at one sitting for men, four or more for women). Even more alarming, half of students who binge do so regularly. Binge drinkers are far more likely than other students to engage in unprotected sex, drive while intoxicated, miss classes, and experience memory lapses. They are also more likely to commit acts of vandalism, get into fights, and injure themselves.

Indeed, drinking too much too fast can be deadly. Each year an estimated 50 students die from bingeing, either because they pass out and choke to death on their own vomit or because their blood becomes so thick that oxygen can't reach their brain (alcohol poisoning). The effects of binge drinking are not limited to participants. At schools with high binge rates, a majority of students who don't drink report such second-hand effects as not being able to sleep or study, enduring insults or unwanted sexual advances, and having to care for drunken friends. Recent studies have found that despite campaigns publicizing the dangers of alcohol abuse, the percentage of binge drinkers on college campuses has been increasing as has the proportion of students who admit they drink specifically to get drunk (not because they enjoy the taste of beer, wine, or whiskey).

The shift from getting high to getting drunk lends support to the functional view that although patterns of deviance change over time, the overall level of deviance remains more or less constant. When frequent use of marijuana on college campuses declined, heavy drinking replaced it. This pattern also suggests that public perception of deviance remains steady. During the marijuana years, alcohol did not disappear on campuses, but most people did not consider college drinking a problem. After all, alcohol wasn't a "drug" in the social sense of being an illicit substance. Likewise, marijuana hasn't disappeared from college campuses, but the public is now somewhat less likely to view cannabis as dangerously addictive and morally subversive. To the contrary, possession of small quantities of marijuana has been decriminalized in a number of states and reduced from a felony to a misdemeanor in others. At the same time, attitudes toward alcohol, and particularly toward drunken drivers, have changed. Once viewed as a matter of personal choice, heavy drinking has been redefined as a public health issue.

Why do college students engage in high levels of deviance? From the functionalist perspective, societies need a certain level of nonconforming behavior in order to test and reaffirm the boundaries of acceptable behavior. College students are well situated to perform this function. As young adults, they are no longer expected to accept their parents' authority without question; nor do they have as many responsibilities as they will when they embark on careers, marry, and become parents. In effect, the college years are a "time out" when the penalties for nonconformity are reduced. Students are expected to question ideas and engage in critical thinking; that some question society's norms and values should not be a surprise. Most people who frequently smoked pot in college do not become life-long drug users; nor do most college binge drinkers continue to abuse alcohol. Having tested the boundaries of acceptable behavior, most choose respectability. But the next generation of college students, and the next, reenact the cycle.

1. Is binge drinking widespread on your campus? How do participants explain and excuse their behavior? What additional interpretations might be suggested by a sociologist?

2. Do you believe that programs like DARE and groups like MADD and SADD are effective in combating alcohol abuse? Discuss.

3. What should be the goals of a sociologically informed campus-based campaign to oppose binge drinking? How would you structure such an effort?

Source: Akers, 1992; Goldberg, 1998; McCormick & Kalb, 1998.

drive on the interstate without getting a ticket? How much can you drink before people will start thinking of you as an alcoholic? In some cases, there are no official rules; in others, there are formal rules but they are enforced with a degree of tolerance, which means that there is a difference between the *formal* and the *actual* boundaries of acceptable behavior.

We learn the real boundaries by observing what happens to people who deviate: We know that we cannot go as far as they do unless we are willing to risk punishment ourselves. In other words, publicly labeled deviants define the range of acceptable behaviors by exceeding that range, and they encourage conformity by showing what happens to people who fail to conform.

It can be argued that one reason why there are so many portrayals of deviance in the mass media is to spread public awareness of the true limits of tolerance. Thus, ironically, one of the principal functions of deviance is to encourage conformity!

2. *The Solidarity Function.* Nothing unites a group of people more strongly than their shared opposition to an enemy; this phenomenon is especially evident in societies engaged in warfare. For example, most Americans experienced a surge of patriotism following the September 11, 2001, terrorist attacks. Deviants provide a domestic equivalent of Osama bin Laden.

3. *The Warning Function.* When any type of deviance becomes substantially more common, it sends a signal that something is wrong in society. Examples include escalations in the frequency of inner-city riots or a sharp increase in the use of illegal drugs by teens. The authorities may respond to the warning in one of two ways: They may modify the rules or laws to fit changing circumstances, or they may simply step up their social control efforts.

4. *The Innovation Function.* Sometimes deviance can be highly functional in promoting social change. For example, the nonviolent tactics employed by the Southern civil rights movement of the 1960s, including sit-ins and freedom rides, were widely viewed at the time as being beyond the conventional limits of political activity, but were nevertheless very effective in bringing about racial integration. Similarly, people in formal organizations sometimes find that they must break some of the formal rules (or "cut through the red tape") in order to achieve important ends.

Chambliss's study of the Saints and the Roughnecks nicely illustrates the boundary setting and solidarity functions of deviance. The official response to

On February 4, 1999, New York City police fired 41 shots into the home of unarmed African immigrant Amadou Diallo, killing him instantly. Shared opposition to this act of apparent police brutality unites the members of this protest crowd.

the misdeeds of the Roughnecks clarified the actual limits of toleration for other youths, and the community clearly was united in condemning the gang's deviance.

The fact that deviance serves positive functions implies that societies may take covert steps to ensure that they do not "run out" of deviants (Erickson, 1962). For example, we claim that prisons are designed to reduce crime. Yet, since there is little emphasis on rehabilitation in modern prisons, what inmates actually learn while incarcerated often consists largely of tips picked up from fellow inmates about how to become better—more effective—offenders. Because of the severe stigma associated with having been incarcerated, ex-prisoners often find it extremely difficult to find honest employment after they are released, strongly pushing them toward illicit sources of income. In light of these facts, it seems possible that prison is really less about reducing crime than about perpetuating it (Reiman, 1995).

Of course, deviance also is dysfunctional for society. In addition to the numerous direct physical and economic injuries that result from acts such as robbery, arson, manufacturing hazardous products, or domestic violence, deviance has at least three important general dysfunctions. First, it makes social life problematic because it reduces our certainty that others will obey the norms. Much like someone driving in the wrong lane of a highway, the presence of criminals and deviants makes our lives less predictable.

Second, if deviance is seen to be rewarded, it reduces people's willingness to play by the rules. If your neighbor gets away with cheating on her income tax, why should you report every penny? If your friends get A's by cheating, why study?

Finally, deviance is dysfunctional because it is very costly. The United States loses more than $450 billion annually due to crime, including both direct costs and social control expenditures (Mandel & Magnusson, 1993). These resources could be used for other, more constructive purposes.

The most important policy implication of the functional approach is to remind the authorities that it is not possible, or even desirable, to attempt to eradicate all deviation. Certainly, we should try to reduce serious predatory crime as much as possible, but at the same time we need to recognize that a certain amount of relatively harmless nonconformity has positive social value. In fact, there is some evidence that if one sort of deviance is sharply reduced, whether by effective social control or by redefinition, some other type of deviance is likely to become more common (Erickson, 1966). This strongly suggests that "zero-tolerance" efforts to completely end drug abuse, juvenile gangs, or other forms of deviance are most unlikely to succeed.

WHY DO PEOPLE DEVIATE?

Through most of history, the usual answer to the question of why people violate important norms was a religious or moralistic one. Thus, deviance might be explained by demonic possession or by a simple declaration that deviants and criminals were "evil" or "sinful" or "bad" people.

But in the late 18th century, Enlightenment thinkers such as Caesare Beccaria and Jeremy Bentham challenged these early explanations by asserting that deviance could best be understood as a consequence of the exercise of free will (Bentham, 1967; Devine, 1982). Deviants, they maintained, consciously assessed the costs and benefits of conformity and nonconformity and chose the latter only when it seemed advantageous to do so. This perspective, known as *classical theory*, has enjoyed renewed popularity in the past two decades under the name **rational choice theory** (Cornish & Clarke, 1986). Early classical theory led to more humane social control efforts than moralistic theories, but it fell into disfavor late in the 19th century with the rise of positivistic thinking in the social sciences.

Positivism is an approach to understanding human behavior grounded in the scientific method.

Positivistic theories are research-based, concentrate on measurable aspects of empirical reality, and aim to identify the causes of behavior. They are strongly oriented toward reducing deviance: If we can identify what causes a behavior pattern, we can use that knowledge to change the behavior. Classical theory simply states that people choose crime because they think such a choice will benefit them. Positivistic theories, in contrast, explore the underlying *reasons* for the choices that people make, thereby allowing us to develop more effective techniques of social control.

It is important to recognize that in contrast to classical theory, positivism does *marginally* reduce the degree to which deviants are considered responsible for their behavior. If deviance is *purely* a result of free will, then deviants are entirely responsible for their actions. If, on the other hand, the decision to deviate is influenced by biological, psychological, or social factors—which are to some extent beyond the deviant's ability to control—then individual responsibility is somewhat lessened. But this does not mean that, in practice, positivists regard criminals as personally blameless.

Positivists therefore see punishment as part of an appropriate response to misbehavior, but they insist that society needs to go beyond negative sanctioning and consider causal factors in order to reduce deviance more effectively. Failing to consider factors that shape the decision to deviate places too much weight on the shoulders of the individual; it is a form of victim-blaming (Ryan, 1971).

Biological Explanations

The first positivistic theories of deviance arose when Darwin's theory of evolution was having a profound influence on European and American intellectual thought and were thus strongly grounded in biology. The most popular of these approaches was a theory developed by Italian criminologist Caesare Lombroso, who maintained that many criminals were born rather than made (Lombroso-Ferreo, 1972). Without altogether denying the importance of other factors, Lombroso argued that some lawbreakers were genetically inferior throwbacks to an earlier, more brutal type of humanity. Defective in reasoning power and physically distinctive, sometimes deformed, these individuals could not be reformed or even reasoned with.

Some early 20th century theorists continued to search for a general genetic cause of deviation that would allow them to put deviants and nondeviants into two distinct categories. However, most of this early work was marred by serious methodological weaknesses, and biological positivism lost popularity early in this century, only to be revived in a more sophisticated form during the last 40 years (Wilson, 1975; Fishbein, 2000).

Instead of arguing that misbehavior is directly caused by biology, modern biological theories generally maintain that certain physical traits, acting in concert with psychological and social factors, increase the chances that an individual will engage in deviance (Ellis & Hoffman, 1990). The key factor is often aggressiveness. The physical factors that may contribute to a violent temperament include dietary deficiencies, hypoglycemia (low blood sugar), allergies, hormonal abnormalities, environmental pollution, abnormal brain wave patterns, and tumors (Siegel, 1995: 138–150).

Other biological research posits a connection between deviance and physiologically based difficulties in learning. Some evidence suggests that offenders are likely to exhibit various forms of learning disorders, often linked to minimal brain dysfunction or to attention deficit disorder (Monroe, 1978; Farone et al., 1993; Hart et al., 1994). Researchers maintain that children who have difficulty learning will become frustrated and consequently hostile in the classroom. This in turn may promote deviance by alienating the child from the conformist world and closing the doors to the educational achievement necessary for economic success.

CRITIQUE While research strongly suggests some link between genetics and deviance, this does not mean that any significant amount of violent crime is caused exclusively by physiological factors. Sociological critics say that biologically oriented theorists overstate the importance of genetics. They also argue convincingly that there are serious methodological problems in many biological studies, including excessively small samples and a tendency to study only in-carcerated male offenders, a nonrandom subset of the larger category of all offenders (Curran & Renzetti, 2001).

In addition, the policy implications of biological theories are potentially disturbing. While some biological problems can be remedied with improved diet and medical treatment, others cannot. Moreover, we are not even close to being able to accurately predict people's future behavior on the basis of inborn physiological variables. If we treat someone like a potential deviant, aren't we running a risk of creating a *self-fulfilling prophecy*? And even if we could accurately identify at-risk individuals, what should we do with them? Psychological therapy or social reform will be, by definition, inadequate. Should we sterilize them? And who decides?

Psychological Explanations

Unlike biological positivism, psychological positivism does not consider deviance inborn. Rather, the tendency toward deviance is seen as developing in infancy or early childhood as a result of abnormal or inadequate socialization by parents and other caregivers (Andrews & Bonta, 1994). Each of the several branches of psychology takes this fundamental insight in a different direction.

The *psychoanalytic approach*, based on the work of Sigmund Freud, holds that criminals typically suffer from weak or damaged egos or from inadequate superegos that are unable to restrain the aggressive and often antisocial drives of the id (Byrne & Kelly, 1981). The *cognitive school* assumes that deviants have failed to reach more advanced stages of moral reasoning (Kohlberg, 1969; Veneziano & Veneziano, 1992)

Children who suffer from biologically-caused learning disorders may become frustrated and even hostile at school. Further deviance becomes more likely if a poor academic record makes it difficult for such children to achieve economic success later in life.

or that they have difficulty properly processing the information they receive. *Social learning* theorists maintain that children learn how to act by observing the kinds of behaviors that are rewarded. If deviance is positively reinforced, whether in real life or in the media, it is likely to be imitated (Bandura, 1973). Finally, *personality theorists* search for personality traits that are disproportionately present among deviants, such as aggressiveness or the inability to defer gratification (Andrews & Warmith, 1989; Curran & Renzetti, 2001).

CRITIQUE Sociologists generally acknowledge the value of psychological positivism, especially in analyzing the origins of some of the more extreme types of deviance. Serial killers, for example, are often diagnosed as *sociopaths*, individuals with highly antisocial personalities lacking any appreciable conscience (McCord & Tremblay, 1992; Hickey, 2002).

However, critics note some serious problems with the psychological approach. The worst may be that there is no one-to-one correspondence between any particular personality pattern and a given type of deviance. Thus some people who are impulsive, immature, defiant, and destructive as youths may grow

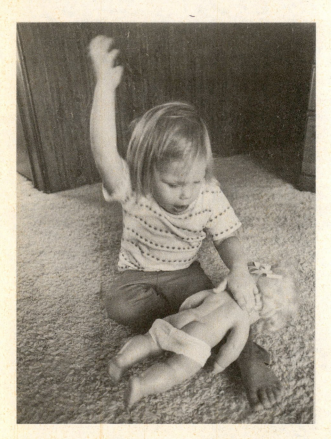

All children act out their aggressive impulses from time to time, but social psychologists have found that those with sociopathic tendencies are unusually prone to violent behavior.

up to be career deviants, but others with the same characteristics as youths become conforming citizens. Conversely, some thieves or drug addicts may display certain distinctive personality patterns, but others do not. As a result, psychologically oriented researchers are rarely able to accurately predict which youths will become seriously deviant, missing some and mislabeling others (Tennenbaum, 1977).

The policy implications of psychological positivism appear humane. Instead of punishing deviants in order to deter them, as classical theory mandates, or subjecting them to medical intervention, as the biological school may suggest, psychologists recommend various forms of therapies, often combined with tranquilizers and antidepressants. Their goal is to reform or rehabilitate deviants. (This approach may not be as progressive as it seems, however; this is a controversial issue that we address toward the end of this chapter). Yet the idea of rehabilitating deviants, widely endorsed by social control agencies through most of this century, is perceived by the general public as not just humane but indeed "soft." Most people appear to believe that the therapeutic approach to criminality has been ineffective, which partially explains the renewed popularity in recent decades of harsher crime-control policies based on biological and free-will understandings.

There are other problems with psychological positivism. Like biological theory, traditional psychological theory tends to ignore the social context in which deviance occurs. Both approaches also accept the definition of crime and deviance as given, meaning that—as conflict theorists are quick to point out—they devote little attention to elite deviance. In sum, both biological and psychological positivism provide useful but incomplete paths to understanding why some people deviate.

Sociological Explanations

Whereas biological and psychological positivism locate the cause of deviation *inside* the individual, sociological approaches focus on the influence of the *external* social environment in the causation of deviance.

There are two major types of sociological theories of deviant behavior. *Social structure theories* explore the reasons why different rates of deviance and criminality are found in different sectors of society. *Social process theories* examine how particular people learn to think about and evaluate deviance within a given social setting (Akers, 1997).

SOCIAL STRUCTURE THEORIES Observers have long noted the heavier involvement in deviance among persons occupying certain social statuses. (see

Figure 8.3). In our society, the highest rates of officially recorded crime occur among young, lower income, minority males. Conflict theorists argue that this pattern is primarily a result of the inability of the relatively powerless segments of society to influence the official definition of deviance or the actions of the criminal justice system. Without necessarily denying the value of this insight, social structural theorists think it is still well worth investigating why so many young, poor, minority males break the law.

The connection between social structure and individual behavior was first explored by the early functionalist Émile Durkheim. As discussed in Chapter 1, Durkheim's study of suicide rates emphasized that people who are strongly integrated into social groupings that disapprove of suicide are unlikely to take their own lives (Durkheim, 1897/1964). But

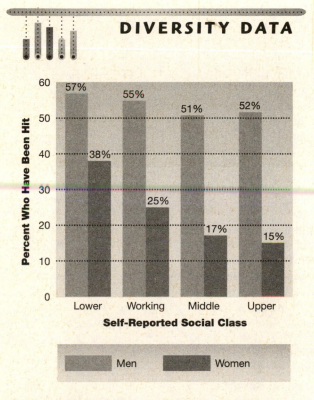

DIVERSITY DATA

FIGURE 8.3 *Chances That Someone Has Ever Been Hit, by Gender and Class.* As the self-reported social class position of women rises, the likelihood that they have been hit declines sharply. A similar pattern is apparent among men, but the differences between the classes are much less substantial. At all class levels, men are considerably more likely than women to have experienced interpersonal violence. What social factors explain why violence seems to be more common among men and the lower classes?

Source: NORC. General Social Surveys, 1972–2000. Chicago: National Opinion Research Center, 2000. Reprinted by permission of NORC, Chicago, IL.

when people become less involved in such groups or when the group's commitment to a particular normative position weakens, the suicide rate rises. In Durkheim's terms, a weakened collective conscience leads to the dysfunctional state of *anomie*, a situation of normative ambiguity in which people are unsure of how they should behave. Society no longer offers adequate guidelines for behavior and, naturally, deviance increases (Durkheim, 1897/1964).

Anomie is generally low in traditional cultures, but industrialization and urbanization break down normative consensus and promote nonconformity. Deviance is particularly likely to occur today among young people, the poor, and minorities precisely because these groups tend to experience significant levels of anomie (Menard, 1995).

Strain Theory In the late 1930s, Robert Merton extended Durkheim's functionalist observations into a widely known sociological theory of deviance (Merton, 1938). He started with the observation that virtually everyone in the United States accepts the desirability of attaining certain "success goals," especially wealth. While some may have stronger needs to succeed than others, almost everyone is socialized in the family, at school, and through the mass media to desire material success. We also learn that only some means are appropriate or legitimate ways to seek this goal. One can properly obtain wealth by inheriting it, working hard, going to school, or perhaps by winning the lottery, but not by selling drugs, holding up banks, or printing hundred dollar bills in the basement.

However, according to Merton, social structural factors limit the ability of many people—especially the poor and minorities—to seek wealth effectively through the approved means. Merton refers to such a situation as a *blocked opportunity structure*. This lack of equal opportunity is dysfunctional and throws society out of balance or equilibrium. People who are blocked experience anomie because they are not sure how to behave; Merton refers to this feeling as strain.

Such people may try to reduce their strain in five different ways (see Table 8.1 on page 208). First, they may continue to slog away in pursuit of success using only the legitimate means despite the fact that their opportunities to succeed are severely limited. Merton terms this response *conformity* and notes that it is fortunately the most common pattern among members of at-risk groups.

Second, individuals experiencing strain sometimes become *innovators:* They continue to desire to attain the success goals but they reject the established ways of doing so and substitute illegitimate means—they embezzle, they kidnap the children of the rich and hold them for ransom, they join an organized crime family. This response is clearly deviant.

TABLE 8.1

Robert Merton's Strain Theory of Deviance

Form of Adaptation	Attitude Toward Conventional Success Goals	Attitude Toward Legitimate Means to Achieve Success Goals	Deviant?	Examples
Conformity	desire	accept	no	work hard; earn a college degree
Innovation	desire	replace	yes	drug dealer; counterfeiter
Retreatism	reject	reject	yes	crack addict; dropout
Ritualism	reject	accept	maybe	Ph.D. in unmarketable discipline; bureaucrat mired in red tape
Rebellion	replace	replace	yes	political revolutionary; full-time environmental activist

Third, people trapped in a blocked opportunity situation may become what Merton calls *retreatists*—they drop out and stop seeking any goals beyond immediate self-indulgence. Retreatists often are heavily involved in drugs and alcohol. They are generally regarded as deviants.

Ritualism is a fourth way of responding to a blocked opportunity structure. Ritualists abandon the idea of achieving economic success, but they still go through the motions of striving for it. They are not seriously deviant, though we may consider them a little eccentric. A graduate student toiling away for a Ph.D. in an obscure discipline with very limited employment possibilities would be a ritualist.

Finally, people may respond to strain by becoming what Merton terms *rebels*. Like retreatists, rebels turn their backs on established goals and the legitimate means to reach them. But, unlike retreatists, they substitute new goals and new ways of attaining these new goals, often in the company of like-minded others. Individuals who channel virtually all of their time into the environmental movement are a good example of what Merton means by rebellion, as are political revolutionaries. Rebels may or may not be considered seriously deviant.

Merton's theory can be applied to the Roughnecks, but strictly speaking, not to the Saints, since the latter group did not have to deal with the strain of blocked opportunities. The Roughnecks, raised in the lower classes, responded to structural strain through innovation, in the form of theft, and retreatism, in their continual truancy from school and frequent indulgence in alcohol.

Critique Merton's theory highlights the importance of social factors and is supported by a good deal of empirical research (Cohen, 1965; Passas & Agnew, 1997). In particular, the finding that deviance thrives where there is a great disparity between rich and poor is in line with his work. This relationship holds both within the United States (D. Jacobs, 1989; Simons & Gray, 1989) and globally (Archer & Gartner, 1984).

However, it is not clear that everyone is equally committed to striving for material success. Some maintain that the working and lower classes aspire to a somewhat different and more realistic set of goals—not to become fabulously wealthy, but simply to own a home and make enough money to live fairly comfortably (Matza, 1969; Messner & Rosenfeld, 1994). Others question whether Merton's theory can be applied to women without substantial modification, since at least traditionally, marriage has been the primary legitimate route by which females have achieved economic success (Pollock, 1999). This is a good example of the androcentric orientation of most traditional theories of crime and deviance (Naffine, 1996).

In addition, Merton does not adequately specify the conditions under which people who are experiencing strain come to choose one or another of the five resolutions. Neither does he explain why most people abandon deviance as they become older. Finally, Merton does not address the deviance that occurs among societal elites like the Saints; he seems to uncritically accept the view that only lower-class deviation needs explanation.

The primary policy implication of Merton's theory is that the structural factors that contribute to deviance by blocking opportunity must be opened up. At a minimum, this means expanding educational opportunities for the lower classes and attacking racist and sexist discrimination.

Lower-Class Focal Value Theory In another influential variation of social structure theory, Walter Miller (1958) agrees with Merton that deviance is concentrated in the lower classes, but he denies that it results from a socially imposed inability to live up to internalized cultural values. Rather, Miller thinks deviance reflects the acceptance by poor young males of a lower-class subculture. The norms and values of this subculture are not entirely distinct from those of the mainstream culture, but the lower class tends to more wholeheartedly accept certain orientations that are less important to members of the higher classes. Accepting these subcultural patterns does not necessarily lead directly to deviance, but it can promote such an outcome. Miller identifies several "focal concerns" as particularly relevant to the lower-class subculture. They include

- *Trouble*—Both getting into trouble and dealing with it effectively are highly valued.
- *Excitement*—Lower class youth put a lot of importance on "kicks" and excitement.
- *Smartness*—Book learning is not necessarily disparaged, but "street smarts," the ability to manipulate others and not be taken advantage of, is strongly emphasized.
- *Fate*—Members of this subculture believe that much of what happens in life is due to factors beyond their control.
- *Autonomy*—Independence from external control is highly valued.
- *Toughness*—Frequently raised in female-dominated families, lower-class boys struggle to affirm their masculinity; this effort often leads to an exaggerated "macho" emphasis on fighting and physical strength.

Both the Saints and the Roughnecks valued excitement, street smarts, trouble, and autonomy. However, the middle-class Saints placed less emphasis on physical toughness and fate than the Roughnecks. As a result, the Saints generally avoided physical confrontations, which reduced their chances of coming into contact with formal agents of social control. Furthermore, believing they were in control of their own destiny, they did a much better job of planning their misbehavior to avoid apprehension.

Critique The key issue in assessing Miller's theory is whether the subculture of the poor is guided by its own relatively distinct set of norms and values. Research on this issue is inconclusive. Some scholars find solid evidence of different norms and values in the lower class (Banfield, 1974; Gaines, 1991), while others reach the opposite conclusion (Cernovich, 1978; Einstadter & Henry, 1995). Critics have also pointed out that Miller's work is focused exclusively on the values of lower-class males; women are again left out of the picture (Pollock, 1999).

The most obvious policy implication of Miller's focal value theory is that if the value system of the lower class could be changed, deviance would decline. However, in order to do this, it would probably be necessary to institute the sorts of reforms implied by Merton's theory. Thus all varieties of social structure theory ultimately lead to the same conclusion: We must reduce inequality and lower the barriers to social mobility in order to combat deviance.

SOCIAL PROCESS THEORIES Social structure theories help explain the higher rates of deviance in some sectors of society, but they do not address the micro-level question of why some individuals growing up in high-crime areas resist temptation and, conversely, why some of the privileged go astray. To answer such questions, we must consider how individuals learn attitudes regarding deviance and conformity from the people around them. Social process theories focus on socialization and incorporate aspects of psychological learning theory, but they also include elements of the symbolic interactionist perspective. They are sometimes called *cultural transmission theories*. We will discuss two representative social process theories: differential association theory and control theory.

Differential Association Theory Writing around the same time as Merton, criminologist Edwin Sutherland addressed the question of how particular individuals, regardless of their place in the social structure, acquire positive attitudes toward crime and learn the skills they need in order to be successful criminals (Sutherland, 1940).

The result was the theory of differential association, which is ultimately based on the everyday observation that deviants and conformists tend to hang around mostly with other people like themselves. Sutherland argued that

- Deviance is learned, not inherited.
- It is learned primarily through interaction in small, intimate groups. Media influence is indirect or filtered through the attitudes of the members of the group.
- A person becomes deviant because he or she encounters more definitions favorable to violation of norms than definitions unfavorable to violation of norms.
- The relationships in which these definitions are transmitted may vary in *frequency* (how regularly a person interacts with a particular individual), *duration* (how long each interaction lasts), *priority* (how early in life the relationship begins), and *intensity* (how important the relationship is to the individual).

Differential association theory clearly applies to the Saints and the Roughnecks. Both groups absorbed definitions favorable to deviance from their peers, but the Saints also learned effective techniques for avoiding social control agents, which the Roughnecks did not acquire.

These children are getting help with their homework from an adult volunteer. Differential association theory suggests that at-risk youths who are exposed to positive role models are less likely to become delinquent.

Critique Differential association theory makes strong intuitive sense. Moreover, unlike social structure theory, it explains both conformity and deviance and applies equally well to both men and women and to members of all social classes. In fact, one of the reasons Sutherland developed it was to explain white-collar crime, which he believed was more likely when cohesive peer groups that endorsed unethical business practices arose in corporations (Sutherland, 1940).

The idea that deviants generally associate with and learn from other deviants has been widely supported by research both in the United States (Short, 1960; Smith et al., 1991; Kandel & Davies, 1991; Heimer, 1997) and abroad (Cheung & Ng, 1988). The major criticism of this theory is that the terms frequency, duration, priority, and intensity are imprecise. For example, it would be difficult to empirically measure the intensity of a relationship. Differential association theory also fails to account for solitary deviants, such as check forgers and embezzlers.

The primary policy implication of Sutherland's theory is that potentially wayward youth need to be encouraged to spend more time with conformist peers. For example, offering recreational programs like basketball leagues potentially weakens the hold of the deviant peer group.

Control Theory Instead of assuming that obeying the rules is normal and that deviance is what must be explained, control theorists think it is *conformity* that must be explained. This perspective is congruent with many nonsociological views of human nature, especially that of Sigmund Freud, but is relatively uncommon within sociology. According to control theory, we all experience strong pushes toward nonconformity. Deviants are people who lack adequate internal or external controls (or containments) against norm violation (Reckless, 1969).

The most widely cited social control theory was developed in the late 1960s by Travis Hirschi (1969) and revised by Hirschi and Michael Gottfredson (Gottfredson & Hirschi, 1990). The original theory suggested that people were more or less successfully insulated from deviance by four types of social bonds:

- *Attachment*, a feeling of emotional connection with parents, teachers, and peers. The desire not to disappoint people one cares about provides a good reason to avoid deviance.
- *Commitment*, a strong interest in achieving goals—for example, attending a good college or becoming a police officer—that might be blocked by a criminal record or a reputation as a deviant.
- *Involvement* in the busy routines of everyday life may not leave youths with enough free time to become deviants.
- *Belief*, the acceptance of conventional values.

Hirschi and Gottfredson's revised theory retains the emphasis on social bonds but adds the idea that these social bonds will be less effective in restraining people whose parents failed to develop in them an adequate level of *self-control*.

The key insight that control theory provides regarding the Saints and the Roughnecks concerns the variable of commitment. While neither group accepted very many conformist beliefs or was tightly bonded to parents or teachers, and both seemed to find time to misbehave, the Saints' middle-class background gave them a reasonable expectation of attending college, a career path that might have been closed off if they had been tagged as serious deviants. In fact, all but one of the Saints completed college, while only two of the Roughnecks were able to do so, both of them on football scholarships.

Critique Researchers have found substantial support for control theory (Grasmick et al., 1993; Nagin & Paternoster, 1993; Free, 1994). Unlike some of the other theories, it has the virtue of explaining why criminality tends to decline as people move past their teenage years: Unlike adolescents, most adults acquire high levels of attachment, commitment, and involvement as they marry, take full-time jobs, and start raising families. Furthermore, like differential association theory, control theory explains both conformity and deviance and applies to everyone regardless of class or gender.

Hirschi and Gottfredson's work suggests that in order to reduce crime, we need to strengthen social bonds with conformist others and improve the quality of child socialization in order to increase people's self-control. Required parenting classes in high school might be a step in this direction.

WHAT IS THE SOCIAL REACTION TO DEVIANCE?

An innovative approach to deviance, called **labeling theory,** emerged in the 1960s. This perspective explores how the label "deviant" is applied to particular people and the ways in which this devalued identity influences their subsequent behavior—a way of thinking that is deeply grounded in the symbolic interactionist perspective that was discussed at length in Chapter 6.

Labeling theorists emphasize the difference between *deviant acts* and a *deviant role* or *deviant identity* (Becker, 1963; Schur, 1971). All of us commit acts that could be defined as deviant from time to time,

but most people do not become publicly known as deviant role players. Thus most students cheat on occasion but only a few acquire the identity of cheaters; many youths experiment with illegal drugs but only some come to be labeled "stoners."

The purpose of labeling is to apply a *stigma*, a powerfully negative public identity, to an individual who is believed to have violated important norms (Goffman, 1963b). The stigma dramatically influences the way others view the labeled individual. Instead of being seen as someone who occasionally has a few drinks or uses drugs now and then, the stigmatized individual becomes a "drunk" or an "addict."

A label may be acquired in three ways. First, some people voluntarily engage in *self-labeling*. Often, they take this step because concealing their true identity requires a great deal of time, energy, and hypocrisy. People may self-label because they may find that it is easier to bear others' negative comments than to continue to hide their deviance.

Others self-label because they have fully rejected the conventional point of view and actively embrace their deviance; examples include some atheists and motorcycle outlaws like the Hell's Angels (Thompson, 1966; Watson, 1988).

Second, people acquire labels *informally*, from family and friends. For example, many prostitutes are labeled as such by their peers long before they come into contact with the criminal justice system. This form of labeling can have a tremendous influence on an individual, since almost everyone cares about the opinions of the people they are close to and with whom they regularly interact (Matsueda, 1992).

Labeling theory has traditionally put the strongest emphasis on the third way that people acquire labels—*formally* (Lerman, 1996). Formal labeling involves a type of public ritual called a **degradation ceremony**

An informal label like "class clown" or "troublemaker," which is acquired in small peer groups like this one, can be an important factor pushing a youth toward criminal or deviant activity.

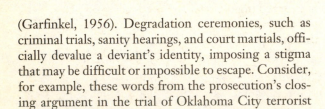

INTERNET CONNECTIONS

Labeling theory is one of a number of theories on deviance. After reading about the theory, go to the Website CrimeTheory.com:

http://www.crimetheory.com/Archive/Response/SR2.htm

Browse through the information but make sure that you click on the parts that are underlined. What sociological question is labeling theory trying to answer? What are some of the weaknesses of the labeling approach to understanding deviance?

(Garfinkel, 1956). Degradation ceremonies, such as criminal trials, sanity hearings, and court martials, officially devalue a deviant's identity, imposing a stigma that may be difficult or impossible to escape. Consider, for example, these words from the prosecution's closing argument in the trial of Oklahoma City terrorist bomber Timothy McVeigh:

> Take a moment and look at Timothy McVeigh. Look into the eyes of a coward and tell him you will have the courage. Tell him you will speak with one unified voice, as the moral conscience of the community, and tell him he is no patriot. He is a traitor, and he deserves to die. (Annin & Morganthau, 1997:41)

What influences the chances that someone will acquire a deviant label? Because we all prefer to believe that we live in a just world, we like to think that people who acquire a stigma must have repeatedly committed serious and harmful deviant acts. Though there is certainly a good deal of truth to this claim, other factors also enter in, principally social power.

Blending themes from the conflict, feminist, and symbolic interactionist perspectives, labeling theorists note that in U.S. society, wealthy, white, male, middle-aged, heterosexual individuals are better able to resist stigmatizing labels than are the less socially empowered (Schur, 1984; Adams et al., 1998). Edwin Schur (1984) was one of the first sociologists to observe the ways in which patriarchal society uses the threat of labeling as an effective means of keeping women from challenging oppressive gender roles.

Other important factors influencing whether a stigmatizing label is applied include (a) how closely a person matches the popular (often media-generated) stereotype of a particular kind of deviant (Surette, 1998; Bailey & Hale, 1998); (b) how concerned formal social control agents currently are about any given type of norm violation (Margolin, 1992); and (c)

how experienced the deviant is—beginners are more likely to be caught, all other factors being equal.

Edwin Lemert (1951) introduced the terms primary and secondary deviance to convey the importance of labeling. **Primary deviance** refers to any deviant act that is not followed by some form of labeling, or to the period of time during which such acts occur. Lemert's point is that primary deviance, even if engaged in for a very long time, rarely affects a person's life very much. You may shoplift, vacuum your apartment naked, smoke crack, or worship the devil for years, but so long as nobody knows about it—or at least nobody who is inclined to publicize this knowledge—it won't have much effect on your life.

On the other hand, once your norm violation is known, you enter into **secondary deviance,** that period of time in which you are compelled to reorganize your life around your devalued identity. Now everything changes. First of all, you may discover that many of your old friends are uncomfortable around you. They may engage in *retrospective reinterpretation* (Scheff, 1984) of their past interactions with you: "Last week she fell asleep in class; I thought she was just tired but now that I know she uses drugs, I realize that she must have been high."

Such reinterpretations may or may not be factually accurate, but once labeled, you have little ability to correct them. You will probably find yourself in the market for new friends, and you are particularly likely to recruit them from fellow deviants who tend not to judge you negatively. Note, however, that in line with Sutherland's differential association theory, deviant friends are likely to propel you toward increased involvement in deviance.

Secondary deviance also requires changes in your major life roles. Labeled deviants frequently lose their jobs, are forced to move, drop out of school, and may become estranged from their families. Such changes combined with the direct effects of stigmatization lower the chances of obtaining legitimate success (Schwartz & Skolnick, 1962). In Merton's terms, your opportunity structure becomes blocked and, again, you are pushed toward deviance.

Finally, secondary deviance also tends to change your self-image, even if you initially resist thinking of yourself as a deviant. A damaged self-image yet again increases the chances that you will move farther into deviance. As a symbolic interactionist would say, the deviant label becomes a self-fulfilling prophecy. The ultimate consequence of secondary deviance is *role engulfment*—deviance becomes your master status (Schur, 1980).

Chambliss's study of the Saints and the Roughnecks is a classic example of the power of labeling. The lower-class Roughnecks were probably no more delinquent than their middle-class counterparts. But, in part because they lacked the social power that would allow them to own cars and hence escape the relentless observation of the police and townspeople, they became known as no-good delinquent punks. This label then affected virtually everything that happened to them. The Saints were also labeled—as basically good kids who occasionally sowed a wild oat or two—a label that also had a great impact on their lives, but in quite the opposite direction.

CRITIQUE One of the most serious criticism of labeling theory is that research has not clearly demonstrated that formal labeling necessarily promotes greater commitment to deviance (Wellford, 1975; Sherman & Smith, 1992; Cavender, 1995). While some studies strongly support this role engulfment thesis (Ageton & Elliott, 1973; Ray & Downs, 1986), others refute it (Tittle, 1975). As Hirschi would argue, it may be that people who have a strong attachment to conformist others and to conformist goals respond to the threat of labeling by reaffirming their commitment to conventional norms, whereas people lacking such controls are pushed toward deviance by labeling.

The primary policy implication of labeling theory is that in order to avoid role engulfment, we should minimize the number of people who are publicly labeled, a policy termed *radical nonintervention* (Schur, 1973). In particular, while we must label and punish serious predatory criminals, we must not create a self-fulfilling prophecy by tagging young people who are not yet committed to crime as juvenile delinquents. In fact, not publically revealing the names of juvenile offenders, a practice now under attack, was originally intended to minimize destructive labeling (Kratcoski & Kratcoski, 1996).

Critics charge that labeling theory's heavy emphasis on the relative nature of deviance and on radical nonintervention seem out of step with the law and order, "lock 'em up" mentality of the United States today. Certainly the notion that a rapist or murderer whose crime goes undetected (that is, who avoids being labeled) is not really a deviant seems to violate the core understandings that most people hold concerning deviance.

Table 8.2 summarizes the principal theories of deviance that have been discussed in this chapter.

TABLE 8.2

Theories of Deviance

Type of Theory	Questions Addressed	Major Observations	Policy Implications	Representative Theorists
Classical Theory/ Rational Choice Theory	Why do individuals deviate?	People calculate the costs and benefits and rationally decide whether or not to deviate. Deviance is freely chosen.	Increase negative sanctions for deviance.	Caesare Beccaria, Jeremy Bentham, Marcus Felson, James Q. Wilson
Conflict Theory	In whose interests is deviance defined?	The rich and powerful define deviance to benefit themselves.	Reduce the power of elites.	Willem Bonger, Richard Quinney, Steven Spitzer
Biological Positivism	Why do individuals deviate?	Deviants are physically different than conformists.	Medical treatment, drugs, perhaps sterilization.	Caesare Lombroso, William Sheldon, Hans Eysenck
Psychological Positivism	Why do individuals deviate?	Deviants are psychologically different than conformists.	Better child rearing; psychological therapy.	Sigmund Freud, Lawrence Kohlberg, Stanton Samenow
Sociological Positivism (*Social Structure Theory*)	Why are some categories of people more deviant than others?	Certain social environments encourage deviance.	Change the social environment; offer more opportunity.	Robert Merton, William Miller, Albert Cohen
Sociological Positivism (*Social Process Theory*)	Why do individuals deviate?	People learn from others around them whether or not to deviate.	Provide more chances to learn from and bond with conformist others.	Edwin Sutherland, Travis Hirschi, Walter Reckless
Labeling Theory	What are the consequences of the ways in which members of society react to deviance?	Labeling people as deviants can reinforce their deviant identity and become a self-fulfilling prophecy.	Minimize labeling; radical nonintervention.	Edwin Lemert, Howard Becker, Harold Garfinkel

LIFE CONNECTIONS

Mental Illness as Deviant Behavior

What is the difference between a mentally healthy person and one who is mentally ill? This is not an easy question to answer, in large part because our understanding of what is and is not normal is heavily influenced by the social and cultural context in which a particular act takes place. For example, members of some religious groups are expected to enter trancelike states in which speaking in tongues is encouraged. So long as such behavior is defined in religious terms, most people in the United States would probably regard it as a little strange but basically normal. If, however, the same behavior were observed in a poorly dressed person standing on a street corner, many of us would have little difficulty labeling that individual "crazy."

The media have a strong influence on our understanding of mental disorders, sometimes in unfortunate ways. Media imagery of the mentally ill tends to stereotype them as violent and dangerous. In fact, the vast majority are neither.

Mental illness is widespread in modern societies. If it is defined as exhibiting severe enough symptoms to require ongoing treatment, then about 15 percent of all people in the United States suffer from mental illness. If it consists of having some difficulty coping with everyday life due to stress, anxiety, or depression, then as much as 80 percent of the population may be affected (Dohrenwend & Dohrenwend, 1974; Gallagher, 1987; Regier, 1991; Coleman & Cressey, 1999). However mental illness is defined, most of the people who suffer from it go untreated (Mechanic, 1989; Barker et al., 1992).

Most people understand mental illness in terms of the *medical model*, which interprets it as a disease with biological or genetic causes that is best treated by a psychiatrist or psychologist. While there is clear evidence that some forms of mental illness, especially the more serious ones such as schizophrenia, are indeed caused partly by biological factors, it is equally clear that many other types do not result from organic defect (Gatchel et al., 1989; Berrios, 1995).

Many sociologists find labeling theory to be more useful than the medical model as a means of understanding psychological disorders (Rosenfeld, 1997). This perspective interprets mental illness as a status with attached role requirements that are first internalized and then acted out. Although most norm violations evoke labels such as strange, eccentric, or criminal if people violate certain basic and taken-for-granted expectations, they are likely to be labeled as mentally ill, an identity that is typically very difficult to change. Examples include people who fail to observe basic principles of personal hygiene or who carry on animated conversations in public with individuals who are not present. Thomas Scheff (1963) refers to such violations of basic social conventions as *residual deviance*.

Some labeling theorists go even further, claiming that the very idea of mental illness is a myth. Thomas Szasz (1961, 1994b) embraces this view, maintaining that the people we call mentally ill are in fact simply experiencing what he calls "unresolved problems in living." He strongly criticizes psychiatrists, who he claims "know little about medicine and less about science," for labeling people as mentally ill and then taking away their freedom in the name of curing them (Szasz, 1994b:36).

D. L. Rosenhan (1973) conducted a classic study that supports the conclusions of labeling theory. Rosenhan and seven of his colleagues presented themselves at a number of different mental hospitals claiming to hear voices. In fact, none of the "pseudopatients" had any history of mental disorder. All were admitted with a diagnosis of schizophrenia; all stopped claiming to hear voices or displaying any other psychiatric symptom immediately upon entering the hospital.

Rosenhan suggested that if psychiatric diagnoses were objective, the pseudopatients would soon be detected by the staff. This did not occur. The researchers' stays in the hospitals varied from 7 to 52 days; all were released with the diagnosis "schizophrenia in remission." The doctors and nurses never detected the deception, although some of the "real" patients did, an outcome Rosenhan attributed to the power of the label of "mental illness" to frame virtually all perceptions of the patients by the medical staff.

In a second stage of the study, Rosenhan told staff members at a prestigious mental hospital who were skeptical of the results of the initial research that he would be sending them more pseudopatients and asked them to identify any they detected. Over the next 3 months, 41 of 193 new patients were identified as fakes with a high degree of confidence by at least one staff member; in fact, Rosenhan sent no pseudopatients!

Sociologists have consistently found an inverse relationship between mental illness and social class. This is true for both treated and untreated populations and has been found in many societies, including Britain and Canada (Turner & Marino, 1994; Armstrong, 1995; Cook & Wright, 1995). Although the connection between class and diagnosed mental disorder is firmly established, there is some disagreement as to whether mental illness is a cause or a consequence of being relatively low in class. The *drift hypothesis* suggests that people move (or "drift") downward on the class ladder because they are mentally ill.

They are unable to function normally, and in particular to hold a job, because of their psychological problems. A number of research studies support this view (Turner & Wagonfeld, 1967; Harkey et al., 1976; Miech et al., 1999). On the other hand, it is intuitively obvious that the strain of living in or near poverty can directly contribute to poor mental health.

Many forms of mental disorder appear to be more common among African Americans, Native Americans, and some other minority groups than among whites, but most research suggests that this is principally a consequence of the generally lower social class ranking of the members of these racial and ethnic groups (Williams et al., 1992; Gaw, 1993; Miech et al., 1999).

There appear to be no significant gender differences in overall *rates* of mental disorder, but there are consistent differences in *type*. Women are more likely to suffer from affective and anxiety disorders, while men are more likely to be diagnosed with personality disorders (Rothblum, 1982; Chino & Funabiki, 1984; Darnton, 1985; Carson et al., 1988). Most sociologists suspect that these differences result more from the ways that therapists perceive men and women than from innate differences between the genders.

It is better for your mental health to be married, especially if you are male. Never-married, divorced, and single men have higher rates of mental illness than those who are married (American Psychological Association, 1985; Steil, 1995). But married women suffer more mental health problems than married men (Gove & Tudor, 1973; Steil & Turetsky, 1987; Rosenfield, 1989; Simon, 1995). For both married men and women, working outside the home contributes to better mental health (Campbell, 1981; Sloan, 1985; Thoits, 1986). Female single parents, especially those who are living in poverty, are particularly likely to suffer from mental illness.

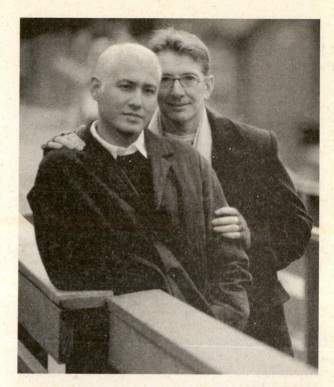

Two generations ago the stigma associated with homosexuality was so strong that the vast majority of gays and lesbians chose to keep their sexual orientation carefully hidden. Today, same-sex couples are an increasingly familiar sight, especially in larger cities, as homosexuality gradually moves through the repression-medicalization-acceptance cycle.

SOCIETY CONNECTIONS

The Repression-Medicalization-Acceptance Cycle

There is a high level of agreement in modern societies concerning most forms of serious, harmful deviance. We may debate exactly how we should respond to acts such as murder, forcible rape, treason, and child abuse, but almost everyone agrees that these behaviors are thoroughly despicable. However, there is much less consensus regarding many other acts that were once more widely condemned, such as alcoholism and homosexuality.

How is it that some behaviors once considered deviant become acceptable? This process is an excellent example of a changing *definition of the situation*, a symbolic interactionist concept that was introduced in Chapter 6 in reference to the issue of sexual harassment. Initially, people *condemn and repress* deviant behaviors, frequently with religious justification. Deviants are seen as evil, sinful people unfit to enjoy normal status in society.

As the values of society become more diverse, however, commitment to traditional forms of religion weakens and a few voices are heard calling for change. Gradually, as moral consensus declines, repression is

GLOBAL CONNECTIONS

The Social Control of Drugs: European Alternatives

For over 80 years, the United States has been guided by these three basic principles in its efforts to control drugs:

- The drug problem is primarily a criminal justice issue.
- The ultimate goal is to end all illicit drug use.
- There are just two kinds of drugs: legal (alcohol, nicotine, caffeine) and illegal. No significant distinctions need to be drawn between different types of illegal drugs.

Policies based on these principles have led to an extremely costly and, in the eyes of many critics, largely futile war against drugs.

On the other hand, many European nations proceed from a very different set of assumptions:

- The drug problem is primarily a public health issue. As Germany's drug czar put it, "Consumers of drugs are not criminals and should be exempt from criminal prosecution. Addiction is a disease and not a crime." (Power, 1999:54)
- Drug use can be minimized but not eliminated; the primary goal is to *reduce the harm* that is done by drug abuse.
- There are profound differences between "soft drugs" (marijuana, hashish) and "hard drugs" (heroin, cocaine, amphetamines) that must be reflected in national drug policies.

These principles have led to a variety of innovative approaches to the drug problem. The policies of the Netherlands have been especially widely publicized. While hard drug sales are severely punished—persons who deal heroin or cocaine may receive 12-year terms in prison—the sale and use of small quantities of soft drugs, while technically illegal, are in fact tolerated. Beginning in 1976, marijuana and hashish could be openly purchased and used in coffee shops in Amsterdam and other Dutch cities.

Dutch policies regarding hard drug users (as opposed to sellers) strongly reflect the harm reduction philosophy. Methadone (a legal heroin substitute) is widely and legally available and there are numerous free needle exchanges designed to reduce the risk of AIDS. There are even ATM-style needle-dispensing machines for use late at night. In addition, the government funds extensive drug education programs and even helps finance the *Junkiebund,* a sort of union of hard drug users.

The results of the Dutch experiment have been generally encouraging. The addict population is small, and few youth seem motivated to try hard drugs; marijuana use is increasing, but still considerably less common, especially among teenagers, than in the United States.

Both Switzerland and the United Kingdom have experimented with supplying not only methadone but also heroin to some hard-core addicts. The Swiss have established 16 clinics where registered long-term addicts who have tried to quit but failed may legally inject heroin as often as three times a day. Both crime rates and unemployment have fallen among patrons of these clinics.

The British also occasionally supply users with heroin, but put much more emphasis on methadone maintenance programs. Addicts obtain methadone prescriptions from their physicians and buy the drug at their corner pharmacy.

Similar policies are in force in some German states, where the government has shifted its drug control efforts from its criminal justice system to its health ministry, and in France, where judges lock up people who sell drugs, but not those who use them. As Nicole Maestracci, director of the French Interministerial Mission Against Drugs and Addiction, puts it, "Sure, a society without drugs would be wonderful. But nobody believes such a society can exist anymore." (Power, 1999:53)

1. What do you think would happen if the United States adopted the European approach to drug control?

2. Do you think it is possible to stop all drug abuse? Explain your answer.

Sources: Trebach, 1989; Beers, 1991; Huber, 1994; Perrine, 1994; Nadelman, 1995; Barnard, 1998; MacCoun & Reuter, 1999; Power, 1999.

---

replaced by medicalization (Conrad & Schneider, 1980). The **medicalization of deviance** involves a redefinition of the character of the deviant from "evil" to "sick." Note that the behavior has not changed— only the label has. Instead of punishing alcoholics and gays, we try to help them "get well." Alcoholics Anonymous has been especially effective in promoting the "disease theory" of alcoholism.

This shift in labels has several consequences. It relocates social control efforts from the criminal justice system to the medical establishment, replacing punishment with therapeutic intervention. Medicalization promotes more humane treatment of deviants, but it also redefines the deviant as less morally responsible for her or his behavior and less personally competent to make decisions about the future. Some critics charge that the medicalization of deviance has simply replaced cops in blue coats with cops in white coats. Furthermore, these critics claim, our society protects the civil rights of "evil" criminals better than the rights of "sick" deviants (Szasz, 1961). In this sense, the medicalization of deviance may be less of a humane advance than it seems at first.

In response to such concerns, some organized groups of deviants have campaigned for yet another redefinition, this time from medicalization to acceptance. John Kitsuse (1980) calls such group efforts to achieve acceptance **tertiary deviance.** This shift has not occurred with alcoholism, but it has regarding homosexuality. In 1974 the American Psychiatric Association formally voted to redefine homosexuality as a variant type of sexual behavior, not a form of mental illness. The general public's attitude toward homosexuality is clearly moving toward toleration if not full acceptance. Figure 8.4 summarizes the repression-medicalization-acceptance cycle.

It is important to note that not all forms of deviance shift smoothly from repression to medicalization and then on to acceptance. Some, like pedophilia, remain in the repression stage despite the best efforts of groups like the North American Man-Boy Love Association. Others, like alcoholism, move only to medicalization. Substantial percentages of the population continue to endorse repression of abortion despite its legalization in the 1973 *Roe v. Wade* decision.

And the popular reaction to a few types of behavior—as we will document shortly—is moving in the opposite direction, toward repression.

The point is not that movement toward acceptance is in any way inevitable, but rather that in modern societies shifting norms make it difficult to define deviance. We conclude this chapter with a brief discussion of some contemporary efforts to reverse the direction of the repression-medicalization-acceptance cycle.

Reversing the Cycle

While the dominant trend in modern society is away from defining various forms of deviance as evil and toward seeing them as signs of sickness or as acceptable alternatives, some behaviors that were accepted in the past are being redefined as more seriously deviant.

For example, campaigns by groups like MADD (Mothers Against Drunk Driving) have had a considerable effect on public attitudes toward driving under the influence of alcohol. While there has been no dramatic reduction in the incidence of drinking and driving (J. B. Jacobs, 1989; Mastrofski & Ritti, 1996), some jurisdictions have made taverns legally liable if they continue to serve obviously intoxicated customers who later have auto accidents. Similarly, naming a "designated driver" who abstains from alcohol in order to drive others home safely is now a widely accepted practice.

Perhaps the most interesting example of the increasing stigmatization of behavior in American society concerns smoking. For centuries, using tobacco has been regarded as acceptable, at least for adult men; since the 1920s it has been generally allowed for women as well. In fact, during much of the 20th century, smoking was widely viewed as a sign of maturity and sophistication. However, this is now changing.

The public's increased willingness to view cigarette smoking as deviant has a number of causes. Chief among them is the great emphasis that an aging population puts on good health combined with an ever-increasing body of research substantiating the damaging effects of smoking. A National Institute of Drug Abuse study found that for every death caused by cocaine, there were 300 tobacco-related deaths (Reinarman & Levine, 1989). People have historically resisted seeing tobacco as an addictive drug, but many are coming to realize that it is in fact just that. Thus, the current "war on drugs" campaign may well be having an anti-tobacco spillover effect.

The signs of this shift in attitude are everywhere. Laws now ban the practice in offices, airplanes, restaurants, and many other public places. A decade or two ago, asking someone to extinguish her or his

FIGURE 8.4 The Repression-Medicalization-Acceptance Cycle.

cigarette in a public place would have been considered pushy and ill-mannered; now it is the smoker who is considered rude. The Clinton administration placed a high priority on trying to keep cigarettes out of the hands of children and adolescents and attempted to give the FDA the power to regulate tobacco as a drug. Spokespersons for the tobacco industry express fears that we may be moving toward some form of legal prohibition of their product.

The bottom line is that smoking is being redefined as mildly deviant behavior. The small clusters of people huddled together just outside the doors of smoke-free buildings are visible proof of this change. It is not clear at present how far this trend will go. The fact that many respectable middle-class people still smoke and the substantial political clout of the tobacco lobby suggest that tobacco users probably do not face full criminalization of their habit. However, they may well have to accept the medicalization of their behavior—they will need to convince the rest of us that they ought to be regarded as nicotine addicts—sick—rather than as immoral devotees of the demon weed.

SUMMARY

1. Sociologists consider deviance a relative concept; therefore, no behavior is seen as inherently deviant. Deviance is found in all societies.

2. Deviance may be interpreted as a negative label established and applied by the socially powerful to a variety of disapproved actions, beliefs, and conditions.

3. Social control consists of actions intended to encourage conformity and to discourage deviance. It may consist of either punishments or rewards. Social control may be exercised by formal or informal agents and is also a consequence of moral socialization.

4. Conflict theory emphasizes the ability of social elites to define what is regarded as deviant in line with their own interests.

5. Although deviance makes social life problematic, erodes trust, and is very costly to control, it also serves several positive functions. It sets the boundaries of what is regarded as acceptable behavior, encourages solidarity, and warns that change is needed.

6. Biological and psychological positivism explain the origins of deviance in terms of internal factors; sociological positivism emphasizes the importance of factors located in the external social environment.

7. Social structure theories, such as Merton's strain theory and Miller's lower-class focal value theory, explain the high rates of deviance among the poor and minorities by reference to broad structural factors such as blocked opportunity and distinctive subcultural values.

8. Social process theories, such as Sutherland's differential association theory and Hirschi's control theory, explain individual decisions to deviate by reference to factors such as social learning and bonds to conventional society.

9. Labeling theory explores the consequences of applying deviant labels to individuals. It assumes that a stigma is likely to become a self-fulfilling prophecy.

10. In modern societies, which are characterized by considerable normative ambiguity, many forms of behavior once considered severely deviant and repressed come to be redefined as illness rather than sin. In some cases, these behaviors are later further reinterpreted as nondeviant and hence worthy of acceptance.

11. However, sometimes the repression-medicalization-acceptance cycle reverses, and previously accepted behaviors such as drunk driving or tobacco smoking come to be seen as deviant.

KEY TERMS

crime 196
degradation ceremony 212
deviance 195
formal social control 198
informal social control 198

labeling theory 211
medicalization of deviance 216
negative sanction 198
positive sanction 198
positivism 204

primary deviance 212
rational choice theory 204
secondary deviance 212
social control 198
tertiary deviance 217

CRITICAL THINKING QUESTIONS

1. Why do many people have trouble accepting the idea that all deviance is relative? Can a person be a good sociologist and at the same time be personally committed to an absolute moral standard? Explain your answer.

2. What sort of social control is usually most effective: formal, informal, or internalized? Similarly, do you think positive or negative sanctions normally work better to reduce deviance?

3. Rational choice and biological theories of deviance seem to be more widely accepted than psychological and especially sociological theories. Why do you think this is the case? How do these preferences affect our social control efforts?

4. Which of the theoretical approaches to deviance strikes you as most useful in interpreting the case of the Saints and the Roughnecks? Explain your choice.

5. What types of behavior, other than those discussed in this chapter, are either becoming more or less accepted in contemporary society? How do you account for these trends?

INVESTIGATE WITH CONTENT SELECT

 Begin your research using Content-Select for this chapter by following the directions found on page 27 of this text to visit Prentice Hall's Research Navigator Website. Enter these search terms into the search field:

Positivism
Medicalization
Strain theory

CHECKING YOUR COMPREHENSION

Choose the best answer for each of the following questions.

1. Which of the following groups would sociologists not classify as deviants?
   a. the physically handicapped
   b. the mentally ill
   c. the HIV-positive
   d. Convicted criminals

2. By conventional standards of behavior in the U.S., jaywalking would be considered
   a. deviant but not criminal.
   b. criminal but not seriously deviant.
   c. both deviant and criminal.
   d. neither criminal nor deviant.

Match the researcher to the learning theory he is associated with

3. Darwin   a. Psychological explanations of deviant behavior

4. Freud   b. Sociological explanations of deviant behavior

5. Durkheim   c. Biological explanations of deviant behavior

                    e. Medical explanations of deviant behavior

Identify the following statements as true or false.

6. The conflict approach to defining deviant behavior enjoys only limited acceptance by sociologists and has had little effect on the general public.

7. It can be argued that one reason there are so many portrayals of deviant behavior in the mass media is to spread public awareness of the true limits of tolerance.

8. Societies may take covert steps to ensure that they do not run out of deviants.

Answer the following questions.

9. What evidence do sociologists point to that supports the notion that deviant behavior is relative in nature?

10. Discuss the three different ways that members of a society can reduce if not eliminate deviant behaviors altogether.

11. Compare and contrast the results of labeling in primary deviance and secondary deviance.

Discussion and Critical Thinking Question

12. Robert Merton maintains that social structural factors limit the ability of many people, especially the poor and minorities, to seek wealth effectively through approved means. This suggests that deviant behavior in these groups is a reaction to the prolonged feeling of the "strain" associated with this condition. Illustrate this "strain theory" with a recent event in our society

Chapter 12

Learning Objectives

Once you have read and studied this chapter, you will have learned:

- The breadth of career opportunities in information technology and for people with IT competency (Section 12-1).

- The rudiments of robots and robotics (Section 12-2)

- Many current and potential applications in information technology and along the information superhighway (Section 12-3).

- The significant challenges posed by information technology as it emerges as a major force in determining how we live, work, and play (Section 12-4).

Technology and Society

Why this chapter is important to you

Contrasting the time line of aviation history to that of computing history, computing is about where the Wright brothers were after their first test flight. Just as it was difficult for the Wright brothers to imagine trans-Atlantic passenger planes, moon landings, and permanently inhabited space stations, it's just as difficult for us to imagine the future of information technology.

The *information technology revolution* is changing our lives in ways humanity has seen only twice before—during the *agricultural revolution* and the *industrial revolution*. You don't have to look very far to see the effects of these revolutions. Everything we do is becoming more tightly integrated with computers—robotics in manufacturing, virtual reality in entertainment, and learning without classrooms.

There is no official name for our wired world. The *information superhighway* metaphor is frequently used as a collective reference to these electronic links that have wired our world. The government talks about a *National Information Infrastructure* (*NII*), and the media continue to create more descriptors for this virtual frontier, such as *I-way, infobahn,* and *cyberspace*. Whatever it is or will be called, it eventually will connect virtually every facet of our society, and we all need some perspective on where it is taking us.

In this chapter you will learn about working in our information society. What people do for a living and how they do it have changed dramatically during your lifetime. The material in this chapter should provide you with a good overview of career opportunities in information technology and for people interested in working with IT.

Also, you will learn about state-of-the-art applications, emerging applications, and applications that we can anticipate in the near future. After reading this chapter, you'll be better prepared to put each new technological innovation into perspective.

If computing capacity continues to double each year, then we can expect computing capacity to be 1000 times that of today within 10 years. Think about the possibilities. You and everyone else will have access to computing capacity roughly equivalent to all of the computers in New York City during the 1960s! And, there is a good chance that we will wear that power, perhaps on our wrists! The twenty-first century is going to be very interesting.

Whether you are seeking employment or a promotion as a teacher, an accountant, a writer, a fashion designer, a lawyer, or in any of hundreds of other jobs, someone is sure to ask, "What do you know about computers?" Today, interacting with a PC is part of the daily routine for millions of knowledge workers and is increasingly common for blue-collar workers. No matter which career you choose, in all likelihood you will be a frequent user of computers and information technology.

Upon completion of this course, you will be part of the IT-competent minority, and you will be able to respond with confidence to any inquiry about your knowledge of computers. But what of that 80% of our society that must answer "nothing" or "very little"? These people are at a career disadvantage and many of them view computers and IT as a continuing source of stress, especially those who work with computers on job-specific tasks.

OPPORTUNITIES FOR IT SPECIALISTS

If you are planning a career as an IT specialist, opportunities remain excellent, even in the face of an economic downturn. Almost every company, no matter how small or large, employs or contracts with IT specialists, and most of these companies are always looking for qualified information technology people. IT specialists have many doors open to them. If they accept employment in an organization's information services department, they often are given the option of working in a traditional office environment or telecommuting to work at least part of the time. Those who prefer working in a variety of environments are working for consulting firms or working as independent contractors. If the trend toward outsourcing (contracting with external personnel to do in-house work) continues, look for the number of consultants and contractors to surpass the number of traditional in-house IT personnel in the near future.

Throughout the past decade, it is estimated that one in every ten jobs for IT specialists was open, waiting to be filled by a qualified applicant. There simply are not enough qualified IT people to fill all jobs. IT workers are in demand not just for their skills but also for what they contribute to the organization. In a recent report, the United States Department of Commerce stated that information technology workers were more than twice as productive as workers in other areas were during most of the 1990s.

Certain IT career fields are in such high demand that an experienced IT specialist can dictate terms of employment including extended vacation time, stock options, telecommuting options, relaxation of dress codes, and, of course, high salaries. The salary table in Figure 12-1 should give you a feel for the salaries that can be expected in familiar IT positions for the year 2004.

The Internet's Impact on the IT Job Picture

The Internet or its predecessor has been around for over three decades, but the World Wide Web and Internet browsers are relatively new (1993). The latter catapulted the Internet into every phase of our information society. The result is that the money flow associated with the Internet industry is growing more than 10 times as fast as the general U.S. economy. The Internet industry is defined by those companies that are wholly online or have a significant presence online in conjunction with traditional bricks-and-mortar companies.

The Internet economy is now larger than the airline industry and is approaching the size of the publishing industry. Over a million new jobs in the U.S. alone can be linked directly to Internet businesses. Tens of thousands of companies are writing job descriptions for the first time for Internet-related jobs. Fortune 500-size companies can have 30 or more job descriptions for Internet-related jobs.

The Growing IT Specialist Fields

For the last decade, people with computer and information technology education have been at or near the top of the "most wanted" list (see Figure 12-2). With millions (yes, millions!) of new computers being purchased and linked to the Internet each year, it is likely that this trend will continue. Of course, the number of people attracted to the booming IT field is also increasing. One of the many reasons for this migration to the IT field is that IT careers are consistently ranked among the most desirable jobs. A recent *Money* magazine article ranked 100 jobs in terms of earnings, long- and short-term job growth, job security, prestige rating, and "stress and strain" rating. The magazine called computer systems analyst the best job in America, with physician, physical therapist, electrical engineer, and civil engineer rounding out the top five. The systems analyst is but one of dozens of IT specialist careers. These are some of the more visible information technology jobs.

THE CRYSTAL BALL:
The Online Doctor Thousands of physicians offer fee-based e-mail consultations for their patients already under their care. The cost of a consultation varies depending on the required response time. Obviously, this form of telemedicine is appropriate only for certain circumstances. The next generation of online patient care will include more sophisticated means of interaction, such as audio/video instant messaging. Used properly, electronic patient care can be just as effective as in-clinic care and can help reduce spiraling medical costs. The electronic patient/physician relation will grow exponentially throughout the decade.

FIGURE 12–1

PROJECTED AVERAGE SALARY AND INDUSTRY SALARY RANGE FOR 2004 (IN $1,000S)

The table shows estimated average salaries (plus bonuses) and salary range for familiar information technology positions. The range is the range of the average salaries by industry. Some industries (for example, high-tech and consulting services) pay higher salaries to IT people than do other industries (for example, education, government, and retail). Actual salaries could be lower or higher. Salaries are projected from year 2002 salary surveys based on historical cost-of-living increases for IT workers and general economic conditions.

TOP MANAGEMENT

Position	Average Salary Range
Chief information officer (CIO)/vice president	$160 ($100–$300)
Chief technology officer	$150 ($95–$180)
Director of systems development	$135 ($90–$172)
Director of IT operations	$115 ($75–$150)
Internet technology strategist	$120 ($60–$140)
Webmaster	$90 ($53–$140)
Director of networks	$120 ($90–$180)

MIDDLE MANAGEMENT

Position	Average Salary Range
Manager of voice and data communications	$85 ($60–$150)
Network manager	$80 ($55–$105)
Manager of Internet/intranet technology	$92 ($55–$134)
Project manager	$96 ($82–$120)
Database manager	$102 ($75–$120)
Computer operations manager	$85 ($67–$125)
Help desk/technical support manager	$82 ($65–$100)

STAFF (INCLUDING ENTRY LEVEL)

Position	Average Salary Range
Network administrator	$70 ($61–$91)
Network engineer	$72 ($55–$85)
Web application developer	$58 ($50–$75)
Senior systems analyst	$85 ($74–$95)
Systems administrator	$71 ($60–$80)
Senior systems programmer	$80 ($69–$95)
Senior programmer	$70 ($55–$90)
Senior programmer/analyst	$80 ($70–$95)
Programmer/analyst	$69 ($60–$82)
Software engineer	$80 ($63–$95)
Database analyst/administrator	$80 ($60–$92)
User liaison	$75 ($60–$90)
Information security specialist	$75 ($49–$90)
Lead computer operator	$55 ($42–$65)
Computer operator	$46 ($38–$55)
PC technical specialist	$60 ($40–$77)
Help desk/technical support specialist	$50 ($40–$60)

FIGURE 12–2 IT-SPECIALIST CAREER OPPORTUNITIES

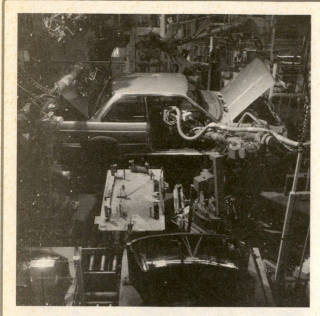

ROBOTICS ENGINEERS AND PROGRAMMERS
Industrial robots now perform many repetitive tasks, such as those on this automobile assembly line. Although the emergence of industrial robots has eliminated some jobs, they have created thousands of jobs for IT specialists who build and program them.

Courtesy of Sun Microsystems, Inc.

NETWORK ADMINISTRATOR AND WEBMASTER
These IT specialists, a network administrator and a Webmaster, develop and maintain a network and a corporate Internet presence. All of these people need a solid foundation of computer knowledge to accomplish their jobs effectively.

Courtesy of Novell

DESIGN ENGINEERS
Computer-aided design (CAD) has revolutionized the way in which engineers and scientists design, draft, and document a product. With CAD, most of the "bugs" can be worked out of a design before a product or plant (in the example) is built.

Courtesy of Intergraph Corporation

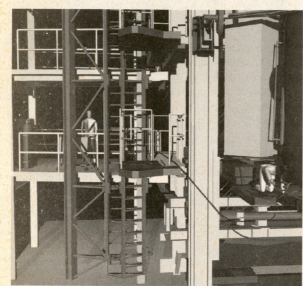

- *Chief information officer.* The director of information services within an organization often is called the **chief information officer** (**CIO**). This person is responsible for all the information services activity in the company, from the organization's Web page to its inventory control system. The CIO, often a vice president, must be somewhat futuristic, predicting what information technologies will become reality so the company can position itself to use them as they become available.

- *Systems analyst.* **Systems analysts** analyze, design, and implement information systems. They work closely with people in the user areas to design information systems that meet their information processing needs. These "problem solvers" are assigned a variety of support tasks, including feasibility studies, system reviews, security assessments, long-range planning, and hardware/software selection.

- *Programmer.* **Applications programmers** translate analyst-prepared system and input/output specifications into programs. Programmers design the logic, then code, debug, test, and document the programs. A person holding a **programmer/analyst** position performs the functions of both a programmer and a systems analyst.

- *Network administrator.* **Network administrators** design and maintain networks: LANs, MANs, and WANs. This work involves selecting and installing appropriate system software and appropriate hardware, such as modems and routers, and selecting the transmission media.

- *System programmer.* **System programmers** design, develop, maintain, and implement system software. System software, such as the operating system and system performance management software, is fundamental to the general operation of the computer; that is, it does not address a specific business or scientific problem.

- *Database administrator.* The **database administrator** (**DBA**) designs, creates, and maintains the integrated database. The DBA coordinates discussions between user groups to determine the content and format of the database so that data redundancy is kept to a minimum. The integrity and the security of the database are also responsibilities of the database administrator.

- *Internet site specialist.* The **Internet site specialist** is responsible for creating and maintaining one or more Internet sites. This specialist uses Internet development tools and source material from throughout the organization to create and maintain World Wide Web sites and pages. Occasionally, people in this job function are also responsible for the hardware required at the server site.

- *Webmaster.* The **Webmaster** is an Internet specialist who, depending on the size of the organization, may have a range of responsibilities. Typically, the Web server and its software are the responsibility of the Webmaster. The Webmaster monitors Internet traffic on the server computer and responds to external inquiries regarding Web site operations. Some Webmasters are actively involved in the design and update of Web site pages.

- *Computer operator.* The **computer operator** performs those hardware-based activities needed to keep enterprise-wide systems operational. The operator is in constant communication with the computer(s) while monitoring the progress of online systems, a number of simultaneous production runs, initiating one-time jobs, and troubleshooting.

- *User liaison.* Computer and information processing activity is very intense in companies that seek to exploit the full potential of information technology. In this environment, someone who is working in a particular functional area (perhaps the marketing department) is told to seek ways to take advantage of available IT resources. More often than not, this person is the user liaison. The **user liaison** is a "live-in" IT specialist who coordinates all computer-related activities within a particular functional area.

Computer-related jobs are not nearly as centralized (for example, in an information services department) as they were during the mainframe era (through 1990). The trend toward client/server computing has resulted in the distribution of IT specialists throughout the organization.

The variety and types of IT specialist jobs are ever changing. For example, there's the *information detective*. Companies and individuals call on these high-tech detectives to help them answer such questions as: Has my child's sitter had any driving accidents? Has my materials supplier ever filed for bankruptcy? Did this applicant for the sales manager position really earn an MBA at Harvard? Another related job is the professional *Internet researcher*. Someone who really knows his or her way around the Internet can do in minutes what might take a Net newbie several days to do. A good detective or researcher can make in excess of $100 an hour and never leave the comfort of home!

Women in Information Technology

The Internet explosion has created a new business culture in which women can more easily climb the corporate ladder. In the IT career field, the number of women in senior management positions is approximately that of men. Factors contributing to this shift away from a male-dominated business world include the enormous demand by Internet companies for knowledgeable, talented employees. Also, the hierarchical structure of Internet and high-tech businesses is more loosely defined and ever changing, enabling significant promotions both laterally and into management. Web companies, especially the smaller ones, are under great pressure to achieve quick success, and they face stiff competition in finding the people who will make that happen. The Internet has made IT employment a new game in which traditional patterns of employment no longer apply.

Licensing and Certification

If you are an IT specialist or your chosen career overlaps directly with information technology, you may be in constant contact with sensitive data and may have the power to control events. An implied responsibility to maintain the integrity of the system and its data accompanies such a job. Failure to do so could have a disastrous effect on the lives of individuals and even on the stability of the organization. Trillions of dollars are handled each day by computer-based systems that are created and

FIGURE 12–3

EXAMS FOR PROFESSIONAL CERTIFICATION
This is an example question for the Windows XP Professional Exam, which is part of several Microsoft certification programs, including the MCP, the MCSE, and the MCSA. The actual exam has 215 questions. Example questions to all Microsoft exams can be found at the Microsoft Web site.

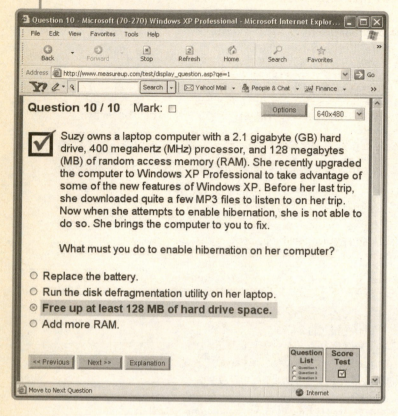

controlled by IT specialists. The lives of millions of air travelers depend on the responsiveness of the computer-based air traffic control system. Life sustaining systems in hospitals are designed, programmed, and maintained by IT specialists.

At present, licensing or certification is usually not a requirement for any IT professional; nor is it required for users of computers. Licensing and certification are hotly debated issues. Many professions require demonstration of performance at a certain level of competence before permission is granted to practice. Through examination, the engineer becomes a registered professional engineer, the attorney becomes a member of the bar, and the accountant becomes a certified public accountant. Many people in the trades, including hairdressers, plumbers, and electricians, must be licensed to practice.

Within the computer community, there are a number of certifications. Several professional organizations provide certification options, including the Institute for Certification of Computer Professionals (ICCP), which awards the *Certified Computing Professional (CCP)* and the *Associate Computing Professional (ACP)*. The CCP and ACP are general certifications in the area of computers and information technology. A growing number of companies whose products have become de facto standards offer certifications. For example, software giants Microsoft and Novell sponsor a range of widely accepted certifications. Microsoft awards these certificates to information technology professionals who have completed a series of rigorous tests (see Figure 12-3).

- *Microsoft Certified Professional*. The MCP credential is for professionals who have the skills to implement successfully a Microsoft product or technology as part of a business solution in an organization.

- *Microsoft Certified Systems Administrators*. MCSAs administer network and systems environments based on the Microsoft Windows platforms.

- *Microsoft Certified Systems Engineer*. The MCSE analyzes business requirements to design and implement an infrastructure solution based on the Windows platform and Microsoft Servers software.

- *Microsoft Certified Database Administrator*. MCDBAs design, implement, and administer Microsoft SQL Server™ databases.

- *Microsoft Certified Trainers*. MCTs are certified by Microsoft to deliver Microsoft training courses to IT professionals and developers.

- *Microsoft Certified Application Developers*. The MCAD uses Microsoft technologies to develop and maintain department-level applications, components, Web or desktop clients, or back-end data services.

- *Microsoft Certified Solution Developer*. MCSDs design and develop business solutions with Microsoft technologies.

- *Microsoft Office Specialist*. Office Specialists are recognized globally for demonstrating advanced skills with Microsoft Office desktop software, such as PowerPoint or Word.

- *Microsoft Office Specialist Master Instructor*. Office Specialist Master Instructors are certified as trainers for Microsoft Office desktop programs.

Novell, a company that specializes in networking products, offers several levels of certification for people who work with its widely used network products.

- *Certified Novell Administrator*. CNAs provide network support for Novell networking products, NetWare and GroupWise.

- *Certified Novell Engineer*. The CNE can provide advanced company-wide networking support, including planning, installation, configuration, troubleshooting, and upgrade.

- *Master CNE.* A Master CNE is a multivendor, multisolution specialist of the network industry.
- *Certified Directory Engineer.* CDEs manage the people, devices, hardware, and applications on a network and the relationships between them.
- *Certified Novell Instructor.* The CNI provides training and performance-based certification for the experienced IT professional on Novell networking products.
- *Novell Authorized Instructor.* The NAI is authorized to teach Novell classes while working toward a CNI.

Novell also awards other IT specialist certificates in such areas as Internet security and database integration.

Sun Microsystems offers several certifications for Java, the "write once, run anywhere" programming language that is so popular with Web-based applications. Certifications are awarded at different skill levels and for Web or enterprise applications. These include the *Sun Certified Programmer for the Java 2 Platform*, the *Sun Certified Developer for the Java 2 Platform*, the *Sun Certified Web Component Developer for the Java 2 Platform (Enterprise Edition)*, and the *Sun Certified Enterprise Architect for J2EE Technology*.

People seeking any of these certifications must pass an array of tests. Generally, recruiters and employers view certifications favorably. Often, being certified results in a higher salary. However, certifications are seldom a requirement for employment.

CAREER OPPORTUNITIES FOR THE IT-COMPETENT MINORITY

Information technology competency is becoming a prerequisite for people pursuing almost any career—from actuaries to zoologists (see Figure 12-4). In fact, most professional jobs come with a telephone, a desk, and a PC. The trend toward greater dependence on technology in the workplace has had a dramatic effect on how we do our jobs.

- The terminal or networked PC has become standard equipment at hospital nursing stations and often is found in operating rooms.
- Draftspeople have traded drawing tables for computer-aided design (CAD) workstations.
- Teachers are integrating the power of computers into their instruction and the students' learning experience.
- Economists would be lost without the predictive capabilities of their decision support system (DSS).
- Truck dispatchers query their information systems, which may include the exact location of fleet trucks (via onboard global positioning systems), before scheduling deliveries.
- Construction contractors keep track of on-site inventory on notebook PCs.
- The PC is the administrative assistant's constant companion for everything from word processing to conference scheduling.
- Stockbrokers often have terminals on both sides of their desks. (Some dedicated brokers stay in touch around the clock via Internet-enabled cell phones.)
- An attorney's law library is no longer on the shelf behind the desk, but on CD-ROM and/or the Internet.
- Professional football coaches rely on their play databases to give them insight into what offense or defense to run for given situations.
- Politicians frequently tap Internet-based polls before casting their votes.

Career mobility is becoming forever intertwined with an individual's current and future knowledge of computers and information technology.

Of course, career advancement ultimately depends on your abilities, imagination, and performance, but understanding computers and IT can open doors to opportunities that might otherwise be shut. All things being equal, the person who has the knowledge of and the will to work with computers and IT will have a tremendous career advantage over those who do not.

Our Jobs Are Changing

Automation is causing the elimination of some jobs. For example, the revenue accounting staff at a major U.S. airline was reduced from 650 to 350 with the implementation of a new computer-based system. Those remaining had to be retrained to work with the new system. Those displaced had to be retrained for other work opportunities in an increasingly automated society.

FIGURE 12–4 CAREER OPPORTUNITIES FOR THOSE WITH IT COMPETENCY

THE KNOWLEDGE WORKER'S TOOLS
Knowledge workers in most industries rely on a networked personal computer and access to enterprise systems and information. Here a knowledge worker joins another worker in two ways, via telephone and via a network link. In the business world, PCs are networked to enable the sharing of information and ideas.

Photo courtesy of Intel Corporation

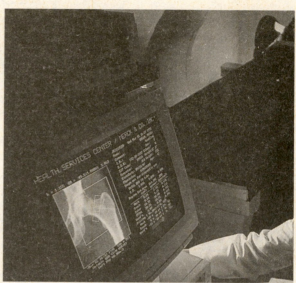

IT IN HEALTH CARE
Hospital and home health care can be easier and more effective when nurses have the patient's complete medical records with them. This nurse reviews the patient's records and updates them on-the-spot as circumstances change, such as a record of tests performed. Here, a nurse is providing a bone densitometry test to detect bone loss, which may indicate osteoporosis.

Courtesy of Merck & Co., Inc.

IT IN EDUCATION
This instructor spends much of his workday interacting with students and computers.

Courtesy of International Business Machines Corporation. Unauthorized use not permitted.

IT solutions have caused all or at least part of many job functions to be replaced with automated systems (see Figure 12-5). Automated telephone systems have eliminated the need for many receptionists. The presence of ATMs means fewer bank tellers are needed. The emergence of e-trading reduces the demand for stockbrokers. E-tailing, much of which is completely automated, affects a variety of retail jobs. Some people get loans from banks online, whereby an expert "loan" system makes the decisions. The explosion of online classes hasn't eliminated the need for professors, but, for some professors, their job function has changed dramatically from in-class instruction to online course development and delivery.

Fortunately, information technology is responsible for the creation of many other jobs. The explosion of information technology has resulted in thousands of new companies that provide a variety of previously unknown products and services. Yahoo! and Netscape were founded in 1994. Dot.com giant America Online was founded in 1985. Many other high-tech companies didn't exist a decade ago. Now they employ hundreds, even tens of thousands, of people in high-paying jobs. Ten years ago, relatively few companies had Web sites. Today, every company desiring to stay in business has a Web site and a site support staff.

As information technology continues to move to the forefront in our society, jobs in every discipline are being redefined. For example, ten years ago sales representatives carried manuals and products to the customer site. Today, they still knock on doors, but to a much lesser extent because much of what used to be personal interaction is now electronic interaction (e-mail, instant messaging, and extranets). When they do make sales calls, they don't carry heavy manuals and products. Instead, they bring their notebook PCs. Thanks to the technology, the sales rep is no longer the sole source of product/service information. Customers can get up-to-date information directly from the vendor via its extranet (an extension of a company's private intranet). Many customers don't deal with sales reps at all. They obtain needed information by browsing the Internet or an extranet, and then they place their orders electronically.

Radical changes in the way we do our jobs are not limited to the business community. Poets, the clergy, politicians, music composers, and others are continually evaluating what they do and how they do it within the context of emerging technology.

FIGURE 12–5 Keeping Score the Electronic Way
The way tennis is played hasn't changed much in the age of information, but the way players train and the way it is tracked and reported have changed. Every point is documented during the Olympics (shown here), during all professional tennis matches, and during many juniors matches, too. The data are analyzed by players and coaches and reported by broadcasters and reporters.

Internet Jobs for Nontechnology People

Contrary to what you might imagine, the glamour and high potential of the high-tech Internet world has plenty of room for people who may not consider themselves techies. Millions of workers have asked these questions: What do I need to do to get an Internet-related job? How can I get that job without returning to entry-level work?

To be sure, all job functions in the technology industries require IT-competent people. Many people, however, have the misconception that all jobs in technology companies require programming knowledge. In fact, many positions require relatively little technical knowledge or experience. Large numbers of jobs deal exclusively with Internet content (from creating artistic Web pages to collection and analysis of online surveys). Other jobs focus more on project management than on the specifics of technology.

The high-tech industries are like other companies in that whatever they do is a team effort, requiring all types of skills, both technical and nontechnical. A Web site that exhibits state-of-the-art technological features may be of little value to the organization if it is not presented artistically and does not contain well-written content.

If you consider yourself a nontechnical IT-competent person and want to become a part of the Internet and high-tech industries, be aware that job titles and descriptions vary enormously between companies. A Webmaster in one company may do the same work as an Internet designer in another company. Positions in high-tech companies are evolving at the same pace as the Internet with new types of jobs and titles coming into existence each month. If you are looking for this type of job, pay close attention to the job description and how it relates to your range of experience and salary history.

Information technology continues to steamroll into our lives. Each of us has a choice: We can resist information technology and hope for the best, or we can embrace it and use it to open new horizons for job opportunities. The fact that you are reading this book indicates that you have chosen the latter.

GETTING A JOB

Whether you are entering the job market for the first time or seeking alternative employment, resources on the Internet can help you land the position you want.

- *Comprehensive career/employment Web sites.* The Internet now has a number of comprehensive career/employment Web sites designed to help employer and candidate find one another. These include sites like Monster.com and CareerMosaic.com, which offer a wide variety of career services.

- *Industry-specific or professional career/employment Web sites.* These sites offer similar services to the comprehensive sites, but their orientation is to a specific industry, such as health care, oil and gas, or airlines. Or, their orientation is to specific professionals, such as accountants, lawyers, engineers, or physicians.

- *Company job opening pages.* Most company Web sites now have a page called something like "career opportunities" or "job seekers." To find this page from the company's home page, click on *About the Company* or *Company Information.* This page and its links will contain detailed information about available openings, often by geographical location, division, or job function.

The career/employment Web sites offer these types of resources and services.

- *Jobs database*. Potential employers post job openings to a searchable job openings database.

- *Candidates database*. You can post a résumé to the site's candidates database. This database is made available to potential employers.

- *Job search*. A comprehensive site may have hundreds of thousands of job openings in its database. You can search the job-openings database by keyword, industry type, job type, and geographic locale to get a listing of jobs that meet your criteria.

- *Candidate search*. Employers continuously search this candidate database, which contains the résumé of those seeking jobs, to find candidates who can fill their job openings.

- *Career resources*. Major career sites have extensive resources for those people who are contemplating a job or career change or are seeking employment for the first time. These could include: interactive tools that help people prepare a résumé and cover letter templates, tips on preparing for an interview, relocation information (including comparisons between cities), compensation statistics, tips on salary negotiation, information on employers, and much more.

The online jobs search has revolutionized the manner in which those seeking employment find jobs and those companies seeking employees find candidates. The tradition of sending a snail mail résumé in response to a help-wanted ad in a newspaper or magazine may have lost its effectiveness in our connected information society. In this new era the jobs search process is made easier for both employer and candidate. Also, some say that the online process results in a better match for both employee and employer.

SECTION SELF-CHECK

12-1.1	At present, less than half of the companies in the United States employ or contract with IT specialists. (T/F)
12-1.2	Because of privacy concerns, companies rarely post their job opportunities to their Internet Web sites. (T/F)
12-1.3	Which of these is not a Microsoft certification: (a) MCP, (b) CNE, (c) MCAD, or (d) MCSA?
12-1.4	America Online was founded in: (a) 1965, (b) 1975, (c) 1985, or (d) 1995.

12-2 Robots and Robotics

WHY THIS SECTION IS IMPORTANT TO YOU

Hollywood's human-like robots have created an erroneous perception of what robots can do. This section helps you separate myth from reality and gives you a better understanding of how modern robots can benefit society, in general, and you, both at home and at work.

To date, the area of artificial intelligence (AI) having the greatest impact on our society and experiencing the greatest commercial success is robotics. **Robotics** is the field of study that deals with creating robots.

R2D2 and the Terminator can do amazing things, but these Hollywood creations are a lifetime away from reality. As you read this section, you will see that today's robots can do amazing things, too, including working tirelessly to make appliances, clothes, automobiles and a thousand other useful products. Most applications of robotics are in manufacturing and the use of *industrial robots*. Industrial robots are quite good at repetitive tasks and tasks that require precision movements, moving heavy loads, and working in hazardous areas. However, robots are emerging as major players not only in manufacturing but also in nonmanufacturing industries, such as health care and other service industries. Already we can give robots crude human sensory capabilities and some degree of artificial intelligence. As these capabilities mature over the next decade, look for robots in other areas of the workplace, in our homes, and even on stage and in museums.

Robotics offers the potential for increased productivity and better service. These benefits have not been overlooked by the manufacturing and service industries. Progressive organizations are rushing to install more and more applications of robotics as a means of staying competitive in the global economy. Industries throughout the world are looking to robots to help them control costs, respond more quickly to market needs, and reduce labor-related costs.

RUDIMENTARY ROBOTICS

The "steel-collar" workforce is made up of hundreds of thousands of industrial robots (see Figure 12-6). The most common industrial robot is a single mechanical arm controlled by a computer. The arm, called a *manipulator*, has a shoulder, forearm, and wrist and is capable of performing the motions of a human arm. The manipulator is fitted with a hand designed to accomplish a specific task, such as painting, welding, picking and placing, and so on.

The automotive industry is the largest user of robots (for painting and welding) and the electronics industry (for circuit testing and connecting chips to circuit boards) is second. General Motors, for example, now has a robot base of over 20,000. Many of these robots perform operations that are

FIGURE 12–6 THE STEEL COLLAR WORKFORCE

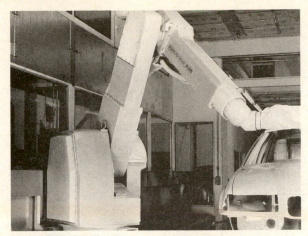

FLEXING MUSCLES

The typical industrial robot has a manipulator arm with a shoulder, forearm, wrist, and hand that is designed for a specific task. Here, this precision industrial robot tirelessly paints automobiles during manufacturing.

Courtesy of FANUC Robotics North America, Inc.

PICK-AND-PLACE

Computer-controlled industrial robots help ensure the flow of work during production. Here a robot transfers boxes between conveyors in a pick-and-place application. This robot can handle 45 boxes up to 130 pounds each per minute.

Courtesy of FANUC Robotics North America, Inc.

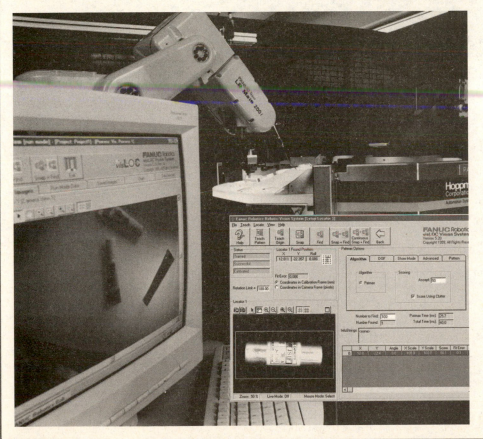

MACHINE VISION

This robotic vision system is used for determining an object's location and orientation. It provides advanced robot guidance capabilities for machine loading/unloading, material handling, packaging, and assembly applications. The robot simplifies the integration of machine vision, as no programming is required to calibrate, train, and run the system (see inset). The system performs visual tasks at a speed and precision unattainable with the human eye.

Courtesy of FANUC Robotics North America, Inc.

FIGURE 12–6 continued

THE ROBOT TEAM
The precise, untiring movement of computer-controlled industrial robots helps assure quality in the assembly of everything from electrical components to automobiles. Here in this DaimlerChrysler Corporation plant, 66 industrial robots apply spot welds. About 300 robots weld, seal, train, paint, clean, and handle material at this plant.

DaimlerChrysler Corporation

difficult or impossible for human workers to perform. For example, robots are used to install sharp windshield glass on cars and trucks. This requires the application of adhesive beads in a precise and uniform manner—something a robot can perform quickly with high repeatability.

TEACHING ROBOTS TO DO THEIR JOB

A computer program is written to control the robot just as one is written to print payroll checks. It includes such commands as when to reach, in which direction to reach, how far to reach, which tool to use, and when to grasp, weld, paint, and so on. Many robots are programmed to reach to a particular location, find a particular item, and then place it somewhere else. This simple application of robotics is called *pick and place*. Instead of a grasping mechanism, other robots are equipped with a variety of industrial tools such as drills, paint guns, welding torches, and so on. Once programmed, robots do not need much attention. One plant manufactures vacuum cleaners 24 hours a day, 7 days a week!

ROBOTS COME TO THEIR SENSES

With the recent innovations in sensor technology, roboticists are outfitting robots with artificial intelligence and human sensory capabilities, such as vision, that enable them to simulate human behavior. A robot with the added dimension of vision can be given some intelligence. Robots without intelligence simply repeat preprogrammed motions. Even though the technology for the vision systems is primitive, a robot can be "taught" to distinguish between dissimilar objects under controlled conditions. With this sensory subsystem, the robot has the capability of making crude but important decisions. For example, a robot equipped with a vision subsystem can distinguish between boxes of differing sizes and shapes as they approach on the conveyor. It can be programmed to place a box of particular dimensions on an adjacent conveyer and let all other boxes pass.

As vision system technology continues to improve, more and more robots will have the ability to move—*navigational capabilities* (see Figure 12-7). Now, most robots are stationary; those that are not

FIGURE 12–7 **ROBOTS WITH NAVIGATIONAL CAPABILITIES**

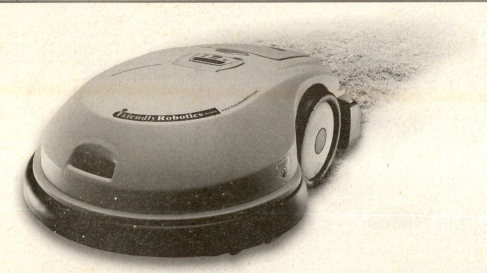

ROBOMOW® AT WORK
It may look like a UFO, but this dual-mode (automatic and manual) hands-free lawn mower from Friendly Machines is one smart little robot. Robomow® is environmentally friendly and doesn't need human help to mow a lawn. When Robomow encounters obstacles, it mows around them. Robomow mows in uniformly straight lines to produce a striped, manicured lawn.

Courtesy of Friendly Machines

MOTORING AROUND MARS
The Mars Pathfinder delivered a stationary lander and a surface rover to the Red Planet on July 4, 1997. The rover vehicle, a mobile robot, was manipulated by controllers some 120,000,000 miles away! The six-wheel rover, named Sojourner, explored the area near the lander, testing the soil and sending back pictures of Mars.

Courtesy NASA

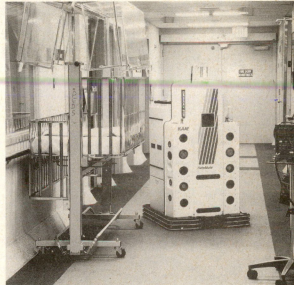

MOBILE ROBOTS CAN DELIVER
The 575 pound HelpMate7 trackless, robotic courier is designed to perform material transport tasks for healthcare facilities. This robot can deliver mail, medication, supplies, and meal trays to the nursing units throughout the hospital. Vision and ultrasonic proximity sensors are used to understand the environment and avoid obstacles as they are encountered. It navigates from point to point by using a map of the building to plan the best route and sensory feedback to follow that route. It can even use the elevator!

Courtesy of HelpMate Robotics, Inc.

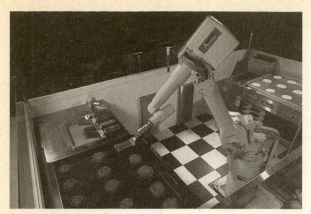

FIGURE 12–8 Flipper the Robot
The number and variety of applications for robots is expanding rapidly. Here, "Flipper," a typical industrial robot, has been programmed to prepare hamburgers and pancakes on two griddles simultaneously. The now famous hamburger-flipping robot was designed originally as a promotional gimmick, but restaurateurs have been so impressed with the speed at which it makes consistently perfect hamburgers and pancakes that we may someday see Flipper and its cousins in commercial kitchens.

Courtesy of AccuTemp Products, Inc.

can only detect the presence of an object in their path or are programmed to operate within a well-defined work area where the positions of all obstacles are known. Service industries using mobile-robot technology applications include hospitals, security and patrol, commercial floor care, hazardous waste handling, bomb disposal, nuclear plant cleanup, janitorial services, rehabilitation programs, and the military.

Autonomous robots can make functional decisions without being guided or remotely piloted by a human operator. These robots can react intuitively to real-world stimuli by using the developing technology of image pattern recognition, mobility, agility, and perceptual cognition. Military self-guided cruise missiles are able to make automatic navigational adjustments in response to changing conditions while constantly reviewing their onboard flight maps. Other potential applications for autonomous robots, especially in situations where human workers would be exposed to great risk, include deep underwater exploration (robots helped in the exploration of the *Titanic*), interior surveillance of nuclear reactors (robots helped clean up after the Chernobyl nuclear incident), and surface navigation of other planets (the Sojourner robot scooted around Mars gathering data).

OPPORTUNITIES FOR ROBOTS ARE GROWING

Each day engineers and entrepreneurs find new ways to use robots (see Figure 12-8). Even surgeons are using robots to help in brain surgery. Robots can be set up to manipulate the surgical drill and biopsy needle with great accuracy, thereby making brain surgery faster, more accurate, and safer. Other surgical applications of robotics include help with hip replacements, knee replacements, and pelvic and spinal surgeries.

Autonomous kinetic sculpture is a new class of robotics and is found in art galleries and in the performing arts. Some robots create works of art, whereas others perform by themselves or with humans. How a performance or robotic sculpture will turn out is often unique because the robots are designed to react in real-time situations and adapt to their environment through their own creative behaviors.

The future of robotics offers exciting opportunities. Companies are sure to take advantage of these opportunities to stay competitive. Robotics suppliers, along with their system integrators, are using Rapid Deployment Automation to expedite the implementation of robotics. This strategy uses computer-aided design (CAD) to shorten the design-to-build cycle and promote a user-friendly "no programming" environment for factory floor personnel. Robotics is being implemented in many nonmanufacturing environments as well (see Figures 12-7 and 12-8). Who knows, we may someday have robots as helpers around the home and as workmates at the office.

SECTION SELF-CHECK

12-2.1 Industrial robots excel at repetitive tasks. (T/F)
12-2.2 Some robots have vision capabilities. (T/F)
12-2.3 Which of these is not a part of a manipulator on an industrial robot: (a) arm, (b) forearm, (c) knuckle, or (d) wrist?
12-2.4 The application where robots find a particular item and then place it somewhere else is called: (a) select and set, (b) move and put, (c) choose and locate, or (d) pick and place.

WHY THIS SECTION IS IMPORTANT TO YOU

It's nice to know what to expect, whether doing a corporate strategic plan, building a house, or considering career options. When you complete this section, you should have a feel for potential applications of information technology, now and in the future.

12-3 Looking Ahead: Future Applications of IT

Let's look down the road at what information technology and the information superhighway might have to offer. The text and the images in this section survey a variety of new and emerging IT applications. Bear in mind that information technology and the Internet are tools. You and other innovators will ultimately determine what applications are created as well as who and what drives along the information superhighway.

Surprisingly, many adults are unaware of the information superhighway, and therefore, the Internet and its impact on society. In fact, millions of people in America and billions worldwide are still waiting at the on ramp. Each day, however, more travelers drive up the ramp and on to the electronic highway. The mode of travel through cyberspace is the computer. A typical Internet session will take you all over the country and often to other countries. The actual traffic along the highway is anything that can be digitized—text (perhaps the morning newspaper), graphic images (an MRI scan of a brain tumor), motion video (a movie), still photographs (a picture of a friend), sound (a radio station in Alaska), and programs (perhaps multiplayer Internet games that load and run on your PC).

The Internet, with its ability to connect people and businesses, will continue to be the basis for innovative new applications of information technology. Some applications will be entirely new to all of us, such as the ability to customize and order automobiles online or the ability to view any previously-aired TV show whenever you want to see it. Other applications will be new to some of us. For example, some of us can shop for groceries online and tap into the online card catalog at the local library. Most of us can't. Eventually shopping for groceries online will be commonplace and you will be able to search a central database that includes the card catalog information for every library in the United States.

A mind-boggling array of information and telecommunication services has been implemented in recent years. Figure 12-9 gives you a feel for the breadth of services, information, and applications currently found on the Net. Many more are planned for the information superhighway, some of which are described in this section.

FIGURE 12–9

CRUISING THE NET
The Internet makes a vast treasure trove of information and services available to people all over the world. This figure contains a sampling of a few of the millions of stops along the Internet.

NEWS ONLINE
The Sept. 11, 2001 terrorist attack on the United States has changed everyone's perspective on life. The event let the Internet flex its muscle and show us the awesome capability of this relatively new vehicle for communication. Information on the attacks, including photos, stories, anecdotes, news, and so on, was posted to CBSNews.com (shown here) and thousands of other sites, many of which had little or nothing to do with news. Almost immediately, the FBI began soliciting information on their Web site and within hours, they had thousands of leads. Sadly, there were many hoaxes perpetuated on netizens during this time of crisis, such as the one that told of a man falling 80 stories and, miraculously, living to tell about it. We now know that the Internet can be a wonderful communications tool during times of disaster. We also know that we need to be vigilant about assessing the validity of all information. Fraud was the saddest Internet note in the aftermath of September 11. Criminals set up Web sites supposedly to raise money for worthy organizations, but their entrepreneurial objective, however, was to take advantage of this crisis and the willingness of people to help the victims.

LOOKING FOR A JOB?
The Net has many places, both commercial and nonprofit, that specialize in matching job applicants with employers. Already, most professional positions are listed on the Net. A good place to start your job search is the Monster Job Search, which offers a comprehensive list of online job services and résumé banks. In the example, the user searches the 800,000-job database for an "Information technology" position in "Florida-Miami."

FIGURE 12–9 continued

WEBCAMS AND NETSCAPE

Shown here within the Netscape browser are the images from several San Francisco Webcams. Webcams, which are cameras that capture a live image every few seconds or minutes, are strategically positioned in interesting locations, both inside and outside, all over the world. Webcam sites let you watch the progress of a pregnant rhinoceros; travel around campus with Mike, Gina, or whoever has the mobile camera; follow the goings-on in a radio station; or enjoy the views around San Francisco (shown here).

INTERNET GREETING CARDS

E-mail messages far outnumber written messages. It may be only a matter of time before online greeting cards overtake traditional greeting cards. Several Web sites, such as Hallmark.com, give you the facilities to create and send your own "greeting cards." In this card, a personal message is displayed after the frogs finish playing Happy Birthday.

PRODUCT INFORMATION AND SUPPORT

Customer service has become the byword of corporate America. Competition demands that companies provide customers with the best possible service, including a comprehensive Web site. Hewlett Packard's Web site provides product information and online troubleshooting help (shown here) for every product.

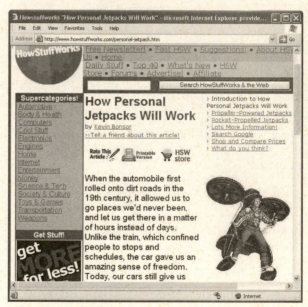

THE BEST OF THE WEB

Cybersurfers are ever vigilant in their search for the best and worst that the Net has to offer. Critics abound on the Internet. People and companies who create Web sites should be aware that cybercritics might eventually pass judgment on the quality of their site, both good and bad. A select few make one of the "best" or "worst" lists. This "How Stuff Works" site is on many "Best of the Web" lists.

FIGURE 12–9 continued

TAKING A VIRTUAL TOUR OF THE WORLD'S GREAT MUSEUMS
Save the plane fare and enjoy virtual museums all over the world, including the Smithsonian's National Air and Space Museum (shown here) and the Louvre.

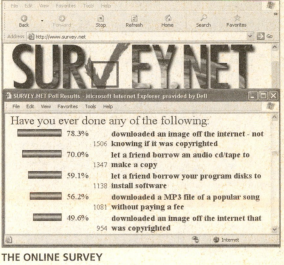

THE ONLINE SURVEY
The Net is a great forum for surveying and polling. Shown here is a survey that taps people's feelings on "Online Intellectual Property." The results of the 17-question survey are continuously updated and made available to online viewers. Many Internet portals have real-time surveys on current events.

SECURITIES ONLINE
Morgan Stanley's brokerage service offers customers quotes, charts, financial planning, online investing, securities research, and more. The Internet has enabled brokerage firms to expand their services and make information accessible to customers that heretofore was available only to brokers. Here, the client requested a chart that compared Wal-Mart's stock performance over the past year with that of the Target Corporation and the Dow Jones Industrial Average.

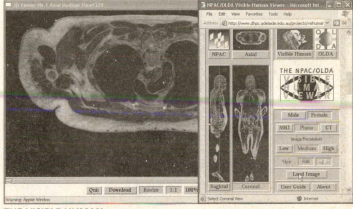

THE VISIBLE HUMAN
This award-winning Visible Human Viewer Web site runs a Java applet that lets you interactively select and view two-dimensional slices of a human body. Selected images can be enlarged (see background image) for viewing.

AT HOME IN 2010

Let's fast forward to the year 2010. Computers are invisible; that is, they are built into our domestic, working, and external environments. Imagine this scenario: B. J. Rogers' invisible computer can be programmed to awaken him to whatever stimulates him to greet the new day. B. J.'s wake up call, which could just as well be yours, can be his favorite music, sports scores, a stock market report, the weather, or a to-do list.

Suppose B. J.'s wake up choice is a *to-do list* for the day. Besides listing the events of the day, his invisible computer, which he calls Rex, might *verbally* emphasize important events (see Figure 12-10). In response to B. J.'s request, the nearest video display, which is prominent in every occupied room in the house, is filled with a list of possible dishes. Just as B. J. notices that all dishes are meatless, Rex, the computer, reminds him of an important consideration. Rex might respond to his inquiry about ingredients by checking the home inventory and ordering as needed (all automatic).

Much of this futuristic scenario is within the grasp of today's technology. Even today, millions of people carry computers with them much of the day, many of which have a wireless link to the Net. Millions more spend most of their day at a computer. Many of these people routinely talk to their PCs via speech-recognition technology. Smart homes now are deemed an economically sound investment. You can shop at thousands of e-tailers from any communications-ready PC. Though expensive, large flat-panel monitors are commercially available. Broadband Internet access is available to most homes in the United States. Hundreds of radio stations now broadcast over the Internet. So you see, we are well on our way to the day when this fictional scenario emerges as reality. The way things are going, the future may be here sooner than we think.

THE ELECTRONIC FAMILY REUNION

Telephones as we know them will probably disappear. In the relatively near future, the function of the telephone will be incorporated into videophones, our PCs, our TVs, our clothing, or perhaps all of these so we can see and hear the person(s) on the other end of the line. The future "telephone" will enable us to pass data and information back and forth, as if we were sitting at the same table. Already some digital cellular telephones permit the sending and receiving of e-mail. Some cell phones have built-in digital cameras that let us take and send pictures.

You will be able to use the Internet, your television, your PC, and multiple videophone hookups to hold an electronic family reunion. Here is how it would work. You would dial, or verbally request, the videophones of your relatives and a real-time video of each family would appear in a window on your wall-size television monitor. The conversation would be in stereo and sound as if all families were in the same room. The members of each family would be able to see the members of the other families. You could even share photos and view family videos. The information superhighway may enable more frequent family reunions, but we will still have to travel on traditional highways to get real hugs and taste grandmother's cherry pie.

Today we have some of these capabilities. Two people with PCs equipped with relatively inexpensive video cameras can hold videophone conversations (see and hear each other) over regular telephone line Internet connections (less than 56 K bps). They can even pass pictures and other still or video images back and forth during the conversation. Only two people can talk to each other at a time, but others can join in the conversation using a chat box (keyed-in text) and share visual information, such as directions to a meeting place.

ENTERTAINMENT EVERYWHERE

Many of the initial e-commerce offerings on the Internet will be aimed at entertaining us. We'll have *video-on-demand;* that is, you will be able to choose what television program or movie you want to watch and when you want to watch it. You will be able to watch any movie, from the classic archives to first runs, at your convenience. The same is true of television programming. If you would prefer to watch this week's edition of *60 Minutes* on Monday, rather than Sunday, you have that option. For that matter, you can elect to watch any past edition of *60 Minutes*. As you might expect, video stores and scheduled TV may become only memories in a few years.

Universal broadband access to the Internet is inevitable and will open the door for a more sophisticated form of entertainment. Already, major television networks are interweaving on-air and online statistics in broadcasts of sporting events. How long will it be before we have interactive soap operas? With the inevitable two-way communication capabilities of your future television/terminal, you can be an active participant in how a story unfolds. The soaps will be shot so they can be pieced together in a variety of ways. Imagine—you can decide whether Michelle marries Clifton or Patrick! You say this sounds far-fetched? Not really. Interactive movies are being produced and shown right now.

Your home entertainment center will become a video arcade, with immediate access to a myriad of games. You can hone your skills on an individual basis or test them, real time, against the best people in the land. Multiplayer games are already very popular on the Internet. Professional players gain

THE CRYSTAL BALL:
Conversations in Multiple Languages
Traveling the world can be difficult, at times, because most of the people cannot speak your language and, chances are, you don't speak theirs. With the increasing sophistication of speech recognition and language translators, it is only a matter of time before we are able to hold conversations in which all parties are speaking a different language. By the end of this decade, our handheld computers will be able to interpret a variety of spoken languages, then either play or display a translation to our native language. Other parties in the conversation will have similar devices. Of course, computer-based translation will always be second best to learning and speaking the language of another culture.

celebrity status and make big money playing games like Quake (from Id Software) and Starcraft™ (from Blizzard Entertainment). Spectators can view the games online. The worldwide gamer community is huge and, in the near future, it is conceivable that online gaming events could have more paying spectators than the Super Bowl or the World Cup.

ELECTRONIC DELIVERY OF NEWSPAPERS, BOOKS, AND OTHER TRADITIONALLY PRINTED MATERIALS

Certainly, books, magazines, newspapers, and the printed word in general will prevail for casual reading and study during the next few years. However, the Internet offers electronic-publishing as an alternative to *hard-copy* publishing. We'll be able to receive virtually any printed matter—books, magazines, newspapers, and reference material—in electronic format. Already you can get online newspapers while the news is hot, with no wait for printing and delivery. This gradual shift to online newspapers is changing the way journalists think and work. Traditionally newspapers have compiled and delivered news once each day, with relatively few exceptions. News, however, happens all day long. Online newspapers post the latest news to the Internet as it happens. Your PC already is a virtual newsstand and it is sure to grow in the future.

Besides having up-to-the-minute online content, online media have several other advantages over print media.

- They are *linked,* enabling related information to be connected via hyperlinks.
- They are interactive.
- They can read to you via *text-to-speech* technology.
- They offer *multimedia* content, such as video and audio.

If people begin to embrace the convenience of dynamically linked, interactive, and multimedia documents, there may be a trend away from print media to online alternatives. Don't be surprised to see novels written specifically for the online market that give readers the flexibility to follow links rather than pages.

The transition to e-publishing is well underway. For example, *The Los Angeles Times* makes "almost the whole newspaper" in an interactive and linked format available for free over the Internet, including the classified ads. Other newspapers make their stories available also, either for free or through an online subscription. The *Encyclopedia Britannica* is now available online—for free. All or part of many traditional magazines, such as *Time* and *People,* and several online only magazines, such as *Slate,* are available to people with access to the Internet. Frequently, stories incorporate text, audio, and video. The trend to e-publishing is evident in other areas also. For example, a number of retailers publish multimedia catalogs on the Internet that are updated almost daily, an option not possible in a print catalog. Any volatile hard-copy document, such as the telephone directory and its yellow pages, is a candidate for e-publishing. Already, continuously updated national white pages and the yellow pages are available online.

Although libraries are far more sophisticated today than they were 50 years ago, we are still in the first generation of libraries. Today's libraries still have shelves of books to be checked out and returned. The new generation of libraries may be all electronic, with no physical facilities for customers. Already thousands of books are made available through traditional libraries and via purely online libraries, such as netLibrary. Each month more and more books are being published in electronic format. The federal government is solidly behind constructing virtual libraries and now, Microsoft, the dominant force in the technology industry, is committed to creating and marketing electronic books. E-books can be viewed on any PC or e-book reader, as well as most handheld PCs. If you wish to purchase a hard-copy version of a book, it will be charged via e-commerce, then printed on your personal high-speed printer.

MAIL AT THE SPEED OF LIGHT

Jokes about the pace of postal delivery will gradually disappear as the Internet matures. Most of what we now know as mail and junk mail will travel electronically over the superhighway. This includes bills, stock summaries, and anything else that can be delivered more cost effectively and quickly over the Net. Personally, we already send e-mail (versus business or personal letters), greeting cards, family photos, and much more over the Internet. Millions of people communicate in real time via instant messaging, which permits real-time interaction via text, audio, and/or video communications. Instant messaging is changing the way people interact in a business environment and is emerging as the preferred means of interoffice communication in many companies.

THE CASHLESS SOCIETY

Each weekday, the financial institutions of the world use business-to-business (B2B) to transfer more than one trillion dollars—that's $1,000,000,000,000! At a more personal level, we use ATMs, have our payroll transferred directly to our bank account, and are beginning to use smart cards (see Figure 12-11). Millions of people now pay utility bills, mortgage payments, and many other bills through automatic electronic bank drafts. E-commerce is exploding. The Internet may be the first step toward a *cashless society*. It provides the necessary link between individuals, businesses, and financial institutions.

If we should move toward a cashless society, the administrative work associated with handling money, checks, and credit transactions would be eliminated. We would no longer need to manufacture or carry money. Each purchase, no matter how small or large, would result in an immediate transfer of funds between buyer and seller. Think of it—rubber checks and counterfeit money would be eliminated. Moreover, with total e-commerce you would have a detailed and accurate record of all monetary transactions.

A cashless society is not feasible until mechanisms are in place to accommodate small retail transactions. That's beginning to happen. A federal task force has been formed to plan for the transition to **electronic money,** or **e-money.** Financial institutions are establishing alliances to prepare for the cashless society. The major players in information technology have agreed on a standard for the *electronic wallet.* The standard, the **electronic-commerce modeling language** (ECML), will enable people to make online purchases as easily as they would make in-store transactions in the retail store. With ECML, consumers will no longer need to enter personal information for each purchase. Appropriate information will be stored in an electronic wallet at controlled server facilities.

The use of e-money opens new doors for barter. For example, when payment is entirely electronic, it is administratively possible to pay for goods and services with very small amounts, called **micropayments.** If micropayments catch on, we might be charged each time we play a song, watch a video, or search a database. Micropayments may be a boon to e-commerce, as there are advantages to both seller and buyer. For example, rather than buy a CD for a single artist, you could subscribe to a plan that would let you pay a small amount, perhaps less than a penny a play, to play the songs of 150 artists.

Every day you see more evidence of the move toward e-money. For example, traditional gas pumps are being replaced with ones that accept credit cards—swipe the card and pump the gas. In Phoenix, bus fares can be paid with VISA or MasterCard. All riders have to do is swipe the card and take a seat. Many college students use prepaid debit cards to pay for sodas, photocopying, and concert tickets. One billion U.S. government entitlement checks are distributed electronically each month. Several banks offer a service that will allow a customer to transfer funds from his or her account to

FIGURE 12–11 THE MOVE TOWARDS A CASHLESS SOCIETY

SMART CARDS

Smart cards with their embedded processors can be "loaded" with e-money at an ATM in much the same way you might withdraw cash. Once loaded with e-money, the stored-value smart card can be used to make purchases. The amount of the purchase is transferred electronically from the card's memory to the retailer, thus reducing the card's stored value.

Courtesy of Samsung Electronics Co., Ltd.

THE FUTURE OF WALK-IN BANKING

This prototype Bank of America Financial Center in an Atlanta neighborhood is redesigned to accommodate the trend to greater use of e-money and with the latest in banking technology, such as Web-enabled ATMs, check imaging, and Automated Business Centers (ABCs), providing a one-stop shop where customers can find advice and solutions to help meet their financial needs.

Courtesy of Bank of America

that of someone else via e-mail. In the near future, credit cards may become obsolete. All we will need to do in the future to purchase a candy bar, whether at a vending machine or a checkout counter, is to press a button on our key ring remote to confirm the transaction and transfer the sale amount from our electronic wallet to the store's account. Any sales taxes will be transferred to the appropriate government agency. It looks like the change in your pocket may become collectible items within a very few years.

SHOP AT HOME

The Internet already provides a direct visual and electronic link to many mail-order companies and retail/wholesale establishments via B2C: business-to-consumer. Sales statistics indicate that more and more people are opting for the convenience and value of electronic shopping. It's no longer necessary to drive from store to store to seek a particular style of sneaker in your size. You can go online and get the sneaker you want, often, at a price that is well below that of the bricks-and-mortar stores. We can use our personal computer in conjunction with the Internet to select and purchase almost anything, from paper clips to airplanes. In some cases the items selected will be automatically picked, packaged, and possibly delivered to our doorstep. This type of service will help speed the completion of routine activities, such as grocery shopping, and leave us more time for leisure, travel, and the things we enjoy.

The Internet offers great promise for the retail and wholesale industry. Consider these advantages: a corner bicycle shop in Pomona, California, has access to millions of customers; stores never have to be closed; transactions are handled electronically; and sales and distribution can be done more cost-effectively. Goods frequently are sent directly from the manufacturer to the customer, eliminating the extra stop in traditional retailing.

E-COMMERCE EXPLOSION

The Internet and networking have made it possible for companies and organizations to cooperate via *business-to-business* (B2B) communication. Also, they are expanding their internal intranets to *extranets* and *VPNs* to better deal with an exploding demand for e-commerce. E-commerce can encourage electronic interchange with customers and suppliers and enable all concerned to do business better and more efficiently. E-commerce fosters intercompany cooperation, which helps all involved save money. E-commerce offers a means of electronic cooperation whereby organizations transfer a wide range of information, including e-money, orders, invoices, medical records, real-time POS sales information, and so on via computer networks.

E-commerce is eliminating the need to produce, send, record, and store billions of paper documents. Companies like Wal-Mart are following the trend to greater electronic communication with suppliers. When Wal-Mart computers detect low inventory for toothpaste, its computers communicate that need directly to supplier computers. Supplier computers then issue shipping orders to warehouse computers, and the supplier computers send invoices directly to Wal-Mart computers. Payment is issued via B2B: computer-to-computer.

E-commerce streamlines administrative duties by linking supplier to manufacturer, manufacturer to retailer, and field sales and retail outlets to corporate headquarters. It provides solutions to many common business problems: mountains of paperwork, lost orders, unnecessary delays, lost opportunities, staff overheads, postage costs, paper costs, and data security. This type of networking also provides organizations with greater control of the production, distribution, and payment processes. As these benefits become more widely known, B2B will eventually become standard in most organizations. This is important because intercompany electronic interchange changes the fundamental way that many people do their jobs. Already most organizations, large and small, are cooperating electronically, some to a greater extent than others.

HIGH-TECH VOTING AND POLLING

Local, state, and federal elections might not require an army of volunteers. Politicians might not have to worry about low voter turnout on a rainy Election Day. In the not-too-distant future we will record our votes over the National Information Infrastructure, or whatever our national network will be called. Such a system will reduce the costs of elections and encourage greater voter participation. Plus, we can avoid the confusion that surfaced in the 2000 election when the U.S. presidency hinged on legal opinions, voter recounts, butterfly ballots, and dimpled chads.

The state of Arizona's success with the Democratic presidential primary shows us that online voting by everyone in all elections may be only a matter of time. There was no confusion with the interface (the ballot), the accounting was computer-accurate, and the number of people voting in the election was five times the number in the previous election, which did not permit online voting.

Already television newscasters routinely sample the thinking of viewers by asking them to respond over the Internet. Eventually they will be able to tap the collective thinking of tens of thousands, even millions, of people in a matter of minutes. After they ask the questions, we at home will register our responses over the national network. Our responses will be sent immediately to a central computer for analysis, and the results reported almost instantaneously. In this way, television news programs will keep us abreast on a day-to-day basis of public opinion on critical issues and on attitudes toward political candidates. Many Web sites conduct ongoing polls, asking visitors to respond to timely questions. Results are updated and posted in real-time.

THE NATIONAL DATABASE

The evolution of the Internet will provide the electronic infrastructure needed to maintain a national database. A national database will be a central repository for all personal data for citizens. An individual would be assigned a unique identification number at birth. This ID number would replace the social security number, the driver's license number, the student identification number, and dozens of others. Eventually the ID number probably will be replaced by some kind of unique digital biometric signature, perhaps a fingerprint or iris scan (eye).

A national database would consolidate the personal data now stored on tens of thousands of manual and computer-based files. It could contain an individual's name, past and present addresses, dependent data, work history, medical history, marital history, tax data, criminal record, military history, credit rating and history, and so on. A national database has certain advantages.

A national database could provide the capability of monitoring the activities of criminal suspects; virtually eliminating welfare and food stamp fraud; quickly identifying illegal aliens; and making an individual's medical history available at any hospital in the country. The taking of the census would be done automatically each year (or even each month), rather than every 10 years. The national database would enable us to generate valuable information. Governments at all levels would have access to up-to-date demographic information they could use to optimize the use of our tax dollars. Medical researchers could use the information to isolate geographical areas with inordinately high incidences of certain illnesses. The Bureau of Labor Statistics could monitor real, as opposed to reported, employment levels on a daily basis. The information possibilities are endless.

The national database is among the most controversial information technology issues in that it offers tremendous benefits to society while posing opportunities for serious abuse. In the aftermath of the September 11, 2001 attack on America, the proposal for a more sophisticated national identification system is gaining momentum. A system with biometric identification, such as a digitized fingerprint, can ensure that you are who you say you are, whether you're attending a football game or checking in for a cross-country flight. Opponents of the national database claim it will lead to abuse and the erosion of personal privacy. However, recent polls have shown that people may be more willing to trade a certain level of their privacy for safety.

VIRTUAL REALITY

Imagine that your job is to monitor the operation of a vast telecommunications network. Cables snake underground and underwater. Data flow between communications satellites and earth and across wiring inside building walls. Now imagine that a graphic image of this vast grid and its data flows could be laid out below you, as you float above, an "infonaut" looking for the kink that is blocking service to millions of customers. Far below, you see a pulsing light. There's the problem. With a gestured command, you fix it—without leaving your office. That's the promise of virtual reality, and it's moving from computer fantasy to computer fact. In fact, telecommunications firms are already experimenting with such systems.

Virtual reality (**VR**) combines computer graphics with special hardware to immerse users in an artificial three-dimensional world, sometimes called a **virtual world**. Instead of passively viewing data or graphics on a screen, users can move about, handle "virtual" representations of data and objects, and get visual, aural, and tactile feedback. The audio, visual, and other stimuli for the virtual world vary, depending on what you do. In the world of computers, the term *virtual* refers to an environment that is *simulated by hardware and software* (for example, virtual memory, virtual department store).

VR Applications

Virtual reality was born in the late 1960s when the U.S. Air Force began experimenting with flight simulators. From there, the technology was picked up by NASA. Today, NASA and a number of universities and corporations are either developing or using virtual reality systems for a variety of applications (see Figure 12-12).

- *Architecture and computer-aided design.* Architects already have access to a number of commercial VR systems that let them conduct electronic "walkthroughs" of proposed buildings.

- *Visualization of data.* NASA has created a virtual wind tunnel that lets a user climb inside an airstream. By gesturing with a data glove, the user can change the airflow and then walk around to experience it from different angles.

- *Exploration of hostile environments.* NASA is using raw data to create a VR version of an Antarctic lake bottom that will let researchers study life forms beneath the frigid waters without risk.

- *Sales.* A Japanese department store uses a "virtual kitchen" for planning custom-designed remodeling projects. After store personnel input a kitchen's existing layout and measurements using CAD software, customers don the VR gear and play around with different appliances, open drawers, turn on faucets, and visualize different arrangements.

- *Exercise.* Exercise bikes and massage chairs are finding a place in the virtual world. With the new lighter headgear, you can add adventure to your exercise as you cycle through virtual towns.

- *Training.* Flight training is one of the most sophisticated and oldest applications of VR. Here is found a world that's almost as realistic as the real world. Pilots can take the controls of a fully loaded passenger plane for their first flight because of the training they received in the simulator. VR researchers are creating VR training systems for firefighters, police officers, and others. Perhaps someday high school drivers' training classes will be conducted in virtual reality.

- *Education.* The learning experience through VR is truly active (versus passive). It allows students to experience first hand such things as life in a medieval village or walking among dinosaurs.

- *Psychology.* A California psychologist is experimenting with VR therapy for acrophobics (those who fear heights). Wearing a VR headset, a patient walks a plank, crosses a bridge, which spans water and hills, and accomplishes other acts that would instill fear. Over 90% of the patients now feel confident enough to climb ladders and cross the Golden Gate Bridge.

- *Virtual weddings.* A bride and groom can join their minister in a virtual world and say their vows amid a virtual re-creation of a significant historical venue, such as the lost city of Atlantis with its palaces, chariots, carousels, and even doves.

FIGURE 12–12 VIRTUAL REALITY IN OUR LIVES

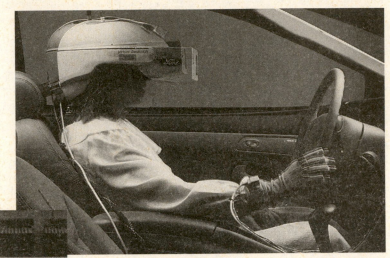

FLIGHT SIMULATORS
This pilot is training in a flight simulator, one of the more mature applications of virtual reality. In the simulator, a pilot can be exposed to many challenging flying situations in a relatively short period of time.

DESIGNING AUTOMOBILES
For this engineer, showing up for work can be as much fun as going to the video arcade. But she's not playing games. She is experimenting with the use of virtual reality to help design cars for the future. This operator wears a helmet and goggles equipped with two small screens (see inset of the 3D image). A special glove fitted with sensors covers her right hand and allows her to manipulate objects during the design process.

Courtesy of Ford Motor Company

THRILLS WITHOUT SPILLS
Virtual reality takes this hang glider to the twenty-first century so he can fly among the skyscrapers of Los Angeles. Virtual hang gliders ride in an actual hang glider harness positioned in front of a box that contains an image generator displaying pictures of a futuristic Los Angeles.

Courtesy of Evans and Sutherland Computer Corporation

Dressing for Cyberspace

To enter the virtual world, users don special hardware for the feeling of total immersion in a three-dimensional world (see Figure 12-12).

- *Headpiece.* The goggles-like head-mounted display (HMD) blocks out visual sensations from the real world and substitutes images presented on *two small video screens*—one for each eye, creating a three-dimensional effect. The headpiece also contains *motion,* or *balance, sensors*—move your head and the computer will shift the view presented on the video screens. Just flip up the visor on your headpiece to see what is going on in the real world. Or, flip it down to enter the virtual world.

- *Headphones.* Headphones block out room noise and substitute three-dimensional *holophononic* sounds. Generally, the headphones are built into the helmet.

- *Data glove.* A data glove outlined with fiber optic sensors and cables completes the ensemble. The glove can be used, like a floating mouse, to "gesture" a command or to grasp and move virtual objects about.

Each piece of hardware is tethered to a computer via wireless or cable links to record the user's movements and provide real-time feedback.

Will the Promise Be Kept?

Virtual reality is still in its infancy, but the breadth and success of existing VR applications have shown us that VR will play an important role in the future. Although some VR applications can be run on PCs, the most realistic experiences are created with sophisticated and expensive computer systems. However, with hardware costs decreasing and software sophistication increasing, virtual reality may emerge as the user interface of the future.

Telemedicine: Networked Health Care

The term **telemedicine** was coined to describe any type of health care administered remotely over communications links. Already, many states are practicing telemedicine (see Figure 12-13). Facilities, such as doctors' offices, nursing homes, and prisons, are networked to regional medical centers. Sophisticated input/output hardware at remote sites, such as digital cameras and medical sensing devices, enable medical personnel and equipment to perform diagnostic procedures on patients.

Federal and state governments are optimistic that telemedicine has the potential to improve health care and reduce its spiraling cost. Recently a consortium of businesses and government agencies demonstrated telemedicine technology for members of Congress. The demonstration simulated a situation in which a car crash victim required doctors in different states to examine medical records, X-rays, and other images quickly. Congress was apparently impressed because millions of federal dollars are being targeted to foster telemedicine. Congress is hopeful that high-tech medicine can reduce overall health-care costs. To realize significant savings, telemedicine must overcome several hurdles. Medical facilities will need to standardize medical records storage and procedures for protection of personal information. Doctors who have been trained in conventional diagnostic methods and are uncomfortable with the high-tech methods will need to be convinced of its value.

Telemedicine has many applications. Mostly it is being used to distribute health-care capabilities to rural areas electronically. Also, it's used in the cities where many ambulances are equipped to administer telemedicine. By the time the ambulance arrives at the hospital, a doctor may have run preliminary diagnostic procedures via telemedicine. The military uses similar systems in the battlefield. As telemedicine matures, look for it to play a major role in home care of the elderly, eliminating the need for costly hospitalization.

THE EDUCATION REVOLUTION

Only recently has information technology begun to have an impact on traditional approaches to education. Our approach to education evolved with the industrial revolution—mass production with students (workers) in rows all doing the same thing at a pace dictated by the teacher (manager). Many

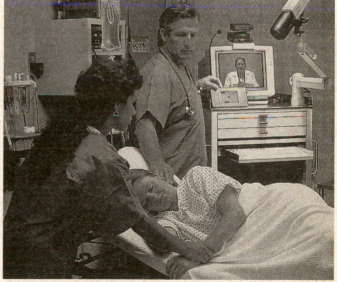

FIGURE 12–13 Telemedicine
This workstation, called F.R.E.D.™ (Friendly Rollabout Engineered for Doctors), is designed for use in health-care facilities such as hospitals, medical centers, clinics, and medical schools. F.R.E.D. provides a telemedicine solution for specialties such as cardiology that gives them virtual bedside access to their patients.

Photo courtesy of VTEL Corporation

educators are questioning the wisdom and effectiveness of traditional techniques in light of recent successes in technology-aided education. The computer has proven a marvelous tool for learning at all levels, from preschool to postgraduate continuing education (see Figure 12-14). The advantages are proving too vivid to ignore.

- Learning is interactive.
- Students can work at their own pace.
- Learning can take place anywhere, anytime, via communications links to available resources.
- Learning materials are more sophisticated (animation, 3-D images, hypermedia links, and so on).

Technology-aided education is being introduced rapidly at all levels of education. Many public school systems are looking to technology-aided education to improve the student/teacher ratio, raise test scores, and ease an ongoing budget crunch. Institutions of higher learning have introduced many ways to leverage information technology in education. Already, the online university is here and growing. You can obtain undergraduate and graduate degrees from reputable colleges and universities through online study. This type of program is sure to appeal to those who are unable to adjust their busy schedules to attend traditional classes. Some universities are using the technology to integrate the teaching of related topics. Rather than teach computers, finance, and ethics in separate courses, they are taught together in concert with applications.

The Internet offers the potential for nationwide uniform testing for elementary and secondary students. With uniform learning standards for each subject at each level, students will be able to advance from one grade to the next based on achievement rather than age. Computer-based uniform testing has another advantage. The system will monitor not only student progress but also the effectiveness of individual teachers and schools.

INTELLIGENT AGENTS AT WORK FOR YOU

Just as we begin to reach electronic saturation with instant messages, voice mail, Internet mailing lists, online newspapers, and so on, along come intelligent agents to help us cope with information overload. We provide *intelligent agents* or *bots,* which are software packages, with instructions detailing what to do. We then give them the authority to act on our behalf, just as we would a human agent. Intelligent agents, which are discussed in more detail in Chapter 10, roam around inside our computer systems, ready to help us whenever they can. They can bring urgent e-mails or instant messages to our attention, page us when our spouse leaves a voice-mail message, alert us to mailing-list messages that contain the keywords *kids* and *games,* and search all East Coast newspapers for articles mentioning *forest conservation.* They can remind us of important birthdays and even order the flowers.

Bots act as intermediaries, filtering the never-ending stream of information to give us only that which we need and want. Today's intelligent agents are still crude, but extremely helpful. We can expect a quantum leap in intelligent agent capabilities in the next five years. In the near future, you will be able to ask your intelligent agent to do some comparison shopping, then make recommendations on which digital camera offers the best value and where to buy it. Intelligent agents will alert us when our favorite music artists release a new album and even download a MP3 sampling of songs from the album. Within a few years, most of us will begin to rely on these cyberbutlers to bring order to our sometimes-hectic lives.

CARS AND THE AUTOMOBILE INDUSTRY GO HI-TECH

Every major manufacturer of automobiles in the world is planning to make computers and Internet access "standard equipment" in the automobile of the future (see Figure 12-15). Some high-end vehicles already have some built-in capabilities, such as the General Motors OnStar global positioning system, which can tell you where you are and how to get to where you are going. OnStar automatically phones police and ambulance services when air bags are deployed. The system can be used to make telephone calls, dinner reservations, and theater reservations, as well.

The soothsayers in Detroit tell us that in the not-too-distant-future we may get in our automobiles and verbally announce ourselves to the car so that it can recall and apply settings from our driver profile. For example, the seat and steering wheel would be repositioned, radio dials would be reset, even selected photographs would be displayed on the dashboard display, and other computer-related settings would be activated such as e-mail preferences, MP3 music play list, and Web site favorites. These automobiles will be continually connected to the Internet, giving us ready access to customized news, weather, stock quotes, thousands of radio stations, and other desired information,

FIGURE 12–14 TECHNOLOGY IN EDUCATION

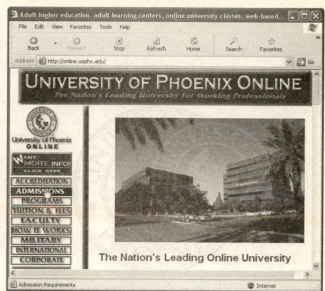

THE VIRTUAL UNIVERSITY

The University of Phoenix exists mostly in cyberspace but it has more students than any other university in the United States. Approximately 150,000 students pursue undergraduate and graduate degree programs via Web-based courses. Hundreds of traditional colleges now offer online courses, and an increasing number are beginning to offer online degrees. The barriers of time and place are eroding and opportunities to learn are everywhere.

THE TOOLS OF EDUCATION

High-tech tools, such as this tablet PC, may never replace paper and scissors in elementary schools; but each year, children spend more time interacting with technology-based learning tools.

Courtesy of Xybernaut

INTERNET2 CLASS

A broadcast technician (inset) controls the picture and sound for an innovative online botany class at Oregon State University. The online class is one of the first in the nation to use the high-speed Internet2 technologies. Internet2, the next generation Internet, is not yet widely available. Students say the class provides a deeper level of understanding because of the interaction between students and professors at several universities.

Copyright 2001 Oregon State University

FIGURE 12–15 **AUTOMOBILE ENTERTAINMENT AND PRODUCTIVITY CENTER**

THE CONNECTED CAR

The world is changing so quickly that it is difficult to speculate on what it will be like in five years. We know we can expect further integration of computers and cars. Automotive, computer, electronics, and communication industries are working together to develop computing platforms that provide drivers and passengers with an environment that is informative (GPS navigation), productive (cellular communications and onboard computer), entertaining (radio and TV data broadcast, video games), and connected via wireless Internet access.

Photos courtesy of Intel Corporation

IN-DASH WINDOWS-BASED COMPUTER

The Clarion AutoPC, shown here, is an in-dash Microsoft Windows CE-based computer system that integrates communication, navigation, information, and entertainment within an automobile. A navigator leads you to your destination through both visual and audio prompting. Clarion AutoPC's voice-activated control listens to you, so your eyes never have to leave the road.

Courtesy Clarion Corporation of America

via either textual/graphic displays or audio response. The onboard system will even read news and e-mails aloud, if you wish. Of course, auto-based systems will have infrared ports to let users share data with handheld PCs.

Automobile dealers and manufacturers are using IT for sales and service, too. It won't be long before you will be able to shop every showroom and new car lot in the country. You and other consumers will use a *configurator* to identify the exact car and features you want. Such an online system will allow you to pick any car, and then select the exact options you desire. Your cost is adjusted as you add and delete options. This inevitable system is more consumer-friendly. Already several Web sites enable consumers to configure cars with dealer suggested retail pricing. It's a natural extension of the system that will let you simultaneously submit your request to all dealers in a particular region. A fully automated response will include the exact price of the car and when you can expect delivery.

Three major automakers in the United States—General Motors, Ford, and DaimlerChrysler—have agreed to cooperate on an online auto parts exchange that will result in a half trillion dollars in spending by these companies and their suppliers.

THE EMERGING INTERNET

The Internet already offers a seemingly endless variety of services, but in reality, these are just the beginning. We can use our PCs to trade securities, but not all companies offer this service. We can take online courses, but not all colleges offer online degrees. We can view many online newspapers and periodicals, but for the most part, they are by-products of the printed version and have little interactivity. In a few years, you will be able to buy and sell securities with any brokerage company and pursue any degree at any major university. Printed versions of magazines may well be by-products of the online versions.

We can only speculate what amazing applications are coming to the cyberworld. We'll be able to adjust the temperature at home from any remote location. We will be able to view any movie ever made at any time. We'll even be able to talk with someone who is speaking a different language through an electronic interpreter (working prototypes are now in operation). Telecommunications, computers, and information services companies are jockeying for position to be a part of what forecasters predict will be the most lucrative industry of the twenty-first century—information technology.

12-3.1	The volume of traditional mail handled by the postal service is expected to decrease as the information superhighway begins to mature. (T/F)
12-3.2	Instant messaging is emerging as the preferred means of interoffice communication in many companies. (T/F)
12-3.3	What software tool can filter available information to give us only that which we want: (a) an intelligent manager, (b) an intelligent agent, (c) an intelligent diplomat, or (d) an intellectual agent?
12-3.4	The application that delivers video upon request is known as: (a) real video, (b) cybervideo, (c) video-on-demand, or (d) at-the-movies.
12-3.5	Typical VR hardware includes all but which of the following: (a) information vest, (b) data glove, (c) headpiece, or (d) headphones?

SECTION SELF-CHECK

12-4   Our Challenge for the Twenty-First Century

The technology revolution is in its infancy. Only recently are we as an information society beginning to comprehend its vast potential and the vast array of challenges we must overcome to realize its potential (see Figure 12-16).

THE VIRTUAL FRONTIER

We are living in and exploring a *virtual frontier*. The virtual frontier encompasses the electronic highways that comprise the Internet, thousands of newsgroups, scores of information services, and millions of private networks. Already this frontier is expanding to embrace other forms of communication, including television, radio, and cellular telephony.

The *virtual frontier* may be the last great frontier. Much of what lies beyond the virtual horizon is uncharted and potentially dangerous territory. Even so, wagon trains filled with brave pioneers set out each day to blaze new electronic trails. The virtual frontier is likened sometimes to the Wild West because there are few rules and people just keep coming. Responsible pioneers accept and live by society's traditional rules of behavior, but the seedier elements of society are quick to observe that there is no virtual sheriff.

It's difficult to fathom the hardships endured by nineteenth-century pioneers who headed West for a better life. Imagine a hardy pioneer woman pushing a Conestoga wagon through the mud while her husband coaxes their oxen to pull harder. The hardships along the electronic trails are not as physical or life-threatening, but they exist. We're still sloshing through the virtual mud in the virtual frontier. When we find a road, it's more like a trail or a roadway under construction than a highway. The highways that exist are narrow, filled with potholes, and have many detours.

The virtual frontier is growing in the same way the Wild West did. In the western frontier, cities grew from nothing overnight. In the virtual frontier, major services or capabilities unheard of a few years ago are becoming mainstream applications in the cyberworld. In the Wild West, many years passed before the ranchers and the farmers could be friends. Similarly, it might be some time before the various telecommunications, hardware, and software industries in the virtual frontier can become friends. Outlaws roamed the Wild West, creating havoc until law and order were established. Electronic outlaws may have their way in the virtual frontier, as well, until cybercops armed with strict cyberlaws drive them out of town.

The opportunity for a better life enticed pioneers to risk all and follow the setting sun. Eventually the Wild West was tamed, and they realized their dreams. The modern-day version of the Wild West presents us with the same opportunity. Bear in mind, though, that the information superhighway is truly a frontier that may not be tamed in the foreseeable future. The fact that it is a frontier, with all the associated risks, makes it even more exciting.

YOUR CHALLENGE

With your newly acquired base of information technology knowledge, you are now positioned to cope with our virtual frontier and enter the mainstream of our information society. However, the IT learning process is ongoing. The dynamics of rapidly advancing IT demands a constant updating of skills and expertise. By their very nature, computers and IT bring about change. With the total amount of computing capacity in the world doubling every two years, we can expect change that is even more dramatic in the future. Someday in the not-too-distant future computers will be as commonplace in the home and office as telephones, and as commonplace on our person as wristwatches.

PERSONAL COMPUTING:
The Notebook PC Goes on a Vacation We don't leave home without our notebook PC, the ultimate vacation accessory. We plan our trips and stops with mapping software. A global positioning system helps us navigate unfamiliar cities and locate sites along the way. Each day, we download pictures from the digital camera to the notebook for storage and viewing. The kids enjoy the notebook's gaming programs and we all enjoy watching DVD movies. Of course, the notebook PC is there for general personal computing tasks, as well. Every few days, we check our e-mail, but we ignore it until we return home.

FIGURE 12–16 SMALLER CHIPS MEANS SMALLER COMPUTERS

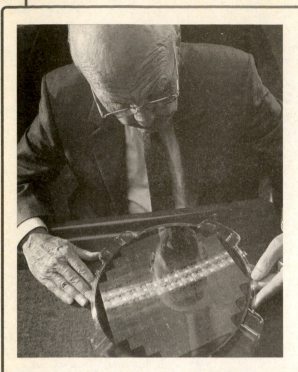

SMALLER, MORE POWERFUL CHIPS
Jack Kilby's first integrated circuit contained a single transistor. Tens of thousands of engineers around the world have built on Mr. Kilby's invention, such that each year our information society is the beneficiary of smaller, more powerful, cheaper chips. Tomorrow's integrated circuits will be manufactured on 300-millimeter wafers, enabling the more powerful chips to be installed in a greater variety of devices, many of which will be smaller, at lower costs.

Texas Instruments Incorporated

FASHIONABLY UNWIRED
This fashion show features runway models sporting wireless Internet technology products. The belt buckle on the model in the foreground is a wearable PC. Voice-recognition and a head-mounted display (over her right eye) enable communication with the PC. According to a recent national poll, more than half of American adults would, if given the choice, gladly carry around multiple wireless devices. The PC featured in this fashion show support digital cameras, GPS receivers, MP3 music files, and broadband streaming audio/video.

Courtesy of Charmed Technology

It's now apparent that we truly live in a global village. Technology has made it possible for us to communicate with someone on the other side of the world as easily as we would with someone in an adjacent building. International project teams work together via telecommunications to create and support products (from automobiles to video games) and services (from banking services to legal services). From now on, any country's national economy must be considered within the context of a world economy.

Many business traditions are vulnerable to IT: More people are telecommuting; company hierarchies are flattening out; the worker has greater visibility via the Internet and therefore greater mobility; methods of compensation are placing greater emphasis on innovation and productivity; the laws that govern commerce and intercompany relationships are under constant review; business processes are continually changing to integrate the latest innovations in technology; and the way we communicate is changing dramatically every few years. Are we that far away from a speech recognition-enabled wristwatch videophone?

So far, the cumulative effects of these changes have altered the basic constructs of society and the way we live, work, and play. PCs have replaced calculators and ledger books; e-mail and videoconferencing facilitate communication; word processing has eliminated typewriters; computer-aided design has rendered the drawing table obsolete; e-commerce may eventually eliminate the need for money; online shopping is affecting consumer buying habits; the Internet has opened the doors of many virtual universities. . . and the list goes on.

We as a society are, in effect, trading a certain level of computer and IT dependence for an improvement in the quality of life. However, this improvement in the way we live is not a foregone conclusion. Just as our highways play host to objectionable billboards, carjackings, and automobile accidents, the information highways are sure to have back roads lined with sleaze, scams, and cyberthiefs. It is our challenge to harness the immense power of information technology and our wired world so we can direct it toward the benefit of society.

Never before has such opportunity presented itself so vividly. This generation, *your generation*, has the technological foundation and capability of changing dreams into reality.

12-4.1 A decade ago the virtual frontier was like the Wild West, but now it is tamed and tightly controlled by law. (T/F)

12-4.2 E-commerce may eventually eliminate the need for: (a) folding money and coins, (b) intercompany networking, (c) e-money, or (d) VPNs.

12-1 CAREERS IN AN INFORMATION SOCIETY

If you are planning a career as an IT specialist, opportunities remain excellent. Almost every company employs or contracts with IT specialists. IT workers are in demand not just for their skills but also for what they contribute to the organization.

Some of the more visible information technology jobs include **chief information officer (CIO)**, **systems analyst, applications programmer, programmer/analyst, network administrator, system programmer, database administrator (DBA), Internet site specialist, Webmaster, computer operator,** and **user liaison.** The variety and types of IT specialist jobs are ever changing.

An implied responsibility to maintain the integrity of a system and its data accompanies IT jobs; however, licensing or certification is usually not a requirement for any IT professional. However, certification offers career advantages. The Institute for Certification of Computer Professionals (ICCP) awards the *Certified Computing Professional (CCP)* and the *Associate Computing Professional (ACP)*. Microsoft Corporation offers these certificates for IT professionals: *Microsoft Certified Professional (MCP), Microsoft Certified Systems Administrators (MCSA), Microsoft Certified Systems Engineer (MCSE), Microsoft Certified Database Administrator (MCDBA), Microsoft Certified Trainers (MCT), Microsoft Certified Application Developers (MCAD), Microsoft Certified Solution Developer (MCSD), Microsoft Office Specialist,* and *Microsoft Office Specialist Master Instructor.* Novell Corporation offers these certifications: *Certified Novell Administrator (CAN), Certified Novell Engineer (CNE), Master CNE, Certified Directory Engineer (CDE), Certified Novell Instructor (CNI),* and *Novell Authorized Instructor (NAI).* Sun Microsystems offers several Java-related certifications.

Information technology competency is becoming a prerequisite for people pursuing almost any career. Career mobility is directly related to an individual's current and future knowledge of computers and IT.

IT solutions have caused all or at least part of many job functions to be replaced with automated systems, but IT is responsible for the creation of many other jobs.

Whether you are entering the job market for the first time or seeking alternative employment, resources on the Internet can help you find work. The online jobs search has revolutionized the way job seekers and companies find each other.

12-2 ROBOTS AND ROBOTICS

To date the area of artificial intelligence (AI) having the greatest impact on our society is **robotics,** the field of study that deals with creating robots. Most applications of robotics are in manufacturing and the use of *industrial robots.* Industrial robots are quite good at repetitive tasks and tasks that require precision movements, moving heavy loads, and working in hazardous areas.

The most common industrial robot has a single mechanical arm, called a manipulator, which can be fitted with a variety of hands for painting, welding, and so on. Roboticists are outfitting robots with artificial intelligence and human sensory capabilities, such as vision, that enable them to simulate human behavior. Some robots have navigational capabilities.

12-3 LOOKING AHEAD: FUTURE APPLICATIONS OF IT

The information superhighway is a network of high-speed data communications links that eventually will connect virtually every facet of our society.

During the next decade, computers will be built into our domestic, working, and external environments. Eventually we will talk to our computers within our smart homes. They will help us perform many duties around the house.

A wide range of information and telecommunication services is now available for the Internet and many more are planned. These applications include video communication, video-on-demand, interactive television, virtual libraries, e-publishing, multimedia catalogs, **electronic money (e-money)**, total e-commerce, electronic voting and polling, a national database, **telemedicine,** using configurators to buy cars online, and much more. Professional gaming is gaining steam. Technology-aided education is being introduced rapidly at all levels of education. Intelligent agents, or bots, act as intermediaries, filtering the never-ending stream of information to give us only that which we need and want.

There is now a standard for the **electronic wallet,** the **electronic-commerce modeling language (ECML)**, which ultimately will let us purchase items electronically from retail stores. When payment is entirely electronic, it is possible to pay for goods and services with very small amounts, called **micropayments.** The cashless society may be on the horizon.

Virtual reality (VR) combines computer graphics with special hardware to immerse users in an artificial three-dimensional world, sometimes called a **virtual world.** In IT parlance, the term "virtual" refers to an environment that is simulated by hardware and software. To enter the three-dimensional virtual world, users don special hardware, including a headpiece, headphones, and a data glove.

Eventually the Internet will enable people of all walks of life to interact with just about anyone else, with institutions, with businesses, and with vast amounts of data and information. However, it must be significantly improved to realize its promise.

12-4 OUR CHALLENGE FOR THE TWENTY-FIRST CENTURY

The virtual frontier encompasses the electronic highways that comprise the Internet, thousands of newsgroups, scores of information services, and millions of private networks. It is likened sometimes to the Wild West because there are no rules. The opportunity for a better life is enticing pioneers to explore the virtual frontier.

The computer and IT offer you the opportunity to improve the quality of your life. It is your challenge to harness the power of the computer and direct it to the benefit of society.

KEY TERMS

applications programmer (p. 450)
chief information officer (CIO) (p. 450)
computer operator (p. 451)
database administrator (DBA) (p. 451)
electronic money (e-money) (p. 466)
electronic-commerce modeling language
  (ECML) (p. 466)

Internet site specialist (p. 451)
micropayment (p. 466)
network administrator (p. 451)
programmer/analyst (p. 450)
robotics (p. 456)
system programmer (p. 451)
systems analyst (p. 450)

telemedicine (p. 471)
user liaison (p. 451)
virtual reality (VR) (p. 469)
virtual world (p. 469)
Webmaster (p. 451)

MATCHING

1. robotics
2. Master CNE
3. e-money
4. America Online
5. industrial robot
6. telemedicine
7. CIO
8. VR
9. manipulator
10. MCP
11. Webmaster
12. online candidates database
13. systems analyst
14. e-publishing
15. user liaison

a. artificial three-dimensional world
b. "live-in" IT specialist
c. remote health care
d. good at repetitive tasks
e. a Novell certification
f. robot arm
g. monitors Internet traffic
h. e-books
i. a Microsoft certification
j. founded in 1985
k. responsible for all the information services activity
l. enables cashless transactions
m. ranked as one of the best jobs
n. contains résumés
o. study that deals with creating robots

CHAPTER SELF-CHECK

12-1.1 In general, IT workers are more productive than workers in other areas. (T/F)

12-1.2 Automation does not eliminate jobs. (T/F)

12-1.3 At present, certification is not a requirement to become an IT professional. (T/F)

12-1.4 The director of information services within an organization is called the: (a) DBA, (b) Webmaster, (c) network administrator, or (d) CIO.

12-1.5 The "live-in" IT specialist who coordinates computer-related activities within a particular functional area is called a: (a) user liaison, (b) computer operator, (c) CIO, or (d) Internet site specialist.

12-1.6 Which certification recognizes advanced skills with Microsoft Office desktop software: (a) MCDBA, (b) CDE, (c) Novell Authorized Instructor, or (d) Microsoft Office Specialist?

12-1.7 The focus of certification programs from Sun Microsystems is what programming language: (a) Visual BASIC, (b) Java, (c) Perl, or (d) COBOL?

12-1.8 The career/employment Web sites offer all but which of these types of resources and services: (a) jobs database, (b) job search capability, (c) career resources, or (d) college degree programs?

12-2.1 Industrial robots offer the potential for increased productivity and better service. (T/F)

12-2.2 All robots are stationary. (T/F)

12-2.3 Robots are used in brain surgery. (T/F)

12-2.4 Robotics is an area of: (a) AI, (b) human factors, (c) ergonomics, or (d) remote navigation.

12-2.5 Industrial robots are equipped with a variety of industrial tools that include all of these except: (a) drills, (b) paint guns, (c) welding torches, or (d) pagers.

12-3.1 A national database was approved by Congress and implemented in 1998. (T/F)

12-3.2 Some cellular phones have built-in digital cameras that let us take and send pictures. (T/F)

12-3.3 Internet gaming has begun its decline now that Generation Xers are entering the work force. (T/F)

12-3.4 E-commerce has actually increased the paper flow between cooperating companies. (T/F)

12-3.5 All of these are advantages of online media over print media except: (a) it is interactive, (b) it is linked, (c) it offers text-to-video, or (d) it offers multimedia content.

12-3.6 When health care is administered remotely over communications links, we call it: (a) telemedicine, (b) cybermedicine, (c) health-care magic, or (d) telehealth.

12-3.7 An artificial environment made possible by hardware and software is known as: (a) virtual planet, (b) near reality, (c) virtual reality, or (d) cyberrealism.

12-3.8 Money as we know it may soon be replaced by: (a) e-money, (b) electronic greenbacks, (c) cybercash, or (d) Eurodollars.

12-3.9 A national database has all but which of the following advantages: (a) virtual elimination of welfare fraud, (b) can monitor criminal suspect activities, (c) enables an annual census, or (d) elimination of all abuse of personal information?

12-4.1 The information highway is well-explored and would no longer be considered a frontier. (T/F)

12-4.2 The total computing capacity in the world is increasing at slightly less than 5% per year. (T/F)

12-4.3 A metaphor frequently used as a reference to the wired world is: (a) cyberway, (b) virtual way, (c) information superhighway, or (d) NINI.

IT ETHICS AND ISSUES

MORAL FILTERING OF INTERNET CONTENT

There has been considerable debate in the cyber community among organizations that set policy for the Internet about whether these organizations should provide some level of moral filtering of Web site content and applications. For example, one site published the names of British Intelligence agents, thus putting their lives at risk. Another lists doctors who perform abortions, then crosses them off as they are killed. Then, of course, there is the issue of easily accessible pornography, which currently comprises 1.5% of Internet content.

Discussion: What role, if any, should be played by Internet policy-making organizations regarding the assessment of the Internet content and applications?

Discussion: If possible, should cooperative international legislation be enacted to better control access to pornographic content on the Internet?

PRESCREENING OF ONLINE COMMUNICATIONS

Millions of people have access to and participate in newsgroups, chat rooms, and online forums. Some sponsors and information services feel obligated to give their subscribers an environment that is free of offensive language. These organizations use an electronic scanner to "read" each message before it is posted to a newsgroup or forum. In a split second the scanner flags those words and phrases that do not comply with the information service's guidelines. The scanner even catches words or phrases that may be disguised with asterisks and so on. Generally, the guidelines are compatible with accepted norms in a moral society. These include the use of grossly repugnant material, obscene material, solicitations, and threats. The scanner also scans for text that may be inappropriate for a public discussion, such as the use of pseudonyms, attempts at trading, presentation of illegal material, and even speaking in foreign languages. Messages that do not pass the prescreening process are returned automatically to the sender.

Some might cry that their rights to freedom of expression are violated. This, of course, is a matter that may ultimately be decided in a court of law. In the meantime, those who wish a more open discussion have plenty of opportunities. On most international newsgroups and information services, anything goes.

Discussion: Is prescreening of electronic communications a violation of freedom of expression?

Discussion: What are the advantages and disadvantages of prescreening online communications from the user's perspective? From the perspective of the organization doing the prescreening?

INAPPROPRIATE USE OF THE INTERNET AT WORK

Internet usage monitoring at the workplace has revealed what many workers already know, at least some of the Internet surfing is not job related (more than half at the U.S. Internal Revenue Service). Most of this surfing is treated much like nonbusiness telephone calls, such as a call home or to confirm a doctor's appointment. However, management is getting involved when abuse is extensive or "inappropriate" material is viewed or downloaded on company PCs. Although corporate policy on such actions may be nonexistent or unclear, some people are losing their jobs.

Discussion: What would be appropriate punishment, if any, for an employee who, against company policy, downloaded and kept "inappropriate" material on his or her PC?

Discussion: What punishment is appropriate for an employee who abuses his or her Internet connection by doing non-job-related surfing at least one hour per day?

DISCUSSION AND PROBLEM SOLVING

12-1.1 Each year, the IT labor shortage places pressure on the U.S. Congress to open the immigration door for more skilled foreign workers. Those who argue for more visas say that companies in the United States will be unable to fill high-tech jobs from the existing pool of college graduates. There is a group of people who want to protect those jobs and salary levels for American workers and they say that the job shortage may be overstated. Argue for or against allowing greater numbers of foreign IT workers into the United States.

12-1.2 If you plan to pursue an IT career, describe your ideal career path. Or, if you plan to pursue a non-IT career, speculate on how being IT competent might affect your level of success in your chosen career.

12-1.3 Contrast the skills needed to be a good systems analyst with those required to be a good Webmaster.

12-1.4 Relatively few computer professionals have any kind of certification. Is certification really necessary?

12-2.1 Industrial robots are performing tasks formerly done by hundreds of thousands of human beings. Should something be done to curtail this worldwide loss of jobs? Explain.

12-2.2 Industrial robots hands can be outfitted with many tools for painting, welding, and so on. Describe at least two other tools appropriate for industrial robots with manipulator arms.

12-2.3 Robots with navigational capabilities are used routinely in health care and warehousing. In what other industry do you envision the use of mobile robots? Describe what they will be doing.

12-3.1 Continue the story line in the scenario depicted in Figure 12-10 by speculating on other futuristic applications.

KEY TERMS

applications programmer (p. 450)
chief information officer (CIO) (p. 450)
computer operator (p. 451)
database administrator (DBA) (p. 451)
electronic money (e-money) (p. 466)
electronic-commerce modeling language
  (ECML) (p. 466)

Internet site specialist (p. 451)
micropayment (p. 466)
network administrator (p. 451)
programmer/analyst (p. 450)
robotics (p. 456)
system programmer (p. 451)
systems analyst (p. 450)

telemedicine (p. 471)
user liaison (p. 451)
virtual reality (VR) (p. 469)
virtual world (p. 469)
Webmaster (p. 451)

MATCHING

1. robotics
2. Master CNE
3. e-money
4. America Online
5. industrial robot
6. telemedicine
7. CIO
8. VR
9. manipulator
10. MCP
11. Webmaster
12. online candidates database
13. systems analyst
14. e-publishing
15. user liaison

a. artificial three-dimensional world
b. "live-in" IT specialist
c. remote health care
d. good at repetitive tasks
e. a Novell certification
f. robot arm
g. monitors Internet traffic
h. e-books
i. a Microsoft certification
j. founded in 1985
k. responsible for all the information services activity
l. enables cashless transactions
m. ranked as one of the best jobs
n. contains résumés
o. study that deals with creating robots

CHAPTER SELF-CHECK

12-1.1 In general, IT workers are more productive than workers in other areas. (T/F)

12-1.2 Automation does not eliminate jobs. (T/F)

12-1.3 At present, certification is not a requirement to become an IT professional. (T/F)

12-1.4 The director of information services within an organization is called the: (a) DBA, (b) Webmaster, (c) network administrator, or (d) CIO.

12-1.5 The "live-in" IT specialist who coordinates computer-related activities within a particular functional area is called a: (a) user liaison, (b) computer operator, (c) CIO, or (d) Internet site specialist.

12-1.6 Which certification recognizes advanced skills with Microsoft Office desktop software: (a) MCDBA, (b) CDE, (c) Novell Authorized Instructor, or (d) Microsoft Office Specialist?

12-1.7 The focus of certification programs from Sun Microsystems is what programming language: (a) Visual BASIC, (b) Java, (c) Perl, or (d) COBOL?

12-1.8 The career/employment Web sites offer all but which of these types of resources and services: (a) jobs database, (b) job search capability, (c) career resources, or (d) college degree programs?

12-2.1 Industrial robots offer the potential for increased productivity and better service. (T/F)

12-2.2 All robots are stationary. (T/F)

12-2.3 Robots are used in brain surgery. (T/F)

12-2.4 Robotics is an area of: (a) AI, (b) human factors, (c) ergonomics, or (d) remote navigation.

12-2.5 Industrial robots are equipped with a variety of industrial tools that include all of these except: (a) drills, (b) paint guns, (c) welding torches, or (d) pagers.

12-3.1 A national database was approved by Congress and implemented in 1998. (T/F)

12-3.2 Some cellular phones have built-in digital cameras that let us take and send pictures. (T/F)

12-3.3 Internet gaming has begun its decline now that Generation Xers are entering the work force. (T/F)

12-3.4 E-commerce has actually increased the paper flow between cooperating companies. (T/F)

12-3.5 All of these are advantages of online media over print media except: (a) it is interactive, (b) it is linked, (c) it offers text-to-video, or (d) it offers multimedia content.

12-3.6 When health care is administered remotely over communications links, we call it: (a) telemedicine, (b) cybermedicine, (c) health-care magic, or (d) telehealth.

12-3.7 An artificial environment made possible by hardware and software is known as: (a) virtual planet, (b) near reality, (c) virtual reality, or (d) cyberrealism.

12-3.8 Money as we know it may soon be replaced by: (a) e-money, (b) electronic greenbacks, (c) cybercash, or (d) Eurodollars.

CHECKING YOUR COMPREHENSION

Choose the best answer for each of the following questions.

1. Which of the following is not an application suited for robotics?
   a. food service
   b. hazardous materials
   c. healthcare
   d. industrial

2. Which of the following communication devices is likely to be incorporated into either your PC or TV?
   a. short wave radios
   b. voice intercoms
   c. telephones
   d. all of these

3. In the world of computers, the term "virtual" refers to which of the following descriptors?
   a. almost new
   b. never used
   c. artificial
   d. simulated

Identify the following statements as true or false.

4. The number of consultants and contractors in the IT industry may surpass the number of traditional in-house IT personnel in the near future.

5. There are more qualified IT specialists than there are jobs available to them.

6. Industries are looking to robotics for the sole purpose of reducing labor-related costs.

Answer the following questions.

7. What are some of the issues unique to IT that a woman should consider when weighing whether or not to choose a career in IT?

8. Discuss some of the advantages of becoming a "cashless" society?

Discussion and Critical Thinking Question

9. Printed materials can be enhanced electronically to include hyperlinks, text-to-speech, and multimedia content such as audio and video. Will these enhancements eliminate the need for conventional printed books in the future?

Chapter 3

Graphs and Functions

Owning your own business is considered by many to be the ultimate American dream. If your business does well, you may be rewarded handsomely for your efforts. However, should your business do poorly then it may be only a matter of time before your business, like many new businesses, no longer exists. On page 185, we use a function to model the salary of a toy store owner. Following this example, in the exercises on pages 189 and 190, we use many other functions to model other real-life situations.

SSM

Study Guide

CD/Video

MathPro 4/5

PH Math Tutor Center

prenhall.com/Angel

147

A Look Ahead

Two primary goals of this book are to provide you with a good understanding of graphing and of functions. Graphing is a key element to this and many mathematics courses. We introduce graphing early in this book, and we use it to model real-life data that you see every day in newspapers and magazines. Functions are closely related to graphing, and graphing functions is a key element to many mathematics courses. We will use both graphing and functions throughout the rest of this book. Additional topics in this chapter will include graphing linear and non-linear equations and linear inequalities. We will revisit each of these topics in later chapters of the book.

3.1 GRAPHS

SSM Study Guide CD/Video

MathPro 4/5 PH Math Tutor Center prenhall.com/Angel

1 Plot points in the Cartesian coordinate system.
2 Draw graphs by plotting points.
3 Graph nonlinear equations.
4 Use a graphing calculator.
5 Interpret graphs.

1 Plot Points in the Cartesian Coordinate System

René Descartes

Many algebraic relationships are easier to understand if we can see a visual picture of them. A graph is a picture that shows the relationship between two or more variables in an equation. Before learning how to construct a graph, you must know the Cartesian coordinate system.

The **Cartesian** (or **rectangular**) **coordinate system**, named after the French mathematician and philosopher René Descartes (1596–1650), consists of two axes (or number lines) in a plane drawn perpendicular to each other (Fig. 3.1). Note how the two axes yield four **quadrants**, labeled with capital Roman numerals I, II, III, and IV.

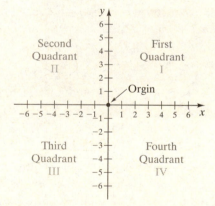

FIGURE 3.1

The horizontal axis is called the **x-axis**. The vertical axis is called the **y-axis**. The point of intersection of the two axes is called the **origin**. Starting from the origin and moving to the right, the numbers increase; moving to the left, the numbers decrease. Starting from the origin and moving up, the numbers increase; moving down, the numbers decrease. Note that the x-axis and y-axis are simply number lines, one horizontal and the other vertical.

An **ordered pair** (x, y) is used to give the two **coordinates** of a point. If, for example, the x-coordinate of a point is 2 and the y-coordinate is 3, the ordered pair representing that point is $(2, 3)$. The x-coordinate is always the first coordinate listed in the ordered pair. To plot a point, find the x-coordinate on the x-axis and the y-coordinate on the y-axis. Then suppose there was an imaginary vertical line from the x-coordinate and an imaginary horizontal line from the y-coordinate. The point is placed where the two imaginary lines intersect.

For example, the point corresponding to the ordered pair $(2, 3)$ is plotted in Figure 3.2. The phrase "the point corresponding to the ordered pair $(2, 3)$" is often abbreviated "the point $(2, 3)$." For example, if we write "the point $(-1, 5)$," it means the point corresponding to the ordered pair $(-1, 5)$. The ordered pairs A at $(-2, 3)$, B at $(0, 2)$, C at $(4, -1)$, and D at $(-4, 0)$ are plotted in Figure 3.3.

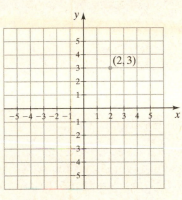

FIGURE 3.2

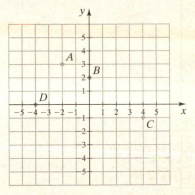

FIGURE 3.3

EXAMPLE 1 Plot the following points on the same set of axes.

a) $A(1, 4)$ b) $B(4, 1)$ c) $C(0, 2)$

d) $D(-3, 0)$ e) $E(-3, -1)$ f) $F(2, -4)$

Solution See Figure 3.4. Notice that point $(1, 4)$ is a different point than $(4, 1)$. Also notice that when the x-coordinate is 0, as in part **c)**, the point is on the y-axis. When the y-coordinate is 0, as in part **d)**, the point is on the x-axis.

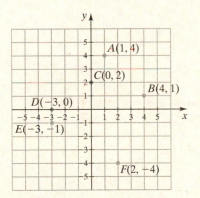

NOW TRY EXERCISE 7   FIGURE 3.4

2 Draw Graphs by Plotting Points

In Chapter 2, we solved equations that contained one variable. Now we will discuss equations that contain two variables. If an equation contains two variables, its solutions are pairs of numbers.

EXAMPLE 2   Determine whether the following ordered pairs are solutions of the equation $y = 2x - 3$.

a) $(1, -1)$ **b)** $\left(\frac{1}{2}, -2\right)$

c) $(3, 4)$ **d)** $(-1, -5)$

Solution   We substitute the first number in the ordered pair for x and the second number for y. If the substitutions result in a true statement, the ordered pair is a solution to the equation. If the substitutions result in a false statement, the ordered pair is not a solution to the equation.

a) $y = 2x - 3$
$-1 \overset{?}{=} 2(1) - 3$
$-1 \overset{?}{=} 2 - 3$
$-1 = -1$ *True*

b) $y = 2x - 3$
$-2 \overset{?}{=} 2\left(\frac{1}{2}\right) - 3$
$-2 \overset{?}{=} 1 - 3$
$-2 = -2$ *True*

c) $y = 2x - 3$
$4 \overset{?}{=} 2(3) - 3$
$4 \overset{?}{=} 6 - 3$
$4 = 3$ *False*

d) $y = 2x - 3$
$-5 \overset{?}{=} 2(-1) - 3$
$-5 \overset{?}{=} -2 - 3$
$-5 \overset{?}{=} -5$ *True*

Thus the ordered pairs $(1, -1)$, $\left(\frac{1}{2}, -2\right)$, and $(-1, -5)$ are solutions to the equation $y = 2x - 3$. The ordered pair $(3, 4)$ is not a solution.   ✳

There are many other solutions to the equation in Example 2. In fact, there are an infinite number of solutions. One method that may be used to find solutions to an equation like $y = 2x - 3$ is to substitute values for x and find the corresponding values of y. For example, to find the solution to the equation $y = 2x - 3$ when $x = 0$ we substitute 0 for x and solve for y.

$$y = 2x - 3$$
$$y = 2(0) - 3$$
$$y = 0 - 3$$
$$y = -3$$

Thus, another solution to the equation is $(0, -3)$.

A **graph** is an illustration of the set of points whose coordinates satisfy the equation. Sometimes when drawing a graph, we list some points that satisfy the equation in a table and then plot those points. We then draw a line through the points to obtain the graph. On the next page is a table of some points that satisfy the equation $y = 2x - 3$. The graph is drawn in Figure 3.5. Note that the equation $y = 2x - 3$ contains an infinite number of solutions and that the line continues indefinitely in both directions (as indicated by the arrows).

In Figure 3.5, the four points are in a straight line. Points that are in a straight line are said to be **collinear**. The graph is said to be **linear** because it is a straight line. Any equation whose graph is a straight line is called a **linear equation**. The equation $y = 2x - 3$ is an example of a linear equation. Linear equations are also called **first-degree equations** since the greatest exponent that appears on any variable is 1. In Examples 3 and 4, we graph linear equations.

TEACHING TIP
Point out that it is not necessary to describe a line as "straight" because all lines are straight. This terminology is used to emphasize this characteristic of lines.

x	y	(x, y)
-1	-5	$(-1, -5)$
0	-3	$(0, -3)$
$\frac{1}{2}$	-2	$(\frac{1}{2}, -2)$
1	-1	$(1, -1)$

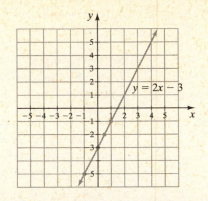

FIGURE 3.5

HELPFUL HINT

STUDY TIP

In this chapter, and in several upcoming chapters, you will be plotting points and drawing graphs using the Cartesian coordinate system. Sometimes students have trouble drawing accurate graphs. The following are some suggestions to improve the quality of the graphs you produce.

1. For your homework, use graph paper to draw your graphs. This will help you maintain a consistent scale throughout your graph. Ask your teacher if you may use graph paper on your tests and quizzes.

2. Use a ruler or straightedge to draw axes and lines. Your axes and lines will look much better and will be much more accurate if drawn with a ruler or straightedge.

3. If you are not using graph paper, use a ruler to make a consistent scale on your axes. It is impossible to get an accurate graph when axes are marked with an uneven scale.

4. Use a pencil instead of a pen. You may make a mistake as you draw your graph. A mistake can often be fixed quickly with a pencil and eraser, and you will not have to start over from the beginning.

5. You will need to practice to improve your graphing skills. Work all of the homework problems that you are assigned. To check your graphs on even-numbered exercises, you may want to use a graphing calculator.

EXAMPLE 3 Graph $y = x$.

Solution We first find some ordered pairs that are solutions by selecting values of x and finding the corresponding values of y. We will select 0, some positive values, and some negative values for x. We will also choose numbers close to 0, so that the ordered pairs will fit on the axes. The graph is illustrated in Figure 3.6.

x	y	(x, y)
-2	-2	$(-2, -2)$
-1	-1	$(-1, -1)$
0	0	$(0, 0)$
1	1	$(1, 1)$
2	2	$(2, 2)$

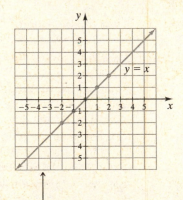

FIGURE 3.6

1. Select values for x.
2. Compute y.
3. Ordered pairs.
4. Plot the points and draw the graph.

EXAMPLE 4   Graph $y = -\frac{1}{3}x + 1$.

Solution   We will select some values for x, find the corresponding values of y, and then draw the graph. When we select values for x, we will select some positive values, some negative values, and 0. The graph is illustrated in Figure 3.7. (To conserve space, we will not always list a column in the table for ordered pairs.)

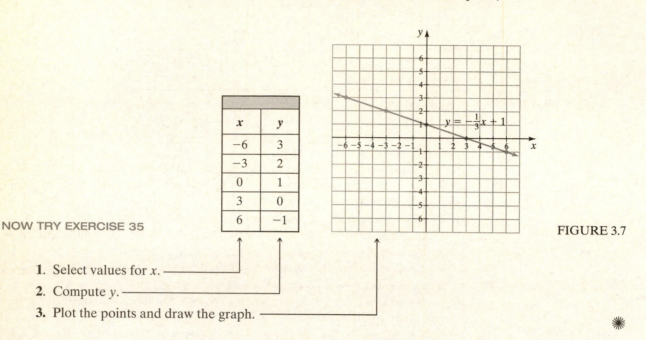

NOW TRY EXERCISE 35

x	y
-6	3
-3	2
0	1
3	0
6	-1

FIGURE 3.7

1. Select values for x.
2. Compute y.
3. Plot the points and draw the graph.

In Example 4, notice that we selected values of x that were multiples of 3 so we would not have to work with fractions.

If we are asked to graph an equation not solved for y, such as $x + 3y = 3$, our first step will be to solve the equation for y. For example, if we solve $x + 3y = 3$ for y using the procedure discussed in Section 2.2, we obtain

$$x + 3y = 3$$
$$3y = -x + 3 \qquad \text{\textit{Subtract x from both sides.}}$$
$$y = \frac{-x + 3}{3} \qquad \text{\textit{Divide both sides by 3.}}$$
$$y = \frac{-x}{3} + \frac{3}{3} = -\frac{1}{3}x + 1$$

The resulting equation, $y = -\frac{1}{3}x + 1$, is the same equation we graphed in Example 4. Therefore, the graph of $x + 3y = 3$ is also illustrated in Figure 3.7.

3 Graph Nonlinear Equations

There are many equations whose graphs are not straight lines. Such equations are called **nonlinear equations**. To graph nonlinear equations by plotting points, we follow the same procedure used to graph linear equations. However, since the graphs are not straight lines, we may need to plot more points to draw the graphs.

EXAMPLE 5 Graph $y = x^2 - 4$.

Solution We select some values for x and find the corresponding values of y. Then we plot the points and connect them with a smooth curve. When we substitute values for x and evaluate the right side of the equation, we follow the order of operations discussed in Section 1.4. For example, if $x = -3$, then $y = (-3)^2 - 4 = 9 - 4 = 5$. The graph is shown in Figure 3.8.

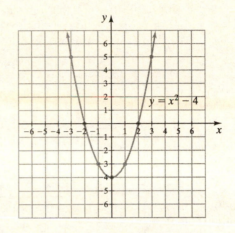

x	y
-3	5
-2	0
-1	-3
0	-4
1	-3
2	0
3	5

FIGURE 3.8

If we substituted 4 for x, y would equal 12. When $x = 5$, $y = 21$. Notice that this graph rises steeply as x moves away from the origin.

NOW TRY EXERCISE 41

EXAMPLE 6 Graph $y = \dfrac{1}{x}$.

Solution We begin by selecting values for x and finding the corresponding values of y. We then plot the points and draw the graph. Notice that if we substitute 0 for x, we obtain $y = \frac{1}{0}$. Since $\frac{1}{0}$ is undefined, we cannot use 0 as a first coordinate. There will be no part of the graph at $x = 0$. We will plot points to the left of $x = 0$, and points to the right of $x = 0$ separately. Select points close to 0 to see what happens to the graph as x gets close to $x = 0$. Note, for example, that when $x = -\frac{1}{2}$, $y = \frac{1}{-1/2} = -2$. This graph has two branches, one to the left of the y-axis and one to the right of the y-axis, as shown in Figure 3.9.

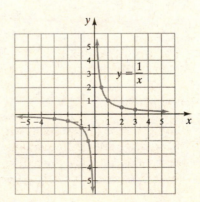

x	y
-3	$-\frac{1}{3}$
-2	$-\frac{1}{2}$
-1	-1
$-\frac{1}{2}$	-2
$\frac{1}{2}$	2
1	1
2	$\frac{1}{2}$
3	$\frac{1}{3}$

NOW TRY EXERCISE 51

FIGURE 3.9

In the graph for Example 6, notice that for values of x far to the right of 0, or far to the left of 0, the graph approaches the x-axis but does not touch it. For example when $x = 1000$, $y = 0.001$ and when $x = -1000$, $y = -0.001$. Can you explain why y can never have a value of 0?

EXAMPLE 7 Graph $y = |x|$.

Solution Recall that $|x|$ is read "the absolute value of x." Absolute values were discussed in Section 1.3. To graph this absolute value equation, we select some values for x and find the corresponding values of y. For example, if $x = -4$, then $y = |-4| = 4$. Then we plot the points and draw the graph.

Notice that this graph is V-shaped, as shown in Figure 3.10.

x	y
-4	4
-3	3
-2	2
-1	1
0	0
1	1
2	2
3	3
4	4

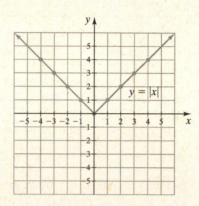

FIGURE 3.10 ✳

AVOIDING COMMON ERRORS

When graphing nonlinear equations, many students do not plot enough points to get a true picture of the graph. For example, when graphing $y = \dfrac{1}{x}$ many students consider only integer values of x. Following is a table of values for the equation and two graphs that contain the points indicated in the table.

x	-3	-2	-1	1	2	3
y	$-\frac{1}{3}$	$-\frac{1}{2}$	-1	1	$\frac{1}{2}$	$\frac{1}{3}$

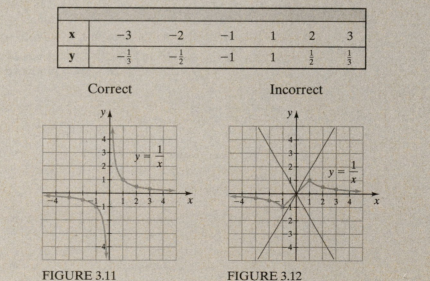

Correct — FIGURE 3.11

Incorrect — FIGURE 3.12

(continued on the next page)

If you select and plot fractional values of x near 0, as was done in Example 6, you get the graph in Figure 3.11. The graph in Figure 3.12 cannot be correct because the equation is not defined when x is 0 and therefore the graph cannot cross the y-axis. Whenever you plot a graph that contains a variable in the denominator, select values for the variable that are very close to the value that makes the denominator 0 and observe what happens. For example, when graphing $y = \dfrac{1}{x-3}$ you should use values of x close to 3, such as 2.9 and 3.1 or 2.99 and 3.01, and see what values you obtain for y.

Also, when graphing nonlinear equations, it is a good idea to consider both positive and negative values. For example, if you used only positive values of x when graphing $y = |x|$, the graph would appear to be a straight line going through the origin, instead of the V-shaped graph shown in Figure 3.10.

4 Use a Graphing Calculator

If an equation is complex, finding ordered pairs can be time consuming. In this section we present a general procedure that can be used to graph equations using a **graphing calculator**.

A primary use of a graphing calculator is to graph equations. A **graphing calculator window** is the rectangular screen in which a graph is displayed. Figure 3.13 shows a TI-83 Plus calculator window with some information illustrated; Figure 3.14 shows the meaning of the information given in Figure 3.13.

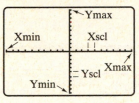

FIGURE 3.13 **FIGURE 3.14**

The x-axis on the *standard calculator screen* goes from -10 (the minimum value of x, Xmin) to 10 (the maximum value of x, Xmax) with a scale of 1. Therefore each tick mark represents 1 unit (Xscl = 1). The y-axis goes from -10 (the minimum value of y, Ymin) to 10 (the maximum value of y, Ymax) with a scale of 1 (Yscl = 1).

Since the window is rectangular, the distances between tick marks on the standard window are greater on the horizontal axis than on the vertical axis.

When graphing you will often need to change these window values. Read your graphing calculator manual to learn how to change the window setting. On the TI-83 Plus, you press the [WINDOW] key and then change the settings.

Since the grapher does not display the x- and y-values in the window, we will occasionally list a set of values below the screen. Figure 3.15 shows a TI-83 Plus calculator window with the equation $y = -\frac{1}{2}x + 4$ graphed. Below the window we show six numbers, which represent in order: Xmin, Xmax, Xscl, Ymin, Ymax, and Yscl. The Xscl and Yscl represent the scale on the x- and y-axes, respectively. When we are showing the standard calculator window, we will generally not show these values below the window.

To graph the equation $y = -\frac{1}{2}x + 4$ on a TI-83 Plus, you would press

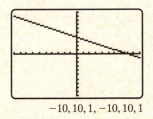

$-10, 10, 1, -10, 10, 1$

FIGURE 3.15

[Y=] [(−)] [(] [1] [÷] [2] [)] [X, T, Θ, n] [+] 4

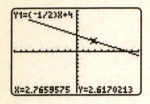

FIGURE 3.16

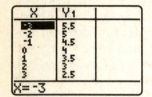

FIGURE 3.17

NOW TRY EXERCISE 93

Then when you press $\boxed{\text{GRAPH}}$, the equation is graphed. The $\boxed{\text{X, T, }\Theta\text{, }n}$ key can be used to enter any of the symbols shown on the key. In this book this key will always be used to enter the variable x.

Most graphing calculators offer a **TRACE feature** that allows you to investigate individual points after a graph is displayed. Often the $\boxed{\text{TRACE}}$ key is pressed to access this feature. After pressing the $\boxed{\text{TRACE}}$ key, you can move the flashing cursor along the line by pressing the arrow keys. As the flashing cursor moves along the line, the values of x and y change to correspond with the position of the cursor. Figure 3.16 shows the graph in Figure 3.15 after the $\boxed{\text{TRACE}}$ key has been pressed and the right arrow key has been pressed a few times.

Many graphing calculators also provide a **TABLE feature** that will illustrate a table of ordered pairs for any equation entered. On the TI-83 Plus, since TABLE appears above the $\boxed{\text{GRAPH}}$ key, to obtain a table you press $\boxed{2^{\text{nd}}}$ $\boxed{\text{GRAPH}}$. Figure 3.17 shows a table of values for the equation $y = -\frac{1}{2}x + 4$. You can scroll up and down the table by using the arrow keys.

Using TBLSET (for Table setup), you can control the x-values that appear in the table. For example, if you want the table to show values of x in tenths, you could do this using TBLSET.

This section is just a brief introduction to graphing equations, the TRACE feature, and the TABLE feature on a graphing calculator. You should read your graphing calculator manual to learn how to fully utilize these features.

5 Interpret Graphs

We see many different types of graphs daily in newspapers, in magazines, on television, and so on. Throughout this book, we present a variety of graphs. Since being able to draw and interpret graphs is very important, we will study this further in Section 3.2. In Example 8 you must understand and interpret graphs to answer the question.

EXAMPLE 8 When Jim Herring went to see his mother in Cincinnati, he boarded a Southwest Airlines plane. The plane sat at the gate for 20 minutes, taxied to the runway, and then took off. The plane flew at about 600 miles per hour for about 2 hours. It then reduced its speed to about 300 miles per hour and circled the Cincinnati Airport for about 15 minutes before it came in for a landing. After landing, the plane taxied to the gate and stopped. Which graph in Figure 3.18a–3.18d best illustrates this situation?

FIGURE 3.18 (*Figure continued on the next page*)

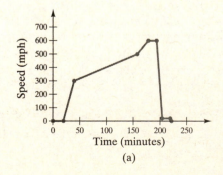

(a)

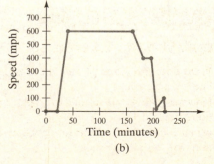

(b)

298

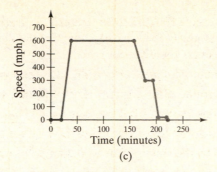

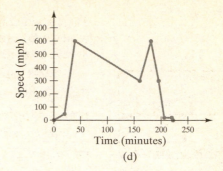

FIGURE 3.18

(c) (d)

Solution The graph that depicts the situation described is (c), reproduced with annotations in Figure 3.19. The graph shows speed versus time, with time on the horizontal axis. While the plane sat at the gate for 20 minutes its speed was 0 miles per hour (the horizontal line at 0 from 0 to 20 minutes). After 20 minutes the plane took off, and its speed increased to 600 miles per hour (the near-vertical line going from 0 to 600 mph). The plane then flew at about 600 miles per hour for 2 hours (the horizontal line at about 600 mph). It then slowed down to about 300 miles per hour (the near-vertical line from 600 mph to 300 mph). Next the plane circled at about 300 miles per hour for about 15 minutes (the horizontal line at about 300 mph). The plane then came in for a landing (the near-vertical line from about 300 mph to about 20 mph). It then taxied to the gate (the horizontal line at about 20 mph). Finally, it stopped at the gate (the near-vertical line when the speed dropped to 0 mph).

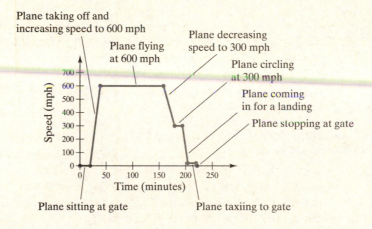

FIGURE 3.19

NOW TRY EXERCISE 81

Exercise Set 3.1

Concept/Writing Exercises

✎ **1. a)** What does the graph of any linear equation look like? a straight line

b) How many points are needed to graph a linear equation? Explain. 2

✎ **2.** How many solutions does a linear equation in two variables have? an infinite number

3. They are in a straight line.

✎ **3.** What does it mean when a set of points is collinear?

✎ **4.** When graphing the equation $y = \dfrac{1}{x}$, what value cannot be substituted for x? Explain. 0

5. $A(3,1), B(-6,0), C(2,-4), D(-2,-4), E(0,3), F(-8,1), G\left(\frac{3}{2},-1\right)$

Practice the Skills   6. $A(8,5), B(14,0), C(6,-15), D(-4,20), E(0,-20), F(-10,-5), G(-5,10)$

List the ordered pairs corresponding to the indicated points.

5.

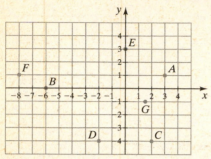

6.

7. Graph the following points on the same axes.

   $A(4,2)\quad B(-6,2)\quad C(0,-1)\quad D(-2,0)$
   See graphing answer section, page G1.

8. Graph the following points on the same axes.

   $A(-4,-2)\quad B(3,2)\quad C(2,-3)\quad D(-3,3)$
   See graphing answer section, page G1.

Determine the quadrant in which each point is located.

9. $(3,5)$ I

10. $(-3,1)$ II

11. $(4,-2)$ IV

12. $(36,41)$ I

13. $(-35,18)$ II

14. $(-24,-8)$ III

15. $(-6,-19)$ III

16. $(8,-120)$ IV

Determine whether the given ordered pair is a solution to the given equation.

17. $(2,21);\ \ y = 2x - 5$ no

18. $(1,1);\ \ 2x + 3y = 6$ no

19. $(-4,-2);\ \ y = |x| + 2$ no

20. $(1,1);\ \ y = x^2 + x - 1$ yes

21. $(-2,5);\ \ s = 2r^2 - r - 5$ yes

22. $\left(\frac{1}{2},\frac{5}{2}\right);\ \ y = |x - 3|$ yes

23. $(2,1);\ \ -a^2 + 2b^2 = -2$ yes

24. $(-10,-2);\ \ |p| - 3|q| = 4$ yes

25. $\left(\frac{1}{2},\frac{3}{2}\right);\ \ 2x^2 + 4x - y = 0$ no

26. $\left(-3,\frac{11}{2}\right);\ \ 2n^2 + 3m = 2$ no

Graph each equation.   See graphing answer section, pages G1 and G2.

27. $y = x$

28. $y = 3x$

29. $y = \frac{1}{2}x$

30. $y = -\frac{1}{3}x$

31. $y = 2x + 4$

32. $y = x + 2$

33. $y = -3x - 5$

34. $y = -2x + 2$

35. $y = \frac{1}{2}x - 1$

36. $y = -\frac{1}{3}x + 2$

37. $y = -\frac{1}{2}x - 3$

38. $y = -\frac{1}{3}x + 4$

39. $y = x^2$

40. $y = x^2 - 4$

41. $y = -x^2$

42. $y = -x^2 + 4$

43. $y = |x| + 1$

44. $y = |x| + 2$

45. $y = -|x|$

46. $y = |x| - 2$

47. $y = x^3$

48. $y = -x^3$

49. $y = x^3 + 1$

50. $y = \frac{1}{x}$

51. $y = -\frac{1}{x}$

52. $x^2 = 1 + y$

53. $x = |y|$

54. $x = y^2$

In Exercises 55–62, use a calculator to obtain at least eight points that are solutions to the equation. Then graph the equation by plotting the points.   See graphing answer section, pages G2 and G3.

55. $y = x^3 - x^2 - x + 1$

56. $y = -x^3 + x^2 + x - 1$

57. $y = \frac{1}{x+1}$

58. $y = \frac{1}{x} + 1$

59. $y = \sqrt{x}$

60. $y = \sqrt{x+4}$

61. $y = \frac{1}{x^2}$

62. $y = \frac{|x^2|}{2}$

300

65. a) See graphing answer section, page G3.   **66. a)** See graphing answer section, page G3.   **67. c)** 2001, 2002, 2003

Problem Solving
68. a) ≈7 million hectares   **b)** ≈33 million hectares

63. Is the point represented by the ordered pair $\left(\dfrac{1}{3}, \dfrac{1}{12}\right)$ on the graph of the equation $y = \dfrac{x^2}{x + 1}$? Explain.   yes

64. Is the point represented by the ordered pair $\left(-\dfrac{1}{2}, -\dfrac{3}{5}\right)$ on the graph of the equation $y = \dfrac{x^2 + 1}{x^2 - 1}$? Explain.   no

65. a) Plot the points $A(2, 7)$, $B(2, 3)$, and $C(6, 3)$, and then draw $\overline{AB}$, $\overline{AC}$, and $\overline{BC}$. ($\overline{AB}$ represents the line segment from A to B.)

   b) Find the area of the figure.   8 sq units

66. a) Plot the points $A(-4, 5)$, $B(2, 5)$, $C(2, -3)$, and $D(-4, -3)$, and then draw $\overline{AB}$, $\overline{BC}$, $\overline{CD}$, and $\overline{DA}$.

   b) Find the area of the figure.   48 sq units

67. *Personal Computer Sales* The following graph shows worldwide shipments of personal computers from 1999 to 2003. Shipments are measured in millions of computers.

Worldwide Shipments of Personal Computers

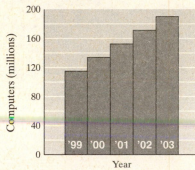

Source: International Data Corporation

a) Estimate the worldwide shipments of computers in 1999.   115 million

b) Estimate the worldwide shipments of computers in 2003.   190 million

c) In which years were the worldwide shipments of personal computers greater than 140 million units?

d) Does the increase in worldwide shipments of personal computers from 1999 to 2003 appear to be approximately linear? Explain.   yes

68. *Genetically Modified Crops* Worldwide production of genetically modified crops—in both developing nations and industrial nations—is rapidly increasing. The graph at the top of the next column shows the land area devoted to genetically modified crops for developing nations, industrial nations, and worldwide from 1995–2000. Land area is given in millions of hectares. A hectare is a metric system unit that is approximately equal to 2.471 acres.

Global Area of Genetically Modified Crops

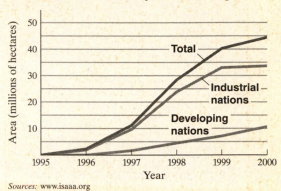

Sources: www.isaaa.org

a) Estimate the area in developing nations devoted to genetically modified crops in 1999.

b) Estimate the area in industrial nations devoted to genetically modified crops in 1999.

c) In what years from 1995 to 2000 was the total area devoted to genetically modified crops less than 20 million hectares?   1995, 1996, 1997

d) In what years from 1995 to 2000 was the total area devoted to genetically modified crops greater than 35 million hectares?   1999, 2000

We will discuss many of the concepts introduced in Exercises 69–76 in Section 3.4.

69. Graph $y = x + 1$, $y = x + 3$, and $y = x - 1$ on the same axes.   See graphing answer section, page G3.

   a) What do you notice about the equations and the values where the graphs intersect the y-axis?

   b) Do all equations seem to have the same slant (or slope)?   yes

70. Graph $y = \dfrac{1}{2}x$, $y = \dfrac{1}{2}x + 3$, and $y = \dfrac{1}{2}x - 4$ on the same axes.   See graphing answer section, page G3.

   a) What do you notice about the equations and the values where the graphs intersect the y-axis?

   b) Do all of these graphs seem to have the same slant (or slope)?   yes

71. Graph $y = 2x$. Determine the *rate of change* of y with respect to x. That is, by how many units does y change compared to each unit change in x?   2

72. Graph $y = 3x$. Determine the rate of change of y with respect to x.   3

73. Graph $y = 3x + 2$. Determine the rate of change of y with respect to x.   3

74. Graph $y = \frac{1}{2}x$. Determine the rate of change of y with respect to x. $\frac{1}{2}$

69. a) The graphs cross at the constants.   **70. a)** The graphs cross at the constants.   **71.–74.** See graphing answer section, page G3.

75. The ordered pair $(3, -6)$ represents one point on the graph of a linear equation. If y increases 4 units for each unit increase in x on the graph, find two other solutions to the equation. $(4, -2), (5, 2)$. *Other answers are possible.*

76. The ordered pair $(1, -4)$ represents one point on the graph of a linear equation. If y increases 3 units for each unit increase in x on the graph, find two other solutions to the equation. $(2, -1), (3, 2)$. *Other answers are possible.*

Match Exercises 77–80 with the corresponding graph of elevation above sea level versus time, labeled a–d, below.

77. Mary Leeseberg walked for 5 minutes on level ground. Then for 5 minutes she climbed a slight hill. Then she walked on level ground for 5 minutes. Then for the next 5 minutes she climbed a steep hill. During the next 10 minutes she descended uniformly until she reached the height at which she had started. c

78. Don Gordon walked on level ground for 5 minutes. Then he walked down a steep hill for 10 minutes. For the next 5 minutes he walked on level ground. For the next 5 minutes he walked back up to his starting height. For the next 5 minutes he walked on level ground. d

79. Nancy Johnson started out by walking up a steep hill for 5 minutes. For the next 5 minutes she walked down a steep hill to an elevation lower than her starting point. For the next 10 minutes she walked on level ground. For the next 10 minutes she walked up a slight hill, at which time she reached her starting elevation. a

80. James Condor started out by walking up a hill for 5 minutes. For the next 10 minutes he walked down a hill to an elevation equal to his starting elevation. For the next 10 minutes he walked on level ground. For the next 5 minutes he walked downhill. b

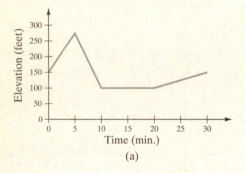

(a)

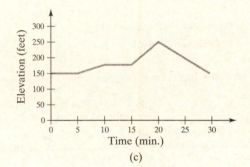

(c)

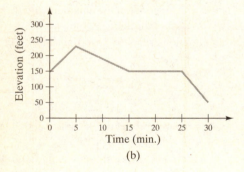

(b)

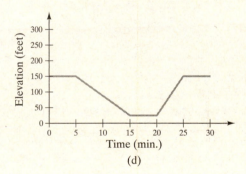

(d)

Match Exercises 81–84 with the corresponding graph of speed versus time, labeled a–d on page 161.

81. To go to work, Cletidus Hunt walked for 3 minutes, waited for the train for 5 minutes, rode the train for 15 minutes, then walked for 7 minutes. d

82. To go to work, Tyrone Williams drove in stop-and-go traffic for 5 minutes, then drove on the expressway for 20 minutes, then drove in stop-and-go traffic for 5 minutes. c

83. To go to work, Sheila Washington drove on a country road for 10 minutes, then drove on a highway for 12 minutes, then drove in stop-and-go traffic for 8 minutes. b

84. To go to work, Brenda Pinkney rode her bike uphill for 10 minutes, then rode downhill for 15 minutes, then rode on a level street for 5 minutes. a

302

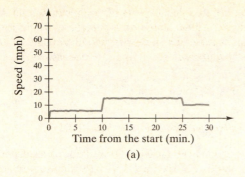

(a)

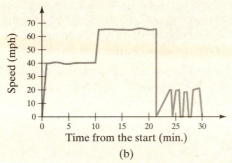

(b)

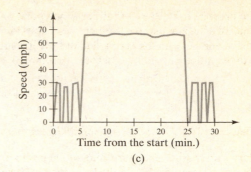

(c)

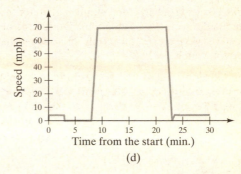

(d)

Match Exercises 85–88 with the corresponding graph of speed versus time, labeled a–d.

85. Christina Dwyer walked for 5 minutes to warm up, jogged for 20 minutes, and then walked for 5 minutes to cool down. b

86. Annie Droullard went for a leisurely bike ride at a constant speed for 30 minutes. a

87. Michael Odu took a 30-minute walk through his neighborhood. He stopped very brietly on 7 occasions to pick up trash. d

88. Richard Dai walked through his neighborhood and stopped 3 times to chat with his neighbors. He was gone from his house a total of 30 minutes. c

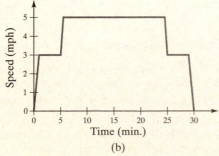

(a)

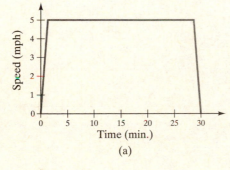

(b)

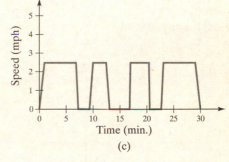

(c)

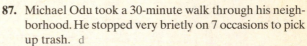

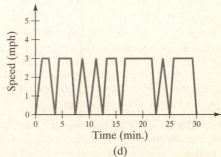

(d)

Match Exercises 89–92 with the corresponding graph of distance traveled versus time, labeled a–d. Recall from Chapter 2 that distance = rate × time. Selected distances are indicated on the graphs.

🔒 **89.** Train A traveled at a speed of 40 mph for 1 hour, then 80 mph for 2 hours, and then 60 mph for 3 hours. b

90. Train C traveled at a speed of 80 mph for 2 hours, then stayed in a station for 1 hour, and then traveled 40 mph for 3 hours. a

91. Train B traveled at a speed of 20 mph for 2 hours, then 60 mph for 3 hours, and then 80 mph for 1 hour. d

92. Train D traveled at 30 mph for 1 hour, then 65 mph for 2 hours, and then 30 mph for 3 hours. c

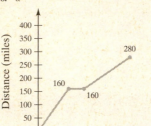

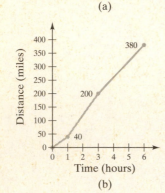

(a)

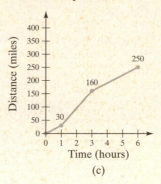

(c)

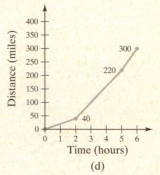

(b)

(d)

🖩 *Use a graphing calculator to graph each function. Make sure you select values for the window that will show the curvature of the graph. Then, if your calculator can display tables, display a table of values in which the x-values extend by units, from 0 to 6.*
See graphing answer section, pages G3 and G4.

93. $y = 2x - 3$

94. $y = \dfrac{1}{3}x + 2$

95. $y = x^2 - 2x - 8$

96. $y = -x^2 + 16$

97. $y = x^3 - 2x + 4$

98. $y = 2x^3 - 6x^2 - 1$

Challenge Problems

Graph each equation.   See graphing answer section, page G4.

99. $y = |x - 2|$

100. $x = y^2 + 2$

Group Activity

101. b) $\left(\dfrac{x_1 + x_2}{2}, \dfrac{y_1 + y_2}{2} \right)$

102. b) 40 sq units **d)** yes, see **a)**; each has area 40 sq units

Discuss and work Exercises 101–102 as a group.

101. a) Group member 1: Plot the points $(-2, 4)$ and $(6, 8)$. Determine the *midpoint* of the line segment connecting these points. $(2, 6)$
Group member 2: Follow the above instructions for the points $(-3, -2)$ and $(5, 6)$. $(1, 2)$
Group member 3: Follow the above instructions for the points $(4, 1)$ and $(-2, 4)$. $\left(1, \dfrac{5}{2}\right)$

  b) As a group, determine a formula for the midpoint of the line segment connecting the points (x_1, y_1) and (x_2, y_2). (*Note*: We will discuss the midpoint formula further in Chapter 10.)

102. Three points on a parallelogram are $A(3, 5)$, $B(8, 5)$, and $C(-1, -3)$.

  a) Individually determine a fourth point D that completes the parallelogram. $(4, -3)$ or $(-6, -3)$ or $(12, 13)$

  b) Individually compute the area of your parallelogram.

  c) Compare your answers. Did you all get the same answers? If not, why not? Answers will vary.

  d) Is there more than one point that can be used to complete the parallelogram? If so, give the points and find the corresponding areas of each parallelogram.

Cumulative Review Exercises

[2.2] 103. Evaluate $\dfrac{-b + \sqrt{b^2 - 4ac}}{2a}$ for $a = 2, b = 7$, and $c = -15$. $\frac{3}{2}$

[2.3] 104. ***Truck Rental*** Hertz Truck Rental charges a daily fee of $60 plus 10¢ a mile. National Automobile Rental Agency charges a daily fee of $50 plus 24¢ a mile for the same truck. What distance would you have to drive in 1 day to make the cost of renting from Hertz equal to the cost of renting from National? ≈ 71 mi

[2.5] 105. Solve the inequality $-4 \le \dfrac{4 - 3x}{2} < 5$. Write the solution in set builder notation. $\{x | -2 < x \le 4\}$

[2.6] 106. Find the solution set for the inequality $|3x + 2| > 5$. $\left\{ x | x < -\frac{7}{3} \text{ or } x > 1 \right\}$

3.2 FUNCTIONS

SSM

Study Guide

CD/Video

MathPro 4/5

PH Math
Tutor Center

prenhall.com/Angel

1   Understand relations.
2   Recognize functions.
3   Use the vertical line test.
4   Understand function notation.
5   Applications of functions in daily life.

1   Understand Relations

In real life we often find that one quantity is related to a second quantity. For example, the amount you spend for oranges is related to the number of oranges you purchase. The speed of a sailboat is related to the speed of the wind. And the income tax you pay is related to the income you earn.

Suppose oranges cost 30 cents apiece. Then one orange costs 30 cents, two oranges cost 60 cents, three oranges cost 90 cents, and so on. We can list this information, or relationship, as a set of ordered pairs by listing the number of oranges first and the cost, in cents, second. The ordered pairs that represent this situation are $(1, 30)$, $(2, 60)$, $(3, 90)$, and so on. An equation that represents this situation is $c = 30n$, where c is the cost, in cents, and n is the number of oranges. Since the cost depends on the number of oranges, we say that the cost is the *dependent variable* and the number of oranges is the *independent variable*.

Now consider the equation $y = 2x + 3$. In this equation, the value obtained for y depends on the value selected for x. Therefore x is the *independent variable* and y is the *dependent variable*. Note that in this example, unlike with the oranges, there is no physical connection between x and y. The variable x is the independent variable and y is the dependent variable simply because of their placement in the equation.

For an equation in variables x and y, if the value of y depends on the value of x, then y is the **dependent variable** and x is the **independent variable**. Since related quantities can be represented as ordered pairs, the concept of a **relation** can be defined as follows.

DEFINITION   A **relation** is any set of ordered pairs.

---

2   Recognize Functions

We now develop the idea of a **function**—one of the most important concepts in mathematics. A function is a special type of relation in which each element in one set (called the domain) corresponds to *exactly one* element in a second set (called the range).

Consider the oranges that cost 30 cents apiece that we just discussed. We can illustrate the number of oranges and the cost of the oranges using Figure 3.20.

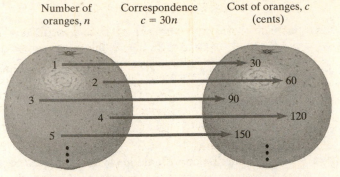

Number of oranges, n Correspondence $c = 30n$ Cost of oranges, c (cents)

FIGURE 3.20

Notice that each number in the set of numbers of oranges corresponds to (or is mapped to) exactly one number in the set of costs. Therefore, this correspondence is a function. The set consisting of the number of oranges, $\{1, 2, 3, 4, 5, \ldots\}$, is called the **domain**. The set consisting of the costs in cents, $\{30, 60, 90, 120, 150, \ldots\}$, is called the **range**. In general, the set of values for the independent variable is called the **domain**. The set of values for the dependent variable is called the **range**, see Figure 3.21.

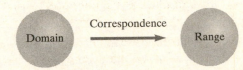

Correspondence

Domain   Range

FIGURE 3.21

EXAMPLE 1 Determine whether each correspondence is a function.

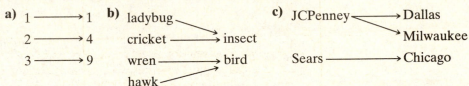

a)
1 ⟶ 1
2 ⟶ 4
3 ⟶ 9

b)
ladybug
cricket ⟶ insect
wren ⟶ bird
hawk

c)
JCPenney ⟶ Dallas
⟶ Milwaukee
Sears ⟶ Chicago

Solution **a)** For a correspondence to be a function, each element in the domain must correspond with exactly one element in the range. Here the domain is $\{1, 2, 3\}$ and the range is $\{1, 4, 9\}$. Since each element in the domain corresponds to exactly one element in the range, this correspondence is a function.

b) Here the domain is {ladybug, cricket, wren, hawk} and the range is {insect, bird}. Even though the domain has four elements and the range has two elements, each element in the domain corresponds with exactly one element in the range. Thus, this correspondence is a function.

c) Here the domain is {JCPenney, Sears} and the range is {Dallas, Milwaukee, Chicago}. Notice that JCPenney corresponds to both Dallas and Milwaukee. Therefore each element in the domain *does not* correspond to exactly one element in the range. Thus, this correspondence is a relation but *not* a function. ✳

NOW TRY EXERCISE 17

Now we will formally define function.

DEFINITION A **function** is a correspondence between a first set of elements, the domain, and a second set of elements, the range, such that each element of the domain corresponds to *exactly one* element in the range.

EXAMPLE 2   Which of the following relations are functions?

a) $\{(1, 4), (2, 3), (3, 5), (-1, 3)(0, 6)\}$

b) $\{(-1, 3)(4, 2), (3, 1), (2, 6), (3, 5)\}$

Solution   **a)** The domain is the set of first coordinates in the set of ordered pairs, $\{1, 2, 3, -1, 0\}$, and the range is the set of second coordinates, $\{4, 3, 5, 6\}$. Notice that when listing the range, we only include the number 3 once, even though it appears in both $(2, 3)$ and $(-1, 3)$. Examining the set of ordered pairs, we see that each number in the domain corresponds with exactly one number in the range. For example, the 1 in the domain corresponds with only the 4 in the range, and so on. No x-value corresponds to more than one y-value. Therefore, this relation *is a function*.

b) The domain is $\{-1, 4, 3, 2\}$ and the range is $\{3, 2, 1, 6, 5\}$. Notice that 3 appears as the first coordinate in two ordered pairs even though it is listed only once in the set of elements that represent the domain. Since the ordered pairs $(3, 1)$ and $(3, 5)$ have *the same first coordinate* and a different second coordinate, each value in the domain does not correspond to exactly one value in the range. Therefore, this relation is *not a function*.

NOW TRY EXERCISE 23

Example 2 leads to an alternate definition of function.

DEFINITION | A **function** is a set of ordered pairs in which no *first* coordinate is repeated.

If the second coordinate in a set of ordered pairs repeats, the set of ordered pairs may still be a function, as in Example 2 **a)**. However, if two or more ordered pairs contain the same first coordinate, as in Example 2 **b)**, the set of ordered pairs is not a function.

3   Use the Vertical Line Test

The **graph of a function or relation** is the graph of its set of ordered pairs. The two sets of ordered pairs in Example 2 are graphed in Figures 3.22a and 3.22b. Notice that in the function in Figure 3.22a it is not possible to draw a vertical line that intersects two points. We should expect this because, in a function, each x-value must correspond to exactly one y-value. In Figure 3.22b we *can* draw a vertical line through the points $(3, 1)$ and $(3, 5)$. This shows that each x-value does not correspond to exactly one y-value, and the graph does not represent a function.

This method of determining whether a graph represents a function is called the **vertical line test**.

Function

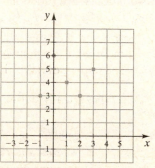

Not a function

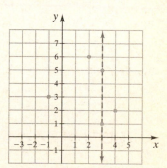

FIGURE 3.22   (a) First set of ordered pairs   (b) Second set of ordered pairs

Vertical Line Test

If a vertical line can be drawn through any part of the graph and the line intersects another part of the graph, the graph does not represent a function. If a vertical line cannot be drawn to intersect the graph at more than one point, the graph represents a function.

We use the vertical line test to show that Figure 3.23b represents a function and Figures 3.23a and 3.23c do not represent functions.

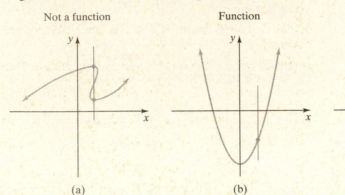

FIGURE 3.23   (a)   (b)   (c)

EXAMPLE 3   Use the vertical line test to determine whether the following graphs represent functions. Also determine the domain and range of each function or relation.

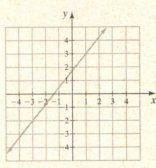

FIGURE 3.24

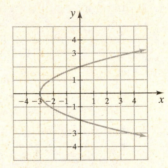

FIGURE 3.25

Solution   **a)** A vertical line cannot be drawn to intersect the graph in Figure 3.24 at more than one point. Thus this is the graph of a function. Since the line extends indefinitely in both directions, every value of x will be included in the domain. The domain is the set of real numbers.

$$\text{Domain: } \mathbb{R} \quad \text{or} \quad (-\infty, \infty)$$

The range is also the set of real numbers since all values of y are included on the graph.

$$\text{Range: } \mathbb{R} \quad \text{or} \quad (-\infty, \infty)$$

b) Since a vertical line can be drawn to intersect the graph in Figure 3.25 at more than one point, this is *not* the graph of a function. The domain of this relation is the set of values greater than or equal to −3.

$$\text{Domain: } \{x | x \geq -3\} \quad \text{or} \quad [-3, \infty)$$

The range is the set of y-values, which can be any real number.

$$\text{Range: } \mathbb{R} \quad \text{or} \quad (-\infty, \infty)$$

EXAMPLE 4   Consider the graph shown in Figure 3.26.

a) What member of the range is paired with 4 in the domain?

b) What members of the domain are paired with −2 in the range?

c) What is the domain of the function?

d) What is the range of the function?

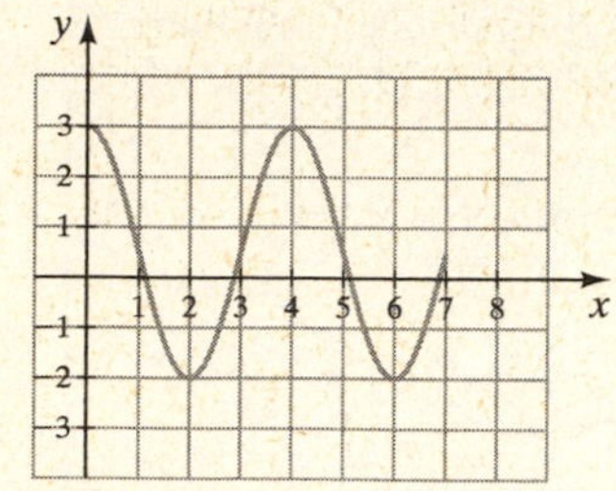

Solution   **a)** The range is the set of *y*-values. The *y*-value paired with the *x*-value of 4 is 3.

b) The domain is the set of *x*-values. The *x*-values paired with the *y*-value of −2 are 2 and 6.

c) The domain is the set of *x*-values, 0 through 7. Thus the domain is

$$\{x|0 \le x \le 7\} \quad \text{or} \quad [0, 7]$$

d) The range is the set of *y*-values, −2 through 3. Thus, the range is

NOW TRY EXERCISE 33

$$\{y|-2 \le y \le 3\} \quad \text{or} \quad [-2, 3]$$

FIGURE 3.26

EXAMPLE 5   Figure 3.27 illustrates a graph of speed versus time of a man out for a walk and jog. Write a story about the man's outing that corresponds to this function.

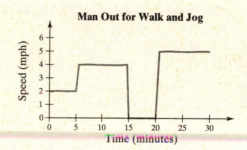

Man Out for Walk and Jog

FIGURE 3.27

Solution   **Understand**   The horizontal axis is time and the vertical axis is speed. When the graph is horizontal it means the person is traveling at the constant speed indicated on the vertical axis. The near-vertical lines that increase with time (or have a positive slope, as will be discussed later) indicate an increase in speed, whereas the near-vertical lines that decrease with time (or have a negative slope) indicate a decrease in speed.

Answer   Here is one possible interpretation of the graph. The man walks for about 5 minutes at a speed of about 2 miles per hour. Then the man speeds up to about 4 miles per hour and walks fast or jogs at about this speed for about 10 minutes. Then the man slows down and stops, and then rests for about 5 minutes. Finally, the man speeds up to about 5 miles per hour and jogs at this speed for about **NOW TRY EXERCISE 65**   10 minutes.

4 Understand Function Notation

In Section 3.1 we graphed a number of equations, as summarized in Table 3.1. If you examine each equation in the table, you will see that they are all functions, since their graphs pass the vertical line test.

TABLE 3.1 Example			
Section 3.1 example	**Equation graphed**	**Graph**	**Does the graph represent a function?**
3	$y = x$		Yes
4	$y = -\dfrac{1}{3}x + 1$		Yes
5	$y = x^2 - 4$		Yes
6	$y = \dfrac{1}{x}$		Yes
7	$y = \lvert x \rvert$		Yes

Since the graph of each equation shown represents a function, we may refer to each equation in the table as a function. When we refer to an equation in variables x and y as a function, it means that the graph of the equation satisfies the criteria for a function. That is, each x-value corresponds to exactly one y-value, and the graph of the equation passes the vertical line test.

Not all equations are functions, as you will see in Chapter 10, where we discuss equations of circles and ellipses. However, until we get to Chapter 10, all equations that we discuss will be functions.

Consider the equation $y = 3x + 2$. By applying the vertical line test to its graph (Fig. 3.28), we can see that the graph represents a function. When an equation in variables x and y is a function, we often write the equation using **function notation**, $f(x)$, read "f of x." Since the equation $y = 3x + 2$ is a function, and the value of y depends on the value of x, we say that **y is a function of x**. When we are given a linear equation in variables x and y, *that is solved for y*, we can write the equation in function notation by substituting $f(x)$ for y. In this case, we can write the equation in function notation as $f(x) = 3x + 2$. The notation $f(x)$ represents the dependent variable *and does not mean f times x*. Other letters may be used to indicate functions. For example, $g(x)$ and $h(x)$ also represent functions of x, and in Section 5.1 we will use $P(x)$ to represent polynomial functions.

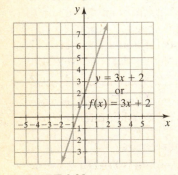

FIGURE 3.28

Functions written in function notation are also equations since they contain an equal sign. We may refer to $y = 3x + 2$ as either an equation or a function. Similarly, we may refer to $f(x) = 3x + 2$ as either a function or an equation.

If y is a function of x, the notation $f(5)$, read "f of 5," means the value of y when x is 5. To evaluate a function for a specific value of x, substitute that value for x in the function. For example, if $f(x) = 3x + 2$, then $f(5)$ is found as follows:

$$f(x) = 3x + 2$$
$$f(5) = 3(5) + 2 = 17$$

Therefore, when x is 5, y is 17. The ordered pair $(5, 17)$ would appear on the graph of $y = 3x + 2$.

HELPFUL HINT

Linear equations that are not solved for y can be written using function notation by solving the equation for y, then replacing y with $f(x)$. For example, the equation $-9x + 3y = 6$ becomes $y = 3x + 2$ when solved for y. We can therefore write $f(x) = 3x + 2$.

EXAMPLE 6 If $f(x) = -4x^2 + 3x - 2$, find

a) $f(2)$ **b)** $f(-1)$ **c)** $f(a)$

Solution **a)** $f(x) = -4x^2 + 3x - 2$

$$f(2) = -4(2)^2 + 3(2) - 2 = -4(4) + 6 - 2 = -16 + 6 - 2 = -12$$

b) $f(-1) = -4(-1)^2 + 3(-1) - 2 = -4(1) - 3 - 2 = -4 - 3 - 2 = -9$

c) To evaluate the function at a, we replace each x in the function with an a.

$$f(x) = -4x^2 + 3x - 2$$
$$f(a) = -4a^2 + 3a - 2$$

EXAMPLE 7 Determine each indicated function value.

a) $g(-2)$ for $g(t) = \dfrac{1}{t + 5}$

b) $h(5)$ for $h(s) = 2|s - 6|$

c) $j(-3)$ for $j(r) = \sqrt{6 - r}$

Solution In each part, substitute the indicated value into the function and evaluate the function.

a) $g(-2) = \dfrac{1}{-2 + 5} = \dfrac{1}{3}$

b) $h(5) = 2|5 - 6| = 2|-1| = 2(1) = 2$

NOW TRY EXERCISE 45 **c)** $j(-3) = \sqrt{6 - (-3)} = \sqrt{6 + 3} = \sqrt{9} = 3$

5 Applications of Functions in Daily Life

Many of the applications that we discussed in Chapter 2 were functions. However, we had not defined a function at that time. Now we examine additional applications of functions.

EXAMPLE 8 **The Masters Golf Tournament** The Masters golf tournament is held every year in April at Augusta National Golf Club in Georgia. The graph in Figure 3.29 shows

Eyes on the Masters

FIGURE 3.29

Source: NTI, Nielsen

Tiger Woods*

the television rating points for the Masters from 1980 through 2001. One rating point represents 1% of the U.S. households with televisions. For example, if a television program receives a rating of 14.1, it means that 14.1% of the U.S. households with televisions are tuned to that program.

a) Explain why the graph in Figure 3.29 represents a function.

b) Determine the television rating for the Masters in 1993.

c) Determine the percent increase in the television rating points from 1993 to 1997.

d) Determine the percent decrease in television rating points from 1997 to 2000.

Solution

a) This graph represents a function because each year corresponds to a specific number of television rating points. Notice that the graph passes the vertical line test.

b) In 1993 the Masters received about 7 television rating points. If we call the function f, then $f(1993) = 7$.

c) We will follow our problem-solving procedure to answer this question.

Understand and Translate We are asked to find the percent increase in television rating points from 1993 to 1997. To do so, we use the formula

$$\text{percent change (increase or decrease)} = \frac{\left(\substack{\text{amount in}\\\text{latest period}}\right) - \left(\substack{\text{amount in}\\\text{previous period}}\right)}{\text{amount in previous period}}$$

The latest period is 1997 and the previous period is 1993. Substituting the corresponding values, we get

$$\text{percent change} = \frac{14.1 - 7.0}{7.0}$$

Carry Out
$$= \frac{7.1}{7.0} \approx 1.0143 \approx 101.4\%$$

Check and Answer Our calculations appear correct. There was about a 101.4% increase in television rating points for the Masters from 1993 to 1997.

---

*It should be noted that in 1997 the extremely high rating was largely due to Tiger Woods winning the event.

d) To find the percent decrease from 1997 to 2000 we follow the same procedure as in part **c)**.

$$\text{percent change (increase or decrease)} = \frac{\left(\begin{array}{c}\text{amount in}\\\text{latest period}\end{array}\right) - \left(\begin{array}{c}\text{amount in}\\\text{previous period}\end{array}\right)}{\text{amount in previous period}}$$

$$= \frac{10.0 - 14.1}{14.1} = \frac{-4.1}{14.1} \approx -0.291 \approx -29.1\%$$

The negative sign preceding the 29.1% indicates a percent decrease. Thus, there was about a 29.1% decrease in television rating points for the Masters from 1997 to 2000.

EXAMPLE 9 **Immigration**   The size of the U.S. foreign-born population is at an all-time high. In 1890 the foreign-born population was 9 million people; in 1910 it was 14 million people; in 1930 it was 14 million people; in 1950 it was 10 million people; in 1970 it was 10 million people; in 1990 it was 20 million people; in 2000 it was 28 million people; and in 2005 it is projected to be 31 million people.

a) Represent this information on a graph.

b) Using your graph, explain why this set of points represents a function.

c) Using your graph, estimate the foreign-born population in 2003.

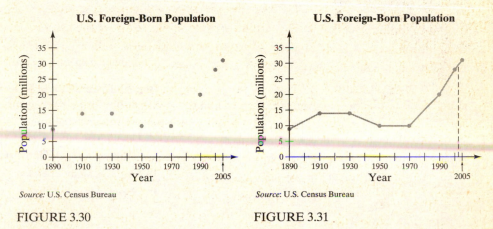

Source: U.S. Census Bureau

FIGURE 3.30   FIGURE 3.31

Solution   **a)** The set of points is plotted in Figure 3.30. We placed the year on the horizontal axis and the foreign-born population, in millions of people, on the vertical axis.

b) Since each year corresponds with exactly one population, this set of points represents a function. Notice that this graph passes the vertical line test.

c) We can connect the points with straight line segments as in Figure 3.31. Then we can estimate from the graph that there were about 30 million foreign-born Americans in 2003. If we call the function f, then $f(2003) = 30$.

NOW TRY EXERCISE 75

In Section 2.2 we learned to use formulas. Consider the formula for the area of a circle, $A = \pi r^2$. In the formula, π is a constant that is approximately 3.14. For each specific value of the radius, r, there corresponds exactly one area, A. Thus the area of a circle is a function of its radius. We may therefore write

$$A(r) = \pi r^2$$

Often formulas are written using function notation like this.

EXAMPLE 10   The Celsius temperature, C, is a function of the Fahrenheit temperature, F.

$$C(F) = \frac{5}{9}(F - 32)$$

Determine the Celsius temperature that corresponds to 50°F.

Solution   We need to find $C(50)$. We do so by substitution.

$$C(F) = \frac{5}{9}(F - 32)$$

$$C(50) = \frac{5}{9}(50 - 32)$$

$$= \frac{5}{9}(18) = 10$$

Therefore, 50°F = 10°C.

In Example 10, F is the independent variable and C is the dependent variable. If we solved the function for F, we would obtain $F(C) = \frac{9}{5}C + 32$. In this formula, C is the independent variable and F is the dependent variable. ✳

NOW TRY EXERCISE 55

1. a correspondence where each member in the domain corresponds to exactly one member of the range

Exercise Set 3.2

5. If a vertical line intersects the graph at more than one point, the graph is not a function.

6. set of values for independent variable   **7.** set of values for dependent variable

Concept/Writing Exercises

10. D: $\mathbb{R}$,   R: $\mathbb{R}$ **12.** If y depends on x, then y is the dependent variable.

1. What is a function?

2. What is a relation?   any set of ordered pairs

3. Are all functions also relations? Explain.   yes

4. Are all relations also functions? Explain.   no

5. Explain how to use the vertical line test to determine if a relation is a function.

6. What is the domain of a function?

7. What is the range of a function?

8. What are the domain and range of the function $f(x) = 2x + 1$? Explain your answer.   D: $\mathbb{R}$,   R: $\mathbb{R}$

9. Consider the function $y = \dfrac{1}{x}$. What is its domain and range? Explain.   D: $\{x \mid x \neq 0\}$, R: $\{y \mid y \neq 0\}$

10. What are the domain and range of a function of the form $f(x) = ax + b, a \neq 0$? Explain your answer.

11. Consider the absolute value function $y = |x|$. What is its domain and range? Explain.   D: $\mathbb{R}$,   R: $\{y \mid y \geq 0\}$

12. What is a dependent variable?

13. What is an independent variable?

14. How is "$f(x)$" read? f of x

13. If y depends on x, then x is the independent variable.

Practice the Skills

*In Exercises 15–20, **a)** determine if the relation illustrated is a function. **b)** Give the domain and range of each function or relation.*

15.   twice a number

$3 \longrightarrow 6$

$5 \longrightarrow 10$

$10 \longrightarrow 20$

15. a) function **b)** D: $\{3, 5, 10\}$, R: $\{6, 10, 20\}$

16. a) not a function

   b) D: $\{$Robert, Margaret$\}$, R: $\{$Bobby, Rob, Peggy, Maggie$\}$

18.   a number squared

$4 \longrightarrow 16$

$5 \longrightarrow 25$

$6 \longrightarrow 36$

a) function

b) D: $\{4, 5, 6\}$,

   R: $\{16, 25, 36\}$

16.   nicknames

Robert $\longrightarrow$ Bobby

        $\searrow$ Rob

Margaret $\longrightarrow$ Peggy

          $\searrow$ Maggie

🔒 **19.**   cost of a stamp

$1990 \longrightarrow 20$

$2001 \longrightarrow 34$

$2002 \longrightarrow 37$

a) not a function

b) D: $\{1990, 2001, 2002\}$,

   R: $\{20, 34, 37\}$

17.   number of siblings

Cameron $\longrightarrow 1$

Tyrone $\longrightarrow 2$

Vishnu

17. a) function **b)** D: $\{$Cameron, Tyrone, Vishnu$\}$, R: $\{1, 2\}$

20. a) function **b)** D: $\{|-3|, |3|, |0|\}$, R: $\{0, 3\}$

20.   absolute value

$|-3| \longrightarrow 3$

$|3|$

$|0| \longrightarrow 0$

In Exercises 21–28, **a)** *determine which of the following relations are also functions.* **b)** *Give the domain and range of each relation or function.*

21. $\{(1,4), (2,2), (3,5), (4,3), (5,1)\}$
   a) function **b)** D: $\{1, 2, 3, 4, 5\}$, R: $\{1, 2, 3, 4, 5\}$

22. $\{(1,1), (4,2), (9,3), (1,-1), (4,-2), (9,-3)\}$
   a) not a function **b)** D: $\{1, 4, 9\}$, R: $\{-3, -2, -1, 1, 2, 3\}$

23. $\{(3,-1), (5,0), (1,2), (4,4), (2,2), (7,5)\}$
   a) function **b)** D: $\{1, 2, 3, 4, 5, 7\}$, R: $\{-1, 0, 2, 4, 5\}$

24. $\{(-1,1), (0,-3), (3,4), (4,5), (-2,-2)\}$
   a) function **b)** D: $\{-2, -1, 0, 3, 4\}$, R: $\{-3, -2, 1, 4, 5\}$

25. $\{(1,4), (2,5), (3,6), (2,2), (1,1)\}$
   a) not a function **b)** D: $\{1, 2, 3\}$, R: $\{1, 2, 4, 5, 6\}$

26. $\{(6,3), (-3,4), (0,3), (5,2), (3,5), (2,5)\}$
   a) function **b)** D: $\{-3, 0, 2, 3, 5, 6\}$, R: $\{2, 3, 4, 5\}$

27. $\{(0,3), (1,3), (2,2), (1,-1), (2,-7)\}$
   a) not a function **b)** D: $\{0, 1, 2\}$, R: $\{-7, -1, 2, 3\}$

28. $\{(3,5), (2,5), (1,5), (0,5), (-1,5)\}$
   a) function **b)** D: $\{-1, 0, 1, 2, 3\}$, R: $\{5\}$

In Exercises 29–40, **a)** *determine whether the graph illustrated represents a function.* **b)** *Give the domain and range of each function or relation.* **c)** *Approximate the value or values of x where y = 2.*

29.
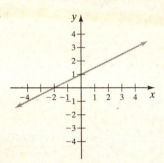
   a) function
   b) D: $\mathbb{R}$, R: $\mathbb{R}$
   c) 2

30.
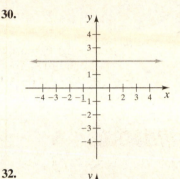
   a) function
   b) D: $\mathbb{R}$, R: $\{2\}$
   c) all real numbers

31.
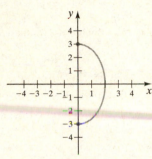
   a) not a function
   b) D: $\{x | 0 \le x \le 2\}$, R: $\{y | -3 \le y \le 3\}$
   c) ≈ 1.5

32.
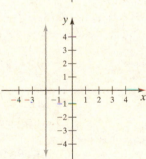
   a) not a function
   b) D: $\{x | -4 \le x \le 4\}$, R: $\{y | -2 \le y \le 2\}$
   c) 0

33.
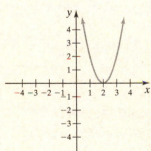
   a) function
   b) D: $\mathbb{R}$, R: $\{y | y \ge 0\}$
   c) 1, 3

34.
   a) not a function
   b) D: $\{-2\}$, R: $\mathbb{R}$
   c) -2

35.
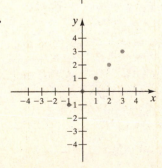
   a) function
   b) D: $\{-1, 0, 1, 2, 3\}$, R: $\{-1, 0, 1, 2, 3\}$
   c) 2

36.
   a) function
   b) D: $\{1, 2, 3\}$, R: $\{1\}$
   c) no values of x

37.

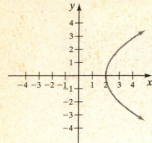

a) not a function
b) D: $\{x|x \geq 2\}$, R: $\mathbb{R}$
c) 3

38.

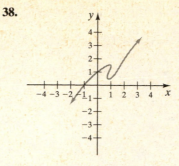

a) not a function
b) D: $\mathbb{R}$, R: $\mathbb{R}$
c) 2

39.

a) function
b) D: $\{x|-2 \leq x \leq 2\}$,
R: $\{y|-1 \leq y \leq 2\}$
c) $-2, 2$

40.

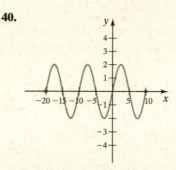

a) function
b) D: $\{x|-20 \leq x \leq 10\}$,
R: $\{y|-2 \leq y \leq 2\}$
c) $-17.5, -7.5, 2.5$

Evaluate each function at the indicated values.

41. $f(x) = -2x + 5$; find

  a) $f(2)$. 1

  b) $f(-3)$. 11

42. $f(a) = \dfrac{1}{3}a + 2$; find

  a) $f(0)$. 2

  b) $f(-6)$. 0

🔒 **43.** $h(x) = x^2 - x - 6$; find

  a) $h(0)$. -6

  b) $h(-1)$. -4

44. $g(x) = -2x^2 + x + 2$; find

  a) $g(2)$. -4

  b) $g\left(\dfrac{1}{2}\right)$. 2

45. $r(t) = -t^3 - 2t^2 + t + 4$; find

  a) $r(1)$. 2

  b) $r(-2)$. 2

46. $g(t) = 4 - 5t + 16t^2 - 2t^3$; find

  a) $g(0)$. 4

  b) $g(3)$. 79

47. $h(z) = |5 - 2z|$; find

  a) $h(6)$. 7

  b) $h\left(\dfrac{5}{2}\right)$. 0

48. $q(x) = -2|x + 3| - 3$; find

  a) $q(0)$. -9

  b) $q(-4)$. -5

49. $s(t) = \sqrt{t + 2}$; find

  a) $s(-2)$. 0

  b) $s(7)$. 3

50. $f(t) = \sqrt{5 - 2t}$; find

  a) $f(-2)$. 3

  b) $f(2)$. 1

51. $g(x) = \dfrac{x^3 - 2}{x - 2}$; find

  a) $g(0)$. 1

  b) $g(2)$. undefined

52. $h(x) = \dfrac{x^2 + 4x}{x + 6}$; find

  a) $h(-3)$. -1

  b) $h\left(\dfrac{2}{5}\right)$. $\dfrac{11}{40}$ or 0.275

Problem Solving   55. **a)** $A(r) = \pi r^2$ **b)** $\approx 314.2 \text{ yd}^2$ 56. **a)** $P(s) = 4s$ 57. **a)** $C(F) = \frac{5}{9}(F - 32)$

53. Area of a Rectangle The formula for the area of a rectangle is $A = lw$. If the length of a rectangle is 6 inches, then the area is a function of its width, $A(w) = 6w$. Find the area when the width is

a) 2 feet.   12 ft²

b) 4.5 feet.   27 ft²

54. Simple Interest The formula for the simple interest earned for a period of 1 year is $i = pr$ where p is the principal invested and r is the simple interest rate. If \$1000 is invested, the simple interest earned in 1 year is a function of the simple interest rate, $i(r) = 1000r$. Determine the simple interest earned in 1 year if the interest rate is

a) 3%.   \$30   **b)** 4.25%.   \$42.50

55. Area of a Circle The formula for the area of a circle is $A = \pi r^2$. The area is a function of the radius.

a) Write this function using function notation.

b) Determine the area when the radius is 10 yards.

56. Perimeter of a Square The formula for the perimeter of a square is $P = 4s$ where s represents the length of any one of the sides of the square.

a) Write this function using function notation.

b) Determine the perimeter of a square with sides of length 3 meters.   12 meters

57. Temperature The formula for changing Fahrenheit temperature into Celsius temperature is $C = \frac{5}{9}(F - 32)$.

The Celsius temperature is a function of Fahrenheit temperature.

a) Write this function using function notation.

b) Find the Celsius temperature that corresponds to $-40°$F. $-40°$C

58. Volume of a Cylinder The formula for the volume of a right circular cylinder is $V = \pi r^2 h$. If the height, h, is 3 feet, then the volume is a function of the radius, r.

a) Write this formula in function notation, where the height is 3 feet. $V(r) = 3\pi r^2$

b) Find the volume if the radius is 2 feet. $\approx 37.7 \text{ ft}^3$

59. Sauna Temperature The temperature, T, in degrees Celsius, in a sauna n minutes after being turned on is given by the function $T(n) = -0.03n^2 + 1.5n + 14$. Find the sauna's temperature after

a) 3 minutes.   18.23°C   **b)** 12 minutes.   27.68°C

60. Stopping Distance The stopping distance, d, in meters for a car traveling v kilometers per hour is given by the function $d(v) = 0.18v + 0.01v^2$. Find the stopping distance for the following speeds:

a) 50 km/hr   34 m   **b)** 25 km/hr   10.75 m

61. Air Conditioning When an air conditioner is turned on maximum in a bedroom at 80°, the temperature, T, in the room after A minutes can be approximated by the function $T(A) = -0.02A^2 - 0.34A + 80$, $0 \le A \le 15$.

a) Estimate the room temperature 4 minutes after the air conditioner is turned on.   78.32°

b) Estimate the room temperature 12 minutes after the air conditioner is turned on.   73.04°

62. Accidents The number of accidents, n, in 1 month involving drivers x years of age can be approximated by the function $n(x) = 2x^2 - 150x + 4000$. Find the approximate number of accidents in 1 month that involved

a) 18-year-olds.   1948   **b)** 25-year-olds.   1500

63. Oranges The total number of oranges, T, in a square pyramid whose base is n by n oranges is given by the function

$$T(n) = \frac{1}{3}n^3 + \frac{1}{2}n^2 + \frac{1}{6}n$$

Find the number of oranges if the base is

a) 6 by 6 oranges.   91   **b)** 8 by 8 oranges.   204

64. Rock Concert If the cost of a ticket to a rock concert is increased by x dollars, the estimated increase in revenue, R, in thousands of dollars is given by the function $R(x) = 24 + 5x - x^2$, $x < 8$. Find the increase in revenue if the cost of the ticket is increased by

a) \$1.   \$28,000   **b)** \$4.   \$28,000

Review Example 5 before working Exercises 65–70

65. Heart Rate The following graph shows a person's heart rate while doing exercise. Write a story that this graph may represent.

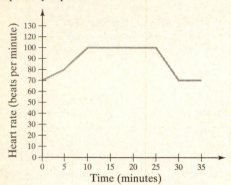

Answers will vary. One possible interpretation: The person warms up slowly, possibly by walking, for 5 min. Then the person begins jogging slowly over a period of 5 min. For the next 15 min the person jogs. For the next 5 min the person walks slowly and his heart rate decreases to his normal resting heart rate. The rate stays the same for the next 5 min.

66. Water Level The following graph shows the water level at a certain point during a flood. Write a story that this graph may represent.

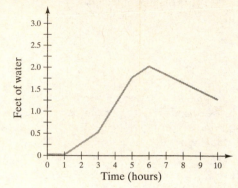

Answers will vary. One possible interpretation: During the first hour there is no water. During the next 2 hours water builds up to about 0.5 feet. During the next 2 hours it rains more heavily and the rain builds up to about 2.0 feet. During the next hour the rain slows down a bit, but the water is still accumulating. During the last 4 hours the rain stops and the water level drops to about 1.5 feet.

67. Height Above Sea Level The following graph shows height above sea level versus time when a man leaves his house and goes for a walk. Write a story that this graph may represent.

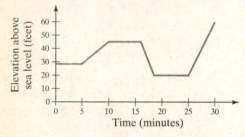

Answers will vary. One possible interpretation: Walks level for 5 min, walks uphill, levels off, walks quickly downhill, levels off, walks quickly uphill.

68. Water Level in a Bathtub The following graph shows the level of water in a bathtub versus time. Write a story that this graph may represent.

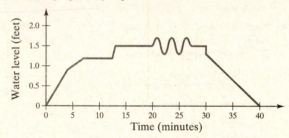

Answers will vary. One possible interpretation: Turn water on full, after 4 min turn down cold or hot water, shut water off, water cools down a few min, someone gets in, after few min makes waves, then gets out and opens drain.

69. Speed of a Car The following graph shows the speed of a car versus time. Write a story that this graph may represent.

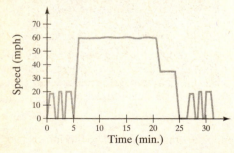

Answers will vary. One possible interpretation: Drives in stop-and-go traffic, then gets on a highway for about 15 min, then gets on a country road for a few min, then stops for a couple of min, then stop-and-go traffic.

70. Distance Traveled The following graph shows the distance traveled by a person in a car versus time. Write a story that this graph may represent.

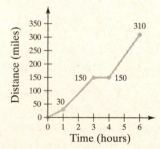

Answers will vary. One possible interpretation: Travels at 30 mph for 1 hr, then 60 mph for 2 hr, then rests for 1 hr, then 80 mph for 2 hr.

71. a) Yes, it passes the vertical line test. **b)** year **c)** ≈$115 billion   **73. e)** 1999 **f)** 2000

\ 71. Computer Sales The following graph shows the amount American businesses have spent on computers and related equipment from 1995 through 2000.

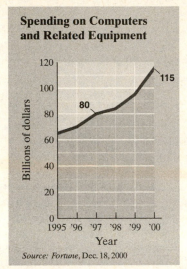

Spending on Computers and Related Equipment

Source: Fortune, Dec. 18, 2000

a) Does this graph represent a function? Explain.

b) In this graph, what is the independent variable?

c) If *f* represents the function, determine *f*(2000).

d) Determine the percent increase in the amount American businesses spent on computers and related equipment from 1997 through 2000. ≈43.75%

\ 72. Computer Exports The following graph shows the U.S. exports of computers and related equipment and parts from 1995 through 2000.

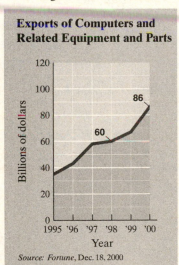

Exports of Computers and Related Equipment and Parts

Source: Fortune, Dec. 18, 2000

a) Does this graph represent a function? Explain.

b) In this graph, what is the independent variable? year

c) If *g* represents the function, determine *g*(2000).

d) Determine the percent increase in exports of computers and related equipment and parts from 1998 through 2000. ≈43.3%

72. a) Yes, it passes the vertical line test. **c)** ≈$86 billion

\ 73. Trade Deficit with China The following graph shows that imports from China to the United States have been rapidly increasing while exports to China from the United States have been rising at a much slower rate.

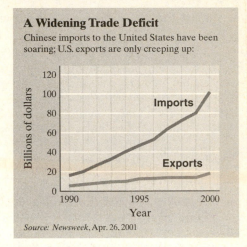

A Widening Trade Deficit
Chinese imports to the United States have been soaring; U.S. exports are only creeping up:

Source: Newsweek, Apr. 26, 2001

a) Does the graph of imports from China represent a function? Explain. Yes, it passes the vertical line test.

b) Does the graph of exports to China represent a function? Explain. Yes, it passes the vertical line test.

c) Does the graph of imports from China appear to be approximately linear? Explain. no

d) Does the graph of exports to China appear to be approximately linear? Explain. yes

e) If *f* represents the function of imports from China and if *t* is the year, determine *t* if *f*(*t*) = $80 billion.

f) If *g* represents the function of exports to China and if *t* is the year, determine *t* if *g*(*t*) = $18 billion.

\ 74. Online Travel The total amount of U.S. online bookings for travel (in billions of dollars) is shown in the following bar graph.

Online Travel is Growing Fast

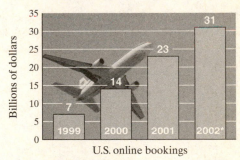

Source: Business Week, June 11, 2001   * Estimate

a) Draw a line graph that displays this information.

b) Does the graph you drew in part **a)** appear to be approximately linear? Explain. yes

74. a) See graphing answer section, page G4.

75. a), 76. a), 77. a) See graphing answer section, page G4.   **76. b)** $23,000   **77. b)** $2.65 per bushel

c) Assuming this trend continues, from the graph you drew, estimate the amount of online bookings for the year 2003. $39 billion

d) Does the bar graph represent a function? yes

e) Does the line graph you drew in part **a)** represent a function? yes

75. *Super Bowl Commercials* The average price of the cost of a 30-second commercial during the Super Bowl has been increasing over the years. The following chart gives the approximate cost of a 30-second commercial for selected years from 1981 through 2001.

Year	Cost ($1000s)
1981	280
1985	500
1989	740
1993	970
1997	1300
2001	2300

a) Draw a line graph that displays this information.

b) Does the graph appear to be approximately linear? Explain. no

c) From the graph, estimate the cost of a 30-second commercial in 2000. $2,000,000

76. *Household Expenditures* The average annual household expenditure is a function of the average annual household income. The average expenditure can be estimated by the function

$$f(i) = 0.6i + 5000 \quad \$3500 \le i \le \$50,000$$

where $f(i)$ is the average household expenditure and i is the average household income.

a) Draw a graph showing the relationship between average household income and the average household expenditure.

b) Estimate the average household expenditure for a family whose average household income is $30,000.

77. *Supply and Demand* The price of commodities, like soybeans, is determined by **supply and demand**. If too many soybeans are produced, the supply will be greater than the demand, and the price will drop. If not enough soybeans are produced, the demand will be greater than the supply, and the price of soybeans will rise. Thus the price of soybeans is a function of the number of bushels of soybeans produced. The price of a bushel of soybeans can be estimated by the function

$$f(Q) = -0.00004Q + 4.25, \quad 10,000 \le Q \le 60,000$$

where $f(Q)$ is the price of a bushel of soybeans and Q is the annual number of bushels of soybeans produced.

a) Construct a graph showing the relationship between the number of bushels of soybeans produced and the price of a bushel of soybeans.

b) Estimate the cost of a bushel of soybeans if 40,000 bushels of soybeans are produced in a given year.

 Group Activity

*In many real-life situations, more than one function may be needed to represent a problem. This often occurs where two or more different rates are involved. For example, when discussing federal income taxes, there are different tax rates. When two or more functions are used to represent a problem, the function is called a **piecewise function**. Following are two examples of piecewise functions and their graphs.*

$$f(x) = \begin{cases} -x + 2, & 0 \le x < 4 \\ 2x - 10, & 4 \le x < 8 \end{cases}$$

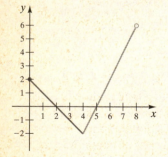

$$f(x) = \begin{cases} 2x - 1, & -2 \le x < 2 \\ x - 2, & 2 \le x < 4 \end{cases}$$

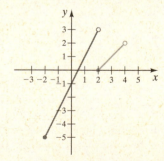

As a group, graph the following piecewise functions. **78., 79.,** See graphing answer section, page G4.

78. $f(x) = \begin{cases} x + 3, & -1 \le x < 2 \\ 7 - x, & 2 \le x < 4 \end{cases}$

79. $g(x) = \begin{cases} 2x + 3, & -3 < x < 0 \\ -3x + 1, & 0 \le x < 2 \end{cases}$

Cumulative Review Exercises

[2.1] **80.** Solve the equation $3x - 2 = \dfrac{1}{3}(3x - 3)$. $\frac{1}{2}$

[2.2] **81.** Solve the following formula for p_2.

$$E = a_1p_1 + a_2p_2 + a_3p_3$$

81. $p_2 = \dfrac{E - a_1p_1 - a_3p_3}{a_2}$

[2.5] **82.** Solve the inequality $\dfrac{3}{5}(x - 3) > \dfrac{1}{4}(3 - x)$ and indicate the solution **a)** on the number line; **b)** in interval notation; and **c)** in set builder notation.

[2.6] **83.** Solve the equation $\left|\dfrac{x-4}{3}\right| + 2 = 4$. $-2, 10$

82. a) ⟵─○──⟶ **b)** $(3, \infty)$ **c)** $\{x \mid x > 3\}$
             3

3.3 LINEAR FUNCTIONS: GRAPHS AND APPLICATIONS

SSM   Study Guide   CD/Video

MathPro 4/5   PH Math Tutor Center   prenhall.com/Angel

1 Graph linear functions.

2 Graph linear functions using intercepts.

3 Graph equations of the form $x = a$ and $y = b$.

4 Study applications of functions.

5 Solve linear equations in one variable graphically.

1 Graph Linear Functions

In Section 3.1 we graphed linear equations. To graph the linear equation $y = 2x + 4$, we can make a table of values, plot the points, and draw the graph, as shown in Figure 3.32. Notice that this graph represents a function since it passes the vertical line test.

x	y
-2	0
0	4
1	6

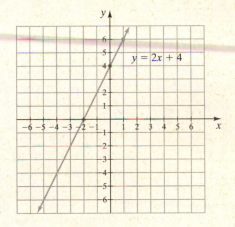

FIGURE 3.32

We may write the equation graphed in Figure 3.32 using function notation as $f(x) = 2x + 4$. This is an example of a linear function. A **linear function** is a function of the form $f(x) = ax + b$. The graph of any linear function is a straight line. The domain of any function is the set of real numbers for which the function is a real number. The domain of any linear function is the set of all real numbers, $\mathbb{R}$: Any real number, x, substituted into a linear function will result in $f(x)$ being a real number. We will discuss domains of functions further in Section 3.6.

To graph a linear function, we treat $f(x)$ as y and follow the same procedure used to graph linear equations.

EXAMPLE 1 Graph $f(x) = \dfrac{1}{2}x - 1$.

Solution We construct a table of values by substituting values for x and finding corresponding values of $f(x)$ or y. Then we plot the points and draw the graph, as illustrated in Figure 3.33.

x	$f(x)$
-2	-2
0	-1
2	0

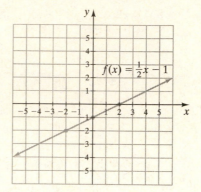

FIGURE 3.33

Note that the vertical axis in Figure 3.33 may also be labeled as $f(x)$ instead of y. In this book we will continue to label it y.

2 Graph Linear Functions Using Intercepts

Linear equations are not always given in the form $y = ax + b$. The equation $2x + 3y = 6$ is an example of a linear equation given in *standard form*.

DEFINITION

> The **standard form of a linear equation** is
>
> $$ax + by = c$$
>
> where a, b, and c are real numbers, and a and b are not both 0.

Examples of Linear Equations in Standard Form

NOW TRY EXERCISE 13
$$2x + 3y = 4 \qquad -x + 5y = -2$$

Sometimes when an equation is given in standard form it may be easier to draw the graph using the x- and y-intercepts. Let's examine two points on the graph shown in Figure 3.32. Note that the graph crosses the x-axis at the point $(-2, 0)$. Therefore, $(-2, 0)$ is called the **x-intercept**. Sometimes we say that the x-intercept is *at* -2 (on the x-axis), the x-coordinate of the ordered pair.

The graph crosses the y-axis at the point $(0, 4)$. Therefore, $(0, 4)$ is called the **y-intercept**. Sometimes we say that the y-intercept is *at* 4 (on the y-axis), the y-coordinate of the ordered pair.

Below we explain how the x- and y-intercepts may be determined algebraically.

To Find the x- and y-Intercepts

To find the y-intercept, set $x = 0$ and solve for y.
To find the x-intercept, set $y = 0$ and solve for x.

To graph a linear equation using the x- and y-intercepts, find the intercepts and plot the points. Then draw a straight line through the points. When graphing linear equations using the intercepts, you must be very careful. If either of your points is plotted wrong, your graph will be wrong.

EXAMPLE 2   Graph the equation $5x = 10y - 20$ by plotting the x- and y-intercepts.

Solution   To find the y-intercept (the point where the graph crosses the y-axis), set $x = 0$ and solve for y.

$$5x = 10y - 20$$
$$5(0) = 10y - 20$$
$$0 = 10y - 20$$
$$20 = 10y$$
$$2 = y$$

The graph crosses the y-axis at $y = 2$. The ordered pair representing the y-intercept is $(0, 2)$.

To find the x-intercept (the point where the graph crosses the x-axis), set $y = 0$ and solve for x.

$$5x = 10y - 20$$
$$5x = 10(0) - 20$$
$$5x = -20$$
$$x = -4$$

The graph crosses the x-axis at $x = -4$. The ordered pair representing the x-intercept is $(-4, 0)$. Now plot the intercepts and draw the graph (Fig. 3.34).

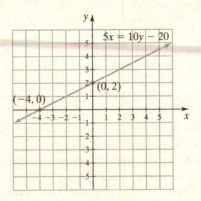

NOW TRY EXERCISE 23   **FIGURE** 3.34

EXAMPLE 3   Graph $f(x) = -\dfrac{1}{3}x - 1$ by plotting the x- and y-intercepts.

Solution   Treat $f(x)$ the same as y. To find the y-intercept, set $x = 0$ and solve for $f(x)$.

$$f(x) = -\frac{1}{3}x - 1$$

$$f(x) = -\frac{1}{3}(0) - 1 = -1$$

The y-intercept is $(0, -1)$.

To find the x-intercept, set $f(x) = 0$ and solve for x.

$$f(x) = -\frac{1}{3}x - 1$$

$$0 = -\frac{1}{3}x - 1$$

$$3(0) = 3\left(-\frac{1}{3}x - 1\right) \qquad \textit{Multiply both sides by 3.}$$

$$0 = -x - 3 \qquad \textit{Distributive property}$$

$$x = -3 \qquad \textit{Add x to both sides.}$$

The x-intercept is $(-3, 0)$. The graph is shown in Figure 3.35.

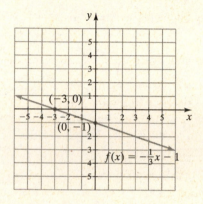

NOW TRY EXERCISE 17   **FIGURE 3.35**

Graphs of the form $ax + by = 0$ go through the origin and have the same x- and y-intercept, $(0, 0)$. To graph such equations we can use the intercept as one point and substitute values for x and find the corresponding values of y to get other points on the graph.

EXAMPLE 4   Graph $-6x + 4y = 0$.

Solution   If we substitute $x = 0$ we find that $y = 0$. Thus the graph goes through the origin. We will select $x = -2$ and $x = 2$ and substitute these values into the equation, one at a time, to find two other points on the graph.

Let $x = -2$.	Let $x = 2$.
$-6x + 4y = 0$	$-6x + 4y = 0$
$-6(-2) + 4y = 0$	$-6(2) + 4y = 0$
$12 + 4y = 0$	$-12 + 4y = 0$
$4y = -12$	$4y = 12$
$y = -3$	$y = 3$
ordered pairs: $(-2, -3)$	$(2, 3)$

Two other points on the graph are at $(-2, -3)$ and $(2, 3)$. The graph of $-6x + 4y = 0$ is shown in Figure 3.36.

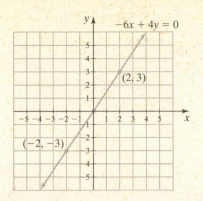

NOW TRY EXERCISE 35   FIGURE 3.36

![calculator icon] **Using Your Graphing Calculator**

Sometimes it may be difficult to estimate the intercepts of a graph accurately. When this occurs, you might want to use a graphing calculator. We demonstrate how in the following example.

EXAMPLE   Determine the x- and y-intercepts of the graph of $y = 1.3(x - 3.2)$.

Solution   Press the $\boxed{\text{Y=}}$ key, and then assign $1.3(x - 3.2)$ to y. Then press the $\boxed{\text{GRAPH}}$ key to graph the function $y_1 = 1.3(x - 3.2)$, as shown in Figure 3.37a.

From the graph it may be difficult to determine the intercepts. One way to find the y-intercept is to use the TRACE feature, which was discussed in Section 3.1. Figure 3.37b shows a TI-83 Plus screen after the $\boxed{\text{TRACE}}$ key is pressed. Notice the y-intercept is at -4.16.

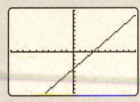

FIGURE 3.37a

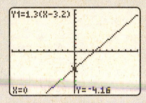

FIGURE 3.37b

Some graphing calculators have the ability to find the x-intercepts of a function by pressing just a few keys. A **zero** (or **root**) of a function is a value of x such that $f(x) = 0$. A zero (or root) of a function is the x-coordinate of the x-intercept of the graph of the function. Read your calculator manual to learn how to find the zeros or roots of a function. On a TI-83 Plus you press the keys $\boxed{\text{2}^{\text{nd}}}$ $\boxed{\text{TRACE}}$ to get to the CALC menu (which stands for calculate). Then you choose option 2, *zero*. Once the zero feature has been selected, the calculator will display

Left bound?

At this time, move the cursor along the curve until it is to the *left* of the zero. Then press $\boxed{\text{ENTER}}$. The calculator now displays

Right bound?

Move the cursor along the curve until it is to the *right* of the zero. Then press $\boxed{\text{ENTER}}$. The calculator now displays

Guess?

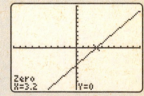

FIGURE 3.38

Now press $\boxed{\text{ENTER}}$ for the third time and the zero is displayed at the bottom of the screen, as in Figure 3.38. Thus the x-intercept of the function is 3.2. For practice at finding the intercepts on your calculator, work Exercises 69–72.

3 Graph Equations of the Form $x = a$ and $y = b$

Examples 5 and 6 illustrate how equations of the form $x = a$ and $y = b$, where a and b are constants, are graphed.

EXAMPLE 5   Graph the equation $y = 3$.

Solution   This equation can be written as $y = 3 + 0x$. Thus, for any value of x selected, y is 3. The graph of $y = 3$ is illustrated in Figure 3.39.   ✳

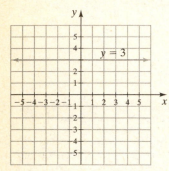

The graph of any equation of the form $y = b$ will always be a horizontal line for any real number b.

Notice that the graph of $y = 3$ is a function since it passes the vertical line test. For each value of x selected, the value of y, or the value of the function, is 3. This is an example of a **constant function**. We may write

$$f(x) = 3$$

FIGURE 3.39

Any equation of the form $y = b$ or $f(x) = b$, where b represents a constant, is a constant function.

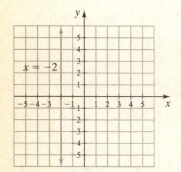

EXAMPLE 6   Graph the equation $x = -2$.

Solution   This equation can be written as $x = -2 + 0y$. Thus, for every value of y selected, x will have a value of -2 (Fig. 3.40).   ✳

The graph of any equation of the form $x = a$ will always be a vertical line for any real number a.

Notice that the graph of $x = -2$ does not represent a function since it does not pass the vertical line test. For $x = -2$ there is more than one value of y. In fact, when $x = -2$ there are an infinite number of values for y.

FIGURE 3.40

NOW TRY EXERCISE 41

4 Study Applications of Functions

Graphs are often used to show the relationship between variables. The axes of a graph do not have to be labeled x and y. They can be any designated variables. Consider the following example.

EXAMPLE 7   **Tire Store Profit**   The yearly profit, p, of a tire store can be estimated by the function $p(n) = 20n - 30,000$, where n is the number of tires sold per year.

a) Draw a graph of profit versus tires sold for up to and including 6000 tires.

b) Estimate the number of tires that must be sold for the company to break even.

c) Estimate the number of tires sold if the company has a $40,000 profit.

Solution   **a)** Understand   The profit, p, is a function of the number of tires sold, n. The horizontal axis will therefore be labeled Number of tires sold (the independent variable) and the vertical axis will be labeled Profit (the dependent variable). Since the minimum number of tires that can be sold is 0, negative values do not have to be listed on the horizontal axis. The horizontal axis will therefore go from 0 to 6000 tires.

We will graph this equation by determining and plotting the intercepts.

Translate and Carry Out   To find the p-intercept, we set $n = 0$ and solve for $p(n)$.

$$p(n) = 20n - 30,000$$
$$p(n) = 20(0) - 30,000 = -30,000$$

Thus, the p-intercept is $(0, -30,000)$.

To find the n-intercept, we set $p(n) = 0$ and solve for n.

$$p(n) = 20n - 30,000$$
$$0 = 20n - 30,000$$
$$30,000 = 20n$$
$$1500 = n$$

Thus the n-intercept is $(1500, 0)$.

Answer   Now we use the p- and n-intercepts to draw the graph (see Fig. 3.41).

b) The break-even point is the number of tires that must be sold for the company to have neither a profit nor a loss. The break-even point is where the graph intersects the n-axis, for this is where the profit, p, is 0. To break even, approximately 1500 tires must be sold.

c) To make $40,000, approximately 3500 tires must be sold (shown by the dashed red line in Fig. 3.41). ✳

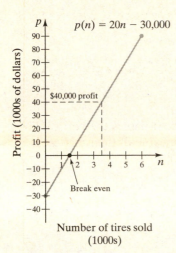

FIGURE 3.41

Sometimes it is difficult to read an exact answer from a graph. To determine the exact number of tires needed to break even in Example 7, substitute 0 for $p(n)$ in the function $p(n) = 20n - 30,000$ and solve for n. To determine the exact number of tires needed to obtain a $40,000 profit, substitute 40,000 for $p(n)$ and solve the equation for n.

EXAMPLE 8   **Toy Store Sales**   Andrew Gestrich is the owner of a toy store. His monthly salary consists of $200 plus 10% of the store's sales for that month.

s	m
0	200
10,000	1200
20,000	2200

a) Write a function expressing his monthly salary, m, in terms of the store's sales, s.

b) Draw a graph of his monthly salary for sales up to and including $20,000.

c) If the store's sales for the month of April are $15,000, what will Andrew's salary be for April?

Solution   **a)** Andrew's monthly salary is a function of sales. His monthly salary, m, consists of $200 plus 10% of the sales, s. Ten percent of s is $0.10s$. Thus the function for finding his salary is

$$m(s) = 200 + 0.10s$$

b) Since monthly salary is a function of sales, Sales will be represented on the horizontal axis and Monthly salary will be represented on the vertical axis. Since sales can never be negative, the monthly salary can never be negative. Thus both axes will be drawn with only positive numbers. We will draw this graph by plotting points. We select values for s, find the corresponding values of m, and then draw the graph. We can select values of s that are between $0 and $20,000 (Fig. 3.42).

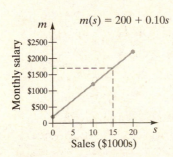

FIGURE 3.42

NOW TRY EXERCISE 53

c) By reading our graph carefully, we can estimate that when the store's sales are $15,000, Andrew's monthly salary is about $1700. ✳

Mathematics in Action

Polluted Air

The relationship between pollutants and heightened levels of respiratory and cardiopulmonary disease has become clearer over the past few years. People living in urban areas with high levels of pollution have a higher risk of mortality than those living in less polluted cities. The pollutants most directly linked to the increased incidence of disease and death include ozone, particulates, carbon monoxide, sulfur dioxide, volatile organic compounds, and oxides of nitrogen.

Particulates—material suspended in the air—with the lowest range in diameter (10 microns or less) are called fine particles. They are able to pass through the natural filtering system of the nose and throat and can penetrate deep into the lungs and do serious damage. Sulfate aerosols constitute the largest percentage of fine particles in the eastern United States; they come from sulfur dioxide produced by coal and oil combustion. Nitrate aerosols, which make up about one-third of fine particles in Los Angeles, come from vehicle emissions.

A study by Harvard University researchers covered six cities over 16 years and tracked the health of more than 8000 people. The results, published in 1993, showed a nearly linear relationship between the concentrations of particles and increased mortality rates; even relatively low levels of fine particle pollution had a measurable effect on health.

Research that correlates disease and mortality with causative factors, such as air pollution in all forms, is critical information for the public and for lawmakers as policy is being formulated with regard to limiting automobile and smokestack emissions. A graph with a straight line essentially matching up thousands of deaths with tons of particulates in the air sends a message that is pretty hard to disregard.

5 Solve Linear Equations in One Variable Graphically

Earlier we discussed the graph of $f(x) = 2x + 4$. In Figure 3.43 on the next page we illustrate the graph of $f(x)$ along with the graph of $g(x) = 0$. Notice that the two graphs intersect at $(-2, 0)$. We can obtain the x-coordinate of the ordered pair by solving the equation $f(x) = g(x)$. Remember $f(x)$ and $g(x)$ both represent y, and by solving this equation for x we are obtaining the value of x where the y's are equal.

$$f(x) = g(x)$$
$$\overbrace{2x + 4} = \overbrace{0}$$
$$2x = -4$$
$$x = -2$$

Note that we obtain -2, the x-coordinate in the ordered pair at the point of intersection.

Now let's find the x-coordinate of the point at which the graphs of $f(x) = 2x + 4$ and $g(x) = 2$ intersect. We solve the equation $f(x) = g(x)$.

$$f(x) = g(x)$$
$$\overbrace{2x + 4} = \overbrace{2}$$
$$2x = -2$$
$$x = -1$$

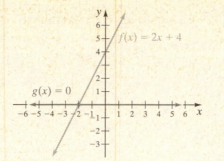

FIGURE 3.43

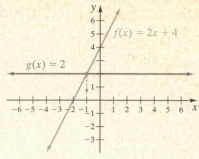

FIGURE 3.44

TEACHING TIP
Point out that this procedure may also be used when the expressions on either side of the equal sign are nonlinear.

The *x*-coordinate of the point of intersection of the two graphs is −1, as shown in Figure 3.44. Notice that $f(-1) = 2(-1) + 4 = 2$.

In general, if we are given an equation in one variable, we can regard each side of the equation as a separate function. To obtain the solution to the equation, we can graph the two functions. The *x*-coordinate of the point of intersection will be the solution to the equation.

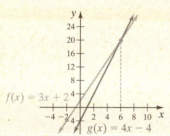

FIGURE 3.45

NOW TRY EXERCISE 65

EXAMPLE 9   Find the solution to the equation $3x + 2 = 4x - 4$ graphically.

Solution   Let $f(x) = 3x + 2$ and $g(x) = 4x - 4$. The graph of these functions is illustrated in Figure 3.45. The *x*-coordinate of the point of intersection is 6. Thus, the solution to the equation is 6. Check the solution now.   ✳

Using Your Graphing Calculator

In Example 9, we solved an equation in one variable by graphing two functions. In the following example, we explain how to find the point of intersection of two functions on a graphing calculator.

EXAMPLE   Use a graphing calculator to find the solution to $2(x + 3) = \frac{1}{2}x + 4$.

Solution   Assign $2(x + 3)$ to Y_1 and assign $\frac{1}{2}x + 4$ to Y_2 to get

$$Y_1 = 2(x + 3)$$

$$Y_2 = \frac{1}{2}x + 4$$

Now press the $\boxed{\text{GRAPH}}$ key to graph the functions. The graph of the functions is shown in Figure 3.46.

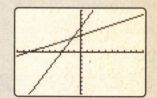

FIGURE 3.46

By examining the graph can you determine the *x*-coordinate of the point of intersection? Is it −1, or −1.5, or some other value? We can determine the point of intersection in a number of different ways. One method involves using the TRACE and **ZOOM** features. Figure 3.47 shows the window of a TI-83 Plus after the TRACE feature has been used and the cursor has been moved close to the point of intersection. (Note that pressing the up and down arrows switches the cursor from one function to the other.)

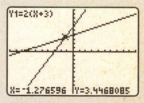

FIGURE 3.47

(continued on the next page)

At the bottom of the screen in Figure 3.47, you see the *x*- and *y*-coordinates at the cursor. To get a closer view around the area of the cursor, you can *zoom in* using the ZOOM key. After you zoom in, you can move the cursor closer to the point of intersection and get a better reading (Fig. 3.48). You can do this over and over until you get as accurate an answer as you need. It appears from Figure 3.48 that the *x*-coordinate of the intersection is about −1.33.

Graphing calculators can also display the intersection of two graphs with the use of certain keys. The keys to press depend on your calculator. Read your calculator manual to determine how to do this. This procedure is generally quicker and easier to use to find the point of intersection of two graphs.

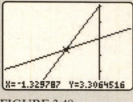

FIGURE 3.48   FIGURE 3.49

On the TI-83 Plus, select option 5: INTERSECT—from the CALC menu to find the intersection. Once the INTERSECT feature has been selected, the calculator will display

First curve?

At this time, move the cursor along the first curve until it is close to the point of intersection. Then press ENTER . The calculator will next display

Second curve?

The cursor will then appear on the second curve. If the cursor is not close to the point of intersection, move it along this curve until this happens. Then press ENTER . Next the calculator will display

Guess?

Now press ENTER again, and the point of intersection will be displayed.

Figure 3.49 shows the window after this procedure has been done. We see that the *x*-coordinate of the point of intersection is −1.333 . . . or $-1\frac{1}{3}$ and the *y*-coordinate of the point of intersection is 3.333 . . . or $3\frac{1}{3}$.

For practice in using a graphing calculator to solve an equation in one variable, work Exercises 65–68.

1. $ax + by = c$ **2.** Solve the equation for *y*, and then substitute $f(x)$ for *y*.   **3.** *x*-intercept: set $y = 0$ and solve for *x*; *y*-intercept: set $x = 0$ and solve for *y*.   **9.** Graph both sides of the equation. The solution is the *x*-coordinate of the point of intersection.
10. Graph $Y_1 = 2(x - 1)$ and $Y_2 = 3x - 5$. The *x*-coordinate of the point of intersection is the solution.

Exercise Set 3.3

Concept/Writing Exercises

1. What is the standard form of a linear equation?

2. If you are given a linear equation in standard form, and wish to write the equation using function notation, how would you do it?

3. Explain how to find the *x*- and *y*-intercepts of the graph of an equation.

4. What terms do graphing calculators use to indicate the *x*-intercepts? zeros or roots

5. What will the graph of $x = a$ look like for any real number *a*? vertical line

6. What will the graph of $y = b$ look like for any real number *b*? horizontal line

7. What will the graph of $f(x) = b$ look like for any real number *b*? horizontal line

8. Is the graph of $x = a$ a function? Explain. no

9. Explain how to solve an equation in one variable graphically.

10. Explain how to solve the equation $2(x - 1) = 3x - 5$ graphically.

Practice the Skills

Write each equation in standard form.

11. $y = -2x + 4$ $2x + y = 4$

12. $2x = 3y - 6$ $2x - 3y = -6$

13. $3(x - 2) = 4(y - 5)$ $3x - 4y = -14$

14. $\frac{1}{3}y = 2(x - 3) + 4$ $2x - \frac{1}{3}y = 2$ or $6x - y = 6$

Graph each equation using the x- and y-intercepts.   *See graphing answer section, pages G5 and G6.*

15. $y = -2x + 4$

16. $y = x - 5$

17. $f(x) = 2x + 3$

18. $f(x) = -6x + 5$

19. $2y = 4x + 6$

20. $x + 2y = 4$

21. $\frac{4}{3}x = y - 3$

22. $\frac{1}{2}x + 2y = 4$

23. $15x + 30y = 60$

24. $0.2x - 0.3y = 1.2$

25. $0.25x + 0.50y = 1.00$

26. $-1.6y = 0.4x + 9.6$

27. $120x - 360y = 720$

28. $125 = 25x - 25y$

29. $\frac{1}{3}x + \frac{1}{4}y = 12$

30. $\frac{1}{6}x + \frac{1}{2}y = -1$

Graph each equation.   *See graphing answer section, page G6.*

31. $y = -2x$

32. $y = \frac{1}{2}x$

33. $f(x) = \frac{1}{3}x$

34. $g(x) = 4x$

35. $2x + 4y = 0$

36. $-6x + 3y = 0$

37. $4x - 6y = 0$

38. $15x + 5y = 0$

Graph each equation.   *See graphing answer section, page G6.*

39. $y = 4$

40. $x = 4$

41. $x = -4$

42. $y = -4$

43. $y = -1.5$

44. $f(x) = -3$

45. $x = \frac{5}{2}$

46. $g(x) = 0$

47. $x = 0$

48. $x = -3.25$

Problem Solving   49., 50., 51. a), 52. b), 53. b) See graphing answer section, page G7.

49. ***Distance*** Using the distance formula

$$\text{distance} = \text{rate} \cdot \text{time, or } d = rt$$

draw a graph of distance versus time for a constant rate of 30 miles per hour.

50. ***Simple Interest*** Using the simple interest formula

$$\text{interest} = \text{principal} \cdot \text{rate} \cdot \text{time, or } i = prt$$

draw a graph of interest versus time for a principal of $500 and a rate of 3%.

51. ***Bicycle Profit*** The profit of a bicycle manufacturer can be approximated by the function $p(x) = 60x - 80,000$, where x is the number of bicycles produced and sold.

   a) Draw a graph of profit versus the number of bicycles sold (for up to 5000 bicycles).

   b) Estimate the number of bicycles that must be sold for the company to break even. 1300

   c) Estimate the number of bicycles that must be sold for the company to make $150,000 profit. 3800

52. ***Taxi Operating Costs*** Raul Lopez's weekly cost of operating a taxi is $75 plus 15¢ per mile.

   a) Write a function expressing Raul's weekly cost, c, in terms of the number of miles, m. $c(m) = 75 + 0.15m$

   b) Draw a graph illustrating weekly cost versus the number of miles, for up to 200, driven per week.

   c) If during 1 week, Raul drove the taxi 150 miles, what would be the cost? $97.50

   d) How many miles would Raul have to drive for the weekly cost to be $147? 480 miles

53. ***Salary Plus Commission*** Jayne Haydack's weekly salary at Charter Network is $500 plus 15% commission on her weekly sales.

   a) Write a function expressing Jayne's weekly salary, s, in terms of her weekly sales, x. $s(x) = 500 + 0.15x$

   b) Draw a graph of Jayne's weekly salary versus her weekly sales, for up to $5000 in sales.

   c) What is Jayne's weekly salary if her sales were $2500? $875

   d) If Jayne's weekly salary for the week was $1025, what were her weekly sales? $3500

54. ***Salary Plus Commission*** Lynn Hicks, a real estate agent, makes $150 per week plus a 1% sales commission on each property she sells.

   a) Write a function expressing her weekly salary, s, in terms of sales, x. $s(x) = 150 + 0.01x$

54. b) See graphing answer section, page G7.

b) Draw a graph of her salary versus her weekly sales, for sales up to $100,000.

c) If she sells one house per week for $80,000, what will her weekly salary be? $950

55. *Weight of Girls* The following graph shows weight, in kilograms, for girls (up to 36 months of age) versus length (or height), in centimeters. The red line is the average weight for all girls of the given length, and the green lines represent the upper and lower limits of the normal range.

Girls: Birth to 36 Months Physical Growth

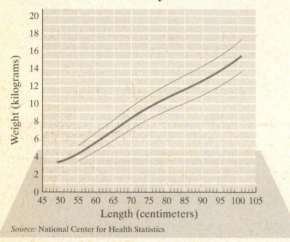

Source: National Center for Health Statistics

a) Explain why the red line represents a function.

b) What is the independent variable? What is the dependent variable?

c) Is the graph of weight versus length approximately linear? yes

d) What is the weight in kilograms of the average girl who is 85 centimeters long? 11.5 kg

e) What is the average length in centimeters of the average girl with a weight of 7 kilograms? 65 cm

f) What weights are considered normal for a girl 95 centimeters long? 12.0–15.5 kg

g) What is happening to the normal range as the lengths increase? Is this what you would expect to happen? Explain. increases

56. *Compound Interest* The graph at the top of the right-hand column illustrates the effect of compound interest.

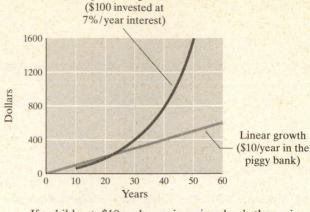

If a child puts $10 each year in a piggy bank, the savings will grow linearly, as shown by the lower curve. If, at age 10, the child invests $100 at 7% interest compounded annually, that $100 will grow exponentially.

a) Explain why both graphs represent functions.

b) What is the independent variable? What is the dependent variable? independent: years, dependent: dollars

c) Using the linear growth curve, determine how long it would take to save $600. 60 yr

d) Using the exponential growth curve, which begins at year 10, determine how long after the account is opened would the amount reach $600?

e) Starting at year 20, how long would it take for the money growing at a linear rate to double? 20 yr

f) Starting at year 20, how long would it take for the money growing exponentially to double? (Exponential growth will be discussed at length in Chapter 9.)

57. When, if ever, will the x- and y-intercepts of a graph be the same? Explain. when the graph goes through origin

58. Write two linear functions whose x- and y-intercepts are both $(0, 0)$. $f(x) = x, g(x) = 2x$

59. Write a function whose graph will have no x-intercept but will have a y-intercept at $(0, 4)$. $f(x) = 4$

60. Write an equation whose graph will have no y-intercept but will have an x-intercept at -2. $x = -2$

61. If the x- and y-intercepts of a linear function are at 1 and -3, respectively, what will be the new x- and y-intercepts if the graph is moved (or translated) up 3 units? both 0

62. If the x- and y-intercepts of a linear function are -1 and 3, respectively, what will be the new x- and y-intercepts if the graph is moved (or translated) down 4 units?

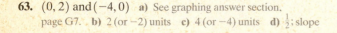

55. a) only one y-value for each x-value **b)** independent: length, dependent: weight

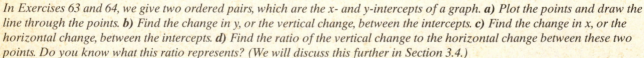

56. a) For each graph, each x-value corresponds to exactly one y-value. **d)** ≈26 yr **f)** ≈10 yr **62.** x-intercept: $\frac{1}{3}$, y-intercept: -1

*In Exercises 63 and 64, we give two ordered pairs, which are the x- and y-intercepts of a graph. **a)** Plot the points and draw the line through the points. **b)** Find the change in y, or the vertical change, between the intercepts. **c)** Find the change in x, or the horizontal change, between the intercepts. **d)** Find the ratio of the vertical change to the horizontal change between these two points. Do you know what this ratio represents? (We will discuss this further in Section 3.4.)*

63. $(0, 2)$ and $(-4, 0)$ **a)** See graphing answer section, page G7. **b)** 2 (or -2) units **c)** 4 (or -4) units **d)** $\frac{1}{2}$; slope

64. $(3, 5)$ and $(-1, -1)$ **a)** See graphing answer section, page G7. **b)** 6 (or -6) units **c)** 4 (or -4) units **d)** $\frac{3}{2}$; slope

Solve each equation for x as done in Example 9. Use a graphing calculator if one is available. If not, draw the graphs yourself.

65. $3x + 2 = 2x + 3$ 1

66. $-2(x - 2) = 3(x + 6) + 1$ -3

67. $0.3(x + 5) = -0.6(x + 2)$ -3

68. $2x + \dfrac{1}{4} = 5x - \dfrac{1}{2}$ 0.25

 Find the x- and y-intercepts of the graph of each equation using your graphing calculator.

69. $y = 2(x + 3.2)$ $(-3.2, 0), (0, 6.4)$

70. $5x - 2y = 7$ $(1.4, 0), (0, -3.5)$

71. $-4x - 3.2y = 8$ $(-2, 0), (0, -2.5)$

72. $y = \dfrac{3}{5}x - \dfrac{1}{2}$ $(0.8\overline{3}, 0), (0, -0.5)$

Cumulative Review Exercises

[1.4] **73.** Evaluate $4\{2 - 3[(1 - 4) - 5]\} - 2$. 102

[2.1] **74.** Solve $\dfrac{1}{3}y - 3y = 6(y + 2)$. $-\dfrac{18}{13}$

[2.6] *In Exercises 75–77* **a)** *explain the procedure to solve the equation or inequality for x (assume that b > 0) and* **b)** *solve the equation or inequality.*

75. a), 76. a), 77. a), 78. a) Answers will vary.   75. b) $x = a + b$ or $x = a - b$

75. $|x - a| = b$

76. $|x - a| < b$ **b)** $a - b < x < a + b$

77. $|x - a| > b$ **b)** $x < a - b$ or $x > a + b$

78. Solve the equation $|x - 4| = |2x - 2|$. $\{2, -2\}$

3.4 THE SLOPE–INTERCEPT FORM OF A LINEAR EQUATION

SSM   Study Guide   CD/Video

MathPro 4/5   PH Math Tutor Center   prenhall.com/Angel

1 Understand translations of graphs.

2 Find the slope of a line.

3 Recognize slope as a rate of change.

4 Write linear equations in slope–intercept form.

5 Graph linear equations using the slope and the y-intercept.

6 Use the slope–intercept form to construct models from graphs.

1 Understand Translations of Graphs

In this section we discuss the translations of graphs, the concept of slope, and the slope–intercept form of a linear equation.

Consider the three equations

$$y = 2x + 3$$
$$y = 2x$$
$$y = 2x - 3$$

Each equation is graphed in Figure 3.50.

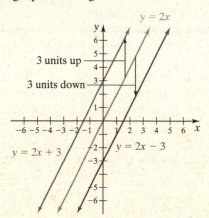

FIGURE 3.50

What are the y-intercepts of $y = 2x + 3$, $y = 2x$ (or $y = 2x + 0$), and $y = 2x - 3$? The y-intercepts are at $(0, 3)$, $(0, 0)$, and $(0, -3)$, respectively. Notice that the graph of $y = 2x + 3$ is the graph of $y = 2x$ shifted, or **translated**, 3 units up and $y = 2x - 3$ is the graph of $y = 2x$ translated 3 units down. All three lines are **parallel**; that is, they do not intersect no matter how far they are extended.

Using this information, can you guess what the y-intercept of $y = 2x + 4$ will be? How about the y-intercept of $y = 2x - \frac{5}{3}$? If you answered $(0, 4)$ and $\left(0, -\frac{5}{3}\right)$, respectively, you answered correctly. In fact, the graph of an equation of the form $y = 2x + b$ will have a y-intercept of $(0, b)$.

Now consider the graphs of the equations $y = -\frac{1}{3}x + 4$, $y = -\frac{1}{3}x$, and $y = -\frac{1}{3}x - 2$, shown in Figure 3.51. The y-intercepts of the three lines are $(0, 4)$, $(0, 0)$, and $(0, -2)$, respectively. The graph of $y = -\frac{1}{3}x + b$ will have a y-intercept of $(0, b)$.

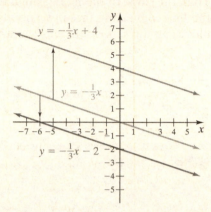

FIGURE 3.51

By looking at the preceding equations, their graphs, and y-intercepts, can you determine the y-intercept of the graph of $y = mx + b$ where m and b are real numbers? If you answered $(0, b)$, you answered correctly. In general, the graph of $y = mx + b$, where m and b are real numbers, has a y-intercept $(0, \boldsymbol{b})$.

If we look at the graphs in Figure 3.50, we see that the slopes (or slants) of the three lines appear to be the same. If we look at the graphs in Figure 3.51, we see that the slopes of those three lines appear to be the same, but their slope is different from the slope of the three lines in Figure 3.50.

If we consider the equation $y = mx + b$, where the b determines the y-intercept of the line, we can reason that the m is responsible for the slope (or the slant) of the line.

2 Find the Slope of a Line

Now let's speak about slope. The **slope of a line** is the ratio of the vertical change (or rise) to the horizontal change (or run) between any two points on a line. Consider the graph of $y = 2x$ (the blue line in Figure 3.50, repeated in Figure 3.52a). Two points on this line are $(1, 2)$ and $(3, 6)$. Let's find the slope of the line through these points. If we draw a line parallel to the x-axis through the point $(1, 2)$ and a line parallel to the y-axis through the point $(3, 6)$, the two lines intersect at $(3, 2)$. (See Fig. 3.52b.)

From Figure 3.52b we can determine the slope of the line. The vertical change (along the y-axis) is $6 - 2$, or 4 units. The horizontal change (along the x-axis) is $3 - 1$, or 2 units.

$$\text{slope} = \frac{\text{vertical change}}{\text{horizontal change}} = \frac{4}{2} = 2$$

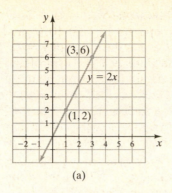

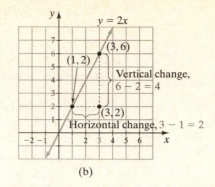

FIGURE 3.52

(a)

(b)

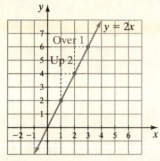

FIGURE 3.53

Thus, the slope of the line through the points $(3, 6)$ and $(1, 2)$ is 2. By examining the line connecting these two points, we can see that for each 2 units the graph moves up the y-axis, it moves 1 unit to the right on the x-axis (Fig. 3.53).

We have determined that the slope of the graph of $y = 2x$ is 2. If you were to compute the slope of the other two lines in Figure 3.50, you would find that the graphs of $y = 2x + 3$ and $y = 2x - 3$ also have a slope of 2.

Can you guess what the slope of the graphs of the equations $y = -3x + 2$, $y = -3x$, and $y = -3x - 2$ is? The slope of all three lines is -3. In general, the slope of an equation of the form $y = mx + b$ is m.*

Now let's determine the procedure to find the slope of a line passing through the two points (x_1, y_1) and (x_2, y_2). Consider Figure 3.54. The vertical change can be found by subtracting y_1 from y_2. The horizontal change can be found by subtracting x_1 from x_2.

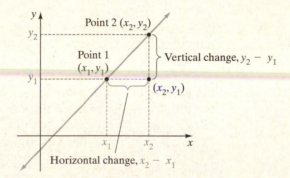

FIGURE 3.54

DEFINITION

The **slope** of the line through the distinct points (x_1, y_1) and (x_2, y_2) is

$$\text{slope} = \frac{\text{change in } y \text{ (vertical change)}}{\text{change in } x \text{ (horizontal change)}} = \frac{y_2 - y_1}{x_2 - x_1}$$

provided that $x_1 \neq x_2$.

It makes no difference which two points on the line are selected when finding the slope of a line. It also makes no difference which point you label (x_1, y_1) or (x_2, y_2). As mentioned before, the letter m is used to represent the slope of a line. The Greek capital letter delta, Δ, is used to represent the words "the change in."

---

*The letter m is traditionally used for slope. It is believed m comes from the French word *monter*, which means to climb.

335

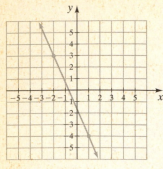

FIGURE 3.55

NOW TRY EXERCISE 35

Thus, the slope is sometimes indicated as

$$m = \frac{\Delta y}{\Delta x} = \frac{y_2 - y_1}{x_2 - x_1}$$

EXAMPLE 1   Find the slope of the line in Figure 3.55.

Solution   Two points on the line are $(-2, 3)$ and $(1, -4)$. Let $(x_2, y_2) = (-2, 3)$ and $(x_1, y_1) = (1, -4)$. Then

$$m = \frac{y_2 - y_1}{x_2 - x_1} = \frac{3 - (-4)}{-2 - 1} = \frac{3 + 4}{-3} = -\frac{7}{3}$$

The slope of the line is $-\frac{7}{3}$. Note that if we had let $(x_1, y_1) = (-2, 3)$ and $(x_2, y_2) = (1, -4)$, the slope would still be $-\frac{7}{3}$. Try it and see.   ✳

A line that rises going from left to right (Fig. 3.56a) has a **positive slope**. A line that neither rises nor falls going from left to right (Fig. 3.56b) has **zero slope**. A line that falls going from left to right (Fig. 3.56c) has a **negative slope**.

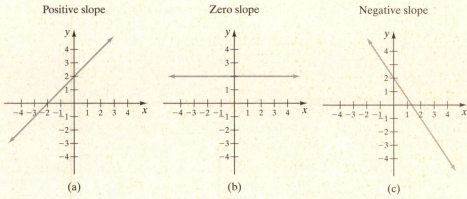

Positive slope   Zero slope   Negative slope

(a)   (b)   (c)

FIGURE 3.56

Slope is undefined.

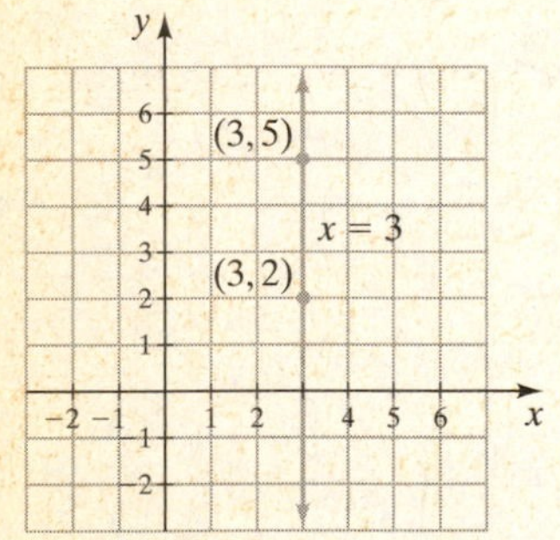

FIGURE 3.57

NOW TRY EXERCISE 19

Consider the graph of $x = 3$ (Fig. 3.57). What is its slope? The graph is a vertical line and goes through the points $(3, 2)$ and $(3, 5)$. Let the point $(3, 5)$ represent (x_2, y_2) and let $(3, 2)$ represent (x_1, y_1). Then the slope of the line is

$$m = \frac{y_2 - y_1}{x_2 - x_1} = \frac{5 - 2}{3 - 3} = \frac{3}{0}$$

Since it is meaningless to divide by 0, we say that the slope of this line is undefined. **The slope of any vertical line is undefined.**

HELPFUL HINT

When students are asked to give the slope of a horizontal or a vertical line, they often answer incorrectly. When asked for the slope of a horizontal line, your response should be "the slope is 0." If you give your answer as "no slope," your instructor may well mark it wrong since these words may have various interpretations. When asked for the slope of a vertical line, your answer should be "the slope is undefined." Again, if you use the words "no slope," this may be interpreted differently by your instructor and marked wrong.

3 Recognize Slope as a Rate of Change

Sometimes it is helpful to describe slope as a *rate of change*. Consider a slope of $\frac{5}{3}$. This means that the *y*-value increases 5 units for each 3-unit increase in *x*. Equivalently, we can say that the *y*-value increases $\frac{5}{3}$ units, or $1.\overline{6}$ units, for each 1-unit increase in *x*. When we give the change in *y* per unit change in *x* we are giving the slope as a **rate of change**. When discussing real-life situations or when creating mathematical models, it is often useful to discuss slope as a rate of change.

EXAMPLE 2   **Public Debt**   The following table of values and the corresponding graph (Fig. 3.58) illustrate the U.S. public debt in billions of dollars from 1910 through 2002.

Year	U.S. public debt (billions of dollars)
1910	1.1
1930	16.1
1950	256.1
1970	370.1
1990	3323.3
2002	5957.2

Source: U.S. Dept. of the Treasury, Bureau of Public Debt.

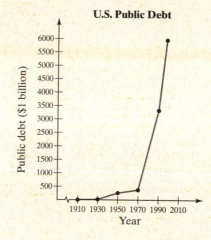

U.S. Public Debt

FIGURE 3.58

a) Determine the slope of the line segments between 1910 and 1930 and between 1990 and 2002.

b) Compare the two slopes found in part **a)** and explain what this means in terms of the U.S. public debt.

Solution   **a)** Understand   To find the slope between any 2 years, find the ratio of the change in debt to the change in years.

Slope from 1910 to 1930

$$m = \frac{16.1 - 1.1}{1930 - 1910} = \frac{15}{20} = 0.75$$

The U.S. public debt from 1910 to 1930 increased at a rate of $0.75 billion per year.

Slope from 1990 to 2002

$$m = \frac{5957.2 - 3323.3}{2002 - 1990} = \frac{2633.9}{12} \approx 219.49$$

The U.S. public debt from 1990 to 2002 increased at a rate of about $219.49 billion per year.

b) Slope measures a rate of change. Comparing the slopes for the two periods shows that there was a much greater increase in the average rate of change in the public debt from 1990 to 2002 than from 1910 to 1930. The slope of the line segment from 1990 to 2002 is greater than the slope of any other line segment on the graph. This indicates that the public debt from 1990 to 2002 grew at a faster rate than at any other time period illustrated.

NOW TRY EXERCISE 67

337

4 Write Linear Equations in Slope–Intercept Form

We have already shown that for an equation of the form $y = mx + b$, m represents the slope and b represents the y-intercept. For this reason a linear equation written in the form $y = mx + b$ is said to be in **slope–intercept form**.

DEFINITION	The **slope–intercept form of a linear equation** is

$$y = mx + b$$

where **m is the slope** of the line and **$(0, b)$ is the y-intercept** of the line.

Examples of Equations in Slope–Intercept Form

$$y = 3x - 6 \qquad y = \frac{1}{2}x + \frac{3}{2}$$

Slope ⟶   ⟵ y-intercept is $(0, b)$

$$y = mx + b$$

Equation	Slope	y-Intercept
$y = 3x - 6$	3	$(0, -6)$
$y = \dfrac{1}{2}x + \dfrac{3}{2}$	$\dfrac{1}{2}$	$\left(0, \dfrac{3}{2}\right)$

To write an equation in slope–intercept form, solve the equation for y.

EXAMPLE 3   Determine the slope and y-intercept of the equation $-5x + 2y = 6$.

Solution   Write the equation in slope–intercept form by solving the equation for y.

$$-5x + 2y = 6$$
$$2y = 5x + 6$$
$$y = \frac{5x + 6}{2}$$
$$y = \frac{5x}{2} + \frac{6}{2}$$
$$y = \frac{5}{2}x + 3$$

NOW TRY EXERCISE 45   The slope is $\dfrac{5}{2}$; the y-intercept is $(0, 3)$.   ✳

5 Graph Linear Equations Using the Slope and the y-Intercept

One reason for studying the slope–intercept form of a line is that it can be useful in drawing the graph of a linear equation, as illustrated in Example 4.

EXAMPLE 4 Graph $2y + 4x = 6$ using the y-intercept and slope.

Solution Begin by solving for y to get the equation in slope–intercept form.

$$2y + 4x = 6$$
$$2y = -4x + 6$$
$$y = -2x + 3$$

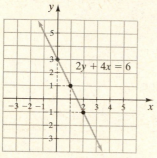

FIGURE 3.59

The slope is -2 and the y-intercept is $(0, 3)$. Place a point at 3 on the y-axis (Fig. 3.59). Then use the slope to obtain a second point. The slope is negative; therefore, the graph must fall as it goes from left to right. Since the slope is -2, the ratio of the vertical change to the horizontal change must be 2 to 1 (remember, 2 means $\frac{2}{1}$). Thus, if you start at $y = 3$ and move down 2 units and to the right 1 unit, you will obtain a second point on the graph.

Continue this process of moving 2 units down and 1 unit to the right to get a third point. Now draw a line through the three points to get the graph. ✳

In Example 4, we chose to move down and to the right to get the second and third points. We could have also chosen to move up and to the left to get the second and third points.

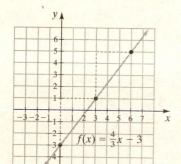

FIGURE 3.60

EXAMPLE 5 Graph $f(x) = \frac{4}{3}x - 3$ using the y-intercept and slope.

Solution Since $f(x)$ is the same as y, this function is in slope–intercept form. The y-intercept is $(0, -3)$ and the slope is $\frac{4}{3}$. Place a point at -3 on the y-axis. Then, since the slope is positive, obtain the second and third points by moving up 4 units and to the right 3 units. The graph is shown in Figure 3.60.

NOW TRY EXERCISE 51 ✳

6 Use the Slope–Intercept Form to Construct Models from Graphs

Often we can use the slope–intercept form of a linear equation to determine a function that models a real-life situation. Example 6 shows how this may be done.

EXAMPLE 6 **Newspapers** Consider the graph in Figure 3.61, which shows the declining number of adults who read the daily newspaper. Notice that the graph is somewhat linear.

a) Write a linear function whose graph approximates the graph shown.

b) Assuming this trend continues, estimate the percent of adults who will read a daily newspaper in 2005 using the function determined in part **a)**.

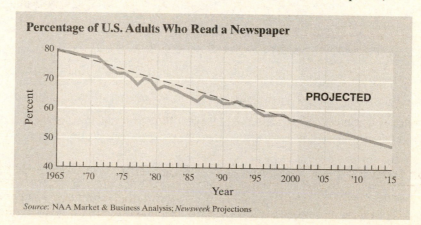

FIGURE 3.61

Solution   **a)** To make the numbers easier to work with, we will select 1965 as a *reference year*. Then we can replace 1965 with 0, 1966 with 1, 1967 with 2, and so on. Then 2001 would be 36 (see Fig. 3.62).

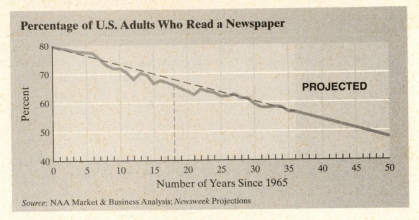

Percentage of U.S. Adults Who Read a Newspaper

PROJECTED

Number of Years Since 1965

FIGURE 3.62   *Source*: NAA Market & Business Analysis; *Newsweek* Projections

If we call the vertical axis y and the horizontal axis x, then the y-intercept is 80. The ordered pair that represents the y-intercept is $(0, 80)$. In 2001 it appears that about 57% of the adult population read a daily newspaper. Let's select $(36, 57)$ as a second point on the graph of the straight line we drew in Figure 3.62. We designate $(36, 57)$ as (x_2, y_2) and $(0, 80)$ as (x_1, y_1).

$$\text{slope} = \frac{\text{change in percent}}{\text{change in year}} = \frac{y_2 - y_1}{x_2 - x_1} = \frac{57 - 80}{36 - 0} = -\frac{23}{36} \approx -0.64$$

Since the slope is approximately -0.64 and the y-intercept is $(0, 80)$, the equation of the straight line is $y = -0.64x + 80$. This equation in function notation is $f(x) = -0.64x + 80$. To use this function remember that $x = 0$ represents 1965, $x = 1$ represents 1966, and so on. Note that $f(x)$, the percent, is a function of x, the number of years since 1965.

b) To determine the approximate percent of readers in 2005, and since $2005 - 1965 = 40$, we substitute 40 for x in the function.

$$f(x) = -0.64x + 80$$
$$f(40) = -0.64(40) + 80$$
$$= -25.6 + 80$$
$$= 54.4$$

Thus, if the current trend continues, about 54% of adults will read a daily newspaper in 2005 (Fig. 3.62).   ✳

NOW TRY EXERCISE 71

Exercise Set 3.4   **1.** Select two points on line; find $\Delta y / \Delta x$.   **5.** Change in x is zero; cannot divide by zero.

Concept/Writing Exercises

↘ **1.** Explain how to find the slope of a line from its graph.

↘ **2.** Explain what it means when the slope of a line is negative.   The line falls going from left to right.

↘ **3.** Explain what it means when the slope of a line is positive.   The line rises going from left to right.

↘ **4.** What is the slope of a horizontal line? Explain. $m = 0$

↘ **5.** Why is the slope of a vertical line undefined?

↘ **6. a)** Using the slope formula, $m = \dfrac{y_2 - y_1}{x_2 - x_1}$, determine the slope of the line that contains the points $(3, 4)$ and $(4, 6)$. Use $(3, 4)$ as (x_1, y_1). $m = 2$

b) Calculate the slope again, but this time use $(4, 6)$ as (x_1, y_1). $m = 2$

c) When finding the slope using the formula, will your answer be the same regardless of which of the two points you designate as (x_1, y_1)? Explain.   yes

7. Explain how to write an equation given in standard form in slope–intercept form. Solve for y.

8. In the equation $y = mx + b$, what does the m represent? What does the b represent? slope, y-intercept

9. a) What does it mean when a graph is translated down 3 units? moved down 3 units
   b) If the y-intercept of a graph is $(0, -3)$ and the graph is translated down 3 units, what will be its new y-intercept? $(0, -6)$

10. a) What does it mean when a graph is translated up 4 units? moved up 4 units
    b) If the y-intercept of a graph is $(0, 2)$ and the graph is translated up 4 units, what will be its new y-intercept? $(0, 6)$

11. What does it mean when slope is given as a rate of change? change in y for a unit change in x

12. Explain how to graph a linear equation using its slope and y-intercept. Plot y-intercept; use m to get second point.

Practice the Skills

Find the slope of the line through the given points. If the slope of the line is undefined, so state.

13. $(2, 5)$ and $(0, 9)$ -2

14. $(2, 3)$ and $(5, 4)$ $\frac{1}{3}$

15. $(5, 2)$ and $(1, 4)$ $-\frac{1}{2}$

16. $(-3, 5)$ and $(5, -3)$ -1

17. $(-3, 5)$ and $(2, 0)$ -1

18. $(2, 3)$ and $(2, -3)$ undefined

19. $(4, 2)$ and $(4, -1)$ undefined

20. $(8, -4)$ and $(-1, -2)$ $-\frac{2}{9}$

21. $(-3, 4)$ and $(-1, 4)$ 0

22. $(2, 3)$ and $(-5, 3)$ 0

23. $(-2, 3)$ and $(7, -3)$ $-\frac{2}{3}$

24. $(2, -4)$ and $(-5, -3)$ $-\frac{1}{7}$

Solve for the given variable if the line through the two given points is to have the given slope.

25. $(3, 2)$ and $(4, b)$, $m = 1$ $b = 3$

26. $(-4, 3)$ and $(-2, b)$, $m = -3$ $b = -3$

27. $(5, 3)$ and $(1, k)$, $m = \frac{1}{2}$ $k = 1$

28. $(5, d)$ and $(9, 2)$, $m = -\frac{3}{4}$ $d = 5$

29. $(x, 2)$ and $(3, -4)$, $m = 2$ $x = 6$

30. $(-2, -3)$ and $(x, 4)$, $m = \frac{1}{2}$ $x = 12$

31. $(2, -2)$ and $(r, -1)$, $m = -\frac{1}{2}$ $r = 0$

32. $(-4, -1)$ and $(x, 2)$, $m = -\frac{3}{5}$ $x = -9$

Find the slope of the line in each of the figures. If the slope of the line is undefined, so state. Then write an equation of the given line.

33.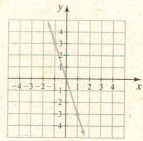
$m = -3$, $y = -3x$

34.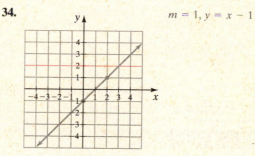
$m = 1$, $y = x - 1$

35.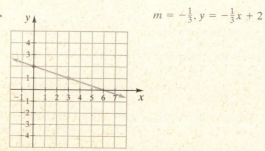
$m = -\frac{1}{3}$, $y = -\frac{1}{3}x + 2$

36.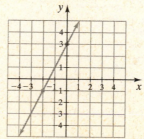
$m = 2$, $y = 2x + 3$

37. 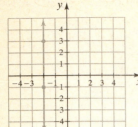 m is undefined, $x = -2$

38. 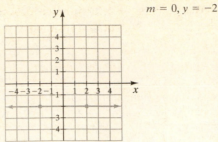 $m = 0, y = -2$

39. 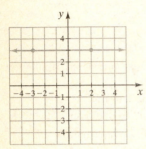 $m = 0, y = 3$

40. 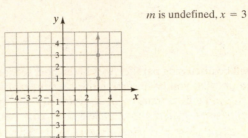 m is undefined, $x = 3$

41. 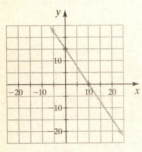 $m = -\frac{3}{2}, y = -\frac{3}{2}x + 15$

42. 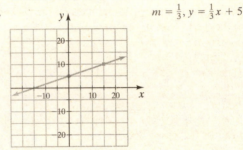 $m = \frac{1}{3}, y = \frac{1}{3}x + 5$

43. $y = -x + 2, -1, (0, 2)$ **44.** $y = 3x + 6, 3, (0, 6)$ **45.** $y = -\frac{1}{3}x + 2, -\frac{1}{3}, (0, 2)$ **46.** $y = -\frac{2}{3}x - 2, -\frac{2}{3}, (0, -2)$

Write each equation in slope–intercept form (if not given in that form). Determine the slope and the y-intercept and use them to draw the graph of the linear equation.   **43.–48.** *See graphing answer section, pages G7 and G8.*

43. $y = -x + 2$

44. $-3x + y = 6$

45. $5x + 15y = 30$

46. $-2x = 3y + 6$

47. $-50x + 20y = 40$
$y = \frac{5}{2}x + 2, \frac{5}{2}, (0, 2)$

48. $60x = -30y + 60$
$y = -2x + 2, -2, (0, 2)$

Use the slope and y-intercept to graph each function.   **49.–52.** *See graphing answer section, page G8.*

49. $f(x) = -2x + 1$

50. $g(x) = \frac{2}{3}x - 4$

51. $h(x) = -\frac{3}{4}x + 2$

52. $h(x) = -\frac{2}{5}x + 4$

Problem Solving

53. Given the equation $y = mx + b$, for the values of m and b given, match parts **a)**–**d)** with the appropriate graphs labeled 1–4.

a) $m > 0, b < 0$ **b)** $m < 0, b < 0$ **c)** $m < 0, b > 0$ **d)** $m > 0, b > 0$

1.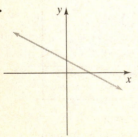

2.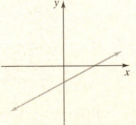

3.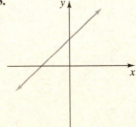

4.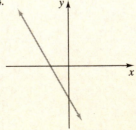

a) 2   b) 4   c) 1   d) 3

55. If the slopes are the same and the y-intercepts are different, the lines are parallel.   **60. a)** $y = -\frac{3}{4}x - 1$

54. Given the equation $y = mx + b$, for the values of m and b given, match parts **a)–d)** with the appropriate graphs labeled 1–4.

a) $m = 0, b > 0$ **b)** $m = 0, b < 0$ **c)** m is undefined, x-intercept < 0 **d)** m is undefined, x-intercept > 0

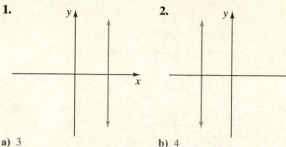

1.   **2.**   **3.**   **4.**

a) 3   **b)** 4   **c)** 2   **d)** 1

55. We will be discussing parallel lines in the next section. Based on what you have read in this section, explain how you could determine (without graphing) that the graphs of two equations are parallel.

56. How can you determine whether two straight lines are parallel?   determine the slope; if same, lines parallel

57. If one point on a graph is $(6, 3)$ and the slope of the line is $\frac{4}{3}$, find the y-intercept of the graph. $(0, -5)$

58. If one point on a graph is $(6, 1)$ and the slope of the line is $m = \frac{2}{3}$, find the y-intercept of the graph. $(0, -3)$

59. In the following graph, the green line is a translation of the blue line.

a) Determine the equation of the blue line. $y = 3x + 1$

b) Use the equation of the blue line to determine the equation of the green line. $y = 3x - 5$

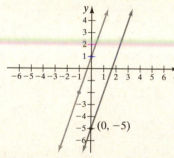

$(0, -5)$

60. In the following graph, the red line is a translation of the blue line.

a) Determine the equation of the blue line.

b) Use the equation of the blue line to determine the equation of the red line. $y = -\frac{3}{4}x + \frac{7}{2}$

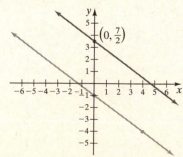

$\left(0, \frac{7}{2}\right)$

61. The graph of $y = x - 1$ is translated up 3 units. Determine

a) the slope of the translated graph.   1

b) the y-intercept of the translated graph. $(0, 2)$

c) the equation of the translated graph. $y = x + 2$

62. The graph of $y = -\frac{3}{2}x + 3$ is translated down 4 units. Determine

a) the slope of the translated graph. $-\frac{3}{2}$

b) the y-intercept of the translated graph. $(0, -1)$

c) the equation of the translated graph. $y = -\frac{3}{2}x - 1$

63. The graph of $3x - 2y = 6$ is translated down 4 units. Find the equation of the translated graph. $y = \frac{3}{2}x - 7$

64. The graph of $-3x - 5y = 10$ is translated up 2 units. Find the equation of the translated graph. $y = -\frac{3}{5}x$

65. If a line passes through the points $(6, 4)$ and $(-4, 2)$, find the change of y with respect to a 1-unit change in x.   0.2

66. If a line passes through the points $(-3, -4)$ and $(5, 2)$, find the change of y with respect to a 1-unit change in x.   0.75

67. *Amtrak Expenses* The National Railroad and Passenger Corporation, better known as Amtrak, continues to face economic struggles. Expenses since 1985 have grown at a much faster rate than revenues. The following table gives the expenses, in millions of dollars, of Amtrak for selected years.

a)–b) See graphing answer section, page G7.

Year	Amtrak expenses (in millions of dollars)
1985	$1600
1990	$2012
1995	$2257
2000	$2876

Source: Amtrak Fiscal Year 2000 Annual Report

a) Plot these points on a graph.

b) Connect these points using line segments.

c) Determine the slopes of each of the three line segments. 82.4, 49.0, 123.8

d) During which period was there the greatest average rate of change? Explain. 1995–2000

68. *Speed of Computers* Each year computers become faster and more powerful. The following table shows the record speed, in billions of operations per second, for supercomputers for selected years.

Year	Operations per second (billions)
1994	143
1996	303
1997	1070
2001	7226

Source: U.S. Dept. of Energy

a)–b) See graphing answer section, page G7.

a) Plot these points on a graph.

b) Connect the points using line segments.

c) Determine the slope of each of the three line segments. 80, 767, 1539

d) During which period was there the greatest average rate of change? Explain. 1997–2001

69. *Heart Rate* The following bar graph shows the maximum recommended heart rate, in beats per minute, under stress for men of different ages. The bars are connected by a straight line.

a) Use the straight line to determine a function that can be used to estimate the maximum recommended heart rate, h, for $0 \leq x \leq 50$, where x is the number of years after age 20. $h(x) = -x + 200$

b) Using the function from part **a)**, determine the maximum recommended heart rate for a 34-year-old man. 186 beats per minute

Heart Rate vs. Age

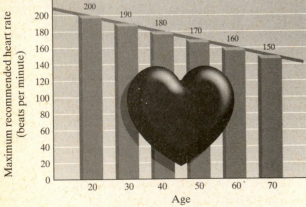

Source: The American Geriatric Society

70. *Poverty Threshold* The federal government defines the poverty threshold as an estimate of the annual family income necessary to have what society defines as a minimally acceptable standard of living. The following bar graph shows the poverty threshold for a family of four for the years 1995 through 2000.

U.S. Poverty Threshold for a Family of Four

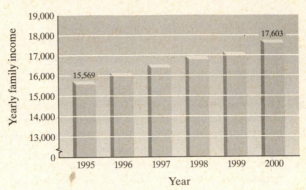

Source: U.S. Bureau of the Census

a) Determine a linear function that can be used to estimate the poverty threshold for a family of four, P, from 1995 through 2000. Let t represent the number of years since 1995. (In other words, 1995 corresponds to $t = 0$, 1996 corresponds to $t = 1$, and so on.) $P(t) = 406.8t + 15{,}569$

b) Using the function from part **a)**, determine the poverty threshold in 1997. Compare your answer with the graph to see whether the graph supports your answer. $16,382.60   **70. c)** $19,637.00

c) Assuming this trend continues, determine the poverty threshold for a family of four in the year 2005.

d) Assuming this trend continues, in which year will the poverty threshold for a family of four reach $20,000? 2005

71. *Number of People Below Poverty Threshold* The poverty threshold was defined in Exercise 70. The following graph shows the number of people in the United States, in millions, who were below the poverty threshold in the years 1996 through 2000.

Persons Below the Poverty Threshold

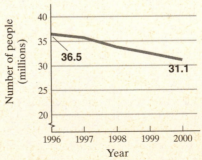

Source: U.S. Bureau of the Census

71. b) 33.8 million people **c)** 24.35 million people   **72. a)** $P(t) = -0.0185t + 0.766$ **73. a)** $n(t) = -50.64t + 7156$ **b)** 6143 hospitals

a) Using 1996 as a reference year, determine a linear function that can be used to estimate the number of people, N, below the poverty threshold for the years 1996 through 2000. In the function, let t represent the number of years since 1996. $N(t) = -1.35t + 36.5$

b) Using the function from part **a)**, estimate the number of people below the poverty threshold for the year 1998. Compare your answer with the graph to see whether the graph supports your answer.

c) Assuming this trend continues, how many people will be below the poverty threshold in 2005?

d) Assuming this trend continues, during what year will the number of people below the poverty threshold reach 25 million people?   2004

72. Purchasing Power of the Dollar The purchasing power of the dollar is measured by comparing the current price of items to the price of those same items in 1982. From the chart below you will see that the purchasing power of the dollar has steadily declined for the years 1990 through 2000. This means that $1 buys less each year.

Purchasing Power of the Dollar

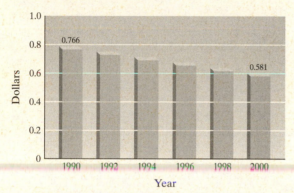

Year

Source: U.S. Bureau of Economic Analysis

a) Using 1990 as the reference year, determine a linear function that can be used to estimate the purchasing power, P, for the years 1990 through 2000. In the function, let t represent the number of years since 1990.

b) Using the function from part **a)**, estimate the purchasing power of the dollar in 1994. Compare your answer with the graph to see whether the graph supports your answer. $0.692

c) Assuming this trend continues, what would be the purchasing power of the dollar in 2006? $0.470

d) Assuming this trend continues, when would the purchasing power of the dollar reach $0.45?   2007

73. U. S. Hospitals The number of hospitals in the United States has been declining approximately linearly since 1975. In 1975 there were 7156 hospitals. In 2000 there were 5890 hospitals. Let n be the number of hospitals in the United States and t be the number of years since 1975. (Let $t = 0$ correspond to 1975 and $t = 25$ correspond to 2000.) *Source:* American Hospital Association

a) Find a linear function $n(t)$ that fits this data.

b) Use the function from part **a)** to estimate the number of hospitals in the United States in 1995.

c) If this trend continues, estimate the number of hospitals in the United States in 2005.   5637 hospitals

d) If this trend continues, in which year will the number of hospitals in the United States reach 5000?   2017

74. Tetanus Decline Largely due to widespread vaccination campaigns, the disease tetanus, commonly called lockjaw, has rapidly declined in the United States. This decline has been approximately linear since 1990. There were 64 reported cases of tetanus in 1990. There were 26 reported cases of tetanus in 2000. Let C be the number of cases of tetanus in the United States and t be the number of years since 1990. *Source:* Centers for Disease Control and Prevention

a) Find a linear function $C(t)$ that fits this data.

b) Use the function found in part **a)** to estimate the number of reported cases in 1998.   34 cases

c) If this trend continues, estimate the number of cases of tetanus that will be reported in 2005.   7 cases

d) If this trend continues, estimate the year in which no cases of tetanus will be reported.   2006

75. Median Home Sale Price The median home sale price in the United States has been rising linearly since 1995. The median home sale price in 1995 was $110,500. The median home sale price in 2000 was $139,000. Let P be the median home sale price and let t be the number of years since 1995. *Source:* National Association of Realtors

a) Determine a function $P(t)$ that fits this data.

b) Use the function from part **a)** to estimate the median home sale price in 1997. $121,900

c) If this trend continues, estimate the median home sale price in 2010. $196,000

d) If this trend continues, in which year will the median home sale price reach $200,000?   2010

76. Social Security The number of workers per social security beneficiary has been declining approximately linearly since 1970. In 1970 there were 3.7 workers per beneficiary. In 2050 it is projected there will be 2.0 workers per beneficiary. Let W be the workers per social security beneficiary and t be the number of years since 1970.

a) Find a function $W(t)$ that fits the data.

b) Estimate the number of workers per beneficiary in 2020.   2.65

74. a) $C(t) = -3.8t + 64$ **75. a)** $P(t) = 5700t + 110,500$ **76. a)** $W(t) = -0.021t + 3.7$

Suppose you are attempting to graph the equations shown and you get the screens shown. Explain how you know that you have made a mistake in entering each equation. The standard window setting is used on each graph.

77. $y = 3x + 6$

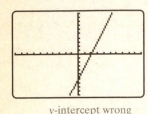

y-intercept wrong

78. $y = -2x - 4$

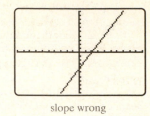

slope wrong

79. $y = \frac{1}{2}x + 4$

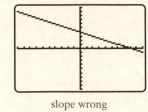

slope wrong

80. $y = -4x - 1$

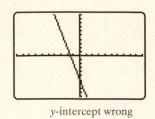

y-intercept wrong

Challenge Problems

81. The photo below is the Castle at Chichén Itzá, Mexico. Each side of the castle has a stairway consisting of 91 steps. The steps of the castle are quite narrow and steep, which makes them hard to climb. The total vertical distance of the 91 steps is 1292.2 inches. If a straight line were to be drawn connecting the tips of the steps, the absolute value of the slope of this line would be 2.21875. Find the average height and width of a step.

height: 14.2 in., width: 6.4 in.

82. A **tangent line** is a straight line that touches a curve at a single point (the tangent line may cross the curve at a different point if extended). Figure 3.63 shows three tangent lines to the curve at points $a, b,$ and c. Note that the tangent line at point a has a positive slope, the tangent line at point b has a slope of 0, and the tangent line at point c has a negative slope. Now consider the curve in Figure 3.64. Imagine that tangent lines are drawn at all points on the curve except at endpoints a and e. Where on the curve in Figure 3.64 would the tangent lines have a positive slope, a slope of 0, and a negative slope?   positive: (b, c) and (d, e), zero: points $b, c,$ and d, negative: (a, b) and (c, d)

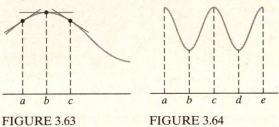

FIGURE 3.63   FIGURE 3.64

Group Activity

83. The following graph from *Consumer Reports* shows the depreciation on a typical car. The initial purchase price is represented as 100%.

a) Group member 1: Determine the 1-year period in which a car depreciates most. Estimate from the graph the percent a car depreciates during this period.

b) Group member 2: Determine between which years the depreciation appears linear or nearly linear.

c) Group member 3: Determine between which 2 years the depreciation is the lowest.

d) As a group, estimate the slope of the line segment from year 0 to year 1. Explain what this means in terms of rate of change.   −0.26

83. a) During the first year, about 25% decrease   **b)** between year 1 and year 3   **c)** between year 4 and year 5

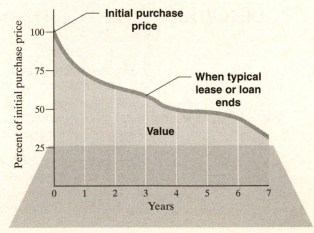

Typical Depreciation Curve

Cumulative Review Exercises

[1.4] **84.** Evaluate $\dfrac{-6^2 - 16 \div 2 \div |-4|}{5 - 3 \cdot 2 - 4 \div 2^2}$. 19

Solve each equation.

[2.1] **85.** $\dfrac{3}{4}x + \dfrac{1}{5} = \dfrac{2}{3}(x - 2)$ $-\dfrac{92}{5}$

86. $2.6x - (-1.4x + 3.4) = 6.2$ 2.4

[2.4] **87.** *Trains* Two trains leave Chicago, Illinois, traveling in the same direction along parallel tracks. The first train leaves 3 hours before the second, and its speed is 15 miles per hour faster than the second. Find the speed of each train if they are 270 miles apart 3 hours after the second train leaves Chicago. First: 75 mph, second: 60 mph

[2.6] **88.** Solve
   a) $|2x + 1| > 3$,   **b)** $|2x + 1| < 3$.
   a) $x < -2$ or $x > 1$ **b)** $-2 < x < 1$

3.5 THE POINT–SLOPE FORM OF A LINEAR EQUATION

SSM   Study Guide   CD/Video

MathPro 4/5 PH Math Tutor Center prenhall.com/Angel

1. Understand the point–slope form of a linear equation.
2. Use the point–slope form to construct models from graphs.
3. Recognize parallel and perpendicular lines.

1 Understand the Point–Slope Form of a Linear Equation

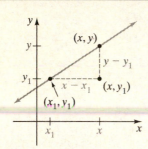

FIGURE 3.65

In the previous section we learned how to use the *slope–intercept form* of a line to determine the equation of a line when the slope and y-intercept of the line are known. In this section we learn how to use the **point–slope form** of a line to determine the equation of a line when the slope and a point on the line are known. The point–slope form can be developed from the expression for the slope between any two points (x, y) and (x_1, y_1) on a line, as shown in Figure 3.65.

$$m = \frac{y - y_1}{x - x_1}$$

Multiplying both sides of the equation by $x - x_1$, we obtain

$$y - y_1 = m(x - x_1)$$

DEFINITION

The **point–slope form of a linear equation** is

$$y - y_1 = m(x - x_1)$$

where m **is the slope** of the line and (x_1, y_1) is a point on the line.

EXAMPLE 1 Write, in slope–intercept form, the equation of the line that passes through the point $(1, 4)$ and has slope -2.

Solution Since we are given the slope of the line and a point on the line, we can write the equation in point–slope form. We can then solve the equation for y to write the equation in slope–intercept form. The slope, m, is -2. The point on the line, (x_1, y_1), is $(1, 4)$. Substitute -2 for m, 1 for x_1, and 4 for y_1 in the point–slope form.

$$y - y_1 = m(x - x_1)$$
$$y - 4 = -2(x - 1) \quad \text{\textit{Point–slope form}}$$
$$y - 4 = -2x + 2$$
$$y = -2x + 6 \quad \text{\textit{Slope–intercept form}}$$

NOW TRY EXERCISE 5

The graph of $y = -2x + 6$ has a slope of -2 and passes through the point $(1, 4)$. ✳

In Example 1 we used the point–slope form to get the equation of a line when we were given a point on the line and the slope of the line. The point–slope form can also be used to find the equation of a line when we are given two points on the line. We show how to do this in Example 2.

EXAMPLE 2 Write, in slope–intercept form, the equation of the line that passes through the points $(2, 3)$ and $(1, 4)$.

Solution Although we are not given the slope of the line, we can use the two given points to determine the slope. We can then proceed as we did in Example 1. We will let $(2, 3)$ be (x_1, y_1) and $(1, 4)$ be (x_2, y_2).

$$m = \frac{y_2 - y_1}{x_2 - x_1} = \frac{4 - 3}{1 - 2} = \frac{1}{-1} = -1$$

The slope, m, is -1. Now we must choose one of the two given points to use as (x_1, y_1) in the point–slope form of the equation of a line. We will choose $(2, 3)$. Substitute -1 for m, 2 for x_1, and 3 for y_1 in the point–slope form.

$$y - y_1 = m(x - x_1)$$
$$y - 3 = -1(x - 2)$$
$$y - 3 = -x + 2$$
$$y = -x + 5$$

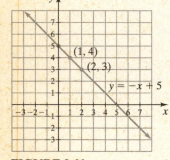

FIGURE 3.66

The graph of $y = -x + 5$ is shown in Figure 3.66. Notice that the y-intercept of this line is at 5, the slope is -1, and the line goes through the points $(2, 3)$ and $(1, 4)$.

Note that we could have also chosen the point $(1, 4)$ to substitute into the point–slope form. Had we done this we would still have obtained the equation $y = -x + 5$. You should verify this now. ✳

NOW TRY EXERCISE 11

2 Use the Point–Slope Form to Construct Models from Graphs

Now let's look at an application where we use the point–slope form to determine a function that models a given situation.

EXAMPLE 3 **Burning Calories** For those trying to burn calories and lose weight, exercise specialists recommend participating in exercise that can be sustained consistently for long periods of time. The number of calories burned in 1 hour riding a bicycle is a linear function of the speed of the bicycle. The average person riding at 12 mph will burn about 564 calories in 1 hour and while riding at 18 mph will burn about 846 calories in 1 hour. This information is shown in the following graph (Fig. 3.67).

a) Determine a linear function that can be used to estimate the number of calories, C, burned in 1 hour when a bicycle is ridden at r mph, for $6 \leq r \leq 24$.

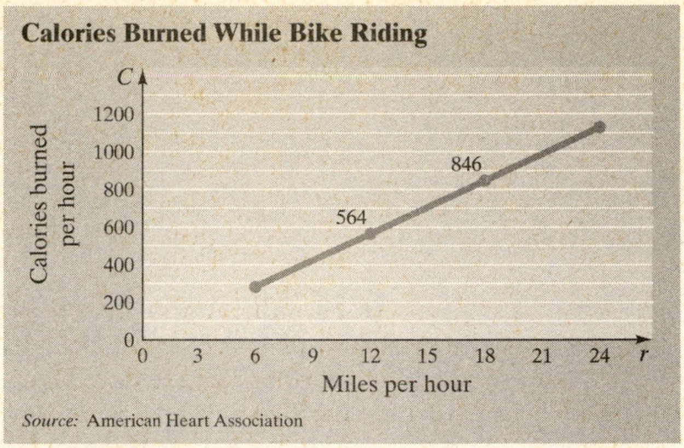

Calories Burned While Bike Riding

Source: American Heart Association

FIGURE 3.67

b) Use the function determined in part **a)** to estimate the number of calories burned in 1 hour when a bicycle is ridden at 20 mph.

c) Use the function determined in part **a)** to estimate the speed at which a bicycle should be ridden to burn 1000 calories in 1 hour.

Solution

a) Understand and Translate   In this example, instead of using the variables x and y as we used in Examples 1 and 2, we use the variables r (for rate or speed) and C (for calories). Regardless of the variables used, the procedure used to determine the equation of the line remains the same. To find the necessary function, we will use the points $(12, 564)$ and $(18, 846)$ and proceed as we did in Example 2. We will first calculate the slope and then use the point–slope form to determine the equation of the line.

Carry Out
$$m = \frac{C_2 - C_1}{r_2 - r_1}$$

$$= \frac{846 - 564}{18 - 12} = \frac{282}{6} = 47$$

Now we write the equation using the point–slope form. We will choose the point $(12, 564)$ for (r_1, C_1).

$$C - C_1 = m(r - r_1)$$
$$C - 564 = 47(r - 12) \quad \text{\textit{Point–slope form}}$$
$$C - 564 = 47r - 564$$
$$C = 47r \quad \text{\textit{Slope–intercept form}}$$

Answer   Since the number of calories burned, C, is a function of the rate, r, the function we are seeking is

$$C(r) = 47r$$

b) To estimate the number of calories burned in 1 hour while riding at 20 mph, we substitute 20 for r in the function.

$$C(r) = 47r$$
$$C(20) = 47(20) = 940$$

Therefore 940 calories are burned while riding at 20 mph for 1 hour.

c) To estimate the speed at which a bicycle should be ridden to burn 1000 calories in 1 hour, we substitute 1000 for $C(r)$ in the function.

$$C(r) = 47r$$
$$1000 = 47r$$
$$\frac{1000}{47} = r$$
$$r \approx 21.28$$

NOW TRY EXERCISE 53

Thus the bicycle would need to be ridden at about 21.28 mph to burn 1000 calories in 1 hour. ✳

In Example 3, the function we determined was $C(r) = 47r$. The graph of this function has a slope of 47 and a y-intercept at $(0, 0)$. If the graph in Figure 3.67 was extended to the left, it would intersect the origin. This makes sense since a rate of 0 miles per hour would result in 0 calories being burned by riding in 1 hour.

3 Recognize Parallel and Perpendicular Lines

Parallel lines

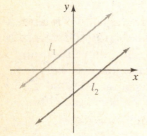

FIGURE 3.68

Figure 3.68 illustrates two *parallel* lines.

> Two lines are **parallel** when they have the same slope.

All vertical lines are parallel even though their slope is undefined.
Figure 3.69 illustrates perpendicular lines. Two lines are *perpendicular* when they cross at right (or 90°) angles.

> Two lines are **perpendicular** when their slopes are *negative reciprocals*.

Perpendicular lines

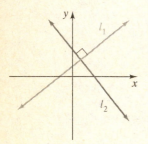

FIGURE 3.69

For any nonzero number a, its **negative reciprocal** is $\frac{-1}{a}$ or $-\frac{1}{a}$. For example, the negative reciprocal of 2 is $\frac{-1}{2}$ or $-\frac{1}{2}$. The product of any nonzero number and its negative reciprocal is -1.

$$a\left(-\frac{1}{a}\right) = -1$$

Note that any vertical line is perpendicular to any horizontal line even though the negative reciprocal cannot be applied. (Why not?)

EXAMPLE 4 Two points on l_1 are $(6, 3)$ and $(2, -3)$. Two points on l_2 are $(0, 2)$ and $(6, -2)$. Determine whether l_1 and l_2 are parallel lines, perpendicular lines, or neither.

Solution Determine the slopes of l_1 and l_2.

$$m_1 = \frac{3 - (-3)}{6 - 2} = \frac{6}{4} = \frac{3}{2} \qquad m_2 = \frac{2 - (-2)}{0 - 6} = \frac{4}{-6} = -\frac{2}{3}$$

Since their slopes are different, l_1 and l_2 are not parallel. To see whether the lines are perpendicular, we need to determine whether the slopes are negative reciprocals. If $m_1 m_2 = -1$, the slopes are negative reciprocals and the lines are perpendicular.

$$m_1 m_2 = \frac{3}{2}\left(-\frac{2}{3}\right) = -1$$

NOW TRY EXERCISE 15   Since the product of the slopes equals -1, the lines are perpendicular.   ✳

EXAMPLE 5   Consider the equation $2x + 4y = 8$. Determine the equation of the line that has a y-intercept of 5 and is **a)** parallel to the given line and **b)** perpendicular to the given line.

Solution   **a)** If we know the slope of a line and its y-intercept, we can use the slope–intercept form, $y = mx + b$, to write the equation. We begin by solving the given equation for y.

$$2x + 4y = 8$$
$$4y = -2x + 8$$
$$y = \frac{-2x + 8}{4}$$
$$y = -\frac{1}{2}x + 2$$

Two lines are parallel when they have the same slope. Therefore, the slope of the line parallel to the given line must be $-\frac{1}{2}$. Since its slope is $-\frac{1}{2}$ and its y-intercept is 5, its equation must be

$$y = -\frac{1}{2}x + 5$$

The graphs of $2x + 4y = 8$ and $y = -\frac{1}{2}x + 5$ are shown in Figure 3.70.

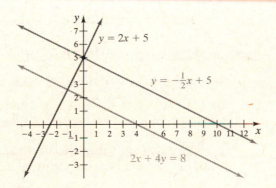

FIGURE 3.70

b) Two lines are perpendicular when their slopes are negative reciprocals. We know that the slope of the given line is $-\frac{1}{2}$. Therefore, the slope of the perpendicular line must be $-1/\left(-\frac{1}{2}\right)$ or 2. The line perpendicular to the given line has a y-intercept of 5. Thus the equation is

$$y = 2x + 5$$

Figure 3.70 also shows the graph of $y = 2x + 5$.   ✳

EXAMPLE 6 Consider the equation $5y = -10x + 7$.

a) Determine the equation of a line that passes through $\left(4, \frac{1}{3}\right)$ that is perpendicular to the graph of the given equation. Write the equation in standard form.

b) Write the equation determined in part **a)** using function notation.

Solution **a)** Determine the slope of the given line by solving the equation for y.

$$5y = -10x + 7$$

$$y = \frac{-10x + 7}{5}$$

$$y = -2x + \frac{7}{5}$$

Since the slope of the given line is -2, the slope of a line perpendicular to it must be the negative reciprocal of -2, which is $\frac{1}{2}$. The line we are seeking must pass through the point $\left(4, \frac{1}{3}\right)$. Using the point–slope form, we obtain

$$y - y_1 = m(x - x_1)$$

$$y - \frac{1}{3} = \frac{1}{2}(x - 4) \qquad \textit{Point–slope form}$$

Now multiply both sides of the equation by the least common denominator, 6, to eliminate fractions.

$$6\left(y - \frac{1}{3}\right) = 6\left[\frac{1}{2}(x - 4)\right]$$

$$6y - 2 = 3(x - 4)$$

$$6y - 2 = 3x - 12$$

Now write the equation in standard form.

$$-3x + 6y - 2 = -12$$

$$-3x + 6y = -10 \qquad \textit{Standard form}$$

FIGURE 3.71

Note that $3x - 6y = 10$ is also an acceptable answer (see Fig. 3.71).

b) To write the equation using function notation, we solve the equation determined in part **a)** for y, and then replace y with $f(x)$.

We will leave it to you to show that the function is $f(x) = \frac{1}{2}x - \frac{5}{3}$. ✳

NOW TRY EXERCISE 39

HELPFUL HINT

The following chart summarizes the three forms of a linear equation we have studied and mentions when each may be useful.

Standard form:	Useful when finding the intercepts of a graph
$ax + by = c$	Will be used in Chapter 4, Systems of Equations and Inequalities

(continued on the next page)

Slope–intercept form:	Used to find the slope and y-intercept of a line
$y = mx + b$	Used to find the equation of a line given its slope and y-intercept
	Used to determine if two lines are parallel or perpendicular
	Used to graph a linear equation
Point–slope form:	Used to find the equation of a line when given the slope of a line and a point on the line
$y - y_1 = m(x - x_1)$	Used to find the equation of a line when given two points on a line

1. $y - y_1 = m(x - x_1)$ **2.** If their slopes are the same and their y-intercepts are different, they are parallel.

Exercise Set 3.5

Concept/Writing Exercises

1. Give the point–slope form of a linear equation.

2. How can we determine whether two lines are parallel?

3. How can we determine whether two lines are perpendicular?

4. Why can't the negative reciprocal test be used to determine whether a vertical line is perpendicular to a horizontal line? cannot divide by 0

3. If their slopes are negative reciprocals, or if one line is vertical and the other is horizontal, the lines are perpendicular.

Practice the Skills

Use the point–slope form to find the equation of a line with the properties given. Then write the equation in slope–intercept form.

5. Slope = 2, through $(1, 1)$ $y = 2x - 1$

6. Slope = −1, through $(-2, 3)$ $y = -x + 1$

7. Slope = $-\dfrac{1}{2}$, through $(4, -1)$ $y = -\dfrac{1}{2}x + 1$

8. Slope = $-\dfrac{7}{8}$, through $(-8, -2)$ $y = -\dfrac{7}{8}x - 9$

9. Slope = $\dfrac{1}{2}$, through $(-1, -5)$ $y = \dfrac{1}{2}x - \dfrac{9}{2}$

10. Slope = $-\dfrac{2}{3}$, through $(-1, -2)$ $y = -\dfrac{2}{3}x - \dfrac{8}{3}$

11. Through $(-4, 6)$ and $(4, -6)$ $y = -\dfrac{3}{2}x$

12. Through $(4, -2)$ and $(1, 9)$ $y = -\dfrac{11}{3}x + \dfrac{38}{3}$

13. Through $(4, -3)$ and $(6, -2)$ $y = \dfrac{1}{2}x - 5$

14. Through $(4, 3)$ and $(-1, 2)$ $y = \dfrac{1}{5}x + \dfrac{11}{5}$

Two points on l_1 and two points on l_2 are given. Determine whether l_1 is parallel to l_2, l_1 is perpendicular to l_2, or neither.

15. l_1: $(2, 0)$ and $(0, 2)$; l_2: $(5, 0)$ and $(0, 5)$ parallel

16. l_1: $(3, 2)$ and $(-1, 5)$; l_2: $(5, -1)$ and $(9, -4)$ parallel

17. l_1: $(1, 1)$ and $(5, 7)$; l_2: $(-1, -1)$ and $(1, 4)$ neither

18. l_1: $(-3, 4)$ and $(4, -3)$; l_2: $(-5, -6)$ and $(6, -5)$ neither

19. l_1: $(3, 2)$ and $(-1, -2)$; l_2: $(2, 0)$ and $(3, -1)$ perpendicular

20. l_1: $(0, 2)$ and $(6, -2)$; l_2: $(4, 0)$ and $(6, 3)$ perpendicular

Determine whether the two equations represent lines that are parallel, perpendicular, or neither. **21., 24., 27.** perpendicular

21. $y = \dfrac{1}{5}x + 1$
$y = -5x + 2$

22. $2x + 3y = 6$
$y = -\dfrac{2}{3}x + 5$ parallel

23. $4x + 2y = 8$
$8x = 4 - 4y$ parallel

24. $2x - y = 4$
$2x + 4y = 8$

25. $4x + 2y = 6$
$-x + 4y = 4$ neither

26. $6x + 2y = 8$
$4x - 9 = -y$ neither

27. $y = \dfrac{1}{2}x - 6$
$-3y = 6x + 9$

28. $2y - 6 = -5x$
$y = -\dfrac{5}{2}x - 2$ parallel

29. $y = \dfrac{1}{2}x + 3$

$-2x + 4y = 8$ parallel

30. $-4x + 6y = 12$

$2x - 3y = 6$ parallel

31. $x - 3y = -9$

$y = 3x + 6$ neither

32. $\dfrac{1}{2}x - \dfrac{3}{4}y = 1$

$\dfrac{3}{5}x + \dfrac{2}{5}y = -1$ perpendicular

Find the equation of a line with the properties given. Write the equation in the form indicated.

33. Through $(2, 5)$ and parallel to the graph of $y = 2x + 4$ (slope–intercept form) $y = 2x + 1$

34. Through $(-3, 2)$ and parallel to the graph of $4x - 2y = 6$ (slope–intercept form) $y = 2x + 8$

35. Through $(-3, -5)$ and parallel to the graph of $2x - 5y = 7$ (standard form) $2x - 5y = 19$

36. Through $(-1, 3)$ and perpendicular to the graph of $y = -2x - 1$ (standard form) $x - 2y = -7$

37. With x-intercept $(3, 0)$ and y-intercept $(0, 5)$ (slope–intercept form) $y = -\frac{5}{3}x + 5$

38. Through $(-2, -1)$ and perpendicular to the graph of $f(x) = -\dfrac{1}{5}x + 1$ (function notation) $f(x) = 5x + 9$

39. Through $(5, -1)$ and perpendicular to the graph of $y = \dfrac{1}{3}x + 1$ (function notation) $f(x) = -3x + 14$

40. Through $(-3, 4)$ and perpendicular to the line with x-intercept $(2, 0)$ and y-intercept $(0, 2)$ (standard form) $x - y = -7$

41. Through $(6, 2)$ and perpendicular to the line with x-intercept $(2, 0)$ and y-intercept $(0, -3)$ (slope–intercept form) $y = -\frac{2}{3}x + 6$

42. Through the point $(2, 1)$ and parallel to the line through the points $(3, 5)$ and $(-2, 3)$ (function notation) $f(x) = \frac{2}{5}x + \frac{1}{5}$

43. a) $C(s) = 45.7s + 95.8$ **44. a)** $C(d) = 35.5d + 347.5$ **45. a)** $d(p) = -0.20p + 90$ **b)** 38 DVD players

Problem Solving

43. *Treadmill* The number of calories burned in 1 hour on a treadmill is a function of the speed of the treadmill. The average person walking on a treadmill (at 0° incline) at a speed of 2.5 miles per hour will burn about 210 calories. At 6 miles per hour the average person will burn about 370 calories. Let C be the calories burned in 1 hour and s be the speed of the treadmill.

a) Determine a linear function $C(s)$ that fits the data.

b) Estimate the calories burned by the average person on a treadmill in 1 hour at a speed of 5 miles per hour. 324.3 calories

44. *Inclined Treadmill* The number of calories burned for 1 hour on a treadmill going at a constant speed is a function of the incline of the treadmill. At 4 miles per hour an average person on a 5° incline will burn 525 calories. At 4 mph on a 15° incline the average person will burn 880 calories. Let C be the calories burned and d be the degrees of incline of the treadmill.

a) Determine a linear function $C(d)$ that fits the data.

b) Determine the number of calories burned by the average person in 1 hour on a treadmill going 4 miles per hour and at a 7° incline. 596

45. *Demand for DVD Players* The *demand* for a product is the number of items the public is willing to buy at a given price. Suppose the demand, d, for DVD players sold in 1 month is a linear function of the price, p, for $\$150 \le p \le \$400$. If the price is $\$200$, then 50 DVD players will be sold each month. If the price is $\$300$, only 30 DVD players will be sold.

a) Using ordered pairs of the form (p, d), write an equation for the demand, d, as a function of price, p.

b) Using the function from part **a)**, determine the demand when the price of the DVD players is $\$260$.

c) Using the function from part **a)**, determine the price charged if the demand for DVD players is 45. $\$225$

46. *Demand for New Sandwiches* The marketing manager of Arby's restaurants determines that the demand, d, for a new chicken sandwich is a linear function of the price, p, for $\$0.80 \le p \le \$4.00$. If the price is $\$1.00$, then 530 chicken sandwiches will be sold each month. If the price is $\$2.00$, only 400 chicken sandwiches will be sold each month.

a) Using ordered pairs of the form (p, d), write an equation for the demand, d, as a function of price, p. $d(p) = -130p + 660$

b) Using the function from part **a)**, determine the demand when the price of the chicken sandwich is $\$1.50$. 465 chicken sandwiches

c) Using the function from part **a)**, determine the price charged if the demand for chicken sandwiches is 205 chicken sandwiches. $\$3.50$

47. *Supply of Kites* The *supply* of a product is the number of items a seller is willing to sell at a given price. The maker of a new kite for children determines that the number of kites she is willing to supply, s, is a linear

49. a) $m(s) = -\frac{1}{3}s + 55$

function of the selling price p for $2.00 \le p \le 4.00$. If a kite sells for $2.00, then 130 per month will be supplied. If a kite sells for $4.00, then 320 per month will be supplied. **a)** $s(p) = 95p - 60$

a) Using ordered pairs of the form (p, s), write an equation for the supply, s, as a function of price, p.

b) Using the function from part **a)**, determine the supply when the price of a kite is $2.80. 206 kites

c) Using the function from part **a)**, determine the price paid if the supply is 225 kites. $3.00

48. *Supply of Baby Strollers* The manufacturer of baby strollers determines that the supply, s, is a linear function of the selling price, p, for $200 \le p \le 300$. If a stroller sells for $210.00, then 20 strollers will be supplied per month. If a stroller sells for $230.00, then 30 strollers will be supplied per month. **a)** $s(p) = 0.5p - 85$

a) Using ordered pairs of the form (p, s), write an equation for the supply, s, as a function of price, p.

b) Using the function from part **a)**, determine the supply when the price of a stroller is $206.00. 18 strollers

c) Using the function from part **a)**, determine the selling price if the supply is 35 strollers. $240.00

49. *Gas Mileage of a Buick Park Avenue* The gas mileage, m, of a Buick Park Avenue is a linear function of the speed, s, at which the car is driven, for $40 \le s \le 90$. If the car is driven at 45 mph, the car's gas mileage is 40 miles per gallon. If the car is driven at 90 mph, the car's gas mileage is 25 miles per gallon.
Source: http://physics.nadn.navy.mil/physics/faculty/schneider/buick.htm

a) Use this data to write the gas mileage, m, of the Buick Park Avenue as a function of speed, s.

b) Using the function from part **a)**, determine the gas mileage of the Buick Park Avenue if the car is driven at a speed of 60 mph. 35 mpg

c) Using the function from part **a)**, determine the speed at which the Buick Park Avenue must be driven to get gas mileage of 30 miles per gallon. 75 mph

50. *Gas Mileage of a Honda Civic* The gas mileage, m, of a Honda Civic is a linear function of the speed, s, at which the car is driven, for $40 \le s \le 90$. If the car is driven at a rate of 45 mph, the car's gas mileage is 50 miles per gallon. If the car is driven at 90 mph, the car's gas mileage is 20 miles per gallon.

a) Use this data to write the gas mileage, m, of the Honda Civic as a function of speed, s. $m(s) = -\frac{2}{3}s + 80$

b) Using the function from part **a)**, determine the gas mileage of the Honda Civic if the car is driven at a speed of 60 mph. 40 mpg

c) Using the function from part **a)**, determine the speed at which the Honda Civic must be driven to get gas mileage of 30 miles per gallon. 75 mph

51. *Chief Warrant Officer Pay* The monthly pay for an Army chief warrant officer, level W-4, is a linear function of the years of service by the officer. An officer with 10 years of service is paid $3477 per month and an officer with 20 years of service is paid $4168 per month.

a) Use this data to write monthly pay, p, as a function of years of service, s. $p(s) = 69.1s + 2786$

b) Using the function from part **a)**, determine the monthly salary of a chief warrant officer with 18 years of service. $4029.80

c) Using the function from part **a)**, determine the number of years of service necessary for a chief warrant officer to have a monthly salary of $4000. ≈ 18 yr

52. *Lecturer Salary* The annual salary of a lecturer at the University of Portsmouth is a linear function of the number of years of teaching experience. A lecturer with 9 years of teaching experience is paid $26,350. A lecturer with 15 years of teaching experience is paid $31,687.

a) Use this data to write the annual salary of a lecturer, s, as a function of the number of years of teaching experience, n. $s(n) = 889.5n + 18{,}344.5$

b) Using the function from part **a)**, determine the annual salary of a lecturer with 10 years of teaching experience. $27,239.50

c) Using the function from part **a)**, estimate the number of years of teaching experience a lecturer must have to obtain an annual salary of $30,000. 13 years

53. *Life Expectancy* As seen in the following graph, the expected number of remaining years of life of a person, y, *approximates* a linear function. The expected number of remaining years is a function of the person's current age, a, for $30 \le a \le 80$. For example, from the graph we see that a person who is currently 50 years old has a life expectancy of 36.0 *more* years.

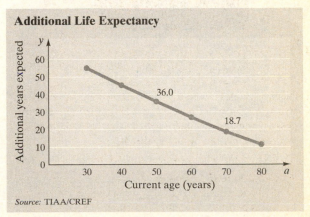

Additional Life Expectancy

Source: TIAA/CREF

53. b) 47.2 yr **c)** 62.7 yr old **55. a)** $w(a) = 0.189a + 10.6$ **b)** 14.758 kg **56. a)** $l(a) = 0.833a + 72$

a) Using the two points on the graph, determine the function $y(a)$ that can be used to approximate the graph. $y(a) = -0.865a + 79.25$

b) Using the function from part **a)**, estimate the life expectancy of a person who is currently 37 years old.

c) Using the function from part **a)**, estimate the current age of a person who has a life expectancy of 25 years.

54. *Guarneri del Gesù Violin* Handcrafted around 1735, Guarneri del Gesù violins are extremely rare and extremely valuable. The graph below shows that the projected value, v, of a Guarneri del Gesù violin is a linear function of the age, a, in years, of the violin, for $261 \le a \le 290$.

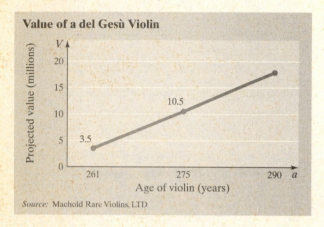

Value of a del Gesù Violin

Source: Machold Rare Violins, LTD

a) Determine the function $v(a)$ represented by this line. $v(a) = 0.5a - 127$

b) Using the function from part **a)**, determine the projected value of a 280-year-old Guarneri del Gesù violin. $13 million

c) Using the function from part **a)**, determine the age of a Guarneri del Gesù violin with a projected value of $15 million. 284 years

Guarneri del Gesù, "Sainton," 1741

55. *Boys' Weights* Parents may recognize the following diagram from visits to the pediatrician's office. The diagram shows percentiles for boys' heights and weights from birth to age 36 months. Overall, the graphs shown are not linear functions. However, certain portions of the graphs can be approximated with a linear function. For example, the graph representing the 95th percentile of boys' weights (the top red line) from age 18 months to age 36 months is approximately linear.

Boys: Birth to 36 months
Length-for-Age and Weight-for-Age Percentiles

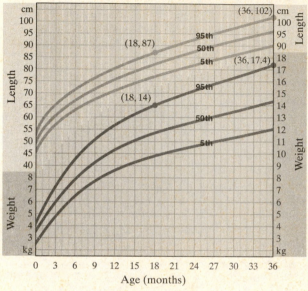

Source: National Center for Health Statistics

a) Use the points shown on the graph of the 95th percentile to write weight, w, as a linear function of age, a, for boys between 18 and 36 months old.

b) Using the function from part **a)**, estimate the weight of a 22-month-old boy who is in the 95th percentile for weight. Compare your answer with the graph to see whether the graph supports your answer.

56. *Boys' Lengths* The diagram in Exercise 55 shows that the graph representing the 95th percentile of boys' lengths (the top yellow line) from age 18 months to age 36 months is approximately linear.

a) Use the points shown on the graph of the 95th percentile to write length, l, as a linear function of age, a, for boys between age 18 and 36 months.

b) Using the function from part **a)**, estimate the length of a 21-month-old boy who is in the 95th percentile. Compare your answer with the graph to see whether the graph supports your answer. 89.493 cm

57. a) Each age has a unique head circumference. **c)** D: $\{a|2 \leq a \leq 18\}$, R: $\{c|48 \leq c \leq 55\}$ **g)** $y = 0.4375x + 47.125$

Group Activity

57. The following graph shows the growth of the circumference of a girl's head. The red line is the average head circumference of all girls for the given age while the green lines represent the upper and lower limits of the normal range. Discuss and answer the following questions as a group.

a) Explain why the graph of the average head circumference represents a function.

b) What is the independent variable? What is the dependent variable? age, head circumference

c) What is the domain of the graph of the average head circumference? What is the range of the average head circumference graph?

d) What interval is considered normal for girls of age 18? 52 to 58 cm

e) For this graph, is head circumference a function of age or is age a function of head circumference? Explain your answer. Circumference is a function of age.

f) Estimate the average girl's head circumference at age 10 and at age 14. 52 cm, 54 cm

g) This graph appears to be nearly linear. Determine an equation or function that can be used to estimate the orange line between $(2, 48)$ and $(18, 55)$.

Head Circumference

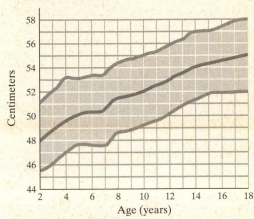

Source: National Center for Health Statistics

Cumulative Review Exercises

[2.5] 58. Solve the inequality $4 - \frac{1}{2}x > 2x + 3$ and indicate the solution in interval notation. $\left(-\infty, \frac{2}{5}\right)$

59. What must you do when multiplying or dividing both sides of an inequality by a negative number?

[3.2] 60. a) What is a relation?

b) What is a function?

c) Draw a graph that is a relation but not a function.

61. Find the domain and range of the function $\{(4, 3), (5, -2), (3, 2), (6, -1)\}$.

59. Reverse the direction of the inequality symbol. **60. a)** any set of ordered pairs **b)** a correspondence where each member of the domain corresponds to a unique member in the range **c)** Answers will vary. **61.** D: $\{3, 4, 5, 6\}$, R: $\{-2, -1, 2, 3\}$

3.6 THE ALGEBRA OF FUNCTIONS

SSM Study Guide CD/Video

MathPro 4/5 PH Math Tutor Center prenhall.com/Angel

1 Find the sum, difference, product, and quotient of functions.

2 Graph the sum of functions.

1 Find the Sum, Difference, Product, and Quotient of Functions

Let's discuss some ways that functions can be combined. If we let $f(x) = x + 2$ and $g(x) = x^2 + 2x$, we can find $f(5)$ and $g(5)$ as follows.

$$f(x) = x + 2 \qquad\qquad g(x) = x^2 + 2x$$
$$f(5) = 5 + 2 = 7 \qquad\qquad g(5) = 5^2 + 2(5) = 35$$

If we add $f(x) + g(x)$, we get

$$f(x) + g(x) = (x + 2) + (x^2 + 2x)$$
$$= x^2 + 3x + 2$$

This new function formed by the sum of $f(x)$ and $g(x)$ is designated as $(f + g)(x)$. Therefore we may write

$$(f + g)(x) = x^2 + 3x + 2$$

We find $(f + g)(5)$ as follows.

$$(f + g)(5) = 5^2 + 3(5) + 2$$
$$= 25 + 15 + 2 = 42$$

Notice that

$$f(5) + g(5) = (f + g)(5)$$
$$7 + 35 = 42 \qquad \textit{True}$$

In fact, for any real number substituted for x you will find that

$$f(x) + g(x) = (f + g)(x)$$

Similar notation exists for subtraction, multiplication, and division of functions.

Operations on Functions

If $f(x)$ represents one function, $g(x)$ represents a second function, and x is in the domain of both functions, then the following operations on functions may be performed:

Sum of functions: $(f + g)(x) = f(x) + g(x)$

Difference of functions: $(f - g)(x) = f(x) - g(x)$

Product of functions: $(f \cdot g)(x) = f(x) \cdot g(x)$

Quotient of functions: $(f/g)(x) = \dfrac{f(x)}{g(x)}$, provided that $g(x) \neq 0$

EXAMPLE 1 If $f(x) = x^2 + x - 6$ and $g(x) = x - 2$, find

a) $(f + g)(x)$
b) $(f - g)(x)$
c) $(g - f)(x)$
d) Does $(f - g)(x) = (g - f)(x)$?

Solution To answer parts **a)–c)**, we perform the indicated operation.

a) $(f + g)(x) = f(x) + g(x)$
$$= (x^2 + x - 6) + (x - 2)$$
$$= x^2 + x - 6 + x - 2$$
$$= x^2 + 2x - 8$$

b) $(f - g)(x) = f(x) - g(x)$
$$= (x^2 + x - 6) - (x - 2)$$
$$= x^2 + x - 6 - x + 2$$
$$= x^2 - 4$$

c) $(g - f)(x) = g(x) - f(x)$
$$= (x - 2) - (x^2 + x - 6)$$
$$= x - 2 - x^2 - x + 6$$
$$= -x^2 + 4$$

d) By comparing the answers to parts **b)** and **c)**, we see that

NOW TRY EXERCISE 11
$$(f - g)(x) \neq (g - f)(x)$$

EXAMPLE 2 If $f(x) = x^2 - 4$ and $g(x) = x - 2$, find

a) $(f - g)(6)$ b) $(f \cdot g)(4)$ c) $(f/g)(8)$

Solution   **a)** $(f - g)(x) = f(x) - g(x)$

$$= (x^2 - 4) - (x - 2)$$
$$= x^2 - x - 2$$

$$(f - g)(6) = 6^2 - 6 - 2$$
$$= 36 - 6 - 2$$
$$= 28$$

We could have also found the solution as follows:

$$f(x) = x^2 - 4 \qquad\qquad g(x) = x - 2$$
$$f(6) = 6^2 - 4 = 32 \qquad\qquad g(6) = 6 - 2 = 4$$
$$(f - g)(6) = f(6) - g(6)$$
$$= 32 - 4 = 28$$

b) We will find $(f \cdot g)(4)$ using the fact that

$$(f \cdot g)(4) = f(4) \cdot g(4)$$
$$f(x) = x^2 - 4 \qquad\qquad g(x) = x - 2$$
$$f(4) = 4^2 - 4 = 12 \qquad\qquad g(4) = 4 - 2 = 2$$

Thus $f(4) \cdot g(4) = 12 \cdot 2 = 24$. Therefore $(f \cdot g)(4) = 24$. We could have also found $(f \cdot g)(4)$ by multiplying $f(x) \cdot g(x)$ and then substituting 4 into the product. We will discuss how to do this in Section 5.2.

c) We will find $(f/g)(8)$ by using the fact that

$$(f/g)(8) = f(8)/g(8)$$
$$f(x) = x^2 - 4 \qquad\qquad g(x) = x - 2$$
$$f(8) = 8^2 - 4 = 60 \qquad\qquad g(8) = 8 - 2 = 6$$

Then $f(8)/g(8) = 60/6 = 10$. Therefore, $(f/g)(8) = 10$. We could have also found $(f/g)(8)$ by dividing $f(x)/g(x)$ and then substituting 8 into the quotient. We will discuss how to do this in Chapter 5.

NOW TRY EXERCISE 31   ✳

Notice that we included the phrase "and x is in the domain of both functions" in the Operations on Functions box on page 216. As we stated earlier, the domain of a function is the set of values that can be used for the independent variable. For example, the domain of the function $f(x) = 2x^2 - 6x + 5$ is all real numbers, because when x is any real number $f(x)$ will also be a real number. The domain of $g(x) = \dfrac{1}{x - 3}$ is all real numbers except 3, because when x is any real number except 3, the function $g(x)$ is a real number. When x is 3, the function is not a real number because $\frac{1}{0}$ is undefined. We will discuss the domain of functions further in Section 6.1.

2   Graph the Sum of Functions

Now we will explain how we can graph the sum, difference, product, or quotient of two functions. Figure 3.72 on page 218 shows two functions, $f(x)$ and $g(x)$.

To graph the sum of $f(x)$ and $g(x)$, or $(f + g)(x)$, we use $(f + g)(x) = f(x) + g(x)$. The table on the next page gives the integer values of x from -2 to 4, the values of $f(-2)$ through $f(4)$, and the values of $g(-2)$ through $g(4)$. These values are taken directly from Figure 3.72. The values of $(f + g)(-2)$ through $(f + g)(4)$ are determined by adding the values of $f(x)$ and $g(x)$. The graph of $(f + g)(x) = f(x) + g(x)$ is illustrated in green in Figure 3.73.

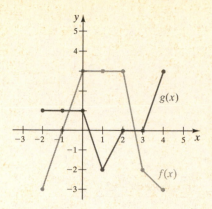

FIGURE 3.72

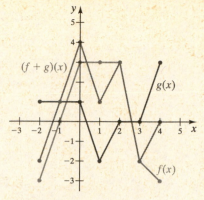

FIGURE 3.73

x	$f(x)$	$g(x)$	$(f + g)(x)$
-2	-3	1	$-3 + 1 = -2$
-1	0	1	$0 + 1 = 1$
0	3	1	$3 + 1 = 4$
1	3	-2	$3 + (-2) = 1$
2	3	0	$3 + 0 = 3$
3	-2	0	$-2 + 0 = -2$
4	-3	3	$-3 + 3 = 0$

We could graph the difference, product, or quotient of the two functions using a similar technique. For example, to graph the product function $(f \cdot g)(x)$, we would evaluate $(f \cdot g)(-2)$ as follows:

$$(f \cdot g)(-2) = f(-2) \cdot g(-2)$$
$$= (-3)(1) = -3$$

NOW TRY EXERCISE 43

Thus, the graph of $(f \cdot g)(x)$ would have an ordered pair at $(-2, -3)$. Other ordered pairs would be determined by the same procedure.

In newspapers and magazines we often find graphs that show the sum of two functions. Graphs that show the sum of two functions are generally illustrated in one of two ways. Example 3 shows one way and Example 4 shows the second way.

EXAMPLE 3   **Mutual Fund Accounts**   The number of mutual fund accounts has risen dramatically since 1980. The graph on the next page shows the number of mutual fund accounts separated into each of three categories, and the total of these three categories for selected years from 1980 through 2000.

a) How is the graph of the total number of accounts, T, determined from the graphs of the stock, S, bond/hybrid, B, and money market, M, accounts?

b) In which 5-year period did the number of stock accounts increase the most?

c) If y represents the year, describe what the function $(B + M)(y)$ represents.

Solution   **a)** In Figure 3.74, the graphs for stock, bond/hybrid, and money market accounts are shown separately on the same axes. The graph for the total of these accounts is obtained by adding the number of stock, bond/hybrid, and money market accounts together. For example, in 1995 there were about 70 million stock accounts,

Mutual Fund Accounts

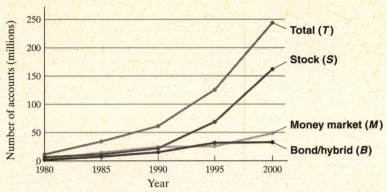

Source: Investment Company Institute

FIGURE 3.74

about 30 million bond/hybrid accounts, and about 25 million money market accounts. The sum of these numbers is 125 million, which is about the total number of accounts shown on the graph for 1995. Other points on the total account graph are determined in the same way.

b) From 1980 to 1985 and from 1985 to 1990, the increase in the number of stock accounts was much less than 50 million. From 1990 to 1995 the increase in the number of stock accounts was about 50 million. From 1995 to 2000 the increase in the number of stock accounts was much higher than 50 million. Therefore, the largest increase in the number of stock accounts took place from 1995 to 2000.

c) If y represents the year, then $B(y)$ represents the number of bond/hybrid accounts and $M(y)$ represents the number of money market accounts, in year y. The function $(B + M)(y)$ is equal to $B(y) + M(y)$. Therefore, $(B + M)(y)$ refers to the sum of the number of bond/hybrid accounts and the number of money market accounts in year y.

NOW TRY EXERCISE 57

In Example 4, which also shows a sum of functions, the categories are "piggy-backed" on top of one another.

EXAMPLE 4 **Natural Gas Use** The graph in Figure 3.75 shows U.S. natural gas use broken down into three categories: residential/commercial, industrial, and utility/transportation for select years from 1950 through 2000. The amount of natural gas used in each category is a function of the year. The total amount of natural gas used, indicated by the red line, is also a function of the year.

U.S. Natural Gas Use

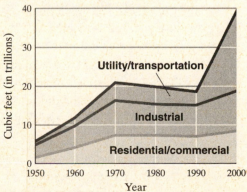

FIGURE 3.75   *Source:* U.S. Dept. of Energy

a) Estimate the amount of natural gas used for residential/commercial purposes in 2000.

b) Estimate the amount of natural gas used for industrial purposes in 2000.

c) Estimate the amount of natural gas used for utility/transportation purposes in 2000.

d) Estimate the total amount of natural gas used in 2000.

Solution   **a)** By reading the graph, we see that the amount of natural gas used for residential purposes in 2000 (the gold color) was about 8 trillion cubic feet.

b) The blue color on the graph represents the amount of natural gas used for industrial purposes. In 2000, the blue shaded area starts at about 8 trillion and ends at about 19 trillion. The difference between these two values, 19 trillion − 8 trillion, is 11 trillion. Therefore, about 11 trillion cubic feet of natural gas was used for industrial purposes in 2000.

c) The peach color on the graph represents the amount of natural gas used for utility/transportation purposes. In 2000, the peach shaded area starts at about 19 trillion and ends at about 39 trillion. The difference between these two values, 39 trillion − 19 trillion, is 20 trillion. Therefore about 20 trillion cubic feet of natural gas was used for utility/transportation purposes in 2000.

d) In 2000, the total amount of natural gas used in the United States was about 39 trillion cubic feet. This can be read directly from the graph. Also notice that 39 trillion is the sum of the quantities determined in parts **a)**, **b)**, and **c)**.

NOW TRY EXERCISE 59

In Example 4, the total amount of natural gas used in any year is the sum of the natural gas used in the three categories. For example, if we add the answers obtained in parts a), b), and c) we get $8 + 11 + 20 = 39$. Thus, in 2000 about 39 trillion cubic feet of natural gas was used. The red line at the top of the graph shows the total amount of natural gas used.

Using Your Graphing Calculator

Graphing calculators can graph the sums, differences, products, and quotients of functions. One way to do this is to enter the individual functions. Then, following the instructions that come with your calculator, you can add, subtract, multiply, or divide the functions. For example, the screen in Figure 3.76 shows a TI-83 Plus ready to graph $Y_1 = x - 3$, $Y_2 = 2x + 4$, and the sum of the functions, $Y_3 = Y_1 + Y_2$. On the TI-83 Plus, to get $Y_3 = Y_1 + Y_2$, you press the $\boxed{\text{VARS}}$ key. Then you move the cursor to Y-VARS, and then you select 1: Function. Next you press $\boxed{1}$ to enter Y_1. Next you press $\boxed{+}$. Then press $\boxed{\text{VARS}}$ and go to Y-VARS, and choose 1: Function. Finally, press $\boxed{2}$ to enter Y_2. Figure 3.77 shows the graphs of the two functions, and the graph of the sum of the functions.

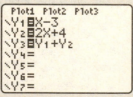

FIGURE 3.76

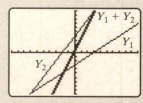

FIGURE 3.77

1. yes   **2.** yes   **4.** Yes, addition is commutative.   **5.** No, subtraction is not commutative.

Exercise Set 3.6

Concept/Writing Exercises

1. Does $f(x) + g(x) = (f + g)(x)$ for all values of x?

2. Does $f(x) - g(x) = (f - g)(x)$ for all values of x?

3. What restriction is placed on the property $f(x)/g(x)$ ⚿ $= (f/g)(x)$? Explain. $g(x) \neq 0$

4. Does $(f + g)(x) = (g + f)(x)$ for all values of x? Explain and give an example to support your answer.

5. Does $(f - g)(x) = (g - f)(x)$ for all values of x? Explain and give an example to support your answer.

6. If $f(2) = 9$ and $g(2) = -3$, determine

  a) $(f + g)(2)$ 6   **b)** $(f - g)(2)$ 12

  c) $(f \cdot g)(2)$ -27 **d)** $(f/g)(2)$ -3

7. If $f(-2) = -3$ and $g(-2) = 5$, find

  a) $(f + g)(-2)$ 2   **b)** $(f - g)(-2)$ -8

  c) $(f \cdot g)(-2)$ -15 **d)** $(f/g)(-2)$ $-\frac{3}{5}$

8. If $f(7) = 6$ and $g(7) = 0$, determine

  a) $(f + g)(7)$ 6   **b)** $(f - g)(7)$ 6

  c) $(f \cdot g)(7)$ 0   **d)** $(f/g)(7)$ undefined

Practice the Skills

*For each pair of functions, find **a)** $(f + g)(x)$, **b)** $(f + g)(a)$, and **c)** $(f + g)(2)$.*

9. $f(x) = x + 1, g(x) = x^2 + x$
  a) $x^2 + 2x + 1$ **b)** $a^2 + 2a + 1$ **c)** 9

10. $f(x) = x^2 - x - 2, g(x) = x^2 + 1$
  a) $2x^2 - x - 1$ **b)** $2a^2 - a - 1$ **c)** 5

11. $f(x) = -3x^2 + x - 4, g(x) = x^3 + 3x^2$
  a) $x^3 + x - 4$ **b)** $a^3 + a - 4$ **c)** 6

12. $f(x) = 4x^3 + 2x^2 - x - 1, g(x) = x^3 - x^2 + 2x + 3$
  a) $5x^3 + x^2 + x + 2$ **b)** $5a^3 + a^2 + a + 2$ **c)** 48

13. $f(x) = 4x^3 - 3x^2 - x, g(x) = 3x^2 + 4$
  a) $4x^3 - x + 4$ **b)** $4a^3 - a + 4$ **c)** 34

14. $f(x) = 3x^2 - x + 4, g(x) = 6 - 4x^2$
  a) $-x^2 - x + 10$ **b)** $-a^2 - a + 10$ **c)** 4

Let $f(x) = x^2 - 4$ and $g(x) = -5x + 3$. Find the following.

15. $f(3) + g(3)$ -7

16. $f(7) + g(7)$ 13

17. $f(-2) - g(-2)$ -13

18. $f\left(\dfrac{1}{4}\right) - g\left(\dfrac{1}{4}\right)$ $-\dfrac{91}{16}$

19. ⚿ $f(3) \cdot g(3)$ -60

20. $f(-4) \cdot g(-4)$ 276

21. $\dfrac{f\left(\frac{3}{5}\right)}{g\left(\frac{3}{5}\right)}$ undefined

22. $f(-2)/g(-2)$ 0

23. $g(-3) - f(-3)$ 13

24. $g(6) \cdot f(6)$ -864

25. $g(0)/f(0)$ $-\frac{3}{4}$

26. $f(2)/g(2)$ 0

Let $f(x) = 2x^2 - x$ and $g(x) = x - 6$. Find the following.

27. $(f + g)(x)$ $2x^2 - 6$

28. $(f + g)(a)$ $2a^2 - 6$

29. $(f + g)(0)$ -6

30. $(f + g)(-1)$ -4

31. $(f - g)(-3)$ 30

32. $(f - g)(1)$ 6

33. $(f \cdot g)(0)$ 0

34. $(f \cdot g)(-5)$ -605

35. $(f/g)(-1)$ $-\frac{3}{7}$

36. $(f/g)(6)$ undefined

37. $(g/f)(5)$ $-\frac{1}{45}$

38. $(g - f)(3)$ -18

39. ⚿ $(g - f)(x)$ $-2x^2 + 2x - 6$

40. $(g - f)(r)$ $-2r^2 + 2r - 6$

Problem Solving

Using the graph, find the value of the following.

41. $(f + g)(0)$ 3

42. $(f - g)(0)$ 1

43. ⚿ $(f \cdot g)(2)$ -4

44. $(f/g)(4)$ 0

45. $(g - f)(-1)$ 1

46. $(g + f)(-3)$ 3

47. $(g/f)(4)$ undefined

48. $(g \cdot f)(-3)$ -4

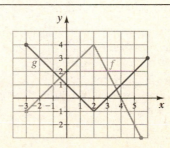

Using the graph below, find the value of the following.

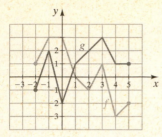

49. $(f + g)(3)$ 4

50. $(f - g)(3)$ −2

51. $(f \cdot g)(1)$ 0

52. $(g - f)(2)$ 3

53. $(f/g)(4)$ −3

54. $(g/f)(5)$ $-\frac{1}{2}$

55. $(g/f)(2)$ −2

56. $(g \cdot f)(0)$ −6

57. *Health Care Expenditures* The following graph shows private, public, and total expenditures for health care in the United States for select years from 1970 through 2000.

National Expenditure for Health Care

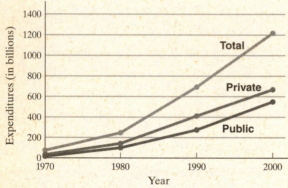

Source: U.S. Department of Health and Human Services

a) How is the graph for the total expenditures determined from the graphs of the private expenditures and the public expenditures?

b) During which 10-year period did the total amount of expenditures for health care increase the least?   1970–1980

c) During which 10-year period did the total amount of expenditures for health care increase the most?   1990–2000

58. *Sources of Electricity* The following graph shows the sources of electricity generated in the United States for select years from 1960 through 2000.

a) How is the graph of the total electricity generated determined from the graphs of electricity generated by fossil fuels, nuclear, and other?

b) During which 10-year period did the amount of electricity generated by nuclear power increase the most?   1980–1990

c) Which of the 4 categories indicated increased the least from 1960 through 2000?   other

Sources of Electricity

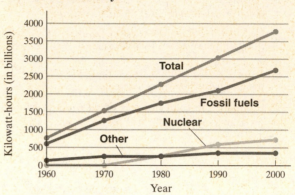

Source: U.S. Department of Energy

59. *Medicare Beneficiaries* The graph below shows the number of Medicare beneficiaries receiving hospital insurance who qualified because they were disabled and who qualified because of age for years 1980 through 2000.

Beneficiaries of Medicare
Hospital Insurance

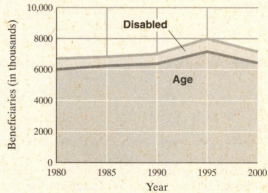

Source: Health Care Financing Administration, Division of Budget

a) Estimate the number of people receiving Medicare hospital insurance who qualified because of age in 2000.   6,500,000 people

b) Estimate the number of people receiving Medicare hospital insurance who qualified because they were disabled in 2000.   700,000 people

c) Estimate the total number of people receiving Medicare hospital insurance in 2000.   7,200,000 people

57. a) Total is the sum of Private and Public.   **58. a)** Total = Fossil + Nuclear + Other

60. *Federal Food Assistance* The graph on the right shows the number of participants in the federal food assistance programs, categorized according to: food stamps, school programs (including lunch, breakfast, and day-care food programs), and women-infants-children (WIC).

a) Estimate the number of participants in the food stamps program in 2000.   17 million people

b) Estimate the number of participants in the school programs in 2000.   37 million people

c) Estimate the number of participants in the WIC programs in 2000.   7 million people

d) Estimate the total number of all food assistance programs in 2000.   about 61 million people

Food Assistance Programs

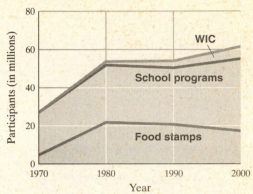

Source: U.S. Department of Agriculture

For Exercises 61–66, let f and g represent two functions that are graphed on the same axes.

61. If, at a, $(f + g)(a) = 0$, what must be true about $f(a)$ and $g(a)$?   They must be opposites or both equal to 0.

62. If, at a, $(f \cdot g)(a) = 0$, what must be true about $f(a)$ and $g(a)$?   Either $f(a)$ or $g(a)$, or both, must be 0.

63. If, at a, $(f - g)(a) = 0$, what must be true about $f(a)$ and $g(a)$? $f(a) = g(a)$

64. If, at a, $(f - g)(a) < 0$, what must be true about $f(a)$ and $g(a)$? $f(a) < g(a)$

65. If, at a, $(f/g)(a) < 0$, what must be true about $f(a)$ and $g(a)$?   They must have opposite signs.

66. If, at a, $(f \cdot g)(a) < 0$, what must be true about $f(a)$ and $g(a)$?   They must have opposite signs.

Graph the following functions on your graphing calculator.   *See graphing answer section, page G8.*

67. $y_1 = 2x + 3$

$y_2 = -x + 4$

$y_3 = y_1 + y_2$

68. $y_1 = x - 3$

$y_2 = 2x$

$y_3 = y_1 - y_2$

69. $y_1 = x$

$y_2 = x + 5$

$y_3 = y_1 \cdot y_2$

70. $y_1 = 2x^2 - 4$

$y_2 = x$

$y_3 = y_1/y_2$

Group Activity

71. *SAT Scores* The following graph shows the average math and verbal scores of entering college classes on the SAT college entrance exam for the years 1992 through 2002. Let f represent the math scores, and g represent the verbal scores, and let t represent the year. As a group, draw a graph that represents $(f + g)(t)$.
See graphing answer section, page G8.

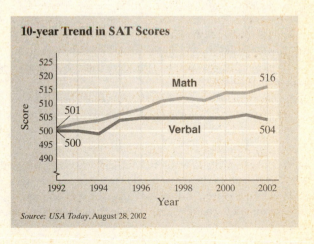

Source: USA Today, August 28, 2002

Cumulative Review Exercises

[1.5] **72.** Evaluate $(-3)^{-3}$. $-\frac{1}{27}$

[1.6] **73.** Express 1,630,000 in scientific notation.

[2.2] **74.** Solve the formula $A = \frac{1}{2}bh$ for h. $h = \frac{2A}{b}$

[2.3] **75.** *Washing Machine* The cost of a washing machine, including a 6% sales tax, is $477. Determine the pre-tax cost of the washing machine.
$450

[3.1] **76.** Graph $y = |x| - 2$.

[3.3] **77.** Graph $3x - 4y = 12$.

73. 1.63×10^6

76. and **77.** See graphing answer section, page G8.

3.7 GRAPHING LINEAR INEQUALITIES

SSM   Study Guide   CD/Video

MathPro 4/5   PH Math Tutor Center   prenhall.com/Angel

1 Graph linear inequalities in two variables.

---

1 Graph Linear Inequalities in Two Variables

A **linear inequality** results when the equal sign in a linear equation is replaced with an inequality sign.

Examples of Linear Inequalities in Two Variables

$$2x + 3y > 2 \qquad\qquad 3y < 4x - 6$$
$$-x - 2y \le 3 \qquad\qquad 5x \ge 2y - 3$$

A line divides a plane into three regions: the line itself and the two **half-planes** on either side of the line. The line is called the **boundary**. Consider the linear equation $2x + 3y = 6$. The graph of this line, the boundary line, divides the plane into the set of points that satisfy the inequality $2x + 3y < 6$ from the set of points that satisfy the inequality $2x + 3y > 6$. An inequality may or may not include the boundary line. Since the inequality $2x + 3y \le 6$ means $2x + 3y < 6$ or $2x + 3y = 6$, the inequality $2x + 3y \le 6$ contains the boundary line. Similarly, the inequality $2x + 3y \ge 6$ contains the boundary line. The graph of the inequalities $2x + 3y < 6$ and $2x + 3y > 6$ do not contain the boundary line. Now let's discuss how to graph linear inequalities.

To Graph a Linear Inequality in Two Variables

1. Replace the inequality symbol with an equal sign.

2. Draw the graph of the equation in step 1. If the original inequality contains a $\ge$ or $\le$ symbol, draw the graph using a solid line. If the original inequality contains a $>$ or $<$ symbol, draw the graph using a dashed line.

3. Select any point not on the line and determine if this point is a solution to the original inequality. If the point selected is a solution, shade the region on the side of the line containing this point. If the selected point does not satisfy the inequality, shade the region on the side of the line not containing this point.

In step 3 we are deciding which set of points satisfies the given inequality.

EXAMPLE 1 Graph the inequality $y < \frac{2}{3}x - 3$.

Solution First graph the equation $y = \frac{2}{3}x - 3$. Since the original inequality contains a less than sign, $<$, use a dashed line when drawing the graph (Fig. 3.78). The dashed line indicates that the points on this line are not solutions to the inequality $y < \frac{2}{3}x - 3$. Select a point not on the line and determine if this point satisfies the inequality. Often the easiest point to use is the origin, $(0, 0)$.

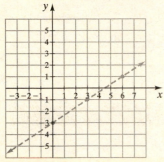

FIGURE 3.78

Check Point $(0, 0)$

$$y < \frac{2}{3}x - 3$$

$$0 \overset{?}{<} \frac{2}{3}(0) - 3$$

$$0 \overset{?}{<} 0 - 3$$

$$0 < -3 \qquad \textit{False}$$

Since 0 is not less than -3, the point $(0, 0)$ does not satisfy the inequality. The solution will be all points on the other side of the line from the point $(0, 0)$. Shade in this region (Fig. 3.79). Every point in the shaded area satisfies the given inequality. Let's check a few selected points $A, B,$ and C.

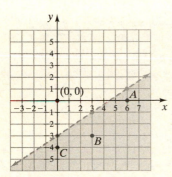

FIGURE 3.79

Point A	Point B	Point C
$(6, 0)$	$(3, -3)$	$(0, -4)$
$y < \frac{2}{3}x - 3$	$y < \frac{2}{3}x - 3$	$y < \frac{2}{3}x - 3$
$0 \overset{?}{<} \frac{2}{3}(6) - 3$	$-3 \overset{?}{<} \frac{2}{3}(3) - 3$	$-4 \overset{?}{<} \frac{2}{3}(0) - 3$
$0 \overset{?}{<} 4 - 3$	$-3 \overset{?}{<} 2 - 3$	$-4 \overset{?}{<} 0 - 3$
$0 < 1$ *True*	$-3 < -1$ *True*	$-4 < -3$ *True*

NOW TRY EXERCISE 15

EXAMPLE 2 Graph the inequality $y \geq -\frac{1}{2}x$.

Solution First, we graph the equation $y = -\frac{1}{2}x$. Since the inequality is $\geq$, we use a solid line to indicate that the points on the line are solutions to the inequality (Fig. 3.80). Since the point $(0, 0)$ is on the line, we cannot select that point to find the solution. Let's arbitrarily select the point $(3, 1)$.

FIGURE 3.80

Checkpoint $(3, 1)$

$$y \geq -\frac{1}{2}x$$

$$1 \overset{?}{\geq} -\frac{1}{2}(3)$$

$$1 \geq -\frac{3}{2} \qquad \textit{True}$$

Since the point $(3, 1)$ satisfies the inequality, every point on the same side of the line as $(3, 1)$ will also satisfy the inequality $y \geq -\frac{1}{2}x$. Shade this region as indicated. Every point in the shaded region, as well as every point on the line, satisfies the inequality.

EXAMPLE 3   Graph the inequality $3x - 2y < -6$.

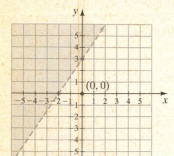

Solution   First, we graph the equation $3x - 2y = -6$. Since the inequality is $<$, we use a dashed line when drawing the graph (Fig. 3.81). Substituting the check-point $(0, 0)$ into the inequality results in a false statement.

$$\text{Checkpoint } (0, 0)$$
$$3x - 2y < -6$$
$$3(0) - 2(0) \overset{?}{<} -6$$
$$0 < -6 \quad \textit{False}$$

FIGURE 3.81

The solution is, therefore, that part of the plane that does not contain the origin.

NOW TRY EXERCISE 23

Using Your Graphing Calculator

Graphers can also display graphs of inequalities. The procedure to display the graphs varies from calculator to calculator. In Figure 3.82, we show the graph of $y > 2x + 3$. Read your graphing calculator manual and learn how to display graphs of inequalities.

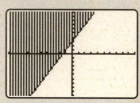

FIGURE 3.82

1. Points on the line are solutions for the corresponding equation, not $<$ or $>$.

2. $\geq$ means greater than or *equal to*; $\leq$ means less than or *equal to*.

3. when the graph goes through the origin.

Exercise Set 3.7

Concept/Writing Exercises

1. When graphing an inequality containing $>$ or $<$, why are points on the line not solutions to the inequality?

2. When graphing an inequality containing $\geq$ or $\leq$, why are points on the line solutions to the inequality?

3. When graphing a linear inequality, when can $(0, 0)$ not be used as a check point?

4. When graphing a linear inequality of the form $y > ax + b$ where a and b are real numbers, will the solution always be above the line? Explain.   yes

Practice the Skills

Graph each inequality.   *See graphing answer section, page G9.*

 5. $x > 1$

6. $x \geq \dfrac{3}{4}$

 7. $y < -2$

8. $y < x$

9. $y \geq -\dfrac{1}{2}x$

10. $y < \dfrac{1}{2}x$

11. $y < 2x + 1$

12. $y \geq 3x - 1$

13. $y > 2x - 1$

14. $y \leq -x + 2$

15. $y \geq \dfrac{1}{2}x - 3$

16. $y < 3x + 5$

17. $2x - 3y \geq 12$ **18.** $2x + 3y > 6$ 🔒 **19.** $y \leq -3x + 5$ **20.** $y \leq \dfrac{2}{3}x + 3$

🔒 **21.** $2x + y < 4$ **22.** $3x - 4y \leq 12$ **23.** $10 \geq 5x - 2y$ **24.** $-x - 2y > 4$

Problem Solving
25.–30. **a)** and **b)** See graphing answer section, page G10. **28. c)** ≈1993

🔒 **25.** *Life Insurance* The monthly rates for $100,000 of life insurance for women from the American General Financial Group increases approximately linearly from age 35 through age 50. The rate for a 35-year-old woman is $10.15 per month and the rate for a 50-year-old woman is $16.45 per month. *Source:* R. K. Reynolds Insurance Services

   a) Draw a graph that fits this data.

   b) On the graph, darken the part of the graph where the rate is less than or equal to $15 per month.

   c) Estimate the age at which the rate first exceeds $15 per month. 47

26. *Consumer Price Index* The consumer price index (CPI) is a measure of inflation. Since 1990, the CPI has been increasing approximately linearly. The CPI in 1990 was 130.7 and in 2000 the CPI was 172.2. *Source:* U.S. Bureau of the Census

   a) Draw a graph that fits this data.

   b) On the graph, darken the part of the graph where the CPI is greater than or equal to 150.

   c) Estimate the first year in which the CPI was greater than or equal to 150. 1995

27. *Hourly Compensation* The hourly compensation is the total annual amount of expenses required to employ an individual divided by the annual number of hours the employee works. In the United States, the average hourly compensation for all employees has been increasing approximately linearly since 1975. In 1975, the average hourly compensation was $6.36 per hour. In 2000, the average hourly compensation was $19.86 per hour. *Source:* U.S. Bureau of Labor Statistics

   a) Draw a graph that fits this data.

   b) On the graph, darken the part of the graph where the average hourly compensation is greater than or equal to $10 per hour.

   c) Estimate the first year that the average hourly compensation exceeded $10 per hour. 1982

28. *California Farmland* The amount of land in California used as farmland has been declining approximately linearly since 1980. In 1980, California had about 34 million acres of farmland. In 2000, California had about 28 million acres of farmland. *Source:* U.S. Dept. of Agriculture

   a) Draw a graph that fits this data.

   b) On the graph, darken the part of the graph where the amount of farmland is less than or equal to 30 million acres.

   c) Estimate the first year in which the amount of farmland was less than or equal to 30 million acres.

29. **a)** Graph $f(x) = 2x - 4$.

   b) On the graph, shade the region bounded by $f(x)$, $x = 2$, $x = 4$, and the x-axis.

30. **a)** Graph $g(x) = -x + 4$.

   b) On the graph, shade the region bounded by $g(x)$, $x = 1$, and the x- and y-axes.

Challenge Problems

Graph each inequality. *See graphing answer section, page G10.*

   31. $y < |x|$ **32.** $y \geq x^2$ **33.** $y < x^2 - 4$

Cumulative Review Exercises

[2.1] **34.** Solve the equation $4 - \dfrac{5x}{3} = -6$. 6

[2.2] **35.** If $C = \bar{x} + Z\dfrac{\sigma}{\sqrt{n}}$, find C when $\bar{x} = 80$, $Z = 1.96$, $\sigma = 3$, and $n = 25$. 81.176

[2.3] **36.** *Store Sale* Olie's Records and Stuff is going out of business. The first week all items are being reduced by 10%. The second week all items are being reduced by an additional $2. If during the

second week Bob Frieble purchases a CD for $12.15, find the original cost of the CD. $15.72

38. $x + 2y = 2$ (other answers are possible)

[3.2] **37.** $f(x) = -x^2 + 3$; find $f(-1)$ 2

[3.3] **38.** Write an equation of the line that passes through the point $(6, -2)$ and is perpendicular to the line whose equation is $2x - y = 4$.

[3.4] **39.** Determine the slope of the line through $(-4, 7)$ and $(2, -1)$. $-\dfrac{4}{3}$

CHAPTER SUMMARY
Key Words and Phrases

3.1
Cartesian coordinate system
Collinear points
Coordinates
First-degree equation
Graph
Graphing calculator
Linear equation
Midpoint
Nonlinear equation
Ordered pair
Origin
Quadrant
Rectangular coordinate system
TABLE feature
TRACE feature
Window of a graphing calculator

x-axis
y-axis

3.2
Dependent variable
Domain
Function
Function notation
Graph of a function or relation
Independent variable
Piecewise function
Range
Relation
Supply and demand
Vertical line test
y is a function of x

3.3
Constant function
Linear function
Root
Standard form of a linear equation
x-intercept
y-intercept
Zero
ZOOM feature

3.4
Negative slope
Parallel lines
Positive slope
Rate of change
Slope of a line
Slope–intercept form of a linear equation

Tangent line
Translated graph
Zero slope

3.5
Negative reciprocal
Perpendicular line
Point–slope form of a linear equation

3.6
Difference of functions
Product of functions
Quotient of functions
Sum of functions

3.7
Linear inequality

IMPORTANT FACTS

Slope of a Line
$$m = \frac{\Delta y}{\Delta x} = \frac{y_2 - y_1}{x_2 - x_1}$$

Forms of a Linear Equation

Standard form: $ax + by = c$
Slope–intercept form: $y = mx + b$
Point–slope form: $y - y_1 = m(x - x_1)$
To find the x-intercept, set $y = 0$ and solve the equation for x.
To find the y-intercept, set $x = 0$ and solve the equation for y.
To write an equation in slope–intercept form, solve the equation for y.

Positive slope
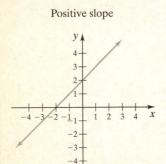

Zero slope
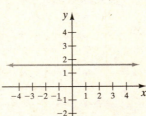

Negative slope
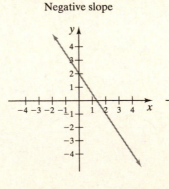

Slope is undefined.
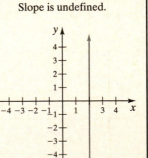

(continued on the next page)

Operations on Functions

Sum of functions: $(f + g)(x) = f(x) + g(x)$
Difference of functions: $(f - g)(x) = f(x) - g(x)$
Product of functions: $(f \cdot g)(x) = f(x) \cdot g(x)$
Quotient of functions: $(f/g)(x) = \dfrac{f(x)}{g(x)}, g(x) \neq 0$

Chapter Review Exercises

[3.1] **1.** Plot the ordered pairs on the same axes. See graphing answer section, page G10.

a) $A(5, 3)$ **b)** $B(0, 4)$ **c)** $C\left(5, \frac{1}{2}\right)$ **d)** $D(-4, 3)$ **e)** $E(-6, -1)$ **f)** $F(-2, 0)$

Graph each equation. *See graphing answer section, pages G10 and G11.*

2. $y = \frac{1}{2}x$ **3.** $y = -2x - 1$ **4.** $y = \frac{1}{2}x + 3$ **5.** $y = -\frac{3}{2}x + 1$ **6.** $y = x^2$

7. $y = x^2 - 1$ **8.** $y = |x|$ **9.** $y = |x| - 1$ **10.** $y = x^3$ **11.** $y = x^3 + 4$

[3.2] **12.** Define function. **12.** a correspondence where each member of the domain corresponds to exactly one member of the range

13. Is every relation a function? Is every function a relation? Explain. no, yes

Determine whether the following relations are functions. Explain your answers.

14.

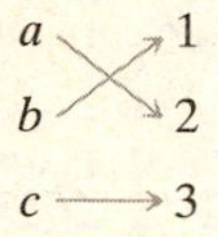

yes

15. $\{(2, 5), (3, -4), (5, 11), (6, -1), (2, -5)\}$ no

For Exercises 16–19, ***a)*** *determine whether the following graphs represent functions;* ***b)*** *determine the domain and range of each.*

16.

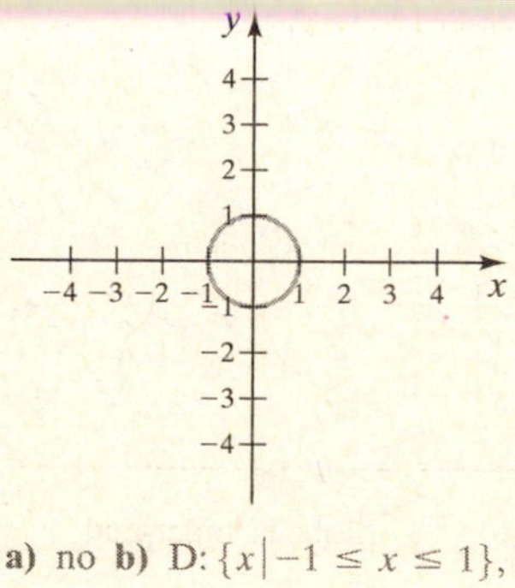

a) no **b)** D: $\{x \mid -1 \le x \le 1\}$, R: $\{y \mid -1 \le y \le 1\}$

17.

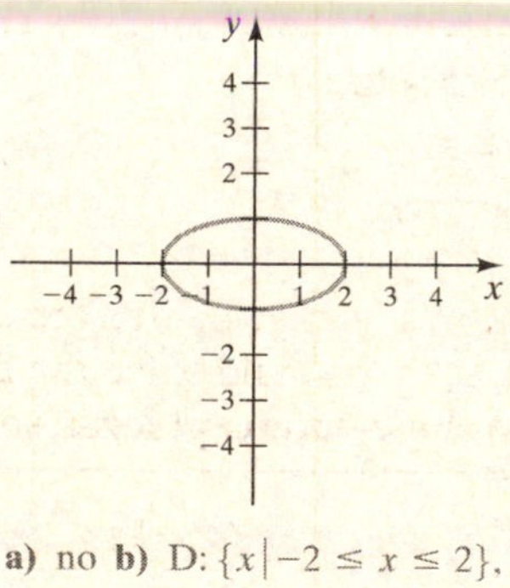

a) no **b)** D: $\{x \mid -2 \le x \le 2\}$, R: $\{y \mid -1 \le y \le 1\}$

18.

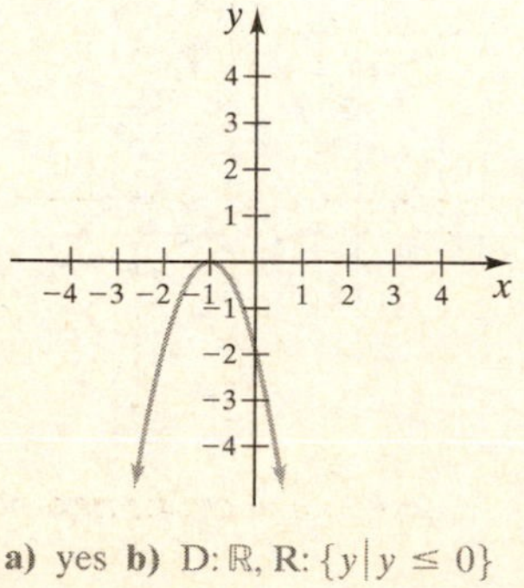

a) yes **b)** D: $\mathbb{R}$, R: $\{y \mid y \le 0\}$

19.

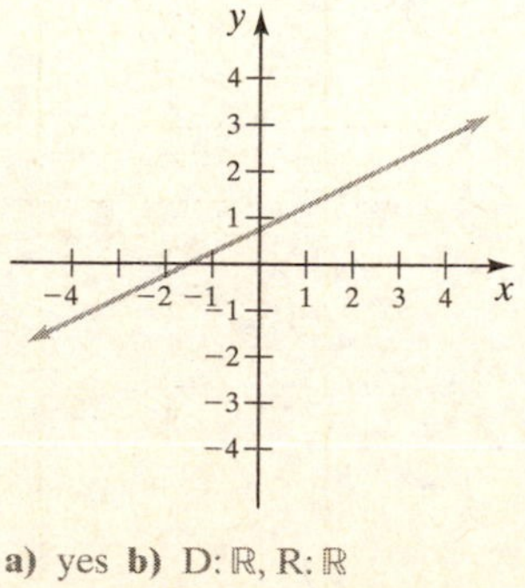

a) yes **b)** D: $\mathbb{R}$, R: $\mathbb{R}$

20. If $f(x) = -x^2 + 3x - 5$, find
   a) $f(2)$ and **b)** $f(h)$. **a)** -3 **b)** $-h^2 + 3h - 5$

21. If $g(t) = 2t^3 - 3t^2 + 1$, find
   a) $g(-1)$ and **b)** $g(a)$. **a)** -4 **b)** $2a^3 - 3a^2 + 1$

22. ***Speed of Car*** Jane Covillion goes for a ride in a car. The following graph shows the car's speed as a function of time. Make up a story that corresponds to this graph.

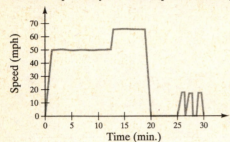

23. ***Apple Orchard*** The number of baskets of apples, N, that are produced by x trees in a small orchard ($x \leq 100$) is given by the function $N(x) = 40x - 0.2x^2$. How many baskets of apples are produced by

   a) 20 trees? 720

   b) 50 trees? 1500

24. ***Falling Ball*** If a ball is dropped from the top of a 100-foot building, its height above the ground, h, at any time, t, can be found by the function $h(t) = -16t^2 + 100$, $0 \leq t \leq 2.5$. Find the height of the ball at

   a) 1 second. 84 ft

   b) 2 seconds. 36 ft

22. Answers will vary. One possible interpretation: car speeds up to 50 mph, stays at 50 mph for about 11 min. Speeds up to about 68 mph, stays at that speed 5 min. Stops quickly. Stopped for 5 min. Then in stop-and-go traffic for 5 min.

[3.3] *Graph each equation using intercepts.* *See graphing answer section, page G11.*

25. $3x - 4y = 6$

26. $\dfrac{2}{3}x = \dfrac{1}{4}y + 20$

Graph each equation or function. **27.**, **28.**, **29. a)**, **30.**, See graphing answer section, page G11.

27. $f(x) = 4$

28. $x = -2$

29. ***Bagel Company*** The yearly profit, p, of a bagel company can be estimated by the function $p(x) = 0.1x - 5000$, where x is the number of bagels sold per year.

   a) Draw a graph of profits versus bagels sold for up to 250,000 bagels.

   b) Estimate the number of bagels that must be sold for the company to break even. 50,000 bagels

   c) Estimate the number of bagels sold if the company has a \$20,000 profit. 250,000 bagels

30. ***Interest*** Draw a graph illustrating the interest on a \$12,000 loan for a 1-year period for various interest rates up to 20%. Use interest = principal · rate · time.

[3.4] *Determine the slope and y-intercept of the graph represented by the given equation.*

31. $y = \dfrac{1}{2}x - 3$ $m = \dfrac{1}{2}, (0, -3)$ **32.** $f(x) = -2x + 1$ $m = -2, (0, 1)$ **33.** $3x + 5y = 12$ $m = -\dfrac{3}{5}, \left(0, \dfrac{12}{5}\right)$

34. $3x + 4y = 10$ $m = -\dfrac{3}{4}, \left(0, \dfrac{5}{2}\right)$ **35.** $x = -2$ m is undefined, no y-intercept   **36.** $f(x) = 6$ $m = 0, (0, 6)$

Determine the slope of the line through the two given points.

37. $(2, 5), (-2, 7)$ $-\dfrac{1}{2}$

38. $(-2, 3)(4, 1)$ $-\dfrac{1}{3}$

Find the slope of each line. If the slope is undefined, so state. Then write the equation of the line.

39.

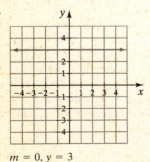

$m = 0, y = 3$

40.

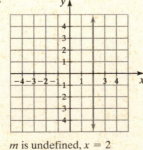

m is undefined, $x = 2$

41.

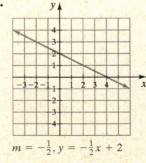

$m = -\dfrac{1}{2}, y = -\dfrac{1}{2}x + 2$

42. If the graph of $y = -2x + 3$ is translated down 4 units, determine
   a) the slope of the translated graph. -2
   b) the y-intercept of the translated graph. $(0, -1)$
   c) the equation of the translated graph. $y = -2x - 1$

43. If one point on a graph is $(-6, -8)$ and the slope is $\frac{4}{3}$, find the y-intercept of the graph. $(0, 0)$

44. *Typhoid Fever* The following chart shows the number of reported cases of typhoid fever in the United States for select years from 1970 through 2000.
   a) Plot each point and draw line segments from point to point. See graphing answer section, page G11.
   b) Compute the slope of the line segments.
   c) During which 10-year period did the number of reported cases of typhoid fever increase the most?

Year	Number of reported typhoid fever cases
1970	346
1980	510
1990	552
2000	317

Source: U.S. Dept. of Health and Human Services

45. *Social Security* The following graph shows the number of social security beneficiaries from 1980 projected through 2070. Use the slope-intercept form to find the function $n(t)$ (represented by the straight line) that can be used to represent this data. $n(t) = 0.7t + 35.6$

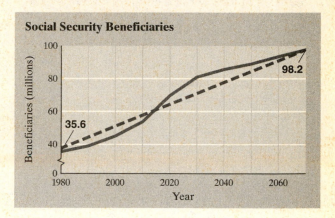

Social Security Beneficiaries

44. **b)** 1970–1980: 16.4, 1980–1990: 4.2, 1990–2000: -23.5
   c) 1970–1980

[3.5] *Determine whether the two given lines are parallel, perpendicular, or neither.*

46. $2x - 3y = 10$
$y = \frac{2}{3}x - 4$ parallel

47. $2x - 3y = 9$
$-3x - 2y = 6$ perpendicular

48. $4x - 2y = 10$
$-2x + 4y = -8$ neither

Find the equation of the line with the properties given. Write each answer in slope–intercept form.

49. Slope $= \frac{1}{2}$, through $(4, 5)$ $y = \frac{1}{2}x + 3$

50. Through $(-3, 1)$ and $(2, -4)$ $y = -x - 2$

51. Through $(0, 4)$ and parallel to the graph of $y = -\frac{2}{3}x + 1$ $y = -\frac{2}{3}x + 4$

52. Through $(2, 3)$ and parallel to the graph whose equation is $5x - 2y = 7$ $y = \frac{5}{2}x - 2$

53. Through $(-3, 1)$ and perpendicular to the graph whose equation is $y = \frac{3}{5}x + 5$ $y = -\frac{5}{3}x - 4$

54. Through $(4, 2)$ and perpendicular to the graph whose equation is $4x - 2y = 8$ $y = -\frac{1}{2}x + 4$

Two points on l_1 and two points on l_2 are given. Determine whether l_1 is parallel to l_2, l_1 is perpendicular to l_2, or neither.

55. l_1: $(4, 3)$ and $(0, -3)$; l_2: $(1, -1)$ and $(2, -2)$ neither

56. l_1: $(3, 2)$ and $(2, 3)$; l_2: $(4, 1)$ and $(1, 4)$ parallel

57. l_1: $(4, 0)$ and $(1, 3)$; l_2: $(5, 2)$ and $(6, 3)$ perpendicular

58. l_1: $(-3, 5)$ and $(2, 3)$; l_2: $(-4, -2)$ and $(-1, 2)$ neither

59. *Insurance Rates* The monthly rates for $100,000 of life insurance from the General Financial Group for men increases approximately linearly from age 35 through age 50. The rate for a 35-year-old man is $10.76 per month and the rate for a 50-year-old man is $19.91 per month. Let r be the rate and let a be the age of a man between 35 and 50 years of age.
   a) Determine a linear function $r(a)$ that fits this data.
   b) Using the function in part **a)**, estimate the monthly rate for a 42-year-old man. $15.03

60. *Burning Calories* The number of calories burned in 1 hour of swimming, when swimming between 20 and 50 yards per minute, is a linear function of the speed of the swimmer. A person swimming at 30 yards per minute will burn about 489 calories in 1 hour. While swimming at 50 yards per minute a person will burn about 525 calories in 1 hour. This information is shown in the graph on page 232.

59. **a)** $r(a) = 0.61a - 10.59$

60. a) $C(r) = 1.8r + 435$

Calories Burned while Swimming

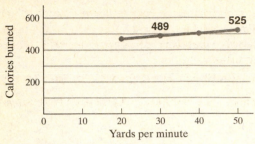

Source: *Health Magazine* Web Site, www.health.com

a) Determine a linear function that can be used to estimate the number of calories, *C*, burned in 1 hour when a person swims at *r* yards per minute.

b) Use the function determined in part **a)** to determine the number of calories burned in 1 hour when a person swims at 40 yards per minute.   507 calories

c) Use the function determined in part **a)** to estimate the speed at which a person needs to swim to burn 600 calories in 1 hour.   91.7 yd/min

[3.6] Given $f(x) = x^2 - 3x + 4$ and $g(x) = 2x - 5$, find the following.

61. $(f + g)(x)$ $x^2 - x - 1$

62. $(f + g)(3)$ 5

63. $(g - f)(x)$ $-x^2 + 5x - 9$

64. $(g - f)(-1)$ -15

65. $(f \cdot g)(-1)$ -56

66. $(f \cdot g)(5)$ 70

67. $(f/g)(1)$ $-\frac{2}{3}$

68. $(f/g)(2)$ -2

69. *Daily Newspapers* The following graph shows the number of daily newspapers in the United States for select years from 1960 through 2000.

Daily U.S. Newspapers

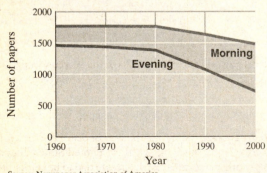

Source: Newspaper Association of America

a) Estimate the number of morning newspapers in 1960.   300

b) Estimate the number of morning newspapers in 2000.   750

c) Estimate the number of evening newspapers in 1960.   1450

d) Estimate the number of evening newspapers in 2000.   750

e) Estimate the total number of daily newspapers in 1960.   1750

f) Estimate the total number of daily newspapers in 2000.   1500

70. *Motor Vehicle Registrations* The following graph shows the number of worldwide car registrations, the number of worldwide truck/bus registrations, and the worldwide total number of motor vehicle registrations for select years from 1970 through 2000. Let function *c* represent the number of car registrations and let function *t* represent the number of truck/bus registrations. Estimate

a) $c(2000)$ 490 million

b) $t(2000)$ 190 million

c) $(c + t)(2000)$ 680 million

World Motor Vehicle Registrations

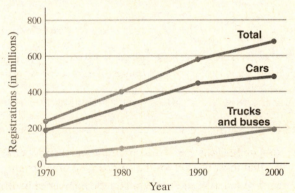

Source: U.S. Dept. of Energy

[3.7] Graph each inequality.   *See graphing answer section, page G11.*

71. $y \geq -3$

72. $x < 4$

73. $y \leq 4x - 3$

74. $y < \frac{1}{3}x - 2$

1.–4., 10–13, 14. a), See graphing answer section, page G12.

Chapter Practice Test

1. Graph $y = -2x + 1$.
2. Graph $y = \sqrt{x}$.
3. Graph $y = x^2 - 4$.
4. Graph $y = |x|$.

In Exercises 7 and 8, determine whether the following graphs represent functions. Give the domain and range of the relation or function.

7.

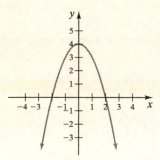

yes, D: $\mathbb{R}$, R: $\{y|y \le 4\}$

9. If $f(x) = 3x^2 - 6x + 2$, find $f(-2)$. 26

In Exercises 10 and 11, graph the equation using the x- and y-intercepts.

10. $-10x + 5y = 20$

11. $\dfrac{x}{5} - \dfrac{y}{4} = 1$

12. Graph $f(x) = -3$.

13. Graph $x = 4$.

14. **Profit Graph** The yearly profit, p, for Zico Publishing Company on the sales of a particular book can be estimated by the function $p(x) = 10.2x - 50{,}000$, where x is the number of books produced and sold.

   a) Draw a graph of profit versus books sold for up to 30,000 books.

   b) Use function $p(x)$ to estimate the number of books that must be sold for the company to break even.

   c) Use function $p(x)$ to estimate the number of books that the company must sell to make a \$100,000 profit.

15. Determine the slope and y-intercept of the graph of the equation $4x - 3y = 9$. $m = \frac{4}{3}, (0, -3)$

16. Determine the equation, in slope–intercept form, of the line that goes through the points $(2, 1)$ and $(3, 4)$. $y = 3x - 5$

17. Determine the equation, in slope–intercept form, of the line that goes through the point $(5, -3)$ and is perpendicular to the graph of $y = \dfrac{1}{2}x + 1$. $y = -2x + 7$

14. b) 4900 books   c) 14,700 books

5. a correspondence where each member in the domain corresponds with exactly one member in the range

5. Define function.

6. Is the following set of ordered pairs a function? Explain your answer.

$\{(3, 1), (-2, 6), (4, 6), (5, 2), (6, 3)\}$ yes

8.

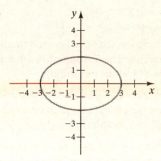

no, D: $\{x|-3 \le x \le 3\}$, R: $\{y|-2 \le y \le 2\}$

18. **U.S. Population Projections** Determine the function represented by the red line on the graph that can be used to estimate the projected U.S. population, p, from 2000 through 2050. Let 2000 be the reference year so that 2000 is represented by $t = 0$. $p(t) = 2.386t + 274.634$

U.S. Population Projections 2000–2050

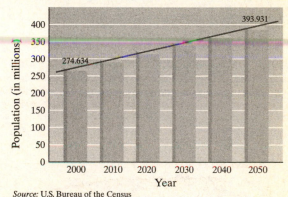

Source: U.S. Bureau of the Census

19. Determine whether the graphs of the two equations are parallel, perpendicular, or neither. Explain your answer.

$2x - 3y = 6$

$4x + 8 = 6y$ parallel

20. **Heart Disease** Although the rate of death due to heart disease is still much higher in the United States than in many other countries, the death rate due to heart disease in the United States has been declining approximately

linearly since about 1970. The bar graph below indicates the number of deaths due to heart disease, per 100,000 deaths, in selected years since 1970.

a) Let r be the number of deaths due to heart disease per 100,000 deaths and let t represent the years since 1970. Write a linear function $r(t)$ that represents this data. $r(t) = -3.2t + 362$

b) Using the function from part **a)**, determine the death rate due to heart disease in 1995.   282 deaths/100,000

c) Assuming that this trend continues, determine the death rate due to heart disease in 2010.   234 deaths/100,000

Heart Disease Death Rate

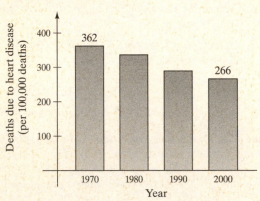

Source: U.S. Dept. of Health and Human Services

---

24. c) 26 million tons

In Exercises 21–23, if $f(x) = 2x^2 - x$ *and* $g(x) = x - 5$, *find*

21. $(f + g)(3)$ 13

22. $(f/g)(-1)$ $-\frac{1}{2}$

23. $f(a)$ $2a^2 - a$

24. *Paper Use*   The following graph shows paper use in 1995 and projected paper use from 1995 through 2015.

a) Estimate the total number of tons of paper to be used in 2010.   44 million tons

b) Estimate the number of tons of paper to be used by businesses in 2010.   18 million tons

c) Estimate the number of tons of paper to be used for reference, print media, and household use in 2010.

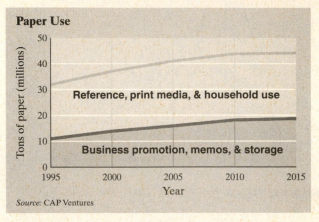

Source: CAP Ventures

25. Graph $y < 3x - 2$.   See graphing answer section, page G12.

Cumulative Review Test

Take the following test and check your answers with those that appear at the end of the test. Review any questions that you answered incorrectly. The section and objective where the material was covered are indicated after the answer.

1. For $A = \{1, 3, 5, 7, 9\}$ and $B = \{2, 3, 5, 7, 11, 13\}$, determine

a) $A \cap B$. $\{3, 5, 7\}$

b) $A \cup B$. $\{1, 2, 3, 5, 7, 9, 11, 13\}$

2. Consider the set $\left\{-6, -4, \frac{1}{3}, 0, \sqrt{3}, 4.67, \frac{37}{2}, -\sqrt{2}\right\}$ List the elements of the set that are

a) natural numbers.   none

b) real numbers. $-6, -4, \frac{1}{3}, 0, \sqrt{3}, 4.67, \frac{37}{2}, -\sqrt{2}$

3. Evaluate $2 - \{3[6 - 4(6^2 \div 4)]\}$.   92

Simplify.

4. $\left(\dfrac{4x^2}{y^{-3}}\right)^2$ $16x^4y^6$

5. $\left(\dfrac{2x^4y^{-2}}{4xy^3}\right)^3$ $\dfrac{x^9}{8y^{15}}$

6. *Baltimore Revenue*   The total amount of revenue available to the city of Baltimore, Maryland, in 2001 was

---

6. a) 4.83832×10^8 or $483,832,000

1.576×10^9. The following graph shows a breakdown of the sources of this money.

a) How much money was obtained from property taxes?

b) How much money was obtained through federal grants? 2.23792×10^8 or $223,792,000

c) How much more money was obtained from state shared taxes than from state grants? 1.4184×10^7 or $14,184,000

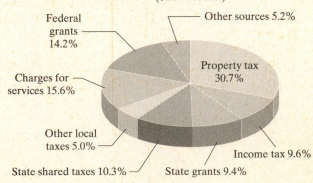

Source: Baltimore City Municipal Dept. of Finance

12. $x > -\frac{10}{3}$ **13.** $1 < x < 5$ **15.** $\{x|-1 \le x \le 2\}$ **16.** See Answers to Cumulative Review Test below.   **17. b)** D: $\{x|x \le 2\}$ R: $\mathbb{R}$

In Exercises 7 and 8, solve the equations.

7. $2(x + 4) - 5 = -3[x - (2x + 1)]$ 0

8. $\frac{4}{5} - \frac{x}{3} = 10$ $-\frac{138}{5}$

9. Simplify $5x - \{4 - [2(x - 4)] - 5\}$. $7x - 7$

10. Solve $A = \frac{1}{2}h(b_1 + b_2)$ for b_1. $b_1 = \frac{2A}{h} - b_2$

11. *Hydrogen Peroxide Solutions* How many gallons of 15% hydrogen peroxide solution must be mixed with 10 gallons of 4% hydrogen peroxide solution to get a 10% hydrogen peroxide solution?   12 gallons

12. Solve the inequality $3(x - 4) < 6(2x + 3)$.

13. Solve the inequality $-4 < 3x - 7 < 8$.

14. Determine the solution set of $|3x + 5| = |2x - 10|$. $\{-15, 1\}$

15. Determine the solution set of $|2x - 1| \le 3$.

16. Graph $y = -\frac{3}{2}x - 4$.

17. a) Determine whether the following graph represents a function.   not a function

b) Find the domain and range of the graph.

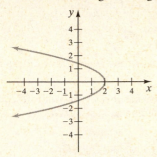

18. Determine the slope of the line through the points $(-5, 3)$ and $(4, -1)$. $-\frac{4}{9}$

19. Determine whether the graphs of the two given equations are parallel, perpendicular, or neither.
$$2x - 5y = 6$$
$$5x - 2y = 9 \quad \text{neither}$$

20. If $f(x) = x^2 + 3x - 2$ and $g(x) = 4x - 6$, find $(f + g)(x)$ $x^2 + 7x - 8$

Answers to Cumulative Review Test

1. a) $\{3, 5, 7\}$ **b)** $\{1, 2, 3, 5, 7, 9, 11, 13\}$; [Sec. 1.2, Obj. 4]   **2. a)** None **b)** $-6, -4, \frac{1}{3}, 0, \sqrt{3}, 4.67, \frac{37}{2}, -\sqrt{2}$; [Sec. 1.2,

Obj. 5]   **3.** 92; [Sec. 1.4, Obj. 3]   **4.** $16x^4y^6$; [Sec. 1.5, Obj. 7]   **5.** $\frac{x^9}{8y^{15}}$; [Sec. 1.5, Obj. 7]   **6. a)** $\$4.83832 \times 10^8$ or $\$483,832,000$

b) $\$2.23792 \times 10^8$ or $\$223,792,000$ **c)** $\$1.4184 \times 10^7$ or $\$14,184,000$; [Sec. 1.5, Obj. 7]   **7.** 0; [Sec. 2.1, Obj. 3]

8. $-\frac{138}{5}$; [Sec. 2.1, Obj. 4]   **9.** $7x - 7$; [Sec. 2.1, Obj. 2]   **10.** $b_1 = \frac{2A}{h} - b_2$; [Sec. 2.2, Obj. 2]   **11.** 12 gal; [Sec. 2.4, Obj. 2]

12. $x > -\frac{10}{3}$; [Sec. 2.5, Obj. 1]   **13.** $1 < x < 5$; [Sec. 2.5, Obj. 3]   **14.** $\{-15, 1\}$; [Sec. 2.6, Obj. 7]

15. $\{x|-1 \le x \le 2\}$; [Sec. 2.6, Obj. 3]   **16.**

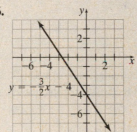

[Sec. 3.1, Obj. 2]

17. a) Not a function **b)** Domain: $\{x|x \le 2\}$; Range: $\mathbb{R}$; [Sec. 3.2, Obj. 3]   **18.** $-\frac{4}{9}$; [Sec. 3.4, Obj. 2]

19. Neither; [Sec. 3.5, Obj. 3]   **20.** $x^2 + 7x - 8$; [Sec. 3.6, Obj. 1]

CHECKING YOUR COMPREHENSION

Choose the best answer for each of the following questions.

1. Which of the equations below would be an example of a linear equation?
    a. $Y = X$
    b. $Y = 2x - 3$
    c. $Y = -1/3x + 1$
    d. all of these

2. A line that rises from left to right on a graph is said to have a
    a. negative slope
    b. positive slope
    c. neutral slope
    d. zero slope

3. Which of the following data would be best illustrated on graph showing the sum of two functions?
    a. annual natural gas use by residential commercial and utility users
    b. projected life expectancy of males in the year 2050
    c. purchasing power of the dollar from 1952 to 2000
    d. average heart rate to age

Identify the following statements as true or false.

4. The x-coordinate is always the first coordinate listed in the ordered pair.

5. A relation is any set of ordered pairs.

6. A function is a set of ordered pairs in which the first coordinate is repeated.

Answer the following questions.

7. Explain how you would plot a point on the Cartesian Coordinate System.

8. Explain what is meant by the vertical line test.

Discussion and Critical Thinking Question

9. Frequently you see data in newspapers, magazines, and on television which is often depicted in some graphic form or another. How do graphs make data and the relationships between sets of data easier to see and understand?

Testing Your Learning:
Answer Key

Unit 1: **Successful and Unsuccessful Paths to Power (1686–1740)**
Chapter 15 of Kagan, *The Western Heritage*, 8th Edition, Prentice Hall, 2004

1. c
2. b
3. b
4. a
5. True
6. True
7. The Ottoman Empire was significant because of its ability to rule over people with great diversity in culture and geographic region, whereas the Habsburg Empire's primary weakness was its inability to rule people of different cultures, language, and geographic region.
8. During the Romanov dynasty, Russia had no warm-water ports from which to easily build and launch ships. Peter the Great was able to build some ships during the warmer months on the shores of the Black Sea, which eventually lead to the acquisition of warm water areas.
9. Answers will vary.

1. c
2. d
3. d
4. c
5. c
6. e
7. d
8. True
9. False
10. If you have learned to fear snakes and you see a rope lying ahead in your path, you may be afraid of the rope because it looks like a snake. This would be an example of generalization. If you were stung by a wasp, it may result in uneasiness around insects that fly. However, if you are not stung every time you encountered a flying insect, you may learn not to be uneasy around butterflies. This is an example of discrimination.
11. Punishment is most effective when it is delivered immediately after the response that is to be eliminated. The punishment needs to be severe enough to deter the response. Punishment must follow every occurrence of the undesired response. There can be no escape or avoidance of the punishment. Those imposing the punishment must be prepared for an aggressive response. Finally, an alternative behavior should be provided at the time of the punishment.
12. Answers will vary.

1. d
2. d
3. c
4. a
5. False
6. True
7. Watchdog groups are often aided by reporters who can expose ethical breaches of responsibility by both government officials and lobbyists. One of the most common breaches of ethical responsibility is the acceptance of money or favors for a vote.
8. Editors of local newspapers are aware that their readers may be more interested in state and national news. Consequently, coverage of local government may be limited and reported by inexperienced reporters. In some cases there might exist a "cozy" relationship between the local newspapers and local government officials that prevents activities from being fairly reported.
9. Answers will vary.

1. c
2. d
3. b
4. True
5. True
6. False
7. Some of the common causes for prison riots are a prison administration that seems insensitive to prisoner's calls for change, living conditions that are perceived as dehumanizing, and the violent tendencies of many of the prisoners. Some of the needed reforms might be a clearer and more widely upheld doctrine of the rights of a prisoner. In addition, upgrading and new construction of modern facilities which can maximize the use of technology for prison administration could also help to curtail the outbreak of riots.
8. One issue facing prisons today are communicable-disease control such as the AIDS virus spread through sexual behavior and intravenous drug paraphernalia. Another issue is geriatrics. The aging of the prison population and crimes committed by the elderly pose special problems for the prison system. Prisoners with special needs (mental illness) increase tension in the prison population which can lead to violence. Education can help diminish high-risk behavior for transmitting disease. More emphasis placed on correcting behavior could lead to earlier releases and less repeat offenders. Psychiatric treatment facilities may have to be part of the prison system. Although expensive, inmates do not have the right to refuse drugs that mitigate the effects of their illness.
9. Answers will vary.

1. **d**
2. **b**
3. **a**
4. **False**
5. **True**
6. **Ohm's Law says that there is a relationship between these three factors, so if you know two of the values you can easily work out the third one:**

   V = I x R

   I = V / R

   R = V / I

   If you know the current and resistance and want to calculate the voltage, you use the first equation. If you know the voltage and resistance and want to calculate the current, you use the second equation. Lastly, if you know the voltage and current and want to calculate the resistance, you use the third equation.
7. **Energy is the ability to do work, while power is the rate at which work is done. In this exhibit, a hand generator is used to create a charge which is stored in large capacitors; the capacitors hold a given amount of energy. The capacitors can then be discharged through one of several different light bulbs that vary in resistance. The energy is consumed at different rates and hence the bulbs have different power ratings (wattage).**
8. **Resistance causes electric energy to be converted into heat energy. The heat is caused by collisions of free electrons within the atomic structure of the resistance. When a collision occurs heat is given off, resulting in the electron giving off some of its acquired energy. Voltage equals energy per charge and the charge is a property of the electrons.**
9. **Answers will vary.**

1. a
2. a
3. c
4. True
5. True
6. False
7. Those who advocated a high tariff believed that tariffs would promote industrial growth, stimulate job growth, lead to higher wages, provide more federal government revenue, and at the same time protect the domestic market for goods. Those who advocated lower tariffs believed that corporate profits would increase; tariffs would restrict competition, increase consumer prices, and restrict foreign trade.
8. The net effect on the political party system was the growth of the Populist party to 42% of the registered voters. There was also tremendous growth in the Republican party while the Democratic party suffered the greatest loss of Congressional seats in American history.
9. Answers will vary.

1. d
2. b
3. c
4. a
5. b
6. True
7. True
8. True
9. Sexuality is far more repressed in some societies than it is in the U.S., and some societies would consider the sexual morays in the U.S. very repressive. Most societies hold completely different expectations of behaviors based solely on gender. Where a behavior takes place may influence its acceptability, for example, language appropriate in locker rooms may not be appropriate in church.
10. Formal social control is exercised by people such as police officers or college deans, who are often part of punishment for disobedience. Informal social control is the influence which can be brought on someone to modify behavior by their peers or family. The desire for approval from these groups is high. Finally, there is an internalizing of normative standards over time. Guilt or positive feelings of self-esteem are powerful forces for conformity.
11. Primary deviance refers to any deviant act that does not result in some form of labeling. Any deviant act that is not somehow made public has little or no effect on the person's life. On the other hand secondary deviance, the violation of normal behavior, becomes known and the person's life can be dramatically affected. Once the person has been labeled, there is little that can be done to rectify it.
12. Answers will vary.

1. a
2. c
3. d
4. True
5. False
6. False
7. Since IT is a very new business culture and women can more easily climb the "corporate ladder," the number of female senior management positions is roughly half that of men. In addition, the hierarchical structure of the Internet and high-tech business is more loosely defined and ever-changing, allowing for opportunities for quick advancement.
8. If we were to move to a cashless society the administrative tasks of handling money, checks, and credit transactions would be eliminated. We would no longer need to manufacture or carry money. Every purchase, regardless of size, would result in an immediate transfer of funds between the buyer and the seller. Finally, in a totally e-commerce world there would be a detailed and accurate record of all monetary transactions.
9. Answers will vary.

Unit 9: **Graphs and Functions**

Chapter 3 of Angel, *Algebra for College Students*, 2nd Edition, Prentice Hall, 2004

1. **d**
2. **b**
3. **a**
4. **True**
5. **True**
6. **False**
7. **To plot a point, find the x-coordinate on the x-axis and the y-coordinate on the y- axis. Then suppose there is an imaginary vertical line from the x-coordinate and an imaginary horizontal line from the y-coordinate. The point is placed where the two imaginary lines intersect.**
8. **A vertical line test is a method of determining whether a graph represents a function. If it is not possible to draw a vertical line between, that intersects two points on a graph, this indicates that each x-value corresponds exactly to each y-value, thus indicating a function. If a vertical line can be drawn between two points on a graph, it indicates that the x-value does not correspond exactly to one y-value and therefore the graph does not represent a function.**
9. **Answers will vary.**